Life and Death Planning
for Retirement Benefits

The Essential Handbook for Estate Planners

Sixth Edition, Completely Revised

2006

Natalie B. Choate

Includes the Pension Protection Act of 2006! See page 575.

Ataxplan Publications, Boston, Massachusetts

Updates for this book are published at our website:

www.ataxplan.com

Life and Death Planning for Retirement Benefits

The Essential Handbook for Estate Planners

Sixth edition, completely revised

By Natalie B. Choate

Published by: Ataxplan Publications
Post Office Box 961093
Boston, Massachusetts 02196-1093

Publisher's Cataloging-in-Publication Data
Choate, Natalie B.
Life and Death Planning for Retirement Benefits: The Essential Handbook for Estate Planners—6th ed. / Natalie B. Choate
    p.   cm.
Includes bibliographical references and index.

ISBN 0-9649440-7-3

1. Estate planning - United States. 2. Tax planning - United States.
3. Retirement income - Taxation - United States. 4. Inheritance and transfer tax - United States. I. Choate, Natalie B. II. Title

KF 6585 .C43 2006

To my mother

Jhan English Choate

who has had to put up with a lot

Warning and Disclaimer

The rules applicable to qualified retirement plan benefits and IRAs are among the most complex in the tax code. I have read few works on this subject that were, in my view, completely accurate; in fact most that I have seen, including, unfortunately, earlier incarnations of this work, contain errors. Furthermore, even accurate information can become outdated quickly as IRS or Congressional policy shifts. Despite my best efforts, it is likely that this book, too, contains errors. Citations are provided so that estate planning practitioners can check any statements made in this book and reach their own conclusions regarding what the law is.

This book is intended to provide general information regarding the tax and other laws applicable to retirement benefits, and to provide suggestions regarding appropriate estate planning actions for different situations. It is not intended as a substitute for the practitioner's own research, or for the advice of a qualified estate planning specialist. The author and publisher shall have neither liability nor responsibility to any person or entity with respect to any loss or damage caused, or alleged to be caused, directly or indirectly by the information contained in this book.

If you do not wish to be bound by the above, you may return this book to the publisher for a full refund.

Summary of Contents

TABLE OF CONTENTS: DETAILED

Introduction

A letter to my Congressman

Dear Barney Frank,

I have a request: Please put me out of business!

The purpose of this book is to explain, for the benefit of my fellow estate planning lawyers, and other tax and financial services professionals involved in helping individuals plan for distribution of their retirement benefits, as many of the applicable rules as I can fit into almost 600 pages. But this book should be much shorter than it is.

For example, Congress should repeal the 10 percent tax on pre-age 59½ distributions (a tax paid mostly by the poor, the desperate, and the unlucky), along with its ~~13~~ make that 14 after you passed the PPA '06! (see p. 575) arbitrary and capricious exceptions. Then I could eliminate Chapter 9.

Congress should also abolish the "life expectancy payout" for distributions of inherited retirement benefits, replacing it with a flat 10- or 20-year payout that would apply to all plans and beneficiaries. And allow nonspouse beneficiaries to roll over inherited QRP benefits into an "inherited" IRA [Barney, you read my mind and included that one in the PPA '06; see ¶ 2.6.03]. And eliminate lifetime required distributions altogether, as you have done already for Roth IRAs. Those changes would let me chop almost all of Chapter 1 and much of Chapter 6.

Also, Barney, it's time to get rid of special income tax breaks for certain people, particularly the "NUA" deal for distributions of employer stock (so I can shorten Chapter 2). Why give employees a big tax incentive to concentrate their portfolios in employer stock? The workers' revolution is not coming, tax rates are reasonable now, and the income tax on a lump sum distribution can be deferred via a tax-free rollover.

Both Congress and the IRS have homework to do in the area of IRAs and prohibited transactions. Big chunks of Chapter 8 are devoted to explaining the contradictions, gaps, and other mysteries in the current rules—most of which have existed since ERISA was passed in 1974. How much longer will you wait to fix them?

By the way, why shouldn't plan administrators honor disclaimers and other standard state-law probate rules? The Supreme Court thinks you guys wanted to take over that field, and has negated (with respect to retirement benefits) state laws developed over centuries to help families transition a decedent's property in sensible fashion. Can't you set the Court straight on this wrong-headed interpretation of ERISA?

Then could you please prod the IRS to issue authoritative rulings (rather than dozens of expensively-obtained but worthless-as-precedent PLRs) confirming that a surviving spouse can roll over benefits she's entitled to receive through a trust or estate, and that a trust or estate can transfer a retirement plan, intact, to the beneficiaries of the trust or estate?

One last request: You definitely should attend to these matters, but since doing so will put me out of business, I do ask that you wait a few more years, until I'm ready to retire. In the meantime, I hope this book will serve as both a handy reference source for the expert and a basic guide for the novice.

Your constituent,
Natalie B. Choate

Limitations of this Book

Many important aspects of planning for retirement distributions are *not* covered in this book, including investment alternatives and financial planning considerations generally. This book also does not cover: 457 plans; qualified domestic relations orders (QDROs); stock options and other nonqualified forms of deferred compensation; ESOPs; creditors' rights; state tax issues; and community property. Other sources for some of these topics are mentioned in the Bibliography.

This book is designed to explain estate planning and tax planning issues for the benefit of estate and financial planners who are counseling individuals (and their beneficiaries) who have assets in retirement plans. It does not cover issues which are of concern to plan administrators, but which do not have a significant impact on planning decisions for the individual participant, such as distribution notice requirements.

This book deals with the *federal* tax law applicable to retirement benefits, but in a few instances state law has a bearing on the subject. When state law has a significant impact, planners will need to determine the law applicable to their clients.

Terminology Used in this Book

In this book:

Section numbers refer to the Internal Revenue Code of 1986, as amended through June 2006, unless otherwise specified. Reg. stands for "Treasury Regulation" unless otherwise specified. Prop. Reg. means "Proposed Treasury Regulation."

Retirement plan means a corporate or self-employed ("Keogh") pension, profit-sharing, or stock bonus plan that is "qualified" under § 401(a), an individual retirement account (IRA) created under § 408, a Roth IRA established under § 408A, or a tax-sheltered annuity (or mutual fund) arrangement established under § 403(b). The narrower term qualified plan or qualified retirement plan (QRP) includes only 401(a) plans. For more description of these plan types see ¶ 10.1.

The participant is the individual whose benefits we are dealing with: the employee who has benefits in a pension or profit-sharing plan, or for whom a tax-sheltered annuity or mutual fund account was purchased; or the account owner in the case of an IRA. For ease of understanding, throughout this book, except in some specific examples and case studies, the "participant" is male and the feminine pronoun refers to the participant's spouse. Of course any statement would apply equally to a female participant and her male spouse. Sometimes, when appropriate, the participant is referred to as "the employee," "the client," or occasionally "the decedent."

How to Use Cross References

The book is divided into numbered Chapters. Chapters are divided into *sections* (which are numbered "x.y"), and sections are divided into *subsections* (which are numbered "x.y.zz"). "X" is the number of the Chapter, "y" is the number of the section, and "zz" is the number of the subsection. Cross references to other parts of the book, indicated by the "¶" symbol, are liberally provided. A cross reference to "¶ 1.7.04" refers to Chapter 1, section 7, subsection .04.

Appendix B provides beneficiary designation forms for some common situations, along with some related trust provisions and other miscellaneous forms suggested in the text. Whenever a drafting suggestion or planning idea in the text is illustrated by a form in Appendix B, that form is cross-referenced. If there is no form reference, you can assume no form is provided.

Other Hints for Using this Book

There are many gray areas in the tax treatment of retirement benefits—questions the regulations do not answer; points of law subject to different interpretations; or regulatory positions that seem contrary to law or for some other reason likely to be changed in the future. When a practitioner encounters one of these in practice, the response may differ depending on whether he is doing advance planning for a client, or is dealing with a *fait accompli*. For this reason, from time to time in this book, in suggesting ways to deal with an issue, I distinguish between "planning mode" and "cleanup mode."

Planning mode deals with advance planning, and suggests a "safe harbor" course of action—the steps that should produce a predictable result and offer peace of mind. **Cleanup mode** deals with the *fait accompli* situation, when it is too late for advance planning, because the participant has already died. In cleanup mode, a more aggressive position may be appropriate on the issue, since there is often nothing to lose.

At the end of each Chapter, there is a summary of the planning principles developed in that Chapter. Bear in mind that most of these are general guidelines and do not apply to every case. The more detailed discussion in the Chapter provides the basis for these principles, and points out limitations and exceptions.

Acknowledgments

I am most grateful to those who took the time to read sections of the book and send me their thoughtful comments, almost all of which were incorporated into the book. For this and other recent editions, these peer reviewers were Alan S. Acker, Esq., of Columbus, OH; Ed Burrows, EA, of Boston; Fred Lindgren, EA, of Boston; Stephan R. Leimberg, Esq., of Bryn Mawr, PA; Barry S. Picker, CPA, of Brooklyn, NY; Ed Slott, CPA, of Rockville Centre, NY; Steven E. Trytten, Esq., of Pasadena, CA; and Mark W. Worthington, Esq., of Worcester, MA. I know that their material reward for this effort (free copies of the book) is trivial in view of the time and effort they expended to help me improve the accuracy and readability of the work.

I also thank, most especially, my personal in-house Harvard Law Review editor, Ian M. Starr, Esq., who pitched in to cite check, and who is also my booking agent, tour-arranger, and husband, and who makes it all worth it.

I am grateful to the many other professionals who on countless occasions have willingly shared their expertise in person, by phone, letter and email, including Jonathan Blattmachr, Frank S. Berall, Don DiCarlo, Guerdon T. Ely, Dave Foster, Seymour Goldberg, Chris Hoyt, Mike Jones, Bob Keebler, Stephen J. Krass, Lou Mezzullo, Dave Snyder of Florida, and Dave Snyder of Indiana. For their comments and insights regarding IRAs and prohibited transactions, I thank lawyers Noel Ice, Ami Givon, and Kevin Wiggins.

The work of many who helped with earlier editions is still evident in this one. Thank you again Ellen K. Harrison, Esq.; Virginia Coleman, Esq.; Paul Frimmer, Esq.; Randall J. Gingiss, Esq.; Zoe M. Hicks, Esq.; Jerold I. Horn, Esq.; Larry Katzenstein, Esq.; James H. Landon, Esq.; George Mair, Esq.; Al Martin, Esq.; Ronald T. Martin, Esq.; David W. Polstra, CFP; Michael G. Riley, Esq.; Kathleen R. Sherby, Esq.; and Lee Slavutin, M.D., C.P.C.

In over thirty years of gathering material for this book, I have talked with, listened to, or read the work of hundreds of estate planners, actuaries, accountants, lawyers, financial planners, retirees, trust officers, mutual fund personnel, plan administrators, IRS and DOL staffers, plan participants, and writers who have studied the subject matter. Since almost everyone who spends time thinking about these issues or working with the actual problems of real life employers and retirees has some interesting and new insight into the subject, I have learned from almost every encounter.

In earlier editions I listed the names of those whose questions and insights had led to something new or better in the book. It is no longer possible to do that, partly because there are now too many, and partly because so often I learn something from a seminar attendee whose name I never get. To all who have shared thoughts, questions, comments, and suggestions for improvement, thank you!

Abbreviations Used in this Book

ADP	Applicable Distribution Period. ¶ 1.2.01, #3.
ASD	Annuity Starting Date. ¶ 10.2.02.
Code	Internal Revenue Code of 1986.
CRT	Charitable Remainder Trust. ¶ 7.5.04.
CSV	Cash surrender value.
DNI	Distributable Net Income. ¶ 6.4.02.
DOL	Department of Labor
DQP	Disqualified person. ¶ 8.6.05.
DRAC	Designated Roth account. ¶ 5.7.
EGTRRA	Economic Growth and Tax Relief Reconciliation Act of 2001 (P.L. 107-16).
ERISA	Employee Retirement Income Security Act of 1974.
FMV	Fair market value.
IRA	Individual Retirement Account. ¶ 10.1.08.
IRD	Income in respect of a decedent. ¶ 2.3.01.
IRS	Internal Revenue Service.
IRT	Individual Retirement Trust. ¶ 6.1.06.
LSD	Lump Sum Distribution. ¶ 2.4.
MRD	Minimum Required Distribution. ¶ 1.2.01.
NUA	Net unrealized appreciation. ¶ 2.5.
PLR	IRS private letter ruling.
PPA '06	Pension Protection Act of 2006. See p. 575.
Prop. Reg.	Proposed Treasury Regulation.
PT	Prohibited transaction. ¶ 8.6, ¶ 8.7.
PTE	Prohibited transaction exemption.
QDRO	Qualified Domestic Relations Order. § 414(p).
QJSA	Qualified Joint and Survivor Annuity. ¶ 3.4.02.
QPSA	Qualified Pre-retirement Survivor Annuity. ¶ 3.4.02.
QRP	Qualified Retirement Plan. ¶ 10.1.12.
RBD	Required Beginning Date. ¶ 1.4.01.
REA	Retirement Equity Act of 1984 (P. L. 98-397). ¶ 3.4.
Reg.	Treasury Regulation.
TAMRA '88	Technical and Miscellaneous Revenue Act of 1988 (P. L. 100-647).
TAPRA '97	Taxpayer Relief Act of 1997 (P. L. 105-34).
TEFRA '82	Tax Equity and Fiscal Responsibility Act of 1982 (P.L. 97-248).
TIPRA '06	Tax Increase Prevention and Reconciliation Act of 2005 (enacted June 2006).
TRA '84	Tax Reform Act of 1984 (P. L. 98-369).
TRA '86	Tax Reform Act of 1986 (P. L. 99-514).
UCA '92	Unemployment Compensation Amendments of 1992 (P. L. 102-318).

1

The Minimum Distribution Rules

*The minimum distribution rules dictate
when benefits must be distributed from
a retirement plan, placing outer limits
on income tax deferral.*

Congress wants tax-favored retirement plans to be *retirement* plans, not estate-building wealth transfer vehicles. To that end, Congress enacted § 401(a)(9), which compels certain annual "minimum required distributions" (MRDs) from plans beginning generally at age 70½ or, if earlier, death. § 401(a)(9) and its related regulations are called the "minimum distribution rules."

This Chapter explains the minimum distribution rules applicable for 2003 and later years under the IRS's final minimum distribution regulations for defined contribution (DC) plans, § 1.401(a)(9)-0 through § 1.401(a)(9)-5, and § 1.401(a)(9)-7 through § 1.401(a)(9)-9. For earlier years, see ¶ 1.9.04. For MRD rules applicable to defined benefit (DB) plans, see ¶ 10.2.

1.1 Introduction to the MRD Rules

1.1.01 *What practitioners must know*

The major attraction of tax-qualified retirement plans is the ability to accumulate funds inside the plan on a tax-deferred basis (or tax-free, in the case of a "Roth" plan). The minimum distribution rules dictate when this tax-sheltered accumulation must end. § 401(a)(9) tells us when benefits must start coming out of a retirement plan, and, once forced distributions start, how much must be distributed each year.

Since these rules set the outer limits on plan accumulations, and since failure to comply with the rules involves substantial penalties, estate planners need to know:

✓   Which plans are subject to the minimum distribution rules. ¶ 1.1.02.

✓   The economics of tax deferral. ¶ 1.1.03.

✓   The 10 Fundamental Laws of the MRD Universe. ¶ 1.2.01.

✓   When the participant must begin taking money out of his plan (the Required Beginning Date or "RBD," which is different for different types of plans; ¶ 1.4), and the special rules that apply during the first year of required lifetime distributions. ¶ 1.4.08.

✓   How to compute MRDs during the participant's lifetime using the Uniform Lifetime Table or the "much-younger-spouse" method. ¶ 1.3.

✓   Once the participant dies, how to determine who the participant's beneficiary is (¶ 1.7.02), and the difference between a beneficiary and a Designated Beneficiary (¶ 1.7.03).

✓   The post-death MRD rules that apply to a beneficiary or Designated Beneficiary, including the life-expectancy-of-the-beneficiary (or "stretch") payout method, the "no-DB rules," and how the plan can override the MRD rules by requiring even faster distribution. ¶ 1.5.

✓   How to calculate post-death MRDs to an individual nonspouse Designated Beneficiary, a surviving spouse, multiple beneficiaries, an estate, or a see-through trust, if the participant died before (¶ 1.5.03) or after (¶ 1.5.04) his RBD.

✓   What changes can be made, after the participant's death, to lengthen the Applicable Distribution Period. ¶ 1.8.

✓   The penalty for violating the rules, how to correct an MRD error, and how to trigger the statute of limitations applicable to MRD mistakes. ¶ 1.9.

✓   The special MRD rules for defined benefit plans. ¶ 10.2.

1.1.02 *Which plans are subject to the MRD rules*

The minimum distribution rules are contained in § 401(a)(9), which applies to Qualified Retirement Plans. The Code specifies that rules "similar to" the rules of § 401(a)(9) shall also apply to IRAs (§ 408(a)(6)); 403(b) plans (§ 403(b)(10)); and 457 plans (§ 457(b)(5), (d)(1)(B), (d)(2)).

Because the minimum distribution regulations were first written for qualified plans, they refer to the participant as the "employee." However, the Treasury has made the same regulations applicable (with certain variations) also to IRAs (Reg. § 1.408-8, A-1(a)); 403(b) plans (Reg. § 1.403(b)-3, A-1(a)); and 457 plans (Reg. § 1.457-6(d)). Thus, even though an IRA owner is not an "employee," he is subject to MRD regulations that call him an employee.

Roth IRAs are also subject to the minimum distribution rules, but only after the participant's death; the lifetime MRD rules do not apply to Roth IRAs. See ¶ 5.1.03 instead of this Chapter.

There are two sets of MRD rules, one for defined contribution (DC) plans (also called "individual account" plans), and another for defined benefit (DB) plans. The DB rules also apply to annuity payouts under DC plans. The DB plan/annuity payout rules are discussed at ¶ 10.2; this Chapter explains the rules for DC/individual account plans.

1.1.03 *MRD economics: The value of deferral*

The most valuable feature of retirement plans is the ability to invest without current taxation of the investment profits. In most cases, investing through a retirement plan defers income tax not only on the investment profits but also on the participant's compensation income that was originally contributed to the plan. The longer this deferral continues, the better, because, generally, the deferral of income tax increases the ultimate value of the benefits.

As long as assets stay in the retirement plan, the participant or beneficiary is investing not just "his own" money, but also "Uncle Sam's share" of the participant's compensation and the plan's investment profits, i.e., the money that otherwise would have been paid to the IRS (and will eventually be paid to the IRS) in income taxes. Keeping the money in the retirement plan enables the participant or beneficiary to reap a profit from investing "the IRS's money" along with his own. Once funds are distributed from the plan, they are included in the gross income of the participant or beneficiary (see ¶ 2.1.06 for exceptions), who then pays the IRS its share. Thereafter the participant (or beneficiary) will no longer enjoy any investment profits from the government's share of the plan.

Despite the apparent goal of the MRD rules (assuring that tax-favored retirement plans are used primarily to provide retirement income), § 401(a)(9) permits tax deferral to continue long past the death of the participant whose work created the benefit—*if* the participant leaves his retirement benefits to the right kind of beneficiary. If various requirements are met, Congress allows the retirement benefits to be paid out gradually, after the worker's death, over the life expectancy of the worker's beneficiary. The financial benefit of the long-term tax deferral permitted by the minimum distribution rules puts a premium on naming a beneficiary who will qualify for this "life expectancy payout method."

Depending on the rate of investment return, if the beneficiary is young, and takes no more than the MRD each year, the value of the inherited plan can mushroom, under the life expectancy payout method, by the time the *beneficiary* reaches retirement age. As an example, a 38 year-old beneficiary who inherits $500,000 IRA and withdraws it using the life expectancy method will have $1,696,000 inside the IRA plus $1,432,000 *outside* the IRA in 30 years; if she cashes out the entire account when she inherits it, she will have (outside the IRA) only $1,517,000. (This example assumes an 8% constant investment return for all assets and 36% tax rate on all plan distributions and investment income; projections were prepared using Brentmark Pension & Roth Analyzer® and NumberCruncher® software; see Appendix C.)

Long-term deferral of distributions also produces greater financial gain with a Roth retirement plan, even though income tax is not being deferred; see Chapter 5.

Deferring income taxes is not always beneficial. One author argues that most people will be subject to higher income taxes when they retire and thus deferral will be a bad deal for many. See Blyskal, Jeff, "Questionable Assumptions," *Worth*, July/August 1993, p. 70. For who should take distributions earlier than required, see ¶ 1.10, #6.

1.2 MRD Fundamentals

1.2.01 *The 10 Fundamental Laws of the MRD Universe*

Here are the basic principles underlying the minimum required distribution (MRD) scheme for defined contribution (DC) plans under the IRS's final minimum distribution regulations. Note that many rules have at least one exception!

1. **MRDs start at a particular time.** The starting point for lifetime required distributions is approximately age 70½ (or upon later retirement in some cases); see ¶ 1.4 for explanation of the "first Distribution Year" and the "Required Beginning Date." The final Distribution Year for lifetime distributions is the year of the participant's death. ¶ 1.5.04(F). The starting point for post-death MRDs is measured from the participant's death. ¶ 1.5.03, ¶ 1.5.04.

2. **Annual distributions must be taken by December 31 each year.** Once MRDs begin, the participant (or beneficiary) must take a distribution every calendar year, no later than December 31. Reg. § 1.401(a)(9)-5, A-1. There are several exceptions to this rule. First, the 5-year rule does not require annual distributions; see ¶ 1.5.06. Second, in the case of certain lifetime MRDs, the distribution for the first Distribution Year can be postponed until the Required Beginning Date; see ¶ 1.4. Finally, see ¶ 1.9.02 for unusual situations in which an MRD can be delayed beyond December 31.

3. **Each year's MRD is determined by dividing the prior year-end account balance by a factor from an IRS table.** MRDs are computed by dividing an annually-revalued account balance by an annually-declining life expectancy factor. Reg. § 1.401(a)(9)-5, A-1(a). (This principle does not apply to post-death distributions computed using the 5-year rule. ¶ 1.5.06.) For how to determine the account balance, see ¶ 1.2.05. For how to find the life expectancy factor, see ¶ 1.2.03. The factor obtained from the applicable IRS table is sometimes called the **Applicable Distribution Period (ADP)** or **divisor**. It is a divisor, not a percentage; see Kenny Example, ¶ 1.3.01.

4.   **There is no maximum distribution.** The formula tells you the *minimum required* distribution. The rules impose no maximum distribution; the participant or beneficiary is always free, as far as the IRS is concerned, to take more than the minimum.

5.   **Taking more than the required amount in one year does not give you a "credit" you can use to reduce distributions in a later year.** Each year stands on it own. Reg. § 1.401(a)(9)-5, A-2. Taking larger distributions in one year *indirectly* reduces later MRDs by reducing the account balance.

6.   **The plan may be stricter than the regulations.** Just because a participant or beneficiary qualifies for the life expectancy payout method under the law does not mean he will actually get to use it; the plan must allow it too. See ¶ 1.5.10.

7.   **The MRD cannot exceed 100 percent of the account balance.** "...[T]he required minimum distribution amount will never exceed the entire account balance on the date of the distribution." Reg. § 1.401(a)(9)-5, A-1(a). This rule helps if investment losses have caused the account to decline in value so much that the total value is less than the MRD for the year.

8.   **Distributions before the first Distribution Year don't count.** The first year for which an MRD is required is called the "first Distribution Year." See ¶ 1.4. Distributions in years prior to that year have no effect on the computation of the MRD for the first (or any other) Distribution Year (other than indirectly, by reducing the account balance). Reg. § 1.401(a)(9)-2, A-6(a).

9.   **Distribution period does not involve an election.** With one exception, determination of the ADP for benefits, either during life or after death, does not involve an "election" on the part of the participant or beneficiary. The ADP is what it is based on the identity of the participant and beneficiary. (This is in contrast to the now-obsolete 1987 proposed regulations, under which the participant had to make various irrevocable elections at his RBD; see ¶ 1.9.04.) The exception is, if the participant dies before his RBD, leaving his benefits to a Designated

Beneficiary, the beneficiary may have to elect between the life expectancy payout method and the 5-year rule; see ¶ 1.5.07.

10.   **The regulations "overrule" the Code.** You cannot compute an MRD simply by following the Internal Revenue Code. The IRS regulations have fundamentally altered the Congressional scheme in several ways. For example, the Code dictates that lifetime distributions must be made over the life expectancy of the participant or the joint life expectancy of the participant and his beneficiary. § 401(a)(9)(A)(ii). The regulations make the identity and life expectancy of the beneficiary almost irrelevant; see ¶ 1.3. For other examples, see "box" after ¶ 1.5.04(F), ¶ 1.5.07, ¶ 1.5.09, ¶ 1.7.04, and ¶ 1.7.05.

1.2.02 Which distributions count towards the MRD

Regs. § 1.401(a)(9)-5, A-9(a), and § 1.408-8, A-11(a), state that, except as otherwise provided in A-9(b) or A-11(b) of such regulations, or as may later be otherwise provided by other IRS pronouncements, "all amounts distributed" from a plan or IRA "are taken into account in determining whether section 401(a)(9) is satisfied...." Here is the MRD status of various types of distributions:

A.   **Distribution of an annuity contract does not count.** When an employee's benefit is used to purchase an annuity contract, distributions under the contract must comply with MRD rules. ¶ 10.2.10. Distribution of the contract itself is a nontaxable event (¶ 2.1.06(G)) and does not count as a distribution for MRD purposes. Reg. § 1.401(a)(9)-8, A-10.

B.   **Corrective and deemed distributions do not count.** Contributions that are returned to the participant because they exceed the 415 limits or the limits on elective deferrals do not count towards the MRD requirement. Reg. § 1.401(a)(9)-5, A-9(b)(1)–(3); § 1.408-8, A-11(b)(1)–(3). Neither do plan loans that are treated as distributions due to failure to comply with the plan loan rules (¶ 2.1.03(F)), or the imputed income arising from life insurance held by a plan (¶ 8.2.01). Reg. § 1.401(a)(9)-5, A-9(b)(4), (6).

C.   ESOP dividends do not count. Dividends on employer stock held in an ESOP can be paid directly to the participant or beneficiary. § 404(k). Such dividend payments do not count towards the MRD requirement. Reg. § 1.401(a)(9)-5, A-9(b)(5).

D.   Nontaxable distributions do count (for exception see "A"). Reg. § 1.401(a)(9)-5, A-9(a), § 1.408-8, A-11(a). See PLR 9840041 in which an employee took a distribution of his entire balance from an employer plan, rolled over the taxable portion of the distribution, and did not roll over the nontaxable amounts. The IRS ruled that the nontaxable distribution, which exceeded the MRD, satisfied the MRD requirement. The nontaxable portion is applied, first, to the MRD. Reg. § 1.402(c)-2, A-8. If the MRD amount exceeds the nontaxable portion of the distribution, then the rest of the MRD is "filled up" from the taxable portion, and any balance of the taxable portion is eligible for rollover. See ¶ 2.1.07–¶ 2.1.11 for how to tell what portion of a particular distribution is nontaxable. See ¶ 1.3.05 if the employee has multiple accounts in a QRP.

E.   Distributions in kind do count. A participant or beneficiary can take MRDs in kind as well as in cash. Plans are permitted to distribute property as well as cash. See Instructions for IRS Forms 1099-R and 5498 (2005), R-6, where the payer is instructed "If you distribute employer securities or other property, include in box 1 [of Form 1099-R] the FMV of the securities or other property on the date of distribution." Regs. § 1.401(a)(9)-5, A-9, and § 1.408-8, A-11, provide that all distributions not specifically excepted there do count towards the MRD requirement; there is no exception for distributions in kind other than as noted at "A" above.

1.2.03 *IRS tables for determining life expectancy (ADP)*

MRDs are determined annually by dividing the prior year-end account balance by a life expectancy factor supplied by the IRS. In the regulations' terminology, the tables supply the ADP or divisor. There are currently three tables in use for this purpose; all are reproduced in full in IRS Publication 590, "Individual Retirement Arrangements."

Lifetime MRDs (¶ 1.3) are calculated using either the **Uniform Lifetime Table** or (if the participant's sole beneficiary is his more-than-10-years-younger spouse) the **Joint and Last Survivor Table**. The Uniform Lifetime Table is found at Reg. § 1.401(a)(9)-9, A-2, and in Appendix A of this book (Table 1). The Joint and Last Survivor Table is found at Reg. § 1.401(a)(9)-9, A-3.

Post-death MRDs, whether based on the life expectancy of the surviving spouse or other Designated Beneficiary, or of the participant, are calculated using the **Single Life Table**. See ¶ 1.5, ¶ 1.6. The only post-death MRDs *not* governed by the Single Life Table are the MRD for the year of the participant's death (¶ 1.5.04(F)) and distributions under the 5-year rule (¶ 1.5.06). The Single Life Table is found at Reg. § 1.401(a)(9)-9, A-1, and in Appendix A of this book (Table 3).

All three tables are "unisex" (life expectancy for men and women is the same). The IRS uses a different set of actuarial tables for estate and gift tax valuations; see § 7520.

1.2.04 *What is a person's "age" for MRD purposes?*

To use the IRS tables, you need to know the participant's or beneficiary's age. Age for MRD purposes means the age the person will attain on his birthday in the applicable Distribution Year. It is the age he will be at the end of the Distribution Year. Reg. § 1.401(a)(9)-5, A-4(a), (b); A-5(c).

The tricky part is that for some MRDs the age is determined only once, at the beginning of the payout period; this is called the "fixed-term" or "reduce-by-one" method. For other MRDs, the age is redetermined annually ("recalculation method"). The participant or beneficiary has no choice in this matter—the regulations dictate which method applies in which situation.

A.   **Recalculation method.** The recalculation method applies for purposes of computing all lifetime MRDs (¶ 1.3), including the MRD for the year of the participant's death if any (¶ 1.5.04(F)), and post-death MRDs when the surviving spouse is the sole beneficiary (¶ 1.6.06(D)).

Under the recalculation method, the individual's age is determined each year, and the divisor used is the divisor applicable to the new age, instead of just deducting one from last year's life expectancy. Under the recalculation method, life expectancy never runs out as long as the distributee is alive: See ¶ 1.3.02, Kenny Example (¶ 1.3.01), and Josephine Example (¶ 1.6.06(D)).

B.   **Fixed-term method.** Under the "fixed-term method," you determine the person's age and the corresponding ADP in the *first* Distribution Year. In subsequent Distribution Years, the divisor is simply the prior year's divisor reduced by one; see Diane Example at ¶ 1.5.05. Some people call this the "reduce-by-one" method. Unlike with the recalculation method, you do not determine a new ADP based on the person's new age. With two exceptions, the fixed-term method is *always* used after the participant's death to determine MRDs to the beneficiary. The two exceptions are: the MRD for the year of the participant's death (¶ 1.5.04(F)); and MRDs during the surviving spouse's life, if she is the participant's sole beneficiary (¶ 1.6.06(D)). The fixed-term method is *never* used to calculate MRDs during the participant's lifetime.

1.2.05 *Which "account balance" the divisor applies to*

Each year, the MRD is determined by dividing the applicable life expectancy factor into the prior year-end account balance. See ¶ 1.2.06(A) regarding a required adjustment to the account balance for a rollover in transit. See ¶ 1.2.07 for how to value the account balance.

If an MRD has been missed, do you deduct the missed MRD from the "prior year-end account balance" when computing the MRDs for subsequent years? It seems that you should be able to do so, since the regulation says that the missed distribution is added to the MRD for the subsequent year, at least for purposes of determining whether a distribution is eligible for rollover. Reg. § 1.402(c)-2, A-7(a), last sentence. However, nothing in the regulations authorizes such an adjustment. See Reg. § 1.401(a)(9)-5, A-3.

Under the 2001 proposed regulations (Prop. Reg. § 1.401(a)(9)-5, A-3(c)), in computing the MRD for a living participant's second Distribution Year, the prior year-end account balance was reduced by the amount of any MRD for the first Distribution Year that had not yet been taken as of the close of the first Distribution Year—provided the participant actually took that first-year MRD no later than the RBD.

The final regulations eliminated this adjustment for 2003 and later years. T.D. 8987, 2002-1 C.B. 852, 858, "Calculation Simplification."

The date as of which the account balance is determined depends on the type of retirement plan:

A.　　**IRAs.** The relevant account balance for an IRA is "the account balance of the IRA as of December 31 of the calendar year immediately preceding the calendar year for which distributions are required to be made." Reg. § 1.408-8, A-6.

B.　　**Qualified plans.** In the case of a qualified retirement plan (QRP), the account value used is "the account balance as of the last valuation date in the calendar year immediately preceding" the Distribution Year. Reg. § 1.401(a)(9)-5, A-3(a). A plan might have only one valuation date per plan year (such as "the last day of the plan year"), or it might have more than one. If the plan's last valuation date in the prior calendar year was December 31, you just use the account value as of that date. Otherwise, see the regulation for required adjustments.

1.2.06 *Rollovers and MRDs*

For how the Required Beginning Date (RBD) is affected by rollovers, see ¶ 1.4.09.

A.　　**Adjustment to account balance for rollovers in transit.** You must increase the prior year-end balance by any amount that was added to the account in the Distribution Year ("Year 2") which represented a rollover from another plan or IRA, if the amount in question was distributed from such other plan or IRA in the *prior* calendar year ("Year 1"). For purposes of MRDs from the *receiving* plan, such a rollover amount is deemed to have been received in the prior calendar year (i.e., Year 1) and not the year it was actually received (Year 2). Reg. § 1.401(a)(9)-7, A-2, last sentence. If this rule did not exist, people could cheat by moving money around from account to account at the end of the year, so as to avoid having the funds count as part of the year-end account balance of *either* plan.

B.   **Other effects on balance, starting date.** Reg. § 1.401(a)(9)-7 contains other rules regarding the effect of rollovers and plan-to-plan transfers on the calculation of MRDs, but (with the exception noted in "A") a rollover *into* a plan or IRA has no effect on MRDs *from* that plan or IRA until the year after the rollover is received. Reg. § 1.401(a)(9)-7, A-2. The rollover has the effect of increasing the plan balance of the receiving plan, which increases the MRD for the year *following* the rollover.

C.   **Using rollovers to stop MRDs.** MRDs are determined under the rules applicable to the plan that holds the benefits, not the plan that the benefits were originally in prior to a rollover. See Reg. § 1.401(a)(9)-7. This means that an individual over age 70½ can stop the flow of MRDs by rolling money from a plan that requires him to take MRDs (such as a traditional IRA, or a QRP where he is a 5-percent owner of the employer) into a plan that would not require him to take MRDs (i.e., a QRP maintained by an employer of which he is not a 5-percent owner). See PLR 2004-53015 for an example of this technique. Similarly, converting a traditional IRA to a Roth IRA stops the flow of MRDs because Roth IRAs are not subject to the lifetime distribution requirements; see ¶ 5.1.03. A surviving spouse can stop (or slow) the flow of MRDs from an inherited retirement plan by rolling over the benefits to her own plan (or, in the case of an IRA of which she is sole beneficiary, electing to treat it as her own). See ¶ 3.2.

1.2.07 *Valuation rules for determining account balance*

The rules in ¶ 1.2.05–¶ 1.2.06 explain which account balance is used and what adjustments to the balance are required or permitted. But the most important thing about that account balance is its value. The value of the account balance is what the ADP is divided into to determine the MRD. IRA providers are required to annually provide the year-end fair market value (FMV) of the IRA to the IRS on Form 5498. See Instructions for Forms 1099-R and 5498 (2005), p. R-13. Surprisingly, there is little guidance on how to determine FMV for MRD purposes.

A.   **How to value annuity contracts.** Reg. § 1.401(a)(9)-6, A-12(a), explains how an annuity contract held inside a defined contribution (DC) plan is to be valued for MRD purposes. The method described here may NOT be used to value a contract for purposes of a Roth IRA conversion; ¶ 5.4.09.

Variable vs. fixed annuities

An "annuity" is an arrangement under which one party (the issuer) is obligated to pay another (the annuitant) a series of periodic payments continuing for a certain period of time; see ¶ 10.2.02. In general, when this book refers to an annuity, a fixed annuity is intended—one in which the payments in the series are fixed in amount—for example, $1,000 per month. However, there is another type of annuity: A variable annuity is similar to a "regular" annuity in that it represents an insurance company's promise to make periodic payments to the annuitant for life or a term of years. Under a variable annuity, however, the periodic payments are not fixed; they fluctuate in tandem with the performance of an investment portfolio. The valuation rules of Reg. § 1.401(a)(9)-6, A-12(a), apply to both kinds of annuity contracts if held in a DC plan. This section discusses "variable annuities" because those are the contracts that raise most of the valuation issues dealt with in the Regulation.

Prior to the Annuity Starting Date (¶ 10.2.02), a variable annuity resembles a mutual fund portfolio held in an annuity "wrapper." A variable annuity contract, until it is annuitized, behaves like a DC plan. The contract has a cash value which is like an account balance in a DC plan; it fluctuates with investment performance.

Not surprisingly, the regulations treat variable annuity contracts as DC plans for purposes of the MRD rules. Reg. § 1.401(a)(9)-6, A-12(a). The participant determines his MRD with respect to the plan-owned variable annuity contract by dividing the value of the contract as of the prior year end by a divisor from the applicable table corresponding to his age at the end of the Distribution Year (see ¶ 1.3).

Generally, the value of the variable annuity contract for MRD purposes is (1) its cash value ("the dollar amount credited to the employee or beneficiary under the contract") plus (2) "the actuarial present value of any additional benefits (such as survivor benefits in excess of the…[cash value]) that will be provided under the contract."

The "actuarial present value" must be "determined using reasonable actuarial assumptions," but without regard to any individual's actual health. Reg. § 1.401(a)(9)-6, A-12(b).

There are two exceptions to this general rule. First, if the *only* additional benefit provided by the contract is a death benefit equal to the total premiums paid (minus prior distributions), such additional benefit can be disregarded in valuing the contract for MRD purposes. Reg. § 1.401(a)(9)-6, A-12(c)(2). Thus, for a variable annuity contract that provides no "extras" besides that return-of-premium guarantee, the "fair market value" of the contract for MRD purposes is its cash value.

If the contract provides additional death and/or life benefit guarantees beyond the mere return of premiums, it may *still* be possible to disregard the contract's additional benefits for MRD purposes—but only if the additional benefits meet complicated tests contained in Reg. § 1.401(a)(9)-6, A-12(c). The problem is that annuity companies must value every contract every year for MRD purposes if held by an individual over 70. The annuity company may not want to go through the elaborate exercises in Reg. § 1.401(a)(9)-6, A-12(c), to determine whether it can exclude additional benefits in valuing the contract. Instead, the annuity company may just play it safe by *including* the value of all additional benefits.

Furthermore, the insurance company may not want to take the time, trouble, and expense to value such additional benefits actuarially. Look at Reg. § 1.401(a)(9)-6, A-12(d), Examples 1 and 2, to see how complicated such actuarial valuation is. The insurance company may decide to simply report such additional benefits at face (rather than actuarial) value.

Connie Example: Connie, age 72, holds, in her IRA, a variable annuity contract which currently provides a death benefit of $50,000 in excess of cash value. Rather than bothering to determine the actuarial value of this death benefit (which is much less than $50,000), or to figure out whether it can exclude that value altogether under Reg. § 1.401(a)(9)-6, A-12(c), the insurance company may simply (and improperly) report the value of that benefit to the IRS as $50,000. That way, the issuer has less work to do, and by overvaluing the contract they do not risk an MRD mistake, because the MRD computed on an inflated value will be too large, not too small.

It remains to be seen what, if anything, the participant can do (short of hiring his own actuary annually to value the contract) to force the company to value the contract correctly. If the plan overvalues the contract and overstates the MRD amount, the participant is entitled to roll over the excess amount, because the MRD is determined based on the actual application of the tax law, not the assumptions of the plan administrator. Reg. § 1.402(c)-2, A-15.

B.   Other assets. Strangely, other than the special valuation rule for annuity contracts discussed above, there is no guidance in the MRD or income tax reporting rules on how to determine the value of an account balance for MRD purposes. Some IRA providers simply report cost basis for illiquid and hard-to-value assets. Most advisers and participants probably use the account value on the year-end statement furnished by the IRA provider.

However, for the record, it should be noted that the typical brokerage account statement would not suffice to establish the fair market value of listed securities for *estate tax* valuation purposes. Most such statements show closing prices, where estate tax regulations require use of the mean between the high and low selling price on the applicable date. Reg. § 20.2031-2(b)(1). Also, most brokerage firms' statements do not show accrued bond interest, or dividends that have been declared but not yet paid, both of which must be included in valuing securities for estate tax purposes.

1.3 MRDs During Participant's Life

An individual (the **participant**) who owns a retirement plan account must start taking annual "minimum required distributions" (MRDs) at a certain point in his life. This general statement does *not* apply to Roth IRAs, which are not subject to the lifetime distribution requirement; see ¶ 5.1.03. This ¶ 1.3 does not apply to Roth IRAs.

Generally the starting point for MRDs is age 70½, but see ¶ 1.4 for full details on the "Required Beginning Date" and the "first Distribution Year."

Once commenced, MRDs continue for the participant's entire lifetime. Although the computation of *post-death* MRDs can be radically different depending who is the beneficiary of the plan (see ¶ 1.5), *lifetime* MRDs are computed the same way for most people.

The lifetime MRD system is designed to assure that the participant will not outlive his retirement plan. This is done by using divisors that liquidate the plan over the joint life expectancy of the participant and a (hypothetical) 10-years-younger individual beneficiary, an approach that assures that the MRD rules will never force the participant to take the last dollar out of his plan.

1.3.01 How to compute MRDs for most participants

Here is how to compute lifetime MRDs for most participants: Each year's MRD is computed by dividing the prior year-end account balance by the Uniform Lifetime Table factor applicable for the participant's age. Reg. § 1.401(a)(9)-5, A-4(a).

Kenny Example: Kenny, a widower, turns age 73 on his birthday in the year 2006. Under the Uniform Lifetime Table, the Applicable Distribution Period (ADP) or divisor for age 73 is 24.7. On December 31, 2005, the value of his IRA was $750,000. Divide $750,000 by 24.7; the result ($30,364) is Kenny's MRD for 2006. Kenny must withdraw $30,364 from his IRA sometime in 2006 (i.e., after December 31, 2005, and before January 1, 2007). In 2007, Kenny will reach age 74. To compute his 2007 MRD, he will use the age 74 factor from the Uniform Lifetime Table. This will be divided into the 2006 year-end account balance to produce the 2007 MRD. Note that Kenny uses the "recalculation method" to determine his MRDs; ¶ 1.2.04(A).

The above rule applies to *most* participants. The exceptions are: a participant whose sole beneficiary is his spouse who is more than 10 years younger than the participant, ¶ 1.3.03; a qualified plan participant who has a pre-1984 TEFRA 242(b) election in effect, ¶ 1.4.10; and a 403(b) plan participant who has a pre-1987 plan balance, ¶ 1.4.06.

For more on the Uniform Lifetime Table, see ¶ 1.3.02. For how to determine the prior year-end account balance, see ¶ 1.2.05–¶ 1.2.07. For how to determine the participant's age, and explanation of the recalculation method see ¶ 1.2.04.

1.3.02 The Uniform Lifetime Table: Good news for retirees

The divisors in the Uniform Lifetime Table represent the joint life expectancy of a participant age 70 (or older) and a hypothetical beneficiary who is 10 years younger than the participant. Thus, the initial divisor under this table (for a participant age 70) is 27.4 years, which is the joint and survivor life expectancy of one person age 70 and another person age 60.

The expectancy factors in the Uniform Lifetime Table are redetermined annually. See ¶ 1.2.04(A). In other words, the table does not start with a 27.4-year distribution period and then reduce it by one each year. If the table used such a "fixed-term method," then all money would have to be distributed out of the plan by the time the participant reached age 97 (70 + 27). Instead, the table's factors are recomputed annually, so the divisor decreases by less than one each year. At age 75, the divisor is 22.9 (not 22.4), at age 89 it is 12.0 (not 8.4). The divisor never goes below 1.9, so if the participant takes only the MRD the account balance will never go to zero, regardless of how long the participant lives (unless it is wiped out by investment losses). (However, the account will start shrinking by the late 90's.)

In fact, depending on the rate of investment return, there may well be more in the account when the participant dies than there was when MRDs began. For example, if the participant takes only the MRD starting at age 70½, and the account has a steady six percent annual investment return, the account will have more dollars in it at his death than it did when he started taking MRDs, if he dies prior to age 89.

How did the IRS come up with this table? The Code requires that benefits be distributed either in full on the RBD, or, "beginning not later than the required beginning date...over the life of such employee or over the lives of such employee and a designated beneficiary (or over a period not extending beyond the life expectancy of such employee or the life expectancy of such employee and a designated beneficiary)." § 401(a)(9)(A)(ii). In its 1987 proposed regulations, the IRS required calculation of MRDs based on the joint life expectancy of the participant and his *actual* beneficiary (if any), determined as of the RBD. This method proved way too complicated, and the IRS ditched it in 2001.

The final regulations implement § 401(a)(9)(A)(ii), instead, by using the joint life expectancy of the participant and a *hypothetical* 10-years-younger beneficiary. T.D. 8987, 2002-1 C.B. 852, 854, "Uniform Lifetime Table." This approach is not only much simpler than the old method, it produces much smaller lifetime MRDs for most people. The Uniform Lifetime Table method is also favorable for the participant's beneficiaries (because it makes it more likely that there will be some benefits left for them to inherit when the participant dies), investment advisor (who will have more IRA assets to manage for a longer period), and estate planner (who will have more assets to plan for).

1.3.03 *Lifetime MRDs: Much-younger-spouse method*

As generous as the Uniform Lifetime Table is, the participant enjoys even smaller MRDs if his sole beneficiary is his more-than-10-years-younger spouse.

"[I]f the sole designated beneficiary of an employee is the employee's surviving spouse, for required minimum distributions during the employee's lifetime, the applicable distribution period is *the longer of* the distribution period determined in accordance with…[the Uniform Lifetime Table] or the joint life expectancy of the employee and spouse using the employee's and spouse's attained ages as of the employee's and the spouse's birthdays in the distribution calendar year." Reg. § 1.401(a)(9)-5, A-4(b) (emphasis added). Note that this formulation mandates annual recalculation (¶ 1.2.04(A)) of the participant's and spouse's life expectancies.

The Joint and Last Survivor Table (¶ 1.2.03) will produce larger divisors and smaller MRDs than the Uniform Lifetime Table if the spouse-beneficiary was born in a year more than ten years later than the year of the participant's birth. For example, if the participant was born in 1931, the joint table will provide larger divisors than the Uniform Lifetime Table if the spouse was born in 1942 or later.

See ¶ 1.3.05 regarding separate accounts; and note the following additional points regarding this method:

A. **No election required.** The participant does not have to elect to use the joint life expectancy of the participant and spouse as his ADP. If the participant's spouse is his sole beneficiary, then the participant's divisor is *automatically* the divisor determined under the Uniform Lifetime Table, or the divisor determined under the Joint and Last Survivor Table, whichever is larger.

B. **Post-RBD changes permitted.** It is not required that the participant and spouse be married on the RBD or any other date prior to the Distribution Year in question. If the participant has named some other beneficiary, he can change the beneficiary to his spouse (or marry after his RBD and name his new spouse as beneficiary); the determination of which table applies is made separately each Distribution Year.

C. **Tests for whether spouse is sole beneficiary.** The spouse is the sole Designated Beneficiary for purposes of determining the participant's MRDs "if the spouse is the sole beneficiary of the employee's entire interest at all times during the distribution calendar year." Reg. § 1.401(a)(9)-5, A-4(b)(1). Marital status is determined on January 1; therefore the death of either spouse, or a divorce, during the year does not cause the spouse to lose her status as "spouse" until the following calendar year. The spouse is deemed to be the "sole beneficiary" for the entire year if she is the sole beneficiary on January 1 of the year *and* the participant does not change his beneficiary designation prior to the end of the calendar year (or prior to the spouse's death, if earlier). Reg. § 1.401(a)(9)-5, A-4(b)(2). "Sole beneficiary" means sole *primary* beneficiary; see ¶ 1.6.02, ¶ 1.7.02.

1.3.04 *Taking distributions from multiple plans*

If the participant has benefits in more than one qualified retirement plan, the MRD must be calculated separately for each such plan, and each such plan must distribute the MRD calculated for that plan. Reg. § 1.401(a)(9)-8, A-1. Thus if he participates in two pension plans and a 401(k) plan, he will receive three separate MRDs.

A different rule applies for IRAs. The MRD must be calculated separately for each IRA, but (subject to the exceptions noted below) the participant is not required to take each IRA's calculated amount from that IRA. He can total up the MRDs required from *all* of his IRAs and then take the total amount all from one of the IRAs, or from any combination of them. Reg. § 1.408-8, A-9.

This aggregation rule applies also to 403(b) accounts. The MRD must be calculated separately for each 403(b) account, but (subject to the exceptions noted below) the participant is not required to take each 403(b) account's calculated amount from that 403(b) account. He can total up the MRDs required from all of his 403(b) arrangements, and then take the total amount all from one of them, or from any combination of them. Reg. § 1.403(b)-3, A-4.

First Exception: An individual's IRAs held as *owner* may not be aggregated with IRAs he holds as *beneficiary*; an individual's 403(b) plans held as *employee* may not be aggregated with such individual's 403(b) plans held as *beneficiary*; and an individual's IRAs (or 403(b) plans) held as beneficiary of one decedent may not be aggregated with IRAs (or 403(b) plans) held as beneficiary of another decedent. Reg. § 1.408-8, A-9, § 1.403(b)-3, A-4. This regulation reversed Notice 88-38, 1988-1 C.B. 524, which stated that an individual could aggregate inherited IRAs with noninherited IRAs for MRD purposes.

Second Exception: If any part of an IRA or 403(b) account has been annuitized, it becomes subject to the DB plan rules and cannot be aggregated with amounts governed by the DC plan rules; see ¶ 10.2.10.

Note that IRAs may be aggregated *only* with other IRAs, and 403(b)s can be aggregated *only* with other 403(b)s.

1.3.05 Separate accounts within a single plan

A QRP may maintain multiple accounts for a particular employee on the plan books, for example a rollover account, an employer contribution account, and an employee contribution account. These multiple accounts within a single QRP are treated as one account for MRD purposes *during the employee's life*. Reg. § 1.401(a)(9)-8, A-2(a). This rule is favorable to the employee, because he can withdraw his MRDs from his employee contribution account (which may contain after-tax dollars) first; see ¶ 1.2.02(D).

Though a single IRA payable to multiple beneficiaries can be divided into "separate accounts" (each payable to a different beneficiary) for MRD purposes after the owner's death (¶ 1.7.06), separate accounts treatment is not available during the participant's life. Thus, it is not possible to use the much-younger-spouse method to calculate the MRD for the fractional portion of the account of which the spouse is the beneficiary if she is not sole beneficiary of the IRA. Reg. § 1.401(a)(9)-8, A-2(a)(2).

1.4 The RBD and First Distribution Year

Computing lifetime minimum required distributions (MRDs; ¶ 1.3) is much easier than figuring out when they start. This ¶ 1.4 explains what the "RBD" and "first Distribution Year" are for various types of retirement plans and looks at the anomalies created by the disconnect between the first Distribution Year and the RBD (¶ 1.4.08).

1.4.01 *Required Beginning Date (RBD): Significance*

A year for which an MRD is required is called a "distribution calendar year" in the regulations, **Distribution Year** in this book. Reg. § 1.401(a)(9)-5, A-1(b). For plans subject to the lifetime MRD rules, the "first Distribution Year" is the year the participant reaches age 70½ (or, in some cases, retires; see ¶ 1.4.03, ¶ 1.4.06).

Normally, the deadline for taking the MRD for a particular Distribution Year is December 31 of such year (¶ 1.2.01, #2), but, for lifetime distributions only, in the case of the first Distribution Year, the deadline is April 1 of the *following* year. Reg. § 1.401(a)(9)-5, A-1(c). That final deadline for the first year's MRD is call the **Required Beginning Date** or **RBD**. § 401(a)(9)(C). This postponement of the MRD for the first year does not apply to death benefits (¶ 1.5), or to the first MRD triggered by a rollover contribution (¶ 1.4.09).

The RBD matters mainly for *compliance* purposes: The participant must start taking MRDs by that date to avoid penalty, and the calculation of post-death MRDs is different depending on whether death occurred before or after the RBD; compare ¶ 1.5.03 with ¶ 1.5.04. The RBD has little significance for *planning* purposes.

The starting point for determining the RBD is the attainment of age 70½, which is "the date six calendar months after the 70th anniversary of the employee's birth." Reg. § 1.401(a)(9)-2, A-3. If the participant's date of birth is December 31, 1935, it is not clear whether he attains age 70½ on June 30, 2006, or July 1, 2006, but it doesn't matter because either way he attains age 70½ in calendar 2006 and his age on his 2006 birthday is 71.

1.4.02 *RBD for IRAs and Roth IRAs*

Roth IRAs have no RBD. The participant is *never* compelled to take distributions from his Roth IRA. Minimum distribution requirements do not apply to a Roth IRA until after the participant's death. See ¶ 5.1.03.

For "traditional" (nonRoth) IRAs, the RBD is April 1 of the calendar year following the year in which the participant reaches age 70½, regardless of whether he is "retired." § 408(a)(6), § 401(a)(9)(C)(i)(I), (ii)(II). There is a different RBD for certain rollover contributions; see ¶ 1.4.09.

1.4.03 Non-5-percent owners: Later of retirement or age 70½

The RBD for a non-5-percent owner (¶ 1.4.04) in a qualified plan, or for any employee in a 403(b) or 457 plan, is generally "April 1 of the calendar year following the *later of* (I) the calendar year in which the employee attains age 70½, or (II) the calendar year in which the employee retires from employment" with the employer maintaining the plan. § 401(a)(9)(C); Reg. § 1.401(a)(9)-2, A-2(a). Emphasis added.

A qualified retirement plan (QRP) may have an *earlier* RBD than is specified in § 401(a)(9)(C); see ¶ 1.4.05. A QRP participant who filed a "TEFRA 242(b) election" may have a *later* RBD than specified in § 401(a)(9)(C); see ¶ 1.4.10.

The ability to postpone the RBD until a post-age 70½ retirement is of no interest to a worker who retires before age 70½; or to the business owner who owns more than 5 percent of his company and thus is not eligible. Typical participants making use of the postponed RBD are executives and professionals who work for large firms, own either no interest or just a small interest (5 percent or less) in the sponsoring employer; and want to keep working past age 70½.

This definition of RBD applies for 1997 and later years. Under the definition that was in effect between 1986 and 1997, postponing the RBD until after a post-age 70½ retirement was allowed *only* for a participant who was born on or before June 30, 1917, and who was not a 5-percent owner (¶ 1.4.04).

1.4.04 Definition of 5-percent owner

Postponement of the RBD until after a post-age 70½ retirement is not available for "an employee who is a 5-percent owner (as defined in section 416) with respect to the plan year ending in the calendar year in which the employee attains age 70½...." § 401(a)(9)(C)(ii)(I); Reg. § 1.401(a)(9)-2, A-2(c). "Once an employee is a 5-percent owner...distributions must continue to such employee even if such employee ceases to own more than 5 percent of the employer in a subsequent year." Notice 97-75, 1997-2 C.B. 337, "Background."

§ 416(i)(1)(B)(i) defines 5-percent owner as someone who owns "*more than* 5 percent of the outstanding stock of the corporation or stock possessing more than 5 percent of the total combined voting power of all stock of the corporation, or (II) if the employer is not a corporation, any person who owns more than 5 percent of the capital or profits interest in the employer" (emphasis added). Note that someone who owns exactly 5 percent is not a 5-percent owner—you must own more than 5 percent to be a 5-percent owner! See ¶ 1.2.06(C) for use of rollovers to stop MRDs in this situation.

In determining ownership percentages under § 416, a modified version of the "constructive ownership" rules of § 318 applies. Under these complicated rules, a participant could be deemed, for purposes of the 5 percent test, to own stock held by various family members, trusts, estates, partnerships, or corporations; and stock options must be taken into account. When advising a participant regarding his eligibility for the postponed RBD, the advisor needs to identify not only ownership interests held by the participant himself but also those held by these related individuals and entities. Explanation of the constructive ownership rules is beyond the scope of this book.

1.4.05 *RBD for QRP; when an MRD is not an MRD*

A QRP is not required to recognize the postponed RBD described at ¶ 1.4.03. A QRP may choose to require *all* employees to commence distributions by April 1 of the calendar year following the year they reach age 70½. Reg. § 1.401(a)(9)-2, A-2(e).

If the plan does require all employees to commence distributions by April 1 of the calendar year following the year they reach age 70½, then things get a little complicated. An employee who has not retired and who is not a 5-percent owner has one RBD for certain purposes, but some of his "required" distributions from the plan are not considered "required" distributions for other purposes. Specifically, for purposes of *determining MRDs from that plan*, and *determining whether the employee died before or after his RBD for that plan*, the employee's RBD is the RBD set by the plan, *not* the RBD described in the statute—regardless of whether he owned 5 percent or less of the sponsoring employer and regardless of whether he had retired. Reg. § 1.401(a)(9)-2, A-6(b).

However, any distributions the employee receives during the period that is after the employee has passed *the plan's* RBD but not the *statutory* RBD are eligible for tax-free rollover. Such distributions are not considered "required distributions" for purposes of the definition of eligible rollover distribution (see ¶ 2.6.04) until after the employee's *statutory* RBD. Somehow the distribution *is* an MRD when the check is cut, but it is *not* an MRD when the check arrives in the employee's mailbox! Notice 97-75, 1997-2 C.B. 337, A-10(c).

1.4.06 *RBD, other grandfather rules, for 403(b) plan*

The RBD for all 403(b) plans is April 1 of the calendar year following the later of the year the participant reaches age 70½ or the year the participant retires. There is no possibility of a different rule for 5-percent owners because all 403(b) plans are maintained by tax-exempt charitable organizations that have no "owners." Reg. § 1.403(b)-3, A-1(c)(1). In contrast to the rule for qualified plans, there is no apparent permission for the plan to establish an RBD earlier than that in the statute (compare ¶ 1.4.05).

A "grandfather rule" applies to certain pre-1987 balances in 403(b) plans if separately identified. See Reg. § 1.403(b)-3, A-2, A-3. The Tax Reform Act of 1986 made the minimum distribution rules applicable, for the first time, to all 403(b) plans, but made this rule prospective only by exempting any pre-1987 403(b) plan balance from the new regime, provided such balance is accounted for separately. The pre-1987 account balance, while not subject to the full panoply of today's minimum distribution rules, is still subject to the more primitive predecessor of today's rules, the **incidental death benefits rule** of Reg. § 1.401-1(b)(1).

Here are the three advantages of qualifying for this grandfather rule: First, the age for starting lifetime required distributions from the pre-1987 balance is actual retirement or, if later, age 75 (not age 70½). See PLR 9345044. Second, required distributions from the grandfathered balance are computed under the **incidental death benefits rule** rather than using the methods described at ¶ 1.3–¶ 1.4, meaning that any mode of distribution to the participant qualifies provided that it is projected to distribute the benefits over the lifetimes of the participant and his spouse, or to distribute at least 50 percent of the benefits during the participant's life. Reg. § 1.403(b)-3, A-3; Rev. Rul. 72-240, 1972-1 C.B. 108; Rev. Rul. 72-241, 1972-1 C.B. 108, ninth paragraph. Third, there were no specific requirements for how rapidly death benefits would have to be distributed if the participant died before commencing distributions.

The significance of this grandfather rule has diminished over the years. The pre-1987 grandfather amount is a frozen, fixed-dollar amount; investment earnings and gains do not increase the grandfathered balance. Reg. § 1.403(b)-3, A-2(a), (c). With the passage of time, additional contributions to the plan and investment growth make the pre-1987 balance an ever-smaller percentage of the overall plan balance, so in most cases it is not a significant planning factor.

To preserve these advantages for the grandfathered balance, the participant should not take any distributions from the 403(b) plan other than MRDs with respect to the post-1986 balance, because any distributions in excess of such MRDs are deemed to come first out of the pre-1987 balance.

If further explanation of the 403(b) grandfather rule is needed, see pages 382–386 of the 1999 edition of this book, or the even fuller explanation at pages 230–238 of the 1996 edition.

1.4.07 *Definition of "retirement"*

For purposes of determining his RBD under a QRP or 403(b) plan, how many hours must the participant work, in what time frame, in order to be considered not "retired?"

The author has found no definition of "retirement" in any IRS publication. Neither the regulations nor Notice 97-75, 1997-2 C.B. 337 (which provides guidance to employers on the tax law changes made by the Small Business Jobs Protection Act of 1996) says anything on this point. Thus it is not clear whether "retirement" means a complete termination of employment, or whether some less drastic reduction of employment would be considered "retirement" for this purpose.

Robin Example: Robin, a non-5-percent owner, age 74, works at Geo Dezik Co. She is a participant in the Geo Dezik Profit Sharing Plan. In 2005, she reduces her hours from full time (40 hours a week) to part time (8 hours a week). The plan provides that an employee is not entitled to withdraw benefits until he "retires." The plan defines retirement for this purpose as a reduction in hours worked to less than

20 hours per week if over age 65. Robin does not want to start taking distributions from the Profit Sharing Plan until she is legally required to. Is she required to start taking distributions on April 1, 2003, because she has met the plan's definition of "retirement"? Or can she wait until she has ceased all employment with this company?

We do know that "retirement" means retirement "from employment with the employer maintaining the plan." Reg. § 1.401(a)(9)-2, A-2(a).

Archibald Example: Archibald, age 73, works at Acme Co. Archibald is not a 5-percent owner of Acme. He is a participant in the Acme Profit Sharing Plan. This plan holds funds contributed to Archibald's account by Acme as well as funds rolled over into this plan from the retirement plan of Archibald's prior employer, Zenith Corp., and funds rolled over from an IRA to which Archibald had contributed $2,000 a year for several years. Even though the funds in Archibald's accounts in the Acme Profit Sharing Plan partly represent funds from a former IRA (which, if they were still held in an IRA, would not be eligible for the postponed RBD), and from the plan of a former employer (from whose employment Archibald has "retired"), Acme is "the employer maintaining the plan" which now holds these funds, and accordingly Archibald is not required to take any distributions from any part of this plan until April 1 following the year in which he retires from Acme.

How this concept applies to some 403(b) plans is not clear. Although some 403(b) plans truly are "plans" maintained by a particular employer, other 403(b) "plans" are merely annuity contracts (or mutual fund custodial accounts) purchased for the employee by the employer, where the employer does not "maintain" the "plan" after the initial funding.

Rolf Example: Rolf, age 75, is a professor who is still working at Y.O.U. He has several 403(b) accounts established for him at Pari Mutual Fund Company by Y.O.U. He also has several 403(b) accounts established for him at the same mutual fund company by his former employer, Eiluv U. Since he no longer works at Eiluv U., it appears he must take distributions from the Eiluv U. 403(b) accounts unless he can roll them over into a "plan" that is "maintained" by his current employer, Y.O.U.

Another mystery: Can a person retire more than once? The statute reads as though there is only one "retirement" per employee. The IRS has issued no guidance on this question.

Carmen Example: Carmen retires from the Royal Cigar Company at age 72 and starts receiving MRDs from the RCC plan. At age 73 she goes back to work for RCC (where she is not and never has been a 5-percent owner). Can her MRDs be suspended until she retires *again*?

1.4.08 *RBD versus first Distribution Year: The limbo period*

The disconnect between the first Distribution Year and the RBD (¶ 1.4.01) creates a "limbo period," beginning January 1 of the first Distribution Year and ending on the RBD. Odd effects occur during this limbo period.

A.   **If the first year's MRD is postponed, two MRDs are required in the second year.** The first odd effect is that if the participant takes advantage of the permitted postponement, and delays his MRD for the first Distribution Year until the following year, he will have two MRDs in the second Distribution Year. The two MRDs in the second year will have different deadlines, be based on different account balances, and use different divisors:

Bernie Example: Bernie turns age 70½ in 2005. 2005 is the first Distribution Year for his IRA. To calculate the 2005 MRD, he uses the 2004 year-end account balance and the Uniform Lifetime Table divisor for the age he attains on his 2005 birthday, which will be 70 if he was born before July 1, or 71 if he was born after June 30. He can take the 2005 MRD at any time from January 1, 2005, through April 1, 2006. Any distribution he takes between January 1, 2005, and April 1, 2006, will count towards that first year's MRD until it has been fully distributed. There will then be *another* MRD for the year 2006, which must be taken between January 1, 2006, and December 31, 2006. The 2006 MRD will be based on the December 31, 2005 account balance and will use the Uniform Lifetime Table factor applicable for the age he attains on his 2006 birthday.

Bernie decides to postpone the 2005 distribution until March 2006. This postponement will mean his MRDs are "bunched up" in

2006 (because he will receive two years' distributions in that one year). It will also mean that his 2006 MRD will be larger than it would be if he took the 2005 distribution in 2005, because the prior year-end account balance used to compute the 2006 MRD will not be reduced by the amount of the 2005 MRD; see ¶ 1.2.05. Bernie doesn't care about these negative aspects of deferring the first year's MRD, because he expects his other income to be much lower in 2006, so deferring the first year's MRD will still lower his overall income taxes.

B.   **No rollovers until first year's MRD has been taken.** See ¶ 2.6.04 regarding attempted rollovers in the first Distribution Year. See ¶ 5.4.03 regarding attempted Roth IRA conversions in the first Distribution Year.

C.   **Death during limbo period is death "before" the RBD, and it "erases" the first year's MRD.**

Otto Example: Otto retired in 2001, and turns age 70½ in 2006. He withdraws nothing from his IRA in 2006 (his first Distribution Year). January 2007 rolls around. Now another MRD (the one for 2007) is triggered, and still Otto has taken nothing out of the IRA, but there is no rush because he has until April 1, 2007. He dies on March 31, 2007. He has died *before* his RBD. The requirement of taking MRDs for 2006 and 2007 is simply erased, because he never reached the RBD. Even if he had taken part or all of his 2006 and 2007 MRDs before his death, his death would still be "before" his RBD for purposes of computing post-death MRDs. Reg. § 1.401(a)(9)-2, A-4, A-6.

1.4.09 *Required distribution date for rollover contributions*

Generally, if a rollover contribution (¶ 2.6) is made into a brand new IRA (an account which contained nothing at the time it received the rollover), there is no distribution required for the year in which the rollover contribution comes into the new account, because the prior year-end account balance was zero. (For an exception to this rule for rollovers that are in transit on the prior-year-end date, see ¶ 1.2.06.) The RBD for the new account will be the later of (1) April 1 of the year after the year the participant reaches age 70½ or (2) December 31 of the year after the year of the rollover. PLRs 2001-23070, 1999-31049.

1.4.10 *Grandfather rule: TEFRA 242(b) elections*

TEFRA (1982) significantly expanded the minimum distribution rules. For years after 1983, § 401(a)(9) would apply to *all* QRPs (previously it had applied only to Keogh plans). Under the pre-TEFRA rules, no distributions were required prior to retirement; TEFRA (and the Tax Reform Act of 1984, "TRA '84," which "cleaned up" the TEFRA changes via many retroactive amendments) added a requirement that 5-percent owners would have to start distributions at age 70½ even if still employed. TEFRA also added requirements for post-death distributions (there had been none previously).

TEFRA contained a grandfather rule, § 242(b)(2), which provided that a plan will not be disqualified "by reason of distributions under a designation (before January 1, 1984) by any employee of a method of distribution...(A) which does not meet the requirements of [§ 401(a)(9)], but (B) which would not have disqualified such [plan] under [§ 401(a)(9)] as in effect before the amendment" made by TEFRA. TRA '84 continued the TEFRA grandfather rule: The TRA '84 changes would not apply to "distributions under a designation (before January 1, 1984) by any employee in accordance with a designation described in section 242(b)(2) of [TEFRA] (as in effect before the amendments made by this Act)." TRA '84, § 521(d)(2)-5. The minimum distribution regulations provide special MRD rules for those with TEFRA 242(b) elections. Reg. § 1.401(a)(9)-8, A-13 A-16.

As a result of the many changes brought by TEFRA, there was a flurry of activity among sophisticated plan participants trying to make a "designation" by December 31, 1983 that would enable them to continue to use the older, more liberal rules. Theoretically, participants with TEFRA 242(b) elections in effect can postpone the start of MRDs past age 70½, until retirement (even if they own more than 5 percent of the employer), and their death benefits are not subject to the "5-year rule" (¶ 1.5.06) or the "at-least-as-rapidly" rule (§ 401(a)(9)(B)(i)). Unfortunately, TEFRA 242(b) elections have not proved as useful as originally expected for several reasons:

1.   The requirements for a valid election, as set forth in Notice 83-23, 1983-2 C.B. 418, 420, are quite restrictive: "The designation must, in and of itself, provide sufficient information to fix the timing, and the formula for the definite determination, of plan payments. The designation must be complete and not allow further

choice." P. 419. This does not mean the designation may not be amendable or revocable. Rather, the designation must be self-executing, requiring no further actions or designations by the participant to determine the size and date of distributions. Some purported TEFRA 242(b) elections do not meet this test.

2.   Rolling over QRP benefits protected by a 242(b) election into an IRA causes loss of the 242(b) protection. However, grandfather protection is not lost if benefits are moved to another QRP without any election on the part of the participant (for example, as a result of a plan merger), if the transferee plan accounts for such benefits separately. Reg. § 1.401(a)(9)-8, A-14, A-15.

3.   TEFRA 242(b) elections generally attempted to defer distributions for as long as possible. This turned out to be counterproductive, because an unrealistically long proposed deferral made it more likely that a participant who had made a 242(b) election would want to make withdrawals sooner than his "designation" indicates. However, "any change in the designation will be considered to be a revocation of the designation." Notice 83-23, p. 420.

4.   If the 242(b) election is revoked, drastic results ensue. In effect the grandfathered status is revoked retroactively, and the participant is required to take make-up distributions—withdraw from the plan all the prior years' distributions he had skipped. Reg. § 1.401(a)(9)-8, A-16. See ¶ 1.9.04 regarding how to compute MRDs for past years.

Thus, a participant relying on a TEFRA 242(b) election lives in a perilous state. The longer he defers his distributions, the larger becomes the make-up distribution that will be required if he ever changes his mind and modifies the designation.

An over-age-70½ participant whose TEFRA 242(b) election called for a lump sum distribution of the benefits at retirement can retire, take the lump sum, roll it over to an IRA, and commence taking MRDs from the IRA in the normal fashion, without being required to take make-up distributions. PLR 2005-10035. If his election had called for instalment or annuity payments rather than a lump sum, taking a lump sum would presumably be considered a modification, but there are no rulings on this point.

1.5 MRDs after the Participant's Death

_____After the participant's death, the minimum distribution rules apply to the beneficiary. The post-death MRD rules are more complicated than the lifetime MRD rules discussed at ¶ 1.3–¶ 1.4.

This ¶ 1.5 applies only to defined contribution (DC) or "individual account" plans. For defined benefit plans or annuity payouts, see ¶ 10.2. Also, if the death benefits are subject to a TEFRA 242(b) election, see ¶ 1.4.10 instead of this section.

Post-death MRDs after 2002 are determined under the final regulations *regardless of when the participant died*. When determining MRDs from the account of a participant who died prior to 2002, "the designated beneficiary must be redetermincd....and the applicable distribution period...must be reconstructed" in accordance with the post-2002 rules described here. Reg. § 1.401(a)(9)-1, A-2(b)(1).

In the Code, "required beginning date" refers only to the starting date for lifetime distributions to the participant. The date by which post-death distributions to the *beneficiary* must begin does not have an official name; compare § 401(a)(9)(A) and (C) with § 401(a)(9)(B). In this book, **Required Commencement Date** is used for the deadline by which a beneficiary must start taking distributions.

1.5.01 *Overview of post-death MRD rules*

The basic concept of the post-death MRD rules is very simple: The participant's retirement benefits can be depleted gradually through annual distributions (beginning the year after the participant's death) over the life expectancy of the participant's "Designated Beneficiary," or by any more rapid means of distribution. This is called the "life expectancy" (or "stretch") payout method, and is generally considered a favorable way to distribute benefits, for reasons explained at ¶ 1.1.03.

This simple concept gets complicated in its application:

First, not every beneficiary is a Designated Beneficiary. Different rules apply to Designated Beneficiaries than apply to other beneficiaries. Only an individual, group of individuals, or qualifying see-through trust can be a Designated Beneficiary. So, after you ascertain who the participant's beneficiary is (¶ 1.7.02), you next must determine whether there is a Designated Beneficiary (¶ 1.7.03). Adding to the fun, not every person or entity who is a beneficiary of the account as of the participant's date of death "counts" in this determination; see ¶ 1.8 for how beneficiaries can be "removed" from the pool through disclaimer or distribution of their benefits after the participant's death.

Second, if there are multiple beneficiaries, then the determination of whether the life expectancy payout method is available to any or all of them, and if so whose life expectancy is the ADP, depends on the IRS's special "separate accounts" rule. See ¶ 1.7.06–¶ 1.7.07.

Third, MRDs are calculated one way if the sole Designated Beneficiary is the participant's surviving spouse (¶ 1.6.06), and an entirely different way if the Designated Beneficiary is someone else (see ¶ 1.5.05). This difference even extends after the beneficiary later dies; see ¶ 1.6.05–¶ 1.6.06 regarding distributions after the death of a surviving spouse-sole beneficiary, ¶ 1.5.14 regarding MRDs after the death of any other beneficiary. The surviving spouse also gets one other special tax deal nobody else gets—the ability to roll over the inherited benefits. See ¶ 3.2.

Fourth, though MRDs normally begin the year *after* the year of the participant's death (or sometimes even later if the surviving spouse is the sole beneficiary), an MRD may also be required for the year of death itself if the participant died after his RBD. See ¶ 1.5.04(F).

Fifth, if the benefits are not left to a Designated Beneficiary, the life-expectancy-of-the-beneficiary payout method is not available, and special "no-designated-beneficiary" (no-DB) rules apply instead…and these rules are different depending on whether the participant died before or after his RBD. See ¶ 1.5.06 for the no-DB rule that applies if the participant died before his RBD, and ¶ 1.5.08 for the no-DB rule that applies if the participant died on or after his RBD.

Sixth, even if the benefits are left to a Designated Beneficiary, the no-DB rule may apply, either as a result of the beneficiary's election or deemed election (in the case of death before the RBD; see ¶ 1.5.07), or because it provides a longer ADP (in the case of death after the RBD; see ¶ 1.5.04).

Seventh, the retirement plan in question is not required to offer the life expectancy form of benefit. See ¶ 1.5.10.

1.5.02 *Information needed to determine post-death MRDs*

Here are the four questions you must answer before you can determine MRDs after the participant's death:

A.   **Did the participant die before, on, or after his RBD?** The calculation of post-death MRDs is somewhat different depending on whether death occurred before (see ¶ 1.5.03) or after (see ¶ 1.5.04) the Required Beginning Date (RBD). This is not always easy to determine, because different types of plans have different RBDs; the participant may have died before his RBD under some of his retirement plans but after the RBD for other plans. If the participant died before April 1 of the year following the year in which he reached (or would have reached) age 70½ then he died before his RBD for all his defined contribution (DC) plans (but see ¶ 10.2.08 for a special rule for defined benefit (DB) plans). If he died later than that, see ¶ 1.4 for how to determine the RBD for each of the decedent's plans. For the most difficult situations, see: ¶ 1.4.05, qualified plan's RBD is earlier than statutory RBD; ¶ 1.4.08, death in the first or second Distribution Year but before the RBD; ¶ 1.4.09, RBD for rollover contributions; and ¶ 1.4.10, TEFRA 242(b) elections. Death *on* the RBD is treated as death *after* the RBD. Reg. § 1.401(a)(9)-2, A-6(a).

B.   **Are there are multiple beneficiaries?** If there are multiple beneficiaries, you need to determine whether the "separate accounts rule" (¶ 1.7.06) applies. If the beneficiaries' interests constitute separate accounts, then the minimum distribution rules apply separately to each such separate account. The distribution options described in ¶ 1.5.03 and ¶ 1.5.04 apply either to the participant's *entire benefit under the plan*, or (if the separate accounts rule applies) to *each separate account*.

C.   **Do the benefits pass to a Designated Beneficiary, and if so who is that Designated Beneficiary?** See ¶ 1.7 for explanation of how to determine who is the participant's "beneficiary" and whether there is a Designated Beneficiary. This Code-defined term does not simply mean any beneficiary who is designated by the participant! Understanding the meaning of Designated

Beneficiary is crucial to both planning for and compliance with the minimum distribution rules. Note that the identity of the beneficiary is not finally fixed, for purposes of these rules, until September 30 of the year following the year of the participant's death; see ¶ 1.8. The rules in ¶ 1.5.03 or ¶ 1.5.04 apply *once the identity of the beneficiary is finalized on September 30 of the year following the year of the participant's death.*

D.   **What distribution options does the plan permit?** The plan may require a faster payout than the minimum distribution rules would require. See ¶ 1.5.10.

1.5.03 *MRDs in case of death BEFORE the RBD*

If the participant died *before his Required Beginning Date* (RBD), here is how to determine the required distributions after his death, depending on who is the beneficiary of the inherited benefits. See ¶ 1.5.02(A) for explanation of the RBD. See ¶ 1.7 to determine who is the beneficiary. Post-death MRDs from a Roth IRA are always determined using rules in this ¶ 1.5.03 (never ¶ 1.5.04); see ¶ 5.1.03.

In *all* cases, see ¶ 1.5.10 for the ability of the plan to require faster distribution of the benefits than the MRD rules would require.

Annual distributions over the life expectancy of a nonspouse beneficiary (paragraph B, D, or E) must begin no later than December 31 of the year after the year of the participant's death. Reg. § 1.401(a)(9)-3, A-3(a). See ¶ 2.6.01, ¶ 2.6.03, regarding whether a nonspouse beneficiary (paragraphs B–E) can transfer inherited benefits to another retirement plan.

A.   **Surviving spouse is sole beneficiary.** The ADP is the surviving spouse's life expectancy, unless the 5-year rule applies. See ¶ 1.5.07 for how to determine whether the 5-year rule applies. See ¶ 1.6.02–¶ 1.6.03, for meaning of "spouse is sole beneficiary." Annual distributions over the spouse's life expectancy must begin no later than December 31 of the year after the year of the participant's death, or, if later, December 31 of the year the participant would have reached age 70½; see ¶ 1.6.04 regarding this special Required Commencement Date for a surviving spouse. See ¶ 1.5.13 and ¶ 1.6.05 for what happens if the spouse, having survived the participant, dies before that Required Commencement Date. See ¶ 1.5.13 and ¶ 1.6.06(E) for what happens if the spouse, having survived the participant and lived beyond the Required Commencement Date, dies before having withdrawn all of the benefits. See ¶ 3.2 for the surviving spouse's ability to roll over the inherited benefits to the spouse's own retirement plan.

B. **Individual beneficiary who is not the surviving spouse.** The ADP is the individual beneficiary's life expectancy, unless the 5-year rule applies. See ¶ 1.5.07 for how to determine whether the 5-year rule applies. See ¶ 1.5.05 for how to calculate annual distributions over the life expectancy of a nonspouse individual beneficiary. See ¶ 1.5.06 for how to calculate distributions under the 5-year rule. See ¶ 1.5.13–¶ 1.5.14, for what happens if the beneficiary, having survived the participant, dies before having withdrawn all of the benefits.

C. **Estate, non-see-through trust, or other nonindividual beneficiary.** If the beneficiary is not an individual or qualifying see-through trust, then the participant has "no Designated Beneficiary," and the no-DB rule applies. The no-DB rule in case of death before the RBD is the 5-year rule. See ¶ 1.5.06 for how to calculate distributions under the 5-year rule. See ¶ 6.1.05 for the ability of an estate or trust to transfer inherited benefits, intact, to the beneficiaries of the estate or trust.

D. **Multiple beneficiaries.** If there are multiple beneficiaries, first determine whether the separate accounts rule applies; see ¶ 1.7.06. If the separate accounts rule does apply determine MRDs for each separate account using the rules in these subparagraphs A–E based on the beneficiary of such separate account. If there are multiple beneficiaries whose interests do not constitute separate accounts, then two special rules apply. First, unless all of the beneficiaries are individuals, the participant is deemed to have "no Designated Beneficiary" and the only available distribution option is the 5-year rule; see ¶ 1.7.05. Second, if all of the beneficiaries are individuals (or qualifying see-through trusts; see ¶ 6.2.03), the ADP is either the life expectancy of the oldest Designated Beneficiary (Reg. § 1.401(a)(9)-5, A-7(a)(1)) or the 5-year rule; see ¶ 1.5.07 to determine which applies. See ¶ 1.5.05 for how to calculate annual distributions over the life expectancy of the oldest individual beneficiary. See ¶ 1.5.06 for how to calculate distributions under the 5-year rule.

E.   **See-through trust.** If the beneficiary is a see-through trust (¶ 6.2.03), then the individual beneficiary(ies) of the trust is (or are) treated (for most but not all purposes) as the participant's Designated Beneficiary(ies). If there are more than one, the "multiple beneficiaries" rules (¶ 1.7.05) apply. If the sole beneficiary of the trust is the participant's surviving spouse, see ¶ 1.6.07. Otherwise, the ADP is the life expectancy of the oldest (or sole) trust beneficiary or the 5-year rule; see ¶ 1.5.07 to determine which applies. See ¶ 1.5.05 for how to calculate annual distributions over the life expectancy of a nonspouse (or the oldest) individual beneficiary. See ¶ 1.5.06 for how to calculate distributions under the 5-year rule. See ¶ 6.1.05 for the ability of an estate or trust to transfer the inherited benefits, intact, to the beneficiaries of the estate or trust.

1.5.04 *MRDs in case of death AFTER the RBD*

If the participant died *on or after his Required Beginning Date* (RBD), here is how to determine required distributions after his death, depending on who is the beneficiary of the inherited benefits. These rules apply if the participant died on or after the RBD, regardless of whether the participant actually took any distributions before he died. Reg. § 1.401(a)(9)-2, A-6(a).

In *all* cases, see ¶ 1.5.10 for the ability of the plan to require faster distribution of the benefits than the MRD rules would require.

Under the final regulations, the life-expectancy-of-the-beneficiary payout method is available to a Designated Beneficiary when the participant died after his RBD, regardless of who (if anyone) was the participant's beneficiary as of the RBD. This is in contrast to prior versions of the regulations, which severely limited post-death payout options once the participant lived past his RBD.

See ¶ 1.5.02(A) and ¶ 1.4 for explanation of the RBD. See ¶ 1.7.02 for how to determine who is the "beneficiary."

Annual MRDs under paragraphs A–E must begin no later than the end of the year after the year of the participant's death. Reg.

§ 1.401(a)(9)-2, A-5. In addition, an MRD for the year of death itself may be required; see "F."

A.   **Surviving spouse is sole beneficiary.** The ADP is the surviving spouse's life expectancy, or what would have been the life expectancy of the deceased participant, whichever is longer. Reg. § 1.401(a)(9)-5, A-5(a)(1). See ¶ 1.6.06 for how to calculate annual distributions over the spouse's life expectancy. See ¶ 1.6.02, ¶ 1.6.03, for meaning of "spouse is sole beneficiary." See ¶ 1.5.08 for how to calculate MRDs using what would have been the participant's life expectancy. See ¶ 1.6.06 for what happens if the spouse, having survived the participant, dies before having withdrawn all of the benefits. The surviving spouse can also roll over the inherited benefits to the spouse's own retirement plan; see ¶ 3.2.

B.   **Individual beneficiary who is not the surviving spouse.** The ADP is the individual beneficiary's life expectancy, or (if greater) the life expectancy of the deceased participant. Reg. § 1.401(a)(9)-5, A-5(a)(1). See ¶ 1.5.05 for how to calculate annual distributions over life expectancy of a nonspouse individual beneficiary. See ¶ 1.5.08 for how to calculate MRDs using what would have been the participant's life expectancy. See ¶ 1.5.13–¶ 1.5.14 for what happens if the beneficiary, having survived the participant, dies before having withdrawn all of the benefits. See ¶ 2.6.03 regarding transfer of an inherited retirement plan by a nonspouse beneficiary.

C.   **Estate, non-see-through trust, or other nonindividual beneficiary.** If the beneficiary is not an individual or qualifying see-through trust, then the participant has "no Designated Beneficiary," and the ADP is what would have been the participant's remaining life expectancy. Reg. § 1.401(a)(9)-5, A-5(a)(2). See ¶ 1.5.08 for how to compute this. See ¶ 6.1.05 for the ability of an estate or trust to transfer inherited benefits, intact, to the beneficiaries of the estate or trust.

D.   **Multiple beneficiaries.** If there are multiple beneficiaries, first determine whether the "separate accounts" rule applies; see ¶ 1.7.06. If the separate accounts rule does apply, then, for years after the year of the participant's death, determine MRDs for each separate account using the rules in these subparagraphs A–E based solely on the beneficiary(ies) of such separate account. If there are multiple beneficiaries whose interests do *not* constitute separate accounts, then two rules apply. First, unless all the beneficiaries are individuals, the participant is deemed to have "no Designated Beneficiary" and the ADP is the participant's remaining life expectancy. Reg. § 1.401(a)(9)-4, A-3 (third sentence), § 1.401(a)(9)-5, A-5(a)(2). See ¶ 1.5.08 for how to compute this. Second, if all of the beneficiaries are individuals (or qualifying see-through trusts; see ¶ 6.2.03), the ADP is either the life expectancy of the oldest Designated Beneficiary (¶ 1.5.05) or (if greater) what would have been the remaining life expectancy of the participant (¶ 1.5.08). Reg. § 1.401(a)(9)-5, A-5(a)(1), A-7(a)(1).

E.　　**See-through trust.** If the beneficiary is a see-through trust (¶ 6.2.03), then the individual beneficiary (or beneficiaries) of the trust is (or are) treated (for most but not all purposes) as the participant's Designated Beneficiary(ies). If the sole beneficiary of the trust is the participant's surviving spouse, see ¶ 1.6.07. Otherwise, the ADP is the life expectancy of the oldest (or sole) trust beneficiary or (if greater) the remaining single life expectancy of the participant. Reg. § 1.401(a)(9)-5, A-5(a)(1), A-7(a)(1). See ¶ 1.5.05 for how to calculate annual distributions over life expectancy of a nonspouse individual beneficiary. See ¶ 1.5.08 for how to compute what would have been the participant's life expectancy. See ¶ 6.1.05 for the ability of an estate or trust to transfer inherited benefits, intact, to the beneficiaries of the estate or trust.

F.　　**MRD for year of death (regardless of who is the beneficiary).** If the participant had not yet taken the entire MRD for the year of death, the balance must be taken by the end of that year by the *beneficiary* of the account. The amount of the MRD for the year of death is whatever the decedent was required to take (because the lifetime distribution rules (¶ 1.3) apply through the year of death); minus what he actually did take in that year prior to his death. Reg. § 1.401(a)(9)-5, A-4(a). The beneficiary owns the account once the participant dies, and the participant's estate has no right to take any distribution from it (unless of course the estate is the beneficiary). See PLR 1999-30052, paragraph [4].

If there are multiple beneficiaries, the MRD rules are satisfied as long as ANY beneficiary takes the balance of the year-of-death distribution; it is not required that each beneficiary take a pro rata share of the year-of-death MRD. This conclusion is based on three IRS pronouncements. First, Reg. § 1.401(a)(9)-5, A-4(a), says that the year-of-death MRD must be distributed to "a" beneficiary, implying "any" beneficiary. Second, the separate accounts rule (¶ 1.7.06) provides that the entire account is treated as a single account for MRD purposes unless and until separate accounts are established, which cannot happen until (at the earliest) the year *after* the year of death. Third, in Rev. Rul. 2005-36 (¶ 4.1.09(A)) the distribution requirement for the year of death was satisfied where the distribution was made to one beneficiary, even though (as a result of that beneficiary's later partial disclaimer) that beneficiary was not the only beneficiary of the account. There is no IRS pronouncement requiring or suggesting that the year-of-death MRD must be paid pro rata to all beneficiaries of the account.

IRS has repealed the "at-least-as-rapidly rule."

The Code provides that, if the participant dies after the RBD, the remaining portion of the participant's benefits "will be distributed at least as rapidly as under the method of distributions being used" to calculate the participant's MRDs during life. § 401(a)(9)(B)(i). This is called the "at-least-as-rapidly rule." The regulations pay lip service to the rule (see Reg. § 1.401(a)(9)-2, A-5), but make no attempt to comply with it. When a participant dies after the RBD the rate at which he was taking (or was required to take) his lifetime MRDs has *no bearing whatever* on the determination of MRDs after his death. The "at-least-as-rapidly rule" has been administratively repealed by the IRS.

1.5.05 *How to compute MRDs: Life expectancy of beneficiary*

Here is how to compute MRDs when the ADP is the life expectancy of an individual (the Designated Beneficiary). Reg. § 1.401(a)(9)-5, A-5(c)(1). This is the so-called "life expectancy payout method" (also called the "life expectancy of the beneficiary" or "stretch" method). This ¶ 1.5.05 does NOT apply if the sole Designated

Beneficiary is the surviving spouse; in that case see ¶ 1.6.06(D) instead.

Annual MRDs over the life expectancy of a Designated Beneficiary are computed similarly to the MRDs to the participant during the participant's life (¶ 1.3.01): Each year's MRD is computed by dividing the prior year-end account balance by a life expectancy factor (called the "Applicable Distribution Period" (ADP) or divisor) obtained from an IRS table, with two significant differences:

A.   **Single Life Table**. The beneficiary's life expectancy is always computed using the Single Life Table (¶ 1.2.03), rather than whichever table was used to compute the participant's MRDs.

B.   **Fixed-term method**. Post-death MRDs are computed using the fixed-term method (¶ 1.2.04(B)), rather than the annual recalculation method used during the participant's life, unless the surviving spouse is the sole beneficiary (see ¶ 1.6.06(D)).

Diane Example: Bonnie died in 2004, after her RBD, leaving her IRA to Diane, who is younger than Bonnie, as Designated Beneficiary. The ADP is Diane's life expectancy as of the first Distribution Year, which is 2005 (the year after Bonnie's death). Diane turns 46 on her birthday in 2005, so her life expectancy (ADP) from the Single Life Table is 37.9. For calculating her MRDs for 2006 (and later years), Diane deducts one from the prior year's ADP, so her 2006 divisor is 36.9, 2007 is 35.9, and so on. She never looks at the table again after the first Distribution Year. See ¶ 1.5.04(F) regarding the 2004 MRD.

A distribution must be taken every year, until the account has been entirely distributed. The "fundamental laws of MRDs" (¶ 1.2.01) continue to apply to the beneficiary just as they applied to the participant during the participant's life.

Calculating MRDs by dividing an annually-revalued account balance by the beneficiary's life expectancy tends to produce gradually increasing payments over the years, so long as the plan has a positive investment return. As long as the beneficiary's remaining life expectancy is greater than [100 ÷ the plan's annual growth rate], the plan balance will be growing faster than the beneficiary is withdrawing it. For example, if the plan is growing at eight percent per year, and the beneficiary's life expectancy is 20 years, the first year's MRD (1/20, or 5%), is less than the plan's earnings for the year (1/12.5, or 8%).

Eventually the beneficiary's life expectancy is reduced to the point that he is withdrawing more than the year's investment return. If the plan is growing at 8 percent per year, the crossover point would be reached 12.5 years before the end of the payout period. Even after this crossover point, the MRDs tend to keep getting larger; though the plan balance is now shrinking, the fraction applied to it grows larger.

When the fixed-term method applies, the distribution period runs out eventually. Diane's final MRD will occur in the 38th year after Bonnie's death and will wipe out the remaining balance of the account. Thus, even though Diane may well live more than 37.9 years after Bonnie's demise, her inherited IRA will run out of money no later than 2042. If Diane dies before her ADP runs out, see ¶ 1.5.13, ¶ 1.5.14.

Note: The discussion above assumes a fixed, unwavering, investment return, which is impossible in real life. See Appendix C for software products available to help make financial projections.

1.5.06 *No-DB rule, death before RBD: The 5-year rule*

The no-DB rule if the participant dies before his RBD is the "5-year rule." § 401(a)(9)(B)(ii), Reg. § 1.401(a)(9)-3, A-4. Under this method of distribution, all benefits must be distributed no later than December 31 of the year that contains the fifth anniversary of the participant's date of death. Reg. § 1.401(a)(9)-3, A-2.

The 5-year rule operates differently from the rest of the minimum distribution rules. Under the 5-year rule, annual distributions are not required. The only requirement is that the entire plan balance must be distributed by December 31 of the year that contains the fifth anniversary of the participant's death. Reg. § 1.401(a)(9)-3, § 54.4974-2, A-3(c). Thus, a beneficiary taking distributions under this rule could spread them over all the years in the period (which could be up to six *taxable* years), or could wait until the end of the period and take out all the money on that date, or anything in between.

The 5-year rule ceases to have any application once the participant reaches his RBD. The 5-year rule is never available as an option in case of death on or after the RBD. § 401(a)(9)(B)(i). (Since Roth IRAs have no RBD, however, the 5-year rule may apply to a Roth IRA even after the participant has passed his RBD on all his other retirement plans; ¶ 5.1.03.)

1.5.07 *Life expectancy or 5-year rule: Which applies?*

Under the Code, it appears that the 5-year rule applies *only* if there is no Designated Beneficiary, and that the life expectancy method automatically applies if there is a Designated Beneficiary. § 401(a)(9)(B)(iii), (iv). The regulations use a different approach.

Under the regulations, the plan can permit the Designated Beneficiary of a participant who died before his RBD to choose between the 5-year rule and the life expectancy payout method. Reg § 1.401(a)(9)-3, A-1. This is the ONLY minimum distribution rule that bases MRDs on an election by the distributee; in all other situations, the computation of the MRD is based on the facts on the ground, not on some choice or election by the participant or beneficiary.

Here are the steps required to determine which method (5-year rule or life expectancy of the Designated Beneficiary) applies to benefits of a pre-RBD decedent:

1.   If the participant died before his RBD with no Designated Beneficiary, you've finished the process: The 5-year rule is the only distribution method available. § 401(a)(9)(B)(ii). Even in that situation, the plan may require a faster payout; see ¶ 1.5.10. If the participant's benefits are left to a Designated Beneficiary, proceed to Step 2.

2.   The retirement plan may provide that one or the other method *must* be used in some or all situations, in which case the plan provision controls. Reg. § 1.401(a)(9)-3, A-4(b). For example, a plan could provide that the 5-year rule applies even if the participant had a Designated Beneficiary.

3.   A retirement plan may (but is not required to) allow its participants and/or their beneficiaries to elect which method will apply. Reg. § 1.401(a)(9)-3, A-4(c), provides that the deadline for making this election is "the earlier of the end of the calendar year in which distribution would be required to commence in order to satisfy the requirements for the life expectancy rule in section 401(a)(9)(B)(iii) and (iv)...or the end of the calendar year which contains the fifth anniversary of the date of death of the employee." This rule produces a different deadline depending on whether 401(a)(9)(B)(iii) or

(iv) applies, i.e., whether or not the surviving spouse is the sole beneficiary:

(a)   If the participant's surviving spouse is the sole beneficiary (¶ 1.6.02), then the deadline is the *earlier* of the end of the year in which the first distribution would be required to be made to her under the life expectancy payout method (¶ 1.6.04) or the end of the year containing the fifth anniversary of the participant's death. This creates a trap for surviving spouses of young decedents, if the plan allows an election but provides the 5-year rule as the default election (see "B," below). For example, if the decedent dies in the year he would have turned age 40, in Year 1, the election period expires in Year 6 (the year that contains the fifth anniversary of the date of death), when the decedent would have reached age 45. Under the life expectancy payout method, the surviving spouse would not have to take any MRDs until the year the decedent would have reached age 70½ (Year 30 or 31; ¶ 1.6.04), but if she is defaulted into the 5-year rule in Year 6 under a QRP, she will receive a nonrollable distribution of the entire balance in Year 6. See ¶ 3.2.06(C) for the effects of this "trap" on the spousal rollover.

(b)   In all other cases, by the end of the year after the year of the participant's death.

If the plan permits participants and/or beneficiaries to choose between the 5-year rule and the life expectancy payout, then the following additional rules apply:

A.   The election becomes irrevocable by the deadline for making the election, and is applicable for all later years.

B.   The plan can provide a default rule, under which the life expectancy method or the 5-year rule will automatically apply if the Designated Beneficiary fails to elect one method or the other by the applicable deadline.

C.   If the plan does not provide a default rule, the default rule is the life expectancy of the Designated Beneficiary. Reg. § 1.401(a)(9)-3, A-4(c).

Gary Example: Gary died in Year 1, before his RBD, leaving his 401(k) plan and his IRA to his daughter Betty as beneficiary. Betty does not find out about either plan until Year 3, too late to take an MRD for Year 2.

The 401(k) plan permits the beneficiary of a participant who dies before his RBD to elect either the life expectancy payout method or the 5-year rule. The plan further provides that if the beneficiary fails to notify the plan of his/her election, and fails to take the first year's entire MRD (computed under the life expectancy method) by the end of the year after the year of the participant's death, the beneficiary is deemed to have elected the 5-year rule. Under the terms of this plan, Betty is deemed to have elected the 5-year rule, and this election is irrevocable and controlling for MRD purposes. She must withdraw the entire plan balance on or before December 31, Year 6.

Gary's IRA also permits the beneficiary of a participant who dies before his RBD to elect either the life expectancy payout method or the 5-year rule. The IRA agreement provides that, if the beneficiary fails to notify the plan of his/her election by the end of the year after the year of the participant's death, the beneficiary is deemed to have elected the life expectancy payout. Since Betty did not notify the IRA provider to the contrary, she is deemed to have elected the life expectancy method. This election is controlling for MRD purposes. However, she has already missed one year's MRD. She will owe a penalty for that missed distribution unless she can get the IRS to waive it (see ¶ 1.9.02(C)) or unless she withdraws the entire IRA balance by December 31, Year 6 (see ¶ 1.5.11(C)).

1.5.08 *No-DB rule, death after RBD: Participant's life expectancy*

The no-DB rule if the participant dies on or after his RBD is the participant's single life expectancy. This is the only payout option available if the participant dies after his RBD with no Designated Beneficiary. Reg. § 1.401(a)(9)-5, A-5(a)(2). (Of course, as always, the plan may require an even faster payout; see ¶ 1.5.10.)

If the benefits are left to a Designated Beneficiary, then the ADP in case of the participant's death on or after the RBD is the longer of the participant's life expectancy or the beneficiary's life expectancy. Reg. § 1.401(a)(9)-5, A-5(a)(1). Note that, in contrast to the situation of death before the RBD, there is no election or choice involved in this situation; the MRDs are calculated based on the beneficiary's life expectancy or the participant's life expectancy, whichever is longer. Compare ¶ 1.5.07.

To calculate the participant's remaining life expectancy, use the IRS's Single Life Table (¶ 1.2.03) and find the divisor or "distribution period" based on the age the participant had attained (or would have attained had he lived long enough) on his birthday in the year of his death. The life expectancy for the year of the participant's death, *reduced by one year*, is the divisor for the first Distribution Year (the year *after* the year of the participant's death). The divisor is reduced by one each year thereafter (fixed-term method; ¶ 1.2.04(B)). Reg. § 1.401(a)(9)-5, A-5(a)(2), (c)(3).

Cookie Example: Cookie died in July, 2005, at age 73, leaving her IRA to her estate. She had already taken her MRD for 2005. The estate's ADP is computed as follows. Cookie was born in November, 1931, so she would have turned age 74 on her 2005 birthday had she lived. The life expectancy factor for age 74 from the Single Life Table is 14.1. Therefore, the estate's divisor for 2006 is 13.1 (14.1 minus one). The first MRD to the estate is the account balance as of December 31, 2005, divided by 13.1. In 2007, the MRD will be the 12/31/06 account balance divided by 12.1, etc.

Here are some points to note about the calculation of MRDs using what would have been the remaining single life expectancy of the deceased participant as the ADP:

A.　**Longest possible payout period is 15 years.** The largest divisor that could apply under this rule is 15.3. If the participant turned 70 in the year he reached age 70½, then died in the following year (but after his RBD), his age on his year-of-death birthday would be 71, for which the life expectancy is 16.3 years, meaning the "divisor" for the first Distribution Year (the year after the year of the participant's death) would be 15.3.

B.　**Requires immediate distribution in case of death after age 104.** If the participant dies later than the year he turns 104, the beneficiary using this no-DB rule will have to take out the entire balance in the year after the participant's death, because after age 103 the single life expectancy declines to less than two, meaning the divisor for the year after the year of the participant's death in the age-104-year would be less than one.

C.   **Cannot use this rule for Roth IRAs or pre-RBD deaths.** The participant's life expectancy is never available as an optional ADP in cases of death before the RBD (and never applies to Roth IRAs, as to which death is always "before the RBD").

D.   **Confusion between Single Life and Uniform Lifetime Tables.** When post-death distributions are computed based on the participant's remaining life expectancy, there is a tendency to get confused and use the Uniform Lifetime Table that the participant was using during his life. The Uniform Lifetime Table applies during the participant's life, and also applies for the year of his death (¶ 1.5.04(F)), but has *no possible application* after that point in computing distributions to a beneficiary. The Single Life Table (which requires much larger MRDs than the Uniform Lifetime Table would require) is the ONLY table used to compute MRDs to a Designated Beneficiary from inherited plans beginning with the year after the year of the participant's death, regardless of whether the ADP is the beneficiary's life expectancy or the participant's.

1.5.09 *Multiple beneficiaries: Must the MRD be prorated?*

This ¶ 1.5.09 discusses whether, beginning with the year after the year of death, MRDs from an account payable to multiple beneficiaries must be prorated when the separate accounts rule (¶ 1.7.06) does not apply. For the same question with regard to the MRD *for the year of death itself*, see ¶ 1.5.04(F) instead of this section.

As explained at ¶ 1.7.05, when there are multiple individual beneficiaries, and separate accounts treatment is not available, the ADP will be the oldest beneficiary's life expectancy (or in some cases the no-DB period, if longer). This is true regardless of whether the surviving spouse is one of the beneficiaries or is the oldest Designated Beneficiary. (However, the spouse may still be able to take her portion of the benefits and roll it over to her own retirement plan to achieve more deferral; see ¶ 3.2.)

When the interests of multiple beneficiaries do not meet the requirements for "separate accounts," then it is unclear whether the distribution requirement is imposed on the collective account (so that the requirement is satisfied as long as the right amount is distributed to any one or more of the account beneficiaries); or whether, alternatively, each beneficiary still has the personal obligation to take his/her pro rata share of the total MRD.

Under § 401(a)(9), the portion of the account payable to a Designated Beneficiary must be distributed over the life expectancy of that beneficiary; this suggests that each beneficiary has a personal obligation to take an annual distribution from his share. However, arguably the IRS has "overruled" this Code provision in its separate account regulations, by providing that: "Except as otherwise provided...[under Reg. § 1.401(a)(9)-8, A-2(a)(2), the separate accounts rule discussed at ¶ 1.7.06], if an employee's benefit under a defined contribution plan is divided into separate accounts under the plan, the separate accounts *will be aggregated* for purposes of satisfying the rules in section 401(a)(9). Thus, except as otherwise provided in this A-2, all separate accounts...*will be aggregated* for purposes of section 401(a)(9)." Reg. § 1.401(a)(9)-8, A-2(a)(1). Emphasis added. If the plan is treated as a single account, then a distribution to any of the beneficiaries would satisfy the distribution requirement. See ¶ 6.3.02 for a planning use of this concept.

1.5.10 *Plan can require even faster payout than MRD rules*

A retirement plan is not required to offer all the payout options that the law allows. Reg. § 1.401(a)(9)-3, A-4(b). While most IRAs permit the life expectancy payout, the situation is just the opposite with qualified plans. Most qualified retirement plans offer death benefits only in the form of lump sum distributions (or in some cases annuities), and do not offer the life expectancy payout method. A plan is not even required, when the 5-year rule applies, to allow the beneficiary to spread out distributions over the five years. Here are suggestions for dealing with such a "lump-sum-only" plan:

A participant in a plan that does not allow beneficiaries to use the life expectancy payout should consider: rolling over the benefits to an IRA for better distribution options, if he is allowed to take the benefits out (¶ 2.6); leaving the benefits to his spouse, who can continue the tax deferral by rolling over the benefits (¶ 3.2); or leaving the benefits to a charitable remainder trust (¶ 7.5.06(C)).

If the participant has already died, and the benefits are left to a Designated Beneficiary, see ¶ 2.6.03 regarding the ability of the beneficiary to transfer the distribution by direct rollover to an inherited IRA after 2006. Distribution of a nontransferable annuity contract is another way to salvage a deferred payout to the beneficiaries while satisfying the plan's desire to get rid of the money. The contract must call for distributions that comply with the minimum distribution rules based on the individual's life expectancy. See ¶ 10.2.09, ¶ 10.2.10, ¶ 2.1.06(G), ¶ 1.2.02(A), and PLRs 2005-48027 and 2005-48028.

1.5.11 *Switching between 5-year rule and life expectancy method*

A beneficiary who has elected or been defaulted into the 5-year rule or the life expectancy method generally cannot later switch to the other method. The only exceptions to this rule are as follows:

A.   If permitted by the plan, any beneficiary can change his or her election prior to the deadline for making the election (¶ 1.5.07, #3). Reg. § 1.401(a)(9)-3, A-4(c), third sentence.

B.   If a beneficiary is using the life expectancy method, then, unless the plan prohibits withdrawing more than the MRD (which would be rare), the beneficiary can take out the entire remaining balance any time, including by the end of the 5-year period if all that is desired is a faster distribution. This has no effect on the penalties unless "C" applies.

C.   If there is *only one* Designated Beneficiary, and he/she withdraws all of the benefits by the end of the 5-year rule period (¶ 1.5.06), the penalty for any missed MRDs in earlier years is automatically waived, so to that limited extent a beneficiary can make a penalty-free switch from the life expectancy method to the 5-year rule even after the initial deadline. Reg. § 54.4974-2, A-7(b). It is not clear why the IRS limits this reasonable provision to the situation in which there is only one individual beneficiary.

1.5.12 *How MRD aggregation applies to inherited IRAs*

Reg. § 1.401(a)(9)-8, A-1, allows a beneficiary who has inherited multiple IRAs from one decedent to aggregate such IRAs with each other (but not with his own IRAs, and not with IRAs inherited from any other decedent, and not with any other type of plan) for the purpose of determining and taking MRDs from such inherited IRAs. Reg. § 1.403(b)-3, A-4, provides similarly for multiple 403(b) plans inherited from the same decedent. See ¶ 1.3.04 for application of these regulations to lifetime MRDs.

Mendel Example: Mendel dies, leaving two 403(b) plans and three IRAs to his daughter Chaya Sora as beneficiary. Assume the MRD rules require that all these retirement plans be distributed to Chaya Sora in annual instalments over her life expectancy. Chaya Sora can treat the two inherited 403(b) plans as one plan for this purpose, so she can take the MRDs for both 403(b) plans from either one or both of the 403(b) plans. Similarly, she take the MRDs for all three inherited IRAs from any one or more of them. However, she cannot aggregate any of these inherited plans with her own 403(b) plans or IRAs for purposes of fulfilling any MRD requirement.

The regulations do not allow multiple IRAs (or 403(b) plans) inherited by *different beneficiaries* from a single participant to be "pooled" so that MRDs paid to *one* beneficiary can fulfill the distribution requirement applicable to *another* beneficiary.

Jeffrey Example: Jeffrey dies, leaving two IRAs. One is payable to a QTIP marital trust (¶ 3.3.02), and one is payable to a credit shelter trust. The IRS's minimum distribution "trust rules" (¶ 6.2) are complied with, so the beneficiaries of the respective trusts are treated as Jeffrey's Designated Beneficiaries, and the life expectancy of the oldest beneficiary of each trust is used to measure the post-death MRDs to that trust. Assume the credit shelter trust permits accumulation of income. To maximize income tax deferral and minimize estate taxes, the family would like to compute one single MRD for both trusts, then take that MRD entirely from the IRA payable to the marital trust. This way, the credit shelter trust would get the maximum available income tax deferral and what income taxes had to be paid would be paid by the marital trust, where at least they could reduce the surviving spouse's future taxable estate. The regulation does NOT allow this maneuver; but see ¶ 6.3.02 for how to possibly achieve the same result by leaving a single IRA to a trust that divides, after the participant's death, into multiple subtrusts.

1.5.13 *Who gets the benefits when the beneficiary dies*

When the participant dies, the beneficiary becomes entitled to the benefits. ¶ 1.7.02. This ¶ 1.5.13 explains who is entitled to receive the inherited benefits if the beneficiary, having survived the participant, and thus become entitled to the benefits, later dies without having withdrawn all of the benefits from the plan.

The person or entity entitled to the benefits after the death of the original beneficiary is called the **successor beneficiary**. Reg. § 1.401(a)(9)-4, A-4(c), § 1.401(a)(9)-5, A-7(c). Who the successor beneficiary is depends on the terms of the plan or IRA agreement. The IRS doesn't really care who the account passes to at that point, since that has no effect on the ADP (see ¶ 1.5.14).

A.   **Beneficiary names successor beneficiary.** Enlightened plans and IRA providers allow the original beneficiary to name his own successor beneficiary. If the original beneficiary has named a successor beneficiary, the successor beneficiary steps into the shoes of the original beneficiary as owner of the account. See ¶ 4.2.08(A) regarding how designating a successor beneficiary affects the original beneficiary's ability to disclaim.

B.   **Beneficiary's estate**. Some plans and IRAs require the benefits to be paid to the original beneficiary's estate in this case. This is also likely to be where the benefits go if the original beneficiary dies without having named a successor beneficiary. In either case, the estate of the original beneficiary steps into the shoes of the original beneficiary as owner of the account. See ¶ 6.1.05 for ability to transfer the account out of the estate.

C.   **Contingent beneficiary named by original owner.** Some practitioners assume that, if the original beneficiary dies after the participant, the account passes to the contingent beneficiary named by the participant. This would typically NOT be true. Usually, the participant's beneficiary designation form provides that the contingent beneficiary will receive the benefits only if the primary beneficiary *predeceases* the participant (or disclaims the benefits). Once the primary beneficiary survives the participant, the primary beneficiary (unless he disclaims the benefits; see Chapter 4) becomes the absolute owner of the account and the contingent beneficiary's interest is completely eliminated. Of course, the plan documents (including the participant's beneficiary designation) could provide otherwise, but typically they don't.

D.   **Participant names successor beneficiary.** Some participants would like to include provisions dictating what happens to the benefits remaining in the account if the original beneficiary dies after the participant but before withdrawing all the benefits. There is nothing illegal about doing this, but it does raise property law and estate tax issues beyond the scope of this discussion. Most IRA providers do not allow this approach, unless the account is an individual retirement trust (IRT; ¶ 6.1.06). See ¶ 3.3.12 for marital deduction effects.

1.5.14 *What is the ADP after the beneficiary's death?*

¶ 1.5.13 explained how to determine who is the successor beneficiary. This ¶ 1.5.14 explains the ADP that applies to the successor beneficiary.

When the ADP is based on the life expectancy of the Designated Beneficiary (see ¶ 1.5.03, ¶ 1.5.04), the subsequent death of the Designated Beneficiary prior to the end of the ADP generally has no effect on MRDs. The ADP is established irrevocably once the Designated Beneficiary is determined (¶ 1.7, ¶ 1.8). Any subsequent beneficiary is merely a "successor" to the original beneficiary's interest and is ignored in determining the ADP. Distributions must continue to be made over the remaining life expectancy of the now-deceased Designated Beneficiary (or at any faster rate required by the plan or desired by the successor beneficiary). Reg. § 1.401(a)(9)-5, A-7(c)(2).

Hugh Example: Hugh, as beneficiary of his mother's IRA, is taking MRDs in annual instalments over his 34-year life expectancy. He dies 10 years into his 34-year ADP. At Hugh's death, ownership of the IRA passes to Regis, a successor beneficiary named by Hugh. MRDs to

Regis continue to be calculated based on Hugh's life expectancy. Regis uses what's left of Hugh's 34-year ADP established at the time of Hugh's mother's death.

This rule holds true even if the Designated Beneficiary, having survived the participant, dies before the Beneficiary Finalization Date; see ¶ 1.8.03. However, there are two situations in which the above rule may not apply. First, if the participant's sole Designated Beneficiary was the participant's surviving spouse, see ¶ 1.6.05–¶ 1.6.06 instead of this section. Second, if the plan documents (or the participant's beneficiary designation form) required the original beneficiary to survive by a certain period of time in order to be entitled to the benefits, and the named beneficiary survived the participant but failed to meet that condition, see ¶ 1.7.02.

1.6 Special Rules for the Surviving Spouse

The Code provides special rules that apply when the beneficiary is the participant's spouse. These rules are intended to provide more favorable treatment when the spouse is the beneficiary, though the effect is not always favorable (see ¶ 1.6.05). For most of the "special deals" the spouse must be the sole beneficiary. In some cases, a trust for the spouse's benefit can qualify for the same treatment available to the spouse individually; see ¶ 1.6.07.

"Spouse" vs. "Surviving Spouse"

The regulations often refer to the spouse as the participant's "surviving spouse" even while they are both alive. Of course, while the participant is alive his spouse is not yet (and may never become) the "surviving" spouse. In this book, as in the regulations, "spouse" and "surviving spouse" are used interchangeably.

1.6.01 Overview of the special spousal rules

There are four special provisions that may apply when the participant's spouse is named as beneficiary:

A.   **Lifetime distributions: Much-younger-spouse method.** If the participant's sole beneficiary is his more-than-10-years-younger spouse, the participant's lifetime MRDs are computed using the Joint and Last Survivor Table rather than the Uniform Lifetime Table. See ¶ 1.3.03.

B. **Postponed Required Commencement Date.** If the participant dies before his RBD leaving benefits to the surviving spouse as sole beneficiary, see ¶ 1.6.04 regarding a possible later Required Commencement Date for MRDs to the spouse, and ¶ 1.6.05 for related rules if the spouse dies after the participant but prior to her Required Commencement Date.

C. **Spouse's life expectancy recalculated.** When the surviving spouse is the sole beneficiary, and withdraws benefits using her life expectancy as the Applicable Distribution Period (ADP), her life expectancy is recalculated annually. See ¶ 1.6.06(D).

D. **Spouse can roll over inherited benefits.** The participant's surviving spouse can roll over to another retirement plan, tax-free, benefits she inherits from the participant. The spouse does NOT have to be the sole beneficiary to have this right (which, unlike A–C, is not a "minimum distribution rule"). A spouse who is the participant's sole beneficiary also has the right to treat an IRA inherited from the deceased spouse as her own IRA. See ¶ 3.2 regarding the spousal rollover and election.

1.6.02 Definition of "sole beneficiary"

For purposes of the special minimum distribution rules applicable to a spouse-beneficiary (though not for purposes of the spousal rollover), the participant's surviving spouse must be the "sole" beneficiary. The spouse is the sole beneficiary if she, alone, will inherit all of the benefits if she survives the participant; in other words if she is the sole *primary* beneficiary. The fact that other beneficiaries are named as *contingent* beneficiaries (who will inherit if the spouse does not survive the participant, or does not survive him for some specified period of time) does not impair her status as "sole" beneficiary.

Bud Example: The beneficiary designation form for Bud's IRA provides: "I name my spouse, Louise, as my sole primary beneficiary, to receive 100 percent of all benefits payable under this Plan on account of my death if she survives me. If she does not survive me, the benefits shall instead be paid to my sister Gladys." The spouse, Louise, is Bud's sole beneficiary so long as both spouses are alive. She is Bud's sole beneficiary at his death if she survives him and does not disclaim the benefits. The fact that Gladys is named as a contingent beneficiary does not impair Louise's status as sole beneficiary.

Reminder: If the retirement benefit in question is divided into "separate accounts" payable to different beneficiaries, then the test of whether the spouse is the "sole beneficiary" (for purposes of the post-death MRD rules at ¶ 1.5.03–¶ 1.5.04) is applied only to the separate account of which the spouse is the beneficiary. Reg. § 1.401(a)(9)-8, A-2. See PLR 2001-21073 and ¶ 1.7.05–¶ 1.7.07.

1.6.03 *When status as sole beneficiary is determined*

The applicable time for determining whether the participant's spouse is the sole beneficiary differs depending on which tax provision is being considered. For purposes of computing *MRDs during the participant's life*, see ¶ 1.3.03.

For purposes of the *post-death minimum distribution rules* (¶ 1.6.04–¶ 1.6.06), to be considered sole beneficiary, the spouse must be "a" beneficiary on the date of death (¶ 1.7.02) and sole beneficiary on September 30 of the year after the year in which the participant died (see ¶ 1.8) of the entire account (or of a "separate account" within the participant's account, if the separate account is established no later than December 31 of the year after the year of the participant's death; Reg. § 1.401(a)(9)-8, A-2(a)(2), ¶ 1.7.06). Thus, in some cases, if the surviving spouse is just one of several beneficiaries on the date of death, and therefore is not the "sole" beneficiary as of that date, it will be possible to "remove" the other beneficiaries (by means of disclaimer or distribution or establishing separate accounts) so that the spouse can become the sole beneficiary by the September 30th deadline. ¶ 1.8.01.

In the case of the spouse's right to elect to treat the deceased spouse's IRA as the spouse's own IRA, she can make this election at any time after the participant's death provided that she is the sole beneficiary as of the Beneficiary Finalization Date. See Reg. § 1.408-8, A-5(a).

1.6.04 *Required Commencement Date: Distributions to spouse*

If the participant dies on or after his RBD (¶ 1.5.02(A)), the Required Commencement Date for distributions to the surviving spouse-beneficiary is the same as the Required Commencement Date for distributions to any other beneficiary: December 31 of the year after the year of the participant's death. Reg. § 1.401(a)(9)-2, A-5. And, as is true for other beneficiaries, the spouse as beneficiary must also withdraw, by the end of the year of the participant's death, any part of the year-of-death MRD not distributed during the participant's life. ¶ 1.5.04(F).

If the participant dies prior to his RBD, and the spouse is the *sole* Designated Beneficiary, annual distributions to the spouse over her life expectancy do not have to begin until the later of: the year following the year in which the participant died, or the year in which the participant would have reached age 70½. § 401(a)(9)(B)(iv)(I); Reg. § 1.401(a)(9)-3, A-3(b). *(However, the spouse may have to make an irrevocable election much earlier than that deadline to preserve her rights; see ¶ 1.5.07, #3(a).)*

This special rule for a spouse who is sole beneficiary applies whenever the participant dies before his RBD; however, it does not actually provide a later-than-normal Required Commencement Date for the spouse unless the participant dies before the year in which he would have reached age 69½. If he dies in the age-69½ year or later, the spouse's Required Commencement Date is the same as the Required Commencement Date of any other beneficiary, i.e., the end of the year after the year of the participant's death. ¶ 1.5.03, ¶ 1.5.04.

1.6.05 *Spouse treated as "participant" if both die young*

If the participant died before his RBD, and his spouse survives him, and the surviving spouse is the sole Designated Beneficiary, § 401(a)(9)(B)(iv)(II) provides an additional rule for what happens on the spouse's later death: If the spouse dies before the date distributions to her are required to commence (see ¶ 1.6.04), then MRDs for years after the year of the spouse's death will not be based on the spouse's remaining life expectancy (even if her life expectancy was the ADP that would have applied for MRDs to her had she lived). Rather, a new distribution period starts: Benefits must be distributed either by the end of the year that contains the fifth anniversary of *the spouse's* death or (if the benefits are payable to a Designated Beneficiary *of the surviving spouse*) in annual instalments over the life expectancy of the spouse's Designated Beneficiary, commencing no later than December 31 of the year following the year of the spouse's death. Reg. § 1.401(a)(9)-3, A-5, A-6, § 1.401(a)(9)-4, A-4(b). As the Code puts it, in these unique circumstances only, the rules are applied "as if the surviving spouse were the employee" for purposes of determining MRDs after her death.

The beneficiary to whom the benefits are paid at the spouse's death could be a successor beneficiary named by the surviving spouse or by the plan; see ¶ 1.5.13, ¶ 1.7.02. The identity and status of the spouse's beneficiary will be determined as of the date of the spouse's death, and finalized on September 30 of the year after the year of the spouse's death (see ¶ 1.8).

Unfortunately, if the surviving spouse dies before designating a successor beneficiary for her interest (see Reg. § 1.401(a)(9)-4, A-2), the benefits (under most plans' and IRAs' default provisions) will pass to the spouse's estate—meaning that, upon the spouse's death during the time this rule applies, the benefits will not pass to a Designated Beneficiary and the 5-year rule will apply. ¶ 1.5.03(C).

Alphonse Example: Alphonse died at age 65, leaving his IRA to his wife Heloise. Heloise died after Alphonse, but before the end of the year in which Alphonse would have reached age 70½, and before she had either rolled the funds over to her own retirement plan (¶ 3.2), elected to treat the IRA as her own (¶ 3.2.04), or named a successor beneficiary for her interest in Alphonse's benefits (¶ 1.5.13(A)). Under the terms of Alphonse's IRA, if a beneficiary has inherited the account, but then dies without having named a successor beneficiary, the account becomes payable to the beneficiary's estate. Under the special rule of § 401(a)(9)(B)(iv)(II), the minimum distribution rules apply as if Heloise were the participant and died before the RBD. Thus, the "new beneficiary" of the account is Heloise's estate and the 5-year rule applies because Heloise did not have a Designated Beneficiary.

1.6.06 *How to determine the spouse's life expectancy*

This is one of the more confusing aspects of the minimum distribution rules. There are several different ways to compute MRDs for benefits left to (or in trust for) a surviving spouse, though there is only one correct method for each particular situation.

A.   **If the spouse rolls over the benefits to her own plan.** Unlike other beneficiaries, the surviving spouse has the option to roll over, tax-free, to her own IRA or other retirement plan, any benefits left to her by her deceased spouse. ¶ 3.2. Once she has rolled over benefits to her own plan, MRDs to her from the rollover plan are calculated using the Uniform Lifetime Table. Reg. § 1.408-8, A-7. The benefits are now in the spouse's own retirement plan, and are no longer in an "inherited plan." Accordingly, she takes MRDs as "participant" (¶ 1.3) rather than as "beneficiary" (¶ 1.5) following the rollover.

B.   **If the spouse elects to treat an inherited IRA as the spouse's own IRA.** Unlike other IRA beneficiaries, the surviving spouse has the option to elect to treat an IRA that she (as sole beneficiary) inherits from the deceased spouse as her own IRA. See ¶ 3.2.04. Once she has made this election, MRDs to her from the elected IRA are calculated using the Uniform Lifetime Table; the IRA is now considered the spouse's own IRA, so she takes MRDs as "participant" (¶ 1.3) rather than as "beneficiary" (¶ 1.5). The exception to this rule is that the MRD *for the year of the participant's death* is still based on the distribution rules applicable to the decedent. Reg. § 1.408-8, A-5(a); ¶ 1.5.04(F). If the surviving spouse makes the election in the same year as the participant died, MRDs will be calculated based on her as the participant beginning the year *after* the year of death. If she makes the election in any later year, her election is retroactive to the beginning of the year the election occurs, meaning that MRDs will be calculated based on her as the participant beginning with the year of the election. Reg. § 1.408-8, A-5(a), fifth and sixth sentences. The "account balance" used for the year of the election is the prior year-end account balance even though the account was not "hers" in such prior year.

C.   **If the spouse is the oldest of multiple Designated Beneficiaries.** If benefits are left to a see-through trust (¶ 6.2) of which the surviving spouse is the oldest beneficiary, but of which the spouse is not the *sole* beneficiary, then MRDs to the trust are calculated using the Single Life Table and the fixed-term method, just as would be true if the oldest Designated Beneficiary was someone other than the spouse. Reg.

§ 1.401(a)(9)-5, A-5(c)(1), (2); see ¶ 1.5.03(E), ¶ 1.5.04(E). The same is true whenever there are multiple Designated Beneficiaries of whom the surviving spouse is the oldest; however, this rule is most likely to apply only when a trust is named as beneficiary, because normally if multiple beneficiaries are named they will arrange to have their respective interests treated as separate accounts (¶ 1.7.06).

D.   **During spouse's life, if the spouse is the sole Designated Beneficiary.** If the spouse is the sole beneficiary of the deceased participant; or if a trust is named as sole beneficiary and the spouse is deemed to be the sole beneficiary of the trust (¶ 1.6.07); and the ADP is the surviving spouse's life expectancy (see ¶ 1.5.07, ¶ 1.5.04(A)); then MRDs to the spouse (or such trust) are computed based the spouse's life expectancy determined using the Single Life Table (¶ 1.2.03) and the spouse's age on her birthday in each year for which a distribution is required (recalculation method; ¶ 1.2.04(A)). Reg. § 1.401(a)(9)-5, A-5(c)(2) (first sentence), A-6. See ¶ 1.6.02, ¶ 1.6.03, for how to determine whether the spouse is the "sole beneficiary."

Josephine Example: Napoleon died after reaching age 70½, leaving his 401(k) plan to his surviving spouse, Josephine, as sole beneficiary. She is taking annual MRDs as Napoleon's beneficiary; she did not roll over the benefits to her own retirement plan. Each year, the plan sends an MRD to Josephine based on her life expectancy (from the Single Life Table) for her attained age on her birthday in the year of the distribution (i.e., her age as of the end of each Distribution Year). Josephine turned 46 in the year after Napoleon's death, so her "divisor" (ADP) for the first Distribution Year was 37.9. For the second Distribution Year, Josephine's divisor is not 36.9 (37.9 minus one—as it would be under the fixed-term method; see Diane Example, ¶ 1.5.05); instead Josephine's second year divisor is 37.0 (the life expectancy of a person age 47). Josephine, as a surviving spouse-sole beneficiary, determines her divisor each year by going back to the Single Life Table and determining her new life expectancy based on her new age (recalculation method).

Note that the spouse does not have to "elect" to use the recalculation method; that's just how her MRDs are determined. If a surviving spouse made a mistake, for example, and computed her MRDs using the fixed-term method, that would not change the amount of her actual MRD; it would just mean that she was taking larger distributions than she was required to take. If she caught her error quickly enough, she could roll the excess back into a tax-deferred account to avoid paying tax on it. ¶ 2.6.06. Or, she could stop (or at least slow) the flow of MRDs altogether by rolling over the inherited plan to her own plan. ¶ 3.2.

E.   **MRDs to spouse's successor beneficiaries.** If "D" above applied during the spouse's life, and the spouse later dies on or after her Required Commencement Date, the MRD for the year of her death must be paid out to the successor beneficiary to the extent the spouse had not already taken it by the time of her death. ¶ 1.5.04(F). Any remaining benefits must be paid out (beginning the year after the year of the spouse's death) over the spouse's remaining life expectancy, using the fixed-term method (¶ 1.2.04(B)). This is computed as of the age she attained (or would have attained if she lived long enough) on her birthday in the year of her death and reduced by one year for each year thereafter. Reg. § 1.401(a)(9)-5, A-5(c)(2). It is not clear whether this rule applies even if the spouse was taking distributions over the participant's remaining life expectancy rather than her own (see ¶ 1.5.04(A)).

1.6.07 *When is a trust for the spouse the same as the spouse?*

A trust for the spouse's sole or primary benefit may be entitled to some of the special privileges that apply when the spouse individually is named as beneficiary:

A.   **Spouse is sole beneficiary: conduit trust.** The spouse is considered the sole trust beneficiary, for minimum distribution purposes, if she is the sole life beneficiary of a conduit trust that is named as sole beneficiary of the benefits. See ¶ 6.3.05. As previewed by Rev. Rul. 2000-2, 2000-1 C.B. 305, the delayed Required Commencement Date of § 401(a)(9)(B)(iv) (¶ 1.6.04) for MRDs (if the participant died before his RBD), and related rules (¶ 1.6.05), apply in this case, as does the special method of computing the spouse's life expectancy (¶ 1.6.06(D)). Reg. § 1.401(a)(9)-5, A-5(c)(2). See ¶ 3.3.10 for planning opportunities. However, the regulations provide that, for purposes of the spouse's right to elect to treat an inherited IRA as her own IRA (¶ 3.2.04), the spouse must be the sole beneficiary of the IRA and this requirement is not satisfied "[i]f a trust is named as beneficiary of the IRA...even if the spouse is the sole beneficiary of the trust." Reg. § 1.408-8, A-5(a). See ¶ 3.2.08 for the spouse's ability, in some cases, to use a rollover through the trust to accomplish the same goal by other means.

B.   **Spouse is sole beneficiary: grantor trust.** If the spouse is treated as owner of all of the trust property under the grantor trust rules (¶ 6.3.08), she *should* be considered the sole beneficiary of that trust and the trust should be entitled to the same privileges as the spouse individually. See "A" for a list of these privileges (and the limitation regarding the spousal election). Unfortunately, the regulations do not discuss grantor trusts and there are no rulings confirming that the grantor trust rules apply in this context. See ¶ 3.2.08 for the spouse's ability, in some cases, to use a rollover through the trust.

C.   **Typical QTIP-type trust: spouse is income beneficiary.** If the spouse does not have the right to demand distribution to herself of *either* (i) the entire amount of the participant's retirement benefits payable to the trust ("B"), *or* (ii) whatever amounts are distributed from the retirement plan to the trust during her lifetime ("A"), the trust is not entitled to any of the privileges of the spouse. A typical example is a QTIP trust (¶ 3.3.02), under which the spouse is entitled only to income for life (with or without limited rights to principal). Many "credit shelter trusts" also fit this model. Even if such a trust qualifies as a see-through trust (¶ 6.2.03), and the spouse's life expectancy is the ADP (because she is the oldest beneficiary of the trust), "some amounts distributed from...[the retirement plan] to [the trust] may be accumulated in [the trust] during [the spouse's] lifetime for the benefit of [the] remaindermen beneficiaries." Therefore the remainder beneficiaries "count" as beneficiaries of the trust, and the spouse is not the sole beneficiary. The delayed Required Commencement Date (and related rules) of § 401(a)(9)(B)(iv) (¶ 1.6.04–¶ 1.6.05) do *not* apply to benefits payable to such a trust. The special method of computing the spouse's life expectancy (¶ 1.6.06(D)) does not apply; the life expectancy of the oldest trust beneficiary is calculated on a fixed-term basis as described at ¶ 1.5.05.

Required *lifetime* distributions to a participant who has named a trust as his sole beneficiary are determined under the Joint and Last Survivor Table or the Uniform Lifetime Table, whichever produces a lower MRD in any particular distribution year, if the trust is either a conduit trust for his spouse, or (presumably) a 100 percent grantor trust for the benefit of his spouse, provided the participant complies with the documentation requirement (¶ 6.2.08) and other trust rules (¶ 6.2.03). A participant who has named a QTIP trust as beneficiary must use the Uniform Lifetime Table.

1.7 The Designated Beneficiary

This ¶ 1.7 explains what a "beneficiary" is (¶ 1.7.02); the difference between a "beneficiary" and a "Designated Beneficiary" (¶ 1.7.03); the problems when an estate is a beneficiary (¶ 1.7.04); the special rules that apply when there are multiple beneficiaries (¶ 1.7.05); and the "separate accounts" rule (¶ 1.7.06–¶ 1.7.07). See ¶ 1.8 for how to modify the selection of beneficiary after the participant's death.

1.7.01 *Significance of having a Designated Beneficiary*

The valuable income tax deferral permitted under the "life-expectancy-of-the-beneficiary" or "stretch" payout method is available only for retirement plan death benefits that pass to a Designated Beneficiary. Not every beneficiary is a Designated Beneficiary. If there is deemed to be no Designated Beneficiary, the payout options (under the applicable "no-DB rule") will generally be less favorable; see ¶ 1.5. Therefore, estate planners must understand the meaning of this term and in most cases will want to take steps to assure that clients have a Designated Beneficiary so as to maximize the value of the client's retirement plans for the benefit of the client's chosen beneficiaries.

However, there are situations in which it doesn't matter whether there is a Designated Beneficiary; see ¶ 6.2.01.

1.7.02 *Who is the participant's beneficiary?*

Like life insurance proceeds, retirement benefits generally pass, as nonprobate property, by contract, to the beneficiary named on the participant's beneficiary designation form for the plan in question. Unless otherwise provided in the beneficiary designation form or plan document, the provisions of the participant's Will are irrelevant in determining who inherits his retirement benefits.

Most retirement plans and IRAs have a printed form they expect the participant to use to name a beneficiary for his death benefits. Some plans and IRA providers will accept attachments to the printed form, or even accept a separate instrument in place of the plan's printed form. For a beneficiary designation form drafting checklist, see Appendix B.

Beneficiary designations offer a vast field for exploration, involving such issues as contradictory, ambiguous, missing or otherwise ineffective beneficiary designations, and which state's law governs the interpretation of a beneficiary designation form. Those subjects are beyond the scope of this book. This Chapter assumes that the identity of the beneficiary is clear.

For purposes of the post-death minimum distribution rules, the **beneficiary** means the person or persons who inherit the plan on the participant's death. For example, a beneficiary designation form typically names a primary beneficiary (such as the participant's spouse) and one or more contingent beneficiaries (such as the participant's issue) who will take the benefits if the primary beneficiary does not survive the participant. If the primary beneficiary survives the participant, the primary beneficiary is "the" beneficiary (unless there is a disclaimer; ¶ 4.1). If the primary beneficiary survives the participant and does not disclaim, the contingent beneficiary ceases to have any relevance to the determination of who is the participant's beneficiary for any purpose. See ¶ 1.5.13(C) and ¶ 1.6.02.

If the primary beneficiary does not survive the participant, the contingent beneficiary becomes "the" beneficiary:

Regina Example: Regina designates her children A, B, and C as beneficiaries of her IRA, with the proviso that, if any child predeceases her, such child's issue take the share such child would have taken if living. B predeceases Regina, leaving two children and no other issue. There are no disclaimers or distributions prior to the Beneficiary

Finalization Date (¶ 1.8). Regina's beneficiaries are A, C, and the two children of B.

If the beneficiary dies *after* the participant, his death usually does not erase his status as beneficiary; see ¶ 1.5.13, ¶ 1.5.14, ¶ 1.6.03. However, some beneficiary designation forms provide that if the named primary beneficiary fails to survive the participant by a particular period of time (typically 30 or 60 days) he loses the rights to the benefits, and the contingent beneficiary becomes "the" beneficiary. The IRS has approved beneficiary designations that contained such a condition, and recognized the primary beneficiary as the Designated Beneficiary, where the primary beneficiary *did* survive for the required period of time. PLR 2006-10026.

There are no IRS pronouncements regarding who is considered the beneficiary for MRD purposes if the original beneficiary failed to survive for the required period so that the formerly-contingent beneficiary becomes the only person entitled to the benefits. Presumably, as long as the required time period of survival was either met or not met prior to the Beneficiary Designation Date (¶ 1.8), the IRS would recognize the formerly-contingent, now-primary beneficiary as "the" Designated Beneficiary, since he is entitled to the benefits "contingent on the employee's death or another specified event" (see ¶ 1.7.03). The IRS should not treat the formerly-contingent-now-primary beneficiary as a mere successor beneficiary (¶ 1.5.13) because the original primary beneficiary never became entitled to the benefits.

1.7.03 *Definition of Designated Beneficiary*

In order for benefits to be distributable over "the life expectancy of the Designated Beneficiary," there must be a Designated Beneficiary. Not every beneficiary is a Designated Beneficiary. The Code defines **Designated Beneficiary** as "any individual designated as a beneficiary by the employee." § 401(a)(9)(E). The regulations substantially expand this definition:

"A designated beneficiary is an individual who is designated as a beneficiary under the plan. An individual may be designated as a beneficiary under the plan either by the terms of the plan or, if the plan so provides, by an affirmative election by the employee...specifying the beneficiary. A beneficiary designated as such under the plan is an individual who is entitled to a portion of an employee's benefit, contingent on the employee's death or another specified event. ... A designated beneficiary need not be specified by name in the plan or by the employee to the plan in order to be a designated beneficiary so long as the individual who is to be the beneficiary is identifiable under the plan. The members of a class of beneficiaries capable of expansion or contraction will be treated as being identifiable if it is possible, to identify the class member with the shortest life expectancy. The fact that an employee's interest under the plan passes to a certain individual under a will or otherwise under applicable state law does not make that individual a designated beneficiary unless the individual is designated as a beneficiary under the plan." Reg. § 1.401(a)(9)-4, A-1.

"Q-2. Must an employee...make an affirmative election specifying a beneficiary for a person to be a designated beneficiary under section 40l(a)(9)(E)?"

"A-2. No, a designated beneficiary is an individual who is designated as a beneficiary under the plan whether or not the designation under the plan was made by the employee." Reg. § 1.401(a)(9)-4, A-2.

So, there are several key elements to achieving Designated Beneficiary status:

1.   Only individuals can be Designated Beneficiaries. An estate does not qualify; ¶ 1.7.04. A trust is not an individual, but, if various rules are complied with, you can look through the trust and treat the individual trust beneficiaries as if the participant had named them directly as his beneficiaries; see ¶ 6.2. A partnership, corporation, or LLC is not an individual for this purpose, even if under some tax rules it is not treated as an entity separate from its individual owners.

2.   If there are multiple beneficiaries, all must be individuals and it must be possible to identify the oldest member of the group. See ¶ 1.7.05. You also must determine whether the separate accounts rule applies. ¶ 1.7.06.

3.   Finally, the beneficiary must be designated either "by the terms of the plan" or (if the plan allows this; almost all plans do) by the participant.

If the participant fills out his beneficiary form naming "my spouse," or "my children," or "my friends Larry, Moe, and Curly," as his death beneficiaries, and the named individual(s) survive the participant, there is no problem. We have individual beneficiaries who have been affirmatively elected by the participant, so there is a Designated Beneficiary whose life expectancy can be used as the ADP after the participant's death.

If the participant does not fill out a beneficiary designation form; or if all the beneficiaries he named fail to survive him; we *still* have a Designated Beneficiary, *if* the plan fills the gap by specifying *individuals* to whom the benefits pass. Most qualified retirement plans, for example, provide that all benefits will be paid to the participant's surviving spouse if the participant fails to designate another beneficiary (see ¶ 3.4). Some plans (see PLR 2005-48027 for an example) and IRAs provide that benefits not effectively disposed of by the beneficiary designation form will pass to the participant's surviving spouse, if any, otherwise to the participant's issue, if any.

In many cases, however, if the participant fails to fill out the beneficiary form (or if his named beneficiaries fail to survive him), the plan or IRA will provide that the benefits are paid to the participant's estate. This will mean loss of the ability to use a beneficiary's life expectancy as the ADP; see ¶ 1.7.04.

If the participant failed to name a beneficiary, the IRS says that a beneficiary named by the participant's executor is not considered a "beneficiary under the plan" and therefore cannot be a Designated Beneficiary. See PLRs 2001-26036, 2005-16021, 2005-20038. However, the IRS has recognized a beneficiary who became such by virtue of post-death judicial reformation of the decedent's beneficiary designation form as a Designated Beneficiary. PLR 2006-16039.

1.7.04 *Estate cannot be a Designated Beneficiary*

If benefits are payable to the participant's "estate," the participant has no Designated Beneficiary, even if all beneficiaries of the estate are individuals. Reg. § 1.401(a)(9)-4, A-3(a), § 1.401(a)(9)-8, A-11; PLR 2001-26041.

This is another example of the regulations' "overruling" the Code (¶ 1.2.01, #10). The Code provides that any portion of the employee's benefit payable "to (*or for the benefit of*)" a designated beneficiary may be distributed over that beneficiary's life expectancy.

§ 401(a)(9)(B)(iii) (emphasis added). Benefits paid to an estate are paid for the benefit of the estate's beneficiaries, and if the beneficiaries of the estate are all individuals, they should be recognized as Designated Beneficiaries and allowed to use the life expectancy method. However, the regulations provide to the contrary.

The executor can transfer the inherited IRA to the estate beneficiaries (see ¶ 6.1.05); however, such a transfer will not have the effect of allowing the estate beneficiaries to use their own life expectancies for computing MRDs, even if completed before the Beneficiary Finalization Date (¶ 1.8).

See ¶ 3.2.08 for whether a spousal rollover may still be available. See ¶ 4.2.07 regarding disclaimers in this situation.

What if the participant, in his beneficiary designation form, does not name "the estate" directly as his beneficiary, but names beneficiaries who are determined indirectly by reference to the participant's Will or estate administration; for example, if the beneficiary designation form names "the beneficiaries of my estate" or "the residuary beneficiaries under my Will" as beneficiaries of his plan? The regulations do not require that beneficiaries be "specified by name...in order to be a designated beneficiary so long as the individual who is to be the beneficiary is identifiable under the plan." Reg. § 1.401(a)(9)-4, A-1. If the beneficiary designation sufficiently identifies the people who are to inherit the benefits, even if this is done by reference to another document such as the Will, this should be sufficient to establish them as Designated Beneficiaries.

1.7.05 *Multiple beneficiary rules and how to escape them*

The IRS has two "multiple beneficiary rules," both of which have a negative effect on post-death payout options, but allows two "escape hatches" whereby post-death actions can mitigate these negative effects.

The two multiple beneficiary rules are: If the participant has more than one beneficiary,

A.　　　The participant has "no designated beneficiary" unless all of the beneficiaries are individuals. Reg. § 1.401(a)(9)-4, A-3; and

B.　　　If all of the beneficiaries are individuals, the ADP is the oldest beneficiary's life expectancy. Reg. § 1.401(a)(9)-5, A-7(a)(1).

Regulation stricter than statute

The regulation appears to be harsher than the Code, which says that (at least in case of death before the RBD) if "*any portion* of the employee's interest is payable to (or for the benefit of) a designated beneficiary," *such portion* may be distributed over the life expectancy of the Designated Beneficiary. § 401(a)(9)(B)(iii) (emphasis added). Thus, the Code appears to permit a life expectancy payout to an individual beneficiary of his portion, even if some *other* portion of the benefit is payable to a nonindividual.

The two escape hatches from these rules are:

1.   The "separate accounts rule," discussed at ¶ 1.7.06–¶ 1.7.07.

2.   The ability to "remove" a beneficiary through disclaimer or distribution of his, her, or its benefits, discussed at ¶ 1.8.

1.7.06 *The separate accounts rule*

If the participant's benefit under a plan "is divided into separate accounts and the beneficiaries with respect to one separate account differ from the beneficiaries with respect to the other separate accounts of the employee under the plan, for years subsequent to the calendar year containing the date as of which the separate accounts were established, or date of death if later, such separate account under the plan is not aggregated with the other separate accounts under the plan in order to determine whether the distributions from such separate account under the plan satisfy section 401(a)(9). Instead, the rules in section 401(a)(9) separately apply to such separate account...." Reg. § 1.401(a)(9)-8, A-2(a)(2).

This regulation does NOT apply to multiple beneficiaries who take their interests through a trust that is named as beneficiary of the plan; see ¶ 6.3.02. Also, separate accounts treatment is NOT available for computing lifetime MRDs. ¶ 1.3.05. Also, though employee contribution accounts in a QRP can be treated as separate accounts for income tax purposes (¶ 2.1.08(A)), they would not be treated as separate accounts for post-death MRD purposes unless they were payable to different beneficiaries. Reg. § 1.401(a)(9)-8, A-2(a).

The separate accounts rule is one of the most useful provisions in planning for retirement benefits. It means that when a retirement plan death benefit or IRA is left to several beneficiaries each beneficiary can use his or her own life expectancy as the ADP, if "separate accounts" are properly established. In order to have separate accounts the following requirements must be met:

A.   **Pro rata sharing in gains and losses.** The beneficiaries' interests must share pro rata in post-death gains and losses. This requirement comes from the definition of separate accounts: "[S]eparate accounts in an employee's account are separate portions of an employee's benefit reflecting the separate interests of the employee's beneficiaries under the plan as of the date of the employee's death for which separate accounting is maintained. The separate accounting must allocate all post-death investment gains and losses, contributions, and forfeitures, for the period prior to the establishment of the separate accounts on a pro rata basis in a reasonable and consistent manner among the separate accounts." Reg. § 1.401(a)(9)-8, A-3.

Chloe Example: Chloe dies in 2002, leaving her IRA to her husband and daughter equally. Chloe's daughter withdraws $15,000 from the account. Between the time Chloe died and the time the husband and daughter divide up the IRA into separate accounts, some assets have declined in value and some have increased. The beneficiaries cannot retroactively decide that (for example) the assets that increased in value belonged to the daughter's separate account and the assets that declined belonged to the father's account. Furthermore, they must treat the $15,000 distribution to the daughter as a reduction in the daughter's interest in the IRA.

Such pro rata sharing would be the norm for fractional or percentage interests in the benefits. A pecuniary gift will not meet this definition of "separate account" unless (under local law or under the terms of the beneficiary designation—see Form 3.5, Appendix B) it will share in post-death gains and losses pro rata with the other beneficiaries' shares. If the beneficiary designation contains any pecuniary gifts that would not so share, the beneficiaries of the pecuniary gifts can be "eliminated" by distributing their gifts to them prior to the Beneficiary Finalization Date (see ¶ 1.8.02). If only fractional or percentage interest beneficiaries remain as beneficiaries on the Beneficiary Finalization Date, then this first requirement is met.

B.   **Accounts must be "established" by 12/31 of year after year of death to determine ADP.** The division of a single account into separate accounts is generally effective for MRD purposes beginning with the year after the year in which the division occurs, and for subsequent years. Reg. § 1.401(a)(9)-8, A-2(a)(2), first sentence. However, if the separate accounts are established either in the year of the participant's death or in the following year, the division will be effective for purposes of calculating MRDs beginning with the year after the year of the participant's death (i.e., for the first year for which distributions are required based on the beneficiaries' life expectancy). T.D. 9130, 2004-26 I.R.B. 1082, "Explanation of Provisions," "Separate accounts under defined contribution plans." If separate accounts are established by that deadline, then the rules in ¶ 1.5.03 or ¶ 1.5.04 (whichever set is applicable) will be applied separately to each separate account to determine the ADP for that account. Note that the deadline for establishing separate accounts is not the same as the Beneficiary Finalization Date (¶ 1.8)!

C.   **If established later, the separate accounts are still effective for all other purposes.** Even after December 31 of the year after the year of the participant's death, multiple beneficiaries who have the appropriate pro rata gain- or loss-sharing interests can establish separate accounts for their respective interests; separate accounts for different beneficiaries can be established "at any time." Reg. § 1.401(a)(9)-8, A-2(a)(2). For Distribution Years following this type of belated "establishment," each beneficiary's MRD will be determined solely based on his or her separate account balance, but the Applicable Distribution Period (ADP) for all the accounts will continue to be the ADP that applied to the combined accounts on the Beneficiary Finalization Date, because the accounts were "established" after the December 31 deadline.

Guerdon Example: Guerdon's IRA beneficiary designation reads as follows: "Upon my death, pay $10,000 each to Natalie Choate, Bob

Keebler, and Mike Jones. The remaining balance shall be paid in equal shares to: Charity X; Ed Slott; Seymour Goldberg; and Barry Picker." Guerdon dies in 2005, before his RBD. Under applicable state law and the terms of the account agreement, the $10,000 pecuniary gifts do not share in gains and losses occurring after Guerdon's demise. Before September 30, 2006, $10,000 is distributed from the account to each of Choate, Keebler, and Jones, thus eliminating the pecuniary gifts from the determination of who is a Designated Beneficiary of the account (¶ 1.8.01). Before December 31, 2006, and before any non-pro rata distributions are made to the remaining ("residuary") beneficiaries, the remaining balance of the IRA is divided into two separate accounts, one equal to 25 percent of the remaining value (which belongs to Charity X) and the other equal to 75 percent (which belongs to Slott, Goldberg, and Picker). The division is exactly 25 percent/75 percent on the date of division (establishment of separate accounts), thus fulfilling the requirement that post-death gains and losses be allocated pro rata. The beneficiaries might agree to take different assets as part of their respective separate accounts—that's ok as long as the overall amount each takes is the correct percentage of the total account.

   For 2006 and later years, the MRD from the separate account belonging to Slott, Goldberg, and Picker will be determined based on the total balance of their combined account, and the life expectancy of the oldest member of that group of three beneficiaries, but without regard to the balance in, or identity of the beneficiary (Charity X) of, the *other* separate account.

   In 2008, Slott, Goldberg, and Picker have a bitter disagreement concerning the RBD for a 457 plan, and decide to go their separate ways. They divide up their combined account into three separate accounts in 2008. For 2009 and later years, Slott's MRD will be based solely on the balance in his separate account, Goldberg's MRD will be based solely on the balance in his separate account, and Picker's MRD will be based solely on the balance in his separate account—but all three will continue to use the life expectancy of the oldest member of their group of three to determine their respective MRDs.

1.7.07 *How do you "establish" separate accounts?*

   It is not clear in all cases what constitutes "establishment" of separate accounts. Clearly a "physical" division of (*e.g.*) an inherited IRA into separate inherited IRAs payable to the individual beneficiaries would work, if the requirements regarding allocation of pre-establishment gains, losses, and distributions are met.

One way to "establish" separate accounts in a QRP is for the plan to purchase, and distribute to each beneficiary, by the applicable deadline, a nontransferable annuity contract payable solely to such beneficiary; see ¶ 1.5.10.

It is not clear whether separate accounts could somehow exist automatically without any post-death action. If a mere fractional bequest (as in "I leave my IRA to my four children equally") were effective to establish separate accounts, then virtually all pro-rata beneficiary designations would be separate accounts "established" as of the date of death. The regulations do not seem to contemplate such a result, since they refer to "establishing" separate accounts, after the participant's death, for the beneficiaries' proportionate shares that exist on the participant's death. Accordingly, if separate accounts treatment is desired, it is recommended to take some step, over and above simply leaving the benefits in fractional or percentage shares, indicating that the parties have "established" separate accounts.

If the IRA provider or the plan administrator tracks each beneficiary's gains, losses, and distributions separately, that should be sufficient to constitute "establishment" of separate accounts. Some IRA providers provide for automatic establishment of separate accounts for multiple beneficiaries upon the participant's death.

Another way to accomplish the objective is for the participant to divide his IRA into separate IRAs payable to the respective beneficiaries while he is still living. For example, a participant leaving his IRA partly to charity and partly to an individual beneficiary could create two totally separate IRAs, one payable to each of the respective beneficiaries. Actual separate IRAs have the nontax advantage of not requiring the beneficiaries to interact with each other after the participant's death. The disadvantages of having multiple IRAs while the participant is still alive include the additional paperwork, the difficulty of keeping the IRAs in the same relative proportion to each other when each contains different investments, and increased investment management fees applicable to multiple smaller accounts compared with one larger account.

1.8 The "Beneficiary Finalization Date"

Establishing separate accounts for multiple beneficiaries (¶ 1.7.06) is one way to improve the MRD situation after the participant's death. Another, discussed in this ¶ 1.8, is to prune the list of beneficiaries (eliminating "undesirable" beneficiaries) by means of distributions, disclaimers, and possibly other methods, prior to the "Beneficiary Finalization Date."

1.8.01 *Beneficiaries can be "removed" up to 9/30 of year after death*

The participant's beneficiaries for minimum distribution purposes are all the beneficiaries who are entitled to inherit his benefits as of the date of the participant's death, *minus* any beneficiary who ceases to have an interest in the benefits by a certain deadline: "[T]he employee's designated beneficiary will be determined based on the beneficiaries designated as of the date of death who remain beneficiaries as of September 30 of the calendar year following the calendar year of the employee's death." Reg. § 1.401(a)(9)-4, A-4(a).

That deadline is called the **Beneficiary Finalization Date** in this book, though that term is not used in the regulations.

Post-death planning cannot somehow designate a new crop of beneficiaries. Rather, "...any person who was a beneficiary as of the date of the employee's death, but is not a beneficiary as of that September 30 (*e.g.*, because the person receives the entire benefit to which the person is entitled before that September 30) is not taken into account in determining the employee's designated beneficiary for purposes of determining the distribution period for required minimum distributions after the employee's death." Reg. § 1.401(a)(9)-4, A-4(a).

So, *if* there are "good" beneficiaries (*e.g.*, individual beneficiaries with long life expectancies) who are *already named* by the deceased participant (*e.g.*, as contingent beneficiaries, or among a group of multiple beneficiaries), it is possible (by disclaimer or distribution or possibly other means) to eliminate other (*e.g.*, older or nonindividual) beneficiaries, so that by September 30 of the year after the year of death only the "good" beneficiaries are left.

1.8.02 *Changing the beneficiaries by disclaimer or distribution*

See ¶ 4.2.01 regarding changing beneficiaries by means of qualified disclaimers made before the Beneficiary Finalization Date.

Another way to cure the multiple beneficiary problem is to distribute, to any nonindividual (or older) beneficiaries, the shares payable to them. If the amounts payable to the nonindividual (or older) beneficiaries are entirely distributed to them by the Beneficiary Finalization Date, then only the remaining (younger, individual) beneficiaries who still have an interest in the benefit will "count" for purposes of determining who is the Designated Beneficiary. Reg. § 1.401(a)(9)-4, A-4(a). This can be helpful if the separate accounts rule (¶ 1.7.06) is not available. See ¶ 7.2.03 for an example.

1.8.03 *Beneficiary's death prior to Finalization Date*

A person who is a beneficiary as of the date of death, but then dies prior to the Beneficiary Finalization Date, does not thereby lose his status as a beneficiary. Reg. § 1.401(a)(9)-4, A-4(c). He will still be considered a beneficiary—unless his benefits are entirely distributed (to him or his estate) or disclaimed (by him or his estate) prior to the Beneficiary Finalization Date. For what happens to the deceased beneficiary's interest at that point, see ¶ 1.5.13–¶ 1.5.14.

(The one exception to the rule in the preceding paragraph would be a beneficiary whose death erased his right to the benefits, due to his failure to survive long enough to meet a minimum survival period stated in the beneficiary designation form; see ¶ 1.7.02.)

1.9 Enforcement of the MRD Rules

1.9.01 *Who enforces the minimum distribution rules*

Compliance with the minimum distribution rules is one of the more than 30 requirements a qualified retirement plan (QRP) must meet to stay "qualified." § 401(a). The plan administrator is the enforcer of the QRP minimum distribution rules. Since disqualification of the plan would be a disaster for all concerned, the plan administrator is extremely concerned to make sure MRDs are distributed—even though the penalty for missing an MRD is imposed on the "payee" rather than on the plan. ¶ 1.9.02.

An IRA does not have to be "qualified" in the same way that QRPs must be qualified; the IRS does not issue individual determination letters for IRAs. Rev. Proc. 87-50, 1987-2 C.B. 647, § 4.03. The penalty for failure to take the MRD falls on the payee, not on the IRA provider.

Nevertheless, the IRS wants IRA providers to help in enforcing the minimum distribution rules. Reg. § 1.408-8, A-10. IRA providers are required to report to the IRS annually, on Form 5498, the year-end account value of each IRA they hold and also whether an MRD is required from the account for the year in question. The IRA provider is also required to inform the IRA account holder that a distribution is required, and to either calculate or offer to calculate the amount of the MRD for the account holder. IRS Notice 2002-27, 2002-16 I.R.B. 0.

1.9.02 *What to do when faced with the 50% penalty*

The Code imposes a penalty for failure to take an MRD. The penalty is 50 percent of the amount that was supposed to be, but was not, distributed. For how to compute the penalty, see Reg. § 54.4974-1. The penalty is imposed on the "payee" (nonpayee?). § 4974(a).

When it appears that a participant or beneficiary may owe the penalty, if looking back at prior years, remember that the MRD rules have changed over the years; it may be that based on prior years' rules the individual did not violate the MRD rules. See ¶ 1.9.04. Here are other ways to escape the penalty:

A.   **MRD deadline extended in certain cases.** MRDs can be delayed beyond the normal deadline in two situations: a review period for QDROs and (in the case of insured plans) delay caused by receivership of the insurance company. Reg. § 1.401(a)(9)-8, A-7, A-8.

B.   **Automatic waiver for sole beneficiary complying with 5-year rule.** See 1.5.11(C).

C.   **Case-by-case waiver of penalty.** The penalty can be waived by the IRS on a case-by-case basis (§ 4974(d)) "if the payee described in section 4974(a) establishes to the satisfaction of the Commissioner" that "(1) The shortfall...in the amount distributed in any taxable year was due to reasonable error; and

(2) Reasonable steps are being taken to remedy the shortfall."
Reg. § 54.4974-2, A-7(a).

Use IRS Form 5329 to report the penalty and request a waiver.
Form 5329 should be attached to the individual's personal income tax
return (Form 1040), or (if the person is not required to file Form 1040),
filed as a stand-alone return. If the person has already filed Form 1040
for the year(s) of the missed distribution(s), he should file an amended
return for each year in which the MRD was not taken just to add the
Form 5329 for such year. A fiduciary should attach Form 5329 to the
estate's or trust's Form 1041; see instructions for Form 1041 (2005),
p. 25 (Schedule G, line 7).

Reminder: The point of filing amended returns is *not* to add the
missed MRDs to your income for those years. The minimum
distribution rules do not create "constructive distributions" of the MRD
amounts; you actually have to take the distribution in order to have
income to report. The income is properly reported only in the year
when the distribution is actually taken. Thus, the amended 1040 or
1041 filed for a year an MRD was missed will show the same income
as the return originally filed for that year, but will show a new higher
tax (because of the 50% penalty).

1.9.03 *Statute of limitations*

If the participant or beneficiary misses his MRD for a particular
year, he is supposed to file Form 5329 for that year to report the missed
distribution and calculate the penalty, and to pay the penalty with that
return. In most cases, of course, the taxpayer who is missing his MRDs
out of ignorance will not know he has missed the MRD until *after* he
has already filed his return for the year.

It is not clear whether filing Form 1040 for a particular year
starts the three-year statute of limitations running on the penalty for
MRDs missed during that year, even if no Form 5329 is attached to the
return, or whether Form 5329 itself is the "return" that must be filed to
start the limitations period running. Since there is NO statute of
limitations if no return is filed (§ 6501(c)(3)), it would appear that all
taxpayers who own an inherited retirement plan, or who are over 70½
and own a regular retirement plan, should file Form 5329 with their
1040s every year, just to establish a statute of limitations period, even
if they didn't (as far as they know) miss any MRDs!

If the taxpayer has filed a return sufficient to start the statute of limitations running with respect to the § 4974 tax (whether that return is Form 1040 or Form 5329), the next question is whether the statute of limitations is three years or six years from the date of filing the return. The normal statute of limitations is three years, but the three years turns into six years "if the return omits an amount of such tax properly includible thereon which exceeds 25 percent of the amount of such tax reported thereon...." § 6501(e)(3). If the taxpayer files a Form 5329 or Form 1040 showing "zero" as the amount of excise tax he owes, and the IRS later decides some tax was owed, it is obvious that the amount "omitted" will always be more than 25 percent of the amount shown on the return.

Fortunately, the Code provides that "In determining the amount of tax omitted on a return, there shall not be taken into account any amount of tax...which is omitted from the return if the transaction giving rise to such tax is disclosed in the return, or in a statement attached to the return, in a manner adequate to apprise the Secretary of the existence and nature of such item." § 6501(e)(3). Therefore, to keep the statute of limitations at three years, an extra step is needed, in addition to filing Form 5329 and/or Form 1040 showing "zero" penalty owed, namely, a disclosure of all the facts. A statement could be attached to the return listing the retirement plans owned by the taxpayer, his age, and other relevant facts, and explaining how the MRD was calculated.

1.9.04 Calculating MRDs for pre-2003 years

Congress established the minimum distribution system of § 401(a)(9) in substantially its present form in the Tax Reform Act of 1986. The final regulations described in this Chapter apply to all defined contribution plan participants and beneficiaries for calendar years beginning after 2002. Reg. § 1.401(a)(9)-1, A-2(a); § 403(b)-3, A-1(b), § 1.408-8, A-1(a). The final regulations are Reg. § 1.401(a)(9)-0 through § 1.401(a)(9)-9; § 1.403(b)-3; § 1.408-8; and § 54.4974-2.

Therefore, for the years 1987–2002, taxpayers took (or failed to take) MRDs without the benefit of final regulations. Looking back, how do we determine what distributions were required in those years? (A few individuals were "grandfathered" from even the 1987 proposed regulations; see ¶ 1.4.06, ¶ 1.4.10.)

MRDs computed *in compliance with* the proposed regulations that were "in effect" at the applicable time are in a safe harbor:

A.   **The 1987 proposed regulations.** In 1987, the IRS issued Prop. Regs. § 1.401(a)(9)-1 and -2, and § 54.4974-2, as amended in December 1997. For explanation of the 1987 proposed regulations see Chapter 1 of the 1999 edition of this book.

B.   **The 2001 proposed regulations.** In January 2001, the IRS issued revised proposed regulations, replacing the 1987 version, and later issued a corrected version of these revised proposed regulations (2001-1 C.B. 865). For explanation of the 2001 proposed regulations, see the 2002 edition of this book. With some changes, these 2001 proposed regulations were re-issued as the final regulations (described in this Chapter) in 2002.

C.   **Year-by-year, which proposed regulations may be relied on.** For years prior to 2001, taxpayers may rely on the 1987 proposed regulations, but may not rely on the 2001 proposed regulations. In determining MRDs for the year 2001, "taxpayers may rely on" either the 2001 or the 1987 proposed regulations. IRS Announcement 2001-23, 2001-1 C.B. 791. For 2002, taxpayers may rely on either the 1987 or the 2001 proposed regulations, or on the final regulations. T.D. 8987, 2002-1 C.B. 852, 859, "Effective Date."

What if the taxpayer's actions prior to 2003 were clearly *not* in compliance with the proposed regulations, but constituted a reasonable interpretation of the statute?

Proposed regulations have a rather lowly legal status. They "are not entitled to judicial deference," *Natomas North America, Inc.*, 90 T.C. 710, at 718, n. 11, (1988), and "are given no greater weight than a position advanced by the Commissioner on brief." *Van Wyk*, 113 T.C. 441 (1999). Therefore failure to comply with proposed regulations *per se* can't be held against you. Furthermore, prior to issuance of regulations the taxpayer "may rely on any reasonable interpretation of the statutory provisions." PLR 9506001. If a particular interpretation of the law was explicitly adopted by the IRS in one or more letter rulings, it is presumably safe to conclude that interpretation is "reasonable."

If pre-2003 distributions were not computed in compliance with the proposed regulations, so the taxpayer is not entitled to the IRS's promised protection for those complying with the proposed regulations, the taxpayer could be liable for a penalty *if* final regulations had been issued with retroactive effect. However, the final regulations were *not* adopted with retroactive effect. Compliance with the final regulations is required only for 2003 and later years. The final regulations make no attempt to dictate how to calculate MRDs for pre-2003 years. Therefore, distributions calculated based on a reasonable interpretation of the statute for the years 1986–2002 are protected even if not in compliance with the proposed *or* final regulations.

Here is a more aggressive position: The statute says that the participant must take MRDs over his lifetime or life expectancy, "beginning not later than the required beginning date, in accordance with regulations...." § 401(a)(9)(A)(ii). Proposed regulations are not "regulations." Only "final regulations" are "regulations." Therefore, since there were no final regulations prior to 2002, and since the 2002 final regulations do not apply to years prior to 2002, the participant was not required to take ANY distribution from ANY plan prior to 2002!

1.10 Putting it All Together

1.　　　　Income tax deferral is the most valuable feature of qualified retirement plans and IRAs. Preserving the option of continued tax deferral is an important goal of estate planning for retirement benefits. The minimum distribution rules set the outer limits on deferral and establish the requirements for reaching those limits.

2.　　　　Naming a beneficiary for retirement benefits does more than determine who will receive the benefits after the participant's death; it also determines the maximum deferral of distributions that will be available for those benefits. Naming the participant's estate as beneficiary generally reduces the opportunities for continued deferral compared with naming an individual beneficiary.

3.　　　　The longest possible deferral for post-death distributions is achieved by either naming the surviving spouse as beneficiary, followed by the spouse's rolling over the benefits to her own account, or by naming a young nonspouse beneficiary (or a qualified "see-through trust" for the benefit of a young beneficiary; see Chapter 6).

4.   The Uniform Lifetime Table gives the participant the ability to defer taxes on a substantial portion of his benefits past his own demise. The life expectancy "stretch" payout to a nonspouse beneficiary provides the beneficiary with a funded retirement plan that will pay him benefits well into old age. The spousal rollover gives the surviving spouse the ability to use the Uniform Lifetime Table, which gives her much longer deferral than she would get using the single life expectancy payout (even though that is the best deal available for nonspouse beneficiaries).

6.   Deferring distributions as long as possible is not always the best choice. A client should consider taking taxable distributions earlier than required if the client does not expect to live a long time, or is "overweighted" in retirement plans, or is temporarily in a low tax bracket or eligible for a special tax deal.

7.   If the client must tap retirement plan funds to pay living expenses or for some other reason, it is usually better to deplete inherited plans before depleting the client's own retirement plan.

2

Income Tax Issues

*How federal income taxes apply to
retirement benefits, including special
income tax deals such as NUA and IRD,
rollovers, and tax withholding rules.*

This Chapter examines the federal income tax treatment of
retirement benefits. This Chapter deals only with "defined
contribution" (individual account) plans. For state income taxes, and
for income tax treatment of annuity payouts, see sources cited in the
Bibliography.

2.1 Income Tax Treatment: In General

Tax-sheltered investment accumulation is the main attraction of
retirement plans. Chapter 1 explained how long that tax-sheltered
accumulation can last. We now turn to how benefits are subjected to
federal income tax once they are distributed (or deemed distributed)
from a qualified retirement plan (QRP), IRA, or 403(b) plan.

2.1.01 *What practitioners must know*

Any practitioner advising clients on investing or planning for
retirement benefits must know:

✓   How the Code taxes retirement plan distributions. ¶ 2.1.02.

✓   The nine "deemed distribution" events that can accelerate tax.
       ¶ 2.1.03.

✓   Special rules for plan overpayments (¶ 2.1.04), and community
       property (¶ 2.1.05).

✓   The 10 reasons a distribution may be either nontaxable, partly
       nontaxable, or taxed at a lower-than-usual rate. ¶ 2.1.06.

✓   How to compute the participant's basis in his retirement plan, and how that basis is recovered tax-free as the participant or beneficiary receives distributions. ¶ 2.1.07–¶ 2.1.11.

✓   How mandatory and voluntary income tax withholding apply to retirement plan distributions. ¶ 2.2.

✓   The rules for "income in respect of a decedent" (IRD), which is what plan distributions become after the participant's death, and how to compute the beneficiaries' income tax deduction for federal estate taxes paid on IRD. ¶ 2.3.

✓   How income taxes can be lowered for certain participants and beneficiaries by taking a "lump sum distribution" from a qualified plan (¶ 2.4), especially a lump sum distribution that contains appreciated employer stock (¶ 2.5).

✓   How to defer income taxes through a tax-free rollover: what a rollover is, which distributions are not eligible for rollover, what types of plans can receive a rollover, and the difference between a rollover and a plan-to-plan transfer. ¶ 2.6.

✓   Planning principles and ideas for dealing with the income tax, including the most common mistakes, reasons why someone would or would not roll benefits over from one type of plan to another, and planning considerations for a client near death. ¶ 2.7.

2.1.02 *Plan distributions includible in gross income*

§ 402(a) governs income taxation of distributions from qualified retirement plans (QRPs). § 402(a) provides that, except as otherwise provided in § 402, "any amount *actually distributed* to any distributee by any employees' trust described in section 401(a)…shall be taxable to the distributee, in the taxable year of the distributee in which distributed, under section 72 (relating to annuities)." Emphasis added.

If *cash* is distributed, the amount of cash distributed is the amount included in gross income. If *property* is distributed, the amount includible in the recipient's gross income is, generally, the fair market value of the property. Reg. § 1.402(a)-1(a)(1)(iii); Notice 89-25, 1989-

1 C.B. 662, A-10. The exceptions are if the property distributed is employer stock (¶ 2.5) or an annuity contract (¶ 2.1.06(G)).

§ 408(d)(1) provides similarly for distributions from IRAs, as § 403(b)(1) does for 403(b) plans. See ¶ 5.2 regarding distributions from Roth retirement plans.

If the distribution occurs after the participant's death, it is *also* subject to the rules of § 691, governing "income in respect of a decedent" (IRD); ¶ 2.3 discusses those additional rules.

§ 72 is one of the most complicated sections of the Code. It has lengthy rules dealing with: taxation of distributions (and deemed distributions) from annuity contracts, employer plans, life insurance contracts, and modified endowment contracts; how the owner's "investment in the contract" (basis) is apportioned among distributions; and various penalties. This ¶ 2.1 covers only nonannuity distributions from QRPs, IRAs, and 403(b) plans, so there is no need to tackle most of the intricacies of § 72. Suffice it to say that all distributions from a QRP, IRA, or 403(b) plan are includible in the distributee's gross income as ordinary income unless an exception applies.

¶ 2.1.03 lists the distributions and other events that trigger income tax; the exceptions (distributions not fully and immediately taxed as ordinary income) are listed in ¶ 2.1.06.

The only parts of § 72 covered in depth in this book are: the penalty for certain distributions before age 59½ (§ 72(t), covered in Chapter 9); and how to compute the participant's "investment in the contract" (basis) that may be distributed tax-free (¶ 2.1.07–¶ 2.1.11).

2.1.03 *Actual distributions and deemed distributions*

Generally, a participant or beneficiary is taxable on QRP, IRA, or 403(b) benefits only if, as, and when such benefits are actually distributed. § 402(a), § 408(d)(1), § 403(b)(1).

On the bright side, this means that the doctrine of "constructive receipt" (holding that income becomes taxable when it is "made available," not just when it is paid) does not apply to these benefits. Compare § 402(b)(2), dealing with tax treatment of distributions from "nonexempt" (nonqualified) employee benefit plans, providing that the employee is taxed on amounts "actually distributed *or made available.*"

On the negative side, this generally means that plan distributions are taxable to the recipient even if the distribution is erroneous (see ¶ 2.1.04), and sometimes (see ¶ 8.3.06), but not always (see ¶ 2.1.05), even if the recipient was someone other than the participant who was entitled to receive the distribution.

Here are the exceptions to the general rule—events that cause a participant or beneficiary to be currently taxable on retirement benefits *without* an actual distribution:

A.   **Pledging IRA as security for a loan.** "If, during any taxable year of the individual for whose benefit an individual retirement account is established, that individual uses the account or any portion thereof as security for a loan, the portion so used is treated as distributed to that individual." § 408(e)(4); see also Reg. § 1.408-4(d)(2). The IRS has allowed an exception to this rule for a pledge of IRA assets to secure a former employee's obligation to repay a pension plan distribution under certain circumstances; PLR 2006-06051.

B.   **Transfer after participant's death.** After the participant's death, certain "assignments" of benefits can trigger immediate realization of the underlying income; see ¶ 2.3.03. Use of plan death benefits to discharge a debt would be considered a taxable assignment; see ¶ 7.1.03.

C.   **Other assignments, pledges.** Assignment of a Roth IRA by the participant to "another individual" causes a deemed distribution of the account to the participant. ¶ 5.8.10. Generally, assigning or pledging an IRA or other retirement plan causes a deemed distribution. § 72(e)(4)(A)(ii); Reg. § 1.408-4(a)(2). See *Coppola v. Beeson*, 2005-2 USTC ¶50,503, 96 AFTR 2d 2005-5375 (5th Cir. 2005), (participant's pledge of his 403(b) account, as security for alimony he owed, treated as a distribution). QRP benefits are nonassignable, so this issue does not arise. § 401(a)(13). The transfer of an IRA or QRP benefit to a 100 percent grantor trust (¶ 6.3.08) should not be treated as an "assignment" of the account, since an individual and his grantor trust are deemed to be in effect "the same person" under Rev. Rul. 85-13, 1985-1 C.B. 184. See PLR 2006-20025.

D.   **Prohibited transaction with IRA.** See ¶ 8.6.06 for how a prohibited transaction involving an IRA can result in a deemed distribution of the entire IRA.

E.   **IRA acquires collectible.** The acquisition by any IRA (or by a self-directed account in a QRP) of a "collectible" (as defined in § 408(m)(2)) is treated as a distribution of the cost of the "collectible." § 408(m)(1).

F.   **QRPs: Certain loan events.** Under § 72(p), certain loans made by a QRP to the participant may be treated as distributions at the time made or if the loan is defaulted. ¶ 9.1.03(D). See ¶ 2.1.08(B) for the effect of a defaulted plan loan on the participant's basis.

G.   **QRP ceases to be qualified.** If a QRP ceases to be qualified under § 401(a), income taxation would cease to be governed by § 402(a), with results that are beyond the scope of this book.

H.   **Sale of life insurance policy.** See ¶ 8.3.03 for how a QRP's sale of a life insurance policy to the participant or beneficiary could be treated as plan distribution for income tax purposes.

I.   **Roth IRA conversion.** Converting an IRA to a Roth IRA causes a deemed distribution of the amount converted. ¶ 5.4.07.

2.1.04 *Plan overpayments; repayments to the plan*

When a plan pays the participant or beneficiary more money than it is supposed to, the recipient must nevertheless include the overpayment in income. If the plan reduces subsequent distributions to make up for the overpayment, the recipient will only have to include the reduced payments in income for the year those are received, but cannot take any type of loss deduction.

If the recipient is required to repay the overpayment to the plan, the proper treatment depends on whether the repayment occurs in the same year as the distribution. If it does, then the repayment is deducted from the gross amount received and the recipient reports only the net amount as income. If the repayment occurs in a different year, the recipient can deduct the repayment (including any interest he is required to pay) from his income under § 165(a); the IRS considers this a loss incurred in the "trade or business" of being an employee. Rev. Rul. 2002-84, 2002-2 C.B. 953. See also § 1341(a), § 67(a), (b)(9).

2.1.05 *Community property: Income tax aspects*

In states that apply community property law, earned income of one spouse generally belongs equally to both spouses. However, community property rules do not affect the income taxation of distributions from QRPs. The federal law giving the worker's spouse certain rights to the worker's QRP benefits (see ¶ 3.4) preempts state-law marital property rights such as community property.

An IRA, in contrast, is not subject to the federal spousal-rights rules, and thus may be community property under applicable state law. However, despite the fact that the spouses are equal owners of the IRA under their state's community property law, the Tax Court has ruled that distributions from the IRA are gross income *to the participant only*, under federal income tax law. *Morris*, 83 TCM 1104, T.C. Memo 2002-17; *Bunney*, 114 T.C. 259 (2000).

2.1.06 *List of no-tax and low-tax distributions*

Though retirement plan distributions are generally taxable to the recipient, upon receipt, as ordinary income, there are exceptions. Here are the situations in which a distribution may be wholly or partly tax-free or may be taxed more favorably than as ordinary income:

A.   **Roth plans.** Qualified distributions (and certain nonqualified distributions) from a Roth retirement plan are tax-free. ¶ 5.2, ¶ 5.7.04–¶ 5.7.05.

B.   **Tax-free rollovers.** Distributions can be "rolled over" tax-free to another retirement plan by either the participant or the surviving spouse, if various requirements are met. ¶ 2.6, ¶ 3.2.

C.   **Life insurance proceeds, contracts.** Distributions of life insurance *proceeds* from a QRP (after the participant's death) are partly tax-free; see ¶ 8.2.06. Distribution of a life insurance *policy* on an employee's life to that employee may be partly tax-free as a return of basis; see ¶ 8.2.05.

D.   **Recovery of basis.** See ¶ 2.1.07–¶ 2.1.11 regarding tax-free return of the participant's nondeductible contributions and other elements of the participant's basis.

E.   Special averaging for lump sum distributions. Certain QRP lump sum distributions to individuals born before January 2, 1936, are eligible for reduced tax. ¶ 2.4.06.

F.   Net unrealized appreciation of employer securities (NUA). Certain distributions of employer stock from a QRP are eligible for deferred taxation at capital gains rates rather than immediate taxation at ordinary income rates. See ¶ 2.5.

G.   No tax on distribution of annuity contract. The distribution of an annuity contract (to either the participant or the beneficiary) is generally nontaxable, provided the annuity contract is nonassignable by the recipient. Reg. § 1.402(a)-1(a)(2). This includes a variable annuity contract. PLR 2005-48027. Instead, the recipient pays income tax on distributions received under the annuity contract.

H.   Return of IRA contribution. An IRA contribution for a particular year may be returned tax-free prior to the extended due date of the individual's income tax return for such year, provided no deduction is allowed for the contribution and that the income that the IRA earned on the contribution is also returned; the income is taxable. § 408(d)(4). See ¶ 5.6.01(A).

I.   Income tax deduction for certain beneficiaries. A beneficiary taking a distribution from an inherited retirement plan is entitled to an income tax deduction for federal estate taxes paid on the benefits, if any. ¶ 2.3.04–¶ 2.3.07.

J.   Distributions to charity. If the beneficiary is income tax-exempt, the beneficiary will not have to pay income tax on the distribution. See ¶ 7.5. See ¶ 7.6.01 for exclusion from gross income of certain IRA-to-charity transfers.

L.   No more $5,000 death benefit exclusion. For beneficiaries of participants who died prior to August 21, 1996, up to $5,000 of employee death benefits could be excluded from the beneficiary's income. This "$5,000 death benefit exclusion" no longer exists. See § 101(b), repealed by the Small Business Job Protection Act of 1996.

2.1.07 *Recovery of participant's basis*

A distribution is nontaxable to the extent it represents the recovery of the participant's "investment in the contract," or what might be more familiarly called his "basis." § 72(b)(2). To apply this rule in any situation requires two separate determinations:

❑   What is the participant's basis? Basis usually results from the participant's nondeductible contributions to the plan, but also (in the case of a QRP) can result from certain "deemed" distributions from the plan.

❑   How much of any particular distribution is treated as a tax-free return of such basis?

To answer these questions with respect to a particular plan, see ¶ 2.1.08 for a QRP or 403(b) plan, ¶ 2.1.09–¶ 2.1.11 for a traditional IRA, ¶ 5.2.03–¶ 5.2.04 for a Roth IRA, and ¶ 5.7.05 for a designated Roth account. For treatment of tax-free return of basis under the minimum distribution rules, see ¶ 1.2.02(D). For the effect of UBTI on basis, see ¶ 8.5.01.

2.1.08 *Participant's basis in a QRP or 403(b) plan*

The participant's basis in a QRP consists of the sum of the following two components, "A" and "B." In addition, some QRP participants may have basis in a life insurance contract held within the plan; see "C." A 403(b) plan participant may have basis attributable to nondeductible contributions; see "A."

A.   **Nondeductible contributions.** Some QRPs permit (or formerly permitted) employees to make after-tax contributions. In a defined contribution plan, usually the employer maintains a separate accounting for the employee contribution account (i.e., the employee's after-tax contributions and the earnings thereon) and the employer contribution account (i.e., the employer's contributions and the earnings thereon). The rules of § 72 may be applied separately to these separate accounts. § 72(d)(2). This rule is favorable to the employee, because typically he has a higher basis in the employee-contribution account, so a distribution from that account might be largely tax-free if it is treated separately from the rest of his plan benefits.

Some 403(b) plans and government plans have mandatory employee contributions or permit participants to contribute their own after-tax money to the plan to purchase "past service credits." These contributions are not kept in a separate account; the plan pays a single benefit based on a defined benefit formula (¶ 10.1.04). A distribution from such a plan (even if it is labeled as a return of the participant's after-tax contribution) is treated as a pro rata distribution of pretax and after-tax money, based on the value of the employee's entire account (see ¶ 2.1.10, ¶ 5.7.05), rather than as a distribution from a separate employee contribution account. However, there are exceptions and grandfather rules, so § 72 must be carefully studied in these cases. See § 72(e)(8)(D), PLRs 2001-15040, 2004-11051, 2004-19036.

B.   **QRP loans that become deemed distributions.** QRPs are permitted to make loans to employees from their accounts in the plan provided various requirements are met. If the loan does not meet these requirements the loan is treated as a "deemed distribution" and included in the employee's income. If, after the loan was treated as a deemed distribution, the employee does in fact repay the loan, then such repayments are treated as employee after-tax contributions to the plan for purposes of computing the employee's investment in the contract. Reg. § 1.72(p)-1, A-21; see IRS Instructions for Forms 1099-R and 5498 (2005), p. R-5, "Loans Treated as Distributions."

C.   **Basis in plan-held life insurance policy.** See ¶ 8.2.05 regarding an employee's basis in life insurance held in a QRP.

It is unusual for an employee to have any basis in a QRP, since most employees do not have defaulted or improper plan loans, plan-held life insurance, or nondeductible employee contributions.

2.1.09 *Determining basis in a traditional IRA*

A participant may have after-tax money in his IRA as the result of nondeductible contributions made to the account after 1986, or because (after 2001) he rolled over, to the IRA, after-tax money distributed from a QRP. Also, a participant who acquires all or part of his ex-spouse's IRA in a divorce pursuant to § 408(d)(6) will thereby acquire some basis, if the ex-spouse had made nondeductible contributions or rolled over after-tax money from a QRP.

A. **Nondeductible IRA contributions after 1986.** The first year for which nondeductible IRA contributions were permitted was 1987. § 408(o), added by § 1102 of TRA '86. As of the end of 2002, therefore, the most basis a person could have in a traditional IRA would be $32,000, the amount of basis a person would have if: he made the maximum $2,000 IRA contribution every year for the years 1987–2002; in every year his contribution was nondeductible (see § 219(g)); and he took no distributions during that time that diminished his basis. Maximum nondeductible contributions for years after 2002 were: for 2003–2004, $3,000 ($3,500 if over 50 by end of year); for 2005, $4,000 ($4,500 if over 50); and for 2006, $4,000 ($5,000 if over 50).

B. **Rollover of after-tax money from a QRP after 2001.** § 401(a)(31) and § 402(c)(2) permit nontaxable as well as taxable amounts to be rolled over from a QRP to a traditional IRA after 2001. See ¶ 2.6.05.

IRS Form 8606 is used to report the participant's basis in his IRAs. A participant is required to file Form 8606 for any year in which he either makes a nondeductible contribution to an IRA, converts any part of an IRA to a Roth IRA (¶ 5.4), takes a distribution from a Roth IRA, or takes a distribution from a traditional IRA at a time when he had after-tax money in any of his traditional IRAs. Form 8606 is attached to the individual's Form 1040, but may be filed separately if the individual is not required to file Form 1040. Part of the information reported on Form 8606 is the participant's basis in his traditional IRAs. To determine a client's basis in his traditional IRAs, therefore, theoretically, you need only look at his most recent Form 8606. Whether everyone who is supposed to file this form has actually done so, or has completed the form accurately, is another question.

2.1.10 *How much of IRA distribution is basis?*

The general rule is that, for purposes of determining how much of a traditional IRA distribution is nontaxable, all of the participant's traditional IRAs are treated as one traditional IRA, and all distributions in one taxable year are treated as one distribution. See § 408(d)(1), which provides that IRA distributions are includible in gross income "in the manner provided under § 72." § 408(d)(2) then provides that: "For purposes of applying section 72 to any amount described in paragraph (1)...(A) all individual retirement plans shall be treated as 1 contract, [and] (B) all distributions during any taxable year shall be treated as 1 distribution...."

Then, each distribution from any IRA is deemed to contain proportionate amounts of the pretax and after-tax money in the aggregated IRAs. § 72(e)(2)(B), (5)(A), (5)(D)(iii), and (8)(B).

Since the conversion of a traditional IRA to a Roth IRA (¶ 5.4) is treated as a distribution from the traditional IRA, the same rules are used to determine how much income a taxpayer realizes when he converts part of his IRA to a Roth. Reg. § 1.408A-4, A-7(a).

Ed Slott: the Cream-in-the-Coffee Rule

Ed Slott, CPA, one of America's leading IRA experts and author of several books on retirement distribution planning and publisher of *Ed Slott's IRA Advisor* newsletter, calls § 408(d)(2) the "cream-in-the-coffee rule." Once after-tax money (cream) has been combined with the pretax money (coffee) in your IRA, there is no way to separate them. Every "sip" (distribution) taken from your IRA will contain some cream and some coffee. (For exceptions, see ¶ 2.1.11.)

The cream-in-the-coffee rule, combined with the rule that all IRAs are treated as one, trips up some taxpayers:

Gibbs Example: Gibbs has made a total of $12,000 in nondeductible contributions to his traditional IRA at X Mutual Fund, which is now worth $30,000. He also has a traditional IRA worth $205,000 at Y Mutual Fund. The larger IRA received no after-tax contributions; it contains only a rollover from a QRP maintained by Gibbs's former employer, plus some deductible IRA contributions Gibbs made prior to 1987. He has no other IRAs. In Year 1, he cashes out the $30,000

IRA. He thinks that, because that particular account contains his $12,000 of after-tax contributions, he will be taxable on only $30,000 - $12,000, or $18,000. Unfortunately, because of § 408(d)(2), Gibbs's $30,000 distribution is *deemed* to come proportionately from *both* of his IRAs (valued as of the end of Year 1), even though it *actually* came from only one of them. Therefore, the amount of the distribution that is deemed to come from his after-tax contributions is A/B x C, where:

A = the total amount of Gibbs's basis in both IRAs, $12,000;

B – the total value of both IRAs as of the end of Year 1, with any amounts distributed out of either traditional IRA in Year 1, including amounts rolled over to a Roth IRA, added back in for this purpose. Assume the Year 1 year-end value of his remaining IRA is $210,000, and there were no distributions from either IRA in Year 1 other than the $30,000 distribution. Therefore, B = $240,000 ($210,000 + $30,000); and

C = the total amount of Year 1 distributions; in this case, the only Year 1 distribution was $30,000, so C is $30,000.

The amount of the $30,000 distribution Gibbs can exclude from his gross income is therefore $12,000/$240,000 x $30,000, or $1,500. The amount of gross income he must report is therefore $28,500 ($30,000 distribution minus $1,500 basis assigned to the distribution). His remaining basis in his traditional IRA is $10,500 ($12,000 total basis, less $1,500 used up in the Year 1 distribution).

2.1.11 *Exceptions to the cream-in-the-coffee rule*

For a temporary exception to the cream-in-the-coffee rule for certain charitable gifts, see ¶ 7.6.01.

Also, the proportionate allocation rule does not apply to rollovers from an IRA to a QRP or 403(b) plan. Instead, a distribution that is rolled from an IRA to a QRP or 403(b) plan is deemed to come entirely out of the *taxable* portion of the IRA. § 408(d)(3)(H)(ii). This exception is necessary because the *nontaxable* portion of an IRA cannot be rolled to a QRP or 403(b) plan. ¶ 2.6.05.

This exception creates the opportunity for a tax-free distribution from a traditional IRA. In the Gibbs Example (¶ 2.1.10), if Gibbs participates in a QRP that accepts rollovers, Gibbs could roll over, from his two IRAs to the QRP, every dollar above his $12,000 basis. Now he is left with one IRA containing just $12,000, all of it after-tax money. He can then close out this IRA, and take a distribution of the $12,000 tax-free. Or he can use the same sequence to create a tax-free Roth IRA conversion for the $12,000 IRA, if he's eligible; see ¶ 5.4.08.

2.2 Income Tax Withholding

For the effect of income tax withholding on the recipient's right to roll over benefits, see ¶ 2.6.02 (first paragraph).

2.2.01 *Federal income tax withholding: Overview*

Retirement plan distributions are subject to withholding of federal income taxes. This fact creates problems and planning opportunities. This book does not cover state or local withholding requirements.

Chapter 24, Subchapter A, of the Code (§ 3401–§ 3406) establishes the withholding of income tax at the source of payment. Though titled "Withholding from Wages," it also deals with income tax withholding for pensions, annuities, and retirement plan distributions. Withholding is voluntary, in the sense that it can be waived by the recipient, for all types of retirement plan distributions *except* "eligible rollover distributions" from QRPs; and participants can usually elect to have additional amounts withheld (see ¶ 2.2.04).

¶ 2.2.02 explains the Code's general scheme for withholding from retirement plan distributions, including the different rules for different types of distributions. Exceptions and special rules are discussed at ¶ 2.2.03. ¶ 2.2.04 explains mutually voluntary withholding. Finally, ¶ 2.2.05 explains how withheld income taxes are applied to the recipient's tax liability for the year.

2.2.02 *Periodic, nonperiodic, and eligible rollover payments*

Here are the Code's opening bids on withholding from retirement distributions, including which ones the recipient can opt out of. (If the recipient wants to have *more* withheld, see ¶ 2.2.04.)

The withholding requirements distinguish between "periodic payments" (§ 3405(e)(2)), "nonperiodic distributions" (§ 3405(e)(3)), and "eligible rollover distributions" (§ 3405(c)(3)).

A. **Periodic payments** from all types of retirement plans, including IRAs, are subject to withholding of taxes at the same rate as wages. § 3405(a)(1). The recipient can elect out of having anything withheld from a periodic payment, so the withholding is voluntary as far as the recipient is concerned. § 3405(a)(2). The Code defines "periodic payment" as a distribution that is "an annuity or similar periodic payment." § 3405(e)(2). The IRS says periodic payments are payments made at regular intervals for more than one year. IRS Publication 15A, "Employer's Supplemental Tax Guide" (01/06), p. 21. An "annuity" is "a series of payments payable over a period greater than one year and taxable under section 72...whether or not the payments are variable in amount." Reg. § 35.3405-1T, A-9.

B. **Nonperiodic distributions** from all types of retirement plans, including IRAs, are subject to withholding at a flat rate of 10 percent, unless they are "eligible rollover distributions" (see "C"). § 3405(b)(1). "Distributions from an IRA that are payable on demand are treated as nonperiodic payments." Instructions for IRS Form W-4P (2006), p. 3. The recipient can elect out of having anything withheld from a nonperiodic distribution, so again the withholding is voluntary. § 3405(b)(2).

C. **Eligible rollover distributions** from QRPs are subject to withholding at a 20 percent rate, and the recipient can *not* elect out. PLR 2000-38055. The only way to avoid the 20 percent withholding is to have the distribution paid directly to an eligible retirement plan (direct rollover; ¶ 2.6.01). § 3405(c). An "eligible rollover distribution" is a defined term meaning basically any distribution from a qualified plan (§ 402(c)(4)) or (after 2001) 403(b) plan that is eligible to be rolled over. § 3405(c)(3); § 402(f)(2)(A); see ¶ 2.6.02. Thus, an IRA distribution cannot be an "eligible rollover distribution" for withholding tax purposes even if it is eligible to be rolled over.

The distinction between periodic payments and nonperiodic distributions is a little vague, but is not terribly important. Both types are subject to withholding by all types of plans, and with both types the recipient can elect out of having anything withheld. The only difference is the rate of withholding that applies if the recipient does not opt out of withholding. The significant distinction is between "eligible rollover distributions" and other payments, because withholding from an eligible rollover distribution is mandatory unless the distribution is sent by direct rollover to another retirement plan.

The mandatory withholding on eligible rollover distributions does not pose a problem if someone simply wants to get the money out of the QRP without paying any income tax until the following April 15. All such person has to do is have his distribution transferred directly (a "direct rollover") into an IRA, so the qualified plan doesn't have to withhold anything; and then take the money out of the IRA (electing out of withholding on the IRA distribution).

The person for whom "mandatory withholding" is *truly* mandatory is the person who wants to take a lump sum distribution from a QRP in order to qualify for special averaging treatment (¶ 2.4.06). This person cannot roll over any part of the distribution, and so will be forced to pay 20 percent income tax on it through withholding. He can get a refund when he files his tax return for the year of the distribution, if his total tax payments (including this withholding) exceed his actual tax liability.

2.2.03 *Exceptions and special rules*

A retirement plan does not have to withhold taxes from a distribution to the extent it is "reasonable to believe" that the distribution is not includible in the payee's income. For some reason this exception is not applicable to a traditional IRA. § 3405(e)(1)(B)(ii); Temp. Reg. § 35.3405-1T, A-2.

If the entire distribution consists of securities of the employer corporation (as defined in § 402(e)(4)(E)) (and up to $200 cash "in lieu of fractional shares"), there is no withholding. If the distribution consists of securities of the employer corporation plus cash and other property, the maximum amount that may be withheld is the value of the cash and other property. § 3405(e)(8). In connection with determining the amount required to be withheld from that sort of mixed distribution, "it is reasonable to believe that all net unrealized appreciation [NUA] from employer securities is not includible in gross income." Temp. Reg. § 35.3405-1T, A-30; see ¶ 2.5 regarding NUA.

There is no withholding on dividends paid to participants on employer securities held in the plan. § 3405(e)(1)(B)(iv); § 404(k)(2).

2.2.04 *Mutually voluntary withholding*

If the plan administrator does not want to withhold from a plan or IRA distribution any income taxes beyond the amount required by § 3405, the participant or beneficiary cannot force him to do so. Temp. Reg. § 35.3405-1T, A-6. However, if the plan administrator or IRA provider is agreeable, the parties can apparently agree to mutually voluntary withholding under § 3402(p)(3)(B) for such payments. Technically, the Code allows mutually voluntary withholding only where authorized by *regulations.* § 3402(p)(3)(B). The only regulation dealing with mutually voluntary withholding on periodic payments and nonperiodic distributions is Temp. Reg. § 35.3405-1T, A-7, which was adopted in 1982 (amended in 2001). A temporary regulation expires three years after its issuance, so this regulation has expired. § 7805(e)(2). Furthermore, this temporary regulation authorized only the continuation of voluntary withholding agreements entered into prior to 1982 (when the current regime for withholding from retirement plan distributions came into effect); it says nothing about *new* mutually voluntary withholding agreements.

Nevertheless, IRS Publication 575, "Pension and Annuity Income" (2005), p. 8, states that the recipient can "ask the payer to withhold an additional amount using Form W-4P" from nonperiodic distributions. The ability to request extra withholding is presumably also implied for periodic payments because ("Unless you choose no withholding") such payments "will be treated like wages for withholding purposes," and mutually voluntary withholding for wages is authorized by Reg. § 31.3402(p)-1. Form W-4P clearly permits the recipient to request withholding of additional amounts for all three types of payments covered by § 3405.

2.2.05 *How withheld income taxes are applied*

In this section, the "taxpayer" is the participant or beneficiary who receives a retirement plan distribution from which federal income tax was withheld.

Withheld income taxes are applied as a credit against the taxpayer's income tax liability for the year of the distribution. § 31(a)(1). Although § 31 is titled "Tax Withheld on Wages," it applies to any amount "withheld as tax under chapter 24," which includes withholding from retirement plan distributions, since § 3402 and § 3405 are part of chapter 24.

§ 6654 (part of Subtitle F of the Code) imposes a penalty for underpayment of estimated income taxes, and also establishes how withheld income tax relates to the taxpayer's obligation to pay estimated taxes. For purposes of determining the penalty, the § 31 credit for withheld income taxes "shall be deemed a payment of estimated tax, and an equal part of such amount shall be deemed paid on each due date for such taxable year, unless the taxpayer establishes the dates on which all amounts were actually withheld...." § 6654(g)(1). This rule can help a taxpayer who has underpaid his estimated taxes "catch up" (and possibly avoid the penalty for underpayment of estimated taxes) through a late-in-the-year distribution for which he elects income tax withholding:

Lincoln Example: Lincoln, age 65, requests a nonperiodic distribution of $101,000 from his IRA in December, Year 1, and also (by filing Form W-4P) asks the IRA provider to withhold $100,000 of this distribution for federal income tax. The IRA provider is willing to do this. Even though the tax is withheld in December, Year 1, it is treated as if it were four $25,000 payments of estimated tax by Lincoln on April 15, June 15, and September 15, Year 1, and January 15, Year 2, for purposes of determining whether Lincoln owes a penalty for underpayment of estimated taxes for Year 1. Lincoln could even avoid income tax on the $101,000 distribution by rolling over $101,000 to the same or another IRA (using other funds to substitute for the money "distributed" to the IRS) within 60 days after the distribution (assuming the distribution is otherwise eligible; ¶ 2.6). Reg. § 1.402(c)-2, A-11.

2.3 Income in Respect of a Decedent (IRD)

When the participant dies, the plan benefits become payable to his beneficiaries. The beneficiaries must pay income tax on the inherited benefits because such benefits are "income in respect of a decedent" (IRD) under § 691.

Generally, the same income tax rules apply to beneficiaries as applied during the participant's life: The benefits are taxable only when they are actually distributed (¶ 2.1.02–¶ 2.1.03), distributions are taxable as ordinary income unless one of the exceptions listed at ¶ 2.1.06 applies, etc. However, three additional considerations apply:

First, the ability to avoid income tax by means of a rollover (¶ 2.6) is eliminated, unless the beneficiary is the participant's surviving spouse; see ¶ 2.6.03, ¶ 3.2. Second, because the plan distributions are IRD, the beneficiary is entitled to an income tax deduction for federal estate taxes paid on the inherited benefits. ¶ 2.3.04–¶ 2.3.07. Third, an "assignment" of the inherited retirement plan would be considered a transfer of the right-to-receive IRD and would trigger immediate tax under § 691(a)(2). ¶ 2.3.03.

2.3.01 *Definition of IRD; why it is taxable*

Income in respect of a decedent (IRD) is not defined in the Code. The IRS defines it as "amounts to which a decedent was entitled as gross income but which were not properly includible in computing his taxable income for the taxable year ending with the date of his death or for a previous taxable year...." Reg. § 1.691(a)-1(b).

Death benefits under qualified plans, 403(b) plans, and IRAs are IRD. Rev. Rul. 92-47, 1992-1 C.B. 198; Reg. § 1.663(c)-5, Example 9; IRS Publication 559, "Survivors, Executors, and Administrators" (2005), p. 10; PLR 9341008. A death benefit under a deferred annuity (Rev. Rul. 2005-30, 2005-20 I.R.B. 1015) or variable annuity (PLR 2000-41018) contract is IRD.

Normally, an individual who inherits property gets a new income tax basis in the property, equal to the value of the property as of the date of death (or other date used to value the decedent's property for estate tax purposes). § 1014(a). The new basis is usually referred to as a stepped-up basis, on the assumption that the property appreciated between the time the decedent acquired it and the date of death.

However, "property which constitutes a right to receive an item of income in respect of a decedent" is an exception: IRD does not get a new basis at death. § 1014(c). Instead, an individual who inherits IRD takes over the decedent's basis (carryover basis).

After 2009, § 1014 is repealed and carryover basis will apply generally to all assets. Therefore, generally, an individual who inherits any asset from someone who dies after 2009 will take the decedent's basis. § 1022(a). This will lessen the relative disadvantage of IRD but will not eliminate it, because:

A.   Even after 2009, there will be a limited stepped-up basis: The decedent's executor will be able to allocate $1.3 million of basis step-up among the decedent's appreciated assets. § 1022(b). Even more step-up can be allocated to assets left to the spouse. § 1022(c). Retirement plans and other IRD will not be eligible for the allocation of basis step-up. § 1022(f).

B.   Retirement plan distributions will be taxable as ordinary income, while the built-in gain in other inherited assets that have carryover basis may be eligible for capital gain treatment.

C.   Section 901 of EGTRRA reinstates § 1014 (as in effect prior to EGTRRA) for deaths after 2010.

2.3.02 When and to whom IRD is taxed

Normally, IRD is includible (when received) in the gross income of the person or entity who acquired, from the decedent, the right to receive such income. § 691(a)(1).

Colin Example: Colin's estate is named as beneficiary of Colin's IRA. The estate withdraws money from the IRA. The withdrawal is includible in the estate's gross income as IRD. § 691(a)(1)(A).

Bill Example: Bill names Ted as beneficiary of his 401(k) plan. Ted withdraws money from the plan after Bill's death. The withdrawal is includible in Ted's gross income as IRD. § 691(a)(1)(B).

Barbara Example: The beneficiary designation for Barbara's 403(b) account provides that the first $20,000 of the account shall be distributed to Lucy, and the balance shall be paid to Tom. Upon Barbara's demise, Lucy withdraws her $20,000; that distribution is includible in her gross income as IRD. Whenever Tom withdraws from the account, such withdrawals will be includible in his gross income as IRD. § 691(a)(1)(B).

2.3.03 *Tax on transfer of right-to-receive IRD*

Although much less common, there is another occasion which can cause IRD to be taxable. If the person or entity who inherited the right-to-receive the IRD from the decedent transfers that right-to-receive-IRD to someone else, § 691(a)(2) provides that the IRD is immediately taxable, to the transferor. A distribution from a retirement plan is IRD; the retirement plan account *itself* is a right-to-receive IRD.

Stokely Example: Stokely is named as beneficiary of his father's IRA. After taking distributions for several years after his father's death (and including such distributions in his income as IRD), Stokely decides he does not need this money and wants his sister to have it. He gives the inherited IRA to his sister. His gift is a transfer of the right to receive IRD, and the full value of the IRA becomes immediately taxable *to Stokely* under § 691(a)(2). This example is not realistic, because it is probable that the IRA provider would not allow such a transfer of the account to even occur. This type of transfer is more likely to occur with other types of "rights-to-receive IRD" (such as an instalment note, which can be legally transferred) than with retirement benefits (which normally cannot be given away or sold by a beneficiary).

Although the Stokely Example is unrealistic, there is one type of transfer of the right-to-receive IRD that is very common, and that is the transfer of an inherited retirement plan by an estate or trust to the individual beneficiary(ies) of the estate or trust. See ¶ 6.1.05. This type of transfer is usually *not* taxable under § 691(a)(2); see ¶ 6.4.07.

Rev. Rul. 85-13, 1985-1 C.B. 184, established that transactions between an individual and trust all of whose assets are deemed owned by such individual under the "grantor trust rules" (see ¶ 6.3.08) are not considered taxable transactions under the income tax Code, because "A transaction cannot be recognized as a sale for federal income tax purposes if the same person is treated as owning the purported consideration both before and after the transaction." If a beneficiary transfers an inherited IRA to a trust of which he is considered the sole owner under § 678 (one of the "grantor trust rules"), the transfer, being a nonevent for income tax purposes, should not trigger deemed income under § 691(a)(2). PLR 2006-20025 confirmed this.

2.3.04 *Income tax deduction for estate tax on IRD*

The beneficiary gets an income tax deduction for federal estate tax paid on IRD he receives. § 691(c). To determine the amount of the deduction, first determine the estate tax due on the entire estate. Next, determine the net value of all items of IRD that were includible in the estate (for definition see § 691(c)(2)(B)). The estate tax attributable to the IRD is the difference between the actual federal estate tax due on the estate, and the federal estate tax that would have been due had the net value of the IRD had been excluded from the estate.

Harvey and Emma Example: Harvey dies in 1999, leaving his $2 million taxable estate (including a $1 million pension plan) to his daughter Emma. The federal estate tax on a $2 million taxable estate, after deducting the unified credit and the maximum credit for state death taxes, is $469,900. If the $1 million IRA were excluded from the taxable estate, the taxable estate would be only $1 million, and the federal estate tax would be $101,300. Thus the amount of federal estate tax attributable to the IRA is $469,900 − $101,300, or $368,600. Emma will be entitled to an income tax deduction of $368,600 which she can claim when she receives the $1 million pension distribution.

Note also:

1.   The deductible portion of the estate tax is computed at the marginal rate, not the average rate; this is favorable to the taxpayer. In the Harvey and Emma Example, even though the IRA constituted only 50 percent of the taxable estate, it accounted for 75 percent of the estate tax, so the IRD deduction equals 75 percent of the total estate tax.

2.   Federal estate taxes are scheduled to be reduced (through increasing exemptions and declining top rates) for deaths in years 2006–2009; the federal estate tax is repealed for deaths in 2010, then reinstated (under EGTRRA's sunset provision, § 901) for deaths in 2011 and later. EGTRRA did not repeal or amend § 691, so if federal estate taxes are paid (because the participant died in a year in which the estate tax was in effect), they can be deducted when the beneficiary receives a

distribution from the plan, even if the distribution occurs when the estate tax no longer exists.

3.   State estate taxes are *not* deductible.

4.   The estate tax does not have to be actually paid before the deduction can be taken, as long as it is owed and attributable to the IRD. PLR 2000-11023.

5.   The computation of the § 691(c) deduction becomes more complex if a marital or charitable deduction is involved; this topic is beyond the scope of this book. See Reg. § 1.691(c)-1(a)(2); *Estate of Cherry v. U.S.*, 133 F. Supp. 2d 949 (W.D. Ky. 2001); Westfall and Mair, *Estate Planning Law and Taxation* (4th ed., Warren, Gorham & Lamont, Boston, 2002–2003), ¶ 14.05[1].

2.3.05 *Who gets the § 691(c) deduction*

The § 691(c) deduction goes to the person who receives the IRD, not the person who paid the estate tax. If there are several beneficiaries who receive the IRD, the deduction is apportioned among them in proportion to the amount of IRD each received. § 691(c)(1)(A).

Jack Example: Jack dies in 2002 with an estate of $3 million. He leaves his $1 million IRA (which is entirely IRD) to his daughters Jill and Holly. He leaves his $2 million probate estate (which is not IRD) to his son Alex. Alex pays the federal estate tax of $897,500. The § 691(c) deduction goes equally to Jill and Holly because they received the IRD, even though Alex is the one who paid the estate tax.

2.3.06 *§ 691(c) deduction: Deferred payouts, multiple plans*

Calculating the § 691(c) deduction is easy when the beneficiary receives a distribution of the entire benefit all at once, but what if the retirement benefit is distributed in installments over the life expectancy of the beneficiary? Clearly the deduction will also be spread out; but how much of the deduction is allocated to each payment? How much of each distribution represents "IRD" that was included in the gross estate, and how much represents income earned by the retirement plan after the date of death?

When IRD is in the form of a joint and survivor *annuity*, the Code requires that the deduction be amortized over the surviving annuitant's life expectancy and apportioned equally to the annuity payments received by the survivor. § 691(d). However, no official source discusses the allocation of the deduction to nonannuity payouts, such as instalment payments. For a list of possible alternative methods, see Christopher Hoyt articles cited in the Bibliography. For possible future developments in this area, keep an eye on regulations and rulings under § 2056A, where which retirement plan distributions constitute IRD and which constitute post-death earnings is critical to application of the deferred estate tax on a "qualified domestic trust" (QDOT).

Meanwhile, the method used by many practitioners could be called the "IRD comes out first" method. All distributions from the retirement plan are assumed to be coming out of the IRD (rather than out of the post-death earnings of the plan) until the § 691(c) deduction has been entirely used up.

Jack Example, continued: In the Jack Example, the total § 691(c) deduction was $427,600, which is 42.76 percent of the total $1 million IRA. Suppose the IRA has grown to be worth $1.2 million by the time Jill and Holly, the beneficiaries, take their first withdrawal of $30,000 each. They assume the distributions come entirely from the $1 million original principal of the IRA (from the IRD, in other words) and none of it from the $200,000 post-death earnings, so each daughter takes a deduction equal to 42.76 percent of her $30,000 distribution, or $12,801. Each daughter keeps doing this until she has received a total of $500,000 of distributions from the IRA, at which point she has used up all of her $218,800 share of the § 691(c) deduction.

Here's another question the regulations don't answer, submitted by Seymour "Sy" Goldberg, JD/CPA, author of numerous books and articles on retirement plan distributions: Suppose a beneficiary inherits an IRA and a 403(b) plan, each worth $100,000, and she is entitled to a § 691(c) deduction of $80,000 for this $200,000 worth of IRD. The IRA experiences investment losses and becomes worthless, while the 403(b) plan doubles in value to $200,000. She cashes out the 403(b) plan. Can she use the entire § 691(c) deduction against the $200,000

403(b) distribution? Or is she required to apportion half the deduction to the now-vanished IRA, so she can never use it?

2.3.07 *§ 691(c) deduction on the income tax return*

On the bright side: Certain miscellaneous itemized deductions are deductible only to the extent the total of such deductions exceeds two percent of the individual's adjusted gross income (AGI). § 67(a). The § 691(c) deduction is *not* one of those, so it may be deducted without regard to the two percent floor. § 67(b)(7). Because it is not subject to the two percent floor, this deduction *is* allowed in computing the alternative minimum tax (AMT). § 56(b)(1)(A)(i).

On the negative side, the § 691(c) deduction is subject to § 68, under which an individual's itemized deductions are reduced by an amount equal to three percent of the individual's AGI in excess of an annually-adjusted threshold amount, or (if less) 80 percent of total itemized deductions. § 68(a), (b). To the extent this reduction applies, the individual gets no benefit from the deduction. However, this reduction is being phased out in the years 2006–2009, so for 2006–2007 the reduction is only 2/3ds of the amount determined under § 68(a); for 2008–2009 it is only 1/3d of that amount. For 2006, the threshold amount is $150,500 ($75,250 for a married taxpayer filing separately). Rev. Proc. 2005-70, 2005-47 I.R.B. 9. EGTRRA repeals § 68 effective in 2010, but EGTRRA's sunset provision reinstates it in 2011 at 2001 levels.

The § 68 reduction of itemized deductions does not apply to trusts or estates; see ¶ 6.4.04.

The impact of the § 68 reduction will vary from beneficiary to beneficiary depending on the size of the distribution and the amount of the beneficiary's other income and deductions. In the case of a high-income taxpayer, with few other itemized deductions, the benefit of the § 691(c) deduction could be substantially reduced by the § 68 adjustment. A high-income beneficiary who inherits a retirement plan that was subject to a large estate tax may want to consider deferring receipt of the income from the plan until 2010, to the extent possible under the plan terms and the minimum distribution rules. Deferring receipt until the complete repeal of § 68 is effective may increase the amount of the § 691(c) deduction such person can take.

2.4 Lump Sum Distributions

See ¶ 2.2.02(C) regarding income tax withholding on lump sum distributions.

2.4.01 *Introduction to lump sum distributions*

Through the years, the Code has provided a special gentle treatment for "lump sum distributions" (LSDs) from qualified retirement plans (QRPs). A person who wishes to obtain this special treatment is confronted with some of the most convoluted requirements known to post-ERISA man.

Congress has changed the rules on LSD treatment so often that the IRS has been unable to keep pace with regulations. There are only assorted proposed and temporary regulations issued in 1975–1979 (under old Code § 402(c)), which became obsolete before they could be finalized. The instructions for IRS Forms 4972 and 1099-R are often the best indication of the IRS's interpretation of the LSD rules.

From 1992 through 1999, the definition of LSD was found in § 402(d); after 1999, it went back to its pre-1992 home, § 402(e). One special LSD deal, five-year forward averaging, ceased to be available for distributions after 1999.

To achieve the favorable tax treatments that are still available for LSDs, the taxpayer must clear various requirement "hurdles," many of which are surrounded by hidden issue "land mines." The requirements that must be met in order for a distribution to qualify as an LSD are summarized at ¶ 2.4.02–¶ 2.4.05. If a distribution clears those hurdles it is an LSD. That doesn't mean much, however, unless it meets further tests to qualify for particular favorable tax treatments:

❑   If the LSD meets numerous *additional* tests, it can qualify for special averaging treatment. ¶ 2.4.06–¶ 2.4.07.

❑   If the LSD includes employer stock, see ¶ 2.5.

The following aspects of LSDs are not treated here: LSDs in connection with a QDRO (§ 402(e)(4)(D)(v), (vii)); interplay with the § 691(c) deduction; an LSD paid to multiple recipients; and distribution of annuity contracts as part of an LSD.

2.4.02 *First hurdle: Type of plan*

Only distributions from § 401(a) "qualified plans" (pension, profit-sharing, or stock bonus) can qualify as LSDs. Both corporate plans and self-employed ("Keogh") plans can give rise to LSDs, but a distribution from an IRA, SEP-IRA, SIMPLE, or 403(b) plan can never qualify for LSD treatment. § 402(e)(4)(D)(i).

2.4.03 *Second hurdle: "Reason" for distribution*

The distribution must be made either:

(i)   On account of the employee's death; or
(ii)   After the employee attains age 59½; or
(iii)   On account of the employee's "separation from service."

§ 402(e)(4)(D)(i), I–III.

Reason (iii) is not available to the self-employed person; a distribution to a self-employed person is eligible for LSD treatment only under reasons (i) or (ii), or after he has become "disabled," which for this purpose means "unable to engage in any substantial gainful activity by reason of any medically determinable physical or mental impairment which can be expected to result in death or to be of long-continued and indefinite duration." § 402(e)(4)(D)(i)(IV); § 72(m)(7).

These LSD "triggering events" are of significance primarily for determining whether there has been a distribution of 100 percent of the balance to the credit of the employee (¶ 2.4.04). Distributions before the triggering event are irrelevant for this purpose; see, *e.g.*, PLR 8541089 (distributions before age 59½ did not adversely affect LSD status of distribution occurring after reaching age 59½).

(a)   Landmine: separation from service

A treatise could be written on the subject of what constitutes "separation from service." "An employee will be considered separated from the service within the meaning of section 402(e)(4)(A) of the Code, only upon the employee's death, retirement, resignation or discharge, and not when the employee continues on the same job for a different employer as a result of the liquidation, merger or consolidation, etc., of the former employer." Rev. Rul. 79-336, 1979-2

C.B. 187. See, *e.g.*, PLRs 9844040, 1999-27048, 2001-48077. See PLR 2000-38050 holding that an executive who transitioned to being a consultant had "separated from service" for LSD purposes. Defining "separation from service" is beyond the scope of this book.

The frustrating technicalities of the term "separation from service" caused Congress to change to a different term—"severance from employment"—in defining when an elective deferral account may properly be distributed from a 401(k) plan (a subject not covered in this book); see § 401(k)(2)(B)(i)(I), effective for distributions after 2001. Unfortunately, Congress did not similarly amend § 402(e), so "separation from service" is still the term applicable in the definition of lump sum distribution. Most cases and rulings on the meaning of separation from service dealt with 401(k) plans; see, *e.g.*, PLR 2001-27053. Post-2001 401(k) pronouncements will no longer help on this question, since the two Code sections now use different terms.

(b)   Landmine: "on account of"

Occasionally taxpayers have had problems asserting that a particular LSD was made "on account of" a triggering event. For example, where the employee died leaving his QRP benefits to his surviving spouse, then she died after taking some distributions from the plan, the children who inherited the remaining QRP benefits at her death were not entitled to LSD treatment, because the payments to them were not "on account of" the employee's death (they were on account of the surviving spouse's death). *Gunnison*, 461 F.2d 496, 499 (7th Cir. 1972). But see PLR 2003-02048, in which a distribution received 10 years after taxpayer's separation from service was ruled to be "on account of" the separation from service.

If the triggering event is reaching age 59½, or becoming disabled, then the distribution does not have to be "on account of" the triggering event; it merely has to be "after" it. PLR 8541089. The treatment is available for someone who has attained age 59½ even if he has not terminated employment; see PLR 2004-10023.

2.4.04 *Third hurdle: Distribution all in one taxable year*

For the distribution to qualify as an LSD, the employee's entire balance must be distributed to him in one calendar year. As the Code puts it, there must be a "distribution or payment within one taxable year of the recipient of the balance to the credit of…[the] employee…" from the plan. § 402(e)(4)(D)(i). The "balance to the credit" includes all the participant's accounts in that plan—employee contribution, employer contribution, rollover, *and* designated Roth (¶ 5.7)!

For exceptions to the all-in-one-year rule, see ¶ 2.4.05.

This hurdle is surrounded by land mines.

Clearly, if an employee takes out, say, one-third of his plan balance in Year 1 and leaves two-thirds in the plan, the distribution of the one-third portion in Year 1 does not qualify for LSD treatment because it is not a distribution of the entire balance. Now suppose the employee takes out the remaining two-thirds of his balance in Year 2. He has taken out 100 percent of his (remaining) plan balance in Year 2. Is the Year 2 distribution an LSD?

It *would* be a distribution of 100 percent of the balance to his credit in one calendar year *if* the "balance to his credit" simply meant the balance as of the date of distribution—but that is not what it means. Rather, the rule means that the balance to the credit of the employee *as of the first distribution following the most recent triggering event* (¶ 2.4.03) must be distributed within one taxable year. See IRS Notice 89-25, 1989-1 C.B. 662, A-6; Prop. Reg. § 1.402(e)-2(d)(1)(ii); Rev. Rul. 69-495, 1969-2 C.B. 100.

Elaine Example: After Elaine retired from Acme in Year 1 at age 64, she withdrew $60,000 from her $800,000 Acme Profit-sharing Plan account in order to fulfill her dream of traveling around the world in a submarine. Returning to the U.S. in Year 2, she withdraws the rest of her account. This final distribution would not qualify for LSD treatment because the entire balance that existed on the date of the most recent triggering event (separation from service) was not distributed all in one calendar year. In contrast, suppose Elaine, upon returning from her cruise, died on her way to the Acme benefits office. Now there is a new triggering event, the employee's death. Her beneficiary can elect LSD treatment for her remaining plan balance even though Elaine, had she lived, could not have done so. Or suppose Elaine had withdrawn the $60,000 for her cruise *before* she retired. Then her later separation from service would have been a new triggering event, and the final distribution would qualify for LSD treatment.

The IRS Instructions for Form 4972 (2005) make no reference to this requirement. Prior distributions from the same plan are referred to only in connection with the rule that if any prior distribution from the same plan was rolled over, subsequent distributions cannot receive special averaging treatment (¶ 2.4.06). These instructions give the impression that the IRS regards the triggering events as obsolete. However, unless the IRS has had an unpublicized change of heart, Notice 89-25 is still in effect. The Code's definition of LSD still includes the requirement that the distribution be of the "balance to the credit" of the employee which becomes payable "after the employee attains age 59½," or "on account of" the participant's death, separation from service (nonowner-employees) or disability (owner-employees).

Failure to distribute the entire balance in one calendar year is a mistake you cannot fix. In PLR 2004-34022, a retiring employee intended to have all of the employer stock in his account in his employer's QRP distributed outright to him and to have all of the other assets in his account distributed directly to his IRA. Through some error of paperwork, the distribution of employer stock occurred in 2002, but the transfer of the other assets did not occur until 2003. He did not have an LSD. The IRS ruled that it could not allow him an extension of the all-in-one-year deadline.

Here are more land mines surrounding this hurdle:

(a)   Landmine: Post-distribution additions

Does a post-distribution addition retroactively destroy the LSD status of the distribution? That depends:

The "balance to the credit" of the employee (which must be distributed "in one taxable year") is determined as of the first distribution following the most recent triggering event. If there is an addition to the account *after* that date (for example, an employer contribution), that new addition is *not* part of the balance that must be distributed within the same taxable year to qualify for LSD treatment. If it *is* distributed within the same year, it is treated as part of the LSD; if it is not distributed within the same year, its existence does not disqualify the LSD. Notice 89-25, 1989-1 C.B. 662, A-6.

The most serious problem is the arrival into the account, after the end of the year in which the supposed LSD occurred, of stray dollars that were overlooked at the time of the LSD, due to a bookkeeping error or some forgotten class action:

Lewis Example: Lewis terminated his Keogh plan and took a distribution of the entire balance in Year 1. He diligently closed every account the plan had and distributed all the assets to himself before the end of Year 1. Then in January, Year 2, he received a notice from a court: Because of certain securities transactions that had occurred in his Keogh plan account in 1993, he (in his capacity as trustee of the plan) was a plaintiff in a class action suit. Enclosed with the notice is a check for $1.98, representing his share of the winnings in the now-settled class action suit. The check is payable to (and presumably constitutes an undistributed asset of) the Keogh plan. The balance of his plan, in other words, was NOT distributed all in one year.

To avoid this problem, when distributing all assets of an account (or when terminating the plan), have the plan trustee sign a blanket assignment of all remaining assets, claims, etc., known and unknown, to the recipient (participant or beneficiary, as the case may be). Thus, the recipient, not the plan trustee, becomes the owner of the stray interest, dividends, and class action claims that seem inevitably to turn up after the plan is liquidated, and the newly-discovered dollars do not upset the LSD status of the terminating distribution.

(b)   Landmine: aggregation of plans

In determining whether the entire balance to the credit of an employee has been distributed, certain plans must be aggregated. Specifically all profit-sharing plans of the same employer are considered to be one plan for this purpose; all pension plans of the employer are treated as one plan; and all stock bonus plans are treated as one. § 402(e)(4)(D)(ii).

Unfortunately it is not always easy to determine what type a particular retirement plan is. The employee is entitled to a summary plan description for each plan; that should tell what type it is.

Finding out what type of plan a particular retirement plan is does not necessarily end the problems with this requirement. For one thing plans may have to be aggregated, even if they are *not* both of the same type, if they have interrelated benefit formulas. Also, it may be impossible to obtain distribution of 100 percent of all similar plans. For example, the employer may have two pension plans (a defined benefit and a money purchase), which must be aggregated for purposes of this requirement, but the employer may permit lump sum distributions from only one of them. See PLR 2002-50036, in which the employer converted part of a pension plan to a stock bonus plan so employees could receive an LSD from the stock bonus plan without having to take anything from the pension plan. If the employer maintains more than one plan, and it is proposed to take an LSD from only one of them, have the employer certify that this requirement is met.

(c)   Landmine: employers under common control

When aggregating "plans of a similar type" of the "employer," who is the "employer"? Must we aggregate separate *employers*, too, if they are under common control?

When two employers are under common control (*e.g.*, a proprietorship and a corporation owned by the same person), § 414 says the two entities will be treated as one "employer" for purposes of certain Code sections relating to retirement plans. § 414(b), (c). § 402 is not among the listed sections. This would suggest that employers are *not* aggregated for purposes of § 402. However, the author is not aware of any authority one way or the other on this question. If your client is taking an LSD from an employer's plan, while he still has a balance in a plan of "similar type" maintained by a different employer that is under common control, this question must be further investigated.

2.4.05 *Exceptions to the all-in-one-year rule*

"[A]ccumulated deductible employee contributions" can be ignored in determining whether the employee has received a distribution of his entire plan balance. § 402(e)(4)(D)(i). This type of contribution, which was permitted under § 72(o) only for the years 1982–1986, is rarely encountered.

Another exception: "Dividends to ESOP participants pursuant to section 404(k)(2)(B) of the Code are not treated as part of the balance to the credit of an employee for purposes of the lump sum distribution rules...Thus, such distribution does not prevent a subsequent distribution of the balance to the credit of an employee from being a lump sum distribution." PLRs 9024083, 1999-47041.

Unfortunately, MRDs are *not* ignored in applying the all-in-one-year rule. If a participant starts taking MRDs from the plan, he must take out the entire plan balance in the same calendar year he takes the first MRD, or he will lose out on LSD treatment (unless there is a subsequent new triggering event).

2.4.06 *Special averaging: Participant born before 1936*

If an LSD (as defined in ¶ 2.4.02–¶ 2.4.05) meets certain additional requirements, the LSD can be taxed separately, using "10-year averaging" and "20 percent capital gain." These two special tax deals are referred to collectively as the "special averaging method." An LSD for which a proper election is made to use these methods is excluded from the recipient's adjusted gross income (AGI), and is instead taxed using special rates. § 402(d)(3); § 62(a)(8). (These Code sections have been repealed for years after 1999, but still apply under the "transition rule" that "grandfathers" participants born before 1936; see effective dates for amendments to § 62 and § 402).

A.   **Exclusion from income.** The fact that an LSD for which special averaging is elected is excluded from AGI can be beneficial, but it can also create problems.

On the good side, it means the distribution will not be included in AGI for purposes of: the income limits for obtaining a Roth IRA (¶ 5.4.04); the threshold for deducting medical expenses (7.5% of AGI; § 213(a)); the threshold for reduction of itemized deductions by a percentage of "excess" AGI (§ 68; see ¶ 2.3.07); the threshold for reducing personal exemptions (§151(d)(3)); or determining how much of the recipient's Social Security benefits will be subject to income tax under § 86. On the negative side, the exclusion of the LSD from AGI may reduce the client's ability to deduct large charitable gifts; the charitable deduction is limited to a certain percentage of AGI. § 170(b).

B.   **Tax using 10-year averaging.** Here is how to determine the tax under the 10-year averaging method:

(i)   Divide the LSD by 10.

(ii)   Determine the tax on 10 percent of the LSD using 1986 rates applicable to single taxpayers (conveniently reproduced in the instructions to IRS Form 4972).

(iii)   Multiply the amount obtained in step (ii) by 10. The result is the 10-year averaging tax applicable to the distribution.

Although maximum tax rates were higher in 1986 than they are now, the effect of the 10-year averaging calculation is to tax the distribution as if it were 10 small distributions rather than one big distribution. The result can be dramatically lower-than-usual taxes, especially on smaller LSDs. See Table 5 in Appendix A. A "minimum distribution allowance" produces an even lower tax on distributions under $70,000; see Form 4972.

Note: No tax is paid currently on the value of certain annuity contracts included in the distribution, though the value is still counted as part of the LSD. Also, the above method determines the tax on the "ordinary income" portion of the LSD. See "C" for possible capital gain treatment of part of the distribution.

C.   **"Capital gain" portion.** If the participant was born before 1936, and was a participant in the plan prior to 1974, part of the LSD for which the "special averaging method" has been elected is eligible to be treated as a "capital gain" taxed at 20 percent. This 20 percent rate applies without regard to the actual tax rate on capital gain in any particular year.

Prop. Reg. § 1.402(e)-2(d) provides that the "capital gain" portion of the distribution is determined by deducting the "ordinary income portion" (OIP) from the "total taxable amount" (TTA). The OIP is determined by multiplying the TTA by the following fraction:

Numerator: Calendar years of active participation after 1973.
Denominator: Total calendar years of active participation.

In the case of pre-1974 years, the employee gets twelve months' credit for each calendar year or partial calendar year of participation. For post-1973 years, he gets one *month's* credit for each calendar month or part of a month in which he is an active participant.

With smaller distributions, the 20 percent "capital gain method" may produce a higher tax than would apply under 10-year averaging. In this case, the participant can elect to have his capital gain portion treated as ordinary income; or rather, technically, to "treat pre-1974 participation as post-1973 participation." See § 402(e)(4)(L) as it existed prior to repeal by TAMRA '88 § 1011A(b)(8)(G). If this election is made, the 20 percent treatment is waived and the entire distribution is taxed under 10-year averaging.

Mike Jones on LSD Anomalies

Mike Jones, CPA *extraordinaire*, who has "dominion over palm and pine" (he practices in California and Minnesota), offers the following observations about the special averaging treatment of LSDs:

1.   Special averaging treatment for an LSD is the only occasion in the Code when a trust or estate gets to use the *individual* income tax rate schedule rather than trust rates.

2.   The exclusion from income means a client can receive (say) a $100,000 LSD, elect special averaging, pay $14,471 of income tax (see Table 5, Appendix A), donate the $100,000 to charity, and (subject to the limits in § 170(b)) take a deduction of $100,000 from his *ordinary* income (saving $35,000 of income tax).

3.   On the negative side, if the LSD is subject to state income tax, it may generate a large deduction for state income tax, which in turn may make the taxpayer subject to the alternative minimum tax if the LSD is excluded from AGI.

2.4.07 *Eligibility for special averaging method*

The special averaging method is available only for individuals "who attained age 50 before 1 - 1 - 86." TRA '86 § 1122(h)(3), (5), (6), as amended by TAMRA '88, § 1011A(b), (13)–(15). The IRS interprets this as applying to anyone born before January 2, 1936; see Instructions to IRS Form 4972 (2005), p. 2. Special averaging may be elected only once with respect to a taxpayer. It must be elected for all lump sum distributions in the same year that qualify for it. *Special averaging cannot be used if any portion of the distribution is rolled over.* The LSD will be subject to mandatory 20 percent income tax withholding; see ¶ 2.2.02(C). Other requirements are listed in Part I of Form 4972 (2005), which can be used as a checklist to determine qualification.

Only individuals, estates, and trusts can elect (by filing Form 4972) the special averaging method. A distribution to a partnership or corporation will not qualify; see former § 402(d)(4)(B). For more details on how to calculate the tax under the special averaging method, see ¶ 2.4.08–¶ 2.4.11 of the 5th edition (2003) of this book.

The 10-year averaging and 20 percent capital gain tax grandfather rules were not repealed by EGTRRA and thus will continue to be available indefinitely for LSDs of benefits of employees born before 1/2/1936; however, EGTRRA did add one new limitation.

EGTRRA substantially liberalized the rollover rules (see ¶ 2.6). Congress intended the new rollover rules to increase the "portability" of pensions, not to increase the amounts eligible for ancient grandfather rules. Accordingly, EGTRRA § 641(f)(3) provides that the benefits of TRA '86 § 1122(h) "shall not apply" to a distribution from an otherwise-eligible retirement plan "if there was a rollover to such plan on behalf of such individual which is permitted solely by reason of any amendment made by this section." Like the new rollover rules themselves, this limitation is permanent as a result of PPA '06.

2.5 Net Unrealized Appreciation of Employer Stock

This ¶ 2.5 describes the special favorable tax treatment available for "lump sum distributions" (and certain other distributions) of employer stock from a retirement plan. For charitable giving with "NUA stock" see ¶ 7.6.04. For 10 percent penalty on distributions of stock prior to the employee's attaining age 59½, see ¶ 9.1.03(A).

2.5.01 NUA: Tax deferral and long-term capital gain

The Code gives special favorable treatment to distributions of employer securities (referred to here as "employer stock," though the "securities" could be stocks or bonds; § 402(e)(4)(E)) from a qualified plan.

Under certain circumstances, the "net unrealized appreciation" (NUA) inherent in the stock is excluded from the employee's gross income at the time the securities are distributed to the employee. § 402(e)(4)(A), (B). NUA is the excess of the stock's fair market value at the time of distribution over the plan's basis in the stock. Reg. § 1.402(a)-1(b)(2). When the stock is later sold, the NUA is taxed as long-term capital gain, regardless of how long the recipient (or the plan) actually held the stock. Reg. § 1.402(a)-1(b)(1)(i); Notice 98-24, 1998-1 C.B. 929; PLR 2004-10023.

Joe Example: Joe, age 61, retires from Baby Bell Corp. in 2005 and receives an LSD of his 401(k) plan, consisting entirely of 10,000 shares of Baby Bell stock. The plan's basis for that stock is $10 per share; the stock is worth $100 a share at the time of the distribution. Joe will receive a 1099-R from Baby Bell for 2005, indicating a "Gross distribution" of $1 million (in Box 1), a "Taxable amount" of $100,000 (in Box 2a), and "Net unrealized appreciation" of $900,000 (in Box 6). In Box 2b, "Total distribution" will be checked.

How Joe reports this distribution: Joe does not have to file any special tax form to report his receipt of NUA stock. He does *not* have to file Form 4972, which is used only by those claiming the special tax treatments for those born before 1936 (¶ 2.4.06). He simply reports the "Gross distribution" amount (from Box 1) on line 16a of his 2005 Form 1040, and the "Taxable amount" (from Box 2a) on line 16b, as a retirement plan distribution.

What happens when Joe sells the stock: If Joe sells the stock immediately for $1 million, he will have long-term capital gain of $900,000. If he waits two months and sells the stock for $125 a share, he has a short-term capital gain of $250,000 ($25 appreciation between date of distribution and date of sale, times 10,000 shares) in addition to his long-term capital gain of $900,000. If he holds the stock for 12 months after receiving the distribution, all gain on any subsequent sale will be long-term capital gain.

The tax deferral/capital gain treatment is not available for all distributions of employer securities. It applies in only two situations:

1.   If the securities are distributed as part of a "lump sum distribution" (¶ 2.4.02–¶ 2.4.05) *all* the NUA is nontaxable at the time of the distribution. § 402(e)(4)(B).

2.   If the distribution is *not* an LSD, then only the NUA attributable to the *employee's* contributions is excludable. § 402(e)(4)(A).

2.5.02 *Determining the amount of NUA*

The employer or plan determines its "cost or other basis" in the plan-held employer securities using one of the methods in Reg. § 1.402(a)-1(b)(2), and thus determines how much of a distribution of employer securities is NUA. Notice 89-25, 1989-1 C.B. 662, A-1. The employer then reports this figure in Form 1099-R (2005), Box 6.

2.5.03 *Distributions after the employee's death*

The favorable tax treatment of NUA also applies when employer stock is distributed to the employee's beneficiary, provided the beneficiary takes an LSD of the employee's balance. If the beneficiary takes distribution of the benefits in some form other than an LSD, then the beneficiary can exclude only the NUA attributable to stock purchased with the employee's contributions. ¶ 2.5.01.

The IRS has held that the NUA, like other post-death retirement plan distributions, constitutes "IRD" (¶ 2.3). Rev. Rul. 69-297, 1969-1 C.B. 131. Accordingly, when the participant's beneficiaries sell the employer stock that is distributed to them from the plan in a qualifying distribution, the NUA portion of the sale proceeds is long-term capital gain. They will get a § 691(c) deduction (¶ 2.3.04) for the estate taxes paid on the NUA; this deduction will reduce the capital gain.

2.5.04 *Basis of stock distributed in life, held until death*

When the employee receives an LSD of employer stock and the NUA is excluded from his income, his basis in the stock going forward is the value that *was* taxed upon distribution, *i.e.*, the plan's original cost basis of the stock. If the employee still holds the stock at death, the IRS has ruled that such stock does *not* receive a stepped-up basis (under § 1014(c)) to the extent the employee benefitted from exclusion of NUA. According to the IRS, the NUA retains its character as NUA even after the employee's death, and will constitute IRD to the employee's heirs when they eventually sell the stock. Only to the extent, if any, that the stock appreciated in value *after* it was distributed to the employee by the plan does it receive a stepped-up basis. Rev. Rul. 75-125, 1975-1 C.B. 254.

Though Rev. Rul. 75-125 has not been revoked, there are indications the IRS has changed its mind since 1975. One indication is that the IRS has allowed NUA-stock recipients to assign their stock and its NUA to charitable remainder trusts; see ¶ 7.6.04. If the NUA represented unrealized income that would be IRD at the participant's death, an assignment of it should trigger income tax. Also, PLR 2000-38050 (eighth ruling) directly contradicts Rev. Rul. 75-125, holding that NUA stock contributed by the employee to a charitable remainder trust gets a stepped-up basis to the extent the CRT is included in the employee's estate.

NUA: Expert Tips

When first advising an employee who holds NUA stock in his retirement plan, consider consulting with a more experienced practitioner. Advisors who counsel numerous NUA stock-holding retirees often know more about the subject than the plan's own counsel and/or an auditing IRS agent. Here are some tips and war stories from three advisors who have counseled hundreds of employees regarding the best disposition of their NUA stock:

Mark Cortazzo, CFP, of Parsippany, NJ, reports that each employer has its own method of calculating the "basis" of the NUA stock; the employee may be able to take advantage of his particular employer's variation to increase his NUA benefit prior to retiring. Mark also has found shocking mistakes by employers, such as reporting periodic distributions as being entitled to NUA treatment even though they clearly don't qualify.

Frank Duke, CPA, of Cincinnati, OH, recommends that the employee consider rolling over stock equal in value to the employer's "basis," and not rolling stock equal in value to the NUA. Using the basis allocation method endorsed by the IRS in PLR 8538062 (¶ 2.5.07(B)), this maximizes the tax benefits to the employee, who can realize long-term capital gain immediately on the NUA portion while deferring income tax on the ordinary income portion that is rolled over.

Bob Keebler, CPA, of Green Bay, WI, and his firm Virchow Kraus, do extensive work with NUA-holding employees and retirees. PLR 2002-15032 (see ¶ 7.6.04), involving gifting NUA stock to a charitable remainder trust, is an example of their creative planning. Much of Bob's work involves computer modeling and hedging strategies to help clients maintain their employer stock (and favorable NUA treatment) while managing the risk of a one-stock portfolio. Bob shares his NUA expertise in seminars and tapes; see Bibliography.

2.5.05 *Election to include NUA in income*

The recipient can elect *out* of the favorable tax treatment, *i.e.*, can elect to have the NUA taxed as income when the distribution is received rather than deferring tax until the stock is sold. This option could be attractive if (i) the distribution qualifies for special averaging (¶ 2.4.06) and (ii) the total distribution is small enough that the tax under the special averaging method is less than the capital gain tax that will otherwise eventually have to be paid. Of course this decision is based on some guesswork, since it involves comparing today's special averaging rate with tomorrow's capital gain rate.

2.5.06 *Should employee keep the LSD or roll it over?*

For most retiring employees, rolling over, to an IRA, a lump sum distribution received from an employer plan is the best tax-saving and financial planning strategy. The opportunity for continued tax-deferred growth of retirement assets inside an IRA offers the greatest financial value for *most* retirees.

An LSD which includes appreciated employer securities often provides an exception to this rule of thumb. Since the NUA is not taxed currently anyway, rolling it over does not defer tax on the NUA. Furthermore, rolling over NUA will convert this unrealized long-term capital gain into ordinary income, since IRA distributions cannot qualify for NUA treatment. Reg. § 1.402(c)-2, A-13(a), last two sentences. So which is best, taking employer stock as part of the LSD (to take advantage of the NUA deal) or rolling over that stock to an IRA? The answer depends on multiple factors (as well as guesswork), and there is no one decision that is right for everyone.

Factors to consider include:

A. **How old is the employee?** If he is under 59½, the currently taxable part of the distribution will be subject to the 10 percent penalty (¶ 9.1.03(A)) unless it qualifies for an exception or unless the tax can be eliminated by a partial rollover (¶ 2.5.07(B)). Also, the younger the employee is, the more attractive continued tax deferral through a total rollover becomes because he has many more years to go until his RBD (¶ 1.4). If he is near or past age 70½, on the other hand, MRDs are starting or have started already, so an immediate distribution at a low tax rate becomes more attractive relative to the limited possibilities for continued deferral.

B. **What other plans does the participant have?** If the employee has substantial other assets in other retirement plans, the chance to cash out some of his benefits at a relatively low tax rate can be appealing. But if this is the employee's only retirement nest egg, rolling it to an IRA could be more attractive.

C.   **How much of the distribution is NUA?** If the NUA is a
substantial portion of the stock's value, taking the NUA deal
becomes more attractive, even irresistible. If the NUA is a
small portion, however, rolling over becomes more attractive.

Thus, the advice to a 45-year-old executive who is switching
jobs, whose employer stock is only 10 percent NUA, and who needs to
save for retirement, may be to roll over the entire distribution (and
forfeit the NUA deal), while the advice to a 71-year-old whose stock
is 90 percent NUA and who has other retirement plans that are funded
beyond his likely needs would be the opposite.

2.5.07 NUA and partial rollovers

Although it is a requirement, when claiming special averaging
(¶ 2.4.06), that no portion of the LSD be rolled over, and indeed that no
other qualifying distribution received in the same year be rolled over,
no such requirement applies to obtaining the exclusion from income of
the NUA portion of an LSD.
For the effect of combining an NUA distribution and a partial
rollover for a year in which a minimum distribution is required, see
Elizabeth Example at ¶ 2.6.04.

A.   **Rolling over everything except the NUA stock.** If the
employee receives a distribution that (i) meets the LSD
requirements (¶ 2.4.02–¶ 2.4.05) and (ii) includes employer
securities, the employee can exclude from his income the NUA
inherent in the securities, while rolling over to an IRA the *rest*
of the distribution, *i.e.*, the assets other than the employer
securities, which otherwise would be included in gross income.
See PLRs 2004-10023, 2001-38030, 2001-38031, 2000-38052,
2000-38057, 9721036. This can even be done by direct rollover
of the nonstock assets to another plan; see PLR 2000-03058.

If the LSD includes other assets besides the NUA stock it is
usually desirable to roll over the nonstock assets, because there is no
special tax advantage to not rolling them over. The only exception
would be, if the LSD also qualifies for special averaging treatment
(¶ 2.4.06), the employee should evaluate whether special-averaging
gives him a low enough tax rate on the LSD to make it worthwhile *not*

to roll over any part of the distribution, then pay tax on the taxable portion using the special averaging method. See Instructions for IRS Form 4972 (2005).

B.   **Rolling over part of the NUA stock.** If the employee rolls over some but not all of the employer stock, the NUA and employer basis must be allocated between the rolled and the nonrolled stock. The employee would like to allocate the NUA, to the maximum extent possible, to the stock that is *not* rolled over, so as to: postpone taxes on that portion until the stock is sold; incur tax on that portion only at capital gain rates; and (if he is under age 59½ and does not qualify for any exception to the premature distributions penalty), avoid the 10 percent penalty (¶ 9.1.03(A)). The employee would like to allocate the ordinary-income employer-basis portion of the distribution, to the maximum extent possible, to the stock that is rolled over to the IRA, so he does not have to pay current tax (or penalty).

        That method of allocation would be correct, according to the IRS in the well-reasoned PLR 8538062, which is the only IRS pronouncement discussing this subject. Though there is no authority directly on point, this approach is consistent with other regulations on similar subjects. See Prop. Reg. § 1.402A-1, A-5(b), dealing with a partial rollover of a nonqualified distribution from a designated Roth account (taxable portion is deemed rolled over first; ¶ 5.7.06); and Reg. § 1.402(c)-2, A-8 (if a partially taxable distribution is received in the same year as a distribution is required under § 401(a)(9), the nontaxable portion is allocated first to the MRD, which cannot be rolled over, and the taxable portion is therefore treated as an eligible rollover distribution to the maximum extent possible).

        Another approach would be to allocate NUA and ordinary income proportionately to the rolled and nonrolled stock; this approach appears possibly to have been used in PLR 2000-38050. Later PLRs do not discuss how basis and NUA are allocated between the rolled and nonrolled shares received in an LSD of employer stock; see, *e.g.*, PLRs 2002-43052, 2002-15032.

2.5.08 *If the employee wants to sell the stock*

If the employee wants to sell the employer stock he is receiving, more complex calculations become necessary in evaluating the rollover-or-not choice. He can take his distribution of employer stock, not roll it over, and sell it; he will then pay tax at long-term capital gain rates, to the extent the sale proceeds consist of NUA.

Or, the employee can roll the stock over to an IRA and sell it inside the IRA and pay *no* current tax. This approach could be attractive if the taxation can be deferred, via the IRA, for a very long period of time. Even if the employee's ordinary income tax bracket at the time of ultimate future distribution will be higher than the capital gain tax he would have to pay today if he sells the stock outside the plan, the advantages of deferral may overcome the bracket differential.

For another approach that may be attractive if the employee wants to sell the stock see ¶ 7.6.04.

2.5.09 *Client with shortened life expectancy*

A client faced with imminent death may want to know what steps can be taken to increase the financial protection of his family if the anticipated event occurs.

If such a client is a participant in a plan that holds appreciated employer stock, consider whether a lump sum distribution (LSD) should be taken before death. By taking an LSD prior to death and rolling over any nonstock assets in the plan to an IRA, the employee gets the following advantages. He preserves the NUA treatment for the stock for himself and/or his beneficiaries (or possibly even gets a stepped-up basis for his beneficiaries? See ¶ 2.5.04); and he allows the beneficiaries to get the life expectancy "stretch" payout for the rollover IRA that is payable to them as beneficiaries.

If the employee dies while all his assets are still in the QRP, the beneficiaries lose any hope of getting a stepped-up basis for the NUA portion of the stock. Also, to get the NUA treatment for the stock, they will have to take an LSD of the entire plan. If this occurs after 2006, then (as a result of PPA '06) they can direct the distribution of the nonstock portion of the LSD to an "inherited IRA" payable to them (see ¶ 2.6.03) if they want to preserve the "stretch" payout for those assets. Thus, after 2006, the importance of the employee's taking a pre-death LSD is greatly diminished if not eliminated.

2.6 Rollovers and Plan-to-Plan Transfers

2.6.01 *Definitions of rollover and plan-to-plan transfer*

A retirement plan distribution is not taxed in the year received if it is "rolled over" to the same or a different retirement plan or IRA, if various requirements are met. § 402(c)(1). A **rollover** means either:

A.   **60-day rollover.** A distribution from one plan or IRA to the participant (or his surviving spouse), followed by the participant's (or spouse's) redepositing the distribution in the same or another plan or IRA; or

B.   **Direct rollover.** The transfer of assets from the participant's account in a qualified retirement plan (QRP) to an IRA in the name of the participant or of his surviving spouse.

This ¶ 2.6 deals primarily with rollovers by the participant. For rollovers by a surviving spouse, see ¶ 3.2.

In an IRA-to-IRA transfer, assets move directly from one IRA to another; there is no distribution. An IRA-to-IRA transfer is also sometimes called a trustee-to-trustee, plan-to-plan, or custodian-to-custodian transfer. Some of the technical rules that apply to rollovers do not apply to IRA-to-IRA transfers. Rev. Rul. 78-406, 1978-2 C.B. 157. IRA-to-IRA transfers are not considered distributions "to" the participant or beneficiary who owns the IRA, nor are they considered "contributions" or "rollovers" to the recipient IRA for IRS reporting purposes. Instructions for IRS Forms 1099-R and 5498 (2005), p. R-12. Therefore, the nonspouse beneficiary of an IRA can direct the transfer of assets from the inherited IRA to another "inherited" IRA payable to such beneficiary. PLR 2005-28031.

Adding to the confusion: The conversion of a traditional IRA to a Roth IRA (¶ 5.4.01), even if it is done by means of an IRA-to-IRA transfer, must meet some (not all) requirements of a true "rollover." Also, some plan administrators carry out an IRA-to-IRA transfer (or direct rollover) by having the transferring plan (1) write a check payable to the transferee plan, but then (2) give the actual check to the participant. See Reg. § 1.401(a)(31)-1, A-4.

Until 1992, the requirements for a valid rollover were almost as difficult and perilous as the LSD rules, but UCA (applicable to distributions after 1992) liberalized the rules, making rollovers easier to accomplish. EGTRRA further eased the rules; pre-2002, a participant could roll a QRP distribution only to another QRP or an IRA. § 402(c)(8)(B) now allows (permanently, as a result of PPA '06; see p. 575) tax-free rollovers of post-2001 distributions from QRPs to 457 and 403(b) plans.

2.6.02 *Distributions that can or cannot be rolled over*

Any distribution from a QRP, IRA, or 403(b) plan can be rolled over except those listed in A–F below. If income taxes have been withheld from a retirement plan distribution, the participant or surviving spouse can nevertheless roll over the withheld amount by substituting other funds. Reg. § 1.402(c)-2, A-11; see PLR 2003-44024.

Here are the distributions that can NOT be rolled over:

A.   **Inherited plans.** A distribution from an inherited retirement plan *generally* may not be rolled over by any beneficiary other than the surviving spouse; see ¶ 2.6.03 for details and new exception created by PPA '06.

B.   **MRD.** A minimum required distribution (MRD; Chapter 1) cannot be rolled over. See ¶ 2.6.04.

C.   **Series payments.** "[A]ny distribution which is one of a series of substantially equal periodic payments" made annually or more often (1) over the life or life expectancy of the participant, (2) over the joint life or life expectancy of the participant and a designated beneficiary, or (3) over a "specified period of 10 years or more" may not be rolled over. § 402(c)(4)(A). Reg. § 1.402(c)-2, A-5, explains how to determine whether a distribution is part of a series of substantially equal payments.

D.   **Corrective and deemed distributions.** Certain corrective or "deemed" distributions, such as the taxable cost of insurance in a QRP (¶ 8.2.01) or the return of an excess 401(k) contribution, cannot be rolled over. Reg. § 1.402(c)-2, A-4.

E.   **Hardship distributions.** Hardship distributions cannot be rolled over. § 402(c)(4). Prior to 2002, this limitation applied only to distributions from 401(k) plans; now it applies to hardship distributions from any type of plan.

F.   **12-month limitation on IRA rollovers.** See ¶ 2.6.07 for a limitation on the number of IRA-to-IRA rollovers that can occur within 12 months of each other.

G.   **Plan loans.** When a participant borrows money from a QRP, the loan amount is deemed distributed to the participant at the time the loan is made unless the loan meets various requirements. § 72(p). ¶ 2.1.03(F). A deemed distribution under § 72(p) is not an eligible rollover distribution. Reg. § 1.402(c)-2, A-4(d). However, if the loan is *not* a deemed distribution (because it meets the requirements of § 72(p)), and the plan later repays itself the loan amount using the participant's plan benefits (for example, upon the participant's termination of employment), the plan's repayment of itself is called a "loan offset," which is treated as a distribution to the participant, and this type of distribution IS an eligible rollover distribution. Reg. § 1.402(c)-2, A-9; PLR 2006-17037.

2.6.03 *Rollovers of inherited benefits*

For rollovers by a surviving spouse-beneficiary, see ¶ 3.2.

A *nonspouse* beneficiary is not allowed to roll over inherited benefits to the beneficiary's own plan. § 402(c)(9), § 408(d)(3)(C).

However, there are two types of transfers permitted for benefits inherited by a nonspouse beneficiary: First, any beneficiary can authorize a plan-to-plan transfer from one IRA inherited from a particular participant to another "inherited IRA" in the name of the same participant and payable to that same beneficiary. This is so because such IRA-to-IRA transfers are not considered "distributions" or "rollovers"; see ¶ 2.6.01. Inherited IRA is defined at § 408(d)(3)(C)(ii).

Second, under § 824 of PPA '06, a Designated Beneficiary who is not the participant's surviving spouse may transfer an inherited QRP benefit, by *direct rollover only*, to a separate "inherited IRA," established specifically to receive the distribution, in the name of the deceased participant and payable to such beneficiary. This option is available *only* for post-2006 distributions, and *only* for "Designated

Beneficiaries" (see ¶ 1.7 for definition). The IRS is to provide rules whereby a trust maintained for the benefit of one or more designated beneficiaries is treated as a designated beneficiary for this purpose. § 402(c)(11), added by PPA '06. This provision increases the importance of naming a "Designated Beneficiary" for QRP benefits.

For pre-2007 distributions, an inherited plan cannot be rolled over by a nonspouse beneficiary even if the participant had requested the distribution and direct rollover prior to his death and done everything necessary to effectuate such distribution/rollover. See PLR 2002-04038 (denying the beneficiaries the right to complete a rollover in those circumstances). However, if (unlike in PLR 2002-04038) the money has actually left the transferor plan, see PLR 2006-08029, in which a surviving spouse, as executor, was allowed to complete the deceased participant's rollover; the decedent had requested a direct rollover to an IRA he had created to receive the distribution, the plan issued the checks, and the participant died before receiving the checks.

A nonspouse beneficiary's taking a distribution from an inherited plan, even if accidental or unintentional, is a mistake that cannot be fixed; the IRS has no power to authorize the contribution of the distributed amount to the same or another plan. PLR 2005-13032. This strict rule will continue to plague beneficiaries even after 2006, because the provision allowing some post-death "rollovers" by nonspouse beneficiaries is available only for direct rollovers; once the money has been distributed by the plan, it's too late for a direct rollover.

Two obscure grandfather rules

Unlike a surviving spouse (see ¶ 3.2.04), a *nonspouse* beneficiary cannot elect to treat the decedent's IRA as the beneficiary's own, with one exception: Any beneficiary of an IRA owner who died *before 1984* could elect to treat the decedent's IRA as his or her own IRA. See 1987 version of Prop. Reg. § 1.408-8, A-4; this grandfather rule is not mentioned in the final regulations.

Another one: A decedent who separated from service before 1983, and dies without having changed the "form of benefit," is entitled to 100 percent exclusion of the retirement benefit from his gross estate for federal estate tax purposes. If he separated from service after 1982 but prior to 1985, the exclusion is limited to $100,000. See § 1852(e)(3) of TRA '86, and PLR 9221030.

2.6.04 *Rollover in a year in which a distribution is required*

A minimum required distribution (MRD) cannot be rolled over. § 402(c)(4)(B), § 408(d)(3)(E). The "trap" is that *the first distribution received in any year* for which a distribution is required (Distribution Year) is considered part of the MRD for that year and thus cannot be rolled over. Reg. § 1.402(c)-2, A-7(a).

Elizabeth Example: Elizabeth, who retired several years ago, turned 70½ in Year 1, so her RBD is April 1, Year 2. Her 401(k) plan with her former employer contains $1 million of employer stock (with basis of $200,000 and NUA (¶ 2.5) of $800,000), plus $500,000 of cash. It is now February, Year 2, and Elizabeth, after consulting with several financial, tax, and estate planning advisors, has decided: to take an LSD in Year 2; keep the NUA stock in her own name (then later selling some of it or giving some to charity); and roll over the $500,000 of cash to her IRA. She wants the stock distribution to satisfy her combined MRD requirement for the 401(k) plan for both Year 1 and Year 2 (which is about $120,000). To make sure this happens, she takes a distribution of all of the NUA stock FIRST, in March, Year 2. Only AFTER that stock has been distributed to her does she request a direct rollover of the cash to her IRA (which of course must be completed by December 31, Year 2, in order to have an "LSD"; ¶ 2.4.04). If she requested the rollover first, the plan would have to distribute her MRDs to her from the cash fund before it could do a direct rollover of the rest; Elizabeth would then have received a nonrollable MRD in cash, and she would IN ADDITION have to pay tax on the basis portion of the NUA stock when that was distributed later in Year 2.

Another "trap" in this rule is that the participant's first Distribution Year is not the year in which the required beginning date (RBD; ¶ 1.4) occurs; it is the year *before* the RBD. Thus the first Distribution Year is the year the participant reaches age 70½ (or retires as the case may be), even though the first MRD does not have to be taken until April 1 of the *following* year. Any distribution received on or after January 1 of the first Distribution Year will be considered part of the MRD for that year (until the entire MRD has been distributed), and thus cannot be rolled over. Reg. § 1.402(c)-2, A-7(a).

Leonard Example: Leonard turns 70½ on January 1, Year 1. On that date, he retires from his job at XYZ Corp. and asks the plan administrator of the retirement plan to send his benefits to his IRA in a direct rollover. The administrator replies that it will make a direct rollover of everything except the MRD for Year 1. Leonard is unhappy because he thought he could postpone all MRDs until his RBD in Year 2. Unfortunately, if he wants to not take any MRD in Year 1, then he also cannot do a rollover in Year 1. Note that a direct rollover IS considered a "distribution" for purposes of the rule that MRDs cannot be rolled over, even though a direct rollover is NOT considered a distribution for income tax or withholding purposes!

For similar problems facing Roth IRA converters, see ¶ 5.4.03(C). For effect of this rule on TEFRA 242(b) electors, see ¶ 1.4.10.

There are three quasi-exceptions to the no-rollover-of-MRDs rule: One is when a plan has an earlier required beginning date than the statute requires; see ¶ 1.4.05. The second is when a surviving spouse named as sole beneficiary of an IRA is deemed to have elected to treat it as her own if she fails to take an MRD, which in effect allows her to roll over that MRD in certain cases; see ¶ 3.2.04(D), #3, ¶ 3.2.06(B), ¶ 1.6.06(B). Finally, it was possible to roll over certain MRDs under transition rules when the final minimum distribution regulations were coming into effect.

2.6.05 *Rollovers of nontaxable distributions*

§ 402(c)(1) provides that an eligible rollover distribution from a QRP is excluded from gross income if it is rolled over to an eligible retirement plan. § 402(c)(2) provides, among other things, that the maximum amount that may be transferred in a rollover is the amount of the distribution that (absent a rollover) would have been includible in the recipient's gross income. However, this limitation (limiting the rollover to pretax amounts) does *not* apply to (1) direct rollovers to another QRP or (2) any rollover to an IRA. § 402(c)(8)(B)(i). Thus, both pretax and after-tax moneys may be rolled over from a QRP to a traditional IRA. (Reg. § 1.402(c)-2, A-3, which provides to the contrary, has not been amended to reflect this 2001 law change.)

However, after-tax money may *not* be rolled in the other direction (from an IRA into a QRP). § 408(d)(3)(A)(ii) generally allows rollovers from any traditional IRA to any other type of plan in years after 2001, but if the rollover is made from an IRA into a QRP, 403(a) or 403(b) plan, or 457 plan, only the *pretax* money in the traditional IRA may be rolled. § 402(c)(8)(B)(iii), (iv), (v), (vi). For planning opportunities created by these rules, see ¶ 2.1.11(A).

(Before 2002, money could be rolled from an IRA to a QRP or 403(b) plan only if the IRA contained no contributions other than one or more distributions rolled from the same or another QRP or 403(b) plan, so-called "conduit IRAs." See § 408(d)(3)(A)(ii)–(iii), prior to repeal by EGTRRA, and Reg. § 1.408(b)(2), which is now obsolete.)

2.6.06 *Deadline for completing a rollover; waivers*

A rollover generally must be completed no later than "the 60th day following the day on which the distributee received the property distributed." § 402(c)(3)(A). There is no automatic extension of this deadline if it falls on a weekend or holiday; see PLR 2006-06055. The deadline is 60 days, not two months. A distribution made on March 12th must be rolled over by May 11th; May 12th is too late. PLR 2005-23032.

There are several exceptions to the 60-day deadline. First, there is a 120-day deadline rather than a 60-day deadline for the rollover of a "first-time homebuyer" distribution (¶ 9.4.09) if the distribution is not used to purchase the residence "solely by reason of a delay or cancellation of the purchase or construction of the residence." § 72(t)(8)(E); PLR 2004-23033. The recontribution of the thwarted homebuyer distribution is also not treated as a rollover for purposes of the once-per-12-months rule (¶ 2.6.07). § 72(t)(8)(E).

Second, the IRS tends to grant blanket extensions for this and other tax deadlines in the case of certain federally-recognized disasters; see the IRS pronouncement applicable to the disaster in question (*e.g.*, IRS News Release IR-2004-115 extending deadlines for taxpayers affect by Hurricane Frances).

Third, regarding qualified reservist distributions, see ¶ 9.4.12.

Finally, for distributions after 2001, the IRS "may waive the 60-day requirement…where the failure to waive such requirement would be against equity or good conscience, including casualty, disaster, or other events beyond the reasonable control of the individual subject to such requirement." § 402(c)(3)(B); § 408(d)(3)(I). The hardship waiver provisions are now a permanent part of the Code, thanks to PPA '06. In Rev. Proc. 2003-16, 2003-1 C.B. 359, the IRS issued the following guidance for such hardship waivers:

A.   Automatic waiver for certain financial institution errors. The deadline is *automatically* waived in the following circumstances: The participant received a distribution after 2001, and (within the 60-day limit) transmitted the funds to a financial institution and did everything else required (under the financial institution's procedures) to deposit the funds in an eligible retirement plan, but "solely due to an error on the part of the financial institution" the funds were not deposited into the eligible retirement plan within 60 days of the original distribution. Provided the funds are actually deposited in the eligible plan within one year of the original distribution, there is an automatic waiver, and no need to seek IRS approval.

B.   Case-by-case waivers in other cases. A participant can request a hardship waiver of the deadline in all other circumstances (including financial institution errors not covered by the automatic waiver) by following the usual procedures for obtaining a private letter ruling. Although the legislative history of EGTRRA indicates that Congress wanted the IRS to issue "objective standards" for granting these waivers, the Rev. Proc. says only that the IRS will consider "all relevant facts and circumstances," such as "death, disability, hospitalization, incarceration, restrictions imposed by a foreign country or postal error;...the use of the amount distributed (for example...whether the check was cashed); and...the time elapsed since the distribution occurred."

Obtaining an IRS letter ruling requires payment of a "user fee" (filing fee). Under Rev. Proc. 2006-8, 2006-1 I.R.B. 245, though the usual fee for a private ruling request (effective for requests on or after February 1, 2006) is $9,000, requests for hardship waivers of the 60-day rollover deadline have their own user fee schedule, which is:

If the rollover is less than $50,000:	$ 500.
If the rollover is $50,000 or more, but less than $100,000:	$1,500.
If the rollover is $100,000 or more:	$3,000.

Prior to February 1, 2006, the fee to apply for a hardship waiver of the 60-day deadline for completing a tax-free rollover was $95, regardless of the amount involved. It looks as though a taxpayer who needs a waiver for a $51,000 distribution should only seek to roll over $49,999 of it; he's better off paying tax on $1,000 of unwanted distribution income than giving the IRS an extra $1,000 of fees!

Following issuance of Rev. Proc. 2003-16, the IRS began issuing a flood of private letter rulings dealing with these deadline waiver requests. Though there are some waiver requests granted where the taxpayer really doesn't have much of an excuse (*e.g.*, taxpayer waited until the 58th day, then found the bank was closed for a long holiday weekend so she couldn't deposit the check; PLR 2004-11052), most successful waiver requests involve one or more of the following facts: processing error or erroneous advice by a professional advisor or financial institution; a distribution that the recipient was unaware of; or illness, disability, or other trauma impairing the individual's ability to complete the rollover or otherwise deal with financial affairs.

Typical are those in which the participant's new financial advisor or institution inadvertently established a regular taxable account instead of an IRA with funds transferred from prior advisor or institution, such as PLRs 2004-02028, 2004-04053, 2004-01023, 2004-20035. In a large number of successful waiver requests, the original distribution was "involuntary," in that the participant hadn't requested it and often did not even realize it had occurred. See PLRs 2004-21009, 2004-21008, 2004-27027, 2004-35017, 2004-36014.

Many successful waiver requests involved participants who were hampered from initiating and/or completing the rollover by mental or physical health problems (of themselves or family members), a death in the family, or other catastrophes. See PLRs 2004-30039, 2004-30040, 2004-36021, 2004-04051, 2004-12002, 2004-26020, 2004-30037, 2004-30038, 2004-36021.

The IRS is most likely to refuse a waiver when the taxpayer deliberately took the distribution (*e.g.*, to allow spouse to qualify for Medicaid, PLR 2005-47024, or to pay medical expenses, PLR 2005-49023, or to complete a house closing, PLR 2005-44025); and/or shows no evidence of intent to roll it over until after the 60-day deadline (typically, when he discovers it is taxable; PLR 2005-46047, 2005-48030, 2005-49017, 2004-33029, 2004-22058); or he deliberately took it, intending to spend it and then replace the funds with other funds, but he did not receive the replacement funds in time to meet the 60-day deadline (PLRs 2004-17033, 2004-22053, 2004-23038, 2004-33022, 2004-36018, 2005-44025).

2.6.07 *Limit of one IRA-to-IRA rollover in 12 months*

A participant or surviving spouse may not roll over an IRA distribution to the same or another IRA "if at any time during the 1-year period ending on the day of...[the receipt of the distribution] such individual received any other amount...from an individual retirement account...which was not includible in his gross income because of the application of this paragraph." § 408(d)(3)(B).

A Roth conversion is not treated as a distribution or tax-free rollover for purposes of this rule. ¶ 5.4.01. For another exception (for thwarted would-be first-time home buyers), see § 72(t)(8)(E), ¶ 2.6.06.

A.   **How rule applies to multiple IRAs.** Under the statute, it appears that the tax-free rollover of a distribution from *any* IRA into the same or any other IRA prevents the tax-free rollover of any *other* IRA distribution that is received less than 12 months after the first distribution—regardless of which IRA the second distribution came from. However, the IRS applies the rule on an account-by-account basis. Once you have rolled over tax-free a distribution from one IRA (IRA #1) into another IRA (IRA #2), you cannot, within 12 months after the date of the distribution that was rolled over, do an IRA-to-IRA rollover of any *other* distribution from either of the two IRAs involved in the first rollover. IRS Publication 590 (2005), p. 23. However, you may roll over a distribution from an IRA that was not involved in the first rollover within that 12-month period.

B.   **Not a calendar year test.** The no-rollover period is twelve months from the date of receipt of the first distribution. Thus it is always necessary to look back into the prior calendar year, as well as to the current calendar year, in determining whether there has been a prior rolled-over distribution that would prevent the rollover of a second distribution.

C.   **Distribution dates count, not rollover dates.** The rule prevents tax-free rollover of a *distribution* that occurs within 12 months of a prior *distribution* that was rolled over. Thus, if Distribution #2 is received less than 12 months after Distribution #1, waiting until 12 months have elapsed since the prior *rollover* does *not* cure the problem. Similarly, there is no prohibition against two tax-free rollovers within 12 months of each other, provided that the *distributions being rolled over* did not occur within 12 months of each other.

Barak Example: Barak received Distribution #1 from IRA "A" on January 2, Year 1, and rolled it into IRA "B" on February 28, Year 1. He received Distribution # 2 from IRA "A" on January 5, Year 2, and rolled it into IRA "B" on February 1, Year 2. Both distributions are tax-free: Even though the second rollover occurred less than 12 months after the first rollover, the second *distribution* did not occur within one year of the first *distribution*.

D.   **Does not apply to plan-to-plan transfers.** The limit of one tax-free rollover per year has no application to a direct transfer of funds or property from one IRA custodian to another IRA custodian (IRA-to-IRA transfer; see ¶ 2.6.01). In most cases, concerns about § 408(d)(3)(B) can be easily avoided by using an IRA-to-IRA transfer rather than a rollover.

E.   **Affects only IRA-to-IRA rollovers.** § 408(d)(3)(B) limits only rollovers from an IRA into an IRA; it does not prevent a tax-free rollover of Distribution #2 into some other kind of eligible retirement plan, nor does it prevent multiple tax-free rollovers *into* an IRA from some other type of plan. Thus it would appear easy to avoid § 408(d)(3)(B) by rolling the second IRA distribution first into a QRP and then rolling it out again to another IRA shortly thereafter; but it has always been easy to avoid § 408(d)(3)(B) anyway (see "D").

F.   **Taxpayer cannot later choose which rollover is tax-free.**

Yoav Example: In July, Yoav withdraws $60,000 from IRA A, intending to roll it over tax-free to another IRA. Then he remembers that in the preceding March he received, and rolled over to IRA B, a $1,000 distribution from IRA A. He would rather pay tax on the $1,000 distribution than on the $60,000 distribution. He now wishes that he had said the $1,000 contribution to IRA B in March was part of his "regular" IRA contribution for the year, not a rollover of the distribution from IRA A. Unfortunately, he can not now retroactively elect to treat the $1,000 he deposited in IRA B in March as a regular rather than a rollover contribution. In order for a contribution to qualify as a tax-free rollover the participant must elect, "at the time the contribution is made, to treat the contribution as a rollover contribution...This election is irrevocable." Reg. § 1.402(c)-2, A-13. Thus, when Yoav made his $1,000 contribution to IRA B in March he was required to irrevocably designate it either as a rollover or a regular contribution. If he said it was a rollover contribution when he made it, he cannot retroactively change that election.

2.6.08 *Must roll over same property received*

A rollover cannot be used to "swap" property out of a retirement plan.

QRP: If property is distributed from a QRP, and tax-free rollover treatment of the distribution is sought, the same property that was received from the first plan must be contributed to the recipient plan. § 402(c)(1)(C). The only exception is that if the participant sells the property after receiving it from the first plan, the sales proceeds can be rolled over rather than the property itself; no income is reportable as a result of the sale (because it is treated as if it had occurred inside a retirement plan). § 402(c)(6). But the participant cannot simply substitute some other asset of equal value; if he still owns the property that was distributed to him from the first plan, that is what he must re-contribute to the same or another plan to have a tax-free rollover. Rev. Rul. 87-77, 1987-2 C.B. 115.

IRA: The Code does not authorize selling distributed property and rolling over the sale proceeds in connection with IRA-to-IRA rollovers. It blesses only rollovers of the "amount received (including money or other property)." § 408(d)(3)(A).

2.7 Putting it All Together

2.7.01 *The biggest income tax mistakes*

Missing the NUA opportunity. Anyone advising an employee (or the beneficiaries of a deceased employee) whose QRP account holds (or could purchase) employer stock MUST impress on the client the importance of considering the favorable NUA deal before the client does any of the following: sells the stock inside the plan; retires; takes a distribution from the plan; or (in the case of the employee or surviving spouse) rolls over anything from the plan to another plan or IRA. Unfortunately, some advisers advise clients to roll over their QRP distributions to an IRA without having evaluated the NUA deal. If the NUA stock is rolled into an IRA, there is no "distribution" of the stock to the employee and the favorable NUA deal is lost. See PLR 2004-42032, in which the client and his advisor agreed that the client should take advantage of the NUA deal when he retired, but when the client called the advisor to ask how to fill out the form requesting the distribution, the advisor said to tell the plan to register the stock in the name of the client's IRA. The advisor realized his mistake and tried to reverse the instructions, but could not because a rollover election is irrevocable. Reg. § 1.402(c)-2, A-13. The employee lost his NUA deal.

Missing the special averaging deal. Similarly, anyone advising a QRP participant (or the beneficiaries of a deceased QRP participant) who was born before January 2, 1936, should impress on the client the importance of considering the favorable special averaging deal (¶ 2.4.06) before the client takes a distribution from the plan or (in the case of the participant or surviving spouse) rolls over anything from the plan to another plan or IRA. Unfortunately, advisers routinely advise clients to roll over their QRP distributions to an IRA without having evaluated special averaging.

Choose beneficiaries without considering their income tax bracket. A grandparent with a modest estate, including retirement benefits, who has wealthy high-income children and young low-income grandchildren, should consider that the benefits will be worth more to the grandchildren. Similarly, if a parent has several children, it is more tax-efficient to leave the benefits to the child who has a medical condition that results in her having a low income and constant high medical expenses, rather than to high-income high-bracket children.

Overlooking the § 691(c) deduction. Planners neglect to consider the impact of the § 691(c) deduction for federal estate taxes paid on IRD. ¶ 2.3.04. The IRD deduction can create an incentive to cash out retirement benefits soon after the participant's death if the IRD is a relatively small part of a large estate. If the estate is large, the marginal estate tax bracket will be high, and that will make a relatively larger share of the IRD tax-free upon distribution. The beneficiary who receives the retirement plan distribution will therefore not lose too much of the distribution to income taxes, and can reinvest the after-tax distribution in property that will produce long-term capital gains and/or dividends, both of which (currently) enjoy relatively low income tax rates. In contrast, if the estate is not so large (so the estate tax and the resulting § 691(c) deduction are low), and/or if the retirement plan is a large portion of the estate (so any particular distribution from the plan will not carry out a large part of the § 691(c) deduction), there is less incentive for beneficiaries to take early distributions.

Even worse is the fact that many beneficiaries never are told they can take this deduction, causing them to waste thousands of dollars on taxes they don't owe.

2.7.02 *Planning for client with short life expectancy*

There are times when an estate planner is called upon to advise a client who, due to accident or illness, has a severely shortened life expectancy. One suggestion to consider is cashing out retirement plan benefits that will have to be cashed out anyway shortly after the client's demise (either because of minimum distribution requirements, or to pay estate taxes, or just because the beneficiaries will want the money). When an income-taxable retirement plan will have to be cashed out shortly after the participant's death, *and* the estate will be subject to estate taxes, there are several reasons why it is better to cash out the account immediately *before* death rather than immediately after:

First, if the plan is cashed out before death, the income taxes on the benefits are thereby removed from the estate for estate tax purposes—in effect, both the federal *and* state income taxes on the benefits become 100 percent deductible for estate tax purposes. If the plan is cashed out *after* death, the recipient of the benefits gets a federal income tax deduction under § 691(c) for the *federal* estate taxes paid on the benefits (¶ 2.3.04)—but *not* for the *state* estate taxes.

Second, the § 691(c) deduction is an itemized deduction, and as such may not be fully deductible; see ¶ 2.3.07. And, the recipient may not be able to take the deduction in determining his *state* income tax.

For all these reasons, paying the income taxes "first" and the estate taxes "second" may produce a lower tax burden overall than doing it the other way round. Another way to get the same advantages is to convert to a Roth IRA if the client is eligible; see ¶ 5.8.09(A).

On the other hand, if the death benefits are going to be paid to charity (so they will not be subject to income taxes—see Chapter 7), or will be paid to a designated beneficiary over a long life expectancy (so the income taxes can be deferred for a long time—see Chapter 1) this arbitrage advantage disappears. Similarly, if the beneficiary is in a lower tax bracket than the participant, that may reduce the arbitrage advantage. Finally, if the estate will not be subject to estate tax, there is no known tax advantage to cashing out the plans before death.

2.7.03 *Reasons to roll over (or stay put)*

Here are some reasons why a participant would or would not want to roll funds over from one type of retirement plan to a different type of plan. For considerations for a surviving spouse, see ¶ 3.2.02.

Roll from a QRP to an IRA to improve death benefit options: Many QRPs offer a lump sum as the only form of death benefit. ¶ 1.5.10. A lump sum is fine if the beneficiary is the spouse (who can roll it over; ¶ 3.2); or a charity (which is tax-exempt; ¶ 7.5); or a Designated Beneficiary (who can transfer it by direct rollover to an inherited IRA after 2006; ¶ 2.6.03). However, if the participant wants to leave his QRP benefits to his estate or to a non-see-through trust (i.e., not to a Designated Beneficiary, ¶ 1.7.03), and wants the beneficiary to be able to use the 5-year rule (¶ 1.5.06) or the participant's life expectancy (¶ 1.5.08) to stretch out the payments somewhat after his death, he needs to roll the benefits to an IRA *before* death, if the QRP requires an immediate lump sum distribution as the only form of death benefit. A beneficiary that is not a Designated Beneficiary cannot roll the lump sum distribution over even to an inherited IRA.

Roll from QRP to IRA to eliminate spousal rights: A person about to marry might roll QRP benefits to an IRA to avoid having federal spousal rights attach to the QRP benefits (see ¶ 3.4.); the IRA could be protected from state-law spousal rights via a prenuptial agreement. A married person can withdraw from a profit sharing plan without spousal consent, and roll the distribution to an IRA that is not subject to federal spousal rights; see ¶ 3.4.03.

Rollover from QRP to IRA: NUA stock: A participant who wants to use the NUA deal can take a lump sum distribution of his plan balance, and use a partial rollover to defer tax on part of the distribution while using the NUA deal for the rest of the distribution. ¶ 2.5.07.

Participant under age 59½: Many of the exceptions to the 10 percent penalty on pre-age-59½ distributions (see Chapter 9) apply only to certain types of plans, or apply differently depending on the type of plan. Thus a participant under age 59½ might roll money from a QRP to an IRA to use the "SOSEPP exception" (¶ 9.2), which is easier to implement in an IRA, or the first-time-homebuyer (¶ 9.4.09) or higher-education-expenses (¶ 9.4.08) exceptions, which are only available for IRAs. However, an employee retiring at age 55 or older would not roll to an IRA if he wanted to use the "early retirement" exception (¶ 9.4.04), which is available only for QRPs.

Participant approaching or past age 70½: For use of a rollover to prevent or stop MRDs, see ¶ 5.7.08 (for designated Roth accounts) or ¶ 1.2.06(C) (for traditional IRAs and other plans). Also for this age bracket, rolling from a QRP to an IRA may improve the person's eligibility to convert a traditional IRA to a Roth IRA; see ¶ 5.4.06.

Reasons to roll from an IRA to a QRP: An IRA cannot own life insurance (¶ 8.4.05) or make a loan to the participant, whereas a QRP can do these things. Also, see ¶ 2.1.11 regarding use of a rollover from an IRA to a QRP to facilitate the tax-free withdrawal (or tax-free Roth conversion) of the individual's after-tax money in the IRA. See ¶ 2.6.07 regarding use of an IRA-to-QRP rollover to evade the once-in-12-months rule.

Universal considerations: Some participants stay in (or leave) a QRP because the investment options and/or maintenance costs are better (or worse) than they would be in an IRA. Also, always consider state income tax effects; a few states offer income or estate/inheritance tax breaks for particular types of retirement plans, so rolling from one type of plan to another could destroy (or improve) the state income tax treatment. An individual concerned about possible creditors' claims should consider which type of plan is best protected; there is no universal answer to that question. While all tax-favored retirement plans receive a complete or nearly complete exemption in federal bankruptcy proceedings, protection varies wildly outside of bankruptcy, depending on state law (for IRA exemptions) and ERISA (which protects some but not all employer plans).

Marital Matters

*Rules and estate planning concerns for
the married participant and the
surviving spouse.*

This Chapter deals with various rules that apply (and planning
options available) to married participants. For convenience, the
participant is referred to as male and the spouse as female. All
statements apply equally to a female participant and her male spouse.

3.1 Considerations for Married Participants

3.1.01 *What practitioners must know*

When planning for disposition of the retirement benefits of a
married participant, whether the participant is leaving those benefits to
his spouse, to a trust for her benefit, or to someone else entirely, the
practitioner needs to know:

✓ How to plan for simultaneous deaths. ¶ 3.1.02.

✓ The advantages of, and rules applicable to, the spousal rollover.
¶ 3.2.

✓ When benefits are left to a marital trust, how to make sure the
disposition qualifies for the marital deduction, if estate taxes
are a concern. ¶ 3.3.

✓ Why leaving benefits to a trust for the spouse's benefit has
substantial income tax drawbacks compared with leaving
benefits to the surviving spouse outright. ¶ 3.3.02.

✓ How federal law ("REA") may prevent the participant from
naming the beneficiary he wants to name, or from taking
benefits out of his plan, without his spouse's consent. ¶ 3.4.

✓ The special minimum distribution provisions that apply to a surviving spouse named as beneficiary. ¶ 1.6.

3.1.02 *Simultaneous death clauses*

If the participant names his spouse as beneficiary, and they die simultaneously, it will be presumed under the Uniform Simultaneous Death Act (1993) that the spouse predeceased the participant. A presumption that the spouse *survived* the participant, if contained in the participant's will or trust, will NOT govern retirement benefits payable directly to the spouse. To be effective, the presumption must be contained in the designation of beneficiary form; see ¶ 1.7.02. Such a presumption may be used, if the spouse's estate is smaller than the participant's, to equalize the estates for estate tax purposes, provided that the plan documents do not create an irrefutable presumption that the participant survives the beneficiary in case of simultaneous deaths.

Although it may be desirable for estate tax purposes, a presumption that the spouse survives the participant, assuming it is recognized for minimum distribution purposes (see ¶ 1.7.02), will often produce bad results under the minimum distribution rules. The IRS's position is that normally the spouse's executor cannot exercise the spouse's right to roll over the benefits; see ¶ 3.2.09. Therefore, in *most* cases, the result of a presumption that the spouse survives in case of simultaneous deaths will be that benefits must be distributed over the remaining single life expectancy of the spouse, or by the end of the fifth year after the spouses' deaths. See ¶ 1.6.05, ¶ 1.6.06(E).

3.2 Spousal Rollover of Inherited Benefits; Election to Treat Inherited IRA as Spouse's IRA

This ¶ 3.2 deals with the surviving spouse's option to roll over, tax-free, to another retirement plan, distributions made to her from the retirement plan of her deceased spouse (the "participant"). ¶ 2.6 explains what a rollover is and the rules governing tax-free rollovers generally; this ¶ 3.2 discusses additional rules and considerations that apply to the rollover of inherited benefits by a surviving spouse.

When the surviving spouse inherits an IRA as sole beneficiary, she has the option to elect to treat it as her own. The effect of such an election is similar to a tax-free rollover. See ¶ 3.2.04.

In this Chapter, spousal rollover generally means a rollover into the spouse's own retirement plan; for rollover into another inherited plan, see ¶ 3.2.07.

3.2.01 *Advantages of spousal rollover*

The surviving spouse's ability to roll over inherited benefits to her own retirement plan gives her a powerful option to defer plan distributions, an option not available to other beneficiaries. By rolling over benefits to her own retirement plan, the spouse becomes "the participant" with regard to those benefits under the minimum distribution rules. By taking distributions as "owner," she gains the following deferral advantages compared with taking the benefits as beneficiary (¶ 1.6):

A.   **Later start for MRDs.** Other beneficiaries must commence taking minimum required distributions (MRDs) by the end of the year after the year of the participant's death (¶ 1.5.03, ¶ 1.5.04). A surviving spouse who is under age 70½ can postpone distributions from the rollover IRA until she reaches her own Required Beginning Date (RBD; ¶ 1.4).

B.   **Slower rate of MRDs (longer ADP).** The Applicable Distribution Period (ADP) for anyone (even the surviving spouse) who takes inherited benefits as *beneficiary* is the beneficiary's *single* life expectancy. ¶ 1.5.03(A),(B), ¶ 1.5.04(A),(B). In contrast to this, the surviving spouse's MRDs from a *rollover* IRA are determined using the Uniform Lifetime Table (¶ 1.3.01), under which her ADP is the *joint* life expectancy of the spouse (as participant) and a hypothetical 10-years-younger beneficiary. With smaller MRDs over a longer period of time, the rollover allows longer deferral of distributions than would taking benefits as beneficiary.

C.   **Start new life expectancy payout after spouse's later death.** The surviving spouse can name her own Designated Beneficiary for the rollover IRA. After her death, MRDs will then be based on the life expectancy of her Designated Beneficiary. ¶ 1.5.03, ¶ 1.5.04. In contrast, when a beneficiary (even the surviving spouse) takes the inherited benefits merely "as beneficiary," the ADP after such beneficiary's death does not change; it will continue to be what's left of the original beneficiary's life expectancy (¶ 1.5.14, ¶ 1.6.06(E)), except in the rare case when both spouses die young (¶ 1.6.05).

This does not mean that naming the spouse as beneficiary is necessarily the way to achieve the longest deferral of distributions. Nevertheless, the spousal rollover is still a valuable deferral tool for three reasons: First, most participants want to name their spouses as beneficiaries, despite the longer deferral that might be available if children or grandchildren were named, so the rollover becomes a way to revive the option of longer deferral if the spouse survives the participant (because she can name younger-generation Designated Beneficiaries for benefits remaining in the rollover IRA at her death).

Second, once the participant has died, the spousal rollover shines as a way to correct problems that exist with the participant's beneficiary designation. See ¶ 4.2.03.

Third, if the only form of distribution permitted by the participant's retirement plan is a lump sum distribution, the spousal rollover preserves the possibility of a life expectancy payout. ¶ 1.5.10.

3.2.02 Rollover if spouse is under age 59½

A surviving spouse who is under age 59½ faces a dilemma. If she leaves the inherited benefits in the deceased participant's plan, she can withdraw the benefits whenever she wishes penalty-free, because the 10 percent penalty on premature distributions does not apply to death benefits. ¶ 9.4.01. However, she may be forced to take annual MRDs as beneficiary (see ¶ 1.6.06(D)), and if she dies while the benefits are still in the deceased participant's account the distribution options after her death will *usually* be less favorable than the options available if she had rolled over the benefits to her own IRA; see ¶ 1.6.05, ¶ 1.6.06(E).

Alternatively, the spouse could take the benefits out of the deceased participant's account and roll them over to her own retirement plan, an action that will usually produce better distribution options for her beneficiaries upon her later death (¶ 3.2.01(C)); but once the benefits are rolled to her own plan, they become "her" benefits, and the death benefit exception no longer applies. She will not be able to withdraw from the rollover account until she reaches age 59½, unless

she pays the 10 percent penalty or qualifies for an exception
(¶ 9.2–¶ 9.4). Here are strategies to deal with this dilemma:

A.   **Leave benefits in decedent's plan until spouse reaches age
      59½, then roll them over.** While she is under age 59½, the
      spouse can withdraw funds as needed penalty-free under the
      death benefits exception. If her death prior to completing the
      rollover would produce undesirable tax results for her
      beneficiaries, she can buy life insurance to protect against that
      risk. If she will reach age 59½ before the end of the year in
      which the deceased participant would have reached age 70½,
      AND the decedent's plan allows her to name her own successor
      beneficiaries, AND she does so, this option does not produce
      bad results EVEN IF the surviving spouse herself dies before
      she reaches age 59½: Her designated beneficiaries' life
      expectancies would be the ADP. See ¶ 1.6.05. But that's not a
      very common scenario. This approach may be best for a poor
      widow and/or the widow of a young decedent.

B.   **Roll to spouse's IRA, use SOSEPP if money later needed.**
      The spouse could roll all of the inherited money over
      immediately to her own IRA, to stop or prevent having to take
      MRDs as beneficiary if applicable, and to assure that the best
      possible distribution options will be available to her
      beneficiaries regardless of when she dies. If she later needs
      funds from the rollover IRA while she is still under age 59½,
      she can use the "series of substantially equal periodic
      payments" exception (¶ 9.2) to avoid the 10 percent penalty.
      This option may be best for a very rich or very ill widow.

C.   **Roll some to spouse's plan, leave some in decedent's plan.**
      Estimate the spouse's needs prior to age 59½, leave that
      amount in the deceased participant's account (so she can
      withdraw it penalty-free), and roll over the rest to the spouse's
      own IRA (so if she happens to die before reaching age 59½ her
      beneficiaries will get the best choice of distribution options).

D.   **Roll to a Beneficiary IRA.** If the spouse wants to leave the
      benefits in the decedent's plan for a while, but the plan in
      question insists that the spouse must take a lump sum

distribution of the benefits immediately (¶ 1.5.10), the spouse can roll over that distribution to an IRA in the name of the decedent, payable to her as beneficiary, in order to preserve its status as a penalty-free death benefit until such later time as she chooses to roll it over to her own plan; see ¶ 3.2.07.

E.   **Comment on doing "some of each."** Note that strategies A, C, and D involve the spouse's taking part of the benefits as beneficiary and rolling over the rest. At one time, the IRS suggested that, by withdrawing *any* benefits penalty-free before she herself attained age 59½, the surviving spouse would be making an irrevocable election not to treat the participant's IRA as her own IRA. The IRS has abandoned this idea. Reg. § 1.408-8, A-5(a), (see ¶ 3.2.04(A)) allows the surviving spouse to treat her interest in an IRA inherited from the participant "or the remaining part of such interest if distribution thereof has commenced to the spouse" as the spouse's own IRA. By specifying that the spousal election can be made even after the spouse has taken one or more distributions as beneficiary, the IRS confirms that taking a distribution as beneficiary does not constitute an election not to treat the remaining benefits as the spouse's own. See PLRs 2001-10033, 2002-42044.

3.2.03 *Spousal rollover of QRP distribution*

§ 402(c)(1) allows a participant in a qualified retirement plan (QRP) to roll over certain plan distributions to another QRP, or to any other eligible plan, if various requirements are met. ¶ 2.6. If death benefits are paid to the participant's surviving spouse, the rollover rules "apply to such distribution in the same manner as if the spouse were" the participant. § 402(c)(9).

The distribution does not have to be the entire account balance. Partial distributions are eligible for rollover, unless they are MRDs or part of a series of substantially equal payments (¶ 2.6.02). The tests for determining whether a distribution is an "eligible rollover distribution," and other rollover rules, are the same for the surviving spouse as they would have been for the deceased participant. See ¶ 2.6, ¶ 3.2.07.

3.2.04 *Rollover (or spousal election) for IRA*

§ 408(d), in a backhanded way, permits a surviving spouse to treat the deceased spouse's IRA that is payable to her as beneficiary as if it were the spouse's *own* IRA:

A.   **Spousal election: Code and regulations.** The Code provides that distributions from an "inherited IRA" may not be treated as tax-free rollovers; but then goes on to say that an "inherited IRA" means an IRA acquired by reason of the death of another individual, if the person who inherited the account is not the surviving spouse of the decedent. § 408(d)(3)(C). Thus an IRA inherited by the surviving spouse is not subject to the restrictions applicable to an "inherited IRA" (¶ 2.6.03) and by negative implication the surviving spouse may roll over distributions she receives from the deceased participant's IRA as if it were the spouse's own IRA.

"Inherited IRA" or "Beneficiary IRA"

In the Code, "inherited IRA" doesn't mean what people normally mean by the term "inherited IRA." It means an IRA inherited by someone other than the surviving spouse; an IRA inherited by the spouse is not an "inherited IRA." This unfortunate phrasing in the Code (and regulations) leads to much confusion, as PLRs "blessing" a spouse's rollover of an IRA proclaim that the IRA is not an "inherited IRA," and therefore the spouse can roll it over. In this book, "inherited IRA" does NOT mean what it means in the Code; it means an IRA that is owned by someone (including the surviving spouse) in his or her capacity as beneficiary of a deceased participant. This book also sometimes uses the term "Beneficiary IRA" rather than "inherited IRA," to avoid the confusion surrounding the term "inherited IRA."

Reg. § 1.408-8, A-5(a), provides that "The surviving spouse of an individual may elect...to treat the spouse's entire interest as a beneficiary in an individual's IRA (or the remaining part of such interest if distribution thereof has commenced to the spouse) as the spouse's own IRA." The effect of such an election is that subsequent MRDs are "determined under section 401(a)(9)(A) with the spouse as IRA owner and not section 401(a)(9)(B) with the surviving spouse as the…beneficiary." See ¶ 1.6.06(B) for how to calculate MRDs when the spouse elects to treat an inherited IRA as her own. See ¶ 1.6.04 for the Required Commencement Date for distributions from an inherited IRA to the surviving spouse.

B.   **When spousal election may be made.** The spousal election may "be made at any time after the individual's date of death," including after the surviving spouse's own RBD. PLR 9311037.

C.   **Conditions that must be met for spouse to be eligible to make this election.** "In order to make this election, the spouse must be the sole beneficiary of the IRA and have an unlimited right to withdraw amounts from the IRA."

The requirement that the spouse be the "sole" beneficiary to make this election is satisfied (as to a "separate account" within the IRA) if the spouse is the sole beneficiary of such separate account, even if she is not the sole beneficiary of the participant's entire interest in the IRA. ¶ 1.7.06. See ¶ 1.6.02 for meaning of "sole beneficiary."

If the spouse has limited her rights to withdraw from the IRA (for example, through a prenuptial agreement), or if the beneficiary designation form limits the spouse's rights to withdraw from the IRA (for example, by specifying that she may withdraw only the income or only the MRD), then the spouse cannot elect to treat the IRA as her own because she does not have the unlimited right to withdraw from the account.

D.   **How spouse makes the election.** Reg. § 1.408-8, A-5(b) provides three ways the surviving spouse can make this election:

1.   **Affirmative election.** Ideally, with proper advice and planning, the spouse makes the election by "redesignating the account as an account in the name of the surviving spouse as IRA owner rather than as beneficiary." However, the election can also get made automatically by the spouse's taking actions deemed inconsistent with "beneficiary" status. This can happen in either of two ways:

2.   **Spouse contributes to the account.** One is if the spouse makes a contribution to the account, other than a rollover contribution of other benefits inherited from the same decedent; since such other contributions to an inherited IRA are not allowed, the spouse is deemed to have elected to treat the account as her own if she contributes to it. Reg. § 1.408-8, A-5(b)(2).

3.   **Failure to take an MRD.** The other way is if the surviving spouse fails to take an MRD that would be required to be made to her as beneficiary. Reg. § 1.408-8, A-5(b)(1); PLR 2001-21073. See ¶ 3.2.06 for the deadline for taking the first MRD after the participant's death. Presumably this means failure to take the *entire* MRD; presumably if the spouse withdraws something less than the entire MRD she is deemed to have elected to treat the IRA as her own.

3.2.05 *Rollover (but no election) for 403(b) plan*

The Code does not permit <u>spousal</u> <u>elections</u> for 403(b) plans. § 403(b) has no provision comparable to § 408(d)(3)(C) (¶ 3.2.04). The regulations confirm that a surviving spouse as beneficiary of a 403(b) plan cannot elect to treat an inherited 403(b) account as her own; that option applies only to IRAs. Reg. § 1.403(b)-3, A-1(c)(2).

§ 403(b)(8) permits <u>rollovers</u> by a 403(b) plan participant, and (by "importing" § 402(c)(9)) also permits rollovers by the participant's surviving spouse. § 403(b)(8)(B). Reg. § 1.403(b)-2. See PLRs 9713018, 2001-01038, 2002-10066, 2002-49008, 2003-14029, and 2003-17040, allowing spousal rollovers of 403(b) benefits.

3.2.06 *Deadline for completing spousal rollover*

There is no deadline, as such, for completing a spousal rollover. Of course, once any benefits are actually distributed to the spouse, they must be rolled over within 60 days (unless a hardship extension is obtained). ¶ 2.6.06. But the Code provides no specific time limit based on the participant's death after which it becomes "too late" for the spouse to roll over distributions. See, *e.g.*, PLR 2002-22033, in which the participant died in 1985 and his surviving spouse was allowed to roll over the benefits to her IRA in 1997.

However, even though there is no deadline as such, other events can diminish or eliminate the spouse's ability to roll over the benefits. For one thing, if the spouse dies before initiating (or completing) the rollover, the spouse's death may make it impossible (or very difficutl) for the rollover to occur (or be completed); see ¶ 3.2.09.

Also, the minimum distribution rules (Chapter 1) can reduce or eliminate the spouse's ability to roll over inherited benefits. As long as the account remains in the name of the deceased participant, the surviving spouse must take minimum required distributions (MRDs) from the account as beneficiary once she reaches her Required Commencement Date (¶ 1.6.04). MRDs cannot be rolled over; see ¶ 2.6.04. The extent to which the MRD rules will limit or extinguish the spouse's rollover rights depends on the circumstances; as the following paragraphs show, there is quite a complex dance among the MRD requirements based on the spouse taking as beneficiary versus rolling over and taking as owner. To minimize problems, the whether-and-when-to-roll-over decision should be reviewed and implemented as soon as possible after the participant's death.

A.   **MRD for year of death.** If the participant died after his RBD, then the beneficiary (including a surviving spouse who is beneficiary) is required to take the MRD for the year of the participant's death to the extent he did not take it himself. See ¶ 1.5.04(F). As an MRD, this distribution cannot be rolled over by a surviving spouse-beneficiary; furthermore, she cannot roll over the inherited plan until after she has taken this MRD. ¶ 2.6.04. Even if the inherited plan is an IRA and the spouse elects to treat the account as her own in the same year as the participant died she still has to take out this distribution. Reg. § 1.408-8, A-5(a). Since this MRD must be taken in any event, it does not reduce the spouse's ability to roll over the inherited plan (unlike the MRDs discussed in "B" through "E" below).

B.   **Other MRDs if participant died after RBD.** If the participant died after his RBD, then the spouse is required to take annual MRDs from the account beginning the year after the year of the participant's death based on her single life expectancy. See ¶ 1.6.04, ¶ 1.6.06(D). The longer she waits to carry out her rollover, the more nonrollable MRDs she will be receiving from the decedent's plan. However, if the plan is an IRA, and the surviving spouse is the sole beneficiary, her failure to take the MRD would be deemed an election to treat the account as her own. ¶ 3.2.04(D), #3. This would cancel out the obligation to take an MRD *as beneficiary* for that year and subsequent years (except that making the election in the year of death does not cancel out the obligation to take the MRD for the year of death; see "A"). See ¶ 1.6.06(B) for how to determine the spouse's MRD for the year of the deemed election if the election is made after the year of the participant's death.

C.   **MRDs if participant died before RBD and 5-year rule applies.** If the participant died before his Required Beginning Date (RBD), and the 5-year rule applies (¶ 1.5.07), then there is no MRD until the year in which the fifth anniversary of the participant's death occurs, but in the fifth year the entire account becomes the "MRD." Reg. § 54.4972-2, A-3(c). If the inherited plan is an IRA of which the spouse is the sole beneficiary her failure to cash out the account by the end of the fifth year would be deemed an election to treat the account as her own, so presumably the "rollover" would take place by default at that time; see ¶ 3.2.04(D), #3. However, under any other type of plan, if the 5-year rule applies, the deadline for completing the spousal rollover would appear to be: December 31 of the year that contains the *fourth* anniversary of the participant's death. See PLR 2002-42044, in which the spouse was allowed to roll over the balance of a decedent's plan in the fourth year after his death.

D.   **Death before RBD: Deadline for electing between 5-year rule and life expectancy method.** Some plans and IRAs provide that the beneficiary of a participant who died before his RBD must elect to use the life expectancy payout method by a certain date, or else be defaulted into the 5-year rule; see ¶ 1.5.07, #3(a). Thus, a surviving spouse of a young decedent could find herself defaulted into the 5-year rule (see "C") years before she would have been required to take any distributions under the life expectancy payout method. Since (except, apparently, in the case of an inherited IRA of which she is the sole beneficiary; see "C") this could mean she is stuck in the fifth year with a nonrollable distribution of the entire account, this once again illustrates the importance of studying the plan documents and the rollover-or-not decision, and having the spouse take the necessary actions to carry out her decision, as soon as possible after the participant dies.

E.   MRDs if participant died before RBD and life expectancy method applies. If the participant died before his RBD, and the life expectancy payout method applies (¶ 1.5.07), then the spouse is required to take MRDs starting the year after the year of the participant's death, or, if later, the year the participant would have reached age 70½. ¶ 1.6.04. See ¶ 1.6.06(C) or (D) for how to calculate these MRDs. The longer she waits after that Required Commencement Date to carry out her rollover, the more nonrollable MRDs she will be receiving from the decedent's plan. However, if the plan is an IRA, and the surviving spouse is the sole beneficiary, her failure to take an MRD as beneficiary would be deemed an election to treat the account as her own, which would cancel out the obligation to take any MRDs as beneficiary beginning with the year of the election. ¶ 3.2.04(D), #3. See ¶ 1.6.06(B) for how to calculate her MRDs as "owner" following such a deemed election.

3.2.07 *Plans the spouse can roll benefits into*

The surviving spouse can roll benefits to a pre-existing plan or IRA that she already owns, or to a new IRA established to receive this rollover. She can establish an IRA just to receive the rollover, even if she is not herself eligible to contribute to an IRA. She can roll over a post-2001 distribution into any type of plan a living participant is permitted to roll into. § 402(c)(9); see ¶ 2.6.01.

Although a spousal rollover usually involves rolling the benefits into the surviving spouse's own retirement plan or IRA, the surviving spouse can also roll a distribution from the deceased spouse's plan into an IRA that is in the name of the deceased participant-spouse and payable to the surviving spouse as beneficiary ("Beneficiary IRA"). Reg. § 1.408-8, A-7, provides that "If the surviving spouse of an employee rolls over a distribution from a qualified plan, such surviving spouse may elect to treat the IRA as the spouse's own IRA...." The fact that the spouse's election to treat the IRA as her own occurs *after* she has rolled over the distribution into that IRA indicates that the IRA into which she rolled the distribution was an IRA in the decedent's name. The PPA '06 provision allowing post-death rollovers from a QRP to an "inherited IRA" (see ¶ 2.6.03) is limited to nonspouse beneficiaries, but this has no effect on rollovers by the surviving spouse; see ¶ 3.2.04.

As with rollovers into her own IRA, a Beneficiary IRA into which the spouse rolls a distribution from the decedent's plan can be either a pre-existing IRA (PLRs 9418034, 9842058, 2006-08029), or a new Beneficiary IRA created for this purpose (PLR 2004-50057). A spouse might roll into a Beneficiary IRA if she is under age 59½ (see ¶ 3.2.02(D)); or to gain more years of total deferral if the decedent was younger than the surviving spouse and died before age 70½ (compare ¶ 1.4.02 with ¶ 1.6.04).

3.2.08 *Spousal rollover through an estate or trust*

If the participant's benefits are left to his estate or a trust as beneficiary, the surviving spouse can roll over benefits that are paid to her as a beneficiary of the estate or trust, provided the spouse has, and exercises, the right to demand payment of the benefits to herself.

There is no statute, regulation, or case stating this principle. Nevertheless, it is the IRS's most well-established, longstanding, consistent, and logical position in the entire field of employee benefit distributions. Dozens of private rulings have affirmed this principle consistently since 1993. Yet in all that time the IRS has never bothered to state its position on this matter in any form that could be cited as precedent (such as a regulation or Revenue Ruling). Thus, every widow who finds herself in this unfortunate position (trauma of losing her spouse, compounded by the stress of the decedent's failure to have a proper estate plan) has her troubles increased by having to seek a ruling to authorize the rollover. This apparently represents a "get tough on widows" policy at the IRS.

The IRS has approved spousal rollovers through an estate or trust wherever the spouse has the right to the benefits, either because she is sole beneficiary of the estate or trust, or because she has the right to and does demand the benefits in fulfilment of her share. The key is that the spouse must have the right to distribute the benefits to herself or to demand distribution of them. If the spouse's receipt of the benefits depends on the discretion of a third party, or meeting a standard for distribution, this approach does not work. See, *e.g.*, PLRs 2003-14029 (403(b) plan payable to the participant's estate; no rollover was allowed for the portion of the plan that the executor could have used to fund the credit shelter trust); 2006-18030 (spouse entitled only to income necessary for health, support, etc.; rollover denied because she was not the sole "payee" of the IRA payable to the trust).

If the surviving spouse is the sole beneficiary and executor of the estate, the spouse can distribute the retirement benefits out of the plan to herself (either directly or through the estate first) and roll them over to her own retirement plan, provided the rollover occurs within 60 days of the distribution (or longer period if hardship extension is obtained; ¶ 2.6.06); see, *e.g.*, PLR 2004-05017.

If the distribution is from a QRP and the plan withholds income taxes from the distribution, the spouse can nevertheless "roll over" the withheld tax money by substituting other funds. PLR 2003-44024, citing Reg. § 1.402(c)-2, A-11.

Here is a list of some recent private letter rulings that permitted a surviving spouse to roll over the deceased spouse's retirement benefits despite the fact that the beneficiary of the plan was the decedent's estate or a trust. In each of these rulings, the IRS recites that benefits may be rolled over by a surviving spouse only if the benefits pass to the spouse *from the decedent*, and that the general rule is that benefits that pass to the spouse through an estate or a trust are *not* deemed to pass to the spouse from the decedent. Then in each and every ruling the IRS goes on to say that, based on the facts of this particular case, the IRS will not apply the general rule.

Estates: IRA payable to estate: PLRs 2004-06048, 2002-36052, 2002-10066; IRA annuity payable to estate: 2004-05017; 403(b) plan or annuity payable to estate: 2003-17040, 2003-14029, 2002-49008, 2002-10066; Defined benefit plan payable to estate: 2003-05030; QRP payable to estate: 2002-12036, 2002-11054.

Trusts: IRA payable to a trust: 2002-42044, 2001-30056; Portion of IRA payable to a trust (where the rest of the IRA was payable, through the same trust, to other beneficiaries): 2004-49040; IRA payable to an estate which passed to a trust: 2001-36031; QRP payable to a trust: 2002-08031.

The IRS in some of the rulings (*e.g.*, PLR 2004-06048) recites that the Preamble to the Final Regulations provides "that a surviving spouse who actually receives a distribution from an IRA is permitted to roll that distribution over...even if the spouse is not the sole beneficiary.... A rollover may be accomplished even if IRA assets pass through either a trust or an estate." However, the cited Preamble does not contain the last sentence "quoted." T.D. 8987, 2002-1 C.B. 852.

Several of these rulings involve benefits under QRPs that were payable to the deceased participant's estate, either as named beneficiary or as a result of the participant's failure to name any beneficiary. In most of these, it is not clear why the benefits did not pass to the surviving spouse directly (rather than indirectly, through the estate) under the federal spousal rights provisions applicable to qualified plans. See ¶ 3.4, and, *e.g.*, PLRs 2003-05030, 2002-11054, 2002-08031. Perhaps that Code section didn't apply because the spouses had been married less than a year (that was the case in PLR 2002-12036), or perhaps the spouse had consented to the decedent's naming the estate as beneficiary; we just don't know.

In most of these rulings, the spouse's right to receive the benefits through the estate or trust was established at the moment of the participant's death. However, in some rulings, other trustees had to resign or refuse to serve, and the spouse had to be appointed as a trustee (by a court or a prior trustee), in order to get the spouse positioned so that she had the right to pay herself these benefits. See PLRs 1999-13048, 2006-15032. Though one might conclude that the benefits were not passing to the spouse "from the decedent" under these circumstances, the IRS nevertheless allowed the rollover.

If the participant's will or trust (or applicable state law) allows or requires debts, expenses, and/or taxes to be paid out of the estate or the trust, and therefore arguably out of the retirement benefits that are payable to that estate or trust, does that potential liability represent a possible limit on the spouse's ability to take the benefits out of the estate or trust? Most of the PLRs don't even mention this subject, but some do mention it and allow the rollover anyway; see PLRs 2001-36030, 2001-30056.

3.2.09 *Rollover or election by spouse's executor*

IRAs: The IRS has not allowed the executor of a surviving spouse's estate to exercise the surviving spouse's "personal" right to treat the deceased participant's IRA as the now-deceased surviving spouse's own IRA. PLRs 2001-26036, 9237038. As one lawyer put it, "She can't roll over in her grave" (Colin S. Marshall, 1997).

All types of plans: If the surviving spouse dies while benefits left to her by the participant are still in the participant's plan (payable to the now-deceased surviving spouse as beneficiary), there is no law or regulation that would permit the surviving spouse's executor to roll over a distribution that such executor takes from the plan. Thus, the surviving spouse's death completely terminates any possibility of a spousal rollover for funds that are still inside the first spouse's retirement plan when the surviving spouse dies.

However, if the surviving spouse, while still living, took a distribution from the decedent's plan, but died without completing the rollover to another plan, her executor *may* be able to complete the rollover, using the procedure for hardship waiver of the 60-day rollover deadline (¶ 2.6.06). See, *e.g.*, PLRs 2004-15012, 2004-20037, and 2004-18045.

3.3 Qualifying for the Marital Deduction

This ¶ 3.3 describes the requirements and effects of qualifying for the federal estate tax marital deduction for retirement benefits left to the participant's surviving spouse, or to a trust for her life benefit, if the surviving spouse is a U.S. citizen. If the participant's spouse is not a U.S. citizen, additional rules apply that are not covered in this book. § 2056A; see Chapter 4 of earlier editions of this book.

This discussion assumes the reader is already familiar with the uses and requirements of the federal estate tax marital deduction, and so explains only how the marital deduction rules apply uniquely to *retirement benefits*. For more on the marital deduction generally, see Chapter 3 of earlier editions of this book, or sources in the Bibliography.

This book does not cover the following forms of marital deduction disposition: the charitable remainder trust of which the surviving spouse is the sole noncharitable beneficiary (§ 2056(b)(8)); insurance or annuity contracts with power of appointment (§ 2056(b)(6)); or the "estate trust" (trust of which the spouse is sole life beneficiary, and the remainder beneficiary is the spouse's estate).

3.3.01 *Leaving benefits to spouse or marital trust: Overview*

§ 2056, which creates the federal estate tax marital deduction, provides a general rule (the deduction is allowed for the value of property "which passes or has passed from the decedent to his surviving spouse"; § 2056(a)), followed by an exception to the general rule (no deduction is allowed if the property that passes to the surviving spouse is a "life estate or other terminable interest"; § 2056(b)(1)), followed by several exceptions to the exception (certain terminable interests do qualify for the marital deduction after all!). The key to qualifying for the marital deduction, therefore, is to make sure that any property left to the surviving spouse either (1) is not a "terminable interest," or (2) if it is a terminable interest, it qualifies for one of the exceptions to the "terminable interest rule."

Here are the steps to follow:

A.   **Choose a method.** Benefits can qualify for the marital deduction if left to the spouse outright (¶ 3.3.12), to a "QTIP" marital trust (¶ 3.3.02), to a "General Power" marital trust (¶ 3.3.09), or in certain forms of annuity (¶ 3.3.11).

B.   **If using a trust, take three extra steps.** If leaving benefits to a QTIP or General Power marital trust, you need to cover three additional points to make sure the benefits qualify for the marital deduction. First, you need to understand the IRS's concept of how the "terminable interest rule" applies to retirement benefits payable to a marital trust; see ¶ 3.3.03. Second, you need to assure that the "income of the retirement plan" is determined correctly for marital deduction purposes; see ¶ 3.3.04. Third, you must make sure the spouse is "entitled" to all that income; see ¶ 3.3.05–¶ 3.3.08.

C.   **Don't forget MRDs.** Work out how the minimum required distribution (MRD) rules will work with the method you have chosen. See comments under each method.

D.   **Pay attention to funding formula.** If the benefits are payable to a trust that is to be divided, at the participant's death, between a "marital trust" and a "credit shelter" (or bypass) trust, it is recommended that either the division be by means of a "fractional" (rather than a "pecuniary") formula, or, if a pecuniary formula is used, that the benefits be made payable directly to the marital trust so they don't become subject to the pecuniary formula; see ¶ 6.4.08.

3.3.02 *Leaving retirement benefits to a QTIP trust*

The most popular method of leaving retirement benefits to benefit the surviving spouse is leaving the benefits to her outright. The second most popular is to leave benefits to a "qualified terminable interest property" (QTIP) trust.

The "classic" QTIP trust provides for all income of the trust to be paid to the surviving spouse for her life, with the principal being paid to the donor's issue on the spouse's death. The spouse may or may not be given access to the principal of the trust during her life (such as through a standard based on need, or in the trustee's discretion, or through a 5-and-5 power). The spouse may or may not be given a limited power to appoint the principal at her death. However, the ultimate choice of remainder beneficiaries remains with the participant-donor; compare the General Power marital trust (¶ 3.3.09).

Leaving retirement benefits to a QTIP trust is no tax bargain. Making benefits payable to a marital trust, as opposed to the spouse individually, often results in forced distribution of the benefits sooner (see "B"), and payment of income taxes at a higher rate (see "C"), than would be the case if the spouse personally were named as beneficiary.

If the client is determined not to leave any assets outright to his spouse, but is unhappy about the adverse MRD and income tax effects of a QTIP trust, consider making the benefits payable to the credit shelter trust, and using other assets to fund the marital trust. Although using this approach with income-taxable benefits is contrary to the usual rule of thumb ("don't waste your credit shelter paying income taxes"), this move could substantially increase the potential deferral if the only beneficiaries of the credit shelter trust are much younger than the spouse, because MRDs will be spread out over a longer life expectancy period if the trust qualifies as a see-through; ¶ 6.2.

A.   How a QTIP trust qualifies for the marital deduction. Property qualifies for the estate tax marital deduction as QTIP if (1) the spouse is entitled for life to all of the income from the property payable at least annually, (2) no person has the power to appoint any of the property to someone other than the spouse during her lifetime, and (3) the decedent's executor irrevocably elects, on the decedent's estate tax return, to treat the property as QTIP. § 2056(b)(7). See ¶ 3.3.04 for how to determine the "income" the spouse is entitled to. See ¶ 3.3.05–¶ 3.3.08 for ways to meet the "entitled" requirement. See ¶ 3.3.03 for requirement of a separate QTIP election for the benefits.

Terminable interests are generally not eligible for the marital deduction, but § 2056(b)(7) allows the marital deduction for this type of trust, even though it definitely is a "terminable interest." To assure the tax is merely deferred not eliminated, § 2044 provides that the surviving spouse's estate includes any property for which the marital deduction was elected at the first spouse's death under § 2056(b)(7).

B.   MRD effects. If the trust qualifies as a see-through trust under the IRS's minimum distribution trust rules, then the Applicable Distribution Period (ADP) for benefits payable to the trust can be based on the life expectancy of the oldest trust beneficiary. See ¶ 6.2 for how to determine if the trust qualifies as a see-through, and ¶ 1.5.03(E) or ¶ 1.5.04(E) for the ADP.

Note that, even if the trust qualifies as a see-through, distributing the benefits over the single life expectancy of the surviving spouse (as the oldest trust beneficiary) results in *substantially less deferral* than would be available if the spouse were named as outright beneficiary and rolled over the benefits to her own plan (compare ¶ 3.2.01). Distribution over the spouse's life expectancy guarantees that the benefits will be entirely distributed out of the plan by the time the spouse reaches (or would have reached) her late 80s. (Slightly better deferral can be obtained with a conduit marital trust; see ¶ 3.3.10.)
In contrast, if benefits are left to the spouse outright and rolled over to her own plan, and she withdraws only the MRDs required under the Uniform Lifetime Table, the benefits are guaranteed to outlive the spouse; in fact they will probably be worth more, when she reaches her late 80s, than they were worth when she inherited the plan!

C.   Other tax considerations. In addition to the loss of deferral, income-taxable retirement plan distributions to the trust (to the extent not passed out to the spouse as "distributable net income"; ¶ 6.4.02) are taxed to the trust. Trust income tax rates reach the top federal bracket at a much lower amount of taxable income than individual rates do; ¶ 6.4.01.

D.   Spousal consent. Finally, under certain types of retirement plans, benefits cannot be left to a trust without the consent of the participant's spouse. See ¶ 3.4.

3.3.03 *IRS regards benefits, trust, as a separate items of QTIP*

Every estate planning lawyer should know how to draft a trust that complies with the marital deduction requirements. Many practitioners assume that, once the standard marital trust is drafted, and the trust is named as beneficiary of the participant's retirement benefits, qualification of those benefits for the estate tax marital deduction is assured (assuming the spouse survives the participant and does not disclaim her interest in the marital trust).

The IRS has a different view. The IRS's position is that, when a retirement plan benefit is payable to a marital trust, both the retirement plan benefit *and* the trust must meet the marital deduction requirements. In the IRS's view, the retirement plan itself is an item of "terminable interest property" separate from the marital trust. Rev. Ruls. 2006-26, 2006-22 I.R.B. 939, and 2000-2, 2000-1 C.B. 305. This IRS positions has two implications:

A.   What to do on the estate tax return. Rev. Ruls. 2006-26 and 2000-2 require the executor, on the estate tax return, to elect QTIP treatment for *both* the retirement benefit *and* the marital trust when retirement benefits are payable to a marital trust, confirming the approach seen in PLR 9442032 as well as Rev. Rul. 89-89, 1989-2 C.B. 231.

B.   How to draft the trust. The IRS does not require that all the marital deduction language must be recited in the beneficiary designation form as well as in the trust instrument. Although that would be one way to comply with the IRS's directive, Rev. Rul. 2000-2 says that the governing instrument requirements are satisfied with respect to a retirement benefit payable to a marital trust if (1) the marital trust document contains the required language (*e.g.*, giving the spouse the right to all the trust's and the plan's income annually) and (2) the retirement plan document does not contain any provisions which would prevent the trustee of the marital trust from complying with the trust's provisions with respect to the plan.

Accordingly it is advisable to specify in the instrument not only that the spouse is entitled to all income *of the trust* (which is the standard marital deduction trust language) but in addition to specify that the spouse is entitled to all income *of any retirement plan payable to the trust*. See ¶ 3.3.04.

3.3.04 *The income the spouse is entitled to*

One requirement a trust must meet if it is to qualify for the marital deduction is that the spouse must be "entitled for life to all of the income" of the trust. This ¶ 3.3.04 explains what "income" the spouse must be entitled to with respect to a retirement plan that is payable to a marital trust. ¶ 3.3.05 explains what it means for the spouse to be "entitled" to that income, and how the income requirement relates to the minimum distribution requirement.

¶ 6.1.02–¶ 6.1.03 explain the problems and options in defining the "income" of a trust that is named as beneficiary of a retirement plan. In Rev. Rul. 2006-26, 2006-22 I.R.B. 939, the IRS explained what it views as the "income" of a retirement plan that the surviving spouse must be entitled to for marital deduction purposes. In the IRS's view, the income of the retirement plan is either the plan's <u>internal investment income</u> ("trust-within-a-trust" concept; see ¶ 6.1.03(B)) or an acceptable (i.e., <u>3%–5%) annual "unitrust" percentage amount</u> (see ¶ 6.1.04). Accordingly, when drafting a marital trust that is to be named as beneficiary of a retirement plan, it would be advisable to specify one of these methods of determining income. See Form 4.5, Appendix B.

In Rev. Rul. 2006-26, the IRS rejected a widely-adopted state law method of determining income with respect to trust-owned retirement benefits, namely, the "10 percent rule" of the 1997 Uniform Principal and Income Act ("UPIA 1997"), under which 10 percent of any MRD is treated as "income" and 90 percent is treated as "principal"; see ¶ 6.1.02(C). As this author predicted would happen in the article "Trustees' Dilemma with Section 643" (*Trusts & Estates*, Vol. 143, No. 7, July 2004, p. 26), the IRS found that this method of determining income "does not satisfy the requirements of § 20.2056(b)-

5(f)(1) and § 1.643(b)-1, because the amount of the...[MRD] is not based on the total return of the IRA (and therefore the amount allocated to income does not reflect a reasonable apportionment of the total return between the income and remainder beneficiaries)." Accordingly, under Rev. Rul. 2006-26, a trust that uses the 10 percent rule to determine the surviving spouse's income under a marital trust will not qualify for the marital deduction.

UPIA 1997, § 409(d), provides that the trustee is to allocate a larger portion of any distribution to income to the extent such larger allocation is necessary for the trust to qualify for the federal estate tax marital deduction. However, the IRS ruled this provision did not overcome the fatal problems with the 10 percent rule because, though such savings clauses may be used to help interpret an ambiguous trust provision, they "are ineffective to reform an instrument for federal transfer tax purposes," citing Rev. Rul. 75-440, 1975-2 C.B. 372.

Does this mean that every marital trust drafted prior to Rev. Rul. 2006-26 must be amended? No, but some must be:

Trusts that need not be amended: Any trust that contains the specific direction that the trustee must pay the surviving spouse *the income of any retirement plan payable to the trust* does not have to be amended to reflect Rev. Rul. 2006-26, for the following reason. Under the IRS's logic, the "income of the retirement plan" means, as noted, either the internal investment income of the account or an acceptable unitrust alternative. In the IRS's view, the 10 percent rule dictates how the trustee is to allocate plan distributions in determining the income *of the trust*, but has nothing whatsoever to do with the income *of the plan*! Therefore if the instrument specifically requires the trustee to pay the spouse the income of the trust's share of the plan, the trustee is required to pay her the internal income of the trust's share of the plan (or unitrust amount, if applicable), *regardless* of whether the UPIA 1997 10 percent rule applies to the trust.

And, the IRS thoughtfully adds, if the trustee pays the spouse the income of the plan plus the income of the trust, the trustee does not have to include 10 percent of the MRD in determining the "income of the trust" that is paid to the spouse (because that would be double counting), regardless of what state law says.

While this IRS interpretation probably makes a hash of the UPIA drafters' intent (it seems clear they thought the "income of the plan" was 10% of the MRD), it is a blessing for estate planners, because it means that most marital trusts drafted since 1989 with retirement benefits in mind will *not* have to be amended due to Rev. Rul. 2006-26, despite the widespread adoption of UPIA 1997 by state legislatures. The IRS view that the benefits and the trust itself constitute separate items of QTIP has been known since Rev. Rul. 1989-89, 1989-2 C.B. 231, and accordingly many estate planners have long included the extra language specifying that the spouse must receive income "of the plan" as well as "of the trust." For example, the requirement that the trustee pay the spouse the income of the plan, not merely of the trust, has been part of the sample forms in Appendix B of this book since its first edition (1996).

Trusts that may require amendment: A marital trust that is named as beneficiary of a retirement plan, and which states that the surviving spouse is entitled to all income "of the trust," but does not specifically state that the spouse is entitled to all income of the trust's interest *in the retirement plan*, may have to be amended if (1) the UPIA 1997 10 percent rule is the state law applicable to the trust and (2) the trust does not have any acceptable definition of income that would supercede the 10 percent rule. Thus, estate planners who have drafted not-yet-operative marital trusts that are named as beneficiaries of retirement benefits, to which the 10 percent rule may apply, and that do not contain the magic words indicating that the spouse is entitled to income of the plan not just of the trust, should consider amending such trusts in light of Rev. Rul. 2006-26.

Trusts that are already irrevocable: Trustees of existing marital trusts that hold inherited retirement benefits, where the participant has already died, do not have the option of amending the trust. If the trust does not contain its own IRS-acceptable definition of income with respect to retirement benefits, and does not contain the magic words that the spouse is entitled to the income of the plan, and is governed by the UPIA 1997 10 percent rule, the trustee faces a dilemma. Rev. Rul. 2006-26 indicates that such a trust may not qualify for the marital deduction. However, if the federal estate tax return has been filed and accepted, with the marital deduction allowed, it's not clear what the IRS can do about it at this stage. Trustees who wish to be released from the 10 percent rule could seek "conversion" of the trust to a unitrust, which is another option under UPIA 1997 and is beyond the scope of this book.

Hopefully, state legislatures will cure the problem uncovered by Rev. Rul. 2006-26 by jettisoning the UPIA 10 percent rule or by legislating that, when retirement benefits are payable to a trust, any rights granted with respect to the trust are granted equally with respect to retirement benefits payable to the trust unless the instrument specifies otherwise. Though this result would appear self-evident to most estate planners, it is not self evident to the IRS and so must be spelled out either in each and every marital trust, or by state law.

3.3.05 The "entitled" requirement; income vs. MRD

We now turn from the "income" aspect to the "entitled" aspect of the requirement that the spouse must be "entitled for life to all of the income" of a marital trust. This ¶ 3.3.05 discusses the general problems of meeting this requirement in connection with retirement benefits payable to a marital trust, and how this requirement relates to the minimum distribution requirement. Particular methods of compliance with the "entitled" requirement are discussed in ¶ 3.3.06–¶ 3.3.08.

Regardless of whether the trustee is required to withdraw "income" from the retirement plan, the trustee must withdraw the minimum required distribution (MRD) annually. Thus, if the trust instrument requires the trustee to withdraw the "income" annually, what it is really requiring is that the trustee withdraw from the retirement plan each year the income or the MRD, whichever is the larger amount; see PLR 2005-22012 for an example of a marital trust that specified the trustee had to withdraw the greater of the two amounts. The trustee must calculate both amounts each year in any case. The MRD may be more or less than the income. The spouse is entitled to the "income," but the marital deduction rules do not require that she receive the entire MRD (if that is larger than the income).

This brings us to the crux of why it matters how a marital trust named as beneficiary of retirement benefits complies with the "entitled to all income" requirement. If the income of the retirement plan benefit is greater than the MRD, it would be desirable not to have to distribute the excess amount out of the retirement plan if such distribution *could* have been deferred until later under the minimum distribution rules. Therefore, if the current distribution of "all income" would result in significant acceleration of distribution, the planner will look for a way to avoid such current distribution.

The planning process on this issue is quite complex, and it is not possible to review every consideration here. A review of the following subsections will reveal that use of any method of compliance other than "distribute all income" (¶ 3.3.06) involves greater complication of the drafting and planning process. These complications are usually worth undertaking only if the result will be significantly improved deferral. Therefore the planner must consider exactly what the difference will be between the amount of the income and the amount of the MRD.

The maximum period of deferral for benefits left to a classic QTIP trust is the life expectancy of the oldest trust beneficiary (¶ 1.5.03(E), ¶ 1.5.04(E)), who is (in most cases) the spouse. If the surviving spouse is age 51 or older at the participant's death, the MRD based on her life expectancy will be more than three percent of the benefits: The "divisor" at age 51 under the Single Life Table is 33.3, which translates to an MRD of three percent of the value of the plan. Each year the divisor declines and the corresponding percentage increases (¶ 1.2.01, #3). Thus, unless the income rate of the retirement benefit is more than three percent, the MRD for a spouse over age 51 will be more than the income—meaning that the trustee will have to withdraw more than the income *even if* the trust allows income to be accumulated in the plan (as discussed at ¶ 3.3.07–¶ 3.3.08). Thus, in many cases, there is no advantage to allowing the trustee to accumulate income inside the retirement plan because the minimum distribution rules will prevent him from doing so.

Another factor to consider when deciding how to comply with the entitled-to-all-income requirement is how cooperative the spouse is likely to be. If the spouse is likely to exercise every demand right given to her, nothing will be achieved by substituting demand rights (¶ 3.3.07–¶ 3.3.08) for mandatory income distributions (¶ 3.3.06).

The next three subsections review three approaches to complying with the requirement that spouse be entitled for life to all income of a marital trust. The same rules apply to both QTIP and General Power marital trusts for purposes of determining whether the spouse is entitled to all income. Reg. § 20.2056(b)-7(d)(2).

Prior to 2000, the IRS's position was that the distribution from the plan of all income annually (¶ 3.3.06) was the *only* method available for a retirement plan benefit payable to a trust to qualify for the marital deduction. Rev. Rul. 89-89, 1989-2 C.B. 231. In Rev. Rul. 2000-2, 2000-1 C.B. 305, the IRS reversed this position and acknowledged that a marital trust funded with retirement benefits can use other methods permitted in its regulations for meeting the "entitled for life to all income" requirement. Rev. Rul. 2000-2 announced that it "obsoleted" Rev. Rul.89-89, which has led to some confusion among practitioners. The method "blessed" in Rev. Rul. 89-89 for complying with the entitled-to-all-income requirement (namely, requiring annual distribution of all plan income to the spouse) still works; Rev. Rul. 2000-2 obsoleted Rev. Rul. 89-89 only to the extent Rev. Rul. 89-89 said this was the *only* method that worked.

3.3.06 *Distribute all income to spouse annually*

The easiest way to comply with the all-income requirement is to require the trustee to withdraw from the retirement plan each year, and distribute to the spouse, the "income" of the retirement plan. Reg. § 20.2056(b)-5(f)(8). This method was "blessed" by the IRS in Rev. Rul. 89-89, 1989-2 C.B. 231, and Rev. Rul. 2006-26, and is believed to be the most commonly used by estate planners. See, *e.g.*, PLRs 9321035, 9321059, 9418026, and 9348025. For an example of a form using this method, see Form 4.4, Appendix B. Unless the "income" substantially exceeds the MRD, this method does not have significant tax drawbacks (beyond the usual drawbacks of leaving retirement benefits to a marital trust in the first place; see ¶ 3.3.02).

Even if use of this method does require distribution to the spouse of an amount significantly greater than the MRD, that would not mean loss of deferral if the spouse is rolls over the excess to her own retirement plan The IRS has repeatedly ruled that a surviving spouse may roll over retirement plan distributions that are made to her through a trust if she was entitled to receive that amount; see ¶ 3.2.08.

While these rulings generally involved the spouse's rolling over a one-time at-death distribution of the entire plan balance, PLR 2005-43064 affirms that the same principle would allow the spouse to roll over, each year, annual distributions she is entitled to receive (through the trust) from the inherited retirement plan (to the extent such distributions exceed the MRD, which cannot be rolled over). In this PLR, decedent named a trust as beneficiary of his IRA. His surviving spouse was entitled to receive all of the trust's net income, plus principal as needed for support, and in addition had the right to withdraw principal from the trust, annually, in an amount not to exceed the greater of $5,000 or five percent of the trust principal ("5-and-5 power"). The trustee by mistake withdrew the entire plan balance shortly after the participant's death. The surviving spouse exercised her 5-and-5 power, and the IRS allowed her to roll over, to her own IRA, an amount equal to the IRA income plus the principal distributed to her under the 5-and-5 power, because she was the "sole, unconditional, named beneficiary of distinct portions or IRA 1," to wit "an annual, non-cumulative 5X5 right to principal, and trust income...as such...she could have elected to roll over said portion(s)...."

3.3.07 Treat the plan as "unproductive property"

A marital trust does not have to forbid the trustee to invest in unproductive (non-income producing) property, but if the trust is *permitted* to invest in unproductive property it must protect the spouse's income rights in one of two ways:

1.   One way is for the instrument to give the spouse the right to require the trustee to make any such property productive or to convert it to productive property within a reasonable time. Reg. § 20.2056(b)-5(f)(4).

2.   If the trust corpus consists substantially of unproductive property and the spouse does *not* have the power to compel the trustee to make it income-producing, the trust will *still* qualify for the marital deduction if the spouse can "require...that the trustee provide the required beneficial enjoyment, such as by payments to the spouse out of other assets of the trust." Reg. § 20.2056(b)-5(f)(5).

If a retirement plan from which annual MRDs are small or nonexistent could be regarded as "unproductive property," current distribution of income could be avoided and income tax deferral enhanced, perhaps with fewer complications than are involved with giving the spouse an income demand right (¶ 3.3.08). The problem is that it is not clear that a retirement plan is "unproductive" just because it isn't *distributing* anything. It is clear (from Rev. Rul. 2006-26) that the IRS does not consider the IRA to be unproductive property if it is invested in income-producing property. Thus, methods #1 and #2 above probably do not apply to a retirement plan payable to the trust unless the *plan's* investments are unproductive.

Even if the IRA is invested in unproductive property, since the IRS regards the retirement plan as a separate item of "terminable interest property" (¶ 3.3.06), it is not clear that distributions to the spouse from *other* (non-retirement plan) assets held by the marital trust (method #2 above) could be used to replace the missing income payments with regard to the retirement plan. This issue can be avoided by giving the spouse the right to demand that the plan be made income-producing (method #1 above) rather than giving the trustee the right to substitute other distributions for the missing income payments.

3.3.08 *Give spouse the right to demand the income*

A spouse is entitled to all income of a trust if she has "the right exercisable annually (or more frequently) to require distribution to herself of the trust income, and otherwise [*i.e.*, if she does not require such distribution in any year] the trust income [for such year] is to be accumulated...." Reg. § 20.2056(b)-5(f)(8).

In Rev. Rul. 2000-2, the IRS ruled that an IRA payable to a marital trust qualified for the marital deduction where the trust gave the spouse "the power, exercisable annually, to compel the trustee to withdraw from the IRA an amount equal to the income earned on the assets held in the IRA" during the year and to distribute that amount through the trust to the surviving spouse, and "[n]othing in the IRA instrument" prohibited the trustee from making such withdrawals.

Use of this method of complying with the entitled-to-all-income requirement involves substantial additional complications not discussed in Rev. Rul. 2000-2. Is the spouse's right to withdraw the income from the retirement plan to be lapsing or nonlapsing? If lapsing, will her failure to withdraw the income constitute a completed gift to the remainder beneficiaries of the trust?

Whether her right is lapsing or not, her failure to withdraw current income could: change the income tax treatment of the trust (by causing it to become partially a "grantor trust" as to the spouse; see § 678(a)(2)); result in inclusion of the different portions of the trust in her estate under different Code sections (§ 2036 versus § 2044), which in turn could make different estate tax apportionment rules applicable to the different parts of the trust at her death (compare § 2207B(a)(1) and § 2207A(a)(1)); and (if a "reverse QTIP" election has been made for the trust; see § 2652(a)(3)) result in the trust's having two transferors for generation skipping transfer tax purposes. These questions are not relevant to marital deduction qualification, nor applicable only to retirement benefits, and are beyond the scope of this book, but need to be considered by a practitioner who uses this method of complying with the entitled-to-all-income requirement. Before undertaking such complications, the practitioner should consider whether the effort will result in significant savings; see ¶ 3.3.05.

3.3.09 *General Power marital trust*

A General Power marital trust is similar to a QTIP marital trust (¶ 3.3.02), in that the surviving spouse must be entitled to all of the trust's income for life. What is different is that the spouse must also have the right to appoint the principal to herself or her estate, which gives the spouse much more control than a QTIP trust gives her. It is used less often than a QTIP, since a client willing to give the spouse this much control would usually be willing to name the spouse as outright beneficiary.

A.   **How a General Power marital trust qualifies for the marital deduction.** Under § 2056(b)(5), property qualifies for the marital deduction if the spouse (1) is "entitled for life to all the income from" the property, payable at least annually, and (2) has the power, exercisable by the spouse alone and in all events, to appoint the property to herself (or to her estate), and (3) there is no power in any other person to appoint any of the property to someone other than the spouse. This type of interest left to a spouse is not a terminable interest because § 2056(b)(5) says that if these conditions are met no part of the property is considered to pass to someone other than the spouse.

When a retirement plan is payable to a General Power marital trust, the IRS would presumably (using the same logic as in its QTIP rulings) require that both the plan and the trust meet the marital deduction requirements. See ¶ 3.3.03–¶ 3.3.08.

B.   **MRD effects.** Generally, the MRD effects (and drawbacks, compared with the spousal rollover) are the same for a General Power marital trust as for a QTIP trust. The fact that the spouse has a general power of appointment at death makes a difference in terms of which Code section the trust qualifies for the marital deduction under, but has no impact on the income tax problems discussed at ¶ 3.3.02(B), (C).

An additional MRD problem is that, if the spouse is given the power to appoint the trust property at her death to her own estate, the trust will be deemed to have a nonindividual beneficiary and accordingly will not qualify as a see-through trust unless it is a conduit trust (¶ 6.3.05) or (possibly) a 100 percent grantor trust (see "C" and ¶ 6.3.08).

C.   **Other tax considerations.** With a General Power marital trust, one way to avoid the high income tax rates applicable to trusts (¶ 3.3.02(C)) is to give the spouse the right to withdraw all of the plan benefits at any time, without restriction, during her life. This would make the trust a grantor trust as to the spouse (¶ 6.3.08), causing the plan distributions to be taxed at her rate rather than the trust's rate. This approach would also enable her to use the spousal rollover. ¶ 3.2.08.

D.   **Spousal consent.** Finally, under certain types of retirement plans, benefits cannot be left to a trust without the consent of the participant's spouse. See ¶ 3.4.

3.3.10 *Combination marital deduction-conduit trust*

A marital trust can also be a conduit trust (¶ 6.3.05). This can be done in either of two ways.

One method is to require the trustee to withdraw from the plan, and distribute to the spouse, the income of the trust's share of the retirement plan for such year or the MRD for such year, whichever is greater (and to distribute to the spouse any additional amounts the trustee withdraws from the plan).

Another method which might be of interest if the participant has many years to go before he will reach age 70½ is to require the trustee to pass all plan distributions out to the spouse (as always is required under a conduit trust), but give the spouse only the right to *demand* income (¶ 3.3.08) rather than requiring the trustee to *distribute* all income regardless of demand. Since such a trust could defer the commencement of distributions until the participant would have reached age 70½ (¶ 1.6.07(A)), this approach could substantially extend the deferral of distributions compared with a standard QTIP trust. *All* plan distributions could be deferred until the year the participant would have reached age 70½. See "Conduit Trust Ironies" at ¶ 6.3.14(A). Since this approach makes a difference only for participants who die relatively young (which most people don't), and since the conduit trust format requires all plan distributions (not just "income") to be distributed immediately to the spouse (which is not what most clients who leave benefits to a QTIP trust want), it seems unlikely this will be a widely used approach.

3.3.11 *Automatic QTIP election for "survivor annuities"*

§ 2056(b)(7)(C) provides that "[i]n the case of an annuity included in the gross estate of the decedent under section 2039...where only the surviving spouse has the right to receive payments before the death of such surviving spouse—(i) the interest of such surviving spouse shall be treated as a qualifying income interest for life, and (ii) the executor shall be treated as having made" a QTIP election for such property unless the executor elects *not* to have QTIP treatment apply. Retirement plan benefits are considered annuities, includible in the participant's estate under § 2039, whether or not paid in the form of true annuities, and thus are subject to this rule. Reg. § 20.2039-1(b).

Electing out of automatic QTIP treatment for a retirement plan death benefit means that the benefit will not subsequently be included in the surviving spouse's estate under § 2044; however, the asset may still be included in the spouse's estate under some *other* Code provision such as § 2033.

The automatic QTIP treatment for "annuities" is a nice backup when benefits are left outright to the spouse (¶ 3.3.12). It also can be helpful when retirement benefits are paid in the form of a true annuity and payments could continue after the surviving spouse's death:

Mona Example: Mona receives a monthly pension of $5,000 for her life, with a minimum guaranteed term of 10 years. She has named her husband Jeff as beneficiary to receive the balance of payments due if she dies before the guaranteed term is up. She has named her child Robin as successor beneficiary to Jeff if he also does not survive until the end of the 10-year guarantee period. On her death the value of the annuity is $400,000. Because this is included in Mona's estate under § 2039, and no one but her spouse has the right to receive any payments until his death, the $400,000 is treated as QTIP unless her executor elects *not* to have it so treated.

What if Mona's estate is not large enough to be taxable, and Jeff's estate is large enough to be taxable, and Jeff (having survived Mona) also dies before the end of the 10-year guarantee period? Normally, if a QTIP election (automatic or otherwise) applied to the annuity in Mona's estate, the remaining value of the payments would be includible in Jeff's estate under § 2044, resulting in estate taxes—even though the QTIP election did not save any estate taxes at Mona's death because her estate was too small to be taxable. However, Rev. Proc. 2001-38, 2001-1 C.B. 1335, makes certain "unnecessary" QTIP elections automatically void. If the automatic QTIP election is voided, the value of the annuity remaining at Jeff's subsequent death is not includible in his estate under § 2044. PLR 2003-18039.

3.3.12 *Marital deduction for benefits left outright to spouse*

Death benefits payable directly to the surviving spouse outright in a lump sum should qualify for the marital deduction, provided the spouse is a U.S. citizen and is entitled to withdraw all the benefits. See, *e.g.*, PLR 8843033. Where the spouse is named as sole beneficiary, with the unrestricted right to withdraw all the benefits, no part of the participant's interest in the plan passes to someone other than the spouse or her estate, so the spouse has not received a "terminable interest" (¶ 3.3.01).

There is one possible quibble with this conclusion. Suppose the participant has also named a successor beneficiary (¶ 1.5.13(D)), to receive the remaining benefits if the spouse survives the participant but dies before having withdrawn all the benefits.

Jerry Example: Jerry leaves his IRA outright to his wife Carol. Jerry's beneficiary designation form names his son Hanson as successor beneficiary to take any remaining benefits if Carol dies after Jerry but before she has withdrawn all the benefits. Since that successor beneficiary is someone other than Carol's own estate, Jerry asks you whether his IRA will qualify for the marital deduction for his estate, or whether it has been transformed into a nondeductible terminable interest. He points out that an interest in the IRA (*i.e.*, the amount remaining in the account at Carol's death) will pass to someone other than Carol or her estate (*i.e.*, Hanson) upon the occurrence of an event or contingency (*i.e.*, Carol's failure to withdraw the benefits during her lifetime), which is the definition of a nondeductible terminable interest under § 2056(b)(1).

The author believes that this scenario does not create a nondeductible interest. For one thing, it meets the description of a deductible interest in § 2056(b)(5), which provides that an interest is deemed to pass to the spouse and only the spouse (and therefore is not a nondeductible terminable interest) if the spouse is entitled to all the income for life, at annual or more frequent intervals, and has the right (exercisable by her alone and in all events) to appoint the principal to herself with no person having the power to appoint it to someone other than her. The spouse has these rights with respect to retirement plan benefits left outright to her, assuming there is nothing in the beneficiary designation form or plan documents that limits her right to withdraw the income or principal of the account.

The fact that the interest will pass to a successor beneficiary *if the spouse chooses not to withdraw the benefits* should not be deemed to transform this into a terminable interest. The situation is analogous to property left by a decedent to his surviving spouse and child as joint tenants. The surviving spouse can seek partition and take her share of the inherited joint property whenever she wishes, but if she chooses not to withdraw her share, it will automatically pass to the child by right of survivorship on the surviving spouse's death. This gift qualifies for the marital deduction. Reg. § 20.2056(b)-5(g)(2).

Furthermore, as explained at ¶ 3.3.11, § 2056(b)(7)(C) treats a surviving spouse's interest in a survivor annuity as QTIP unless the decedent's executor elects otherwise, if the spouse is the sole beneficiary during her lifetime. Therefore, even if it were determined (wrongly, in the author's view) that Jerry's IRA in the example above *was* a terminable interest, the interest would qualify for the automatic QTIP marital deduction under § 2056(b)(7)(C).

To sidestep the issue altogether, one could include additional language such as that in Section 3.07, Forms 2.1, 2.2, Appendix B, when (1) the participant is naming his spouse outright as beneficiary and (2) the participant names a successor beneficiary (other than the spouse's estate) who will be entitled to receive the benefits that the spouse does not withdraw during her lifetime. This language explicitly recites that the spouse has the right to withdraw all income and principal of the benefits, tracking the wording of § 2056(b)(5) and Reg. § 20.2056(b)-5(f)(8).

For why it may be desirable for the participant to name a successor beneficiary see ¶ 1.6.05.

3.4 REA '84 and Spousal Consent

For the interaction of REA and qualified disclaimers, see ¶ 4.2.10. This book does not cover state law spousal rights such as community property.

3.4.01 *Introduction to the Retirement Equity Act of 1984*

This ¶ 3.4 describes the federal rights granted to spouses of retirement plan participants by the "Retirement Equity Act of 1984" ("REA" or "REACT"; P.L. 98-397), and discusses the estate planning implications of these rights. The applicable law is in IRC § 401(a)(11) and § 417, and the virtually identical ERISA § 205 (29 U.S.C. § 1055); and Regs. § 1.401(a)-20 and § 1.417(e)-1.

The purpose of this ¶ 3.4 is to provide estate planners with an overview of REA's requirements and exemptions, with emphasis on aspects that affect estate planning. This essay by no means exhausts REA's intricacies. Practitioners who have studied the spousal consent requirements are bedeviled by such problems as precisely when (relative to the distribution date) spousal consent must be obtained in order to be valid; whether a new spousal consent is required for every distribution paid prior to the Required Beginning Date (RBD; ¶ 1.4); and whether the consent requirements limit the ability of the participant and spouse to change the form of benefits after the RBD.

This Chapter should not be relied upon for purposes of design or administration of a retirement plan. For an explanation of REA aimed at the plan designer or administrator, see *The Pension Answer Book* by Stephen J. Krass (Panel Publications). See Bibliography.

Retirement plans fall into three categories with respect to REA's requirements: plans that are subject to the full panoply of REA requirements (all pension plans, some profit-sharing plans, some 403(b) plans; ¶ 3.4.02); plans that are subject to a modified version of the REA requirements (some profit-sharing plans and some 403(b) plans; ¶ 3.4.03); and plans that are totally exempt from REA's requirements (IRAs, Roth IRAs, and some 403(b) plans; ¶ 3.4.04).

3.4.02 Plans subject to full-scale REA requirements

If a plan is fully subject to REA, then, generally (for exceptions see ¶ 3.4.05), ANY benefits distributed by that plan to a married employee MUST be distributed in the form of a "qualified joint and survivor annuity" (QJSA), unless the employee has waived that form of benefit and the employee's spouse consents to the waiver. If a married employee covered by such a plan dies before retirement, then the plan MUST pay his surviving spouse a "qualified pre-retirement survivor annuity" (QPSA) unless she has waived the right to receive the QPSA. The spousal consent or waiver must meet certain requirements; see ¶ 3.4.07, ¶ 3.4.08. The plan must offer additional joint annuity options after 2007 as a result of PPA '06; see § 417(a).

A QJSA is an annuity (1) for the life of the participant with a survivor annuity for the life of his spouse which is not less than 50 percent of (and is not greater than 100 percent of) the amount of the annuity which is payable during the joint lives of the participant and spouse, and (2) which is the actuarial equivalent of a single annuity for the life of the participant.

The definition of a QPSA is even more elaborate. Basically, it is supposed to be the annuity the spouse would have received under the QJSA had the employee lived to retirement, retired with a QJSA, then died. In the case of a defined contribution plan (such as a money purchase pension plan or "nonexempt" profit-sharing plan), the value of the QPSA is defined as an annuity equal in value to 50 percent of the employee's account balance. § 417(c)(2).

All *pension plans* are subject to the QJSA/QPSA requirements that are described in this ¶ 3.4.02. Defined benefit plans and money purchase pension plans are in this category. § 401(a)(11)(B).

Other types of qualified retirement plans (*e.g.*, profit-sharing, stock bonus) may or may not be subject to the rules described in this ¶ 3.4.02, depending on whether they fit into the "exemption" (which is not really an exemption, just a modified version of the requirements) described at ¶ 3.4.03.

3.4.03 REA requirements for "exempt" profit-sharing plans

Certain qualified plans are exempt from the QJSA/QPSA requirements of REA described at ¶ 3.4.02. Although this type of plan could be any type of QRP other than a "pension" plan, i.e., it could be a profit-sharing or stock bonus plan, these plans are called here "exempt profit-sharing plans." However, these plans are not "exempt" from *REA*, because (as a condition of being exempt from the QJSA/QPSA requirements) they still have to provide a spousal benefit.

A qualified retirement plan that is not a pension plan is not subject to the QJSA/QPSA requirements described at ¶ 3.4.02 if it meets tests A, B, and C described below, and, most significantly for estate planning, "The plan provides that the participant's nonforfeitable accrued benefit is payable in full, upon the participant's death, to the participant's surviving spouse (unless the participant elects, with spousal consent that satisfies the requirements of section 417(a)(2), that such benefit be provided instead to a designated beneficiary)." Thus, the only way a profit-sharing plan can be "exempt" from the QJSA/QPSA requirements is by (among other requirements) paying 100 percent of the participant's account to the participant's spouse at the participant's death unless the spouse consents to waive this right.

Even though it must comply with REA, an exempt profit-sharing plan is still critically different from a pension plan. Under an exempt profit-sharing plan, the employee can withdraw ALL his benefits from the plan whenever the plan permits him to do so (typically, upon separation from service, although some profit-sharing plans permit in-service distributions) WITHOUT the consent of his spouse. He can then roll the benefits over to an IRA (¶ 2.6) and continue to enjoy tax deferral without any further obligations to his spouse under federal law (¶ 3.4.04).

The trade-off is that, if the employee dies BEFORE having withdrawn the benefits from the plan, 100 percent of his benefits (including proceeds of any life insurance policy held in the plan) must be paid to the surviving spouse, unless she has consented to waive this right. Reg. § 1.401(a)-20, A-12(b).

In addition to providing that 100 percent of the participant's death benefits are paid to the spouse, a profit-sharing plan must meet the following three tests in order to be exempt from providing QJSA/QPSA benefits for any particular participant:

A.   **Participant must not elect to have his benefits paid in the form of a life annuity.** As a practical matter, this means that a plan cannot *offer* annuities as a form of retirement benefit if it wants to avoid the QJSA/QPSA requirements, because if the plan offers retirement annuities some participants will elect them, and then the plan will be in the QJSA/QPSA business. See Reg. § 1.401(a)-20, A-4. Many profit-sharing plans choose not to offer an annuity retirement benefit for this reason. However, offering annuities solely as a form of *death benefit* (¶ 1.5.10) would not trigger the QJSA/QPSA requirement.

B.   **The plan must not contain money transferred to it from a pension plan.** This refers to direct transfers, for example, if an employer terminates its pension plan and transfers its funds into a profit-sharing plan. Amounts rolled over into the profit-sharing plan by employees are not considered transfers for this purpose, even if the amount rolled over originally came from a pension plan. If a profit-sharing plan does contain money that was transferred from a pension plan, there is a way of keeping the pension money (subject to REA) separate from the "pure" profit-sharing plan money and avoiding the QPSA/QJSA requirements as to the latter. Reg. § 1.401(a)-20, A-5.

C.   **No interrelated benefit formula.** The employees' benefits under the profit-sharing plan are not taken into account as part of an interrelated benefit formula of a pension plan; Reg. § 1.401(a)-20, A-5(a)(3) (next to last sentence).

3.4.04 *IRAs, Roth IRAs, and 403(b) plans*

IRAs and Roth IRAs are not subject to REA; neither ERISA § 205 nor IRC § 401(a)(11) applies to IRAs or Roth IRAs (with the possible exception of SEP-IRAs and SIMPLEs).

Finally, we come to the special case of 403(b) plans. Although 403(b) plans are subject to some of the same § 401(a) requirements as qualified plans (see § 403(b)(10), (12)), § 401(a)(11) is not one of the 401(a) provisions "imported" into § 403(b), which would make it at first appear that 403(b) plans are not subject to REA. However, even though the Internal Revenue Code REA provisions don't apply, *some* 403(b) plans are subject to ERISA—which has its own set of QJSA/QPSA requirements. Therefore, "to the extent that section 205 [of ERISA] covers section 403(b) contracts and custodial accounts they are treated as section 401(a) plans" for purposes of the QJSA/QPSA requirements. Reg. § 1.401(a)-20, A-3(d). Therefore, some 403(b) plans are subject to REA and some are not.

The 403(b) plans NOT covered by ERISA (and therefore not subject to REA) are those funded exclusively by means of elective employee deferrals (salary reduction agreements). 403(b) plans funded in whole or in part by employer contributions are subject to ERISA and therefore also to the REA requirements. DOL Reg. § 2510.3-2(f).

403(b) plans that are subject to ERISA and offer annuity benefits to the participant will be subject to REA's full QJSA/QPSA requirements, just like a pension plan (¶ 3.4.02). A 403(b) plan that is subject to ERISA but that does *not* offer annuity benefits (*i.e.*, a plan funded exclusively with mutual fund custodial accounts pursuant to § 403(b)(7)) can use the alternative compliance procedure available to "exempt" profit-sharing plans (¶ 3.4.03).

3.4.05 *Various REA exceptions and miscellaneous points*

There are exceptions to the REA requirements, even for covered plans. These exceptions, though usually not significant in estate planning, may be significant in your particular client's situation (but see ¶ 3.4.06).

A.   No spousal consent is required for distribution of benefits to the participant when the total value of his benefits is under $5,000. Reg. § 1.411(a)-11(c)(3).

B.   REA does not require that a QPSA, or 100 percent-death-benefit-in-lieu-of-QPSA, be paid to a spouse who was married to the participant for less than a year prior to the date of death. § 417(d); § 401(a)(11)(D).

C.   No spousal consent is required if "it is established to the satisfaction of a plan representative that the consent...may not be obtained because there is no spouse, because the spouse cannot be located, or because of such other circumstances as the Secretary may by regulations prescribe." § 417(a)(2)(B).

D.   Plan benefits may not be used as security for a plan loan to the employee unless the spouse consents. § 417(a)(4).

E.   There are modified rules for ESOPs. § 401(a)(11)(C).

F.   There are exceptions for plans terminated (or employees retired) before REA's effective date.

G.   The spouse loses her REA rights upon divorce or legal separation or her "abandonment" of the participant. Reg. § 1.401(a)-20, A-27. (Instead, she may receive a share of the benefits through a "qualified domestic relations order" issued in connection with the divorce; see § 414(p).)

3.4.06 *Plan may be more generous than REA requires*

For reasons of administrative convenience or other reasons, a retirement plan may give spouses more rights than REA requires. For example, REA does not require that a QPSA, or (in the case of an "exempt" profit-sharing plan) the 100 percent-death-benefit-in-lieu-of-QPSA, be paid to a spouse who was married to the participant for less than a year prior to the date of death. § 417(d); § 401(a)(11)(D). However, many retirement plan designers decided it was easier to grant the same rights to *all* spouses, regardless of the length of the marriage.

Similarly, the value of the legally-required QPSA (which is supposed to be equivalent only to the survivor pension the spouse would have received under a QJSA) is less than the total value of the employee's accrued benefit in the plan. However, some plans simply award every nonconsenting spouse 100 percent of the value of the participant's benefit, presumably because that is administratively easier than figuring out for each individual employee and spouse what would have been the relative values of their shares under a QJSA.

3.4.07 *Requirements for spousal consent or waiver*

The spouse's consent to waive REA-mandated benefits cannot be in any old form done at any old time. § 417 contains elaborate rules for the spousal consent, including as to its form (¶ 3.4.08) and:

A.   **Timing.** The participant's waiver of a QPSA, and the spouse's consent to such waiver, must be given after the beginning of the plan year in which the participant reaches age 35, and prior to the employee's death. § 417(a)(6)(B). The IRS, unlike the Code itself, permits waiver of the QPSA even *before* the participant reaches age 35, provided the participant goes through the waiver/consent process *again* after reaching age 35. Reg. § 1.401(a)-20, A-33. For exempt profit-sharing plans (¶ 3.4.03), the spousal consent for waiver of the 100 percent-death-benefit may be provided "at any time," including before the participant reaches age 35. Reg. § 1.401(a)-20, A-33(a).

B. **Disclosure.** "No consent is valid unless the participant has received a general description of the material features, and an explanation of the relative values of, the optional forms of benefit available under the plan in a manner which would satisfy the notice requirements of section 417(a)(3)." Reg. § 1.417(e)-1(b)(2)(i). Although this disclosure must be provided to the *participant* rather than to the spouse, the spouse's consent to the participant's waiver of the QJSA or QPSA must "acknowledge the effect" of the election. § 417(a)(2)A)(i). This probably means that the spouse should see the same disclosures provided to the participant, in order that the spouse may understand the effect of the waiver.

3.4.08 *Form of spousal consent or waiver; later changes*

An election in proper form "designates a beneficiary (or a form of benefits) which may not be changed without spousal consent (or the consent of the spouse expressly permits designations by the participant without any requirement of further consent by the spouse), and...the spouse's consent acknowledges the effect of such election and is witnessed by a plan representative or a notary public...." § 417(a)(2)(A). See Reg. § 1.401(a)-20, A-31, for more on the form of spousal consent.

Note that there are two ways the spouse can consent: She can say "I am consenting to this *particular* beneficiary designation; if you change the beneficiary designation hereafter you need to get a new consent from me"; or the consent can expressly permit further changes ("designations") by the participant without the requirement of further spousal consents.

If the spouse consents to the participant's naming a trust as beneficiary, later amendments to the trust do not require a subsequent spousal consent. Reg. § 1.401(a)-20, A-31(a).

The IRS has published sample spousal consent forms. Notice 97-10, 1997-1 C.B. 370.

3.4.09 *Key points for estate planners*

REA poses many challenges to estate planners, including:

1. REA creates serious, and sad, difficulties when a mentally disabled spouse is unable to consent to the desired estate plan. In that case the consent must be provided by the spouse's legal guardian. Reg. § 1.401(a)-20, A-27. The author has seen the following situation more than once: The participant has a mentally disabled spouse, whose life expectancy is shortened due to the disability. A survivor annuity would probably never provide a dime to the disabled spouse (because of the shortened life expectancy), but *would* reduce the participant's pension (because the plan's actuarial formula for determining the amount of benefits does not take into account the health of the individual participant or spouse). Through hard work and loving care the participant has avoided the expense and humiliation of legal guardianship proceedings for the disabled spouse. Thanks to REA, said expense and humiliation must be incurred when the participant reaches retirement age. Although the regulations say that the participant may be the guardian of a disabled spouse for the purpose of providing the needed consent, the court (perceiving a conflict of interest) either does not allow the participant to serve as guardian or requires appointment of a guardian ad litem with attendant expense.

2. If there is any question about the spouse's willingness to consent, or to honor a consent once given, it becomes especially important to adhere strictly to the statutory requirements regarding the form of the consent. There is no guarantee that the plan's standard printed spousal consent form complies with REA. Consider supplying your own form, using the IRS-provided sample spousal consent forms (¶ 3.4.08).

3. Waiver of the QJSA benefit must occur not more than 90 days prior to the annuity starting date, so it is impossible to lock in spousal consent in advance.

4. The Supreme Court has held that REA preempts state spousal rights laws such as community property; *Boggs v. Boggs*, 570

U.S. 833 (1997). The interrelation of REA and state spousal rights laws baffles the nation's estate planning gurus.

5.   REA rights cannot be waived in a prenuptial agreement, because the employee's affianced is not at that point the "spouse," even if the agreement is executed within the applicable election period. Reg. § 1.401(a)-20, A-28.

6.   If the spouse is being asked to waive a QPSA or QJSA, consider whether the spouse needs to be advised of the option of retaining separate counsel. The spouse might for example wish to consent to a waiver of the QJSA (and allow the participant to roll over the benefits to an IRA) only if the participant agrees to name the spouse as beneficiary of the IRA.

3.5 Putting it All Together

1.   The tax laws generally, though not always, favor naming the participant's surviving spouse, personally, as Designated Beneficiary of retirement benefits and using other assets to fund a credit shelter trust.

2.   IRS rulings provide clear instructions for qualifying retirement benefits payable to QTIP trusts for the estate tax marital deduction. Wise practitioners heed these instructions.

3.   Making benefits payable to a QTIP trust often results in a substantial loss of potential income tax deferral compared with leaving benefits to the surviving spouse outright.

4.   Upon the participant's death it is extremely important for the surviving spouse to consider her options immediately, and to roll over the benefits quickly if that is the chosen option.

4

Disclaimers of Retirement Benefits

The uses of qualified disclaimers in planning for retirement benefits.

A disclaimer is the refusal to accept a gift or inheritance. Federal tax law recognizes that a person cannot be forced to accept a gift or inheritance. Therefore, a disclaimer (provided it meets the requirements of § 2518; ¶ 4.1.02) is not treated as, itself, a taxable transfer. § 2518(a). Since the person making the disclaimer never accepted the property in the first place, the theory goes, he never owned it and therefore he could not have given it away.

Disclaimers of inherited retirement benefits can be very useful in *post mortem* planning. Unfortunately, not every refusal to accept an inheritance is a qualified disclaimer, entitled to the blessings of § 2518.

4.1 Qualified Disclaimers of Retirement Benefits

4.1.01 *What practitioners must know*

Estate planners need to know:

✓ The requirements for a qualified disclaimer under § 2518. ¶ 4.1.02, ¶ 4.1.11–¶ 4.1.12, ¶ 4.2.05–¶ 4.2.06.

✓ The income tax effects of qualified and nonqualified disclaimers of retirement benefits. ¶ 4.1.03–¶ 4.1.04.

✓ What constitutes "acceptance" of an inherited retirement plan by the beneficiary which would preclude a qualified disclaimer. ¶ 4.1.05–¶ 4.1.10.

✓ The rules for disclaimers by fiduciaries, and the effect of other fiduciary actions on the ability to disclaim. ¶ 4.1.06, ¶ 4.2.07–¶ 4.2.08.

✓ Pre- and post-mortem planning uses of disclaimers of retirement plan benefits. ¶ 4.2.01–¶ 4.2.03.

✓ Drafting concerns, problems with REA, ERISA, and plan administrators, and other practical issues involved in disclaimers of retirement benefits. ¶ 4.2.04, ¶ 4.2.09–¶ 4.2.11.

✓ Planning checklist for disclaimers. ¶ 4.3.

4.1.02 Requirements for qualified disclaimer: § 2518

Here are the requirements for a qualified disclaimer under § 2518:

A. The disclaimer must be irrevocable, unqualified (unconditional), and in writing. § 2518(b). Yes that's right: In order to be qualified, the disclaimer must be unqualified! Verbal, revocable, and conditional disclaimers are not qualified disclaimers.

B. The disclaimant must not have "accepted the interest disclaimed or any of its benefits." § 2518(b)(3). See ¶ 4.1.05–¶ 4.1.10.

C. The disclaimer must be delivered by a certain deadline. For retirement plan death benefits, the deadline is normally nine months after the participant's date of death. ¶ 4.1.11, ¶ 4.2.10.

D. The disclaimer must be delivered to the correct party(ies). ¶ 4.1.12.

E. The property must pass, as a result of the disclaimer, *to someone other than the disclaimant.* See ¶ 4.2.05. Exception: Property can pass to the decedent's spouse as a result of the disclaimer, even if she is also the person making the disclaimer (the "disclaimant"). § 2518(b)(4).

F. The property must pass, as a result of the disclaimer, to whoever it passes to *without any direction on the part of the disclaimant.* Disclaimers in favor of the spouse are NOT excepted from this rule. § 2518(b)(4). See ¶ 4.2.06.

G.   A disclaimer can be qualified under § 2518 even if it is not valid under state law. § 2518(c)(3). The income tax effects of a qualified disclaimer that is not valid under state law are uncertain; see ¶ 4.1.03–¶ 4.1.04.

4.1.03 *Income tax treatment of qualified disclaimers*

§ 2518 recognizes qualified disclaimers "for purposes of this subtitle." § 2518 is part of Subtitle B of the Code, "Estate and Gift Taxes." Income taxes are governed by Subtitle A. Except for a minor provision dealing with disclaimers of powers by a trust beneficiary (§ 678(d)), there is no Code provision dealing with the effectiveness of disclaimers *for purposes of Subtitle A.*

The IRS Chief Counsel's office has filled the statutory gap, at least with respect to certain disclaimers. GCM 39858 (¶ 4.2.10(B)) ruled that a disclaimer of retirement benefits, if it met the requirements of § 2518 and applicable state law, shifts the income tax burden of the benefits from the disclaimant to the person who receives the benefits as a result of the disclaimer. This GCM also held that such a disclaimer is not an "assignment or alienation" of plan benefits of the type forbidden by § 401(a)(13).

Thus, at least for qualified disclaimers that are valid under applicable state law, we can be sure that a disclaimer will not be treated as an assignment of the benefits (which could cause immediate taxation of the income inherent in the plan; see ¶ 2.3.03).

4.1.04 *Nonqualified disclaimers*

GCM 39858 did not purport to decide the income tax effects of a disclaimer that was either *not qualified* under § 2518 or *not valid under state law.*

The IRS has at least once treated a nonqualified disclaimer of qualified retirement plan (QRP) benefits as effective to transfer the income tax burden of the benefits to the person who took the benefits as a result of the disclaimer. See PLR 9450041. Nevertheless, a nonqualified disclaimer is clearly outside the safe harbor of GCM 39858.

There are cases in which it does not matter, for *gift tax purposes*, whether a disclaimer is qualified. However, when the disclaimed property is a retirement plan, it is normally vital to have the disclaimer not be treated as an assignment, since assignment of a retirement plan generally results in loss of the income tax-sheltered status of the benefits. ¶ 2.3.03. If the disclaimer does not meet the requirements of § 2518, the benefits might be treated as immediately distributed to the disclaimant. See Donna Example, ¶ 4.2.05.

While the income tax effect of nonqualified disclaimers and disclaimers that are not valid under state law is uncertain, we have a safe harbor regarding the income tax treatment of a disclaimer that is valid under state law and qualified under § 2518. The rest of this ¶ 4.1 discusses how to meet the requirements of § 2518 in connection with disclaimers of retirement benefits. ¶ 4.2 discusses the planning uses (and pitfalls) of such disclaimers.

4.1.05 What constitutes "acceptance": Overview

One requirement of a qualified disclaimer is that the disclaimant must not "have accepted the interest disclaimed or any of its benefits." § 2518(b)(3). For what this means in connection with actions taken in a fiduciary capacity, see ¶ 4.1.06. Acceptance must involve some action on the part of the beneficiary. Mere passive title-holding is not acceptance. Reg. § 25.2518-2(d)(1). See ¶ 4.1.07–¶ 4.1.08 for how this concept applies to retirement benefits.

Under Reg. § 25.2518-2(d)(1), "Acceptance is manifested by an affirmative act which is consistent with ownership...," such as:

A.   **Accepting income.** Accepting "dividends, interest or rent from the property" constitutes acceptance of the property. See Reg. § 25.2518-2(d)(4), Examples (6), (11). The proper way to disclaim an income payment in the form of a check is to return the check uncashed along with a written disclaimer. Reg. § 25.2518-2(c)(5), Example (6).

B.   **Exercising control.** "[D]irecting others to act with respect to the property" constitutes acceptance. See Reg. § 25.2518-2(d)(4), Example (4), and ¶ 4.2.04, #1. However, see PLR 2005-03024, in which a surviving spouse exercised control by selling some securities in a joint account that had passed to her by right of survivorship but was not thereby deemed to have accepted the *entire* account (just the securities she had traded), and was accordingly allowed to disclaim the rest of the account.

C.   **Accepting consideration.** "[A]cceptance of any consideration in return for making the disclaimer" is treated as acceptance of the property. Reg. § 25.2518-2(d)(1), last sentence; (d)(4), Example (2). Thus, the beneficiary will not have made a qualified disclaimer if he has contracted with someone to receive consideration for disclaiming.

4.1.06 *Limited exception for certain fiduciary actions*

This ¶ 4.1.06 discusses whether a person who is both a beneficiary and a fiduciary of the property can disclaim an interest *as beneficiary* despite having taken certain actions regarding the property in his capacity *as fiduciary*. For disclaimers by a fiduciary *in his capacity as fiduciary* see ¶ 4.2.07–¶ 4.2.08.

Actions taken by a person who is both a beneficiary and a fiduciary "in the exercise of fiduciary powers to preserve or maintain the disclaimed property" do not constitute acceptance *as beneficiary*. Reg. § 25.2518-2(d)(2).

Shirley Example: Shirley dies. Her will leaves her house to her three children A, B, and C, and names C as executor. To fulfill his duties as executor under applicable state law, C arranges for insurance, security, and maintenance for the house. These actions taken as executor would not preclude his disclaiming his interest as beneficiary.

This exception can lead practitioners astray. This is a very limited exception for which the IRS provides no examples in the regulations. The only fiduciary powers blessed are "to preserve or maintain the disclaimed property." Any exercise of discretionary powers *to direct the enjoyment of the property*, even if exercised in a fiduciary capacity, would preclude a qualified disclaimer of the property by the individual in his personal capacity, unless the exercise of discretion is limited by an ascertainable standard. ¶ 4.2.06.

Now we turn to how these rules apply to retirement benefits. When there are no rulings dealing with retirement benefits, we must analogize from rulings dealing with other assets.

4.1.07 *Titling of account does not determine acceptance*

The fact that a retirement plan account is retitled in the name of the beneficiary after the death of the participant does not in and of itself mean the beneficiary has accepted the account. See Reg. § 25.2518-2(d)(4), Example (6); PLR 8817061 (a surviving spouse's filing an election to take a statutory share of the decedent's estate did not constitute acceptance of the statutory share; the spouse could disclaim part of the statutory share); PLR 9214022.

Rachel Example: Rachel dies, leaving her IRA (which is held at Brokerage Firm X) to her husband Isaac. Isaac informs Brokerage Firm X of Rachel's death. Firm X retitles the account "Rachel, deceased, IRA, for the benefit of Isaac, beneficiary." Firm X sends Isaac paperwork explaining the account agreement, its fees, and his rights regarding rollover and investments. If this is all that happens, Isaac has not accepted the IRA. But: If Isaac gives Firm X any instructions regarding the account, such as buying or selling investments, he has accepted the account (or at least those investments; see ¶ 4.1.05(B)). If he takes a withdrawal from the account, see ¶ 4.1.09. If he names a successor beneficiary for his interest, see ¶ 4.1.10.

4.1.08 *Automatic deposit of benefits not acceptance*

It is common for a participant to arrange his retirement plan so that periodic distributions are automatically deposited in his bank account. If the bank account is a joint account co-owned with the retirement plan beneficiary, the mere continuation of the automatic deposits after the participant's death would not, *in itself*, constitute acceptance of the retirement plan, or even of the amounts deposited, by the beneficiary, since there has been no action by the beneficiary.

George Example: George receives monthly distributions of $2,500 from his IRA. These are automatically transferred, by the IRA provider, by electronic means, to the bank account George owns jointly with Martha, who is also the beneficiary of the IRA. George dies. Two more monthly payments of $2,500 are transferred from the IRA to the bank account after George's death. When the IRA provider is notified of George's death, it ceases making the transfers. Martha is not deemed to have accepted George's IRA just because of the continuation of the monthly automatic deposits, even though they were transferred into an account in her name, because she is not the one who directed that they be so transferred. These deposits were initiated by George, not Martha.

Although the continuation of automatic distributions does not itself create "acceptance" by the beneficiary, the waters get muddy if the surviving account owner/beneficiary exercises control over the joint bank account funds after the participant's death. For example, suppose Martha in the above example writes some checks on the (formerly) joint bank account, or withdraws some cash from it, after George's death, and later decides she wants to disclaim the IRA distributions that were placed in the account after George's death. (If she wants to keep those payments but disclaim the *rest* of the IRA, see ¶ 4.1.09.)

If she wants to say she never accepted the post-death automatic distributions from George's IRA, she presumably has to prove that the money she spent from that account after George's death did *not* come out of the post-mortem IRA distributions. If, after George's death and prior to the disclaimer, the balance in the account ever dipped below the then-cumulative total of the post-death transfers from the IRA, then Martha will not be able to argue that she did not accept the IRA distributions. So, for example, if, after the first $2,500 post-death automatic deposit came in from the IRA, the balance in the account dipped below $2,500, that would mean Martha must have spent some of the money from the IRA distribution. If she spent it, she accepted it.

On the other hand, if the account balance always stayed equal to or higher than the cumulative total of post-death IRA distributions, Martha should succeed in her claim that she never touched those distributions and so never accepted them. See PLR 2000-03023.

4.1.09 *Effect of taking a distribution; partial disclaimers*

If the beneficiary accepts a distribution from the plan, that does not necessarily constitute acceptance of the entire plan.

A.   **Taking the MRD for the year of death is not acceptance of the entire plan.** The IRS has issued a safe-harbor ruling that a beneficiary can receive and keep the minimum required distribution (MRD) for the year of the participant's death (¶ 1.5.04(F)) and still disclaim all or part of the rest of such beneficiary's interest in the decedent's plan. Rev. Rul. 2005-36,

2005-26 I.R.B. 1368. There is one minor limitation: By taking the MRD, the beneficiary is deemed to have accepted not only the MRD itself but also the income that the plan earned on that "pecuniary amount" (as the IRS calls it) between the date of death and the date the MRD is distributed to the beneficiary. See the Ruling for how to compute this income.

B. **Taking other distributions from the plan.** If the beneficiary takes out more than just the year-of-death MRD (and income thereon), such excess distribution is not within the safe harbor of Rev. Rul. 2005-36. However, he has still not necessarily accepted the entire plan; the Code permits a beneficiary to disclaim part of an inheritance while accepting other parts of it.

A person may disclaim "any interest" in property. § 2518(a). Reg. § 25.2518-3 is entirely devoted to disclaimers of "less than an entire interest." Several types of partial disclaimers are recognized, including a disclaimer relating to "severable property."

Severable property is "property which can be divided into separate parts each of which, after severance, maintains a complete and independent existence. For example, a legatee of shares of corporate stock may accept some shares of the stock and make a qualified disclaimer of the remaining shares." Reg. § 25.2518-3(a)(1)(ii). When a beneficiary inherits an estate, or a joint securities account, the beneficiary has inherited in effect a collection of severable property. The beneficiary can take some assets from the inherited collection and disclaim others. See Reg. § 25.2518-3(d), Example (17).

The IRS has in rulings allowed beneficiaries to accept some assets from an estate, trust, or joint investment account and later disclaim other assets. The favorable rulings (PLRs 8113061, 8619002, 9036028, and 2005-03024) support the conclusion that a beneficiary may take a distribution from a typical self-directed IRA (which is, like an estate or a joint investment account, essentially a collection of severable property) without being deemed to have accepted the entire account and therefore without being precluded from disclaiming all or part of the rest of the account. (The only exception would be if the distributions taken could somehow be construed as representing the "income" of the entire account; see ¶ 4.1.05(A).) Rev. Rul. 2005-36 supports this conclusion, in that it created a safe harbor for one type of partial acceptance (taking the MRD for the year of death), and did not rule out the possibility of a qualified disclaimer even if other distributions had been taken.

If the beneficiary thinks of this issue in advance, he can either execute a partial disclaimer before taking the distribution, or at least send in to the IRA provider, along with the request for a distribution, a written statement that the beneficiary is not accepting the entire account, just the amount of this distribution.

If the beneficiary does disclaim part of the account, see Rev. Rul. 2005-36 for elaborate rules regarding how the income of the retirement plan must be apportioned between the portions disclaimed and not disclaimed.

Taking a distribution *would* preclude a later disclaimer if the retirement benefit is not a collection of "severable" property. For example, if the plan in question is a Defined Benefit plan (¶ 10.1.04), and the death benefit is a life annuity of $100 per month, as soon as the beneficiary accepts the first $100 check, he has accepted the entire benefit, because there is no way to "sever" the annuity. The only exception would be if the check was part of the MRD for the year of death and therefore within the safe harbor of Rev. Rul. 2005-36.

4.1.10 *Naming a successor beneficiary as acceptance*

A beneficiary's designating a successor beneficiary for his interest in the account is probably not "acceptance," *unless* the beneficiary dies while that designation is in effect (i.e., before he disclaims), in which case see ¶ 4.2.08(A). "The exercise of a power of appointment to any extent by the donee of the power is an acceptance of its benefits," says Reg. § 25.2518-2(d)(1), but this apparently does not include an executory exercise: See Reg. § 25.2518-2(d)(4), Example (7), in which B has a testamentary power of appointment under A's trust, and signs a will which would exercise the power, but then makes a qualified disclaimer of the power before he dies.

4.1.11 *Deadline for qualified disclaimer*

At one level the deadline for disclaimers of retirement benefits is simply stated ("nine months after the participant's death"). When stated with all its exceptions and wrinkles the rule is more complicated. § 2518(b)(2) states that the disclaimer must be delivered "not later than the date which is 9 months after the later of--(A) the day on which the transfer creating the interest in such person is made, or (B) the day on which such person attains age 21." See PLR 2003-33023 for an example of the latter. Now the wrinkles:

First, the deadline is measured from *the date of the transfer* that created the interest being disclaimed. Normally, in the case of retirement plan death benefits, the date of transfer is the date of the participant's death, but there are cases in which the transfer arguably occurred prior to the participant's death; see ¶ 4.2.10.

Second, the fact that the deadline for finalizing the identity of the designated beneficiary for MRD purposes is September 30 of the year after the participant's death (¶ 1.8) does NOT mean that the deadline for making a qualified disclaimer is extended to that date; the MRD rules have no effect whatever on the deadline for a qualified disclaimer. ¶ 4.2.01.

Third, if the deadline for delivering the disclaimer falls on a Saturday, Sunday, or legal holiday (see Reg. § 301.7503-1(b) for definition), the deadline is extended to the next day which is not a Saturday, Sunday, or legal holiday. Reg. § 25.2518-2(c)(2).

Fourth, in rules borrowed from the deadline for filing tax returns, the IRS provides that "a timely mailing of a disclaimer" to the correct person (¶ 4.1.12) "is treated as a timely delivery." Reg. § 25.2518-2(c)(2). See Reg. § 301.7502-1(c)(1), (2), and (d), for requirements of "timely mailing."

4.1.12 *To whom is the disclaimer delivered?*

§ 2518(b)(2) requires that the disclaimer be "received by the transferor of the interest, his legal representative, or the holder of the legal title to the property to which the interest relates." Reg. § 25.2518-2(b)(2) adds one more candidate, "the person in possession of such property," but adds no further elucidation and no examples.

In the case of retirement benefits, the disclaimer cannot be delivered to "the transferor" (the participant) because he is dead, so that leaves "his legal representative" (i.e., the executor or administrator of the participant's estate), "the holder of the legal title to the property," and "the person in possession." The legal title to retirement benefits is generally held by the trustee (of a QRP or individual retirement trust) or custodian (of an individual retirement account or 403(b) mutual fund account), who also has "possession" of the retirement plan's assets.

The "or" in the Code and Regulation makes it appear that § 2518(b)(2) would be satisfied if the disclaimer is delivered *either* to the executor of the participant's estate *or* to the trustee or custodian of the retirement plan, i.e., that you have a choice regarding where to send the disclaimer. However, it is possible that, without specifically so stating, the government intends that the correct person to send the disclaimer to depends on the type of property; in other words, you can't just send it to any of the above, you have to send it to the right recipient. See Reg. § 25.2518-2(a)(3) and § 25.2518-2(c)(2), both of which speak of delivery to "*the person*" described in Reg. § 25.2518-2(b)(2), as though in the case of any particular asset there is only one correct recipient of the disclaimer.

Regardless of which destination would satisfy § 2518(b)(2), it is normally *also* necessary to comply with applicable state law, which may have different requirements about where the disclaimer must be delivered. Also, in the case of a QRP, check whether the plan has its own requirements for disclaimers and comply with those (see ¶ 4.2.09).

For what it's worth, in PLR 9016026 a qualified disclaimer of QRP benefits was filed with the employer and the plan trustee; in PLR 9226058, a qualified disclaimer of an IRA was filed with the Probate Court. Other letter rulings discussing qualified disclaimers of retirement benefits don't say where the disclaimers were filed.

4.2 Planning with Disclaimers

Disclaimers have proven to be of great value in cleaning up beneficiary designations where the deceased participant named the "wrong" beneficiary. Disclaimers have been used to redirect benefits to the surviving spouse (so she can roll them over), and to create funding for a credit shelter trust that would otherwise have no assets. *Post mortem* planning flexibility can be increased if the possibility of disclaimers is planned for in the drafting stage, although excessive reliance on possible future disclaimers is discouraged.

4.2.01 *Changing the Designated Beneficiary*

A qualified disclaimer made by September 30 of the year after the year of the participant's death (the "Beneficiary Finalization Date"; see ¶ 1.8) is effective to "remove" the disclaimant as a beneficiary for purposes of determining who is the participant's Designated

Beneficiary under the minimum distribution rules. If "a person disclaims entitlement to the employee's benefit, pursuant to a disclaimer that satisfies section 2518 by that September 30 thereby allowing other beneficiaries to receive the benefit in lieu of that person, the disclaiming person is not taken into account in determining the employee's designated beneficiary." Reg. § 1.401(a)(9)-4, A-4(a).

The fact that the Beneficiary Finalization Date is not until September 30 of the year after the year of death does *not* extend the deadline for making a qualified disclaimer; the disclaimer deadline is still nine months after the date of death. ¶ 4.1.11.

By means of a qualified disclaimer, an older beneficiary (such as a surviving spouse or child) can disclaim the benefits and allow them to pass to a younger contingent beneficiary (such as a child or grandchild) and the younger beneficiary will then be "the" Designated Beneficiary whose life expectancy becomes the Applicable Distribution Period for MRD purposes (¶ 1.5). MRDs will then be determined based on the identity of the beneficiary who takes as a result of the disclaimer rather than on the identity of the original beneficiary who disclaimed.

Clancy Example: Clancy named his wife Nancy as primary beneficiary of his IRA, and named his child as contingent beneficiary. Clancy died on June 1, Year 1, before his Required Beginning Date (¶ 1.5.03). Nancy disclaims the IRA by means of a qualified disclaimer on February 1, Year 2, which is within nine months after Clancy's death. Because her qualified disclaimer occurred prior to the Beneficiary Finalization Date for Clancy's IRA (September 30, Year 2), the child now becomes "the" beneficiary of the IRA for purposes of applying the minimum distribution rules, and the child's life expectancy is the Applicable Distribution Period for the IRA.

Trust beneficiaries can disclaim interests or powers they have under the trust, to help the trust qualify as a "see-through trust" under the IRS's minimum distribution trust rules. See ¶ 6.3.03(B).

A qualified disclaimer made after the Beneficiary Finalization Date is not effective to "remove" the disclaiming beneficiary for purposes of determining the Applicable Distribution Period. For example, a minor beneficiary can disclaim as late as nine months after he reaches age 21, which might be many years after the participant's death. See ¶ 4.1.11. Even though such a disclaimer could be qualified disclaimer, it would not be effective to change the Designated

Beneficiary for minimum distribution purposes if it occurs after the Beneficiary Finalization Date.

4.2.02 *Funding credit shelter trust*

In PLR 9442032, the participant named his surviving spouse as primary beneficiary and his trust as contingent beneficiary. The trust provided that all IRA benefits had to be allocated to the marital trust, over which the spouse had a general power of appointment (¶ 3.3.09). No assets passed to the credit shelter trust. "To enable [the] estate to fully utilize the available unified credit," the spouse, as beneficiary of the IRA, disclaimed her interest in the IRA, and then, as beneficiary of the marital trust, disclaimed her general power over the marital trust. As a result of these disclaimers, the IRA was now payable to a trust of which she was merely the life income beneficiary, with no general power of appointment. Then, as executor, she made a fractional QTIP election for the IRA and the trust (¶ 3.3.03). The nonelected portion of the IRA and marital trust became in effect the credit shelter trust.

See ¶ 4.2.04 regarding incorporating disclaimer-activated credit shelter trust funding in the estate plan.

4.2.03 *Salvaging spousal rollover*

If the participant dies having named the "wrong" beneficiary, it may be possible to get the benefits to the spouse (so she can roll them over) by having the named beneficiary disclaim the benefits. This strategy works if, as a result of the disclaimer, the benefits pass outright to the spouse either as contingent beneficiary, or as the default beneficiary under the plan (¶ 1.7.02).

If the default beneficiary under the plan is the participant's estate, this strategy still works *if* (as a result of the disclaimer) the benefits will pass outright to the spouse as residuary beneficiary under the participant's will or by intestacy. See ¶ 3.2.08. Unfortunately, this strategy does not work if the spouse will not get the benefits as a result of the disclaimer (for example, if the benefits will pass to the estate as a result of the disclaimer, and the participant's Will or the state intestacy law would cause the estate to pass to the participant's children rather than to the spouse).

In PLR 9045050, the participant named a trust as his beneficiary. The spouse was a trustee of the trust. Upon the participant's death, the spouse, as trustee, made a qualified disclaimer of the benefits. As a result of the disclaimer, the benefits passed to the spouse outright rather than to the trust, and she rolled them over. PLR 1999-13048 (discussed at ¶ 3.2.08) was similar.

In PLR 9450041, benefits were redirected from a marital trust to the spouse via a chain of qualified and nonqualified disclaimers; the rollover was allowed.

In PLR 2005-05030, a participant died without having named a beneficiary for his Defined Benefit and 457 plans. The benefits therefore became payable to his estate, which in turn was left to "Trust #2." The beneficiaries of Trust #2 were the participant's spouse, issue, sister, sister's issue, sister-in-law, and sister-in-law's issue. Qualified disclaimers were filed by the spouse, and all the then-living issue (two daughters and two grandchildren), and by the sister and sister-in-law and *their* then-living issue (seven nieces and nephews). As a result of these disclaimers, the trust passed to the surviving spouse under applicable state law, and the IRS approved the spousal rollover.

4.2.04 *Building disclaimers into the estate plan: Pitfalls*

It is wise, at the planning stage, to anticipate the possibility of disclaimers. For example, the participant may be trying to choose between naming his spouse as beneficiary, to achieve deferral of income taxes via a spousal rollover, on the one hand, and naming a credit shelter trust as beneficiary, on the other hand, to take advantage of his unified credit. Each choice has its merits and a clear "winner" may not be apparent during the planning phase.

The participant may decide to make the benefits payable to the spouse as primary beneficiary, because his main goal is to provide for the spouse's financial security, but provide that, if the spouse disclaims the benefits, the benefits will pass to the credit shelter trust. If funding the credit shelter trust appears to be the more attractive alternative at the time of the participant's death, the spouse can activate the credit shelter plan by disclaiming the benefits, which will then pass to the credit shelter trust as contingent beneficiary. PLR 9320015 illustrates this type of planning. See also PLR 2005-22012 (benefits payable to spouse as primary beneficiary, with marital trust as contingent beneficiary if spouse disclaimed, and family trust as second contingent beneficiary if spouse also disclaimed the marital trust, and participant's children as third contingent beneficiaries if spouse also disclaimed the family trust); PLR 2005-21033 is identical.

While it is wise to consider the possibility of disclaimers, the apparent flexibility of disclaimers can tempt planners to rely excessively on future disclaimers as a way of carrying out the estate plan. One justification offered for this approach is that it avoids the need to spend time analyzing the choices at the planning stage. Thus, professional fees are lower—at the planning stage. The estate plan relies on the fiduciaries and beneficiaries to make the decisions later, when a more informed choice can be made.

Before making important estate planning goals dependent on prospective disclaimers by beneficiaries or fiduciaries, the planner needs to weigh carefully the risks and drawbacks of relying on disclaimers. Disclaimers are not a simple solution. This ¶ 4.2.04 describes several issues that exist with disclaimers of any type of property. ¶ 4.2.05 and ¶ 4.2.06 explain two essential elements of a qualified disclaimer that are often misunderstood or overlooked. ¶ 4.2.08–¶ 4.2.10 discuss particular problems that arise with disclaimers of retirement benefits.

1.   One requirement of a qualified disclaimer is that the disclaimant must not have "accepted" the disclaimed property. See ¶ 4.1.05–¶ 4.1.10. If the surviving spouse is the sole beneficiary, and is considering a disclaimer, no one can exercise investment authority over the account pending her decision, unless the benefits are in a trusteed plan under which the trustee can exercise such authority. Assets in a custodial or self-directed plan would essentially be frozen, since the participant's powers of attorney or grants of investment authority would expire at his death and the spouse could not grant new authority without accepting the account. ¶ 4.1.05(B).

2.   Disclaimers generally have an inexorable deadline of nine months after the date of death. ¶ 4.1.11. Thus, an estate plan that depends on disclaimers requires rapid action *post mortem*.

3.   No matter how cooperative and disclaimer-friendly the proposed disclaimant may have been in the planning stage, he could have a change of heart (or suffer emotional paralysis due to the death) and not sign a disclaimer when the time comes.

4.   If estate taxes will be due on the disclaimed property, who will pay them? The decedent's will may contain a tax payment clause that does not operate correctly if there is a disclaimer.

4.2.05 *Property must pass to "someone other than" disclaimant*

§ 2518(b)(4) requires that the property must pass, as a result of the disclaimer, either to the transferor's (i.e., the participant's) *surviving spouse* or to *someone other than the disclaimant.*

Donna Example: Donna, named as primary beneficiary of her late brother's IRA, disclaims the IRA. As a result of her disclaimer, the IRA passes to the contingent beneficiary, a charitable remainder trust (CRT; ¶ 7.5.04) of which Donna is the life beneficiary. Because of her life interest in the CRT, the IRA is not passing to "someone other than the disclaimant." Since Donna is not the spouse of the IRA owner, her disclaimer is therefore not a qualified disclaimer (unless she first disclaims all interests in the CRT). Her nonqualified disclaimer is treated as a gift for gift tax purposes; however, there are no adverse *gift tax* consequences, because the "donee" is a CRT of which the only beneficiaries are herself and a charity. Gifts to yourself or to charity are not subject to gift tax. However, her nonqualified disclaimer is not within the safe harbor of GCM 39858 for *income tax* purposes. ¶ 4.1.03. If the disclaimer is treated as an assignment of the right to receive income in respect of a decedent, Donna would be liable for income taxes on the full value of the IRA, and the IRA would lose its qualification. ¶ 2.1.03(C), ¶ 2.3.03.

This requirement is frequently overlooked, as planners cheerfully expect (*e.g.*) children to disclaim benefits that will then pass to a trust of which the same children are beneficiaries. Passing the benefits by disclaimer from the outright beneficiary to a trust only works if the outright beneficiary is (1) the surviving spouse or (2) not a beneficiary of the trust. See ¶ 4.2.07 for how this rule applies to disclaimers by fiduciaries.

4.2.06 *Property must pass "without direction" by disclaimant*

§ 2518(b)(4) also requires that the property pass, as a result of the disclaimer, to whoever it passes to *without any direction on the part of the disclaimant.* Disclaimers in favor of the spouse are NOT excepted from this rule.

If a surviving spouse named as outright beneficiary is to disclaim, she cannot thereafter retain any discretionary distribution powers over the disclaimed benefits (unless limited by an ascertainable standard; Reg. § 25.2518-2(e)(1)). For example, if the spouse is disclaiming benefits which will then pass to a credit shelter trust for issue, she cannot be a trustee of that trust if the trustee has, say, discretionary power to "spray" the trust among the participant's issue; nor can she have a power of appointment enabling her to, *e.g.*, decide which issue of the participant will receive the trust after her death. See PLR 2005-22012, in which the surviving spouse (to avoid this rule) disclaimed her testamentary power of appointment under a trust with respect to an IRA that flowed to such trust by virtue of her disclaiming the IRA as beneficiary. Thus, taking advantage of the flexibility of disclaimers may eliminate the use of other, *post mortem,* planning tools, such as a spousal power of appointment.

4.2.07 *Disclaimer by fiduciary of participant's estate or trust*

This ¶ 4.2.07 deals with the disclaimer by an executor (or trustee), in his fiduciary capacity on behalf of the estate (or trust), where the estate (or trust) is the beneficiary (¶ 1.7.02) of the benefits. For disclaimers by a fiduciary in his *personal* capacity, see ¶ 4.1.06. When an individual is named as beneficiary, and survives the participant, but dies before withdrawing the benefits, see ¶ 4.2.08 for the possibility of a disclaimer by the beneficiary's executor.

There is scant authority on the subject of fiduciaries' disclaiming. There can be state law obstacles, such as a requirement of court approval or a requirement of specific language in the document authorizing disclaimers. For examples of disclaimers by trusts or estates to facilitate a spousal rollover, see ¶ 4.2.03.

The requirement that property must pass "without any direction" on the part of the disclaimant (¶ 4.2.06) would presumably preclude a disclaimer from one discretionary trust to a second discretionary trust with the same trustees.

When retirement benefits are payable to the *participant's own estate*, the IRS has ruled that the participant's executor may not disclaim the benefits because the participant had "accepted" his own retirement benefits. PLR 9437042.

4.2.08 *Disclaimer by executor of beneficiary's estate*

If the beneficiary of a retirement plan dies after becoming entitled to the benefits, the beneficiary's executor generally can disclaim the benefits on the beneficiary's behalf if permitted by state law. Here are two issues to consider with respect to such disclaimers:

A.   **Who is the successor beneficiary?** When a beneficiary dies after becoming entitled to the benefits, the person who succeeds to the deceased beneficiary's interest is called the successor beneficiary. ¶ 1.5.13. If the successor beneficiary is not the deceased beneficiary's own estate there are two potential obstacles to a disclaimer by the beneficiary's executor:

First, if the beneficiary himself had designated a successor beneficiary (¶ 1.5.13(A)), then a qualified disclaimer by the beneficiary's executor is probably not possible. The beneficiary's death would cause his "executory" designation of a successor beneficiary (¶ 4.1.10) to be considered "executed," and this would be deemed acceptance by the beneficiary, precluding disclaimer. *Estate of Engelman*, 121 T.C. 54 (2003).

Second, if there is a successor beneficiary (other than the participant's own estate) who has been designated by the participant (¶ 1.5.13(D)), one case held that the successor beneficiary is automatically entitled to ownership of the benefits upon the death of the original beneficiary, so the estate of the original beneficiary has no standing to disclaim. *Nickel v. Estate of Estes*, 122 F. 3d 294 (5ᵗʰ Cir. 1997). Though this case has been criticized (and might not be followed by other courts), if there is a designated successor beneficiary, that successor beneficiary is likely to claim the benefits, citing this case.

B.   **If the fiduciary is also a beneficiary.** When the beneficiary's executor disclaims benefits that are payable to the estate as a result of the beneficiary's death, the interest he is disclaiming is the *decedent's* interest in those benefits. Thus, an executor can make such a disclaimer on behalf of the deceased beneficiary even if the executor in his *individual* capacity (1) is a beneficiary of the decedent's estate and (2) will receive the benefits personally as a result of the estate's disclaimer.

Such a disclaimer *appears* to violate the rule that the benefits must pass to someone other than the disclaimant (¶ 4.2.05), since the beneficial interest in the benefits is owned by the same individual both before and as a result of the disclaimer; however, it does not violate that rule, because when he disclaims in his capacity as executor he is not deemed to be disclaiming on behalf of himself.

This situation arises most commonly when a husband and wife die within a short time of each other. See *Dancy*, 872 F. 2d 84 (4th Cir. 1989), in which a son, as executor of his mother's estate (of which he was also the sole beneficiary), was allowed, on her behalf, to make a qualified disclaimer of her interest as surviving joint owner of certain property she held with her husband, even though the son was also the beneficiary of the husband's estate which would receive the property as a result of the disclaimer; and PLRs 9015017 and 8749041 (involving similar situations).

4.2.09 *Disclaimers and the plan administrator*

One concern is whether a plan administrator of a qualified retirement plan (QRP) might cite ERISA requirements in refusing to recognize a disclaimer. A plan administrator might take the position that the plan requires the benefits to be paid to the beneficiary named by the participant, and the plan has no authority to pay the benefits to someone else if the named beneficiary is in fact living; that ERISA requires the plan to be administered in accordance with its terms; and that ERISA preempts state laws including disclaimer statutes.

In the author's view, this is not a correct interpretation of ERISA. QRP documents generally provide that the interpretation of the plan and administration of the trust are governed by state law to the extent not contrary to (or preempted by) ERISA. If the applicable state law permits disclaimers, the plan is required to give effect to them, in the author's view, unless the plan contains a specific provision to the contrary. All trustees, not just ERISA trustees, are required to administer their trusts in accordance with the terms of the trust instrument; most nonERISA trust instruments also say nothing about disclaimers, but no one argues that trustees generally are entitled (let alone required) to ignore valid disclaimers. An ERISA trust is not different from any other trust except to the extent federal law requires it to be. In GCM 39858 (¶ 4.2.10(B)), the IRS recognized that disclaimers do not violate ERISA. The IRS has blessed disclaimers of

QRP benefits in numerous letter rulings; see, *e.g.*, PLRs 9016026, 9247026, and 2001-05058. In a similar vein, the IRS has recognized that a plan must conform to a state's "slayer" statute, and not pay benefits to the person who murdered the participant, even if that person is named as beneficiary under the plan. PLR 8908063.

On the other hand, the Supreme Court has upheld a QRP's refusal to follow a state statute that would have voided a beneficiary designation in favor of an ex-spouse, citing ERISA's preemption of state laws and the need for uniform national rules for plan administration. *Egelhoff v. Egelhoff*, 121 S. Ct. 1322, 532 U.S. 141 (2000). Note that an employer that wanted to help (rather than frustrate) employees and their families could easily eliminate any possible ERISA-state law conflict by providing in the plan document that disclaimers would be given effect, and establishing reasonable procedures for verifying and implementing disclaimers.

These issues are of no concern to IRA administrators, since IRAs are not subject to ERISA and its preemption rule.

4.2.10 *REA and deadline for qualified disclaimers*

A qualified disclaimer must be made within a certain time period "after the...date of the transfer creating the interest" being disclaimed. ¶ 4.1.11. The period is measured "with reference to the transfer creating the interest in the disclaimant." A transfer occurs when there is a "completed gift" (in the case of an inter vivos transfer), or (in the case of a transfer at death, or a transfer that becomes irrevocable at death) as of the date of death. Reg. § 25.2518-2(c)(3)(i).

So far, we have assumed that the participant's date of death is the starting point for measuring the time period during which a qualified disclaimer must be made. However, if a beneficiary acquires rights in the participant's benefits earlier than the date of death we need to consider whether the time starts earlier.

Federal law gives married persons certain rights in each other's retirement benefits. See ¶ 3.4. Thus, under a pension plan, the participant's spouse acquires vested rights in the participant's benefits at the same moment the participant does (or upon their marriage, if the marriage occurred when the participant was already in the plan). If the spouse acquired these rights in the participant's benefits more than nine months before the date of death, is it too late for her to disclaim these benefits when the participant dies?

§ 2503(f) provides that *certain* spousal waivers of retirement benefits are exempt from gift tax. Specifically, § 2503(f) says that, "If any individual waives, *before the death of a participant*, any survivor benefit, or right to such benefit, *under § 401(a)(11) or 417* [REA benefits, in other words], such waiver shall not be treated as a transfer of property by gift for purposes of this chapter" (emphasis added). Thus, the Code has an exemption from gift tax for *certain* spousal waivers, namely, waivers (1) of REA-guaranteed survivor benefits (2) that occur before the death of the participant. Does this mean that:

A.   **Waivers of *other* spousal plan benefits *are* taxable gifts?** Many plans give spouses more rights than REA requires. ¶ 3.4.06. Although the statutory exemption is limited to REA-guaranteed benefits, presumably the IRS would not attempt, in the case of a spousal waiver, to assess gift tax on the enhanced value of spousal benefits over the REA-guaranteed minimum.

B.   **Spousal waivers that occur *after* the participant's death *are* taxable gifts?** No. GCM 39858 (which was issued in 1989, though it is inexplicably dated 9/9/81) provides that § 2503(f) creates "no inference" that Congress intended to impose gift tax on spousal waivers that occur *after* the participant's death.

GCM 39858 involved a spousal disclaimer of REA-guaranteed benefits and does not mention any deadline for such a disclaimer earlier than nine months after the participant's death, holding that: "There is no evidence that Congress intended to preclude a spouse from disclaiming or renouncing benefits under a qualified plan payable after the participant's death." In view of the IRS's strong policy statement in this GCM, it appears that REA-guaranteed benefits can be the object of a qualified disclaimer up to nine months after the participant's death.

4.2.11 *Practical issues in disclaimers of retirement benefits*

Here are some tips for dealing with and planning for qualified disclaimers of benefits:

A.   **How to do partial disclaimers.** If making a partial disclaimer, review Reg. § 25.2518-3, which discusses and gives examples of disclaimers of part of an inheritance by: disclaiming one or more separate interests in property while retaining others (Reg. § 25.2518-3(a)(1)(i); § 25.2518-3(d), Example (21)); disclaiming some "severable" property and accepting other severable property (see ¶ 4.1.09 and Reg. § 25.2518-3(a)(1)(ii); § 25.2518-3(d), Examples (1), (3)); disclaimer of an undivided portion (Reg. § 25.2518-3(b); § 25.2518-3(d), Example (20)); and disclaimer of a pecuniary amount (or of everything except a pecuniary amount) (Reg. § 25.2518-3(c); § 25.2518-3(d), Examples (16) (19)). Follow the "successful" examples, and the rules stated in Rev. Rul. 2005-36, as closely as possible, and comply with state law requirements.

B.   Keep the disclaimer short. It's tempting to recite, in the disclaimer, who will receive the property as a result of the disclaimer, but it's a bad idea. If you mention who the property will pass to, it looks as if the disclaimant is trying to direct who will receive the property, or to make the disclaimer conditional on the property passing to those recipients, either of which actions would make the disclaimer not qualified under § 2518.

C.   Know where the property will go before you disclaim it. Investigate THOROUGHLY who will receive the property as a result of the disclaimer. A child (*e.g.*) may assume that if he disclaims an inheritance from his father this will cause the inheritance to pass to his mother, only to find out later that the disclaimer caused the property to pass to some distant relatives of the father. In the case of a retirement plan, *usually*, a disclaimer by the primary beneficiary will cause the property to pass to the contingent beneficiary, and a disclaimer by all named beneficiaries will cause the benefits to pass to the default beneficiary under the plan document.

D.   Consider having the disclaimer occur at the trust level. If it is anticipated that a beneficiary might want to make a "formula" disclaimer (*e.g.*, a surviving spouse as primary beneficiary disclaiming an amount sufficient to fully fund the participant's credit shelter trust), consider the practicalities of drafting such a formula, getting the plan administrator to accept it, and carrying out its terms all within a brief nine-month window after the participant's death.

If that looks like it might be difficult to accomplish, or if there is any other reason to anticipate that the plan administrator may pose obstacles to the disclaimer (see ¶ 4.2.08), consider naming, as primary beneficiary, a trust which gives the surviving spouse the right to (1) all income for life, plus (2) principal if needed for health or support, plus (3) an unrestricted power to withdraw all principal during her life, plus (4) a general power of appointment at death (see ¶ 3.3.09). If she wants to keep the benefits, she can withdraw them from this trust and roll them over; see ¶ 3.2.08. If she wants to convert the trust to a "credit shelter trust" for her life benefit, she can disclaim rights (3) and (4); see ¶ 4.2.02. If she wants to disclaim all interests, she can do that too (see "E"). She can disclaim any of these rights as to all or a fractional portion of the trust, if the trust contains the proper language. In doing all this, she will need to deal only (or primarily) with the (friendly, expert, understanding) trustee, and you sidestep the problems of dealing with the (cold, bureaucratic, nonexpert) plan administrator.

E.   **Naming different contingent beneficiaries to take in case of primary beneficiary's death or disclaimer.** The most common use of this dual designation of contingent beneficiary is where: (1) the primary beneficiary is the spouse and (2) the contingent beneficiary in case of the spouse's disclaimer is a trust of which the spouse is a life beneficiary, and (3) the contingent beneficiary in case of the spouse's death is the same person (or group of people) who is the remainder beneficiary of the trust at the spouse's death.

The purpose of the dual contingent-beneficiary-designation is simply to allow the spouse to disclaim as outright beneficiary, while keeping her interest as beneficiary of the trust.

Even though it appears that the participant is naming "different" contingent beneficiaries depending on whether the spouse predeceases him or disclaims the benefits, he really isn't. He's just allowing the spouse to decide whether she wants to take the benefits as outright beneficiary or as life beneficiary of a trust, which is permitted under § 2518. There would be no point in providing that the Trust is also contingent beneficiary *in case of the spouse's death*, because the Trust won't even exist if the spouse predeceases the participant. See Form 3.1, Appendix B.

4.3 Putting it All Together

Here is a checklist of pre- and post-mortem planning considerations regarding disclaimers.

1.   Upon the death of a client, all plan and IRA beneficiary designations should be reviewed as soon as possible. Either (1) no benefits should be distributed to any beneficiary until this review is completed or (2) if a beneficiary wants to take a distribution (other than the MRD for the year of death) the request for the distribution should be accompanied by a statement that the beneficiary is not thereby accepting the entire account (just the amount distributed). No beneficiary should exercise investment (or other) control over inherited plan benefits until this review is completed. If any beneficiary designation appears undesirable, consider the use of qualified disclaimers to redirect benefits to the "right" beneficiary.

2.   When preparing beneficiary designations as part of the estate planning process, name a contingent as well as a primary beneficiary. Consider whether a different contingent beneficiary should be named in case of a disclaimer by, as opposed to the death of, the primary beneficiary. ¶ 4.2.11(E).

3.   When choosing among competing considerations in naming a primary beneficiary (such as "financial security of spouse" versus "saving estate taxes for children"), name the primary beneficiary based on the relative priorities the client assigns to the choices. For maximum flexibility after the client's death, name the second choice as contingent beneficiary.

4.   When a disclaimer is anticipated at the estate planning stage, take steps beforehand to facilitate that process, including: spousal waiver of REA rights (¶ 3.4), if needed; instructions to the beneficiaries regarding the choices that will be available to them and what considerations should be applied in making the choices; granting disclaimer authority to fiduciaries, along with guidelines for exercise of the power to disclaim; and review the plan documents, § 2518 requirements, and state law to make sure these pose no obstacles to the proposed disclaimers.

5

Roth Retirement Plans

Roth retirement plans offer the possibility of tax-free distributions to those who are eligible (and can afford) to adopt them.

Prior to the debut of the Roth IRA in 1998, all retirement plans had the same basic tax structure: Contributions to the plan might or might not be tax deductible; and all distributions from the plan in excess of the participant's after-tax contributions would be includible in the recipient's gross income. § 408A established a new kind of IRA, called a Roth IRA, effective in 1998. Roth IRA contributions are never deductible, but distributions are normally tax-free. Thus, income tax on the plan's investment returns is not merely deferred, it is eliminated, at the cost of payment of income taxes up front on the plan contributions.

In 2001, EGTRRA added two more "Roth" retirement plans, the "deemed Roth IRA" (effective in 2003 and later years; ¶ 5.1.04) and the "Designated Roth Account" (beginning in 2006; ¶ 5.7).

5.1 Introduction to Roth Retirement Plans

5.1.01 *What practitioners must know*

Estate planners need to know:

✓   Roth IRA basics. ¶ 5.1.

✓   The income tax treatment of qualified and nonqualified Roth IRA distributions. ¶ 5.2.

✓   How to create a Roth IRA through "regular contributions" (¶ 5.3) or "conversion" of a traditional IRA (¶ 5.4), including the different eligibility tests.

✓   How the 10 percent penalty on pre-age 59½ distributions applies to Roth IRA conversions and distributions. ¶ 5.5.

✓   How to "undo" a Roth IRA conversion. ¶ 5.6.

✓   What a "designated Roth account" (DRAC) is, and how DRACs differ from Roth IRAs. ¶ 5.7.

✓   Which clients should consider Roth IRAs and DRACs. ¶ 5.8.01–¶ 5.8.09.

✓   How to handle Roth benefits in a client's estate plan. ¶ 5.8.10.

✓   Which Roth IRA transactions are abusive. ¶ 5.4.09, ¶ 8.6, ¶ 8.7.

5.1.02 *Overview of Roth IRAs*

For federal income tax purposes, Roth IRAs are treated just like traditional IRAs except where the Code specifies different treatment. § 408A(a); Reg. § 1.408A-1, A-1(b). Thus, if any question about Roth IRAs is not specifically answered in § 408A or the Roth IRA regulations, the answer should be the same as for a traditional IRA.

Final regulations for Roth IRAs were issued February 3, 1999, effective for taxable years beginning after 1997. TD 8816, 64 FR 5597.

In addition to tax-free distributions, the Roth IRA offers two other advantages over traditional IRAs: no minimum required distributions during life (¶ 5.1.03(A)); and no maximum age for making contributions (¶ 5.3.03(B)).

There are three ways to create a Roth IRA. Each method has its own rules and eligibility requirements. One is by nondeductible "regular contributions" on behalf of an individual who has compensation income; see ¶ 5.3. Another is by "conversion" of a traditional IRA to a Roth IRA; see ¶ 5.4. The third is by rollover from a DRAC; see ¶ 5.7.08.

5.1.03 *Roth IRAs and the minimum distribution rules*

Here is how the minimum distribution rules (Chapter 1) apply to Roth IRAs:

A.   **No lifetime required distributions.** The lifetime minimum required distribution (MRD) rules (¶ 1.3) do not apply to Roth IRAs. § 408A(c)(5) provides that § 401(a)(9)(A) (which contains the lifetime minimum distribution rules) and the "incidental death benefits" rule (¶ 1.4.06) do not apply to Roth IRAs. Therefore, a person who reaches age 70½ does not have to start taking distributions from his Roth IRA as he does from his traditional IRA. There is no "required beginning date" (RBD; ¶ 1.4) for a Roth IRA. This is a major advantage of the Roth IRA; see ¶ 5.8.08(A).

B.   **Post-death MRD rules do apply.** Once death occurs, the minimum distribution rules do apply to Roth IRAs. The Roth IRA is not exempted from any minimum distribution rules other than § 401(a)(9)(A) and the incidental death benefits rule, both of which apply only during the participant's life, so distributions must begin coming out of the Roth IRA after his death. Since there is no RBD for a Roth IRA, the post-death minimum distribution rules will *always* be applied "as though the Roth IRA owner died before his" RBD, regardless of when he dies. Reg. § 1.408A-6, A-14(b). For how to compute MRDs from a Roth IRA after the participant's death, see ¶ 1.5.03.

C.   **Roth distributions, conversions, do not fulfill MRD requirement for traditional IRA.** Distributions from a Roth IRA cannot be used to fulfill a distribution requirement with respect to any other kind of IRA. Reg. § 1.408A-6, A-15. A Roth IRA conversion may not be used to fulfill the distribution requirement for a traditional IRA, because the conversion is considered a rollover, and as such it cannot take place until after the MRD for the year of the conversion has actually been distributed from the traditional IRA to the participant. ¶ 5.4.03(C).

5.1.04 *Deemed IRAs and deemed Roth IRAs*

An employer who maintains a qualified retirement plan may permit employees to make voluntary contributions to "a separate account or annuity established under the plan." § 408(q)(1)(A). The separate account must meet the requirements of § 408 (traditional IRA) or § 408A (Roth IRA). The separate account (the deemed traditional IRA or deemed Roth IRA) is then treated in all respects the same as a traditional IRA or Roth IRA, as the case may be, and is generally not subject to the qualified plan requirements.

Since a "deemed" Roth IRA is treated in all respects the same as a "real" Roth IRA, all discussion in this Chapter about Roth IRAs applies equally to deemed Roth IRAs.

5.2 Tax Treatment of Roth IRA Distributions

Not all Roth IRA distributions are automatically tax free; only "qualified distributions" from a Roth IRA are income tax-free. ¶ 5.2.01. It is relatively easy to qualify for "qualified" distributions, and even nonqualified distributions from Roth IRAs (¶ 5.2.03) get favorable treatment compared with distributions from traditional IRAs.

The basis of property distributed from a Roth IRA is its fair market value on the date of the distribution. Reg. § 1.408A-6, A-16.

§ 408A(d)(4)(A) provides that § "408(d)(2) shall be applied separately with respect to Roth IRAs and other individual retirement plans." This means that the taxation of distributions from *traditional* IRAs is computed without regard to the existence of, or distributions from, *Roth* IRAs in the same year; and that all of the participant's Roth IRAs are treated as one single account for purposes of applying the Ordering Rules (¶ 5.2.04).

5.2.01 *Qualified distributions: Definition, tax treatment*

"Qualified distributions" from a Roth IRA are not included in the recipient's gross income for federal income tax purposes, regardless of whether the recipient is the participant or a beneficiary. § 408A(d)(1). A qualified distribution is one that is made after the Five-Year Period (¶ 5.2.02); and which *in addition* (§ 408A(d)(2)(A)):

1.   Is made on or after the date the participant attains age 59½; or

2.   Is made after the participant's death; or

3.   Is "attributable to" the participant's being totally disabled (as defined in § 72(m)(7); see ¶ 9.4.02); or

4.   Is a "qualified special purpose distribution," i.e., a distribution of up to $10,000 for certain purchases of a "first home" (see ¶ 9.4.09). § 408A(d)(5); § 72(t)(2)(F), (t)(8).

These conditions for a qualified distribution from a Roth IRA resemble the requirements for avoiding the premature-distributions penalty of § 72(t) (Chapter 9), but are not identical. For example, withdrawals from a Roth IRA to pay higher education expenses are not qualified distributions, even though such withdrawals from a traditional IRA would be exempt from the 10 percent penalty (¶ 9.4.08).

5.2.02 *Computing Five-Year Period for qualified distributions*

The Five-Year Period (called in the statute the "nonexclusion period") for *all* of a participant's Roth IRAs begins on January 1 of the first year for which a contribution was made to *any* Roth IRA maintained for that participant. § 408A(d)(2)(B); Reg. § 1.408A-6, A-2.

Fred Example: On August 3, 1999, Fred put $1,000 into his Roth IRA. Fred's Five-Year Period starts January 1, 1999, and is completed on December 31, 2003. The first year in which he can possibly have a qualified distribution is 2004. If he makes further contributions (either regular or rollover) to the same (or any other) Roth IRA, those contributions do NOT start a new Five-Year Period running. In 2006, Fred converts his $100,000 traditional IRA to a Roth IRA. This new Roth IRA instantly meets the Five-Year Period requirement, because Fred has already completed the Five-Year Period for every Roth IRA he will ever own. If Fred is already over age 59½, he can immediately take qualified distributions from his newly-created Roth IRA in 2006.

Note the following points regarding calculation of the Five-Year Period for a Roth IRA:

❏   If a Roth IRA contribution is recharacterized (¶ 5.6.02), it is treated as if it had never been made. Thus, in the Fred Example, if Fred had recharacterized his 1999 Roth IRA contribution, that contribution would not start the Five-Year Period running.

❏   The Five-Year Period is computed differently for a designated Roth account (DRAC). ¶ 5.7.04(B).

❑   The method of computing the Five-Year Period for a Roth IRA does not change just because the Roth IRA receives a rollover from a DRAC, regardless of how long the DRAC had been in existence. ¶ 5.7.08.

5.2.03 *Tax treatment of nonqualified distributions*

A nonqualified distribution is one made before the Five-Year Period is up; or which is made after expiration of the Five-Year Period but not for one of the specified reasons (age 59½, disability, death, etc.; ¶ 5.2.01). A nonqualified distribution is not *per se* excludible from gross income. However, even if a distribution is not "qualified" it receives favorable tax treatment compared with distributions from a traditional IRA.

A Roth IRA contains two types of money. First, it contains the participant's contributions; since these amounts were *already* included in the participant's gross income, these originally-contributed funds will not be included in his income *again* when they are later distributed. Thus, the amount of the participant's original contribution(s) to the Roth IRA constitutes the participant's basis (or "investment in the contract") in the Roth IRA. ¶ 2.1.07. If the account has grown to be worth more than this basis, the rest of the account value (which represents the earnings and growth that have occurred since the original contribution) has not yet been taxed (and may *never* be taxed if it is distributed in the form of a qualified distribution).

The general rule is that all distributions from a Roth IRA are deemed to come *first* out of the participant's contributions. ¶ 5.2.04, #1. Thus, if the participant or beneficiary wants to get money out of the Roth IRA, but does not meet the requirements for a qualified distribution, he can still take out money income tax-free, up to the amount the participant contributed.

In contrast to this favorable treatment afforded to Roth IRAs, all distributions from a *traditional* IRA are deemed to come *proportionately* from the "basis" (nontaxable) portion and the post-contribution earnings of all of the participant's aggregated IRAs. ¶ 2.1.10. This same unfavorable proportionate rule also applies to nonqualified distributions from DRACs. ¶ 5.7.05.

5.2.04 *The Ordering Rules*

Any distribution from a Roth IRA (*except* a "returned contribution"—see ¶ 5.6.01(A); Reg. § 1.408A-6, A-9(e)) is deemed to come from the following sources, in the order indicated. § 408A(d)(4)(B); Reg. § 1.408A-6, A-9. These rules are referred to in this chapter as the Ordering Rules.

1.   Any distribution is deemed to come, first, from the participant's contributions to his Roth IRA(s), to the extent that all previous distributions from his Roth IRA(s) have not yet exceeded the contributions; and

2.   If the participant has made both "regular" (¶ 5.3) and "rollover" (conversion) (¶ 5.4) contributions, the distributions are deemed to come, first, from the regular contributions (with no rule specifying in what order contributions made in different years are deemed distributed), then from rollover contributions on a first-in, first-out, basis; and

3.   Once it is determined that the distribution is deemed to come from a particular rollover contribution, the dollars that were includible in gross income by virtue of that rollover (¶ 5.4.07) are deemed distributed first; and

4.   Finally, once all contributions have been distributed, the balance of the distribution comes out of earnings. Whew!

Fortunately, the Ordering Rules will have to be consulted only in certain unusual situations, namely:

❑   For most people, the Ordering Rules matter only for purposes of determining whether a nonqualified distribution is subject to income tax; the Ordering Rules essentially mean that the distribution is NOT taxable until all contributions have been distributed.

❑   The Ordering Rules matter also for someone who converts a traditional IRA to a Roth IRA before reaching age 59½, and then takes a distribution within five years of the conversion and before reaching age 59½. The Ordering Rules will apply in determining whether the 10 percent penalty applies to the distribution. See ¶ 5.5.02.

5.3 "Regular Contributions" to a Roth IRA

One way to fund a Roth IRA is by making what the IRS calls "regular" (as opposed to "rollover"; ¶ 5.4) contributions. This ¶ 5.3 discusses the requirements for making a regular contribution to a Roth IRA, as contrasted with the rules governing regular contributions to a traditional IRA. See ¶ 5.6.02 for how to change your mind about which type of IRA you want to contribute to after you've already contributed.

As with traditional IRAs, only cash may be contributed. § 408A(a), § 408(a)(1). See ¶ 5.6.03 regarding the deadline for making a regular Roth IRA contribution.

5.3.01 *Definition of compensation*

The first requirement an individual must meet in order to make a regular contribution to either a traditional or a Roth IRA is that the individual must have compensation income. Reg. § 1.408A-3, A-3. The individual's contributions to either type of IRA for a particular year may not exceed the amount of such individual's compensation income for such year (or, if less, the dollar limit described in ¶ 5.3.02).

"Compensation" is partly defined in § 219(f)(1). It includes self-employment income (§ 401(c)(2)), and does *not* include pension, annuity, or deferred compensation payments. It includes taxable alimony and separate maintenance payments (§ 71). It includes "wages, commissions, professional fees, tips, and other amounts received for personal services...." Reg. § 1.408A-3, A-4. See Rev. Proc. 91-18, 1991-1 C.B. 522, for further detail on the definition. See also ¶ 5.8.07.

5.3.02 *How much may be contributed annually*

The maximum annual regular *Roth* IRA contribution derives from the maximum annual regular *traditional* IRA contribution.

The maximum amount that may be contributed to all of a person's traditional IRAs for a particular year is the lesser of the applicable dollar limit or the individual's compensation income (¶ 5.3.01) for the year. The maximum regular contribution for a particular year to all of a person's *Roth* IRAs is the exact same amount—minus the amount of regular contributions made to any traditional IRA(s) for that person for that year. § 408A(c)(2).

So, an individual who has compensation income (¶ 5.3.01), and who meets the other eligibility requirements (see ¶ 5.3.03 for Roth IRAs, § 219 for traditional IRAs) may contribute to either a traditional IRA or a Roth IRA (whichever he is eligible to contribute to), provided that the total contributed to both types of accounts for the year does not exceed the lesser of (1) the applicable dollar limit or (2) the individual's compensation income for the year.

Contributions made on the individual's behalf to a SEP-IRA or a SIMPLE are ignored for this purpose; these are considered employer contributions, and as such have no effect on the maximum the individual may contribute to a traditional or Roth IRA. § 408A(f).

The applicable dollar limit (ADL) was $2,000 for the years 1998–2001. § 219(b)(1)(A) (pre-2002). Under § 219(b)(5), the ADL is the sum of the basic dollar limit and (if applicable) the add-on:

Year	Basic Dollar Limit	Add-on for Participant over 50
2002–2004	$3,000	$ 500
2005	$4,000	$ 500
2006–2007	$4,000	$1,000
2008–2010	$5,000	$1,000

The $500 or $1,000 add-on to the basic dollar limit ("catch-up contribution") is available to a participant who has attained age 50 by the end of the taxable year. § 219(b)(5)(B). After 2008, § 219(b)(5)(C) applies a cost-of-living adjustment (COLA) to the basic dollar limit (but NOT to the over-50 add-on amount) in $500 increments. As a result of PPA '06, the above contribution limits will not "sunset" after 2010, even though they were enacted as part of EGTRRA. See p. 575.

5.3.03 *Who may make a "regular" Roth IRA contribution*

A.   **Income must be below certain levels.** Not just anyone who has compensation income may contribute to a Roth IRA. There is an income limit. A specially calculated version of "adjusted gross income" (see ¶ 5.4.04) cannot exceed the following levels. In order to be able to contribute the full dollar limit to a

Roth IRA, AGI may not exceed $95,000 for a single taxpayer, $150,000 for a married taxpayer filing a joint return, or zero for a married taxpayer filing a separate return. Under § 833(b) of PPA '06, these dollar amounts will be adjusted upwards, after 2006, for post-2005 inflation.

The ADL is reduced if AGI exceeds these levels. The ADL goes to zero if AGI exceeds the ADL by $15,000 (single) or $10,000 (married). § 408A(c)(3)(A), (C)(ii). Note that the reduction applies to the ENTIRE ADL (including the over-50 add-on amount), not just to the basic dollar limit.

For this purpose, "a married individual who has lived apart from his or her spouse for the entire taxable year and who files separately is treated as not married." Reg. § 1.408A-3, A-3(b).

An individual who is prevented from contributing the ADL to a Roth IRA because of these income limits can contribute his reduced ADL to the Roth and the balance of the "normal" ADL to a traditional IRA (assuming he otherwise meets the requirements for contributing to a traditional IRA). Reg. § 1.408A-3, A-3(d), Example 4.

B.   **No age limit.** There is no maximum age for contributing to a Roth IRA, as there is for contributions to a traditional IRA; a taxpayer can contribute to a Roth IRA even after age 70½. § 408A(c)(4); compare § 219(d)(1); § 408(o)(2)(B)(i).

C.   **Participation in an employer plan is irrelevant.** A person who meets the income test (¶ 5.3.03(A)) and has compensation income (¶ 5.3.01) may contribute to a Roth IRA regardless of whether he participates in a "workplace" retirement plan in the same year.

5.4 Conversion of Traditional IRA to Roth IRA

See ¶ 5.5 for how a Roth conversion interacts with the 10 percent penalty on premature distributions. See ¶ 5.6.03 regarding the deadline for completing a Roth IRA conversion. The term **conversion** of a traditional IRA to a Roth IRA includes a rollover from a traditional IRA to a Roth IRA. Conversion contributions and rollover contributions to Roth IRAs mean the same thing: a transfer, rollover or conversion of funds from a traditional IRA to a Roth IRA.

5.4.01 *Rollover (conversion) contributions to a Roth IRA*

The second way to create a Roth IRA is to transfer funds to it from a traditional IRA. The amount so transferred is included in the participant's gross income. ¶ 5.4.07. Thereafter the account will enjoy the favorable tax treatment afforded to Roth IRAs. § 408A(d)(3)(A)–(C). Since there is no limit on the amount that can be converted from a traditional to a Roth IRA, a conversion contribution can be a much more substantial amount than the few thousand dollars per year maximum regular Roth IRA contribution (¶ 5.3.02).

Manuel Example: Manuel is 60 years old. He rolls over [or transfers, or converts—all these terms are used interchangeably] $300,000 from his traditional IRA to a Roth IRA in 2005. The entire $300,000 is included in his gross income for 2005. This is the first Roth IRA he has ever had. When he retires at age 65, in 2010, the Roth IRA has increased to $1.2 million. All subsequent distributions from the Roth IRA (whether made to Manuel or to his beneficiaries) will be income tax-free (because they are "qualified distributions"; see ¶ 5.2.01).

There are three ways to make this type of contribution to a Roth IRA:

1.   A distribution from a traditional IRA may be contributed (rolled over) to a Roth IRA within 60 days after the distribution is made. § 408(d)(3)(A)(i); see ¶ 5.6.03 regarding the deadline.

2.   Money in a traditional IRA may be transferred in a plan-to-plan transfer directly from the trustee (or custodian) of the traditional IRA to the trustee (or custodian) of the Roth IRA.

3.   All or part of a traditional IRA can simply be "redesignated" as a Roth IRA maintained by the same trustee or custodian. Reg. § 1.408A-4, A-1(b)(3).

All three of these transactions are considered rollovers ("a distribution from the traditional IRA and a qualified rollover contribution to the Roth IRA"). Reg. § 1.408A-4, A-1(c). Prior to the arrival of Roth IRAs, "rollovers" were always tax-free, and most people still associate that word with tax-free transfers from one retirement plan to another (¶ 2.6). In contrast, the rollover of funds from a traditional IRA to a Roth IRA is taxable. The term "conversion" is often used (including in § 408A) for the rollover of funds from a traditional IRA to a Roth IRA, which is a taxable event, just as a handy way to distinguish that type of rollover from a "normal" rollover, which is nontaxable.

Both partial and total conversions are allowed. An eligible individual (¶ 5.4.03) may choose to convert all, part, or none of his traditional IRA to a Roth IRA. There is no minimum or maximum dollar or percentage amount that must or may be converted.

Generally, there is no limit on the number of times an individual may convert traditional IRA funds to Roth IRA status. A person who converts part of his traditional IRA to a Roth IRA is free at any later time (in the same or a later year) to convert more of the same or another IRA to a Roth IRA. The one exception applies to someone who did a Roth IRA conversion, then later "unconverted"; see ¶ 5.6.07.

The one-rollover-per-year limitation in § 408(d)(3)(B) (¶ 2.6.07) does not apply to a conversion to a Roth IRA, so such conversion may occur even if it is within 12 months of a tax-free traditional IRA-to-IRA rollover. Reg. § 1.408A-4, A-1(a).

5.4.02 *What type of plan may be converted to a Roth IRA*

An "individual retirement plan" may be converted to a Roth IRA. § 408A(d)(3)(B), (C); Reg. § 1.408A-4, A-5. "Individual retirement plans" include individual retirement accounts (IRAs) and individual retirement trusts (IRTs) under § 408(a), (h).

However, an *inherited* IRA may NOT be converted to a Roth IRA. § 408(d)(3)(C).

A SEP-IRA (§ 408(k)) or SIMPLE IRA (§ 408(p)) cannot be "redesignated" as a Roth IRA (§ 408A(f)). However, an eligible individual (¶ 5.4.03) can roll a distribution from either of these types of IRAs into a Roth IRA, subject to one limit: A SIMPLE IRA distribution "is not eligible to be rolled over into" a Roth IRA "during the 2-year period...which begins on the date that the individual first participated in any SIMPLE IRA Plan maintained by the individual's employer...." Reg. § 1.408A-4, A-4(b). Once a SEP or SIMPLE IRA account has been converted to a Roth IRA, the account is not eligible to receive further contributions under the SEP or SIMPLE plan. Reg. § 1.408A-4, A-4(c).

A distribution from a designated Roth account (DRAC) may be rolled into a Roth IRA; see ¶ 5.7.08. Except for such DRAC distributions, however, there is no way to transfer funds directly from a qualified retirement plan (QRP) or 403(b) plan to a Roth IRA, or to roll over a distribution from such a plan directly into a Roth IRA, prior to 2008. § 408A(e); see also Reg. § 1.408A-4, A-5. Any rollover-eligible distribution *after 2007* from a QRP or 403(b) plan may be rolled over to a Roth IRA, either by direct or 60-day rollover. PPA '06, § 824. In this book, references to converting an IRA to a Roth IRA should be read to include the rollover of any eligible post-2007 nonDRAC QRP or 403(b) distribution to a Roth IRA. In the meantime, a participant in a QRP or 403(b) plan who receives a pre-2008 distribution eligible to be rolled to a traditional IRA can roll the distribution to a traditional IRA and then convert *that* to a Roth IRA.

In order to roll from any type of plan or IRA to a Roth IRA, the individual must meet certain requirements; see next section.

5.4.03　Who may convert: Income, age, filing status, MRDs

The following paragraphs (A)–(C) describe the eligibility requirements for converting to a Roth IRA for the years 1998–2009. If a person converts his IRA to a Roth IRA and does not meet the eligibility tests described here, see ¶ 5.6.02 for consequences and remedies.

Under TIPRA 2006, paragraphs (A) and (B) will cease to apply for years after 2009. Accordingly, after 2009, even high-income taxpayers and married-filing-separately taxpayers will be eligible to do Roth IRA conversions.

A.　　　**Income limit.** No conversion is permitted if the taxpayer's modified adjusted gross income (MAGI; ¶ 5.4.04) exceeds $100,000 for the taxable year. § 408A(c)(3)(B). In the case of a *married couple filing jointly*, the $100,000 limit applies to the MAGI of the *couple*, not of each *spouse*. Reg. § 1.408A-4, A-2(b). See ¶ 5.4.04–¶ 5.4.06 for definition of MAGI.

The year you look at for applying this income limit is the year in which the distribution from the traditional IRA occurs (*i.e.*, the distribution that is rolled over to a Roth IRA), *not* the year that the contribution to the Roth IRA occurs. Reg. § 1.408A-4, A-2(a). Usually, the distribution from the traditional IRA and its recontribution to the Roth IRA occur simultaneously; this rule covers the case of a distribution from the traditional IRA that occurs in one taxable year, and is rolled over in the *next* taxable year (but still within 60 days of the distribution; ¶ 2.6.06).

B.   **Filing status.** Generally, no conversion is permitted if the taxpayer is *married filing a separate return* for the year. § 408A(c)(3)(B). However, if a "married individual has lived apart from his or her spouse for the entire taxable year, then such individual can treat himself or herself as not married for purposes of...[the income test], file a separate return and be subject to the $100,000 limit on his or her separate modified AGI." Reg. § 1 408A-4, A-2(b).

C.   **Age.** A participant who meets the income and filing status tests can convert his traditional IRA to a Roth regardless of his age; you are never too young or too old to convert to a Roth IRA.

However, if the participant is under <u>age 59½</u>, see ¶ 5.5 regarding how the 10 percent penalty on premature distributions applies. Also, beginning in the year the participant reaches <u>age 70½</u>, he will not be able to convert his IRA to a Roth IRA until *after* he has withdrawn the minimum required distribution (MRD) for the year of the conversion from the IRA, because of the rules explained at ¶ 2.6.04. This is true even though, in the year he reaches age 70½, he normally would not be required to take any MRD from his IRA until April 1 of the following year. Thus, if a participant wants to convert his entire traditional IRA to a Roth without ever having to take an MRD from the IRA, he needs to take full distribution of the IRA no later than the year he reaches age 69½ (and complete the rollover/conversion within 60 days thereafter).

5.4.04 *Definition of AGI for Roth IRA eligibility*

For the years 1998–2004, the definition of MAGI was the same for purposes of determining a person's eligibility for both regular Roth IRA contributions (¶ 5.3) and Roth IRA conversions (¶ 5.4), though the maximum permitted *amount* of MAGI has always differed depending on which type of Roth IRA contribution you're talking about; compare

¶ 5.3.03 with ¶ 5.4.03. For years after 2004, an additional adjustment is required for purposes of the conversion eligibility test that does not apply for purposes of regular contribution eligibility. See ¶ 5.4.06.

"Adjusted gross income" (AGI) is a defined term in the Code (§ 62); however, for purposes of determining Roth IRA eligibility you do not simply look at the AGI line on the person's Form 1040. Rather, the definition of MAGI for purposes of the Roth IRA income limits starts with the modified definition of AGI used under § 219(g)(3) (income limits for making a deductible contribution to a traditional IRA when the individual is also a participant in an employer plan). § 408A(c)(3)(C)(i).

The § 219(g)(3) definition of AGI includes the individual's taxable Social Security benefits (§ 86), and takes into account the disallowance of "passive activity losses" (§ 469) if applicable, then requires the following further adjustments:

1.   Certain income normally *excluded* from AGI is added back in, namely: income resulting from redemption of U.S. savings bonds to pay higher education expenses (§ 135); qualified adoption expenses paid by the individual's employer (§ 137); the deduction for domestic production activities (§ 199); and foreign earned income and housing costs (§ 911).

2.   Certain deductions otherwise allowed for purposes of computing AGI are not allowed for this purpose, namely the deductions for: education loan interest expenses (§ 221); tuition expenses (§ 222); and IRA contributions (§ 219).

After completing the adjustments described in #1 and #2, make *one* further modification (¶ 5.4.05) to determine eligibility to make a regular Roth IRA contribution (¶ 5.3), or *two* further modifications (¶ 5.4.05–¶ 5.4.06) to determine eligibility for a Roth IRA conversion.

5.4.05 *Conversion income does not count for AGI test*

For purposes of the income limits applicable to both regular Roth IRA contributions and Roth IRA conversions, MAGI does not include the deemed distribution amount (¶ 5.4.07) that results from converting a traditional IRA to a Roth IRA. § 408A(c)(3)(C)(i). So, if, in the year being tested, the participant converts a traditional IRA to a

Roth IRA, resulting in the inclusion of some or all of the conversion amount in his gross income, the gross income resulting from the conversion is disregarded *solely for purpose of determining whether the taxpayer's MAGI is low enough to make him eligible to contribute to a Roth IRA.*

This aspect of Roth IRA conversions is the downfall of many taxpayers and tax preparers. Determining AGI is no easy task because it involves many interrelated computations, such as how much of the individual's Social Security payments are taxable, and how much passive activity loss is deductible. Yet all these computations must be done twice: First, for purposes of determining the individual's eligibility to contribute to a Roth IRA, all gross income resulting from traditional-to-Roth IRA conversions is ignored (and all adjustments dependent on AGI are determined in accordance with this reduced income figure). This fictional AGI has *no relevance* to the taxpayer's actual tax burden—it is a pro forma number used solely to determine eligibility to contribute to a Roth IRA. Reg. § 1.408A-4, A-9.

Then, for purposes of determining the individual's *actual* tax owed, income resulting from conversions to a Roth IRA *is* included in gross income; and all computations dependent on AGI—such as taxability of Social Security benefits, deductibility of medical expenses, etc.—are redetermined based on this true AGI figure.

5.4.06 *Post-2004 MRDs from IRAs also do not count*

Effective for 2005 and later years, some MRDs are excluded in determining MAGI.

For example, if a 72-year old person has AGI of $110,000 in 2005, but that AGI includes $15,000 of MRDs from her IRA, her MAGI is only $95,000, and she qualifies to do a Roth conversion. In 2004, she would not have qualified on these facts, because (prior to 2005) the MRD would have been included in her MAGI. This change should make Roth IRA conversion an option for more people.

Note the limitations of this rule:

1.   The participant is not exempted from taking the MRD. She still must still *take* all MRDs from her traditional IRA and every other applicable plan, and she must still *pay tax on* all such MRDs that she has taken.

2.   This exclusion applies only for the $100,000 income ceiling test for determining eligibility to do a Roth IRA conversion (§ 408A(c)(3)(B)(i)). It does NOT apply to the income test for determining eligibility to make a "regular" Roth IRA contribution! § 408A(c)(3)(C)(ii).

The big question is: Exactly *which* MRDs are excluded? The statute (§ 408A(c)(3)(C)(i)(II)) is ambiguous. The legislative history published at the time the statute was enacted suggested that Congress was thinking of lifetime MRDs from every type of plan, but not necessarily MRDs from an *inherited* plan. Then the Joint Committee on Taxation published a revised legislative history, indicating that only MRDs from IRAs were intended to be excluded. Reg. § 1.408A-3, A-6, specifically mentions only MRDs from *IRAs*.

IRS Publication 590 (2005), p. 55, states that "Minimum required distributions from qualified retirement plans, including IRAs" are excluded from MAGI for purposes of determining eligibility to convert an IRA to a Roth IRA. This appears to be a mistake; and Publication 590 is not legal authority and cannot be relied upon. In view of the ambiguous statute and revised "legislative history," taxpayers would be wise to assume that only MRDs *from IRAs* (including inherited IRAs) are excluded from MAGI for purposes of determining eligibility for a Roth IRA conversion.

5.4.07 *Tax treatment of converting to a Roth IRA*

The rollover from a traditional IRA to a Roth IRA is generally treated, for income tax purposes, as a distribution from the traditional IRA. § 408A(d)(3)(A)–(C). Thus, the rollover amount is generally included in the participant's gross income, to the extent an actual distribution of the same amount from his traditional IRA would have been taxable (¶ 2.1.02), with one exception: If the converted property includes an annuity contract, a special valuation rule applies; see ¶ 5.4.09.

The conversion may result in an increase in the taxpayer's required estimated tax payments for the year of the conversion.

For rollovers in 1998 ONLY, the inclusion in gross income could be spread equally over the four taxable years 1998–2001. § 408A(d)(3)(A)(iii). For details on this election, and on the acceleration of taxation in case of actual distributions prior to 2001, see

"1998 Conversions: The Four-Year Spread," in Chapter 5 of the 1999 edition of this book. Under TIPRA, for certain conversions after 2009, income resulting from a Roth conversion can be spread over two years.

5.4.08 *Conversion of nontaxable amounts*

Since conversion of a traditional IRA to a Roth IRA is treated (for income tax purposes) as a distribution of the converted amount (¶ 5.4.07), the amount converted is includible in the participant's gross income except to the extent it is excluded from income as a return of the participant's basis. To the extent the amount converted represents the participant's basis in the traditional IRA it is nontaxable; see ¶ 2.1.10. Reg. § 1.408A-4, A-7(a).

Whit Example: Whit's only IRA is a traditional IRA worth $70,000. He has made a total of $6,000 of nondeductible contributions to his traditional IRA over the years and has never taken a distribution from any IRA. If he converts the entire traditional IRA to a Roth IRA in 2006, he will have to include only $64,000 in gross income on account of the conversion ($70,000 total IRA value minus $6,000 basis).

Someone with after-tax money in an IRA or QRP who is able to roll money between the two types of plans can use the sequence described at ¶ 2.1.11 to achieve a tax-free Roth IRA conversion.

5.4.09 *Conversion of annuity contract*

If one of the IRA assets converted to a Roth IRA is an annuity contract, a special valuation rule applies.

Until Roth IRA conversions came along, it made little difference how annuity contracts were valued upon distribution from a retirement plan, because distribution of an annuity contract is not a taxable event. ¶ 2.1.06(G). The arrival of the Roth IRA conversion changed the landscape. The lower an IRA-owned annuity contract can be valued when the IRA is converted to a Roth IRA, the less income tax the participant must pay on the conversion. Subsequent distributions from the annuity contract will go into the Roth IRA, distributions from which will be tax-free.

According to the IRS, "some advisers" sought to take advantage of this loophole, and marketed, to IRA owners, "a single premium annuity contract with significant artificial penalties that apply in the" early years, "causing the annuity to have a low cash surrender value...." The IRA owner would then convert his IRA to a Roth IRA, and report the contract's artificially low cash surrender value (CSV) as the gross income resulting from the conversion. T.D. 9220, 2005-39 I.R.B. 596, "Explanation of Provisions."

To stop such abuses, the IRS issued a temporary and proposed regulation providing that fair market value (FMV), not CSV, must be used to determine the participant's gross income resulting from conversion of an IRA-owned annuity contract to a Roth IRA, effective for conversions on or after (and perhaps even before) August 19, 2005.

Reg. § 1.408A-4 governs Roth IRA conversions. Reg. § 1.408A-4T adds a new section A-14 to Reg. § 1.408A-4, providing a special rule for the valuation of an IRA-owned annuity contract that is converted to a Roth IRA. This is not the same valuation that applies when an annuity contract is simply distributed to the IRA owner (¶ 2.1.06(G)), nor is it the same as the special rule for valuing annuity contracts for purposes of the minimum distribution rules (¶ 1.2.07(A)). Rather, A-14 provides that the amount treated as distributed "is the fair market value of the annuity contract" on the date of the Roth IRA conversion, and provides guidelines (to be used pending IRS issuance of further more detailed guidance, probably to be similar to Rev. Proc. 2005-25; see ¶ 8.3.02) for determining such fair market value.

5.5 10% Penalty For Pre-Age 59½ Distributions

This section discusses the 10 percent penalty on "premature distributions" as it applies to Roth IRAs; for background and all other details on the penalty, see Chapter 9.

5.5.01 Penalty applies to certain Roth IRA distributions

The 10 percent penalty applies to pre-age 59½ distributions from Roth IRAs, the same as to such distributions from traditional IRAs, under the rule that Roth IRAs are treated the same as traditional IRAs unless § 408A provides otherwise. Reg. § 1.408A-6, A-5.

A.   **Distribution eligible for exception.** If the distribution is eligible for an exception from the penalty (¶ 9.2–¶ 9.4), there is no 10 percent penalty. If no exception applies, then:

B. **Nonqualified distributions.** If the distribution is a nonqualified distribution (¶ 5.2.03), the portion of the distribution allocable, under the Ordering Rules (¶ 5.2.04), to the earnings of the Roth IRA would be includible in the participant's gross income and would be subject to the penalty (Reg. § 1.408A-6, A-5(a)); and

C. **Conversion followed by distribution within five years.** See ¶ 5.5.02 for a special rule that may result in a penalty being applied to the return of the participant's own contribution.

5.5.02 *Roth conversion prior to reaching age 59½*

The 10 percent penalty does not apply to the deemed distribution (¶ 5.4.07) that results from converting a traditional IRA to a Roth IRA. § 408A(d)(3)(A)(ii); Reg. § 1.408A-4, A-7(b). Thus a young person who meets the eligibility requirements (¶ 5.4.03) may convert his traditional IRA to a Roth IRA without penalty. However, this does not mean he can forget about the 10 percent penalty.

A person who is under age 59½, although he can convert to a Roth IRA without penalty, has to come up with the money to pay the income tax on the conversion from some source *other* than the IRA, because he will owe the penalty to the extent he taps his newly-converted Roth IRA for this money, under the following special rule:

If a participant who is under age 59½ receives a distribution from a Roth IRA; and if "any portion" of that distribution is allocable under the Ordering Rules (¶ 5.2.04) to funds that were rolled over to the Roth from a traditional IRA and that were includible in gross income; and "the distribution is made within the 5-taxable-year period beginning with the first day of the individual's taxable year in which the conversion contribution was made"; then the § 72(t) penalty will apply to the distribution (unless an exception applies; see last paragraph below). Reg. § 1.408A-6, A-5(b); § 408A(d)(3)(F).

This provision was not included in the original Roth IRA legislation (TAPRA '97), but was added by the IRS Restructuring and Reform Act of 1998, effective retroactively to January 1, 1998. This retroactive imposition of the penalty was held to be constitutional in *Kitt v. U.S.*, 288 F. 3d 1355 (2002).

Note that this five-year period is *not the same* as the Five-Year Period for determining "qualified distributions" (¶ 5.2.02). The latter begins in the first year *any* contribution is made to any Roth IRA; the former begins, as to any conversion of a traditional IRA to a Roth IRA, with the year of that *particular* conversion. Reg. § 1.408A-6, A-5(c). Note also that this penalty applies regardless of whether the distribution is included in gross income in the year it occurs.

Rand Example: Rand, age 32, converts his $100,000 traditional IRA to a Roth IRA in 1999. He has no basis in the traditional IRA, so the entire $100,000 is includible in his gross income in 1999. He has no other Roth IRAs, and makes no other contributions to this one. In 2002, at age 35 (i.e., before the end of the Five-Year Period, and while he is still under age 59½) he withdraws $20,000 from the Roth IRA in order to buy a rare *Spiderman* comic book. Under the Ordering Rules, this distribution is deemed to come out of the portion of the 1999 conversion-contribution that was includible in gross income, and therefore it is subject to the 10 percent penalty in 2002.

"The exceptions under § 72(t) also apply to such a distribution," so there should be no penalty if the distribution is made after the death (or on account of the total disability) of the participant, for example. Reg. § 1.408A-6, A-5(b).

5.5.03 *Conversion while receiving "series of equal payments"*

The 10 percent penalty does not apply to IRA distributions that are part of a "series of substantially equal periodic payments" (SOSEPP; ¶ 9.2). If a participant who is receiving such a series of payments from a traditional IRA converts the traditional IRA to a Roth IRA, the conversion is "not treated as a distribution for purposes of determining whether a modification" of the series (¶ 9.3.01) has occurred, so the conversion itself does not trigger the loss of the penalty-exempt status of the series. Reg. § 1.408A-4, A-12.

However, the conversion does not mean that the participant can stop taking his periodic payments. "[I]f the original series...does not continue to be distributed in substantially equal periodic payments *from the Roth IRA* after the conversion, the series of payments will have been modified and, if this modification occurs within 5 years of the first payment or prior to the individual [sic] becoming disabled or attaining age 59½, the taxpayer will be subject to the recapture tax of section 72(t)(4)(A)." Reg. § 1.408A-4, A-12; emphasis added.

This statement in Reg. § 1.408A-4 seems to assume that the participant converted the entire traditional IRA to a Roth IRA. If he converted only part of the traditional IRA to a Roth IRA, it is not clear whether the rest of his "series" payments would have to come all from the Roth IRA, or proportionately from the new Roth IRA and the (now-diminished) traditional IRA; or whether the participant could take the payments from whichever of the two accounts he chooses.

5.6 Corrective Distributions; Recharacterizations

A taxpayer who is unhappy with the IRA contribution choices he made for a particular year, or who discovers that he was not eligible to contribute to the type of IRA he contributed to, or who contributed more than he was entitled to contribute, has some ability to remedy the problem through return, "absorption," and/or recharacterization of the contribution.

5.6.01 *How to undo a regular Roth IRA contribution*

There is an excise tax of six percent imposed on contributions to Roth IRAs in excess of the applicable limits, just as there is for excess contributions to traditional IRAs. § 4973; Reg. § 1.408A-3, A-7. This excise is imposed *annually* on the excess contribution. § 4973(a).

There are two ways to make an excess "regular" Roth IRA contribution. One is by contributing an amount to the account that is in excess of the limits on IRA contributions (¶ 5.3.02). This type of excess contribution can be corrected by means of a corrective distribution ("A") or by "absorption" ("B").

The other way to make an excess regular Roth IRA contribution is to contribute to a Roth IRA an amount that could legally have been contributed to a traditional IRA, but that is not eligible to be contributed to a Roth IRA because the participant's income is too high (¶ 5.3.03(A)). This type of excess contribution can be corrected by corrective distribution ("A"), "absorption" ("B"), or recharacterization (¶ 5.6.02).

A.   **Return the contribution.** One way to correct mistakes (or simply act on a change of heart) is for the participant to distribute the contribution back to himself. If any Roth IRA contribution (together with its net income; ¶ 5.6.06) is distributed before the extended due date (¶ 5.6.04) of the tax return for the year for which the contribution was made, then (1) the contribution is treated, for purposes of the six percent penalty, as not having been contributed, and (2) the net income on the contribution is "includible in gross income for the taxable year in which the contribution is made...." Reg. § 1.408A-3, A-7, § 1.408A-6, A-1(d); see also § 408(d)(4).

This book refers to regular IRA/Roth IRA contributions that are returned to the participant prior to the due date of his tax return as **corrective distributions**, regardless of the reason for the return.

Wayne Example: Wayne contributed $3,000 to a new Roth IRA in 2004. By 2005, the investments in the Roth IRA had earned $75 of interest, so the account was worth $3,075. Wayne then changed his mind and decided he would rather spend the money on a new gas grill. He closes the account, and the $3,075 is distributed to him in 2005. The $75 of taxable income is included in his gross income for the year of the contribution (2004). If Wayne is under 59½, see ¶ 9.1.03(B). If cashing out the Roth IRA resulted in a loss, see ¶ 8.1.03.

B.   Absorbing the contribution. Once the deadline for a returned contribution (see "A") has passed, if the participant did not withdraw the excess contribution and its associated income, the participant owes the penalty for the year for which the excess contribution was made. The penalty will continue to accrue annually until the excess contribution is either withdrawn from the account or treated as a proper contribution for a later year (to the extent the participant is eligible to make a contribution in a later year but does not do so). Reg. § 1.408A-3, A-7.

5.6.02 *How to recharacterize any Roth IRA contribution*

The regulations provide broad relief to taxpayers who wish to "amend" their IRA contributions by switching the contribution from a Roth IRA to a traditional IRA or vice versa. This relief is for anyone who changes his mind about which type of IRA he wants his contribution to go to, as well as for those who need to correct Roth IRA conversions for which they were ineligible (¶ 5.4.03). Reg. § 1.408A-5, A-10, Example 2.

A regular contribution to either type of IRA may be recharacterized as a contribution to the other type (by transferring it to the other type) at any time up to the "extended due date" (¶ 5.6.04) of the person's tax return for such year (assuming the individual is eligible to contribute the amount to the other type). § 408A(d)(6), (7).

If a person converted a traditional IRA to a Roth IRA but was not eligible to do so, the result is a "failed" conversion. A failed conversion would be treated as a taxable distribution from the traditional IRA (subject to the 10% penalty if the individual is under 59½; see PLR 2001-48051), followed by an excess contribution to the Roth IRA, generating a six percent penalty under § 4973 (¶ 5.6.01). PLR 2001-48051. To avoid the penalties, the person would have to recharacterize the contribution by the applicable deadline. ¶ 5.6.04.

A timely corrective distribution (¶ 5.6.01(A)) can be useful for undoing *regular* Roth IRA contributions, but it is not much help for someone who has *converted* a traditional IRA to a Roth IRA and then wishes he hadn't (or who discovers after the fact that he wasn't eligible; ¶ 5.4.03). This person usually does not want to distribute the money out to himself, he just wants to restore the pre-conversion status quo. His Roth IRA contribution may be transferred back to a traditional IRA before the "extended due date" (¶ 5.6.04) of his tax return for the year the distribution from the traditional IRA occurred. The contribution will be treated as a contribution to the *transferee* IRA for tax purposes. § 408A(d)(6), (7).

For example, if a person converts a traditional IRA to a Roth IRA in 2005, and then discovers that his income for 2005 exceeded the $100,000 limit so he was ineligible to do that conversion, he can move the money back to a traditional IRA before the extended due date of his tax return for 2005, and it will be treated as a rollover contribution to the traditional IRA. In effect, the Roth conversion is "undone," so the taxpayer does not realize any income on account of the Roth conversion.

Partial recharacterizations are permitted. Reg. § 1.408A-5, A-2(c)(5), (c)(6), Example 2.

Here are the significant requirements for effecting a recharacterization:

1.   The transfer from the Roth IRA back to the traditional IRA (or vice versa) must be by plan-to-plan transfer, *not* by a rollover. Reg. § 1.408A-5, A-1(a). See ¶ 2.6.01 for the difference.

2.   Not only the original contribution but "any net income allocable to such contribution" must be retransferred. See ¶ 5.6.06.

3.   The election to recharacterize is made by providing notice and directions to the IRA sponsors involved. The election to recharacterize "cannot be revoked" after the transfer back to the traditional IRA has occurred. Reg. § 1.408A-5, A-6(b).

A recharacterized contribution will be treated for Federal income tax purposes as having been contributed to the transferee IRA (rather than the transferor IRA) "on the same date and (in the case of a regular contribution) for the same taxable year that the contribution was made to the" transferor IRA. Reg. § 1.408A-5, A-3. A recharacterization is "never treated as a rollover for purposes of the one-rollover-per-year limitation of § 408(d)(3)(B) [¶ 2.6.07], even if the contribution would have been treated as a rollover contribution by the…[transferee] IRA if it had been made directly to the" transferee IRA in the first place. Reg. § 1.408A-5, A-8.

5.6.03 *Deadline for Roth IRA contributions and conversions*

The various deadlines for contributions, conversions, corrective distributions, and recharacterizations are extremely confusing. Some deadlines are based on the calendar year end, some on the extended due date of the return, and some on the unextended due date; and some of the deadlines qualify for an automatic extension—but you do not get the "automatic" extension unless you ask for it!

Starting with the easiest one: The deadline for making a regular contribution to a Roth IRA (¶ 5.3) for a particular year is the same as the deadline for contributing to a traditional IRA, i.e., the *unextended* due date of the tax return for that year, in other words, for most people, April 15 following the year in question. Reg. § 1.408A-3, A-2(b), § 219(f)(3). For example, a contribution "for" the year 2006 may be made at any time after December 31, 2005, and on or before April 15, 2007. When a participant makes a contribution between January 1 and April 15, the IRA provider must ask which year it is for, since between those dates it could be for either the year in which the contribution occurs or the prior year.

> **Meaning of "April 15"**
>
> The deadline for filing an individual's income tax return is the 15th day of the fourth month following the end of the individual's taxable year. § 6072(a). That means April 15th for most people. However, the actual deadline will be later if April 15th falls on a weekend or holiday. § 7503. Also, the deadline may be extended (by IRS proclamation) for individuals in an area affected by a natural disaster; and of course the deadline is different for an individual whose taxable year is not the calendar year. In this book, "April 15" is used as shorthand for "the unextended due date of the individual's income tax return for the year in question, whatever that may be."

Conversions are slightly more complicated. Because the conversion is technically a "rollover" (¶ 2.6), a conversion contribution is tied to the traditional IRA distribution that is being "rolled over." Therefore a Roth IRA conversion that is supposed to be "for" the year 2006 must be tied to a *distribution that occurred in the calendar year 2006*. The due date of the 2006 return is *irrelevant*.

A distribution made from a traditional IRA in the calendar year 2006, if it is to be contributed to a Roth IRA, must be so contributed within 60 days after the date of the distribution. Reg. § 1.408A-4, A-1(b)(1). January 1, 2006, would be the first date in calendar 2006 on which an amount could be distributed out of a traditional IRA; therefore the earliest possible date for a "2006 Roth IRA conversion" would be January 1, 2006 (same-day conversion of a January 1 distribution). The last possible date in calendar 2006 on which an amount could be distributed out of a traditional IRA would be December 31, 2006; therefore the last possible date for a "2006 conversion" would be the 60th day after December 31, 2006 (the deadline for rolling over a traditional IRA distribution made on December 31, 2006; § 408(d)(3)(A)(i)). ¶ 2.6.06.

Note that:

A.   Roth IRA conversions are usually accomplished by transferring sums directly from a traditional IRA to a Roth IRA. If both accounts are with the same IRA provider, the traditional IRA distribution and the Roth IRA contribution would normally occur simultaneously. Thus in this typical situation there would be no need to calculate the 60-day period.

B.   The IRS can extend the 60-day rollover deadline in cases of hardship. ¶ 2.6.06. To date there are no PLRs in which this provision has been used to allow a longer period to complete a Roth IRA conversion.

5.6.04 Recharacterization deadline: Meaning of "extended due date"

Generally, the deadline for recharacterizing an IRA contribution is the due date of the tax return for the year of the contribution that is being recharacterized, *including extensions.* § 408A(d)(6), (7). So:

1.   A regular contribution to either a Roth IRA or a traditional IRA for a particular year, that was made by the *unextended* due date of the return for that year, can be recharacterized by the *extended* due date of the return for that year.

2.   A conversion contribution to a Roth IRA that was made within 60 days after a distribution from a traditional IRA may be recharacterized by the extended due date of the return for the taxable year in which the distribution occurred.

"Due date including extensions" or "extended due date" has a special meaning under IRS regulations. The taxpayer does not actually have to get an extension of his income tax return in order to go beyond April 15 for his recharacterization decision. Reg. § 301.9100-2(b) provides an automatic six-months extension (from the *unextended* due date of the return) for all "regulatory or statutory elections whose due dates are the...due date of the return including extensions *provided* the taxpayer timely filed its return for the year the election should have been made and the taxpayer takes" necessary corrective actions (such as filing an amended return if necessary). Emphasis added.

What's confusing is there are two different "automatic" six-months extensions, neither of which is totally automatic. Any taxpayer can obtain a "automatic" six-months' extension of time to file his income tax return (i.e., to October 15 instead of April 15)—but it's not truly automatic because to get this extension the taxpayer has to request it by April 15th, usually by filing Form 4868. Reg. § 1.6081-4T.

Then there's the "automatic" six-months' extension of time to recharacterize an IRA contribution. This extension *is* automatic in the sense that the taxpayer doesn't have to request it; but to qualify for this automatic extension he has to "timely" file his income tax return. "Timely" filing the income tax return means filing the return on or before April 15 (*or* getting an extension of time to file from the IRS and then filing the return on or before the extended due date).

Putting all these rules together, we find that if a taxpayer wants to recharacterize a Roth IRA contribution made in Year 1 he must complete the necessary actions (¶ 5.6.02) by whichever one of the following deadlines applies:

A. **October 15 if return is timely filed.** If he files his income tax return for Year 1 on or before its due date, he has until October 15 of Year 2 to complete the recharacterization. The "due date" of the Year 1 income tax return is April 15, Year 2, *unless* he obtained an extension of time to file the return, in which case the due date is whatever date the return was extended to. For example, if, on or before April 15, Year 2, he filed Form 4868 with the IRS requesting the "automatic" six-months' extension, the due date of his Year 1 return is October 15, Year 2. However, *regardless* of whether he got an extension of time to file his income tax return, as long as he filed the income tax return by whatever date it was due, the deadline for recharacterizing his IRA contribution is October 15, Year 2, under the automatic extension rule of Reg. § 301.9100-2(b).

B. **April 15 if return is filed late.** If the individual does not file his income tax return for Year 1 on or before the date it is due (whether that due date is April 15 or a later date he qualified for by requesting an extension from the IRS), he must complete the recharacterization by April 15 of Year 2.

For the unfortunate taxpayer who converts to a Roth IRA, then belatedly discovers that he was not eligible to convert to a Roth IRA, but misses the deadline for recharacterizing, there is still hope.

First, there are procedures for applying to the IRS for relief in cases of good faith errors. See Reg. § 301.9100-1 *et seq.* In dozens of private letter rulings, the IRS has been generous in using these relief provisions to grant extensions for recharacterizations of erroneous Roth conversions, where the taxpayers requested relief before the IRS caught the mistake. See, *e.g.*, PLRs 2001-16053 (taxpayer erroneously believed that due date of her return was October 15 and that capital gain did not count toward $100,000 Roth conversion income limit); 2001-16057 (recharacterization of improper Roth conversion was late due to financial institution error); 2001-16058, 2001-19059, 2001-20040, 2001-22050, 2001-28058, and 2001-30058 (taxpayers unaware they didn't qualify for Roth conversion and unaware of recharacterization deadline); 2001-26040 (taxpayers had been erroneously advised that the Roth IRA conversion income limit was $150,000, that the deadline for a 1998 conversion was 4/15/99, etc.); and 2001-29040 (taxpayer ineligible to convert, and thought she had timely recharacterized all her Roth IRAs, but missed the deadline on one of them because she forgot about that account).

Second, Congress and the IRS sometimes grant blanket extensions of time and other relief to the victims of particular disasters. If the taxpayer is affected by such a disaster he may be entitled to complete a Roth recharacterization later than other taxpayers.

5.6.05 *Confusion: Conversions vs. recharacterizations*

While it is nice that taxpayers have been given a way to undo Roth IRA conversions, so they need not be punished for (*e.g.*) making an incorrect prediction of their income, the addition of the recharacterization option is bound to create confusion among IRA owners and their advisors. Here are some points that will need to be constantly restated:

First, the ability to recharacterize a "Year 1" IRA contribution until October 15 of "Year 2" does *not* create a new extended right to do Roth IRA conversions between January 1 and October 15 of Year 2 that will count as Year 1 conversions. If, in Year 1, there was no traditional IRA distribution that was properly converted to a Roth IRA, there is nothing to "recharacterize."

Second, not every type of contribution to a *traditional* IRA may be recharacterized—only "regular" contributions (¶ 5.3) may be. A tax-free rollover from an employer plan (or from another traditional IRA) to a traditional IRA may not be recharacterized as a Roth IRA conversion or contribution, because "an amount contributed to an IRA in a tax-free transfer cannot be recharacterized." Reg. § 1.408A-5, A-10, Example 4.

Similarly, employer contributions to a SEP or SIMPLE may not be recharacterized as contributions to a Roth IRA, because the employer could not have made direct contributions to a Roth IRA in the first place. Reg. § 1.408A-5, A-5. But the employee may be able to roll over the SEP or SIMPLE account to a Roth IRA; ¶ 5.4.02.

5.6.06 *Determining net income attributable to contribution*

To effect a recharacterization, not only the original contribution but also any net income attributable to such contribution must be retransferred. Reg. § 1.408A-5, A-2(a). This requirement may be met in one of two ways. Note that the "net income" may be a negative amount—a loss, in other words.

Method 1: If the contribution in question was made to a separate Roth IRA that contained no other funds, *and* there have been no other contributions to or distributions from that separate Roth IRA, *and* the entire contribution is being recharacterized, then simply transferring the entire account balance to a traditional IRA satisfies the requirement. Reg. § 1.408A-5, A-2(b). This method being so much simpler than Method 2, there is an advantage to keeping each year's contributions in a separate Roth IRA account (not commingled with any pre-existing Roth IRA), until the period has expired for recharacterizing such contributions.

Method 2: If Method 1 is not available, then the net income attributable to the contribution must be calculated by a formula that is contained in Reg. § 1.408-4(c)(2)(ii), Reg. § 1.408A-5, A-2(c), or Notice 2000-39, 2000-2 C.B. 132.

5.6.07 *Same-year reconversions outlawed*

The IRS has imposed various limits on the ability to use the recharacterization rules to flip back and forth between traditional IRA and Roth IRA status. For the limits applicable to reconversions in 1998 and 1999, see *"Limit on the number of 'reconversions' in 1998 and 1999: IRS Notice 98-50"* at page 225 of the 1999 edition of this book.

In Reg. § 1.408A-5, A-9, the IRS banned same-year reconversions, effective in 2000 and later years. Once a recharacterization of a Roth IRA conversion occurs, the individual may not reconvert the amount to a Roth IRA until the taxable year following the taxable year of the original conversion, or until at least 30 days have elapsed since the recharacterization, *whichever is later*. If the individual defies this rule and attempts to reconvert before the prescribed time period ends, the result is a failed conversion (¶ 5.6.02).

5.7 Designated Roth Accounts

5.7.01 *Meet the DRAC: Roth 401(k)s, 403(b)s*

Employees have long been permitted to make "elective deferral" (also called "salary reduction") contributions to workplace retirement plans. Under such a "cash-or-deferred arrangement" (CODA), the participant can choose either to receive a certain amount of his salary in cash or to have such amount contributed to a vested account for his benefit in a retirement plan. See ¶ 10.1.02.

Needless to say, elective deferrals are subject to many complicated tax rules. Through 2005, the reward for successfully complying with these rules was that the amount of the elective deferral would be excluded from the participant's income (except for FICA tax purposes; ¶ 5.7.02(E)). The deferred salary (and earnings thereon) would not be taxed until they were later distributed to the participant or his beneficiaries (typically after retirement or death).

Starting in 2006, the participant has an additional option for his elective deferrals under a 401(k) or 403(b) plan: Instead of deferring income tax on the deferred compensation income, he can pay tax on the deferred compensation currently and have the deferred compensation contributed to a **designated Roth account** (**DRAC**) within the plan, later qualified distributions from which will be tax-free. § 402A(d)(1). The portion of the elective deferral that the participant elects to have contributed to a DRAC is called a "designated Roth contribution." § 402A(a)(1). DRACs are also called "Roth 401(k)" or "Roth 403(b)" plans. This Chapter will refer only to 401(k) plans; unless specifically otherwise indicated the same rules apply to 403(b) plans. Prop. Reg. § 1.403(b)-3(c)(1).

The IRS issued proposed regulations on contributions to DRACs in 2005. Later, the IRS issued *final* regulations on DRAC contributions and *proposed* regulations on DRAC distributions and reporting rules. See T.D. 9237, 2006-6 I.R.B. 394, containing Preamble and final regulations; proposed amendments to Reg. § 1.402(g)-1, § 1.403(b)-3, § 1.403(b)-5, and § 1.403(b)-7; and Prop. Regs. § 1.402A-1, § 1.402A-2, and § 1.408A-10.

5.7.02 *DRAC contributions: Who, how much, how, etc.*

A.   **Who may contribute.** After 2005, any participant in a 401(k) or 403(b) plan can elect to have all or part of his elective deferral go into a DRAC, provided his employer has adopted the necessary plan amendments to permit designated Roth contributions. A self-employed individual who has a self-employed (Keogh) 401(k) plan can have all or part of his elective deferral contributed to a DRAC once he adopts the necessary plan amendments.

In contrast to Roth IRAs (¶ 5.3.03(A), ¶ 5.4.03(A)), there is <u>no income ceiling</u> above which the participant is not allowed to make designated Roth contributions. § 402A. This is the first Roth retirement plan that does not limit contributions to individuals with income below certain levels.

There is <u>no age limit</u> above which the participant cannot contribute to a Roth 401(k). Traditional IRAs are the only plans which do not allow contributions after the participant has reached age 70½ (see ¶ 5.3.03(B)).

An individual can contribute to a Roth 401(k) <u>even if he is also a participant in other retirement plans</u> offered by the same or another employer. Though the deductibility of traditional IRA contributions for a high-income individual depends on whether he participates in another retirement plan offered by the employer, no such limitation applies to Roth (or regular) 401(k)s. Participation in another plan may limit the *amount* that may be contributed; see "B."

B.   **How much may be contributed.** The maximum amount that may be contributed to a DRAC is whatever is the maximum amount of elective deferral contribution the participant may make to his 401(k) plan for the year in question. § 402(g)(1)(B).

The dollar limit for elective deferrals in 2006 and later years is $15,000, plus an additional $5,000 "catch-up" contribution if the participant is 50 or older by the end of the year. § 402(g)(1)(B), (C). Cost-of-living adjustments will increase both the base amount (§ 402(g)(4)) and the maximum permitted catch-up contribution

(§ 414(v)(2)(C)) after 2006. A long-term employee in a 403(b) plan may have even higher limits.

The DRAC option does not increase the amount the participant may contribute to a plan through elective deferrals. Rather, the participant may choose to put his total permitted elective deferral into a DRAC, or into a "regular" 401(k) account, or partly into each. For example, in 2006 an over-50 participant with sufficient compensation can (if permitted by his plan) contribute $20,000 to his regular 401(k) account, or $20,000 to a DRAC; or he can send part of his elective deferrals to a DRAC and part to a regular account, as long as the combined total so contributed does not exceed $20,000.

As a reminder, as is true for a "regular" 401(k) plan, the elective deferral limits apply to an individual based on *all* elective deferral plans he participates in (with this or any other employer; § 402(g)); and § 415 also limits the amount that may be contributed.

C.   **Election is irrevocable once the money is contributed.** The election to have part of one's compensation contributed to a DRAC is irrevocable to the same extent the normal § 401(k) deferral election is irrevocable. Thus, a participant cannot retroactively designate a DRAC contribution as a regular contribution or vice versa. Reg. § 1.401(k)-1(f)(1)(i).

In this, the decision is the same as the decision to make a "regular" elective deferral contribution to a 401(k) plan has always been: The decision is made in advance, prior to earning the money, and is irrevocable. This is unlike a Roth IRA, contributions to which can be withdrawn (¶ 5.6.01) or recharacterized (¶ 5.6.02) for a certain period of time, if he changes his mind.

Under the typical 401(k) plan, an employee would elect in advance to have a particular dollar or percentage amount of his paycheck (or all or part of a forthcoming bonus) contributed to the plan. Though this election is irrevocable, the employer may permit the employee to change the election *prospectively* at one or more times during the year. For plan years beginning after 2005, the plan *must* permit the employee to change his election *prospectively* at least once each plan year. Reg. § 1.401(k)-1(e)(2)(ii).

The irrevocability of the DRAC decision will make planning more difficult; a participant might prefer to wait until the end of the year (when he has a better idea of his income and tax situation) to decide whether he wants a tax deduction now or tax-free income later.

D. **What may be contributed.** The ONLY contributions that can go into a DRAC are: (1) the participant's post-2005 elective deferrals and (2) certain rollovers from other DRACs (see ¶ 5.7.07).

The employer cannot make matching (or any other) contributions to a DRAC. The employer's matching contribution (if any), and any other employer contributions, must be made to the participant's regular 401(k) account, regardless of whether the participant's contribution that is being "matched" was made to a regular 401(k) account or to a DRAC. Forfeitures cannot be allocated to DRACs. Reg. § 1.401(k)-1(f)(2). Existing 401(k) balances cannot be converted to DRACs. Money cannot be rolled from a Roth IRA into a DRAC, even if that Roth IRA contains nothing but money rolled into it from the same or another DRAC. Prop. Reg. § 1.408A-10, A-5.

E. **FICA taxes.** Elective deferral contributions are treated as "wages" for purposes of the Federal Insurance Contributions Act (FICA). See ¶ 10.1.02. Since these contributions are subject to FICA taxes in any event, the employee's decision to have his elective deferral paid into a DRAC, into a regular 401(k) account, or to himself in cash will have no effect on either the employee's or the employer's FICA tax obligations.

5.7.03 *MRDs and other contrasts with Roth IRAs*

A DRAC (unlike a Roth IRA) is part of a 401(k) or 403(b) plan. As such it is subject to all the same rules that apply to other 401(k) or 403(b) plans, except to the extent § 402A provides otherwise.

For example (unlike Roth IRAs, which are not subject to the lifetime MRD rules; see ¶ 5.1.03), DRACs are subject to the same lifetime and post-death minimum distribution rules as other 401(k) plans. Reg. § 1.401(k)-1(f)(3). Once a DRAC participant reaches age 70½, or (in the case of a non-5%-owner; ¶ 1.4.03) retires, if later, he can stop or prevent MRDs only by rolling the DRAC over to a Roth IRA; see ¶ 5.7.08.

DRAC distributions are subject to the income tax withholding rules applicable to qualified plan distributions. DRACs are also subject to federally granted spousal rights (¶ 3.4), and the rules restricting distributions from elective deferral accounts. Roth IRAs are subject to none of these. Other differences include the irrevocability of contributions (¶ 5.7.02(C)), the definition of qualified distributions (¶ 5.7.04), the treatment of nonqualified distributions (¶ 5.7.05), and the rollover rules (¶¶ 5.7.06–¶ 5.7.08).

5.7.04 *DRACs: Definition of "qualified distribution"*

As with a Roth IRA, there are two types of distributions from a DRAC, qualified distributions and other (nonqualified) distributions. Qualified distributions from a DRAC, like qualified distributions from a Roth IRA, are income tax-free. § 402A(d)(1), § 408A(d)(1); Prop. Reg. § 1.402A-1, A-2(a). However, the definition of qualified distribution is different for the two types of Roth plan. Each involves a five-year waiting period and a triggering event, but the computation of the Five-Year Period, and the triggering events, are not the same.

The following DRAC distributions and deemed distributions can NOT be qualified distributions, even if the five-year and triggering event tests are met: return of excess deferrals and other corrective distributions; loans treated as deemed distributions; the deemed income resulting from plan-owned life insurance; and dividends on employer securities distributed under § 404(k). Prop. Reg. § 1.402A-1, A-2(c), A-11; Reg. § 1.402(c)-2, A-4.

A.   **Qualified distribution triggering events.** A DRAC distribution is a qualified distribution only if it is either (1) made on or after the date the participant reaches age 59½, (2) made after his death, or (3) attributable to the participant's being disabled "within the meaning of section 72(m)(7)." An additional category of qualified distribution from a Roth IRA, the first-time homebuyer distribution, does NOT apply to DRACs; compare ¶ 5.2.01, #4. § 402A(d)(2)(A); § 408A(d)(2)(A).

B.   **How the Five-Year Period is computed for a DRAC.** As with Roth IRAs, DRACs have a five-year waiting period (called the "nonexclusion period" in the statute, the "Five-Year Period" in this Chapter) before a qualified distribution can occur. § 402A(d)(2)(B). However, there is a difference in the way the Five-Year Period is calculated. With a Roth IRA, the Five-Year Period begins with the first year of contribution to *any* Roth IRA; see ¶ 5.2.02.

For a DRAC, in contrast, the Five-Year Period is five consecutive years beginning with the first year the employee made a contribution to a DRAC *in that particular plan* (i.e., the year the elective deferral was included in his income). § 402A(d)(2)(B)(i). The Five-Year Period is computed plan-by-plan even for two plans maintained by the same employer. Prop. Reg. § 1.402A-1, A-4(a), (b). For the only exception to this rule, see ¶ 5.7.07(B).

5.7.05 *Nonqualified DRAC distributions*

Though not automatically entitled to 100 percent tax-free treatment the way a qualified distribution is, a nonqualified distribution may be partly or wholly tax-free. However, the treatment of nonqualified distributions is one of the big differences between Roth IRAs and DRACs.

As is true with a Roth IRA, if the DRAC has appreciated since the original contribution(s), then the DRAC contains two kinds of money: the participant's contributions (which are the participant's basis in the account—the money he has already paid tax on; the IRS calls this the participant's "investment in the contract"), plus the appreciation (which is pretax money; the IRS calls this the "earnings"). Hopefully, the appreciation/earnings will NEVER be taxed, because they will come out eventually in the form of a tax-free qualified distribution (¶ 5.7.04).

But if there is a nonqualified distribution, the earnings cannot come out tax-free. Accordingly, we need to determine how much of any nonqualified distribution represents the participant's investment in the contract (tax-free) and how much is considered earnings (taxable), and here's where we find the difference between Roth IRAs and DRACs. With a Roth IRA, basis comes out first. ¶ 5.2.03. Accordingly, even nonqualified Roth IRA distributions are tax-free until the entire basis has been distributed.

With DRACs, in contrast, there is no special rule in the Code allowing the participant's basis to come out first. So, the regular rule of § 72(e)(8) will apply, under which any nonqualified distribution carries out proportionate amounts of the participant's investment in the contract (after-tax money) and earnings (pretax money). Prop. Reg. § 1.402A-1, A-3; see ¶ 2.1.10. Thus, every nonqualified distribution from a DRAC will be partly taxable unless either (1) there has been no appreciation in the account since the original contributions or (2) the earnings portion is rolled over (¶ 5.7.06).

The good news is that the participant's DRAC is treated as a separate account from the participant's "regular" accounts in the plan for income tax purposes. § 402A(d)(4). Thus, distributions can be taken (and taxed) from each one separately. However, if the participant has more than one DRAC inside a single 401(k) plan (for example, an elective deferral account and a rollover account), these are treated as a single account for purposes of § 72. Prop. Reg. § 1.402A-1, A-9(a).

Also, interestingly, the plan can split the DRAC into multiple separate accounts for the participant's multiple beneficiaries after the participant's death, and each such account will be treated as a separate "contract" under § 72. Prop. Reg. § 1.402A-1, A-9(b).

5.7.06 *Rollovers of DRAC distributions: General rules*

Distributions from a DRAC may be rolled over to another DRAC (¶ 5.7.07) or to a Roth IRA (¶ 5.7.08), either by direct rollover or within the usual 60-day deadline (¶ 2.6.06). Prop. Reg. § 1.402A-1, A-5. If the distribution was not a qualified distribution (¶ 5.7.04), so part of it would be includible in income if not rolled over (¶ 5.7.05), and the participant rolls over only part of the distribution, the part rolled over is deemed to come first out of the *taxable* portion of the distribution, according to Prop. Reg. § 1.402A-1, A-5(b)...however, the Preamble to the Proposed Regulation says exactly the opposite! 71 FR 4320 (1/26/06). Hopefully the IRS will tell us its "final answer" on this subject in the near future.

5.7.07 *DRAC-to-DRAC rollovers*

For general rules regarding rollovers of DRAC distributions, see ¶ 5.7.06. DRAC-to-DRAC rollovers are subject to several additional complicated rules.

A.   Must roll to same type of plan. A 401(k) DRAC can be rolled to another 401(k) DRAC, but not to a 403(b) DRAC. See Prop. Reg. § 1.402A-1, A-5(a), in which the IRS asserts there is a comparable rule for 403(b) plans at Prop. Reg. § 1.403(b)-7(a).

B.   Direct rollover: all or nothing. The participant can do a DRAC-to-DRAC rollover by means of a direct rollover (¶ 2.6.01(B)) of the entire account.

If any portion of the distribution from the first plan would not be includible in the participant's income, the ONLY way the nontaxable portion can be rolled to another DRAC is if the ENTIRE DRAC is rolled to the new DRAC by direct rollover. Prop. Reg. § 1.402A-1, A-5(a). Since every DRAC distribution is at least partly nontaxable, in effect this rule is saying that a partial DRAC-to-DRAC direct rollover is not permitted.

The advantage of doing a direct DRAC-to-DRAC rollover of the entire account is that the participant's holding period from the transferor plan is tacked on to the holding period in the transferee plan for purposes of computing the Five-Year Period (¶ 5.7.04(B)). § 402A(d)(2)(B); Prop. Reg. § 1.402A-1, A-4(b), last sentence. With any other type of rollover, the years in the prior plan will not count in computing the Five-Year Period for the transferee plan; see "C," and examples at ¶ 5.7.08.

If the distribution from the first DRAC was a qualified distribution, then the entire amount of the distribution is allocated to the participant's "investment in the contract" (basis) in the transferee DRAC. Prop. Reg. § 1.402A-1, A-6.

C.   60-day rollover. If the participant actually receives the distribution (i.e., he did not arrange for a direct rollover), then he has 60 days to roll all or part of that distribution into another plan. ¶ 2.6.06. The IRS calls this type of rollover a "60-day rollover," to contrast it with a direct rollover. There are three rules regarding 60-day DRAC-to-DRAC rollovers:

1.   The participant can roll the earnings (pretax) portion of the distribution to another DRAC. This is consistent with the rule that, in case of a partial rollover, the portion rolled is deemed to come first out of the part of

the DRAC distribution that would be taxable if not rolled over. See ¶ 5.7.06.

2.   The nontaxable portion of a DRAC distribution cannot be rolled to another DRAC by means of a 60-day rollover. See "B."

3.   With a 60-day rollover, the transferee DRAC does NOT tack on the participant's holding period from the prior DRAC. The participant's Five-Year Period for the DRAC that receives the rollover is based on the first year he made a contribution to that particular DRAC (whether that first contribution was the rollover contribution or some earlier contribution). Prop. Reg. § 1.402A-1, A-5(c).

5.7.08 *DRAC-to-Roth-IRA rollovers*

For general rules regarding rollovers of DRAC distributions, see ¶ 5.7.06.

A DRAC-to-Roth-IRA rollover may be accomplished by either direct rollover or "60-day rollover." Prop. Reg. § 1.402A-1, A-5(a).

Rollover from a DRAC to a Roth IRA is permitted even if the participant is not eligible to make annual contributions to a Roth IRA or to convert his traditional IRA to a Roth IRA. Prop. Reg. § 1.408A-10, A-2. Thus, he can establish a Roth IRA purely for the purpose of receiving a rollover from his DRAC, even if his income is too high to otherwise allow him to contribute to a Roth IRA.

Rolling over from a DRAC to a Roth IRA has several effects. One advantage is that the rollover will end the requirement of lifetime minimum required distributions. ¶ 5.7.03. Another is that the Roth IRA has more favorable rules for recovery of basis than a DRAC. Compare ¶ 5.2.03 with ¶ 5.7.05.

Another effect of such a rollover, if it occurs after the participant's Required Beginning Date (RBD; ¶ 1.4), is to change the method of computing the Applicable Distribution Period that will apply to the participant's beneficiaries from the "death post-RBD rules" (¶ 1.5.04) to the "death pre-RBD rules" (¶ 1.5.03). For other pros and cons of rolling from a qualified plan to an IRA, see ¶ 2.7.03.

A disadvantage of rolling from a DRAC to a Roth IRA is that the participant may have to start the Five-Year Period all over again. With DRAC-to-DRAC rollovers, Congress specified that the employee's holding period carries over from one DRAC to the other. § 402A(d)(2)(B). However, Congress said nothing about a carryover of holding period in the case of a DRAC-to-Roth-IRA rollover, so the Proposed Regulations allow no such carryover.

The Five-Year Period for a Roth IRA begins January 1 of the first year the individual has any Roth IRA (¶ 5.2.02), *regardless* of whether the Roth IRA holds money rolled over from a DRAC; whatever holding period the DRAC owner had established in the plan that originally held the DRAC does NOT carry over to the Roth IRA, regardless of whether the DRAC-to-Roth-IRA rollover is a "direct rollover" or a "60-day rollover." Prop. Reg. § 1.408A-10, A-4.

This rule will adversely affect some (see "C"), but is not the total disaster it at first appears (see "A" and "B").

A.   **Rollover of a qualified distribution.** If the DRAC distribution that was rolled over to the Roth IRA was *itself* a qualified distribution (i.e., the DRAC had been in existence for more than five years and the distributee was either the participant who was over 59½ or disabled, or the surviving spouse), then the entire rollover amount is treated as a "regular contribution" to the Roth IRA. Prop. Reg. § 1.408A-10, A-3. A regular contribution can be withdrawn from a Roth IRA at any time, tax-free. ¶ 5.2.03. Thus, only the post-rollover earnings on the rollover amount will be subject to the "fresh start" Five-Year Period in order to become tax-free qualified distributions. Prop. Reg. § 1.408A-10, A-4(b), Example 3.

Denny Example: Denny, age 60, receives a qualified distribution of $40,000 from his DRAC in 2011 and rolls it over to a Roth IRA. This is the first Roth IRA Denny has ever had. He cannot have a qualified distribution from the Roth IRA until 2016. Any distributions he takes from the Roth IRA before 2016 will be nonqualified distributions. However, he can take out up to $40,000 of nonqualified distributions tax-free as recovery of basis, because the $40,000 contribution is deemed to be his tax-paid "regular contribution" to the account, and that comes out first under the Roth IRA ordering rules. ¶ 5.2.04. Only post-rollover appreciation will be taxable if withdrawn prior to 2016.

B.   **Rollover to a pre-existing Roth IRA.** If the participant had already established a Roth IRA prior to the rollover, the money rolled from the DRAC gets the benefit of the years already completed towards the Roth IRA Five-Year Period. If the participant has already fulfilled the 5-year requirement for his Roth IRA, then the rollover from the DRAC gets the benefit of that—even if the money was in the DRAC for less than five years. See Prop. Reg. § 1.408A-10, A-4(b), Example 1.

Amanda Example: Amanda, age 60, started a Roth IRA in 1998 with $1,000. In 2006 she makes a $20,000 DRAC contribution to her proprietorship's "self-employed 401(k) plan." In 2008 she retires and rolls the DRAC over to a Roth IRA (either the existing one or a new one—it doesn't matter). Even though her holding period for the DRAC was only two years, so the DRAC distribution is a nonqualified distribution, it "instantly" becomes qualified once she rolls it to a Roth IRA, because she has already met the 5-year requirement for any Roth IRAs she may ever own. Since she is over 59½, she can withdraw as much as she likes from the Roth IRA tax-free at any time.

C.   **Danger: Rolling a nonqualified distribution to a new Roth IRA.** The person who is hurt by this rule is the person who had no prior Roth IRA, and had completed one or more years in his DRAC at the time he rolls a nonqualified distribution from the DRAC to a Roth IRA. He loses the years he had completed, and starts the 5-year clock over again. Because his rollover was NOT of a qualified distribution, only his basis in the DRAC (i.e., the amount of his original elective deferral contribution(s)) is treated as a "regular contribution" to the Roth IRA. The rest of the rollover is treated as "earnings," meaning that it cannot be distributed tax-free except in a qualified distribution. See Prop. Reg. § 1.408A-10, A-4(b), Example 2.

This will make little difference to a person who is rolling from the DRAC to a Roth IRA when he is under age 54½ (because, absent disability, he will have to wait five or more years ANYWAY before he can have a qualified distribution from the Roth IRA). However, it could be tough for a person who has accumulated many years in the DRAC and then rolls to a Roth IRA shortly before reaching age 59½. If the first year for which he has ever owned a Roth IRA is the year he establishes a Roth IRA with his DRAC rollover, then he will have to wait five years to have a qualified distribution from that Roth IRA.

Bryon Example: Bryon, age 38, establishes a $15,000 DRAC in 2006 in his employer's 401(k) plan. He makes no further contributions to the DRAC. In 2026, he retires at age 58 and rolls over the DRAC (now worth $45,000) to a Roth IRA. This is his first Roth IRA; accordingly, computation of his Five-Year Period for the Roth IRA starts with the year of the rollover (2026), so he cannot have a qualified distribution from the Roth IRA until 2031. His basis in the DRAC ($15,000) will be treated as his only "investment in the contract" in the Roth IRA. Though he can withdraw that basis tax-free at any time, he cannot withdraw the post-2006 earnings tax-free until 2031. If he had just waited until he had reached age 59½ before rolling the DRAC to a Roth IRA, the rolled distribution would have been a qualified distribution and the fresh-start rule would have applied only to post-rollover earnings (see "A"), not to ALL earnings.

5.7.09 *The employer's obligations; other DRAC details*

A designated Roth contribution is includible in the employee's income and thus is subject to income tax withholding. Reg. § 1.401(k)-1(f)(1)(ii); Prop. Reg. § 1.199-2(f)(i). Presumably the income tax on the contribution would have to be withheld from the nondeferred portion of the employee's salary, to avoid diminishing the plan contribution.

The plan must maintain separate records for the participant's Roth and "regular" accounts. § 402A(b)(2). The separate accounting must be maintained until the DRAC has been completely distributed by the plan. Reg. § 1.401(k)-1(f)(2). The IRS is concerned that employers will try to arrange the plan accounting so that profits are shifted unduly into the DRAC; the regulation provides that any transaction or methodology that has the effect of transferring value into a DRAC from another account violates the requirements of § 402A. However, swapping assets between accounts at fair market value is permitted. Prop. Reg. § 1.402A-1, A-13.

A plan that holds a DRAC must keep track of each participant's investment in the contract and also the Five-Year Period for such participant. Prop. Reg. § 1.402A-2, A-1; see the Proposed Regulation for more details on reporting requirements.

The reporting requirements generally are effective in 2007. The rest of the regulations are effective variously in 2006 and 2007, but most purport to be effective for 2006. The proposed regulations may be relied upon until final regulations are issued.

As a result of PPA '06, DRACs are now a permanent part of the Code; they will NOT "sunset" after 2010, even though they were enacted as part of EGTRRA (see page 575).

5.8 Putting it All Together

"Tax-free compounding is the best thing in the world."

–Jonathan G. Blattmachr, Esq.

¶ 5.8.01 discusses the Roth decision process generally. ¶ 5.8.02 lists factors that favor adoption of a Roth plan. ¶ 5.8.03 lists contrary factors. ¶ 5.8.04–¶ 5.8.09 look at how the Roth decision applies in some particular typical client situations. Finally, ¶ 5.8.10 discusses how to deal with Roth accounts in the client's estate plan.

5.8.01 *Which is better, a Roth plan or a regular plan?*

A Roth retirement plan is a nice asset to own. It offers the ability to invest in the stock and (nonmunicipal) bond markets and generate totally income tax-free investment accumulations that can be spent in retirement or left to heirs. The Roth IRA offers the additional advantage of no required distributions during the participant's life.

The question is what price must be paid to acquire this wonderful asset. Generally, the price is payment of income taxes on the amount going *in* to the Roth retirement plan—taxes that could have been deferred (via a traditional retirement plan) until the money in question was taken *out* of the retirement plan.

So which is better: to pay the taxes up front and get tax-free distributions later or to defer the taxes?

One thing is sure: If you take $A, pay income tax on it at B percent, deposit the net after-tax amount in a Roth IRA, earn an investment return of C percent and withdraw the accumulated funds ($D) on date E, the amount of money you will have ($D) will be *exactly the same* as if you had deposited $A in a traditional IRA, earned a return of C percent, withdrawn the accumulated funds on date

E, and paid income tax on that distribution at B percent. For the Roth approach to *produce more dollars* than the traditional plan one or more of the factors in the equation must be different as between the Roth and traditional options. See ¶ 5.8.02(A)–(D), ¶ 5.8.08, ¶ 5.8.09.

Some clients considering a Roth plan will evaluate the financial impact using computer projections (see "Software," Appendix D). Computer projections of the benefits of converting an existing IRA to a Roth IRA are based on assumptions as to future tax rates, investment returns, and withdrawal amounts. Most such projections assume a constant rate of investment return; that today's tax rates will last forever; and that participants and beneficiaries will withdraw from the account no more than required by today's minimum distribution rules. Other possible scenarios should be considered; see ¶ 5.8.03.

One might conclude that financial projections regarding the profitability of a Roth contribution are too speculative to be useful, or the projections may indicate that the Roth choice is financially neutral. There are several reasons one might choose a Roth despite the lack of a clear projected profit. See ¶ 5.8.02(E)–(F), ¶ 5.8.05, ¶ 5.8.09(C).

5.8.02 *Reasons to adopt a Roth retirement plan*

Here are factors in the equation that can tilt the balance in favor of a Roth plan.

A.   **Best: Pay taxes neither now nor later.** If you can duck the "pay now or pay later?" question by not paying taxes *either* when the money goes into the Roth plan *or* when it comes out, then you can get the advantages of a Roth retirement plan "free." That deal is irresistible. An otherwise eligible individual can get that deal if he is in a zero tax bracket, either "naturally" (see ¶ 5.8.07) or temporarily (due, for example, to a net operating loss from a business); or in some cases through a series of rollovers leaving after-tax money as the only money in his traditional IRA (see ¶ 5.4.08).

B.   **Future tax rate expected to be higher.** Someone convinced that income tax rates must go up in the future to finance the retirement benefits and medical expenses of poverty stricken aging baby boomers will want to pay taxes at today's "cheap" rate and get it over with. This factor is also at work in setting up

Roth IRAs for young family members (¶ 5.8.07) and converting an IRA to a Roth for the benefit of heirs (¶ 5.8.09(B)).

C.   **No required lifetime distributions.** Money can stay in a Roth IRA much longer than in a traditional IRA, because of the different minimum distribution rules that apply (¶ 5.1.03). Thus more tax-free compounding can occur in a Roth IRA during the owner's life than is possible with a traditional IRA (from which the owner must take lifetime distributions; ¶ 1.3).

D.   **Pay tax with assets outside the plan.** Since taxes on a Roth plan contribution can be paid with money that is not in a retirement plan, outside assets can in effect be used to increase the amount inside the retirement plan.

Eric Example: Eric wants to maximize his retirement savings. He figures that by contributing $15,000 to a "regular" 401(k), he's really only stashing away about $10,000 in the plan, because the plan "owes" the government roughly 33 percent income taxes on the contribution. He'll have to pay that "debt" when he withdraws money from the regular 401(k) plan. With a Roth account, he's in effect increasing his plan contribution. Contributing $15,000 to a Roth plan is equivalent to contributing $22,500 to a regular plan.

E.   **Diversification:** "A" has substantial funds accumulated in several traditional retirement plans. He wants to hedge his bets. Since he is already heavily weighted in pretax retirement plans, he wants to place a bet on the Roth.

F.   **Cash flow:** "B" has her retirement income (including income taxes) carefully projected for the next 10 years. If she needs a chunk of extra cash, it would be nice to be able to take it out of a Roth plan tax-free so as not to upset the income tax projections. "C" does not want to be forced to start liquidating her retirement savings at age 70½. The Roth IRA appeals to her because it does not require any distributions prior to the owner's death. She plans to contribute to a Roth 403(b) plan at her job, then roll that to a Roth IRA at retirement.

5.8.03 *Risks, drawbacks, of Roth retirement plans*

It would be a shame to pay income tax on today's stock values, only to find out later that this was the all-time market high. This exact scenario happened to many who converted to Roth IRAs in the halcyon investment era of 1998–1999, then endured the stock market declines of 2000–2001.

The Roth deal also turns bad if the benefits would be subject to income taxes at a substantially lower rate when they come out than the rate the participant paid when he contributed to the plan. Prepaying the income tax would also presumably turn out to be a bad deal if the income tax is replaced by a value-added tax. One skeptic won't "Roth" because he expects that retired baby boomers will use their electoral clout to cause Congress to make *all* pensions wholly or largely tax-free.

Also, Congress could change the minimum distribution rules to require that all benefits be distributed within some much shorter period of time after the deaths of the participant and spouse. Or Congress could decide that the Roth IRA was too good a deal, and take away some of its favorable tax features (presumably only prospectively).

5.8.04 *Annual contributions: Traditional IRA vs. Roth IRA*

An individual who has compensation income and whose AGI is under the limits described at ¶ 5.3.03(A) has the option to contribute to a Roth IRA. If he is under age 70½ (as of the end of the tax year) he also has the option to contribute to a traditional IRA instead of to a Roth IRA, or to contribute part of his maximum permitted "regular" contribution amount (¶ 5.3.02) to each type of IRA. Assuming he wants to contribute to an IRA, which type should he contribute to?

The decision is easy if the individual (or his spouse) is an active participant in an employer plan, and his (or their) AGI exceeds the amounts specified in § 219(g)(3)(B); then his only choice is between a nondeductible traditional IRA and a Roth IRA. Since he can't get a tax deduction for his contribution no matter which kind of IRA he contributes to, he gives up nothing by choosing the Roth IRA. The decision is also easy if the individual's taxable income is so low he is not subject to income tax, since, again, he gives up nothing by opting to contribute to the Roth IRA.

If neither the individual (nor his spouse) is an active participant in an employer plan; or, if he (or his spouse) is an active participant in an employer plan, but his (or their) AGI is low enough that he can get a tax deduction for a contribution to a traditional IRA; *and* his (or their) tax bracket is higher than zero; then his choice is between a *deductible* traditional IRA contribution (which could save him some current income taxes) and the nondeductible Roth IRA contribution, considering the factors discussed at ¶ 5.8.02–¶ 5.8.03.

5.8.05 *Choosing between a DRAC and a regular 401(k)/403(b)*

Which 401(k) participants should choose the DRAC (¶ 5.7)?

By choosing the DRAC, the individual gives up the immediate tax savings of having the contribution excluded from his income. The savings could be as high as 35 percent of the contribution amount (maximum regular federal income tax rate as of 2006). If the individual is subject to the alternative minimum tax (AMT; § 55), contributing to a regular 401(k) plan saves income taxes at the AMT rate (26%–28%) rather than at the individual's theoretical usual tax rate.

However, for many, the choice will not be based on elaborate projections regarding whether taxes are higher or lower now than they will be later. Rather, the choice will be based on how badly the individual wants a Roth account versus an immediate tax deduction:

Bunny and Honey are both 55-year-old lawyers with incomes over $500,000, looking to maximize savings for a planned retirement in five to ten years. Both are in 401(k) plans that offer DRACs.

Bunny is a partner in large firm. The only tax-deferred retirement savings plan she has is the firm's 401(k) plan, where her account is now worth $600,000. Her only "tax shelter" is her annual 401(k) salary deferral contribution, which will be $20,000 in 2006. She does not want to give up the tax deduction. She opts for a regular 401(k) account contribution.

Honey is a solo practitioner with a defined benefit pension plan now worth $1 million. She also has a self-employed 401(k) plan worth $50,000 and a traditional IRA worth $600,000. Her contribution to the defined benefit plan in 2006 will be $120,000, tax deductible. She feels that the tax-deferred side of her balance sheet is already large enough and it will only get larger through internal growth and future plan contributions. She opts for a DRAC, to start building up a different type of tax-advantaged retirement plan.

5.8.06 *Clients who may profit from Roth conversion*

The client most likely to profit from converting to a Roth IRA is one who: has sufficient other wealth that he will never need to draw from the account during life (not drawing anything out of the account is the way to maximize the tax-free accumulations of the Roth IRA); plans to leave the account to young generation beneficiaries, to be drawn down over their life expectancy after the client's death (again, the long life expectancy payout available for distributions to a young designated beneficiary maximizes the tax-free build-up of the Roth IRA); and can afford to pay the income tax on the conversion, and the estate tax on the account's date-of-death value, from other assets, without sacrificing other goals such as his own financial security (so that the income tax-free Roth IRA is not depleted by paying tax bills). Add steady to rising income tax rates, no negative tax law changes, and positive investment returns and the conversion is a definite winner.

5.8.07 *Establishing Roth IRAs for low-income relatives*

Establishing a Roth IRA for teenage children, grandchildren, etc., has great appeal. Typically these young family members have summer or after-school jobs that generate compensation income on which an IRA contribution can be based, but have little enough income that they are in a low or zero tax bracket. The projections of what a humble $4,000 contribution will grow to by the time the 15-year-old child reaches age 65 can be staggering. What gives pause is that there is no way to prevent the donee from taking the money out of the account once he reaches the age of majority.

For this idea to work, the child must have compensation income. ¶ 5.3.01. Gifts are not compensation. If a parent pays his toddler a salary for performing household chores, the IRS might maintain that the child has received a gift, not compensation, and that Roth IRA contributions based on this "compensation" are excess contributions subject to the six percent excise tax (§ 4973).

5.8.08 *How Roth conversions can help retirees*

A.   Take advantage of lower brackets; reduce future MRDs. This is an idea for the retired individual who has not yet reached age 70½ and has a substantial IRA; whose income dropped significantly following retirement; and who is living comfortably on his Social Security benefits or other minuscule taxable income.

This person is now in a very low tax bracket. In a few years, when he turns 70½, he will be in a high tax bracket again, when the minimum required distribution (MRD; Chapter 1) rules start forcing distributions out of his IRA. He will not be happy when his IRA starts shrinking (and his taxable income skyrockets) once MRDs start. Now is the time to blunt the future force of MRDs (and take advantage of the low income tax brackets) by doing partial Roth IRA conversions each year. For example, if the retiree's taxable income (before Roth conversion) is $25,000, he is only in the 15 percent tax bracket (2005 rates). He could convert $300,000 of his IRA to a Roth IRA without getting into the top 35 percent bracket (which applies to taxable income in excess of $326,450). This will reduce future MRDs from the traditional IRA (thus saving income taxes in the future), allow greater in-plan asset accumulation (since Roth IRAs do not have lifetime MRDs), and give the retiree a financial safety valve for tax-free later distributions (from the Roth IRA) for extra needs in later retirement.

B.   Above average life expectancy. Roth IRAs have appeal for retirees who expect to live well beyond the average life expectancy due to their genetic heritage and/or health.

A traditional IRA participant approaching age 70½ faces forced distributions that may substantially diminish the account over a long life span. ¶ 1.3. With a traditional IRA, the way to maximize tax deferral is to die prematurely, leaving benefits to a young beneficiary. By converting the traditional IRA to a Roth IRA, this person can eliminate the forced lifetime distributions and reverse the usual rule of thumb: The way to maximize tax deferral with a *Roth* IRA is to live as long as humanly possible, deferring the commencement of ANY distributions until that way-later-than-normal death (and then leave the benefits to a young beneficiary to get the long life expectancy payout).

C.   Control taxable income levels. Under an extremely elaborate formula, part of an individual's Social Security (SS) benefits may be taxable if his "provisional income" exceeds a certain base amount. "Provisional income" means the individual's adjusted gross income (with certain modifications), plus his tax-exempt interest income, plus one-half of his SS benefits.

If provisional income exceeds $25,000 for a single person ($32,000 for married taxpayers filing jointly), then half of the SS benefits (or, if less, half the excess of provisional income over the base amount) must be included in the individual's gross income. If provisional income exceeds $34,000 for a single person ($44,000 for married taxpayers filing jointly), then 85 percent of the SS benefits (or, if less, 85% of the excess of provisional income over the base amount) must be included in the individual's gross income. MRDs from a traditional IRA can cause an individual year after year to pay more taxes on his SS benefits. If he can convert to a Roth IRA, however, he will get the income taxation of the IRA over with, and negatively impact the taxation of his SS benefits for only one year. Thereafter, he can use tax-free Roth IRA distributions for his cash needs without increasing his provisional income (and without increasing his AGI for other purposes such as deductibility of medical expenses).

5.8.09 *How participant's conversion helps beneficiaries*

Beneficiaries of a traditional IRA can NOT convert that inherited IRA to a Roth. ¶ 2.6.03. If the participant converts his IRA to a Roth IRA prior to death, that conversion can benefit his beneficiaries:

A.   **Reduce estate taxes.** Converting to a Roth IRA just before death can reduce *estate taxes* by removing the income taxes due on the Roth conversion from the gross estate.

B.   **Low bracket parent, high bracket children.** A participant may do a Roth conversion to save *income taxes* for his beneficiaries:

Rhonda Example: Rhonda is a widow, age 65, living happily on her Social Security payments plus $25,000 a year withdrawn from a substantial traditional IRA. Her children are all in the highest income tax bracket, and some day those high brackets will apply to distributions the children take from the traditional IRA they inherit at her death. She can convert some of the traditional IRA to a Roth IRA each year to use up her lower income tax brackets. The high-bracket children will pay no income tax on distributions from the inherited Roth IRA.

C.   **Simplify beneficiaries' lives.** Even if the pure mathematics indicate no advantage to having the participant pay the income tax now rather than having the beneficiaries pay it later, it would be a convenience to the beneficiaries to inherit a Roth IRA (distributions from which are tax-free) rather than a traditional IRA, so they do not to have to wrestle with the valuable but complicated IRD deduction every year (¶ 2.3.07).

5.8.10 *Roth plans and the estate, gift, and GST taxes*

Roth benefits generally should not be left to charity; there is no point in prepaying the income taxes on money being left to a tax-exempt entity. This principle may require an individual who participates in a 401(k) or 403(b) plan to designate different beneficiaries for his DRAC and regular 401(k)/403(b) accounts.

A Roth plan could ease the problems of leaving retirement benefits to a "qualified domestic trust" (QDOT; § 2056A) for the benefit of a noncitizen spouse, as compared with leaving traditional (taxable) benefits to such a trust. Many of the problems of leaving traditional retirement benefits to benefit a noncitizen spouse arise from the fact that such benefits are taxable as income in respect of a decedent (¶ 2.3). The Roth plan eliminates this problem.

By leaving Roth plan death benefits (rather than traditional plan death benefits) to his grandchildren (or to a see-through trust for their benefit; ¶ 6.2.03), the participant gives his beneficiaries the advantage of long-term tax-free investment accumulations and does not "waste" any of the GST exemption paying income taxes.

Assigning a Roth IRA by lifetime gift "to another individual" causes the Roth IRA to be "deemed" distributed to the owner-donor, and accordingly it ceases to be a Roth IRA. Reg. § 1.408A-6, A-19. Needless to say, this treatment eliminates the advantages of such a gift.

6

Leaving Retirement Benefits to a Trust

Minimum distribution, income tax, and trust accounting considerations when a trust is named as beneficiary of retirement benefits.

Estate planning often requires naming a trust rather than an individual as beneficiary of a retirement plan. Leaving retirement benefits to a trust involves clearing numerous income tax, minimum required distribution, and trust accounting hurdles.

6.1 Trust as Beneficiary: in General

6.1.01 *What practitioners must know*

When a trust is named as beneficiary of an IRA or other retirement plan, the practitioner needs to know:

✓ How trust accounting concepts of "income" and "principal" will apply to the benefits. ¶ 6.1.02–¶ 6.1.04.

✓ How the trust can transfer the retirement benefits, intact, to the trust beneficiaries. ¶ 6.1.05.

✓ What a "trusteed IRA" (or "individual retirement trust") is, and how it differs from a custodial IRA payable to a trust as beneficiary. ¶ 6.1.06.

✓ Whether the trust qualifies as a "see-through trust" for purposes of the minimum distribution rules (¶ 6.2–¶ 6.3), and how to determine whether such qualification even matters (¶ 6.2.01).

✓ How retirement plan distributions will be subjected to federal income tax as they pass to a trust, or through a trust, including the special "DNI" rules applicable to income in respect of a decedent. ¶ 6.4.

✓   When a trust for the benefit of the participant's spouse is entitled to the special tax deals that apply when the participant names the spouse individually as beneficiary. ¶ 1.6.07.

6.1.02 Trust accounting for retirement benefits

Suppose a trust is the beneficiary of a deceased client's $1 million IRA. The trust provides that the trustee is to pay all income of the trust to the client's surviving spouse for life, and at the spouse's death the trustee is to distribute the principal of the trust to the client's children. The trust receives a $50,000 minimum required distribution (MRD) from the IRA. Is that distribution "income" that the trustee is required to pay to the spouse? Or is it "principal" that the trustee must hold for future distribution to the client's children? Or some of each?

A.   **Trust income ≠ federal gross income.** A retirement plan distribution generally will constitute gross income to the trust for federal income tax purposes (¶ 6.4.01), but that same distribution may be "principal" (or "corpus," to use the IRS's preferred term) for trust accounting purposes:

Jorge Example: Jorge dies leaving his $1 million 401(k) plan to a trust for his son. The trustee is to pay the trust "income" to the son annually, and distribute the trust "principal" to the son when he reaches age 35. The 401(k) plan distributes a $1 million lump sum to the trustee a few days after Jorge's death. Barring an unusual provision in the trust instrument or applicable state law, the entire $1 million distribution is the trust's "corpus." On the federal income tax return for the trust's first year, the trust must report the $1 million distribution as gross income, because it is "income" for income tax purposes even though it is "principal" for trust accounting purposes. The trustee invests what's left (about $650,000) after paying income taxes and pays the income (interest and dividends) from the investments to Jorge's son.

B.   **Trust income ≠ MRD.** "Income" for trust accounting purposes also does not mean the same thing as MRD. MRDs and trust accounting income are totally different and unrelated concepts.

C.   State law; the 10 percent rule of UPIA 1997. If the "trust accounting income" attributable to a retirement plan held by the trust is not the same as federal gross income, and is not the same as the MRD, what is it? Unless the trust has its own definition (which is the preferred solution; see ¶ 6.1.03(B)), the answer is determined by state law.

For example, the 1997 Uniform Principal and Income Act ("UPIA"), which has been adopted by a majority of states, provides trust accounting rules for retirement plan distributions. UPIA § 409 governs the trust accounting treatment of (among other things) any "payment" from an IRA or pension plan.

UPIA § 409(b) provides, first, that, to the extent a payment from a retirement plan "is characterized as interest or a dividend or a payment made in lieu of interest or a dividend, a trustee shall allocate it to income." The balance of any payment that is partly so characterized is allocated to principal. The official Comment to § 409(b) indicates that the drafters envisioned § 409(b) as applying to a very narrow set of circumstances, namely, an employee benefit plan "whose terms characterize payments made under the plan as dividends, interest, or payments in lieu of dividends or interest." For example, under an employee stock ownership plan (ESOP; § 409), the employee's plan account owns shares of company stock; when the stock pays a dividend, it is immediately distributed out of the plan to the employee (or, if he is deceased, to the beneficiary, in this case the trust). See § 404(k). The Comment makes it clear that § 409(b) was intended to apply *only* to a plan that, by its terms, distributes dividends and interest directly to the participant or beneficiary, and not to the typical IRA or other self-directed retirement plan: "Section 409(b) *does not apply to an IRA* or an arrangement with payment provisions similar to an IRA. IRAs and similar arrangements are subject to the provisions in Section 409(c)." Emphasis added.

UPIA § 409(c) governs retirement plan distributions not covered by § 409(b), and accordingly is the provision that will govern the vast majority of retirement plan distributions received by trusts. Here is what § 409(c) provides: If "all or part of the payment is required to be made, a trustee shall allocate to income 10 percent of the part that is required to be made during the accounting period and the balance to principal." A nonrequired payment is allocated entirely to principal. This is known as "the **10 percent rule**."

Unfortunately, the 10 percent rule will provide too little income in most cases, especially if the benefits are being paid out over a long life expectancy. For example, if the trust's Applicable Distribution Period (ADP; ¶ 1.2.01, #3) is the 40-year life expectancy of the oldest trust beneficiary (¶ 6.2.01), the first year's MRD will be only 2.5 percent of the value of the retirement benefits, which is already a low percentage, and the MRD under UPIA § 409(c) will be only 10 percent of that, a minuscule amount. It seems unlikely that a trust donor would choose this particular formula for determining the amount of "income" distributed to the life beneficiary.

The IRS has given notice that it will NOT respect the 10 percent rule as sufficient to establish the "income" of a retirement plan for federal tax purposes; see ¶ 3.3.04. Some states that have adopted the UPIA have modified § 409, and other states have not adopted the 1997 UPIA at all, so all trustees will have to look at their particular states' laws and their particular trust instruments to determine trust accounting income with respect to a retirement plan payable to a trust.

6.1.03 *Trust accounting: Drafting solutions*

There are three ways to avoid the problem discussed in ¶ 6.1.02(C): draft a totally discretionary trust ("A"); define income as it applies to retirement plan benefits ("B"); or use the "unitrust" approach (¶ 6.1.04). For a marital deduction trust (¶ 3.3.02), use "B" or the "unitrust" approach; do not use the "A" approach.

This ¶ 6.1.03 gives an overview of this subject; it does not provide sufficient detail to enable the drafter to prepare a trust instrument without studying the applicable state law and IRS standards set forth in regulations under § 643 and in Rev. Rul. 2006-26. Also, this discussion deals with planning approaches; the trustee of a trust that is *already operative* needs to comply with the terms of the instrument and applicable state law to determine the trust's income, and does not have the option to simply adopt whatever method is appealing.

A.   **Draft so "income" definition doesn't matter.** The trust accounting question may be unimportant in a totally discretionary trust. For example, if the trust provides that the trustee shall pay to the life beneficiary "such amounts of the income and/or principal of the trust, including all thereof, as the trustee deems advisable in its discretion from time to time," it will make no difference whether a particular retirement plan distribution is treated as income or principal for trust accounting purposes. The beneficiaries' substantive rights do not depend on whether a particular asset or receipt is characterized as income or principal.

However, if the trustee's compensation is based on differing percentages of trust income and principal, even a totally discretionary trust will have to resolve the income/principal question regarding the retirement benefits. Also, total-discretion trusts cannot be used in every situation; such a trust would not qualify for the marital deduction (¶ 3.3), for example.

B.   **Draft your own definition of income.** Another way to deal with the trust accounting problem is to provide, in the trust instrument, how retirement plan benefits are to be accounted for. This solution is recommended because even if the applicable state law definition at the time the trust is drafted suits the client's needs perfectly, the state law could change.

What should such a trust accounting provision say? First determine what the client is trying to accomplish. If the client wantshis beneficiary to receive the "income," find out what the client thinks that means with respect to the retirement benefits. The client may want the beneficiary to receive the entire MRD. Most likely the client will have no idea what he wants until you walk him through the alternatives.

Second, see "C" if the trust must comply with the IRS's definition of income.

One approach, which works for IRAs and other "transparent" defined contribution plans where the trustee controls the plan's investments, and can readily determine exactly how much income those investments earn and when, is to treat the retirement plan as a trust-within-a-trust. Investment income earned inside the plan is treated as trust income just as if it had been earned in the trust's taxable investment account. The IRS has approved this approach for marital deduction trusts. ¶ 3.3.04. See Form 4.5, Appendix B.

The trust-within-a-trust approach will not work for a defined benefit plan (¶ 10.1.04), or any other plan where the trustee cannot readily get the information needed to compute the plan's internal income. Thus, there must be some type of default rule to cover these plans. A unitrust approach is recommended for the default rule, if permitted by applicable state law; see ¶ 6.1.04.

C.   **IRS not bound by trust instrument's definition.** There are some situations in which it matters to the IRS whether an item is considered income or corpus for trust accounting purposes. The most important of these situations is the marital deduction trust; the effect of the determination of trust accounting income on qualification for the estate tax marital deduction is discussed at ¶ 3.3.04. The IRS also "cares" about this question in the case of a qualified domestic trust (QDOT) for the benefit of a noncitizen spouse, because distributions of "corpus" from a QDOT are subject to the deferred estate tax, while "income" distributions are not (§ 2056A(b)(3)(A), (B)); and in the determination of whether a trust is required to distribute all income currently so that it is taxed as a simple trust under § 651 rather than as a complex trust under § 661. Reg. § 1.651(a)-1. The IRS's rules for whether it will respect the governing instrument's or state law's definition of income are in Reg. § 1.643(b)-1; see also Rev. Rul. 2006-26, 2006-22 I.R.B. 939.

6.1.04 *"Total return" or "unitrust" concept*

A trend in trust drafting is to eschew "income" and "principal" concepts in favor of a "total return" (also called "unitrust") approach: The life beneficiary receives a fixed percentage (unitrust percentage) of the value of the trust's assets each year, rather than receiving the traditional trust accounting income of rents, interest, and dividends. For an excellent, readable, and practical analysis of the reasons for this trend, the methods of implementing the idea, and its pros, cons, and pitfalls, see Al Golden article cited in the Bibliography. The UPIA 1997 permits the unitrust method of trust accounting.

The IRS will accept a state-law definition of income based on the unitrust method if the annual fixed percentage that the income beneficiary is entitled to is not less than three nor more than five percent of the trust's value (as determined annually or averaged on a multiple year basis). Reg. § 1.643(b)-1.

Retirement benefits pose a valuation problem for the unitrust approach: Should the built-in income tax liability be deducted from the nominal value of the benefits? That issue can be avoided by distributing, each year, the required percentage of the retirement plan assets and the required percentage of the nonretirement assets. This method of implementing the unitrust method was blessed, for a marital deduction trust, in Rev. Rul. 2006-26 (¶ 3.3.04).

6.1.05 *Transferring a retirement plan out of a trust or estate*

When a trust terminates, the trustee can transfer, intact, to the beneficiaries of the trust, any IRA or other retirement plan then held by the trust. The same applies to the participant's estate (if the benefits pass to the estate as either named or default beneficiary), and to the estate of a beneficiary who dies prior to withdrawing all the benefits from an inherited retirement plan (¶ 1.5.13(B)): The estate can transfer the IRA or plan to its beneficiaries.

The transfer of an inherited retirement plan or IRA from a trust or estate to the beneficiary(ies) of the trust or estate has no effect on the Applicable Distribution Period for the benefits. Such a transfer is solely for the purpose of allowing the trust or estate to terminate or otherwise cease to have control of the benefits. See ¶ 6.4.07 for income tax effects, and Form 5.2, Appendix B, for how to do the transfer.

A.   Examples of fiduciary transfers of inherited retirement plans. Here are some common examples of such transfers:

Foster Example: Foster names the Foster Revocable Trust as beneficiary of his IRA. The Foster Revocable Trust provides that, upon Foster's death, the trustee is to divide all assets of the trust into two separate trusts, the Marital Trust and the Credit Shelter Trust, pursuant to a fractional formula. All retirement benefits are to be allocated to the Marital Trust. The trustee instructs the IRA provider to change the name of the owner of the IRA from "Foster Revocable Trust, as beneficiary of Foster, deceased," to "Marital Trust, as beneficiary of Foster, deceased." The trustee has transferred the IRA from the Foster Revocable Trust to the Marital Trust.

Stanley Example: Stanley names his testamentary trust as beneficiary of his IRA. The trust provides that, after Stanley's death, the trustee is to pay income of the trust to Mrs. Stanley for life. On her death, the trust is to terminate, with the principal of the trust passing to Stanley's two children, A and B. The trustee takes annual MRDs from Stanley's

IRA computed using the life expectancy of Mrs. Stanley, which is 18 years, as the ADP (¶ 6.2.01). Mrs. Stanley dies 12 years later. It is now time for the trust to terminate. There are still six years left in the ADP. The trustee instructs the IRA provider to divide the inherited IRA (which is now titled in the name of "Stanley Testamentary Trust, as beneficiary of Stanley, deceased") into two equal inherited IRAs, one titled in the name of "Child A as successor beneficiary of Stanley, deceased," and the other similarly titled for Child B. The trustee has transferred the IRA from the testamentary trust to the two children.

B.	**Income tax effects.** Generally, the transfer of an inherited retirement plan from a trust or estate to the beneficiaries of the trust or estate is a neutral (nontaxable) event for income tax purposes, and the transferee-beneficiary will be taxable on plan distributions occurring after the transfer. See ¶ 6.4.02(E), ¶ 6.4.07, and ¶ 6.4.08.

C.	**PLRs and IRA providers.** Countless private letter rulings have approved the transfer of inherited IRAs and other plans from the trust named as beneficiary of the plan to the individual trust beneficiaries. PLR 2001-31033 (Rulings 5, 6, and 7) is typical. This ruling allowed the transfer of "IRA Y" from a terminating trust to the participant's children, C and D. From the ruling: "The provision of Trust X which provides for its termination does not change either the identity of the individuals who will receive the IRA Y proceeds or the identity of the designated beneficiary of IRA Y.... Furthermore, the Trust X termination language which results in distributions from IRA Y being made directly to Taxpayers C and D instead of initially to Trust X and then to Taxpayers C and D was language in Trust X approved by [the participant] during his lifetime which reflects [the participant's] intent to pay his children directly instead of through Trust X."

Other rulings approving the transfer of a retirement plan from a trust to the trust beneficiaries (without requiring termination of the plan account, or otherwise triggering immediate income tax) are: regarding IRAs, PLRs 2001-09051; 2003-29048 (IRA payable to a trust divided into four "sub-IRAs," each to be held by one of the individual former trust beneficiaries); 2004-33019; 2004-49040–2004-49042.

For rulings permitting Beneficiary IRAs to be opened directly in the name of the individual trust beneficiaries (rather than first in the name of the trust), where the IRA was payable to a trust that was to terminate immediately upon the participant's death and be distributed outright to the individual beneficiaries, see PLRs 2005-38030, -38031, -38033, and -38044, and M. Jones article cited in the Bibliography.

Unfortunately, PLRs cannot be cited as authority. ¶ 6.5.03. The PLRs cite Rev. Rul. 78-406, 1978-2 C.B. 157, which established the rule that a custodian-to-custodian transfer of an IRA does not have to meet the requirements of a rollover, and that such a transfer can be initiated by the beneficiary after the participant's death. However, Rev. Rul. 78-406 did not deal specifically with transferring an IRA from a terminating trust (or estate) to the trust (or estate) beneficiaries.

Sophisticated IRA providers (see list posted at www.ataxplan.com/bulletin board/ira providers.htm) readily permit these transfers, upon receipt of proper instructions from the fiduciary of the trust or estate, plus (in some cases) an opinion of counsel. However, some IRA providers balk at permitting these transfers.

A trustee or executor faced with an IRA provider's refusal to allow transfer of the inherited IRA to the trust or estate beneficiaries has four choices. #1. Cash out the plan and pay the income tax, giving up further deferral. #2. Keep the trust or estate open until the end of the ADP, to preserve continued deferral of distributions, but at the cost of ongoing administration expenses. #3. Get a private letter ruling from the IRS; see ¶ 6.5.03. #4. Move the account (still in the name of the estate or trust), by means of a plan-to-plan transfer (¶ 2.6.01) to a more cooperative financial institution, and *then* transfer it to the beneficiaries. Since options #1–#3 involve substantially increased taxes or costs, #4 is encouraged. Estate-plan friendly IRA providers welcome such transfers because they know the purpose of the transfer is to allow the beneficiaries to keep the account alive for many more years.

D.   Qualified plans; anti-alienation rule. If the benefits are in a qualified plan rather than an IRA, the question arises whether a transfer of the benefits from a trust (or estate) to the beneficiaries violates the rule that "benefits provided under the plan may not be assigned or alienated." § 401(a)(13)(A).

§ 401(a)(13) should have no application to this type of transfer. § 401(a)(13) prohibits arrangements (such as pledges and garnishments of benefits) "whereby a party acquires...a right... enforceable against the plan in, or to, all or any part of a plan benefit which...may become payable to the participant or beneficiary." § 1.401(a)-13(c)(1)(ii). The transfer of an inherited plan from a terminating trust or estate is a transfer *to* the participant's beneficiary(ies), not a transfer to a "party" that takes benefits *away* from the beneficiary. See PLR 2005-20004, approving the transfer of a 401(k) plan from the participant's estate to a charitable residuary beneficiary (without mentioning § 401(a)(13)).

6.1.06 *Individual retirement trusts (trusteed IRAs)*

Individual retirement arrangements can be established in either of two legal forms, a custodial account (§ 408(h)) or a trust (§ 408(a)). These two types of IRAs are treated identically for all tax purposes. For some reason, most IRAs are established as custodial accounts rather than as trusts. This Chapter deals with naming a trust as beneficiary of an IRA or other retirement plan; however, it should be noted that in some cases an IRA owner can use a "trusteed IRA" (also called an "individual retirement trust," or "IRT") in place of a standard custodial IRA payable to a separate trust as beneficiary.

An IRT can combine the *substantive terms* of a trust and the *tax deferral* of an IRA. The client (IRA owner) puts the trust terms and conditions into the IRT document. The document must comply with the minimum distribution rules and all other requirements of § 408, but otherwise there's no limit on what it may provide, other than what the IRT provider is willing to accept.

Regarding disclaimer of an IRT, see ¶ 4.1.12; regarding Roth conversion, see ¶ 5.4.02.

Here are some reasons a client might consider using an IRT instead of the more common custodial IRA. Keep in mind that not every provider's IRT necessarily provides all these advantages:

A. **Disability**. The IRT agreement can authorize the trustee to use the IRT assets for the participant's benefit during disability. An IRA custodian will not perform those duties.

B. **Limit beneficiary's access**. An IRA beneficiary can generally withdraw the entire account at will. An IRT can limit the beneficiary's access to MRDs, or MRDs plus additional payments (such as for health or support). Thus, it may be used in place of a conduit trust in some cases. See ¶ 6.3.05(F), ¶ 6.3.12.

C.   **Limit beneficiary's control at beneficiary's death**. Under an IRT, but not under most custodial IRAs, the *participant* can specify the successor beneficiary. See ¶ 1.5.13(D).

D.   **Avoid complications of MRD trust rules.** A trust named as beneficiary of a custodial IRA must meet complicated IRS requirements to qualify as a "see-through trust" (¶ 6.2–¶ 6.3). An IRT does not have to jump through these hoops.

E.   **Possibly, better creditor protection.** An IRT may have better protection from the owner's or beneficiary's creditors, because it may be treated as a spendthrift trust under some states' laws.

F.   **Reduce legal fees**. An IRT typically offers the participant a limited menu of the most popular post-death payout options, such as: outright to the beneficiary; beneficiary limited to MRDs (or spouse-beneficiary limited to greater of income or MRDs), with or without additional payments in the trustee's discretion. If the participant's estate planning goal is met by one of these "canned" options, the participant can avoid paying a legal fee to draft a trust agreement, because the trust terms are pre-drafted and included in the IRT document.

An IRT has some drawbacks: The provider's fee (or minimum account size) is typically higher than for a custodial IRA because more services are provided, but that may be appropriate if the client needs the services; see Beneficiary Designation Drafting Checklist, p. 531, #4(B). Also, since the IRT must pass all MRDs out to the IRT beneficiary directly, the IRT is not suitable for a client who wants MRDs accumulated and held in the trust for future distribution to the same or another beneficiary.

The IRT normally is not drafted by the participant's estate planning lawyer; it is a printed form pre-drafted by the IRA sponsor, for which the IRA sponsor has obtained IRS approval (similar to a "prototype" pension plan), and which the participant then adopts, typically by making check-the-box choices in, and signing, a printed adoption agreement. Not all IRA sponsors offer IRTs.

6.2 The Minimum Distribution Trust Rules

Chapter 1 explains the minimum distribution rules. This ¶ 6.2 explains how those rules apply when a trust is named as beneficiary of a retirement plan.

6.2.01 *When and why see-through trust status matters*

If retirement benefits are left to a "see-through trust" (¶ 6.2.03), the benefits can be distributed in annual instalments over the life expectancy of the oldest trust beneficiary, just as if the benefits had been left to an individual human Designated Beneficiary (¶ 1.7). In contrast, if the trust does not qualify as a see-through trust under the rules explained here, the retirement benefits must be distributed under the "no-DB rules" (¶ 1.5.03(C), ¶ 1.5.04(C)). Usually, distribution over the life expectancy of a beneficiary provides substantially longer deferral than distribution under the no-DB rules.

However, the mere fact that a trust qualifies as a see-through trust does not mean that the trust is the best choice as beneficiary of the retirement benefits. For example, making benefits payable to a trust of which the spouse is the life beneficiary results in substantially less income tax deferral than would be available (via the spousal rollover) for benefits left to the spouse outright *even if* the trust qualifies as a see-through; see ¶ 3.3.02. Also, complying with the trust rules does not solve the problem of high trust income tax rates (¶ 6.4.01).

Another reminder: Complying with the IRS's minimum distribution trust rules is not a requirement of making retirement benefits payable to a trust. If a trust named as beneficiary of a retirement plan flunks the rules, the trust still receives the benefits; it just does not get to use the life expectancy of the oldest trust beneficiary as the Applicable Distribution Period (ADP).

There are some situations in which it makes little or no difference whether the trust complies with the trust rules:

A.   **Plan offers only lump sum distributions.** Many qualified retirement plans (QRPs) do not permit the life expectancy payout. ¶ 1.5.10. For distributions prior to 2007, if the client's benefits are in this type of plan, the life expectancy payout will not be available regardless of whether the trust passes the rules. However, as a result of PPA '06, if the trust qualifies as a see-through, it should be able to transfer the lump sum by direct rollover to an "inherited IRA"; see ¶ 2.6.03.

B.   **Oldest trust beneficiary same age as participant.** If the participant dies after his Required Beginning Date, leaving benefits to a see-through trust (¶ 6.2.03), the ADP is the life expectancy of the participant or of the oldest trust beneficiary, whichever is longer. ¶ 1.5.04(E). If the trust is not a see-through, the ADP is the participant's life expectancy. ¶ 1.5.04(C). If the oldest trust beneficiary is the same age as (or older than) the participant, the ADP will be the same whether or not the trust qualifies as a see-through (but see ¶ 2.7.03, first bold paragraph, if the plan requires lump sum distribution).

C.   **Charitable trust.** Passing the trust rules is irrelevant for an income tax-exempt charitable remainder trust (¶ 7.5.04).

D.   **Lump sum is best form of distribution.** There is no need to comply with the MRD trust rules if the trust qualifies for and plans to take advantage of a lump sum distribution income tax deal. See ¶ 2.4, ¶ 2.5.

E.   **Client's goals; beneficiaries' needs.** It may be appropriate to sacrifice the deferral possibilities of the life expectancy payout method in order to realize the client's other goals. See ¶ 6.3.12(H) for an example. Similarly, if it is expected that the retirement plan will have to be cashed out shortly after the participant's death to pay estate taxes or for other reasons, there is no point in making the trust qualify as a see-through.

6.2.02 *MRD trust rules: Ground rules*

Here are introductory points regarding the MRD trust rules.

A.   **Do you discuss MRDs in the trust instrument?** The MRD trust rules do NOT require the trust instrument to specify that the trustee must withdraw the annual MRD from the retirement plan. § 401(a)(9)(B) requires the MRD to be distributed from the plan or IRA to the trust-named-as-beneficiary whether or not the trust instrument mentions the subject.

Nevertheless, practitioners frequently do mention the requirement of withdrawing the MRD in the trust instrument itself, for various reasons, such as: In a conduit trust (¶ 6.3.05), the minimum distribution rules are essentially incorporated into the substantive provisions of the trust, so they should be mentioned in that case. In other types of trusts it doesn't hurt to remind the trustee that he is supposed to comply with the minimum distribution rules.

Also, including language dealing with the minimum distribution rules makes it clear that the drafter was aware of these rules and that the dispositive terms of the trust are not meant to conflict with the minimum distribution rules. In a marital deduction trust (¶ 3.3.03) it is advisable to specify that the trustee must withdraw from the retirement plan "the greater of" the income (that the spouse is entitled to under the marital deduction rules) and the MRD.

Finally, specifying that the donor intends the trust to qualify as a see-through should help if qualification turns on the interpretation of some trust provision.

B.   **Benefits and proceeds thereof.** For purposes of minimum distribution rule testing, a trust's interest in a retirement plan includes not just the retirement plan itself and the distributions from the retirement plan, but also the proceeds resulting from the trust's reinvestment of the retirement plan distributions.

C.   **Benefits pass from one trust to another.** If the beneficiary of the trust is *another* trust, then *both* trusts must qualify under the trust rules (though the IRS in letter rulings seems to ignore this requirement). Reg. § 1.401(a)(9)-4, A-5(d).

However, if the second trust can be disregarded under the rules discussed at ¶ 6.3, the second trust does *not* need to comply with the trust rules. Under a conduit trust, for example, the trust's remainder beneficiaries are disregarded. Thus, the remainder beneficiary of a conduit trust can be a trust that does *not* comply with the trust rules.

6.2.03 *What a "see-through trust" is; the five "trust rules"*

As explained at ¶ 1.5, the Code allows retirement plan death benefits to be distributed in annual instalments over the life expectancy of the participant's Designated Beneficiary (¶ 1.7). Although the general rule is that a Designated Beneficiary must be an *individual*, the regulations allow you to name a *trust* as beneficiary and still have a Designated Beneficiary for purposes of the minimum distribution rules. Reg. § 1.401(a)(9)-4, A-5(b), contains the IRS's four "minimum distribution trust rules" (also called the MRD trust rules):

1.   The trust must be valid under state law. ¶ 6.2.05.

2.   "The trust is irrevocable or will, by its terms, become irrevocable upon the death of the" participant. ¶ 6.2.06.

3.   "The beneficiaries of the trust who are beneficiaries with respect to the trust's interest in the employee's benefit" must be "identifiable...from the trust instrument." ¶ 6.2.07.

4.   Certain documentation must be provided to "the plan administrator." ¶ 6.2.08.

If the participant dies leaving his retirement benefits to a trust that satisfies the above four requirements, then, for most (not all!) purposes of § 401(a)(9), the beneficiaries of the trust (and not the trust itself) "will be treated as having been designated as beneficiaries of the employee under the plan...." Reg. § 1.401(a)(9)-4, A-5(a).

However, treating the trust beneficiaries as if they had been named as beneficiaries directly does not get you very far if the trust beneficiaries themselves do not qualify as Designated Beneficiaries. Accordingly, Rule 5 is that:

5.   All trust beneficiaries must be individuals. ¶ 6.2.09–¶ 6.2.10.

The IRS calls a trust that passes these rules a **see-through trust**, because the effect of passing the rules is that the IRS will look through, or see through, the trust, and treat the trust beneficiaries as the participant's Designated Beneficiaries, just as if they had been named directly as beneficiaries of the retirement plan, with two significant exceptions: "Separate accounts" treatment (¶ 6.3.02) and the spousal rollover (¶ 1.6.07) are not available to any trust, even a see-through.

6.2.04 *Dates for testing trust's compliance with rules*

The regulations give no specific testing date for the requirement that the trust must be <u>valid under state law</u>, but the examples in the regulation refer to a trust that is valid under state law *as of the date of death*. ¶ 6.2.05. The <u>irrevocability requirement</u> must be met as of the date of death. ¶ 6.2.06.

The <u>documentation requirement</u> must be met by October 31 of the year after the year of the participant's death. ¶ 6.2.08.

The requirement that the <u>beneficiaries be identifiable</u> must be met as of the date of death. However, if the trust flunks this requirement as of the date of death, it *may* be possible to cure the problem by disclaimers and/or distributions prior to the Beneficiary Finalization Date (¶ 1.8). See ¶ 6.3.03.

The <u>all beneficiaries must be individuals</u> test must be met as of the Beneficiary Finalization Date. See ¶ 6.2.10(C), ¶ 6.3.03.

6.2.05 *Rule 1: Trust must be valid under state law*

The first rule is that "The trust is a valid trust under state law, or would be but for the fact that there is no corpus." Reg. §1.401(a)(9)-4, A-5(b)(1). There is no PLR, regulation, or other IRS pronouncement giving an example of a trust that would flunk this requirement.

A testamentary trust can pass this test, despite the fact that, at the moment of the participant's death, the trust is not yet in existence; see Reg. §1.401(a)(9)-5, A-7(c)(3), Examples 1 and 2. There is no requirement that the trust be "in existence" or be funded at the time it is named as beneficiary or at the participant's death. The requirement is that the trust, once it is funded with the retirement benefits after the participant's death, must be valid under state law.

6.2.06 *Rule 2: Trust must be irrevocable*

The second rule is: "The trust is irrevocable or will, by its terms, become irrevocable upon the death of the employee." Reg. § 1.401(a)(9)-4, A-5(b)(2).

Including in the trust the statement "This trust shall be irrevocable upon my death" is not necessary, since any testamentary trust or "living trust" automatically becomes irrevocable upon the testator's or donor's death, and therefore passes this test. On the other hand it does no harm to include this sentence, and inclusion may avoid the necessity of argument with possible future plan administrators and auditing IRS agents who may not be familiar with estate planning.

A trustee's power, after the participant's death, to amend administrative provisions of the trust should not be considered a power to "revoke." The IRS seems to smile on post-death amendments; see PLRs 2005-37044 (discussed at ¶ 6.3.10(B)), and 2005-22012.

Unfortunately, it is not clear what the IRS is driving at with Rule 2. The IRS has never given an example of a trust that does not become irrevocable at the participant's death. Perhaps the regulation-writers are thinking of a situation where someone *other than* the participant has a power to "revoke" the trust after the participant's death, as in some community property trusts:

Steve Example: Steve owns a $1 million IRA that is community property. Under the law of Steve's state, all property of both spouses, as an aggregate, is treated as community property, and the surviving spouse is permitted to satisfy her community property interest in the decedent's assets by withdrawing any assets she chooses, up to the value of half the total value of all community property. Steve dies and leaves the IRA to a trust. The trust also holds $600,000 of other assets, all of which are community property. Steve's surviving spouse, Imelda, has the power to revoke the trust with respect to her community property interest in any property in the trust. Assume that her one-half community property interest in the $1.6 million trust is $800,000. That power would allow her to cancel ("revoke") the trust with respect to as much as $800,000 worth of the IRA. It appears that the trust is not irrevocable as to the IRA proceeds up to the maximum amount that is subject to the spouse's power. Thus, the trust "flunks" the irrevocability rule to the extent of $800,000 worth of the IRA.

However, flunking this trust rule doesn't matter if Imelda *exercises* her power by withdrawing $800,000 of the IRA from the trust. Since that portion of the IRA is no longer part of the trust, we don't care whether the trust passes the trust rules as to that portion.

Also, the spouse's power of revocation is not a problem to the extent that the IRA exceeds the spouse's 50 percent interest; if her power is to revoke only 50 percent of the trust, and the IRA represents more than 50 percent, the excess is not subject to the power, and so the rule is not violated as to that excess portion. If Imelda withdraws $800,000 from the IRA, which is the maximum amount she can take out of Steve's trust, then the remaining $200,000 of the IRA that is still in the trust is not subject to Imelda's power to revoke and so the trust is irrevocable as to that part.

Thus Rule 2 matters for Steve's trust, if at all, only to the extent that Imelda could, *but chooses not to*, satisfy her community property interest by withdrawing the IRA. If Imelda takes her $800,000 by withdrawing $200,000 from the IRA plus $600,000 from the other assets, that leaves $800,000 of the IRA still in the trust. Since Imelda *could* have revoked the trust as to an additional $600,000 of the IRA that is still in the trust, the IRS might say the trust flunks Rule 2 as to $600,000 worth of the IRA. There are no rulings on point.

6.2.07 *Rule 3: Beneficiaries must be identifiable*

"The beneficiaries of the trust who are beneficiaries with respect to the trust's interest in the employee's benefit" must be "identifiable within the meaning of A-1 of this section from the trust instrument." Reg. §1.401(a)(9)-4, A-5(b)(3). The entirety of what "A-1 of this section" provides on the meaning of the word "identifiable" is the following: "A designated beneficiary need not be specified by name in the plan or by the employee to the plan...so long as the individual who is to be the beneficiary is identifiable under the plan. The members of a class of beneficiaries capable of expansion or contraction will be treated as being identifiable if it is possible to identify the class member with the shortest life expectancy." Reg. § 1.401(a)(9)-4, A-1.

A.   **Must be possible to identify the oldest trust beneficiary.** One meaning of this rule is that it must be possible to determine who is the oldest person who could ever possibly be a beneficiary of the trust, because that's whose life expectancy is used as the ADP after the participant's death. ¶ 1.5.03(E), ¶ 1.5.04(E).

Thus, if the trust beneficiaries are "all my issue living from time to time," the members of that class of potential beneficiaries are considered "identifiable," even though the class is not closed as of the applicable date, because no person with a shorter life expectancy can be added later. The oldest member of the class can be determined with certainty, because the participant's issue who are born after his death must be younger than the oldest issue of the participant who is living at his death. Reg. § 1.401(a)(9)-4, A-1.

Actually, there *is* theoretically a problem even with this common provision. If people who are issue by virtue of adoption are to be included on the same basis as "natural" issue, there is a potential for violating the rule. After the participant's death, one of his issue could adopt someone who was born earlier than the person who was the oldest beneficiary of the trust when the participant died. It is not known whether the IRS would ever raise this "issue," but to avoid the problem the trust should provide that older individuals cannot be later added to the class of beneficiaries by adoption. See Form 4.3, Appendix B.

The rule that it must be possible to identify the oldest member of a class of beneficiaries is similar to the rule against perpetuities, in that the mere *possibility* that an older beneficiary could be added to the trust after the applicable date is enough to make the trust flunk this rule, regardless of whether any such older beneficiary ever is *actually* added (unless the potential older beneficiary can be disregarded under the rules explained at ¶ 6.3.04).

Kit and Julia Example: Kit leaves his IRA to a trust that is to pay income to his daughter Julia for life, and after her death is to pay income to her widower (if any) for his life, with remainder to Kit's grandchildren. Kit dies, survived by Julia and several grandchildren, none of whom disclaims his or her interest in the trust. Kit's trust flunks Rule 3, because Julia, after Kit's death, *could* marry a new husband who is older than she. Thus an older beneficiary *could* be added to this trust after the applicable date, and we cannot tell with certainty who is the oldest beneficiary of the trust.

For the effect of a power of appointment on the question of whether there are unidentifiable beneficiaries, see ¶ 6.3.09.

The "identifiable" test is applied, first, as of the date of death. If the trust flunks the requirement as of the date of death, but the "unidentifiable" beneficiaries can be "removed" by disclaimer (as in PLR 2004-38044; see ¶ 6.3.09(B)), prior to the Beneficiary Finalization Date, the trust would "pass." Unfortunately, if a trust flunks this test as of the date of death it often is not the type of mistake that can be fixed by a disclaimer or distribution. In the Kit and Julia Example, Julia's future husband(s) can't disclaim (and we can't pay them their share of the benefits) because we don't know who they are yet—that's the whole problem!

B.　　**What does "oldest beneficiary" mean?** Older does not necessarily mean born first; it means having a shorter life expectancy for MRD purposes. Paul dies leaving his IRA to a trust that provides income per stirpes to his issue. Each issue has a separate share of the trust, with a testamentary power of appointment to appoint to any individual *other than* someone born before the year of birth of Paul's oldest issue living at Paul's death. Suppose Judy, born December 30, 1945, was Paul's oldest issue living at Paul's death. She can appoint her share to anyone born in 1945 or later, even if the appointee was born January 1, 1945, and so is almost a full year older than Judy. This power of appointment does not make the beneficiary "unidentifiable," because Judy still has the shortest life expectancy. For MRD purposes, everyone born in 1945 has the same life expectancy! PLR 2002-35038.

B.　　**Identifying who the beneficiaries are.** Sometimes it appears the IRS thinks that "identifiable" means that "…the identity of the beneficiaries…can be determined by perusing…[the trusts'] terms." PLRs 2005-21033, 2005-22012, and 2005-28031 use that exact phrase, and PLR 2002-09057 uses similar wording. What this phrase means, if anything, has yet to be established.

If the benefits are payable to a trust under which the trustee has absolute discretion to pay the benefits to "my son John and/or any individual in the world who is younger than John," are the beneficiaries identifiable? Not in the normal sense of the word; though we know who the oldest *potential* beneficiary is, we cannot determine the identity of the beneficiaries by "perusing" the trust. We cannot know who is entitled to the benefits until the trustee makes his selection.

To date, however, the IRS has not used Rule 3 in any published ruling to disqualify trusts that are payable to broad or amorphous classes of unknown future beneficiaries or where access to the benefits is dependent on the trustee's discretion. In fact, the rulings indicate exactly the opposite: In PLR 2002-35038, the IRS approved a trust where the remainder interest could be appointed to any individual in the world who was not born in a year prior to the birth of the donor's oldest issue living at the donor's death. PLR 2006-08032 is similar.

6.2.08 *Rule 4: Documentation requirement*

The trustee of the trust that is named as beneficiary must supply certain documentation to the **plan administrator**. Reg. § 1.401(a)(9)-4, A-5(b)(4). In the case of a qualified plan, "plan administrator" is the statutory title of the person responsible for carrying out the plan provisions and complying with the minimum distribution rules; the employer must provide the name, address, and phone number of the plan administrator to all employees in the Summary Plan Description. In the case of an IRA, the IRA trustee, custodian, or issuer is the party to whom the documentation must be delivered. Reg. § 1.408-8, A-1(b).

A.   **Post-death distributions.** The <u>deadline</u> for supplying this documentation with respect to post-death distributions is October 31 of the year after the year of the participant's death (or October 31, 2003, if later). Reg. § 1.401(a)(9)-4, A-6(b). This deadline is one month after the Beneficiary Finalization Date (¶ 1.8). The idea is that, once it is settled, on September 30 of the year after the year of the participant's death, exactly who the Designated Beneficiaries are, the trustee then has another month to certify this information to the plan administrator.

It is not necessary to wait until after September 30 to send the documentation to the Plan Administrator. Unless there is some reason to believe the information will change between the date of death and September 30, the trustee might as well send in the documentation as soon as possible; the trustee can always send amended documentation after September 30 (and before October 31) if a change does occur.

Here is the <u>documentation required</u> to be supplied to the plan administrator by that deadline. The trustee of the trust must *either*:

1.   "Provide the plan administrator with a final list of all beneficiaries of the trust (including contingent and remaindermen beneficiaries with a description of the conditions on their entitlement) as of September 30 of the calendar year following the calendar year of the employee's death; certify that, to the best of the trustee's knowledge, this list is correct and complete and that the [other "trust rules"] are satisfied; and agree to provide a copy of the trust instrument to the plan administrator upon demand...."; or

2.   "Provide the plan administrator with a copy of the actual trust document for the trust that is named as a beneficiary of the employee under the plan as of the employee's date of death."

Supplying a copy of the trust (#2) is an easier way to comply than providing a summary of the trust (#1). However, some retirement plans may require the alternative method of compliance, since it relieves the plan administrator of the burden of reading the trust and determining whether it complies with the trust rules.

B.   **Lifetime distributions.** The identity of the beneficiaries is irrelevant to the calculation of lifetime MRDs if the participant is using the Uniform Lifetime Table (¶ 1.3.01). Therefore, the participant has no need to comply with the documentation requirement or other trust rules for his lifetime distributions *unless*: (1) the participant has named a trust as his sole beneficiary; (2) the participant's more-than-10-years-younger spouse is the sole beneficiary of the trust (¶ 1.6.07); and (3) the participant wants to use the spouses' joint life expectancy (rather than the Uniform Lifetime Table) to measure his MRDs. ¶ 1.3.03. In such cases, see Reg. § 1.401(a)(9)-4, A-6(a), regarding the documentation to be supplied.

No deadline is specified for supplying documentation in the case of lifetime MRDs. The conservative assumption would be that the deadline is the beginning of the distribution year in which the spouses' joint life expectancy is to be used as the ADP. Note that in the case of lifetime MRDs the person who must fulfill this requirement is *the participant* (not the trustee, as is the case when the participant dies).

C.   **If incorrect trust documentation is supplied.** If the participant (in the case of lifetime MRDs) or the trustee (in the case of post-death MRDs) completed the certifications incorrectly, or sent a copy of the wrong trust instrument to the plan administrator, the regulations let the *plan* off the hook.

The plan will not be disqualified "merely" because of these errors, provided "the plan administrator reasonably relied on the information provided and the required minimum distributions for calendar years after the calendar year in which the discrepancy is discovered are determined based on the actual terms of the trust instrument." Reg. § 1.401(a)(9)-4, A-6(c)(1).

However, the penalty tax (which is payable by the person required to *take* the MRD; see ¶ 1.9) will be still be based on what should have been distributed "based on the actual terms of the trust in effect." Reg. § 1.401(a)(9)-4, A-6(c)(2).

6.2.09 *Rule 5: All beneficiaries must be individuals*

The result of compliance with the first four rules is that the trust beneficiaries will be treated (except for purposes of the separate accounts rule, ¶ 6.2.03, and spousal rollover, ¶ 1.6.07) as if the participant had named them directly as beneficiaries. The next step, therefore, is to make sure that these trust beneficiaries qualify as Designated Beneficiaries, *i.e.*, that they are individuals.

The first pitfall under this rule is that an estate is not an individual and therefore an estate cannot be a Designated Beneficiary. ¶ 1.7.04. Therefore, if any part of the trust's interest in the benefits will pass to an estate, there is a risk that the participant has no Designated Beneficiary; see ¶ 6.2.10. Once that hurdle is cleared we move on to other tough questions regarding which trust beneficiaries, if any, can be disregarded in applying this rule. See ¶ 6.3.

6.2.10 *Payments to estate for expenses, taxes*

Typically, a trust provides that the trust must or may contribute funds to the decedent-trustor's estate for payment of his debts, expenses, and taxes. Despite suggestions in several PLRs (see, *e.g.*, PLR 9809059) that such a provision might disqualify a trust from having see-through status, there is no evidence that the IRS really does (or ever did) take this position. There is no published instance of any trust's ever having lost see-through status on account of such a clause.

If this type of clause *is* a problem, the risks of disqualification can easily be avoided either at the planning stage or (with a bit more care) in the post-mortem stage.

Many PLRs blessing see-through trusts do not even mention the subject; see PLRs 2003-17044, 2003-17043, 2003-17041; 2002-18039; 2002-11047; and 2002-08031. Every letter ruling that *does* mention such a clause in a trust finds some reason why the trust nevertheless qualifies as a see-through, based on one of the following rationales:

A.   Document prohibits use of benefits for this purpose. The IRS has recognized trusts as see-throughs, despite a trust clause calling for payments to the estate for debts, expenses, and/or taxes, where the trust in question forbade the distribution of *retirement benefits* to the participant's estate (PLRs 2002-35038–2002-35041) or to any nonindividual beneficiary (PLRs 2004-10019–2004-10020). PLR 2004-53023 refers favorably to trust language that would "wall off" the benefits from being used to pay the decedent's debts and expenses (though the trust in question did not contain such language).

B.   State law protects the benefits. The IRS has recognized trusts as see-throughs, despite a trust clause calling for payments to the estate for debts, expenses, and/or taxes, where the trustees asserted either that applicable state law prohibited use of the retirement benefits for this purpose (either directly, or indirectly through the application of some fiduciary standard), or that state law exempted such benefits from creditors' claims. See PLRs 2002-23065, 2002-28025, for examples of this language; other PLRs with similar language and holdings are 2001-31033; 2002-21056, 2002-21059, 2002-21061; 2002-35038; 2002-44023; 2004-10019–2004-10020; and 2005-38030.

C.   Benefits will not be so used after Beneficiary Finalization Date. PLRs 2004-32027–2004-32029 confirm that, even if the participant's estate is deemed to be a beneficiary of the trust as of the date of death (by virtue of the estate's right to receive funds from the trust for payment of debts, expenses, and/or taxes), the estate can be "removed" as a beneficiary by complete distribution of its share prior to (or "as of") the Beneficiary Finalization Date (¶ 1.8).

In these PLRs, "as of" September 30 of the year after the year of the participant's death, the trustee had withdrawn, from the IRA that was payable to the trust, sufficient funds to pay all anticipated debts, expenses, and taxes of the participant's estate, including a reserve for income taxes that would be due on the IRA distributions themselves. The IRS blessed the trust as a see-through, ruling that on the applicable September 30 the only remaining beneficiaries of the trust were the participant's three children.

D.   There are no other assets available. In PLRs 2004-32027–2004-32029, the IRS conceded that the trust's contingent liability to pay additional estate taxes after the Beneficiary Finalization Date (for example, if the tax bill went higher as a result of audit) did not disqualify the trust, despite the fact that such additional tax payments would have to come out of the IRA. The IRS does not give any particular rationale for this conclusion, just the conclusion.

In PLR 2004-40031, section 8.7(v) of the trust named as beneficiary of the participant's plans gave the trustee discretion to pay the participant's expenses of last illness, estate taxes, and probate costs. The estate was insolvent, so the trustee and an estate creditor sought a court order to pay some of the estate's expenses from the trust. Applicable state law exempted the benefits from claims of the participant's and beneficiary's creditors, but the court nevertheless ordered the trust to use plan benefits to pay the estate's liabilities "because no other assets existed" to defray these expenses. The IRS ruled that it would not treat "the creditors referenced in section 8.7(v)" of the trust as potential beneficiaries of the trust for MRD purposes.

The bottom line here is that there is no PLR or other IRS pronouncement in which the IRS has disqualified a trust either on the basis of a trust clause permitting the trustee to make payments to the participant's estate, or on the basis of the trust's actually making such payments. The IRS seems to understand that it would be absurd to disqualify a trust because the retirement benefits payable to it may be liable for the participant's debts, administration expenses, and estate taxes. All retirement benefits are potentially subject to those liabilities regardless of whether a trust is the named beneficiary. While the threatening IRS hints on the subject make it worthwhile to draft to avoid the issue (see Form 4.2, Appendix B), there is little to fear even if a trust does contain this clause.

6.2.11 *Effect of § 645 election on see-through status*

A deceased participant's estate and revocable trust can make an election to be treated as a single combined entity for income tax purposes during the administration period. § 645. Even though the effect of such election is that the estate and trust are treated as one entity "for all purposes of Subtitle A" of the Code (Reg. § 1.645-

1(e)(2)(i), (3)(i)), "...the IRS and Treasury intend that a revocable trust will not fail to be a trust for purposes of section 401(a)(9) merely because the trust elects to be treated as an estate under section 645, as long as the trust continues to be a trust under state law." TD 8987, 67 FR 35731, 2002-1 C.B. 852, 857 ("Trust as Beneficiary").

6.3 MRD Rules: Which Beneficiaries Count?

There is no special difficulty in determining whether the trust is valid under state law (Rule 1; ¶ 6.2.05), and irrevocable at the participant's death (Rule 2; ¶ 6.2.06), and that proper documentation has been supplied to the plan administrator (Rule 4; ¶ 6.2.08). The hard part of testing a trust under the MRD trust rules is determining whether all trust beneficiaries are individuals (Rule 5; ¶ 6.2.09), and which trust beneficiary is the oldest (Rule 3; ¶ 6.2.07). The difficulty is determining which trust beneficiaries "count" for purposes of these two rules, and which may be disregarded. This involves a two-step process.

The first step is to determine whether certain beneficiaries may be disregarded because, even though they are beneficiaries of the overall trust, they will not share in the retirement benefits that are payable to that trust. See ¶ 6.3.01–¶ 6.3.02.

The second step is to look at the beneficiaries who *could* potentially share in the retirement benefits and see whether any of them can be disregarded for some other reason, such as distribution or disclaimer of their benefits prior to the Beneficiary Finalization Date (¶ 6.3.03), or because they are "mere potential successors" to other beneficiaries (¶ 6.3.04–¶ 6.3.10).

6.3.01 *If benefits are allocated to a particular share of the trust*

This ¶ 6.3.01 deals with the following situation: Retirement benefits are payable to a trust. Upon the participant's death, that trust is divided or split into separate shares or trusts, and the retirement benefits are allocated only to one of such shares or "subtrusts." The question discussed here is whether the "identifiable" and "all-beneficiaries-must-be-individuals" tests (MRD trust Rules 3 and 5) are applied to the entire trust (i.e., all possible beneficiaries of all subtrusts created by the trust instrument), or rather are applied only to the beneficiary, share, or subtrust that ends up with the retirement benefits.

One typical example would be a trust that divides, upon the participant's death, into a marital and credit shelter trust and under which the benefits are allocated entirely to the marital trust; see Foster Example, ¶ 6.1.05(A). Another common case is a trust under which the benefits are entirely allocated to the share of one of multiple beneficiaries, or may not be used to fund a particular beneficiary's share. As the following discussion shows, it should not be assumed, that, merely because the benefits are allocated to one particular beneficiary, share, or subtrust, other trust beneficiaries, or beneficiaries of other shares or subtrusts, will be disregarded in applying the MRD trust rules.

A.   **The principle that *should* govern: "Beneficiaries with respect to the trust's interest in the benefits."** Reg. § 1.401(a)(9)-4, A-5(a), tells us that, if the trust rules are complied with, "the beneficiaries of the trust (and not the trust itself)" will be treated as having been designated as beneficiaries by the employee. Although A-5(a) uses the phrase "beneficiaries of the trust," all other references to the see-through trust rules make clear that it is not *all* beneficiaries of the trust who are so treated, but rather only the beneficiaries of a trust *with respect to the trust's interest in* the employee's benefit. Reg. § 1.401(a)(9)-4, Q-5; A-5(b)(3), (c); § 1.401(a)(9)-8, A-11 (last sentence).

Thus, the regulations seem to state that, even if the benefits are payable to a funding trust (such as the participant's revocable living trust), we are not required to test all potential beneficiaries of the *funding trust,* if the benefits are allocated only to certain beneficiaries or to particular subtrusts created under the funding trust. Instead, this wording suggests, we look only at the beneficiaries of the subtrust that actually receives the retirement benefits, because they are the only beneficiaries "with respect to the trust's interest in the benefits."

Does the IRS agree with this interpretation? The few IRS pronouncements (all of which are in private letter rulings) are inconsistent. Sometimes the IRS seems to confuse this question with the entirely different issue of "separate accounts" treatment (¶ 6.3.02).

B.   Subtrust is named directly as beneficiary of the benefits.
One thing is clear: If the participant's beneficiary designation
form names the subtrust directly as beneficiary of the plan,
rather than naming the funding trust, then the only beneficiaries
who "count" for purposes of the trust rules are the beneficiaries
of the subtrust named as beneficiary. PLR 2006-07031.

C.   Benefits allocated pursuant to trustee's discretion. If the
trustee has discretion to decide which assets to use to fund
which subtrust, and exercises its discretion by allocating the
benefits to one particular beneficiary or share, can other
beneficiaries or beneficiaries of other shares be disregarded in
applying the MRD trust rules?

This seems like the worst case for convincing the IRS that other
beneficiaries of the trust should be ignored, yet ironically it is the one
situation in which there is a favorable PLR squarely on point! See PLR
2002-21061 (issued under the proposed regulations), in which all pre-
residuary beneficiaries of a trust (including charities) were ignored in
determining the ADP for retirement benefits payable to the trust,
because the trustees (although they *could* have used the benefits to fund
the pre-residuary bequests) were legally and financially able to, and
did, satisfy the pre-residuary bequests out of other assets of the trust,
and the pre-residuary beneficiaries did not have the right under state
law to demand that they be paid out of the retirement benefits.

D.   Instrument mandates allocation; no formula. If the trust
instrument requires that the benefits be allocated to a certain
subtrust or to certain beneficiaries, or that the benefits cannot
be paid to certain beneficiaries or shares, regardless of the
amount of the benefits or any other factors, beneficiaries of the
shares to which the benefits absolutely cannot under any
circumstances be allocated *should* be disregarded.

Scott Example: Scott's IRA is payable to the Scott Trust. At his death
the assets of the Scott Trust are to be divided between a marital trust
and a credit shelter trust. The trust requires that all retirement benefits
are to be allocated to the marital trust, even if that means the credit
shelter trust is underfunded. Can the beneficiaries of the credit shelter
trust be disregarded in applying the MRD trust rules?

It appears the answer to this should be yes, in view of PLR 2006-20026 (see "E") and the language of the regulation. However, in view of the IRS vagueness on these issues, if it is important to Scott that the credit shelter trust beneficiaries be disregarded, he should name the marital trust directly as beneficiary of his IRA (see "B").

In PLR 2004-40031, "A" left his qualified retirement plan (QRP) benefits to Trust T. Trust T required that the proceeds of any QRP be held in Subtrust U, which benefitted A's grandchildren and younger issue. In determining that Trust T qualified as a see-through trust, of which the oldest grandchild was the oldest beneficiary, the IRS did not discuss the beneficiaries of any part of Trust T other than Subtrust U. While this *suggests* that the mandatory allocation to Subtrust U required that beneficiaries of other subtrusts be disregarded, the ruling does not actually state that there *were* any other subtrusts, or any beneficiaries of Trust T who were not beneficiaries of Subtrust U, so this ruling is not helpful.

Some PLRs mention, as part of a favorable ruling on see-through trust status, the fact that the trust in question forbade the distribution of retirement benefits to the participant's estate; see ¶ 6.2.10(A). These PLRs *imply* that the IRS will disregard trust beneficiaries who are forbidden, by the terms of the trust, to share in the retirement benefits, but are not conclusive, because the IRS has never on the record ruled that a trust was not a see-through trust merely because the benefits were subject to an obligation to contribute to payment of the deceased participant's debts, expenses, or estate taxes.

E.   **Mandated allocation pursuant to formula.** Many trusts that create a marital and credit shelter trust (or other subtrusts) by means of a formula specify that retirement benefits are to be allocated to a particular subtrust to the extent possible, and only used to fund other subtrusts if there are no other assets that can be used for such purpose. If the formula and the "to the extent possible" language compel the trustee to allocate the benefits entirely to (say) the marital trust, can the credit shelter trust beneficiaries be disregarded in applying the trust rules?

The PLRs on point are contradictory. PLR 1999-03050, decided under the proposed regulations, dealt with a three-share trust involving community property. The trustee was required to allocate the surviving spouse's share of community property (including pension benefits) to

"Trust A," of which the surviving spouse was sole beneficiary (because she had the absolute right to withdraw all its assets; see ¶ 6.3.08). The trustee was required to allocate the decedent's interest in any qualified plans to "Trust B," unless there were insufficient other assets to fund Trust C. Because there were sufficient other assets to fund Trust C, the trustee was required to allocate those benefits to Trust B. The taxpayers sought a ruling on who were the beneficiaries for MRD purposes.

The IRS treated this as a "separate accounts" issue (¶ 6.3.02): "Because the separation of plan benefits among Trusts A, B, and C occurred under the terms of Trust M rather than under the beneficiary designation form, the determination of Individual A's designated beneficiary can not be done on a separate account basis.…Thus, all beneficiaries of the trusts created under Trust M must be considered in determining the applicable distribution period." Thus, the IRS failed to distinguish between the separate accounts rule and the question of who are the beneficiaries "with respect to the trust's interest in the benefits."

However, in PLR 2006-20026, involving an IRA and QRP payable to "Trust T," the IRS ruled exactly the opposite way. Trust T was to be divided into Subtrust A and Subtrust B upon the participant's death by means of a formula. As a result of applying the formula, the benefits "had to be allocated to Subtrust B." The ruling then proceeded to analyze only Subtrust B, with no mention of the terms or beneficiaries of Subtrust A. This suggests that the IRS has changed its mind since PLR 1999-03050, and is willing to ignore the beneficiaries of other trust shares, where the funding formula forces the trustee to allocate the benefits to one particular share.

F.   Mandatory allocation under state law. If applicable state law mandates that the benefits be allocated to one particular beneficiary, subtrust, or share, do we disregard beneficiaries of all other shares in applying the MRD trust rules?

In PLRs 2005-28031–2005-28035, the IRS said "no." Unfortunately, these rulings offer no argument or basis for the conclusion. Slightly comforting is the rulings' statement that the allocation to a particular subtrust "was accomplished by the trustee(s) of Trust T and was not done by" the participant. An allocation to a particular share that is mandated by the trust instrument (see "D" and "E"), i.e. by the participant himself, may be distinguishable from the state law-caused allocation in these PLRs.

6.3.02 *Separate accounts rule not applicable*

Normally, if the participant's benefit under a plan "is divided into separate accounts and the beneficiaries with respect to one separate account differ from the beneficiaries with respect to the other separate accounts of the employee under the plan...the rules in section 401(a)(9) separately apply to such separate account...." Reg. § 1.401(a)(9)-8, A-2(a)(2). See ¶ 1.7.06.

It is clear from the regulations that the separate accounts concept applies at the *plan level*, not at the *trust level*. The *plan benefit* is not considered divided into separate accounts merely because it is payable to a *trust* that has multiple beneficiaries, even if the beneficiaries' shares constitute "separate shares" for purposes of allocating the income of the trust (¶ 6.4.05). Reg. § 1.401(a)(9)-4, A-5(c); PLR 9809059. The problem can be avoided (if separate accounts treatment is desired) by naming the subtrusts directly as beneficiaries in the participant's beneficiary designation form, rather than naming the single funding trust as beneficiary. PLR 2005-37044; ¶ 6.3.01(B).

Prior to issuance of the final minimum distribution regulations, separate accounts treatment was available for trust *beneficiaries* under certain circumstances. In PLR 2002-34074 (issued in May 2002, after the final regulations were issued, though this PLR was decided under the proposed regulations), the benefits were payable to a trust that terminated and was distributed in equal shares to the participant's children immediately upon his death. In one of its best-reasoned PLRs ever, the IRS stated that the MRD trust rules require treating the trust beneficiaries as if they had been named directly as the participant's beneficiaries, so the children's interests qualified as separate accounts even though the named beneficiary was a trust.

Perhaps because this result was so clear and logical the IRS promptly abandoned it. The following new sentence appeared for the first time in the final regulations (it was not contained in either set of proposed regulations, so there was no opportunity for public comment on this 180° change in the IRS's position): "...the separate account rules under A-2 of § 1.401(a)(9)-8 are not available to beneficiaries of a trust with respect to the trust's interest in the employee's benefit." Reg. § 1.401(a)(9)-4, A-5(c). Unfortunately, it is now clear that the IRS regards Reg. § 1.401(a)(9)-4, A-5(c), as precluding separate accounts treatment for any benefits that are payable to a single trust.

PLRs 2003-17041, 2003-17043, and 2003-17044, issued under the final regulations, are almost identical in relevant facts to PLR 2002-34074, but here the IRS reached exactly the opposite result of PLR 2002-34074. The 2003 rulings provided that *each child had to use the oldest child's life expectancy as the ADP*, because the IRA had been payable to the trust as named beneficiary and separate accounts could not be established for the beneficiaries of a trust (citing the new sentence in the regulation). This IRS position was confirmed in PLRs 2004-32027–2004-32029 and PLR 2006-08032. (However, for the record, PLRs 2002-35038–2002-35041 are to the contrary—they allowed separate accounts treatment for benefits left to a trust.)

Taking Advantage of "No Separate Accounts" Rule

Reg. § 1.401(a)(9)-4, A-5(c), creates a planning opportunity. Suppose a $3 million IRA is left to a funding trust that is divided, upon the participant's death, in a manner that does not trigger immediate realization of income (¶ 6.3.08). Following the division of the IRA, the trustee is administering a $1 million IRA held by the marital trust and $2 million IRA held by the credit shelter trust. The marital trust's terms are "income to spouse, plus principal in the trustee's discretion, remainder to issue at spouse's death." The credit shelter trust's terms are "pay income and/or principal to spouse and/or issue in trustee's discretion, remainder to issue at spouse's death." Assume the trust qualifies as a see-through, and the ADP is the spouse's life expectancy.

Because of the rule, the trustee can withdraw each year's MRD for the entire $3 million IRA ENTIRELY from the share payable to the marital trust, allowing the credit shelter trust's share of the inherited IRA to continue to grow tax-deferred. The trustee does not have to withdraw a separate MRD for each subtrust, because (even though the trustee has divided the IRA into separate accounts for its internal trust accounting purposes), "the separate accounts *will be aggregated for purposes of satisfying the rules in section 401(a)(9)*. Thus, ...*all separate accounts...will be aggregated* for purposes of section 401(a)(9)." Reg. § 1.401(a)(9)-8, A-2(a)(1) (emphasis added). If all beneficiaries' accounts *must be aggregated* for purposes of § 401(a)(9), then as long as the year's MRD for the *unified account* is distributed to *some one or more of the beneficiaries*, the distribution requirement would appear to be satisfied. However, there is no ruling on point. See ¶ 1.5.09.

6.3.03 *Beneficiaries "removed" by Finalization Date*

As explained at ¶ 1.8, the participant's Designated Beneficiary "will be determined based on the beneficiaries designated as of the date of death who remain beneficiaries as of September 30 of the calendar year following the calendar year of the employee's death." Reg. § 1.401(a)(9)-4, A-4(a). This regulation gives two examples of how a date-of-death beneficiary can be "removed" by this Beneficiary Finalization Date. One example is by complete distribution of the entire benefit to which such beneficiary is entitled; the other is by a qualified disclaimer of the benefit. However, a beneficiary's death does not "remove" him as a beneficiary; see ¶ 1.8.03.

A.   **Distribution on or before September 30.** If a trust beneficiary's share of the retirement benefits that are payable to the trust has been entirely distributed to him as of the Beneficiary Finalization Date, that beneficiary is disregarded. He no longer "counts" for purposes of the MRD trust rules.

In PLRs 2004-49041–2004-49042, the participant left his IRA to a trust that was to be distributed, in specified percentages, to his wife and two daughters. The wife took distribution of her percentage in full by the Beneficiary Finalization Date (and rolled it over tax-free to her own IRA; see ¶ 3.2.08). Therefore she was disregarded in determining who was the oldest beneficiary of the trust, and the older daughter's life expectancy was the ADP for both daughters' shares of the IRA.

Nonindividual trust beneficiaries (i.e., charities) are disregarded if their interest in the trust is distributed to them prior to the Beneficiary Finalization Date. PLR 2006-08032.

B.   **Qualified disclaimer by September 30.** A qualified disclaimer can change the ADP by removing an older beneficiary. ¶ 4.2.01. See PLRs 2004-44033 and 2004-44034, in which "A" died leaving her IRA to a trust for the life benefit of her sister, with remainder to A's two nieces. The sister disclaimed her interest in the trust, so that the two nieces became the sole beneficiaries, and the older niece's life expectancy became the ADP. Similarly, disclaiming a power of appointment can eliminate potential appointees who would otherwise be "unidentifiable" and cause the trust to flunk Rule 3 (¶ 6.2.07). See PLR 2004-38044, discussed at ¶ 6.3.09(B).

C.   **Are there other ways to "remove" a trust beneficiary?** The regulation seems to cite the beneficiary's receipt (or disclaimer) of his share of the benefits simply as *examples* of ways in which a person who was a beneficiary as of the date of death could cease to be a beneficiary as of the Beneficiary Finalization Date, not necessarily as the *only* ways this could be accomplished.

Certain post-death amendments of the trust, made before the Beneficiary Finalization Date pursuant to express provisions included in the trust instrument, have been recognized by the IRS; see PLR 2005-37044 (discussed at ¶ 6.3.10(B)), and PLR 2005-22012. See also discussion of post-death judicial reformations, ¶ 1.7.03. No other permitted method has yet come to light. The trustee's allocation of the benefits to the trust share of certain beneficiaries by the Beneficiary Finalization Date, though consistent with the trust instrument and required by state law, was not sufficient to allow the beneficiaries of other trust shares to be disregarded; see PLRs 2005-28031–2005-28035, discussed at ¶ 6.3.01(F).

6.3.04 *Disregarding "mere potential successors"*

We now come to the last stand: trust beneficiaries who either definitely will, or someday may, receive a share of the retirement benefits that are payable to the trust, and who have not been "removed" as of the Beneficiary Finalization Date. Which members of this group can we disregard, if any?

Reg. § 1.401(a)(9)-5, A-7(c), the "mere potential successor rule," tells us which beneficiaries in this group can be disregarded in applying the trust rules. Reg. § 1.401(a)(9)-4, A-5(c). The mere potential successor rule has been stated differently in each version of the regulations (1987 and 2001 proposed, 2002 final), without improving clarity. The final regulation's version is as follows:

"(c). Successor beneficiary–(1) A person will not be considered a beneficiary for purposes of determining who is the beneficiary with the shortest life expectancy...or whether a person who is not an individual is a beneficiary, *merely because the person could become the successor* to the interest of one of the employee's beneficiaries after that beneficiary's death. However, the preceding sentence does not apply to a person who has any right (including a contingent right) to an employee's benefit beyond being a *mere potential successor* to the interest of one of the employee's beneficiaries upon that beneficiary's death." Reg. § 1.401(a)(9)-5, A-7(c). Emphasis added.

How does the mere potential successor rule apply to a trust? The IRS recognizes two types of trusts, called in this book "conduit trusts" (¶ 6.3.05) and "accumulation trusts" (¶ 6.3.06–¶ 6.3.09).

Under a <u>conduit trust</u>, because the trustee is required to pass all plan distributions out to the individual trust beneficiary, the IRS regards the conduit beneficiary as the sole beneficiary of the trust; all beneficiaries other than the conduit beneficiary are considered mere potential successors and are disregarded.

Any trust that is not a conduit trust is an <u>accumulation trust</u>, meaning that the trustee has the power to accumulate plan distributions in the trust. Under an accumulation trust (except, probably, in the case of a 100% grantor trust; ¶ 6.3.08) some or all of the potential remainder beneficiaries *do* "count" (i.e., they are not disregarded) for purposes of the MRD trust rules.

From Reg. § 1.401(a)(9)-5, A-7(c): "Thus, for example, if the first beneficiary has a right to all income with respect to an employee's individual account during that beneficiary's life and a second beneficiary has a right to the principal but only after the death of the first income beneficiary (any portion of the principal distributed during the life of the first income beneficiary to be held in trust until that first beneficiary's death), *both beneficiaries must be taken into account* in determining the beneficiary with the shortest life expectancy and whether only individuals are beneficiaries." Emphasis added.

While a conduit trust is guaranteed to pass the IRS trust rules, an accumulation trust may or may not pass the trust rules. Under an accumulation trust, it may or may not be easy to figure out which beneficiaries may be disregarded as mere potential successors, because the meaning of this term is clear in certain situations but unclear in others. The regulations offer no other guiding principles and contain only two examples, one of which is a conduit trust (¶ 6.3.05).

The other example, which is the only example the IRS provides of an accumulation trust that passes the rules, is the following ambiguous Example 1 of Reg. § 1.401(a)(9)-5, A-7(c)(3): "Under the terms of Trust P, all trust income is payable annually to B [spouse of the deceased participant, A], and no one has the power to appoint Trust P principal to any person other than B. A's children, who are all younger than B, are the sole remainder beneficiaries of Trust P. *No other person has a beneficial interest in Trust* P." Emphasis added. In this example, the IRS is making the point that B and the children of A are all considered "beneficiaries" of Trust P, so the surviving spouse is not the sole beneficiary, but her life expectancy is used as the ADP because she is the oldest beneficiary.

This example is defective, however, because it does not explain what happens under "Trust P" if all of A's children predecease B. Either the trust document or state law must have something to say on that point, but the IRS's example is silent. Yet the only way we would be entitled to disregard the beneficiaries ("contingent beneficiaries") who take in that case is if they are considered "mere potential successors" to the interests of A's children. The ambiguity is repeated in the IRS's use of the same example in Rev. Rul. 2006-26 (¶ 3.3.04).

The IRS has resolved this ambiguity in several private letter rulings (which of course are not authoritative); see ¶ 6.3.06.

6.3.05 *Conduit trusts*

"Conduit trust" is not an official term. It is a nickname for a trust under which the trustee has no power to accumulate plan distributions in the trust.

A.   **What a conduit trust is**. Under a **conduit trust**, the trustee is required, by the terms of the governing instrument, to distribute to the individual trust beneficiary or beneficiaries any distribution the trustee receives from the retirement plan. The trustee has no power to hold and retain inside the trust ("accumulate," in IRS terminology) *any* plan distribution made during the lifetime of the individual conduit trust beneficiary.

Under the conduit trust approach, the conduit beneficiary is in the same position as if he had been named directly, individually, as beneficiary of the benefits, but with a variation: It is as if the participant, instead of leaving it up to the beneficiary to decide when and how to take out the benefits, had specified a payout mode as well as a beneficiary. In this case, it is as if the participant had specified that distributions would be paid in instalments over the life expectancy of the Designated Beneficiary.

If the Designated Beneficiary (or life beneficiary of the conduit trust) lives to his life expectancy, he will have received 100 percent of the benefits and the remainder beneficiary will receive nothing. (The exception to this statement is a conduit trust for the surviving spouse. Because the spouse's life expectancy is recalculated annually for MRD purposes, the benefits will last beyond her lifetime, even under a conduit trust; see ¶ 6.3.14.)

B.   How a conduit trust is treated under the MRD rules. With a conduit trust, the retirement benefits are deemed paid "to" the individual conduit trust beneficiary for purposes of the minimum distribution rules, and accordingly the "all beneficiaries must be individuals" test is met. All potential remainder beneficiaries (the persons who would take the remaining benefits if the conduit beneficiary died before the benefits had been entirely distributed) are disregarded because the IRS regards them as mere potential successors to the conduit beneficiary's interest. Reg. § 1.401(a)(9)-5, A-7(c)(3), Example 2.

The conduit trust is a safe harbor. It is guaranteed to qualify as a see-through trust, and it is guaranteed that all remainder beneficiaries (even if they are charities, an estate, or older individuals) are disregarded under the MRD trust rules.

See ¶ 6.3.11(A) for using a conduit trust for a disabled beneficiary, ¶ 6.3.12(A) for a minors' trust, ¶ 6.3.14(A) for a life trust for the benefit of the participant's surviving spouse. See Forms 4.7, 4.8, Appendix B, for sample conduit trust forms.

C.   Payments for beneficiary's benefit. Payment to the legal guardian of a minor or disabled beneficiary would be considered payment "to" the beneficiary for this purpose. See ¶ 6.3.11(A) regarding payment to another trust.

D.   Payment of trust expenses. In PLRs 2004-32027–2004-32029 (discussed at ¶ 6.2.10), the IRS conceded that "The use of Trust T assets to pay expenses associated with the administration of

Trust T (in effect, expenses associated with the administration of the Trust T assets for the benefit of [the participant's three children]...does not change" the conclusion that the trust had only individual beneficiaries.

E.   **Drawbacks of the conduit trust.** The conduit trust is not suitable for every estate planning situation, because it lessens the trustee's control considerably. Also, to work as intended, the conduit trust depends entirely upon the minimum distribution rules staying exactly as they are under present law. If changes in the law require or encourage faster distributions the trust beneficiary will receive the money much sooner than the participant intended.

F.   **Conduit trust drafting pointers.** A participant considering leaving benefits to a stand-alone conduit trust might consider using an "individual retirement trust" (IRT) instead. ¶ 6.1.06.

In drafting a conduit trust, be sure your definition of retirement benefits that are subject to the conduit requirement applies only to benefit plans that allow the stretchout. See Form 4.7, Appendix B.

Also, the life expectancy payout period under a conduit trust could last longer than the Rule Against Perpetuities would permit the trust to last. Even though the maximum payout period for post-death MRDs is an individual beneficiary's single life expectancy, the beneficiary whose life expectancy is being used as a measuring period could die more than 21 years before the end of his IRS-defined life expectancy, in which case (if his was the only measuring life), the trust could (depending on exactly what the dispositive terms are at that point) be in existence more than 21 years after the termination of "lives in being" at the commencement of the trust. The trust drafter should take care that the payout period required by the trust does not exceed the "perpetuities" period under applicable state law.

6.3.06 Accumulation trust: O/R-2-NLP

As explained at ¶ 6.3.04, the only example of a qualified see-through trust in the regulations besides the conduit trust is ambiguous. In PLR 2004-38044, the IRS for the first time resolved that ambiguity by approving an "outright-to-now-living-persons" (O/R-2-NLP) trust.

In this PLR, "A" died, leaving his IRA payable to a trust. The trust benefitted the participant's spouse, B, for her life. Upon B's death the principal would be divided among the participant's "lineal descendants then living," with each descendant's share held in trust for him until he had attained age 30.

At the time of the participant's death, his spouse survived him, and he had three living children, C, D, and E, and apparently no deceased children. The three children had *already attained age 30* at the time of the participant's death. Thus, if the spouse had died immediately after the trust's establishment, the three children would have taken the trust principal (including the remaining retirement benefits) *outright*.

Since the spouse's interest in the trust was "not unlimited" (she was entitled only to a life income interest, plus principal in the trustee's discretion), it was "necessary to determine which other beneficiaries of Trust Y must be considered in determining who, if anyone, may be treated as Taxpayer A's designated beneficiary...." In other words, if a trust beneficiary is *not* entitled to outright distribution of the entire trust, or even of all distributions the trustee receives from the retirement plan, we must keep looking; we must also count as beneficiaries (for purposes of applying the tests in the IRS's MRD trust rules) the beneficiary(ies) who will take the trust when the first beneficiary dies.

However, the ruling goes on to say that we can stop our search once we reach the children who are the apparent remainder beneficiaries. *Because they will take their shares outright when the prior beneficiary dies*, we do not need to go further and find out who would take the benefits if any of these three children predecease the surviving spouse. From the ruling: "Since the right of each child to his/her remainder interest in the...[trust] was unrestricted at the death of Taxpayer A, it is necessary to consider only Taxpayers B through E [i.e., the spouse and the three children] to determine which of them shall be treated as the designated beneficiary of Taxpayer A's interest in" the IRA.

Under the approach exemplified in this PLR, and in PLRs 2005-22012 and 2006-10026 to the same effect, once you find a now-living person who is entitled to outright ownership of the benefits on the death(s) of the prior limited-interest beneficiary(ies), all other potential subsequent beneficiaries are disregarded as mere potential successors to the "outright ownership" remainder beneficiary. This type of trust is called O/R-2-NLP in this book.

It is recommended that practitioners use conduit trusts and O/R-2-NLP trusts as often as possible when drafting trusts that are to be named as beneficiary of retirement benefits, since these are among the few types of trusts where we have clear guidance that it "works." However, the O/R-2-NLP is not a panacea. Here are some limitations of the IRS approach enunciated in PLR 2004-38044:

❑   If any of the participant's children had been under age 30 at the time of the participant's death, it would have been necessary also to count, as trust beneficiaries, anyone who would inherit the trust if a child died before reaching age 30. See PLRs 2002-28025 and 2006-10026; ¶ 6.3.12(C)–(F), ¶ 6.3.13.

❑   The O/R-2-NLP trust requires the existence of at least one now-living person who would be entitled to outright distribution of the benefits upon the prior beneficiary's death. If outright distribution is to be made to some remote future yet-unborn generation, for example if it is to be made to the then-living issue of someone who now has no living issue, it is not clear how if at all the O/R-2-NLP approach applies. See ¶ 6.3.15(A).

For how to have an O/R-2-NLP trust for a disabled beneficiary, see ¶ 6.3.11(B); for minors, see ¶ 6.3.12(C)–(F); for the participant's surviving spouse, see ¶ 6.3.14(B).

6.3.07 Accumulation trust: "Circle" trust

One way to deal with the mystery of which beneficiaries are disregarded is to draft the trust so there are no beneficiaries you *need* to disregard. If the trust property cannot under any circumstances be distributed to a nonindividual beneficiary, then it passes Rule 5.

For example, if the trust provides "income to spouse for life, remainder outright to our issue living at spouse's death; provided, if at any time during spouse's life there are no issue of ours living, the trust shall terminate and be distributed to spouse," it is impossible for the trust assets to pass to anyone other than spouse or issue, all of whom are individuals. If spouse dies before issue, issue get the benefits. If issue die before spouse, spouse gets the benefits. This is nicknamed a "circle trust" because the group of beneficiaries is a closed circle.

Why would anyone use a circle trust rather than an O/R-2-NLP trust? Because the validity of the O/R-2-NLP trust concept depends on private letter rulings interpreting an ambiguous regulation. See ¶ 6.3.06. A circle trust complies with the regulation without the necessity of relying on PLRs.

6.3.08 *Accumulation trust: 100 percent grantor trust*

Under the so-called "grantor trust rules," a trust beneficiary who is a U.S. citizen or resident is treated for purposes of the federal income tax as the "owner" of trust assets if such beneficiary has the sole unrestricted right to withdraw those assets from the trust. See § 678(a)(1), § 672(f), Reg. § 1.671-3. If an individual is deemed the owner of all of the trust's assets under § 678(a)(1) (or any other of the grantor trust rules, § 671–§ 677), then retirement benefits payable to such trust are deemed paid "to" such individual beneficiary for purposes of the minimum distribution rules, and the "all beneficiaries must be individuals" test is met. See, *e.g.*, PLR 2000-23030, in which the decedent's IRAs were payable to a trust that was a grantor trust as to the surviving spouse under § 676. The IRS ruled that a transfer of the decedent's IRAs to or from this trust was deemed a transfer to or from the surviving spouse.

See also PLR 2003-23012, in which the surviving spouse was recognized as the participant's designated beneficiary under the annuity rules of § 72 when benefits were payable to a trust deemed owned by the spouse under the grantor trust rules.

Treating the trust beneficiary as the "owner" of the benefits for income tax purposes would have two significant results: Income taxes on the trust's income would be imposed at the beneficiary's rate; and the remainder beneficiary should not be considered a beneficiary of the trust for purposes of the minimum distribution rules. Thus an estate, older individuals, or charities could be named as remainder beneficiaries (to succeed to whatever part of the trust was not distributed to or withdrawn by the owner-beneficiary during his/her life) without loss of the use of the owner-beneficiary's life expectancy as the ADP. Similarly, a power of appointment that affected the trust property only after the death of the owner-beneficiary could be disregarded; see ¶ 6.3.09.

Under this model, the trust beneficiary would be given the unlimited right to withdraw the benefits (and any proceeds thereof) from the trust at any time. Until the beneficiary chooses to exercise this right, the trustee exercises ownership rights and responsibilities on the beneficiary's behalf, for example, by investing the trust funds, choosing distribution options, and distributing income and/or principal to or for the benefit of the beneficiary.

This type of trust would be uncommon, since anyone wanting to give such broad rights to the beneficiary would presumably leave the benefits outright to the beneficiary rather than in trust. However, this model could be useful for a QDOT for the benefit of a non-citizen spouse (§ 2056(d)), or for certain disabled beneficiaries (¶ 6.3.11(C)).

6.3.09 *Powers of appointment*

If a remainder interest is subject to a power of appointment upon the death of the life beneficiary, all potential appointees, as well as those who take in default of exercise of the power, are considered "beneficiaries," unless they can be disregarded under the rules discussed in this ¶ 6.3.

Under a conduit trust, the trust's remainder beneficiaries are disregarded. ¶ 6.3.05(B). Thus, the conduit beneficiary (or the trustee or anyone) can be given the power to appoint the trust assets remaining at the conduit beneficiary's death to anyone, even a charity (i.e., a nonindividual), a nonqualifying trust, an estate, or an older individual, and the trust will still qualify as a see-through with the ADP based on the conduit beneficiary's life expectancy.

However, with an accumulation trust, remainder beneficiaries generally must be counted. (The exception is the 100 percent grantor trust; see ¶ 6.3.08.) Thus, if an accumulation trust (other than a 100 percent grantor trust) is to qualify as a see-through, all such potential appointees (and default takers) should be (1) identifiable (¶ 6.2.07) (2) individuals (¶ 6.2.09) who are (3) younger than the beneficiary whose life expectancy is the one that the parties want to use as the ADP. The following examples illustrate the possibilities:

A.   **Power to appoint to "issue" apparently is acceptable.** A trust that says "The trustee shall pay income to my spouse for life, and upon my spouse's death the principal shall be paid to such persons *among the class consisting of our issue* as my spouse shall appoint by her will" does not create a problem under this rule because the power is limited to a small, clearly-defined group of "identifiable" younger individuals. See, *e.g.*, PLRs 1999-03050 ("Trust B") and 1999-18065 ("Trust 2") approving trusts that contained powers to appoint principal among the participant's issue. Presumably in these PLRs the participant had some issue living at the time of his death; see ¶ 6.3.06.

B.   **Power to appoint to spouses of issue.** A power to appoint property to someone's "spouse" is a classic example of creating a nonidentifiable beneficiary (unless it is limited to a particular identified spouse). See Kit and Julia Example, ¶ 6.2.07(A). In PLR 2004-38044, the participant's surviving spouse had the power to appoint the trust at her death to the participant's issue *and their spouses*; she disclaimed this power to enable the trust to qualify as a see-through. See ¶ 4.2.01.

C.   **Power to appoint to charity.** A trust that says "The trustee shall pay income to my spouse for life, and upon my spouse's death the principal shall be paid to such members of *the class consisting of our issue and any charity* as my spouse shall appoint by her will," would flunk this rule, because the benefits could pass under the power to a nonindividual beneficiary.

D.   **Power limited to younger individuals.** If the class of potential appointees is limited to *younger individuals*, the power of appointment will not create a problem because all remainder beneficiaries must be individuals and it is possible to identify the oldest beneficiary of the trust. See PLR 2002-35038.

E.   **Implied power to appoint to another trust.** Under many states' laws, a power to appoint to individuals includes the power to appoint *in trust for* such individuals. The IRS has never commented on the effect of such a state law. Since the regulations require that, if benefits are distributable under one trust to another trust, *both* trusts must comply with the rules (¶ 6.2.02(C)), it would appear that any power of appointment that could be exercised by appointing in trust would cause a trust to flunk the trust rules unless the power is limited to appointing only to other trusts that comply with the rules.

6.3.10 *Combining two types of qualifying trusts*

If the trust beneficiary has the right to demand distribution of the entire trust to himself, it appears the trust qualifies as a see-through because it is a 100 percent grantor trust; see ¶ 6.3.08. A trust also qualifies as a see-through if the trustee is required to pass all plan distributions out to the beneficiary immediately (conduit trust; ¶ 6.3.05). What if the trustee is not required to automatically distribute all plan distributions to the beneficiary, but beneficiary has the right to demand immediate payment to himself of all distributions the trustee receives from the plan? The IRS position regarding such a hybrid grantor-conduit trust is not known.

Can one trust instrument contain both an accumulation trust and a conduit trust and still qualify as a see-through? Yes and no.

A.   **Stacking does not work.** Suppose a trust provides income to the participant's spouse for life, with remainder passing to the participant's issue, but with each issue's share to be held in trust until the beneficiary reaches age 30. The trust is clearly an accumulation trust during the spouse's life; assume the trust otherwise passes the trust rules, and the trust's ADP is the spouse's life expectancy.

To make the trust "pass" the trust rules, can the trust become a conduit trust for the issue on the surviving spouse's death? I.e., can it provide that, during the spouse's life, only *income* is distributed to the spouse, but after the spouse's death the trustee must distribute to the issue all distributions the trustee receives from the plan? No: A trust cannot start out as an accumulation trust (say, during the life of the spouse), then flip to being a conduit trust for the remainder beneficiary after the life beneficiary's death and still qualify as a see-through. The reason is that the trust may have *already* accumulated plan distributions (during the spouse's lifetime), so the trust does not meet the definition of a conduit trust at the participant's death.

B.   **"Toggle" trusts.** PLR 2005-37044, involving an IRA that was payable to several trusts as named beneficiaries, illustrates an innovative planning idea, the "toggle trust." In this PLR, the decedent's beneficiary designation form left "IRA W" to nine separate conduit trusts for nine individuals. Upon the death of the individual conduit beneficiary, his or her separate trust would be paid partly to the other trust beneficiaries' shares and partly to beneficiaries appointed by the conduit beneficiary.

The remainder beneficiaries of the trusts included charities and older individuals as potential appointees; however, since the conduit beneficiary is considered the sole trust beneficiary, these remainder beneficiaries are disregarded for MRD purposes. ¶ 6.3.05(B).

However, the trust also provided for a "Trust Protector," who had the power to make certain amendments to any of the nine trusts. One amendment he could make would be to take away the "conduit" provision, and change the trust to an accumulation trust, with the beneficiary receiving distributions only in the discretion of the trustee. Another amendment the Trust Protector could adopt was to limit the remainder beneficiaries of any trust to only individuals younger than the life beneficiary of that trust.

There was no time limit mentioned in the ruling after which the Trust Protector could no longer exercise these amendment powers. However, there may have been such a time limit in the trust, since the ruling mentions that there was "additional language" in the trust referring to the exercise of the amendment power "after September 30 of the year following the calendar year of Decedent's death." It is hard to see how the IRS could have approved these trusts as see-throughs without such a time limit, because otherwise the Trust Protector could further amend the trusts, after the ruling was issued, in ways that would cause them not to qualify as see-throughs.

The Trust Protector exercised its power to amend one of the nine trusts, "Trust J." First, he converted Trust J from a conduit to an accumulation trust. Second, he limited the potential remainder beneficiaries of Trust J to individuals younger than the life beneficiary.

Interestingly, the ruling request submitted to the IRS was whether the Trust Protector's *amendment* of the trust negatively affected the see-through trust status of any of the trusts. The IRS considered the matter from that point of view only, and did not get into the question of whether the Trust Protector's mere *power* to amend the trusts negatively affected the trusts' see-through status.

From this limited point of view the IRS was able to rule that the trusts, including the one trust that was amended by the Trust Protector, were see-throughs, because the Trust Protector's actions: carried out specific provisions adopted by the participant (i.e., the Trust Protector did not simply substitute some provisions of its own devising); were effective retroactively to the date of death, and accordingly "may be treated as a part of" the original trust instrument; and were "treated as a disclaimer under the laws of" the applicable state. (The taxpayers had represented to the IRS that the Trust Protector's actions were "treated as a disclaimer for all purposes associated with this ruling request.")

The finding that state law treated this trust amendment as a "disclaimer" is critical to the IRS's favorable ruling. Since the MRD regulations explicitly approve "changes of beneficiary" made by means of a qualified disclaimer, so long as the disclaimer occurs prior to the Beneficiary Finalization Date (¶ 4.2.01), anything that state law explicitly recognizes as equivalent to a disclaimer is highly likely to win IRS approval. However, the Trust Protector's action was not a disclaimer, and was nothing like a disclaimer. It is hard to imagine what the state law provision could have been that would "treat" this transaction as a disclaimer for any purpose.

As quoted in the ruling, the trust in PLR 2005-37044 was fatally defective and could not, without amendment, have qualified for see-through status. The conduit trusts were valid see-through conduit trusts—except for one thing: The Trust Protector had the power to amend those trusts to make them NOT conduit trusts. The Trust Protector had the power to turn the conduit trusts into accumulation trusts. As accumulation trusts, the trusts were defective, because the beneficiaries had the power to appoint the plan accumulations to charity (i.e., to a nonindividual beneficiary) or to older individuals. The Trust Protector had the power to modify those powers of appointment, to limit the appointees to individuals younger than the life beneficiary; but the Trust Protector apparently also had the power NOT to so limit the identity of the remainder beneficiaries.

Did the IRS simply miss this issue? Or was there additional trust language not quote in the ruling, indicating that the trustee could not convert a trust to an accumulation trust unless he ALSO limited the remainder beneficiaries to younger beneficiaries? Or, is the IRS truly signaling that there is more room than previously suspected to amend and "clean up" a trust by the September 30th deadline?

Though the trust in this ruling appears (based on what is quoted in the ruling) to have been defectively drafted, the concept of a "toggle" trust is both innovative and valid, PROVIDED it is not implemented in the manner that PLR 2005-37044 seems to suggest was used in "Trust T." For the toggle concept to work (unless the IRS has had an unannounced change of heart regarding the MRD trust rules), both sides of the "toggle" must be qualifying see-through trusts, and the trust instrument should establish the Beneficiary Finalization Date (¶ 1.8.01) as the deadline for exercise of the amendment power.

6.3.11 *Planning choices: Trust for disabled beneficiary*

Here are options available for a trust intended to provide for a disabled beneficiary, when qualifying for see-through trust status is an important goal (¶ 6.2.01). Which type is best depends on whether the beneficiary needs to qualify for need-based government benefit programs and on who the remainder beneficiary is. If qualification for benefit programs is a goal, the donor should hire an attorney who specializes in this type of trust to draft the trust; such an attorney can be found through the National Academy of Elder Law Attorneys (NAELA), www.naela.org.

A.   **Conduit trust.** A conduit trust (¶ 6.3.05) is not suitable if the beneficiary must qualify for welfare. The MRDs would have to be distributed to the beneficiary, and would be considered available income or assets to the beneficiary, thus forfeiting eligibility for welfare benefits. However, if qualification for these benefits is not an issue (for example, because the family is wealthy and intends to provide for all of the beneficiary's care), a conduit trust could be suitable, especially if the donor wants the remainder interest to pass to charity.

A conduit trust, of course, requires that all plan distributions be immediately passed out to the individual trust beneficiary (or his guardian or custodian). Under a charitable remainder trust (¶ 7.5.04), where the Code requires an annual unitrust or annuity payment to be made "to" a beneficiary, the IRS has ruled that a payment to a trust for the benefit of a disabled individual can be treated as a payment "to" that individual, if various requirements are met (both as to the disability and as to the trust). Rev. Rul. 2002-20, 2002-1 I.R.B. 794. To date there is no ruling comparable to Rev. Rul. 2002-20 that would allow conduit trust payments to be made to a trust for the benefit of a disabled beneficiary rather than to the beneficiary (or his guardian or custodian).

B.   **Accumulation O/R-2-NLP Trust.** Under most forms of "supplemental needs" trusts (designed to benefit a disabled beneficiary without causing loss of the beneficiary's eligibility for need-based government benefit programs), the trustee has discretion regarding whether to distribute trust funds to or for the benefit of the disabled individual, but is prohibited from distributing funds for needs that are provided by the government programs such as support and health care. Such a trust would be considered an accumulation trust for MRD purposes, but would still qualify as a see-through if the trust principal passes outright at the disabled beneficiary's death to other now-living individuals, such as the disabled beneficiary's siblings. See ¶ 6.3.06.

If an O/R-2-NLP trust is used, a charity cannot be named as remainder beneficiary. The chosen remainder beneficiaries should be (as siblings typically are) individuals close in age to (or younger than) the disabled beneficiary, since the life expectancy of the oldest member of the group will be the ADP. Thus, drafting this type of trust is "easy" if the disabled individual has living siblings who are younger or close in age, but impossible if there are no such suitable younger or close-in-age individual remainder beneficiaries.

C.   **Accumulation 100 percent grantor trust.** A trust that gives the beneficiary the unlimited right to withdraw all the trust property at any time would be treated as a 100 percent grantor trust (¶ 6.3.08). It could be a suitable way to provide for a mentally handicapped beneficiary who (1) does not need to qualify for need-based government benefits (because this type of trust would disqualify him) and (2) can exercise the right of withdrawal only through a legal guardian, especially if the guardian is also the trustee. For this type of beneficiary, this type of trust provides the benefits of a discretionary trust while allowing the life expectancy of the handicapped beneficiary to be the ADP. This can be particularly helpful if the beneficiary has no siblings or issue, and is not likely to have issue, where the only likely remainder beneficiaries are either much older individuals, the beneficiary's own estate, or charities.

6.3.12 *Planning choices: Trusts for minors*

Here are options available for a trust intended to provide for minor beneficiaries, when qualifying for see-through trust status is an important goal (¶ 6.2.01). Which type is best depends on the purpose of the trust: Is the trust to be the major source of support for an orphaned family, or is it just providing extra spending money for well-to-do children whose support is otherwise taken care of? Is the donor's main goal to be sure that the "stretchout" payout method is available, so the benefits become the minors' own retirement plans eventually? Or is the money most likely to be spent during the beneficiaries' childhood, for their support and care? Are the benefits and nonbenefit assets each substantial enough to justify establishing separate trusts, one for the benefits and one for the other assets? Are the benefits substantial enough to justify establishing a separate trust for each minor beneficiary, or is the "family pot trust" approach better?

Naming a minor directly as beneficiary of a retirement plan is not recommended. This approach will cause the plan administrator not to release the benefits to anyone other than a legal guardian of the minor. In some states, subjecting property to legal guardianship is not only time consuming and expensive, it restricts how the money can be spent for the minor's benefit.

Trusts for minors often provide for a staged distribution of principal, *e.g.*, half at age 25, balance at age 30, or one third at 30, one-half at 35, balance at 40. In view of the complications of transferring a retirement plan out of a trust (see ¶ 6.1.05), consider not using such staged distribution for retirement benefits, so as to minimize the number of times this issue has to be dealt with.

Here are ideas regarding different ways to leave retirement benefits for the benefit of minor beneficiaries:

A.   **Conduit trust (or IRT) for supplemental money.** Aunt Emily believes that leaving her IRA to her young nephews is a fine way to provide them with a nest egg, but knows that, if she names them directly as beneficiaries, they will simply cash out the account immediately upon her death. So she leaves the IRA to a conduit trust for them. ¶ 6.3.05. The purpose of the trust is to make sure that the nephews take advantage of the "life expectancy payout," whether they want to or not, and to provide professional management for the undistributed portion of the IRA. The nephews' support and education is paid for by their wealthy parents. The trustee is instructed to withdraw from the IRA, each year, the MRD (based on the life expectancy of the oldest nephew) and distribute it equally to the surviving nephews. Aunt Emily could also use an IRT in this situation. ¶ 6.1.06.

B.   **Conduit trust for a primary support trust.** If the retirement benefits are a significant part of a trust fund that will be providing the primary source of support and education for an orphaned family, a conduit trust may not be a good match. The trustee would be required to distribute to one or more of the children, each year, all distributions the trustee receives from the retirement plan. Even assuming the trustee can pick and choose, each year, which member of the group will receive that year's distributions, the trustee has no discretion to accumulate distributions for possible later needs. If later changes in the minimum distribution rules, or in the income tax laws, make accelerated distributions either mandatory or desirable (*e.g.*, because tax rates are about to go up substantially), the trustee cannot comply with (or take advantage of) the changed tax rules without losing control of the funds.

On the other hand, if the retirement benefits are not substantial enough to justify establishing a separate trust, the conduit approach can make sense for benefits that are part of the corpus of a larger trust. The benefits are left to the same trust as all the other assets, but that trust contains the special "conduit" provisions requiring the trustee to pass through all retirement plan distributions. See Form 4.7, Appendix B.

Even though a conduit trust partly defeats the purpose of leaving money in trust for a young beneficiary, some practitioners opt for this because it is a safe harbor, and does not require a letter ruling, on the theory that the MRDs that would have to be passed out to the minor beneficiary (or his guardian or custodian) would be very small because of his young age.

C.   **O/R-2-NLP: The problem: Who will be the NLP remainder beneficiary?** To avoid using a conduit trust, and still qualify as a see-through, practitioners look for ways to make the minors' trust an O/R-2-NLP trust (¶ 6.3.06).

The typical minors' trust calls for the trust to terminate and be distributed outright to the minors as each reaches a certain age (for example, age 35), or when all of the siblings have either reached that age or died. To be a see-through under the O/R-2-NLP approach it is necessary to have a younger individual remainder beneficiary who will inherit the benefits outright if all of the minor children die *before* reaching the stated age.

With a trust for an adult beneficiary, the outright remainder beneficiary can usually be the then-living issue of the primary beneficiary, but that approach won't work with minor children who have no issue at the time of the participant's death. D, E, and F below provide examples of ways to implement the O/R-2-NLP trust concept for a minors' trust; with each, a separate trust just for the retirement benefits will be required, since the remainder beneficiary provisions would be different for the benefits than for the other assets.

D.   **O/R-2-NLP: Last man standing.** One solution is to provide that if, at any time, there is only one child living among the original group of minor beneficiaries, the trust terminates at that time and all assets are distributed outright to that one. Thus, the living person who will receive the benefits outright on the death of all other beneficiaries is one of the minors.

This approach makes it unnecessary to name some remainder beneficiary the donor doesn't really want to name (see E and F). The drawback is obviously that if the provision is triggered the benefits could pass outright to a two-year old (through his legal guardian or a custodian for his benefit).

E.   **O/R-2-NLP: Fill in the blank.** Typically, the donor of a minors' trust would name a "wipe-out" beneficiary, to take the trust property if all of the minor children die without issue while there is still money in the trust.

The problem is, if the wipe-out beneficiary is a charity or other nonindividual, the trust will flunk Rule 5; if the wipe-out beneficiary is simply "my heirs at law," the trust would flunk Rule 3 (because the oldest beneficiary is not identifiable); and if the wipe-out beneficiary is an individual who is older than the oldest minor child, the wipe-out beneficiary's life expectancy will be the ADP.

See PLR 2002-28025, which involved a trust for the benefit of two minors. The trust was to terminate and be distributed outright to the minors as each reached age 30, but if they both died before reaching that age, the trust would pass to other relatives, the oldest of whom was age 67 at the participant's death. The IRS ruled that the 67-year-old's life expectancy was the ADP because he was the "oldest trust beneficiary." So one approach is for the donor to plug in the name of a younger individual as the wipe-out beneficiary, perhaps a young niece, nephew, or other relative.

F.   **O/R-2-NLP: Leave it blank.** Another approach, used successfully in PLR 2002-35038, is to give the trustee the power to distribute the remainder to any individual beneficiary who was born in the same year as the donor's oldest child or in a later year (or give the minor children the power to appoint to any younger beneficiaries). The problem with the leave-it-blank approach is that the IRS's rulings approving this approach are seriously defective in reasoning, in that the rulings fail to mention what would happen to the benefits if the power of appointment was not exercised; realistically, the donor would still have to "fill in the blank" ("E") to cover this possibility.

G.   **Whether to have a separate trust for each minor.** If the benefits are left to the typical "family pot" trust for the benefit of all of the donor's children collectively, then (assuming that trust qualifies as a see-through) the ADP will be the life expectancy of the oldest child. The donor could leave the benefits to separate trusts, one for the benefit of each child, to enable each child's trust to use that child's life expectancy as the ADP. This would work if each trust was a conduit trust.

The drawbacks of this approach are: the money is divided into rigid predetermined shares, without the ability of the trustee to "spray" more money in the direction of a child who needs it more; and, unless the trusts are conduit trusts, you still have the problem of finding a younger remainder beneficiary if the child dies before reaching the age for outright distribution. If the remainder beneficiaries are the other siblings, you are right back with the oldest child's life expectancy being the ADP for all the trusts.

H.   Dump the stretch; buy life insurance. Young parents of young children might consider drafting the trust to say exactly what they want it to say, ignoring the see-through trust requirements, and purchasing term life insurance to assure adequate funds for payment of any extra income taxes caused by loss of see-through status. This may make more sense than accepting the drawbacks of a conduit trust, or naming wipe-out beneficiaries the donors don't want to name.

I.   Custodianship under UTMA. For parents of minors where there are not enough assets to justify a trustee's fee, another choice is to leave the benefits to a custodian for the child under the Uniform Transfers to Minors Act ("UTMA"). § 3(a) of UTMA permits a "person having the right to designate the recipient of property transferable upon the occurrence of a future event" to nominate ("in a writing designating a beneficiary of contractual rights") a custodian to hold such property under the Act on behalf of a minor beneficiary.

The main drawbacks of leaving benefits to a custodian under UTMA are that the beneficiary becomes entitled to the money outright at a certain age (typically 18 or 21, depending on state law), and that age may be younger than the age the parents would ideally like. Also, the benefits must be left to specific individuals (such as, typically, equal shares to the surviving children). You lose the flexibility of leaving benefits to a "family pot" trust where the trustee has discretion to spend more for one child than another depending on their needs.

The IRS has never ruled on the question of who is considered the designated beneficiary when benefits are paid to a custodian under UTMA. Presumably the IRS would recognize that the minor is the "beneficiary." There would be no basis for the IRS to claim that the custodian is the beneficiary. Even though UTMA permits funds to be disbursed from a custodial account for the support of the minor (regardless of whether someone else is obligated to support that minor), the IRS presumably would not claim that the person(s) obligated to support the minor are somehow co-beneficiaries along with the minor.

The IRS recognizes that the minor is the sole owner of property held in custodianship when determining who is the "stockholder" for purposes of qualifying as an "S corporation" (Reg. § 1.1361-1(e)(1)), and presumably would do so also in the case of retirement benefits held by a custodian for a minor beneficiary. Income (including retirement plan distributions) paid to a custodian is taxable to the minor unless used to discharge someone else's legal obligation to support that minor. Rev. Rul. 56-484, 1956-2 C.B. 23. If leaving benefits to a custodian for a minor, check applicable state law for format required, eligible custodians, and age at which the custodianship terminates.

6.3.13 Minors' Trusts: What the IRS should do

The IRS position on O/R-2-NLP trusts produces absurd results.

Watson Trust Example: Watson dies at age 70, leaving his IRA to a trust. The trust provides that Watson's son Jackson is to receive income from the trust for life. On Jackson's death, the trust is to pass to Jackson's children, but each child's share is to be held in trust for such child until he or she reaches age 35. If all Jackson's children die without issue at a time when there is still money in the trust, the remaining trust funds pass to Watson's sister Dickie. At the time of Watson's death, Jackson is age 45, Dickie is age 68, and Jackson has two children living, who are ages 8 and 10. Under the current apparent IRS O/R-2-NLP concept, Jackson and his children are "limited" beneficiaries of the trust. The first "unlimited" beneficiary is Dickie. Therefore the trust beneficiaries for MRD purposes are Jackson, Dickie, and the two minor children, and 68 year-old Dickie is the oldest trust beneficiary. See PLR 2002-28025. This produces the utterly absurd result that we are required to ignore the over 95 percent actuarial likelihood that at least one of the two minor children will reach age 35; and we are required to treat Dickie as a trust beneficiary even though under the IRS's own actuarial tables Dickie's chance of surviving the other three beneficiaries approaches zero!

The IRS could easily eliminate this absurdity, and solve the headache of providing for minor beneficiaries, by adopting a simple convention as an add-on to the O/R-2-NLP concept. The IRS could make a rule that an individual will be considered an "unlimited" trust beneficiary (so successors to his interest can be disregarded as "mere potential successors") if the interest in the benefits and trust is to pass to him outright either (1) immediately upon the death of the donor or of another beneficiary or (2) upon the beneficiary's attainment of a certain age that is not older than age 45 (or age 35, or age 30, or whatever age the IRS likes). By adopting that rule, the IRS would immediately make legal the most standard and normal trust provision for minor beneficiaries, which is that they will come into outright possession upon attaining a certain age—an age that (under the vast majority of trust instruments) they have an overwhelming actuarial likelihood of attaining, according to the IRS's own actuarial tables.

6.3.14 *Practical options: trust for spouse*

Here are options to consider for a trust intended to provide life income to the participant's surviving spouse, including a credit shelter or QTIP trust, when qualifying for see-through trust status is an important goal (¶ 6.2.01).

A.   **Conduit trust as credit shelter or QTIP substitute.** The drawback of a conduit-credit shelter trust is that, if the spouse lives long enough, MRDs will eventually cause most of the benefits to be distributed outright to her. Benefits distributed outright to the spouse will not "bypass" her estate.

Conduit Trust Ironies

If the spouse is the conduit trust beneficiary, she is considered the "sole beneficiary," so nothing needs to be distributed from the plan until the deceased participant would have reached age 70½. ¶ 1.6.07(A). Thus, ironically, a conduit credit shelter trust can be used to keep money *away from* the surviving spouse of a young decedent!

When MRDs do commence, the spouse's life expectancy will be determined using recalculation (¶ 1.6.06(D))...meaning that she is guaranteed *not* to receive all of the benefits during her lifetime (if the trustee is limited to distributing to her only the MRD amount). Finally, a conduit trust for the life of the spouse, with remainder to a charity, "passes" the MRD trust rules (because the nonindividual remainder beneficiary is ignored), even though some of the benefits are *guaranteed* to pass to a nonindividual—which is the result the trust rules were supposed to prevent!

Similarly, if the purpose of leaving benefits to a QTIP trust is to preserve the asset for the younger generation, a conduit trust will defeat that purpose, since most of the benefits will be distributed outright to the surviving spouse if she lives long enough. A conduit trust may be fine if the participant just wants to make sure the spouse doesn't spend the entire fund at once. Because the spouse will be considered the "sole beneficiary" of the trust (¶ 1.6.07(A)), the trust can use the special minimum distribution rules available to a surviving spouse who is sole beneficiary (though not the spousal rollover).

B.   **Accumulation O/R-2-NLP trust.** The typical QTIP or credit shelter trust is an accumulation trust, meaning that the remainder beneficiaries "count" for purposes of the all-beneficiaries-must-be-individuals rule and the oldest-beneficiary's-life-expectancy-is-the-ADP rule. See, *e.g.*, PLR 9322005 (marital trust to a spouse for life, remainder to children; spouse *and children* regarded as beneficiaries).

If the trust terminates and passes outright to the participant's then-living issue on the spouse's death, the trust passes the rules as an O/R-2-NLP trust, as long as at least one issue survives the participant. ¶ 6.3.06. The trust can provide whatever the participant wants it to provide regarding disposition of the trust assets if all the issue predecease the spouse. If using this format, it is advisable to name the issue directly as contingent beneficiaries of the retirement plan if the spouse does not survive or to the extent she disclaims her interest in the benefits as trust beneficiary; see ¶ 6.3.02 and Form 3.1, Appendix B.

C.   **Accumulation trust: issues' shares held until certain ages.** If the trust does not pass outright to the participant's issue upon the surviving spouse's death, but rather is to be held in trust for some or all of the issue until they reach certain ages, the trust will not qualify as an O/R-2-NLP trust unless further steps are taken to assure that the benefits must pass outright to younger beneficiaries if all the issue die before reaching the specified ages. The options here are the same as for a minors' trust; see ¶ 6.3.12(C)–(F). Having the trust "convert" to conduit trusts for the young issues' shares will NOT work; see ¶ 6.3.10(A).

D.   **Accumulation circle trust.** Alternatively, provide that the trust terminates at such time during the participant's spouse's life as there are no issue of the donor living and passes outright to the surviving spouse (circle trust; ¶ 6.3.07). The circle trust would be appropriate for a client who is leaving benefits to a credit shelter trust for the spouse only to save estate taxes for his issue, and who would just as soon leave it outright to the spouse if it should happen that all issue predecease the spouse.

If naming any type of trust for the spouse as beneficiary, be sure the client understands the income tax drawbacks of leaving benefits to a trust for the spouse as opposed to outright to the spouse. ¶ 3.3.02. Also, if qualifying for the marital deduction is important, see ¶ 3.3.

6.3.15 Generation-skipping and "dynasty" trusts

The MRD trust rules pose unique challenges whether you are trying to avoid the generation-skipping transfer (GST) tax or take advantage of the GST exemption. For details on the GST tax, see § 2601–§ 2664 and sources in the Bibliography.

A.   **Perpetual or multi-generation trusts.** Leaving retirement benefits to a generation-skipping trust is usually not considered advisable because part of the GST exemption will be "wasted" paying income taxes. However, it is appropriate in some cases, particularly if the client has no other assets suitable for a generation-skipping gift. Leaving the benefits directly to grandchildren outright, or to conduit trusts or O/R-2-NLP trusts for the benefit of "skip persons," poses no particular problems.

Too date, there is no IRS pronouncement either favorable or unfavorable regarding whether a trust that is not to vest in any member of any now-living generation (sometimes called a "dynasty" or "perpetual" trust) can qualify as a see-through. A multi-generation trust for the exclusive benefit of the participant's issue appears to satisfy the IRS's "identifiable" rule, which seems to require nothing beyond the ability to identify the oldest beneficiary. Although it does not seem to quite jibe with the Code's requirement that the benefits be paid out over the life expectancy of "the" designated beneficiary (since no living individual ever has the right to receive the benefits), the IRS's minimum distribution regulations overrule the Code in several respects (¶ 1.2.01, #10) and perhaps this is one of them.

B.   **Leaving benefits to a "GST nonexempt" share.** A common estate planning technique for larger estates is for a parent to leave the amount of his GST exemption to a generation-skipping trust, and the rest of his estate to "GST nonexempt" trusts for his children. Since leaving taxable retirement benefits to the GST-exempt trust wastes GST exemption (see "A"), it is usually considered preferable to leave the benefits to the GST nonexempt shares.

If the benefits are left outright to the children, or to GST nonexempt trusts that are conduit trusts for the children (¶ 6.3.05), there is no problem—the children are recognized as the Designated Beneficiaries. If the benefits are left to an accumulation trust there can be a problem: The GST nonexempt trust is by definition not sheltered by the parent's GST exemption. Therefore to avoid having a GST tax imposed on the trust at the child's death (when the trust passes to the child's issue, who are grandchildren of the original donor) it is common practice to give the child a general power of appointment by Will over the GST nonexempt share. This causes the child to be treated as the "transferor" of the GST nonexempt share for GST tax purposes, so there is no generation-skipping transfer when the share passes to the child's issue at the child's death.

However, a general power of appointment at death requires that the child have the ability to appoint the trust to the child's estate, which is a nonindividual. § 2041(b)(1), ¶ 1.7.04. Thus, if the child has a general power of appointment at death the trust will flunk the MRD trust rules, unless it is a conduit trust. One solution is to give the child the right to withdraw all of the trust principal during life with the consent of a trustee who does not have a substantial adverse interest to the child's exercise of such power, instead of giving the child a general power of appointment at death. This causes the trust to be included in the child's estate under § 2041(a)(2), (b)(1)(C), making the child the transferor for GST tax purposes, without causing the trust to have a nonindividual beneficiary.

6.4 Trust Income Taxes: DNI Meets IRD

This ¶ 6.4 deals with the income tax treatment of retirement benefits that are paid to a trust and includible in the trust's gross income. The discussion here does not apply to a nontaxable distribution from a retirement plan; see ¶ 2.1.06 for a catalogue of no-tax and low-tax retirement plan distributions.

Fiduciary income taxation is an extremely complex topic. The purpose of this discussion is solely to explain how the trust income tax rules apply uniquely to retirement plan distributions. For complete explanation of trust income taxation, see sources in the Bibliography. See ¶ 7.4.01 for income tax considerations in connection with a trust's distributions to charity.

Income taxation of retirement benefits paid to an *estate* is generally the same as the treatment described here for *trusts*: A retirement plan distribution to an estate is IRD and is DNI; see PLR 2002-09026. One exception is in computation of the income tax charitable deduction; see ¶ 7.4.04.

6.4.01 *Income tax on retirement benefits paid to a trust*

When retirement benefits are distributed after the participant's death to a trust that is named as beneficiary of the plan, the distribution is includible in the trust's gross income just as it would have been included in the gross income of an individual beneficiary. ¶ 2.3. However, there are several differences between trust income taxes and individual income taxes. On the bright side, the trust may be able to reduce its tax by passing the income out to the individual trust beneficiaries (¶ 6.4.02); and a trust is not subject to the reduction of itemized deductions under § 68 (¶ 6.4.04).

On the negative side, trusts are generally in a higher income tax bracket than human beneficiaries. A trust (unless its existence as a separate entity is ignored under the "grantor trust rules" of § 671–§ 678; ¶ 6.3.08) or estate is a separate taxpayer and pays tax on its taxable income at the rate prescribed for trusts and estates. A trust or estate goes into the highest tax bracket (35%) for taxable income in excess of $10,050 (2006 rates). For an individual, the top income tax bracket applies only to taxable income above $336,550. § 641(a); § 1; Rev. Proc. 2005-70, 2005-47 I.R.B. 979. Thus, in all but the wealthiest families, income paid to a trust will be taxed at a higher rate than would apply to the individual family members, unless the high trust tax rates can be avoided or mitigated by one of the following means:

A.   **Pass income out to individual beneficiaries.** A trust is entitled to an income tax deduction for distributions it makes from the trust's "distributable net income" (DNI) to individual trust beneficiaries, if various requirements are met. See ¶ 6.4.02.

B.   **Charitable deduction.** A trust is entitled to an income tax deduction for certain distributions it makes to charity. ¶ 7.4.01.

C.   **Transfer the retirement plan to a beneficiary.** A trust can transfer the retirement benefits, intact, to the trust beneficiary. Following such a transfer, distributions will be made directly to (and taxed to) the individual former trust beneficiary. ¶ 6.4.07.

D.   **Grantor trust rules.** If the individual trust beneficiary is a U.S. citizen or resident, and has the unlimited right to take the retirement benefits out of the trust, the trust is considered a "grantor trust" as to that beneficiary, and distributions from the retirement plan to the trust would be taxed at the beneficiary's rate rather than at the trust's rate. ¶ 6.3.08.

E.   **Use the IRD deduction.** If the participant's estate was liable for federal estate taxes, the trust gets an income tax deduction for the estate taxes paid on the retirement benefits. ¶ 6.4.04.

Qualifying as a see-through trust under the minimum distribution rules (¶ 6.2.03) makes no difference to the trust's income tax treatment. See-through trust status matters only for purposes of determining when the trust must take distribution of the benefits; it has no effect on the tax treatment of those distributions once they arrive in the trust's bank account.

6.4.02 *Trust passes out taxable income as part of "DNI"*

A trust gets a unique deduction on its way from "gross income" to "taxable income": The trust can deduct certain distributions it makes to the trust's beneficiaries. § 651, § 661. The beneficiaries then pay the income tax on these distributions. § 652, § 662. This "DNI deduction" is limited to the amount of the trust's **distributable net income** or **DNI**. § 651, § 661.

If the trust's income resulting from retirement plan distributions can be passed out to the individual beneficiaries of the trust as part of DNI, the income tax burden is shifted to the individual beneficiaries, and overall income taxes will be lowered if they are in a lower tax bracket than the trust. Unfortunately, the DNI deduction is not as simple as some practitioners might wish.

First the good news: Retirement plan distributions received by a trust, like other items of "income in respect of a decedent" (IRD; ¶ 2.3) become part of the trust's DNI. See definition of DNI at § 643(a); Reg. § 1.663(c)-5, Example 6. Accordingly, distributions of such IRD are eligible for the DNI deduction when passed out to the trust beneficiary, and are includible in the beneficiary's income. § 661(a); § 662(a)(2); Reg. § 1.662(a)-3. See ¶ 6.4.04 regarding the IRD deduction.

Even though IRD, like capital gain, is a form of gross income that is usually allocated to "principal" for trust accounting purposes (¶ 6.1.02), IRD is not subject to the special rules that limit a trustee's ability to pass out capital gain as part of DNI. IRD goes straight into DNI just as dividends, interest, and other ordinary income items do. In contrast, capital gains are not included in DNI (and accordingly cannot be passed through to the trust beneficiary) unless the governing instrument, state law, or established trustee practice calls for such gain to be allocated to trust income or certain other elaborate tests are met. Reg. § 1.643(a)-3(a), (b).

Now the bad news: The mere fact that a trustee receives a retirement plan distribution and later makes a distribution to a trust beneficiary does *not* automatically mean that the distribution to the beneficiary carries with it the gross income arising from the retirement plan distribution. The trust might still be liable for the income tax on the retirement plan distribution it received. The question is (in trust administration lingo) whether such distribution "carries out DNI."

Here are the six hurdles the trustee must clear in order for the trust's distribution of IRD to carry out the income tax burden to the trust beneficiary as part of DNI:

A.   **Trust must authorize the distribution.** The DNI deduction will not be available unless the beneficiary is entitled to receive the money; thus, obtaining this deduction requires attention at the trust drafting stage. See ¶ 6.4.03.

B.   **Income must be required to be, or must actually be, distributed, in year received.** The DNI deduction is available only for gross income that either is required to be distributed, or is actually distributed, to the individual beneficiary *in the same taxable year it is received by the trust* (or within 65 days after the end of such taxable year, if the trustee elects under § 663(b) to have such distribution treated as made during such taxable year). § 651(a), § 661(a). Thus, in the case of discretionary distributions, the trustee must take action prior to the deadline; if no one considers the problem until it is time to prepare the trust's tax return, it will be too late.

C.   **No DNI deduction for certain pecuniary bequests.** The DNI deduction is not available for distributions in fulfillment of a bequest of a specific sum of money ("straight" pecuniary bequest) unless the governing instrument requires that such distribution is to be paid in more than three instalments (which would be quite unusual). § 663(a)(1), Reg. § 1.663(a)-1.

Thus a trustee's distribution in fulfilment of a typical pecuniary bequest such as "pay $10,000 to my grandchild" will not "carry out DNI" to the grandchild. However, a "formula" pecuniary bequest is *not* considered a bequest of a specific sum of money for this purpose, and so a formula pecuniary bequest *can* "carry out DNI." Reg. § 1.663(a)-1(b)(1). A "formula pecuniary bequest" does not mean any pecuniary amount determined by a formula; it means a bequest of a sum of money determined by a formula where the amount of the bequest cannot be determined as of the date of death. Many marital deduction bequests are of this type. See PLR 2002-10002 for an example of a formula pecuniary bequest to a credit shelter trust.

D.   **No DNI deduction for distribution to charity.** The trust does not get a DNI deduction for a distribution to a charity; instead, such a distribution will be deductible only if it qualifies for a charitable deduction. See ¶ 7.4.01.

E.   **Transfer of the retirement plan does not carry out DNI.** Though a retirement plan *distribution* received by the trust is IRD, and becomes part of DNI just like any other ordinary income, the retirement *plan* itself, which is a "right to receive IRD," is outside the normal DNI rules. Accordingly, transferring the *plan* to the beneficiary does not "carry out DNI." See ¶ 6.4.07–¶ 6.4.08.

F.   Allocation of DNI when separate share rule applies. Finally, if there are two or more beneficiaries, and they have "substantially separate and independent shares," a distribution to one beneficiary will not carry out DNI that is allocated under the "separate share" rule to a different beneficiary. See ¶ 6.4.05–¶ 6.4.06 for how this extremely important rule applies to retirement benefits.

6.4.03 *Trust must authorize the distribution*

The trustee can distribute to the beneficiary only what the trust authorizes the trustee to distribute. This is not an income tax rule; it is part of the law of trusts.

If the trust instrument requires the trustee to distribute to the individual trust beneficiary all retirement plan distributions received by the trust (without regard to whether such plan distributions are considered income or corpus for trust accounting purposes), the DNI resulting from the plan distributions would be carried out and taxable to the beneficiary. § 643(a), § 661(a), § 662(a)(2); Reg. § 1.662(a)-3.

The problem is that often trusts are drafted without adequate thought being given to the income tax consequences of the retirement plan distributions. Trustees often find themselves in the unhappy situation of not being able to pass out retirement plan distributions to the beneficiary because the trust instrument docs not authorize it:

Arthur Example: Arthur leaves his IRA to a credit shelter trust that requires the trustee to pay all income of the trust to Arthur's wife for life, and hold the principal in trust for distribution to Arthur's issue upon his wife's death. The trustee receives a minimum required distribution (MRD) from the IRA. Under the state law applicable to Arthur's trust, 10 percent of the MRD is allocated to trust income and the balance to principal; see ¶ 6.1.02(C). The trustee has no authority to distribute more than 10 percent of the MRD to Arthur's wife; the other 90 percent must be retained in the trust, and will be taxed at trust income tax rates. Even if the trust says the trustee can distribute principal to Arthur's wife "if her income is not sufficient for her support," the trustee cannot give her more than the 10-percent "income" amount unless she actually needs more for her support.

Accordingly, when drafting a trust that may receive retirement benefits, if you want the trust to be permitted to take advantage of the DNI deduction to reduce income taxes on distributions from the retirement plan, the trust instrument must give the trustee discretion to distribute principal (or at least the part of principal that consists of distributions from retirement plans) to the individual beneficiaries. If you want the trust to be *forced* to take advantage of this deduction, see "conduit trusts" at ¶ 6.3.05.

6.4.04 *Trusts and the IRD deduction*

If a retirement plan distribution to the trust is IRD when received, the trust is entitled to the applicable § 691(c) deduction, if any (¶ 2.3.04), unless the IRD is passed out to the trust beneficiary(ies) in the same year it is received, as part of DNI, in which case the deduction also passes to the beneficiaries. Reg. § 1.691(c)-2. A different rule applies to charitable remainder trusts; ¶ 7.5.05(C).

If the IRD is not passed out to the trust beneficiaries as part of DNI, then the IRD and the IRD deduction stay in the trust.

Under § 68, the itemized deductions of a high-income taxpayer may be reduced. ¶ 2.3.07. Since the deduction for federal estate taxes paid on IRD is an itemized deduction, it is adversely affected by § 68. § 68 does not apply to trusts or estates, however, only individuals. This creates an incentive to name a trust or estate as beneficiary of benefits that will need to be cashed out shortly after the participant's death.

6.4.05 *IRD and the separate share rule*

So far we have spoken of the trustee's receiving a retirement plan distribution, including it in the trust's gross income, then paying it out to the trust beneficiary and taking a DNI deduction. This simple pattern becomes more complex if the "separate share rule" of § 663(c) applies. Under this rule, "in the case of a single trust having more than one beneficiary, substantially separate and independent shares of different beneficiaries in the trust shall be treated as separate trusts."

When the separate share rule applies, if a fiduciary distributes money to a beneficiary, that distribution will carry out DNI only to the extent there is DNI that is properly allocable to that particular beneficiary's "separate share."

Separate Accounts Vs. Separate Shares

The separate *share* rule of § 663(c) governs the allocation of DNI among multiple beneficiaries of a trust or estate. Do not confuse this rule with the separate *accounts* rule that dictates when multiple beneficiaries of a retirement plan are treated separately for purposes of the minimum distribution rules. ¶ 1.7.06, ¶ 6.3.02. These are completely different and unrelated rules!

The separate share regulations have the following special rule regarding the allocation of IRD that is "corpus" (principal) for trust accounting purposes: "(3) Income in respect of a decedent. This paragraph (b)(3) governs the allocation of the portion of gross income includible in distributable net income that is income in respect of a decedent within the meaning of section 691(a) and is not...[trust accounting income]. Such gross income is allocated *among the separate shares that could potentially be funded with these amounts....* based on the relative value of each share that could potentially be funded with such amounts." Reg. § 1.663(c)-2(b)(3). Emphasis added.

Here's how the separate share rule would apply to a retirement plan distribution that is corpus for trust accounting purposes:

Jody Example: Jody dies in Year 1, leaving his $1 million 401(k) plan, $1 million of real estate, and $1 million of marketable securities to a trust. At Jody's death, the trust is to be divided into two equal shares, one for each of Jody's children Brad and Angelina, so each child is to receive a total of $1.5 million. Each child's share is to be distributed outright to the child upon attaining the age of 35. Angelina is already age 36; Brad is 33. In Year 1, the 401(k) plan sends the trustee a check for the entire plan balance of $1 million, creating $1 million of gross income to the trust. The trustee immediately distributes the $1 million it received from the 401(k) plan to Angelina in partial fulfillment of her 50 percent share. The trust has no other income, and makes no other distributions, in Year 1. What is the trust's DNI deduction for the distribution to Angelina?

Step 1: Does the separate share rule apply? The separate share rule applies here because distributions to Jody's children are made "in substantially the same manner as if separate trusts had been created" for them. Reg. § 1.663(c)-3(a). If, instead, this had been a "spray" trust, with the trustee having discretion to pay income and/or principal of the entire fund to either child at any time, and not having to give each an equal amount, the separate share rule would not apply.

Step 2: Is the plan distribution corpus? The regulation next requires that we determine whether the 401(k) plan is "corpus" for trust accounting purposes. Assume that it is; see ¶ 6.1.02.

Step 3: Does the trust instrument or state law dictate to which share(s) this plan distribution shall be allocated? If either the trust instrument or state law mandates that the plan distribution be allocated to a particular share, that allocation will be followed for purposes of allocating the resulting DNI among the separate shares. To carry out Step 3, therefore, we must look at the terms of Jody's particular trust and/or state law:

Scenario 1: If Jody's trust *required* the trustee to allocate the 401(k) plan proceeds to Angelina's share, then all the income arising from that plan distribution is allocated to Angelina's "separate share" and the $1 million distribution carries out $1 million of DNI to Angelina. Reg. § 1.663(c)-5, Example 9.

Allocation Respected Despite No Economic Effect

Under the regulation, a trust instrument's allocation of an IRD-corpus item to a particular beneficiary's share is given effect for income tax purposes, even if such allocation has no "economic effect" (i.e., it does not change the amount each beneficiary receives, it affects only the taxability of what each beneficiary receives). In other contexts, the regulations give effect to the allocation of a particular class of income to one beneficiary or another "only to the extent that it has an economic effect independent of the income tax consequences of the allocation." Reg. § 1.652(b)-2(b).

Scenario 2: Alternatively, if Jody's trust requires that each beneficiary receive an equal share of each asset; or if the trust is silent on that topic, but applicable state law requires such pro rata funding of the beneficiaries' shares; the separate share rule will require that the DNI resulting from the retirement plan distribution be allocated equally to Brad's and Angelina's shares.

Thus, under Scenario 2, even though the trust distributed $1 million to Angelina, the trust's income tax deduction is only $500,000, and Angelina includes only that much in her gross income for Year 1. The trust will have taxable income of $500,000 for Year 1. This is the fair result the separate share rule was designed to bring about: No one beneficiary bears a disproportionate share of income tax just because he/she happened to receive more distributions in a particular year.

6.4.06 *IRD, separate shares, and discretionary funding*

Scenario 3: Continuing the Jody Example from ¶ 6.4.05, suppose Jody's trust provides that "The Trustee shall not be obligated to allocate each asset equally to the two shares, but rather may allocate different assets to each child's share, provided that the total amount allocated to each child's share is equal." The trust thus authorizes discretionary pick-and-choose (non-pro rata) funding.

The trustee has exercised its authority to choose which assets to use to fund each beneficiary's share: The trustee, in proper exercise of its discretion, allocated the entire $1 million 401(k) plan distribution to Angelina's share. Does this enable the trustee to deduct the entire distribution as DNI?

Probably not. There are two possible interpretations of the separate share regulation in this situation. The first interpretation, which is apparently the most widely accepted, is that, since the trustee *could* have elected to fund either beneficiary's share of the trust with the IRD, the trustee *must* (in computing its taxable income and DNI) allocate the IRD equally to the two shares. Under this interpretation, discretionary pick-and-choose funding produces the same result as mandatory pro rata funding.

While this is certainly the most obvious interpretation of the words "could potentially be funded," it has a defect, namely, that it overrides a specific provision of the governing instrument. A second possible interpretation would be that, if the fiduciary has, and exercises, a power to allocate the IRD to a particular share, there is no longer an open question of which shares could "potentially be" funded, because one particular share *has* been funded with the IRD, and that is therefore the only share that can "potentially be" funded with the IRD. Under this interpretation, the regulation would not trample on the fiduciary's rights under the instrument. Though the author is fond of this interpretation, she has not found anyone else who shares it.

If the trustee of a trust that (1) is subject to the separate share rule and (2) permits discretionary pick-and-choose funding wants the gross income arising from a retirement plan to be allocated disproportionately, there are two ways to avoid the separate share rule and its apparently-mandatory pro rata allocation of IRD-corpus:

A.   **Transfer the plan itself, rather than a distribution.** In the Jody Example, the trustee could transfer the 401(k) plan itself to Angelina, rather than withdrawing money from the plan and distributing the money to Angelina. Such a transfer generates no gross income at the trust level and accordingly the separate share rule for allocation of DNI never comes into play. The problem of Reg. § 1.663(c)-2(b)(3) is avoided. See ¶ 6.4.07.

This approach was blessed in PLR 2002-34019, in which IRAs were payable to the participant's estate. The residuary beneficiaries of the estate were charities and individuals. The executor (pursuant to power granted in the Will to make disproportionate distributions in kind) distributed cash to the individual beneficiaries in satisfaction of their shares, and proposed to transfer the IRA to the charities in payment of their shares. The IRS ruled that transfer of the IRAs to the charities would not be a taxable assignment of IRD under § 691, or create taxable income to the estate or the individual beneficiaries. PLR 2004-52004 is similar.

B.   **Fund other shares first.** If the trustee wants to allocate a particular IRD-corpus item to one beneficiary's share, the trustee can distribute all the other assets first, fully funding all the other beneficiaries' shares before withdrawing funds from the plan. Then he is left with only one asset, the retirement plan, which he cashes out. This cash can only be used to fund one beneficiary's share because all other beneficiaries have received their shares in full.

6.4.07 *Income tax effect of transferring plan*

See ¶ 6.1.05 regarding the ability of a trust or estate to transfer an inherited IRA or plan to the beneficiaries of the trust or estate. This ¶ 6.4.07 discusses the income tax effects of such a transfer.

The general rule is that the transfer of an inherited retirement plan would trigger immediate realization of the income represented by the retirement plan, because it is the transfer of a right to receive "income in respect of a decedent" (IRD). ¶ 2.3.03. However, this general rule does not apply to a "transfer to a person pursuant to the right of such person to receive such amount by reason of the death of the decedent or by bequest, devise, or inheritance from the decedent." § 691(a)(2). Instead, the transferee is taxable on the IRD as and when it is paid to him or her. § 691(a)(1)(C).

Clothier Example: Clothier's IRA is payable to his estate. Clothier's will leaves his personal effects, automobile, and IRA to his sister Wanda. Clothier's executor transfers the personal effects, automobile, and IRA to Wanda. The transfer to Wanda is not a taxable event. Wanda withdraws money from the IRA. The withdrawal is taxable to Wanda as IRD. § 691(a)(1)(C); Reg. § 1.691(a)-4(b)(2).

This exception applies to the transfer of the right to receive IRD by a terminating trust to the trust beneficiaries; such a transfer does not cause realization of income. Reg. § 1.691(a)-4(b)(3); PLR 9537005 (Ruling 7), PLR 9537011.

The same is true for a transfer of a retirement plan by an estate to the estate's residuary beneficiaries. See PLR 2005-20004, in which the participant died leaving his IRAs and a 401(k) plan to his estate. The executor (who was authorized by the will to make distributions in kind) transferred the IRAs and plan to the estate's residuary beneficiary, a charity, in partial satisfaction of the charity's residuary bequest. This was ruled not to be an income-triggering assignment under § 691(a)(2); accordingly, only the charity realized gross income from the IRAs and plans (when later distributions were received by it). See also PLR 2002-34019 (discussed at ¶ 6.4.06(A)); 2006-188023 (nonqualified annuity transferred to residuary beneficiaries).

If the right-to-receive IRD is distributed as a specific bequest from a trust, or upon termination of the trust, the beneficiary who is entitled to the item, and not the trust, bears the income tax. Reg. § 1.691(a)-2(a)(3), (b), Example 1; § 1.691(a)-4(b)(2), (3).

If the right-to-receive is transferred to the trust beneficiaries under a discretionary power to distribute principal, the beneficiaries pay the income tax; although Reg. § 1.691(a)-4(b)(3) provides only that the beneficiaries pay the tax if a trust *terminates* and distributes the right-to-receive to the beneficiaries, Professor Jeffrey Pennell points out that a discretionary distribution of principal could be considered a partial termination of the trust and thus fit within the regulation cited.

6.4.08 *Funding pecuniary bequest with right-to-receive IRD*

It is axiomatic among estate planners that a distribution of the right-to-receive IRD in fulfillment of a pecuniary bequest triggers immediate realization of income by the estate or other funding entity. Most commentators assume that transferring the right to receive IRD in fulfillment of a pecuniary bequest is exactly the same as fulfilling such a bequest with appreciated property in kind. In view of the universality of this belief, it is surprising to learn that this result is not specified in the Code, or in any regulation or Revenue Ruling, nor has any reported case ever so held.

However, this widely held belief does not spring out of thin air. It derives partly from the regulations under § 691(a)(2). The IRS, in its regulations, does not come right out and say that transferring the right-to-receive IRD in fulfilment of a pecuniary bequest is treated as a nonexempt transfer of the right-to-receive, but implies it. Reg. § 1.691(a)-4(b)(2) says that, if the right-to-receive IRD is transferred to "a *specific* or *residuary* legatee" (emphasis added), only the legatee includes the IRD in income. The negative implication is that fulfilling a *pecuniary* bequest with the right-to-receive IRD does *not* carry out the income tax burden to the legatee. The regulation implies that satisfying a pecuniary bequest with the right-to-receive IRD should be treated as a "sale," just as (under Reg. § 1.661(a)-2(f)) satisfying a pecuniary bequest with appreciated property is treated as a "sale."

Furthermore, the IRS has indicated in some private letter rulings that it considers the "sale" principle of §1.661(a)-2(f) applicable to funding a pecuniary bequest with the right-to-receive IRD. See PLRs 9123036 (using an installment obligation to fund a pecuniary credit shelter gift would trigger realization of gain); and 9315016 and 9507008 (satisfying pecuniary legacies with Series E or H bonds triggers realization by the funding entity of the untaxed interest accruals on the bonds, which were IRD).

IRD, however, is taxed under § 691, not § 661–§ 663. It is taxed only when § 691 says it is taxed. § 691's standards for carrying out the income tax burden to the beneficiaries are not the same as the "DNI" rules of §§ 661–663. Thus, it is quite logical, under the Code, that a pecuniary bequest funded with *IRD* could carry the income tax burden to the beneficiary when funding the same bequest with *appreciated property* would not.

Ron Example: Ron dies, leaving his $1 million IRA payable to his trust as beneficiary. The trust contains a pecuniary formula marital bequest, under which the marital trust is entitled to $400,000. The trust holds no other assets except the IRA. Ron's trustee transfers $400,000 of the IRA to the marital trust and keeps the rest for the residuary credit shelter trust. In this example, the IRA is transferred to the marital trust "by bequest from the decedent." The funding trust is not "selling" or "exchanging" the IRA—it is fulfilling the pecuniary marital bequest, and a transfer in fulfillment of a bequest is not taxable under § 691(a)(2). The trust has no choice regarding which asset to use to fund the marital trust—the IRA is the only asset available.

Although the precise question discussed here has never been decided, the principle that § 691 overrides the § 661–§ 662 scheme is established in other contexts. On the question of whether an estate can take a DNI deduction (¶ 6.4.02) for distributing the right-to-receive IRD, the Tax Court (in holding that the estate can not take such a deduction despite the specific language of § 661(a), which appears to allow deduction) has stated that, "We hold as a general principle that section 691 overrides sections 661 and 662" (*Edward D. Rollert Residuary Trust*, 80 T.C. 619, 648 (1983), aff'd 752 F2d 1128 (6th Cir. 1985)), and "...the transfer by an estate of section 691 property is treated as a neutral event, and is not subject to the distribution rules of section 661 and 662" (*Estate of Jack Dean*, 46 TCM 184 (1983)). As one source put it, "the general distribution rules of subchapter J...do not apply to distributions of rights to [IRD]...[the DNI] scheme is antagonistic to the rules of section 691...Section 691...prevails over the rules relating generally to distributions, and a transfer to a beneficiary of property representing [IRD] is treated as a neutral event." James J. Freeland, *et al.,* "Estate and Trust Distribution of Property in Kind After the Tax Reform Act of 1984," 38 Tax L. Rev. 449, 463 (1985).

Note: *Rollert* and other sources indicating that § 691 overrides § 661–§ 662 are referring only to transfers of the right-to-receive IRD. Once a retirement plan distribution has been received by the trust or estate, it becomes DNI just like any other income. See ¶ 6.4.02.

Letter rulings indicate that the IRS *may* have recognized that transferring retirement benefits in fulfillment of a pecuniary marital bequest is not a § 691(a)(2) transfer. In PLRs 9524020, 9608036, 9623056, and 9808043, an estate or trust transferred an IRA to the participant's surviving spouse in fulfilment of a pecuniary bequest or share, and in each case the IRS permitted a tax-free rollover by the spouse of the portion of the IRA so transferred to her, citing the fact that these amounts were transferred to the surviving spouse "from the decedent," not "from the trust" or estate. In none of these rulings did the IRS say that the transfer of the IRA generated current income to the funding entity, although the IRS did not mention IRD or § 691(a)(2).

A possible explanation, which would make these rulings consistent with the otherwise apparently inconsistent letter rulings (holding that Reg. § 661(a)-2(f) applies to funding a pecuniary bequest with the right-to-receive IRD), *may* be found in the statutory conflict between § 402 and § 408, on the one hand, and § 691(a)(2) on the other. The Code provides that the income represented by qualified plans and IRAs is included in gross income only when it is actually distributed by the plan. See ¶ 2.1.02. These provisions override other normal income tax rules such as the doctrine of constructive receipt. Perhaps they also override § 691(a)(2).

For more on this issue, see Choate, N., "Mysteries of IRD," *Tax Management Memorandum*, Vol. 38, No. 20, p. 235 (Tax Management Inc., Washington, D.C., 9/29/97). See also PLR 1999-25033 in which the IRS ruled that a non-pro rata division of community property, in which a surviving spouse took the decedent's IRA as part of the surviving spouse's share of the community property, did *not* constitute a § 691(a)(2) "assignment," and PLR 2006-08032 (partial interests in IRAs transferred to charities in fulfilment of pecuniary gifts) in which the IRS refused to rule on this issue.

6.5 Putting it All Together

6.5.01 *Trust as beneficiary: Checklist*

When the estate plan calls for naming a trust as beneficiary of retirement benefits, use this checklist to review planning and drafting considerations:

1.   Does the client really need to name a trust as beneficiary, or is there a way to achieve the planning goals without incurring the risks and complications of naming a trust as beneficiary?

In view of the substantial complications and other disadvantages involved in making retirement benefits payable to a trust, the bias is in favor of leaving the benefits outright to the intended beneficiaries unless there is a compelling reason to leave them in trust. The rest of this checklist deals with drafting the trust, once you have determined that you will need to name a trust as beneficiary.

2.   If any trust provisions deal with retirement benefits, you need to define "retirement benefits." See Form 4.7, Appendix B, which uses three different definitions for three different purposes.

3.   If the trust is intended to qualify for the federal estate tax marital deduction, see ¶ 3.3.

4.   If the trust's dispositive terms will distinguish between "income" and "principal," or if the trustee's compensation will be based on specified percentages of income and principal, consider how these terms will apply to the retirement plan and to distributions from it and draft accordingly. ¶ 6.1.02.

5.   If see-through trust status is important, make sure the trust complies with IRS's MRD trust rules. ¶ 6.2–¶ 6.3.

6.   If the trust is to be divided into shares or subtrusts upon the client's death, see ¶ 6.3.01 regarding whether, if benefits may be allocated only to one share, beneficiaries of the other shares are disregarded for MRD purposes, and ¶ 6.3.02 regarding how the "separate accounts" rule applies to trusts. If the benefits are to pass to multiple beneficiaries, and separate accounts treatment is important, leave the benefits to the various beneficiaries directly (i.e., do not leave the benefits to a trust to be divided among the multiple beneficiaries) in the beneficiary designation form. For the same reason, if leaving benefits to a trust for the participant's surviving spouse, and the trust is to pass outright to the participant's issue on the death of the surviving spouse, name the trust as beneficiary only if the participant's spouse survives the participant; name the issue directly as contingent beneficiary if the spouse does not survive. See ¶ 6.3.02 and Form 3.1, Appendix B.

7.   To avoid the issue of whether funding a pecuniary bequest with IRD is a taxable transfer (¶ 6.4.08), avoid having retirement benefits pass through a pecuniary funding formula. If benefits must pass to a trust, make them payable to a trust that will not be divided up. If benefits are going to a trust that will be divided, either specify clearly (in both the beneficiary designation form and the trust instrument) which trust share these retirement benefits go to (so that the benefits pass to the chosen share directly, rather than through the funding formula), or use a fractional formula (fulfillment of which does not trigger immediate realization of IRD) rather than a pecuniary formula (which may).

8.   Including a spendthrift clause poses no MRD issues, even in a conduit trust. Since the Code itself imposes spendthrift restrictions on retirement plans (see § 401(a)(13)), such clauses are favored by government policy.

6.5.02 *Boilerplate provisions for trusts named as beneficiary*

Many practitioners would like to have a blanket trust form that will work for all clients' situations without further fine tuning. This approach can be hazardous when dealing with retirement benefits.

It certainly makes sense, if qualification for see-through trust status is important, to include the "boilerplate" provision either prohibiting the use of the retirement benefits for payments to the estate for debts, expenses, or taxes, or to require that no such payments may be made from the retirement benefits on or after the Beneficiary Finalization Date. See ¶ 6.2.10(A), (C), and Form 4.2, Appendix B.

If there are no assets available to pay debts, expenses and taxes other than retirement benefits, consider specifying that only certain plans may be used for this purpose, so that only the plans authorized to be used to pay the debts and expenses will be "tainted," and the other(s) can be exempted from this problem; or have the participant take withdrawals during life so his estate will have sufficient nonretirement assets to pay these items (and to remove the income tax money from the gross estate for estate tax purposes).

Similarly, include a provision that the trust will be irrevocable at the participant's death (¶ 6.2.06) and that (in determining who are a person's children or issue) adult adoptions occurring after the participant's death will be ignored (¶ 6.2.07). See Forms 4.1, 4.3, Appendix B. Beyond these few limited clauses, however, there is no boilerplate provision that can assure that the trust will qualify as a see-through. Qualification depends on the substantive terms of the trust.

6.5.03 *Advance rulings on see-through trust status*

One expensive and time-consuming way to achieve certainty regarding the see-through status of a trust would be to seek a private letter ruling on this point while the client is still living. The IRS will not rule on "hypothetical" questions, but once the trust is named as the participant's beneficiary, the IRS should be willing to rule on whether the trust complies with the trust rules, as it did for a living taxpayer in PLR 2003-24018. However, the IRS stated that in that PLR that it was "unable" to rule on the Applicable Distribution Period that would apply after the taxpayer's death until after the taxpayer had actually died.

The IRS certainly does not limit rulings to completed transactions; see, *e.g.*, PLR 2002-42044, in which a surviving spouse proposed (as co-trustee of the trust named as beneficiary of participant's IRA) to demand that the IRA be distributed to the trust, and then (as beneficiary of the trust) to withdraw the distribution from the trust and roll it over to her own plan. The IRS granted her requested rulings on these proposed transactions, even though these were just as "hypothetical" as the future death of the taxpayer in PLR 2003-24018.

In this chapter, PLRs are cited as "authority" for various propositions because of the IRS's failure to issue any authoritative guidance. Of course, a PLR cannot be relied upon as authority by anyone other than the taxpayer who obtained it. Furthermore, the fact that the IRS approved a particular trust instrument in a PLR is not equivalent to an IRS endorsement of that form of trust. The firm that obtained the ruling should not attempt to sell the trust form to other taxpayers as, in effect, an IRA-approved prototype document.

However, a PLR can serve as "substantial authority" for a position taken on a tax return for purposes of avoiding a penalty. Reg. § 1.6662-4(d)(3)(iii). Also, a court *might* hold the IRS bound by a position that the IRS has taken consistently in numerous PLRs.

7

Charitable Giving

Charitable giving is a tax-efficient way for the charitably-inclined client to dispose of retirement plan benefits, but is not always easy to implement.

7.1 Charitable Giving with Retirement Benefits

Leaving retirement benefits to charity is an ideal way to fulfill a client's charitable intent. Because the charity is income tax-exempt, it receives the benefits free of income tax. Thus the benefits are worth more to the charity than they are to the client's other beneficiaries. This Chapter explains the pros, cons, and mechanics of donating retirement benefits to charity.

This Chapter discusses charitable gifts of retirement benefits under traditional IRAs, qualified retirement plans, and 403(b) plans. This discussion does not apply to Roth retirement plans (Chapter 5). Distributions from Roth plans are generally income tax-free, so there is no income tax advantage to leaving a Roth plan to charity.

7.1.01 *What practitioners must know*

Estate planning practitioners need to know:

✓ The reasons to leave retirement benefits to charity. ¶ 7.1.02.

✓ The seven ways to leave retirement plan death benefits to charity, and the advantages and pitfalls of each. ¶ 7.2.

✓ Minimum distribution problems that occur when benefits are paid to a charity under a trust that also has individual beneficiaries. ¶ 7.3.

✓ Income tax issues that arise when benefits pass through a trust or estate on their way to the charitable beneficiary. ¶ 7.4.

✓   Which types of charitable entities are suitable to be named as beneficiaries of retirement benefits. ¶ 7.5.

✓   Obstacles and planning opportunities in lifetime charitable giving with retirement benefits. ¶ 7.6.

This Chapter assumes the reader is generally familiar with the tax rules of charitable giving. For more information about charitable giving, see the Bibliography.

7.1.02 *Reasons to leave retirement benefits to charity*

There are three reasons a client should consider leaving his retirement plan benefits to charity.

A.   **To benefit charity.** The main reason to leave retirement benefits (or any other asset) to charity is to help the charitable organization achieve its charitable goals. There is no advantage to giving retirement benefits to charity if the donor does not want to benefit that charity!

This Chapter explains how tax savings can help finance the cost of passing retirement benefits to charity, but the "cost" is never zero. In all the ideas discussed here, a substantial financial benefit is provided to the charity. Unfortunately, some promoters try to take advantage of the tax-exempt status of a charity to reap gains for private individuals. They devise schemes which provide only a token or speculative benefit to the charity, while profiting individuals who have no charitable intent. This Chapter does not discuss that type of "planning idea." The ideas here are for *charitably-minded clients only*.

B.   **Most tax-efficient use of retirement plan dollars.** If a client wishes to leave some of his estate to charity and some to family members or other noncharitable beneficiaries, the most tax-efficient allocation of his assets generally is to fund the charitable gifts with retirement benefits and leave other assets to the noncharitable beneficiaries. Retirement plan assets are *worth more* to the charity than to the family members, while other types of assets are *worth the same* to a charity as to an individual, for the following reason:

Retirement plan distributions to a beneficiary generally are "income in respect of a decedent" (IRD). Unlike other inherited assets, IRD does not get a "stepped up basis" at the donor's death, and accordingly will generally constitute taxable income to the beneficiary when received after the participant's death. See ¶ 2.3. For a family member or other individual beneficiary, the income tax reduces the value of the inherited benefits. A charity is income tax-exempt, and thus does not lose any part of the inherited benefits to income taxes.

Note: Not everyone agrees that family members would necessarily be better off inheriting the nonretirement assets. Some practitioners argue that a "stretch" payout of an inherited IRA over the long life expectancy of a young beneficiary will eventually produce more dollars for that beneficiary than he would have if he merely inherited after-tax assets of the same amount. See ¶ 1.1.03.

C.   **Accomplish other estate planning goals.** Judicious use of charitable giving with retirement benefits can help the client accomplish other estate planning goals at the same time as he fulfills his charitable intentions. See ¶ 7.5.06.

7.1.03 *Charitable pledges (and other debts)*

If the client names a creditor as beneficiary of his retirement benefits, so that the benefits will be used to satisfy the client's debt to that creditor, paying the benefits to the creditor would generate taxable income *to the client's estate*. Although generally retirement benefits are taxed to the person who receives them (¶ 2.1.03), the IRS would say that the estate "received" the IRD, because the estate's debt was canceled when the benefits passed to the creditor.

A charitable pledge that remains unfulfilled at death may, depending on applicable state law, constitute a debt enforceable against the estate. See, *e.g.*, *Robinson v. Nutt*, 185 Mass. 345, 70 N.E. 198 (1904) (unpaid written charitable subscription enforced as a debt against the estate due to charity's reliance), and *King v. Trustees of Boston University*, 420 Mass. 52, 647 N.E. 2d 1196 (1995). However, a charitable pledge is *not* considered a debt for federal income tax purposes. Rev. Rul. 64-240, 1964-2 C.B. 172. Therefore, leaving retirement benefits to a charity, in fulfilment of the decedent's lifetime charitable pledge, will not cause the estate to realize income when the charity collects the benefits, regardless of whether the pledge was enforceable as a debt against the participant's estate.

7.2 Seven Ways to Leave Benefits to Charity

Here are the seven ways retirement benefits can pass, upon the participant's death, to a charitable beneficiary.

7.2.01 Name charity as sole plan beneficiary

The method of leaving retirement plan benefits to charity that involves the fewest difficulties is simply to name the charity directly as the beneficiary of 100 percent of the death benefit payable under the particular retirement plan. Because the benefits are paid directly to the charity under the beneficiary designation form, income tax on the benefits is easily avoided. § 691(a) causes the benefits to be included directly in the income of the charitable recipient as named beneficiary, and the charity's income tax exemption (§ 501(c)) makes the distribution nontaxable. The estate tax charitable deduction (§ 2055(a)) is available for the full value of the charity's interest.

This format works equally well for gifts to multiple charitable beneficiaries: If all beneficiaries of the plan are charities, the problems discussed in the rest of this ¶ 7.2 do not arise.

7.2.02 Leave benefits to charity, others, in fractional shares

A charity can be named as one of several beneficiaries receiving fractional shares of the retirement plan, with other fractional shares passing to noncharitable beneficiaries, as in "I name as beneficiary of my IRA My Favorite Charity and my son Junior in equal shares."

The problem with this approach is that it risks losing the option of a "life expectancy payout" for the noncharitable beneficiary(ies). As explained at ¶ 1.5, a Designated Beneficiary can withdraw inherited retirement benefits in annual instalments over his life expectancy, thus achieving significant income tax deferral. However, this favorable life expectancy or "stretch" payout option is available only to individual beneficiaries; a charity, as a nonindividual, cannot be a Designated Beneficiary. ¶ 1.7.03.

If there are multiple beneficiaries, all of them must be individuals or none of them can use the life expectancy payout method, unless an exception applies. ¶ 1.7.05. Thus, if Junior and the charity are both named as beneficiary, the IRS's "opening bid" is that Junior cannot use the stretch payout method. There are two exceptions to this harsh rule. Because of these exceptions, it is still feasible to name both charities and humans as beneficiaries of the same account (though it may still not be *desirable*; see "C").

A.   **First exception: separate accounts.** If there are multiple beneficiaries, but the respective beneficiaries' interests in the retirement plan constitute "separate accounts," each separate account is treated as a separate retirement plan for purposes of the minimum distribution rules. Thus, the Applicable Distribution Period (ADP) for each individual beneficiary will be his life expectancy, and he can use the life expectancy payout method for his "separate account." He is considered the sole beneficiary of that separate account. ¶ 1.7.06.

The drawback of relying on this exception is that the beneficiaries may not meet the deadline for establishing separate accounts. ¶ 1.7.06(B). If they miss that deadline, the beneficiaries will be limited to taking benefits under whichever no-Designated Beneficiary rule applies; see ¶ 1.5.03(C), ¶ 1.5.04(C).

B.   **Second exception: distribution or disclaimer by Sept. 30.** The other exception is that a beneficiary is "disregarded" (doesn't count as a beneficiary for purposes of determining the ADP) if its interest is entirely distributed (or disclaimed) by September 30 of the year after the year of the participant's death (Beneficiary Finalization Date). See ¶ 1.8. Thus, the charity's share can be paid out immediately after the participant's death, or at any time up to the Beneficiary Finalization Date, and the remaining beneficiaries (assuming they are all individuals) will be entitled to use the life expectancy payout method. As of the magic date there is no nonindividual beneficiary on the account, so the plan complies with the "all-beneficiaries-must-be-individuals" rule.

Frank Example: Frank's beneficiary designation for his $1 million IRA provides that "$10,000 shall be paid to Charity X and the balance shall be paid to my son." If the charity's share is distributed to it in full by the Beneficiary Finalization Date, the son is left as the sole beneficiary. As an individual, the son is a Designated Beneficiary, and MRDs will be determined based on the son's life expectancy.

The drawback of relying on this exception is that time passes quickly and people miss deadlines. If for any reason the charity's interest is not entirely distributed by the deadline, the charity still "counts" as a beneficiary and the individuals would lose out on the life expectancy payout method.

C.   **When to rely (or not rely) on the exceptions.** As explained at "A" and "B," it is possible to name both individuals and charities as co-beneficiaries of one IRA, without necessarily losing the option for the individual beneficiaries to use the life expectancy payout method, because of the two exceptions to the multiple-beneficiaries rule. The next question is whether it is advisable to rely on these exceptions, or to avoid the whole problem by not using this approach.

Relying on the exceptions makes sense in some cases but not in others. If use of the life expectancy payout method would be extremely desirable and advantageous for the individual beneficiaries, it may not be wise to rely on the exceptions. Instead, consider establishing separate IRAs during the participant's life, one payable to the charitable beneficiaries and one payable to the individual beneficiaries, rather than putting both types of beneficiaries on the same account and risking loss of the life expectancy payout method through the beneficiaries' failure to meet the deadlines for establishing separate accounts (or paying out the charities' share).

On the other hand, if establishing separate IRAs prior to death would be disproportionately burdensome compared to the benefits gained thereby, it makes sense to rely on the exceptions.

D.   **If the spouse is the only noncharitable beneficiary.** The concern about multiple beneficiaries does not arise when the only beneficiaries are the participant's spouse and one or more charities, if *the spouse in fact survives the participant*, because the spouse does not need to take an installment payout of the benefits over her life expectancy in order to defer income taxes;

she can simply roll over her share of the benefits to her own retirement plan. ¶ 3.2.

However, even when the spouse is named as the sole noncharitable primary beneficiary, consider the possibility of the spouse's disclaimer (Chapter 4), simultaneous death (¶ 3.1.02), or predeceasing the participant *if* the contingent beneficiary in that case would be another individual, because in that case you are right back in the situation of having both individual and nonindividual beneficiaries.

7.2.03 *Leave pecuniary gift to charity, residue to individuals*

Another way to leave part of the benefits to charity is to name it as beneficiary of a **pecuniary** (fixed-dollar) portion of the account, with the balance (residue) going to individual beneficiaries.

Nora Example: Nora's beneficiary designation for her $1 million IRA reads as follows: "Pay $100,000 to the Topeka Maritime Museum and pay the balance of the account to my daughter Diana."

According to anecdotal evidence, some IRA providers will not accept pecuniary gifts in a beneficiary designation form. Assuming the IRA provider will accept it, the pecuniary gift presents some of the same problems as leaving benefits to charitable and individual beneficiaries in fractional shares, and some additional problems:

A.   **Pecuniary gift may not qualify as a "separate account."** Under one approach to funding a pecuniary gift, the IRA provider would create two shares as of the date of death, one with $100,000 and the other containing the rest of the account's assets. Then both shares would share pro rata in gains and losses occurring after the date of death. This treatment could be required by the beneficiary designation form, or (if the beneficiary designation form does not address this question) this treatment might be required as part of the IRA provider's standard procedures.

On the other hand, the beneficiary designation form, or the IRA provider's documents, might indicate that the charity is to receive a flat $100,000, regardless of what appreciation or depreciation occurs in the

IRA after the date of death. The planner needs to determine what the client's wishes are and spell out the desired result in the beneficiary designation form.

The interpretation of the pecuniary gift will affect not only how much each beneficiary receives, but also what options will be available for preserving the availability of the life expectancy payout option for Diana. If the beneficiary designation creates two separate shares as of the date of death, with the Museum's portion sharing pro rata in gains and losses that occur after Nora's death, then the same options will be available as discussed under ¶ 7.2.02(A) and (B) above (establish separate accounts by 12/31 of the year after the year of Nora's death, or pay out the charity's share to it in full by 9/30 of the year after the year of Nora's death).

If the Museum is to receive a flat $100,000, regardless of any post-death fluctuations in the account value, then the option of establishing separate accounts will not be available. ¶ 1.7.06(A). However, the option of paying out the charity's entire share by 9/30 of the year after the year of Nora's death is available either way. If the Museum receives its full share of the account by that date, the Museum does not count as a beneficiary of the account for minimum required distribution (MRD) purposes, and Diana can use the life expectancy payout method for her share of the IRA.

B.   **Consider separate IRAs for large pecuniary bequests.** For example, Nora might divide her IRA into two separate IRAs while she is still living, one containing something more than $100,000 (perhaps $200,000?) of which the beneficiary is "$100,000 to the Topeka Maritime Museum, residue to Diana," and the other containing the balance of the IRA ($800,000?) payable solely to Diana. That way, she can have her pecuniary bequest to the charity just as she wants it in the smaller IRA. Meanwhile, the bulk of the assets are in a separate IRA payable solely to the individual beneficiary, and *this* IRA is not subject to any risk of losing the life expectancy payout method due to failure to comply with the post-death deadlines.

C.   **Put small pecuniary bequest in will?** If the pecuniary bequest to charity is modest, consider ignoring the usual rule of thumb ("use retirement benefits to fund charitable bequests") and put the charitable bequest in the will. Though it is more tax-advantageous to fund the charitable bequest from the retirement plan, the advantage (if the bequest is very small) may not be worth incurring the risk of jeopardizing the life expectancy payout for the individual beneficiaries.

Richard Example: Richard has a $1 million IRA and many other assets. He wants to leave $10,000 to a charity that cares for abandoned emus, and the rest of his estate to his children. Richard's lawyer suggests that it does not make sense to jeopardize the children's ability to use the life expectancy payout method for their $990,000 share of the IRA by putting this small charitable bequest in the beneficiary designation, nor is it worth creating a separate IRA for this amount. Accordingly, Richard's lawyer recommends putting the bequest into Richard's will, rather than in the beneficiary designation, despite the fact that it would be more tax-efficient to fund it from the IRA.

D.   **Make charity's gift conditional on payment by 9/30?** Richard in the preceding example tells his lawyer that she's too chicken. Richard wants to put the $10,000 charitable bequest in the beneficiary designation form for his $1 million IRA; he is confident his children are sufficiently competent that they would pay out the charity's share before the Beneficiary Finalization Date.

However, just to be on the safe side, he makes the charity's IRA gift *conditional* on the charity's taking its entire $10,000 share of the IRA prior to the Beneficiary Finalization Date. The beneficiary designation form says, "Pay to Charity X the sum of $10,000 before September 30 of the year after the year of my death; and pay the balance (including any portion or all of said $10,000 that Charity X has failed to withdraw from the account by September 30 of the year after the year of my death) to my issue surviving me by right of representation." Thus, he has guaranteed that the life expectancy payout method will be available for his children, because (as of the Beneficiary Finalization Date) they are the only beneficiaries of the IRA (because the charity has either received or forfeited its share).

Now Richard has one more concern: This conditional IRA gift to charity may not entitle his estate to an estate tax charitable deduction. To cover that gap, he puts the following bequest in his Will: "I bequeath to Charity X the sum of $10,000, reduced by any amounts paid to the said Charity from my IRA." Thus, the estate tax deduction is assured, because the charity is guaranteed to receive the $10,000 either from the IRA or from the probate estate. This is a complicated way to deal with the problem, but every method has its drawbacks.

7.2.04 *Formula bequest in beneficiary designation*

Often, the amount a client wants to leave to charity is neither a fixed dollar amount nor a fractional share of the retirement plan, but rather is derived from a formula based on the size of the client's estate and/or adjustments for other amounts passing to the charity.

Corey Example: Corey wants to leave 10 percent of his estate to his church and the balance to his issue. His assets are a $2 million IRA, a home worth $1 million, and other investments worth $3 million. Thus, based on present values, he would expect the church to receive about $600,000. One way to accomplish that goal is to leave the charity 10 percent of the IRA and 10 percent of the rest of the estate. That approach exactly carries out Corey's intent of leaving 10 percent of all his assets to the church. However, that is not the most tax-efficient way to fund the church's share. As explained at ¶ 7.1.02(B), without reducing the amount the church receives, Corey could leave more to his children by funding the church's share entirely from the IRA. His lawyer drafts a beneficiary designation formula leaving the church a fractional share of the IRA equal to 10 percent of Corey's total estate, and leaving the balance of the IRA (if any) to Corey's issue.

The first problem with a formula beneficiary designation is that the typical IRA provider will not accept it. For one thing, the IRA provider does not have the information needed to apply the formula. The IRA provider has no way to determine what assets are in Corey's estate; all it knows is what is in the IRA. Second, the IRA provider typically charges a nominal fee for providing custodial duties, and its services do not include calculating elaborate formula amounts.

Both these problems can be overcome, with some IRA providers, by specifying that the participant's executor or some other fiduciary will provide the formula amount to the IRA provider, and that the IRA provider has no responsibility for verifying that the fiduciary's figures are correct. For example, one IRA provider requires any IRA holder who files a "customized beneficiary designation" to give the provider, along with the beneficiary designation, an authorization that allows the IRA provider to rely on certificates and representations by the participant's executor. If using this approach, make sure that the related trust document or will specifies that this task is part of the duties the fiduciary undertakes by agreeing to be executor or trustee.

7.2.05 *Leave benefits to charity through a trust*

In many cases it is not feasible to name the intended charitable recipient directly as beneficiary of the retirement benefits. The most common reason for this is that some additional actions must be taken, after the client's death, to carry out the charitable gift. For example:

❑   The intended charitable recipient may be a charitable foundation that has not been created yet;

❑   The amount going to various charities may be based on a formula that depends on facts that cannot be determined until after the client's death; or

❑   The client may want the charitable recipients to be selected after his death, with a designation such as "The benefits shall be distributed to such one or more educational institutions located in Indiana as my executor shall select from among those that are exempt from federal income taxes under § 501, and gifts to which qualify for the federal estate tax charitable deduction under § 2055."

In all of these cases, the plan administrator may not be willing to accept a beneficiary designation under which the plan administrator would not be able to tell, at the participant's death, who is entitled to the benefits.

If the only problem is that the actual charitable recipients are to be selected after the participant's death, consider leaving the retirement benefits to a "donor-advised fund" (¶ 7.5.03). The participant should create the fund prior to death, name it as beneficiary, designate who will be responsible for allocating the fund's assets to charities after his death, and provide the allocators with the guidelines they are to follow. Because the donor-advised fund is itself tax-exempt, the problems discussed in the rest of this section do not arise—and the plan administrator is happy because it knows to whom it must make the check payable.

In some situations, however, the benefits may have to be made payable to the participant's estate (or trust) as beneficiary of the retirement plan, with the Will (or trust instrument) specifying that the benefits are to be paid to the not-yet-created (or not-yet-selected) charitable beneficiaries. The executor or trustee is then responsible for carrying out the post-death actions (such as forming the charitable foundation, calculating the formula distributions, or selecting the charities), and the plan administrator can then simply follow the instructions of the executor (or trustee) in distributing the benefits.

Unfortunately, this approach involves substantial additional complexity due to the need to avoid having income tax imposed on the benefits at the estate (or trust) level; see ¶ 7.4.

7.2.06 *Leave benefits to charity through an estate*

When it is not feasible to name a charity directly as beneficiary, there is an advantage to leaving the benefits to the charity through the participant's estate, rather than through a trust. An estate is entitled to an income tax deduction for amounts "set aside" for charity, whereas generally a trust is entitled to an income tax deduction only for amounts "paid" to charity. ¶ 7.4.04(B), (C). Thus, an estate has a slight edge; but otherwise the income tax complications of passing retirement benefits through an estate on their way to the charity are the same as for a trust, and require expert knowledge, both at the drafting and administration stages. See ¶ 7.4.

7.2.07 *Disclaimer-activated gift*

This approach may appeal to a client who would like to encourage his individual beneficiary to be philanthropic. The participant names an individual (such as a son or daughter) as primary beneficiary of the plan, and names a charity as contingent beneficiary, specifying that the charity is to receive any benefits disclaimed by the primary beneficiary. See PLR 2001-49015 for an example of this type of planning. The participant might express a wish (preferably in a separate letter, to avoid the necessity of getting the plan administrator to deal with a nonstandard beneficiary designation form) that the child disclaim all or part of the benefits.

See Chapter 4 regarding disclaimers of retirement benefits.

Why not just leave the benefits to the child, along with a letter expressing the parent's wish that the child give the funds to charity? The disclaimer route is preferable because of the income tax consequences. If the child is the beneficiary of the account and does not disclaim it, the child cannot later assign the benefits to a charity without first paying income tax on them. The child may not be able to eliminate the income tax on the distribution through the charitable deduction. ¶ 7.6.01. In contrast, if the charity receives the benefits as the result of the child's qualified disclaimer, the income associated with the benefits is shifted to the tax-exempt charity. ¶ 4.1.03.

The contingent beneficiary that will receive the benefits upon the primary beneficiary's disclaimer can be any type of charity that is suitable to receive retirement benefits (¶ 7.5.01–¶ 7.5.07), EXCEPT that it CANNOT be:

1.   A charitable remainder trust (¶ 7.5.04) or gift annuity (¶ 7.5.07) of which the disclaimant is an income beneficiary (unless the disclaimant is the participant's surviving spouse), because of the requirement that disclaimed property must pass, as a result of the disclaimer, either to the participant's surviving spouse or to someone other than the disclaimant. See ¶ 4.2.05.

2.   A private foundation (¶ 7.5.02) of which the disclaimant is a trustee or manager having power to choose recipients of the foundation's funds, unless the foundation is legally required to hold the disclaimed assets in a separate fund over which the disclaimant does not have such powers. This is because of the requirement that disclaimed assets must pass "without any direction on the part of" the disclaimant. ¶ 4.2.06.

A disclaimer in favor of a donor-advised fund (DAF; ¶ 7.5.03) does not violate requirement #2, even if the disclaimant is an "advisor" to the DAF, because the advisor merely advises; he cannot "direct" distribution of the DAF's funds. PLR 2005-18012.

7.3 MRDs and Charitable Gifts Under Trusts

7.3.01 *Trust with charitable and human beneficiaries*

Suppose a client wants to name a trust as beneficiary of his retirement plan. His children are intended to be the primary beneficiaries of the trust, but the trust also has one or more charitable beneficiaries. He wants the plan benefits that pass to this trust to be paid out in installments over the life expectancy of his oldest child. To achieve the desired result, the "MRD trust rules" (¶ 6.2) must be complied with. One of these rules is that all trust beneficiaries must be individuals. ¶ 6.2.09. This rule creates two problems in common estate planning situations involving charities.

First, *any* charitable gift that is to be paid from the trust at the participant's death, no matter how small, would cause the trust to flunk this requirement. (The only possible exception to this rule would be if the trustee is forbidden to use the retirement benefits to fund the charitable bequest; see ¶ 6.3.01(D)). Even the normally innocuous statement "this trust shall pay any bequests under my Will, if my estate is not adequate to pay the same," could make the trust "flunk" if the Will contains charitable bequests. However, the problem of such payable-at-death charitable gifts can be cured by distributing the charitable bequests prior to the Beneficiary Finalization Date. ¶ 7.3.02.

The second problem is that, generally, remainder beneficiaries are considered "beneficiaries" for this purpose. ¶ 6.3; PLR 9820021. Thus, if a trust is the beneficiary of the retirement plan, and any part of the remainder interest in the trust passes to charity (or could be appointed to charity under a power of appointment), the trust will flunk (unless the charitable remainder beneficiary can be disregarded under the IRS's MRD trust rules; ¶ 6.3). This is not a problem with a true "charitable remainder trust" (¶ 7.5.04), because such trusts are income tax-exempt. The problem is with a trust that is primarily a family trust but which definitely or even possibly has charitable gifts that will be made after the family members' deaths.

Thus, when drafting a trust that is to make charitable gifts, or that may be used to fund charitable bequests under the will, it is important to determine whether any retirement benefits may be payable to that trust, and, if so, to either:

A.   In the beneficiary designation form and in the trust, make the benefits payable directly to the trust shares that benefit only individuals (¶ 6.3.01(B)), if qualifying for the life expectancy payout is an important goal (¶ 6.2.01); or

B.   Match the retirement benefits to the charitable gifts, if the goal is to have the benefits pass to the charity free of income taxes (¶ 7.4.02). Under this approach you are giving up on using the life expectancy payout method for the benefits.

7.3.02 *If charitable gifts occur at the participant's death*

Russ Example: Russ leaves his $3 million IRA to a trust. The trust provides that, upon Russ's death, the trustee is to pay $10,000 to Russ's favorite charity, and hold the rest of the funds in trust for the life of Russ's wife with remainder to Russ's issue.

The trustee can "eliminate" the charitable beneficiary by paying to the charity its $10,000 bequest before the Beneficiary Finalization Date (¶ 1.8). If the charity is paid in full prior to the Beneficiary Finalization Date, then it is no longer a "beneficiary" of the trust as of the Beneficiary Finalization Date, and (assuming that the one $10,000 bequest to a noncharitable beneficiary was the only defect of the trust under the minimum distribution trust rules) the trust has only individual beneficiaries and qualifies as a "see-through trust." ¶ 6.3.03.

If the trust does not contain a prohibition against paying retirement benefits to charity, and the trustee has authority to pay any asset to any beneficiary, the trustee could choose whether to use the IRA proceeds or other assets to pay the $10,000 bequest. It would make no difference, under the minimum distribution rules, which assets were used, as long as the charity has no further interest in the benefits after the Beneficiary Finalization Date. See ¶ 7.4 regarding income tax treatment of the trust's distribution.

7.3.03 *If charitable gifts occur later*

Heather Example: Heather's trust provides that, upon Heather's death, the trust is divided into equal shares for her four children. Each child receives income for life from his or her share, plus principal in the trustee's discretion for the child's health, education and support. At death, each child can appoint the principal of such child's share among Heather's issue and any charity. If the child fails to exercise this power of appointment, such child's share is paid to such child's issue if any, or otherwise to the other children. Assets coming to this trust at Heather's death include Heather's $2 million IRA and $3 million of other assets. The existence of potential charitable remainder beneficiaries (as appointees under the children's powers of appointment) would mean that, under the multiple beneficiary rule, this trust would flunk the IRS's minimum distribution trust rules. ¶ 6.3. The trust would not be able to use the life expectancy of the oldest child to measure MRDs from the IRA to the trust after Heather's death. It would be stuck with the "no-DB rule." ¶ 1.5.06, ¶ 1.5.08.

Adding a blanket prohibition against paying retirement benefits to charity is not the best way to solve the problem in Heather's trust. For one thing, it is not totally clear that such prohibitions "work" under the MRD trust rules; see ¶ 6.3.01(D).

For another, because the potential charitable gifts do not occur until each child dies, the trustee, in order to carry out a blanket prohibition against using retirement benefits to fund any charitable gift, would have to segregate the IRA (and all distributions from the IRA) from the other assets of the trust immediately upon Heather's death and keep them segregated for the duration of the trust. So instead of administering four trusts (one for each child) the trustee would end up administering eight trusts (one trust for each child's share of the IRA and IRA distributions, which could not be appointed to charity on the child's death, plus a separate trust for each child's share of the non-IRA assets, which *could* be appointed to charity on the child's death). That is the only way the trustee will be able to tell, when the child dies many years from now, which assets can be appointed to charity and which assets cannot be. If the trust instrument or local law does not clearly give the trustee authority to establish two separate trusts for each beneficiary, the trustee might have to go to court to get such authority.

Suppose the trustee sets up the eight separate trust shares. Now Child A needs a discretionary distribution of principal. Does it come out of the retirement assets trust for Child A? or the nonretirement assets trust for Child A? Again, this is a question that must be covered in the trust instrument (or, if it is not, the trustee might have to go to court for authority to pay out of one share or the other).

If there may be charitable remainder interests in a trust that is being created primarily for individual beneficiaries, and the trust may receive retirement benefits, here are the options to consider instead of the "catchall clause" used in Heather's trust:

A.   **Jettison the less important goal.** Determine which is a more important goal to the client, the charitable remainders or the life expectancy payout for the retirement benefits, then give up whichever one is less important. If the charitable gifts are high priority, consider giving up the life expectancy payout. In the Heather Example, if the total value of Heather's retirement plan had been $100,000 out of her total estate of $5 million, she might decide the life expectancy payout was not of significant value, and therefore not bother taking steps to try to preserve it.

B.   **Create separate trusts.** Consider creating separate trusts to receive the retirement benefits and the nonretirement assets. If Heather places high priority on *both* the deferred payout of her $2 million IRA over the life expectancy of her children, *and* on allowing the children to appoint their shares of the other $3 million of assets to charity, she could direct the trustee to establish two separate trusts for each child, one for the child's share of the IRA and one for the child's share of the other assets. The power to appoint to charity would apply only to the trusts that held no retirement benefits. The drawback of this approach is the administrative inconvenience and cost of extra trust bookkeeping.

C.   **Use a Charitable Remainder Trust.** Consider whether an income tax-exempt Charitable Remainder Trust (CRT; ¶ 7.5.04) would be a better choice of beneficiary than the client's "regular" trust.

Hilda Example: Hilda, age 68, has a $3 million IRA. Her goal is to provide a life income to her sister (age 71) and remainder to a charitable foundation. Assuming the income stream from a CRT would fulfill the noncharitable objective, it would make no sense to sacrifice her charitable objectives in order to get a life expectancy payout of the IRA (especially since her sister does not have a multi-decade life expectancy). The CRT would provide far greater tax advantages: no income tax on distribution of the benefits from the IRA to the CRT, and an estate tax deduction for the value of the charitable remainder.

D.   Use a Conduit Trust. Under a Conduit Trust, each time the trust receives any distribution from the retirement plan, the trustee must immediately pass that distribution out to the life beneficiary. See ¶ 6.3.05. For MRD purposes, the remainder beneficiary of a Conduit Trust does not "count" as a beneficiary; thus, having a charity as remainder beneficiary of a Conduit Trust does not violate the rule that "all trust beneficiaries must be individuals." ¶ 6.3.05(B).

Luigi Example: Luigi wants his daughter Lavinia, age 41, to receive a stream of income from his $3 million IRA. A stream of minimum required IRA distributions over her life expectancy would be just right. However, he does not want her to have outright control of the entire IRA after his death. Although a stream of MRD payments from the IRA would not be guaranteed to last for Lavinia's entire life (it would last only until the end of her IRS-defined life expectancy; ¶ 1.5.05), he thinks a stream of MRD payments probably *would* last for her lifetime because she has a below-average life expectancy due to her medical condition. If she does die prematurely, he wants any money left in the IRA goes to the charity that funds research into Lavinia's illness. He could leave the benefits to a Conduit Trust for Lavinia with remainder to the charity. There would be no estate tax charitable deduction (because this is not a Charitable Remainder Trust; ¶ 7.5.04), but, as a Conduit Trust, the trust would be able to use Lavinia's life expectancy as the ADP (because the charitable beneficiary can be disregarded).

7.4 Income Tax Treatment of Charitable Gifts From a Trust or Estate

This ¶ 7.4 discusses whether and how an estate or noncharitable trust can avoid income taxes on retirement plan benefits that are paid to it and used to fund charitable gifts under the instrument.

The following discussion assumes that the fiduciary receives a distribution from the retirement plan and, in the same year, funds a fractional or residuary gift to a "public" charity (¶ 7.5.01) or private foundation (¶ 7.5.02). If the charitable gift is not funded in the same year the distribution is received from the retirement plan, see ¶ 7.4.04. If, instead of taking a distribution from the plan and passing the distributed property out to the charity, the fiduciary assigns the retirement plan itself to the charity, see ¶ 7.4.03. If the bequest is of a pecuniary amount (as opposed to a fractional or residuary bequest), see ¶ 7.4.02, which also covers how the separate share rules apply.

In the rest of this ¶ 7.4, "trust" means a trust that is not income tax-exempt.

7.4.01 *Charitable deduction; no DNI deduction*

The general scheme of income taxation of trusts and estates is explained at ¶ 6.4. As explained at ¶ 6.4.02, a trust generally gets a "DNI deduction" when it distributes income (including gross income resulting from the distribution of funds from a retirement plan to the trust) to the individual trust beneficiaries.

However, there is no DNI deduction allowed for a distribution from an estate or trust to *a charity*. § 651(a)(2), § 663(a)(2). A distribution to a charity from an estate or trust is deductible, if at all, only as a charitable deduction under § 642(c). (Although the Code could be interpreted to mean that a trust can take a DNI deduction for any distributions to charity that do not qualify for the deduction under § 642, the IRS has not interpreted it that way, and the courts have supported the IRS; see *Blattmachr* [Bibliography], § 2:6.1[J].)

§ 642(c) allows an estate or trust "a deduction in computing its taxable income…[for] any amount of the gross income, without limitation, which pursuant to the terms of the governing instrument is, during the taxable year, paid for a" permitted charitable purpose. For meaning of "pursuant to the governing instrument" in this context, see *Zaritsky* [Bibliography], ¶ 4.07.

The charitable deduction for a trust or estate is unlimited, unlike the income tax charitable deduction for individual taxpayers. On the other hand, the gift must be paid out of the trust's gross income (which requires tracing where the gift was paid from); an individual taxpayer does not have to prove that he paid his charitable gifts out of income to qualify for the income tax charitable deduction.

A distribution to a Charitable Remainder Trust (¶ 7.5.04) is *not* eligible for the charitable deduction; it is deductible, if at all, as DNI (¶ 6.4.02). GCM 39707 (3/14/88).

7.4.02 *Which distributions are deductible*

As explained at ¶ 7.4.01, a trust can take a charitable deduction under § 642(c) for a distribution to charity that is paid, pursuant to the governing instrument, out of the trust's gross income.

If the trustee withdraws money from the retirement plan, then turns around and distributes that money to the trust's charitable beneficiaries, how does he know whether the distribution is deductible under § 642? If the distribution to the charity is not made in the same year as the trustee receives the gross income, see ¶ 7.4.04. Here are two other problem situations; for ways to avoid the problems, see ¶ 7.4.03.

A.   **Separate share rules.** The separate share rules of § 663(c) generally tell us when a single trust must be treated as separate trusts for purposes of allocating gross income among the various beneficiaries of the trust, with specific rules for allocation of trust income that is treated a corpus, including retirement benefits. See ¶ 6.4.05.

Even though § 663(c) applies "For the sole purpose of determining the amount of distributable net income in the application of sections 661 and 662," it appears that the separate share rules *also* apply to determine allocation of DNI among the separate shares allocable to charitable as well as noncharitable beneficiaries (even though, after all the allocating is done, there will be no DNI deduction for distributions to charity). See Reg. § 1.663(c)-5, Example 11.

Thus, if the trust is to pass to multiple beneficiaries in fractional shares, and the governing instrument specifies that the retirement benefits are to be used to fund the fractional shares of the charitable beneficiaries, that specification should be sufficient to enable the trustee to deduct amounts withdrawn from the retirement plan and passed out to the charities in the same year received; see ¶ 6.4.05. If the document does NOT specify which beneficiary receives the retirement benefits, see ¶ 7.4.03.

B.   **Pecuniary gifts.** Suppose the trust instrument contains pecuniary charitable gifts and directs that these are to be funded with retirement benefits. In this case it would appear that the *charitable* deduction should be available (because of the specific direction that the gifts be funded out of the gross income arising from the plan distributions), even though there generally is no *DNI* deduction for distributions in fulfilment of noncharitable pecuniary bequests (see ¶ 6.4.02(C)).

Ivan Example: Ivan dies, leaving his $1 million IRA (all distributions from which are includible in the trust's gross income) and $2 million of other assets to his revocable trust. The trust instrument directs the trustee to pay $100,000 to each of three charities and two aunts immediately upon Ivan's death, and to fund these gifts, to the maximum extent possible, from the IRA. The trustee withdraws $500,000 from the IRA and distributes $100,000 to each of the five beneficiaries. There is no DNI deduction for the distributions to the aunts (¶ 6.4.02(C)) or for the distributions to the charities (¶ 7.4.01), but the distributions to the charities may be deductible under § 642.

7.4.03 *Transferring benefits, intact, to the charity*

The trustee of a trust that is named as beneficiary of retirement benefits does not want to get stuck paying income taxes on retirement plan distributions intended for charitable beneficiaries. That situation can arise for various reasons if the trustee cashes out the retirement plan, intending to distribute the proceeds to the charitable beneficiaries of the trust; see ¶ 7.4.02, ¶ 7.4.04. All of these problems can usually be avoided by simply transferring the charity's proper share of the retirement plan to the charity, intact, without first withdrawing from the plan. See ¶ 6.1.05. Then the charity withdraws the funds from the plan, and pays no income tax on the plan distributions because it is tax-exempt. Here are examples of how to use this approach:

If the document requires the trustee to fund pecuniary bequests with retirement benefits (see ¶ 7.4.02), the assignment of a share of the benefits, intact, to the charitable (or other pecuniary) beneficiary in fulfilment of its bequest should be a nontaxable event under § 691(a)(2); see ¶ 6.4.08. This approach would probably not work, however, in the IRS's view, if the document did NOT require those pecuniary bequests to be funded with the benefits.

If the document leaves fractional shares to multiple charitable and noncharitable beneficiaries, but does NOT specify that the charities' shares are to be funded with the benefits, the trustee will run afoul of the separate share rule if he cashes out the plan at a time when the plan distributions could be used to fund shares of either charitable or noncharitable beneficiaries. ¶ 6.4.06. Instead, if:

1.   The trust (or applicable state law) gives the trustee authority to pick and choose which asset will be used to fund the charity's share; and

2.   The trust (or applicable state law) gives the trustee authority to distribute in kind;

the trustee, instead of taking distribution of the retirement benefits, can assign the retirement plan itself to the charity (¶ 6.1.05).

Following the assignment, the charity can take distributions directly from the retirement plan. The distributions do not have to be included in the gross income of the trust because the benefits are never paid to the trust. The assignment itself does not trigger realization of income; ¶ 6.4.07. See PLRs discussed at ¶ 6.4.06(A) for examples of successful use of this technique.

7.4.04 *Estate rules, and delayed distributions*

¶ 7.4.02 dealt with retirement plan distributions that are paid to a trust and distributed by the trustee to the trust beneficiaries, where the plan-to-trust distribution and the trust-to-beneficiary distribution occur *in the same taxable year of the trust.* The exact same rules apply when a retirement plan distribution is paid to an estate and is distributed by the executor to the estate beneficiaries, where the plan-to-estate distribution and the estate-to-beneficiary distribution occur *in the same taxable year of the estate.*

If the plan distribution is received in one year, but nothing is distributed to the charity until a later year, then different rules apply (and the results may differ depending on whether the plan distribution was received by a trust or by an estate):

A.   **Distribution to charity in the next year.** If the amount is distributed to the charity in the year (Year 2) *following* the year the income was received (Year 1), the fiduciary can elect to treat the payment to the charity as if it had been made in Year 1 (and so can deduct it in Year 1). § 642(c)(1). This rule applies to both estates and trusts.

B.   Estate gets a set-aside deduction. If the distribution to the charity does not occur until even later than that, things get tougher. An *estate* can take a charitable deduction for amounts "permanently set aside for" charity as well as for amounts "paid to" charity. § 642(c)(2). Note: There is no set-aside deduction, even for an estate, for amounts set aside for future distribution to a Charitable Remainder Trust. GCM 37076 (3/31/77).

C.   Trust may or may not get set-aside deduction. Trusts, unlike estates, generally *cannot* take a deduction for amounts that are merely "set aside for" charity; a trust generally gets a deduction only for amounts *paid* to charity. There are two exceptions (cases in which a trust does get a set-aside deduction): First, if the trust is treated as part of the estate pursuant to a § 645 election (see Reg. § 1.645-1(e)(2)(i)). Second, if the trust is eligible for a grandfather exception for certain pre-10/9/69 instruments (see § 642(c)(2)). PLR 2004-18040.

7.5 Types of Charitable Entities

The Tax Code recognizes various types of charities and "split-interest" partially-charitable entities, not all of which are income tax-exempt. This ¶ 7.5 explains which charitable entities are and are not suitable to be named as beneficiaries of retirement plan death benefits.

7.5.01 *Suitable: Public charity*

§ 501 provides an income tax exemption for a lengthy list of organizations, including clubs, burial societies, employee benefit plans and, in § 501(c)(3), the type of organization people usually mean when they refer to "charities": "Corporations, and any community chest, fund, or foundation, organized and operated exclusively for religious, charitable, scientific, testing for public safety, literary, or educational purposes, or to foster national or international amateur sports competition (but only if no part of its activities involve [sic] the provision of athletic facilities or equipment), or for the prevention of cruelty to children or animals, no part of the net earnings of which inures to the benefit of any private shareholder or individual," and which does not engage in certain proscribed political activities. The definition is similar, though not identical, for § 2055(a)(2) (estate tax deduction for bequests to charity). These organizations are referred to in this Chapter as "public charities," meaning 501(c)(3) organizations that are not private foundations (¶ 7.5.02).

A public charity is exempt from income tax (except for the tax on "unrelated business income" or "UBTI"; ¶ 8.5). § 501(a), (b). Bequests to public charities qualify for the estate tax deduction, up to the value of such property included in the gross estate. § 2055(a).

Lifetime gifts to such charities are deductible for gift tax purposes (§ 2522(a)). Lifetime gifts to domestic charities qualify for the income tax charitable deduction. § 170(a). Gifts to some charities qualify for a larger deduction (as a percentage of the donor's gross income) than others, but this distinction is irrelevant to at-death gifts.

Making a bequest of retirement plan death benefits directly to a public charity presents the fewest problems. The planner needs to verify that the organization is an exempt organization under § 501(c)(3) and for a major gift the planner should review each of the Code sections under which a deduction will be claimed, to make sure that the organization in question meets the requirements. This is not generally a problem in the case of gift by a U.S. citizen to typical charities.

7.5.02 *Suitable: Private foundation*

In general, a private foundation is a "501(c)(3) organization" (¶ 7.5.01) that is primarily supported by contributions of one donor or family. However, the definition of a private foundation is notoriously convoluted (see § 509), especially since there are several different types and not all are subject to the same restrictions. Untangling the various definitions and subsets of private foundations is beyond the scope of this book.

Certain private foundations, although exempt from "regular" income taxes (except the tax on UBTI; ¶ 8.5), are subject to a two percent excise tax on net investment income. § 4940. The § 4940 tax "is a limited excise tax that applies only to the specific types of income listed in that section. Amounts from retirement accounts are deferred compensation income," not part of "the gross investment income" of a foundation, and therefore are *not* subject to the tax. PLR 9838028; PLR 2000-03055 is similar. These PLRs evidently supercede the prior PLR 9633006, which ruled that a distribution from a Keogh plan to a foundation was subject to the two percent tax to the extent it represented investment income and gains accumulated inside the retirement plan, but not to the extent it represented contributions to the plan by the decedent or his employer—despite the IRS's contrary earlier PLR 9341008, holding that the tax does not apply to any property a foundation receives as a gift, including IRA death benefits. See Timothy W. Mulcahy, CPA (criticizing PLR 9633006), "Is a Bequest of a Retirement Account to a Private Foundation Subject to Excise Tax?," 85 *Journal of Taxation* 2 (August 1996), p. 108.

7.5.03 *Suitable: Donor-advised fund*

A donor-advised fund (DAF) is not one of the types of charitable entity defined in the Code. It is a "public" (501(c)(3)) charity that receives contributions from many individual donors, invests those contributions as separate accounts (one per donor), and distributes the account funds at a later time to "real" charities such as schools, museums, and aid organizations. The donor of the gift (or other individuals appointed by the donor) "advise" the DAF which charities to distribute the funds to. The DAF is not obligated to follow the advisor's suggestions but normally does so.

Originally offered by community foundations, DAFs are now run also by mutual fund families and some more questionable organizations as well. Some problems have led Congress to impose more regulations and penalties on DAF abuses; see § 4966 and § 4977, added by PPA '06. However, most use of DAFs is entirely benign and DAFs are very useful for donors, so hopefully they will continue to exist, and donors will avoid the abusive transactions.

One legitimate use of the DAF is to involve family members (the donor's children, typically) in philanthropy. By leaving assets to a DAF where his children are the advisors, the donor provides a philanthropic role for them. Because a DAF is a § 501(c)(3) charity, funding it with retirement plan death benefits is highly suitable.

7.5.04 *Suitable: Charitable remainder trust*

A Charitable Remainder Trust (CRT), as that term is used in this book, means a charitable remainder trust that meets the requirements of § 664. The general idea of a CRT is that the trust pays out an annual income to one or more noncharitable beneficiaries (such as the donor and/or the donor's spouse or children) either for life or for a term of not more than 20 years. At the end of the life (or term) interest, the remaining trust assets are paid to charity.

A CRT must meet rigid requirements set forth in § 664: The annual payout to the noncharitable beneficiary is specified in the trust instrument and must be either a fixed dollar amount, in which case the trust is a "charitable remainder annuity trust" or CRAT, or a fixed percentage of the annually-determined value of the trust, in which case the trust is a "charitable remainder unitrust" or CRUT. The annual payout rate of a CRUT must be at least 5 percent (but not more than 50%). A CRUT is more flexible than a CRAT because it can provide that the annual payout to the noncharitable beneficiary is the unitrust percentage or the net income of the trust if less, and can even provide for "makeup" distributions to the noncharitable beneficiary if in later years the trust's income exceeds the unitrust percentage. However, neither type of CRT can permit the noncharitable beneficiary to receive anything other than the unitrust or annuity payout amount.

The attraction of leaving retirement plan death benefits to a CRT is that the benefits are paid to the CRT with no income tax. Thus, the client's human beneficiaries can receive a life income from reinvestment of the *entire amount* of the retirement benefit. In contrast, if the individuals inherited the benefits as named beneficiaries under the plan, they would have to pay income taxes on the benefits as those were distributed to them, meaning that (once distribution of the benefits is complete) the amount left over for the beneficiaries to invest is substantially reduced. Thus they could expect a larger annual income from the CRT than they would receive by investing the after-tax value of any retirement benefits distributed to them directly.

Another attraction is that the decedent's estate is entitled to an estate tax charitable deduction for the value of the charitable remainder gift. This value is determined using IRS-prescribed actuarial tables and interest rates, and must be at least 10 percent of the date-of-death value of the trust. § 664(d)(1)(D); § 7520.

This is not to suggest that the client's human beneficiaries will receive more money as life beneficiaries of a CRT than they would receive if they were named directly as beneficiaries of the plan. Normally the opposite is true, because an individual named directly as beneficiary of a retirement plan receives the *entire* benefit, not just the income from the benefit. The income beneficiary of a CRT receives only the income from the reinvested plan proceeds; the proceeds themselves (the principal of the CRT) eventually go to the charity.

Also, the economic advantage of deferral of distributions over the life expectancy of the beneficiary, if the life expectancy payout method is available, reduces the negative effects of the fact that the distributions are taxable income to the beneficiary; see ¶ 1.1.03.

On the other hand, the payout from a CRT may be more attractive than naming the individual beneficiaries directly as beneficiaries of the retirement plan if long-term deferral is not available (for example, if the retirement plan in question does not offer a life expectancy payout; ¶ 1.5.10), especially when the estate tax benefits of the charitable deduction are taken into account.

Caution: When retirement benefits are left to a CRT, the entire value of the benefit is included in the decedent's gross estate for estate tax purposes. The charitable deduction will not shelter the entire value from estate taxes. Rather, only the actuarial value of the charitable remainder is allowed as a charitable deduction. Unless the surviving spouse is the sole noncharitable beneficiary of the CRT (in which case her interest qualifies for the marital deduction; § 2056(b)(8)), the noncharitable beneficiary's interest in the CRT will in effect be subject to estate tax. The question of who is going to pay that tax and with what funds needs to be settled as part of the estate plan.

7.5.05 *Income tax rules for CRTs; IRD deduction*

A CRT generally pays no income tax itself (see ¶ 7.5.04), but:

A.   **Retirement benefits and UBTI.** A CRT that receives unrelated business taxable income (UBTI; ¶ 8.5) loses its income tax exemption for the year of such receipt. § 664(c). PLRs 9237020 and 9253038 involved CRTs that were to be named as beneficiaries of retirement benefits. The IRS ruled that the trusts in question qualified as CRTs (and thus were tax-exempt as long as they did not have UBTI), and that retirement plan death benefits payable to the trusts would be IRD and have the same character as the income would have had if it had been paid to the deceased participant. These rulings thus imply that retirement plan distributions are *not* UBTI.

B.   **The multi-tier CRT accounting system.** A CRT has a unique internal accounting system, under which every dollar that the CRT receives is allocated to one of several "tiers" based on its federal income tax character (such as ordinary income, capital gain, tax-exempt income, or principal). § 664(b).

In effect, the CRT "remembers" what types of income it has received. Then, when the CRT makes a distribution to the human beneficiary, the distribution is deemed to come out of one of these tiers, and the federal income tax character of the amount is revived. If the distribution to the noncharitable beneficiary is deemed to come out of the ordinary income tier, the beneficiary will have to include that distribution in his gross income as ordinary income.

Distributions to the noncharitable beneficiary are assigned to tiers on a "worst-first" basis, so (for example) the noncharitable beneficiary cannot receive any capital gain income from the CRT until the CRT has distributed everything it held in its ordinary income tier.

Some people mistakenly believe that, if they leave a retirement plan to a CRT, the CRT could take a distribution of the entire plan tax-free (correct so far), reinvest the proceeds in municipal bonds (that's ok too), and then pay the tax-exempt municipal bond interest to the noncharitable beneficiary. This maneuver does not work, because the retirement plan distribution (to the extent it is "ordinary income"; see ¶ 2.1.06) all goes into the "ordinary income" tier. Even if the trustee *did* invest the proceeds in municipal bonds, no distribution to the human beneficiary would be treated as coming from the tax-exempt bond interest "tier" until the ordinary income "tier" had been used up.

So, although the CRT pays no income tax when it receives a distribution from a retirement plan, the beneficiary of the CRT will have to pay income tax on the distributions *from* the CRT, to the extent those are deemed to represent the CRT's regurgitation of the retirement plan benefit (or other taxable income) under the tier system.

C.   **CRTs and the IRD deduction.** Generally, when the beneficiary of a retirement plan receives a distribution from the plan, he must include it in his gross income as income in respect of a decedent (IRD), but he is entitled to an income tax deduction for the federal estate taxes that were paid on those benefits. § 691(c); ¶ 2.3.04. If retirement benefits are paid to a Charitable Remainder Trust, that deduction for practical purposes disappears—nobody gets to use it. There is no mechanism by which a CRT can pass out the IRD deduction to the CRT's human beneficiaries.

The § 691(c) deduction reduces the taxable income of the CRT (i.e., income assigned to the trust's "first tier") in the year the distribution is received from the plan. Reg. § 1.664-1(d)(2). Distributions to the individual beneficiary would be deemed to come out of the "net taxable income" of the CRT (first tier) until it had all been used up. The income of the CRT that was sheltered by the 691(c) deduction would become "principal" that could eventually be distributed to the individual beneficiary tax-free as part of the last tier. However, the tax-free principal of the CRT is not deemed distributed until after all net *taxable* income has been distributed. This point would never be reached in most CRTs funded with retirement benefits.

The IRS confirmed this explanation of how § 691(c) applies to a CRT in PLR 1999-01023. Some practitioners disagree with the result in this ruling and argue that the unitrust distributions to the noncharitable beneficiary from the CRT should retain their character as IRD and therefore carry out the IRD deduction to the noncharitable beneficiary along with the taxable income, citing Reg. § 1.691(c)-1(d).

7.5.06 *Solving planning problems with a CRT*

For a client with any charitable inclination, naming a charitable remainder trust as beneficiary of retirement benefits can help solve estate planning problems in addition to satisfying the charitable intent.

A.   **CRT to benefit an older individual.** Naming an older nonspouse individual outright as beneficiary of retirement benefits has the effect of dumping the benefits out of the plan and into the beneficiary's gross income rapidly (over the beneficiary's short life expectancy), so the income taxes get paid up front and the elderly person will have less money available in his later years. In contrast, if the benefits are left to a CRT for the life benefit of that person, he will enjoy a more-or-less steady income from the CRT that will last for his entire life (not run out at the end of some artificial life expectancy from an IRS table).

In addition, the participant's estate will get an estate tax charitable deduction which may free up some other funds that can be given to the same or other beneficiaries. A charitable gift annuity could also be used in this situation; ¶ 7.5.07. The downside is that the individual beneficiary cannot take out more than the pre-set income stream from the CRT (or gift annuity) regardless of need.

B.   CRT to provide life income for multiple adults. Naming a noncharitable trust for multiple adult beneficiaries of varying ages produces a nightmare from the point of view of minimum required distributions (MRDs): Either the trust must use the oldest beneficiary's life expectancy to measure MRDs, or the participant must name multiple separate trusts, one for each beneficiary, which could have the effect of chopping up the assets into too many too-small pots. ¶ 6.2.01, ¶ 6.3.02.

By naming as beneficiary, instead, one CRT that pays a unitrust payout for life to several adult beneficiaries, the participant avoids all MRD problems (because the tax-exempt CRT can cash out the plan benefits immediately upon the participant's death, with no income taxes). The trust produces a more-or-less steady income which can be split among the human beneficiaries. As the older ones die, their income share passes to the younger members of the group, thus providing a crude form of inflation protection. Because the value of the charity's remainder interest (determined actuarially using IRS tables) must exceed 10 percent of the total trust value as of the date of the participant's death, this approach will only work with a small group of adult beneficiaries (*e.g.*, a group of 50-something siblings or friends and 80-something parents). § 664(d(1)(D).

C.   CRT for lump sum distribution-only plan. Many qualified retirement plans offer a lump sum distribution as the only permitted form of death benefit. See ¶ 1.5.10. A CRT is a good choice of beneficiary for a lump sum distribution-only plan. By receiving the lump sum distribution tax-free, then paying a unitrust payout for life to, *e.g.*, the participant's adult children, the CRT approximates the life expectancy payout that is not available under the retirement plan. If the human beneficiaries live a long time, the life payout they receive from the CRT, plus the estate tax charitable deduction the participant's estate gets by having the plan benefits pass to a CRT, may add up to a greater value than the human beneficiaries would have received by being named outright as beneficiaries of a lump sum distribution!

D.   **CRT as a QTIP alternative.** For a charitably inclined participant, leaving retirement benefits to a CRT for the life benefit of his surviving spouse can sidestep the drawbacks and risks involved in leaving such benefits outright to the spouse or to a noncharitable trust for her benefit.

Leaving benefits outright to the spouse has major tax advantages (primarily the spousal rollover, ¶ 3.2), but only if the spouse rolls the benefits over to her own retirement plan after the participant's death, and there is no way to guarantee that she will actually do that. Also, the spouse might blow money left to her outright on expenditures the participant wouldn't approve of, and/or leave what's left of it at her death to a beneficiary the participant wouldn't approve of. If the participant leaves the benefit to a QTIP trust to head off these outcomes, there are major income tax drawbacks (¶ 3.3.02).

In contrast, if benefits are left to a CRT for the spouse's life benefit, the spouse will get an income stream for life, without the drawbacks of leaving benefits to a QTIP trust. There will be no need for the spouse to roll benefits over on the participant's death. The participant can choose the ultimate beneficiary (which has to be a charity of course). If the spouse is the only noncharitable beneficiary (strongly recommended), there will be no estate tax on the benefits either at the participant's death or at the spouse's death (due to the combination of the charitable and marital deductions). § 2056(b)(8).

7.5.07 *Suitable: Charitable gift annuity*

Under a charitable gift annuity, a sum is left to a charity and the charity agrees to pay a fixed income to a human beneficiary for life. This could be a good way to provide an income for an older beneficiary. The participant's estate gets an estate tax deduction for the value of the retirement benefits left to the charity minus the value of the annuity (determined using IRS tables). The benefits are paid to the charity free of income tax. See PLR 2002-30018.

This approach has several advantages compared with the charitable remainder trust (¶ 7.5.06(A)) or a life expectancy payout directly from the retirement plan: The human beneficiary would receive a fixed predictable income (which many beneficiaries prefer to the fluctuating income provided by a charitable remainder unitrust or a life expectancy payout from a retirement plan). There is no need to draft a

CRT. The income is guaranteed to last for the beneficiary's life, not run out at the end of her IRS-defined life expectancy.

For an excellent explanation of charitable gift annuities, including what is known about funding this type of transfer with retirement benefits, see "Charitable Gift Annuities" by William Finestone, 29 *ACTEC Journal* 37 (Vol. 29, No. 1), Summer 2003.

7.5.08 *Usually unsuitable: Charitable lead trust*

A charitable lead trust (CLT) is the mirror image of a charitable remainder trust: A "unitrust" or "annuity" income stream is paid to a charity for a term of years, then the underlying property passes to the donor's individual beneficiaries at the end of the term. § 170(f)(2)(B).

Unlike a CRT, however, the CLT is not exempt from income taxes. Thus a CLT named as beneficiary must pay income tax on the benefits as they are distributed from the retirement plan. Because of this, leaving retirement benefits to a CLT appears generally to be a disadvantageous way to fund such a trust.

Generally, the planning advantage of a CLT funded at death is that, in addition to satisfying the donor's charitable intentions, it may allow funds to pass to the donor's descendants free of gift or estate taxes. This phenomenon occurs if the investment performance of the trust "beats" the IRS's § 7520 rate. When the initial bequest is made to the CLT, the IRS § 7520 tables are used to value the charity's and family's respective interests in the trust. The decedent's estate then pays estate tax on the value of the interest passing to the family. If the trust's investments outperform the § 7520 rate, the amount by which the investments outperform the § 7520 rate eventually passes to the family beneficiaries. Since the IRS rates did not predict that this value would exist, the excess value is never subjected to estate tax.

If the CLT is funded with retirement benefits, however, the CLT will generally start out at a disadvantage, since some of the principal that the IRS assumed the trust would have has been used up paying income taxes. This makes it *less* likely that the trust will "beat" the IRS's § 7520 rate, because in effect the trust starts out with a loss. The client may well end up paying estate tax on *more* than the family beneficiaries eventually receive. The CLT thus appears generally an unattractive choice as beneficiary of retirement benefits, though there could be some unique circumstances in which it would work.

7.5.09 *Unsuitable: Pooled income fund*

With a pooled income fund (§ 642(c)(5)), the donor makes his gift to a fund maintained by the charitable organization that will ultimately receive the gift. The fund invests the gift collectively with gifts from other donors, and pays back to the donor (or to another beneficiary named by the donor) a share of the fund's income corresponding to the relative value of the donor's gift. When the donor (and/or the beneficiary he nominated) dies, the share of the fund attributable to that donor's gift is removed from the fund and transferred to the charitable organization.

The pooled income fund has been called "a poor man's charitable remainder trust," because it provides approximately the same benefits as a CRT (irrevocable gift of remainder interest to charity generates an estate tax charitable deduction, while providing a life income to the donor's human beneficiaries), without the expense of creating and operating a stand-alone CRT. Unlike CRTs, however, pooled income funds are not exempt from income tax. Reg. § 1.642(c)-5(a)(2); compare § 664(c). Therefore, generally retirement plan death benefits paid to a pooled income fund will be subject to income tax in the year received by the fund to the same extent they would be taxable to an individual beneficiary. Accordingly a pooled income fund is not an attractive choice as beneficiary of retirement benefits.

7.6 Lifetime Gifts of Retirement Benefits

This ¶ 7.6 discusses charitable giving options for individuals who have more money in their retirement plans than they need, and would like to give some of the excess to charity. Unfortunately, as of mid-2006, there is no way to move assets *directly* from the retirement plan to the charitable recipient (see ¶ 7.6.07). In order to give plan funds to charity, the donor must first remove the funds from the plan.

7.6.01 *Lifetime gifts from distributions*

A client who has more money in his retirement plan than he needs may wish to give some of it to charity. Generally the only way that can be done under present law is to first withdraw assets from the plan and then give them to charity (see below for temporary exception created by PPA '06). Withdrawing assets from a retirement plan causes the value of the withdrawn property to be included in the recipient's income. (There are exceptions; see ¶ 2.1.06.)

If the recipient then donates the withdrawn assets to charity in the same year that he took the distribution, the income tax charitable deduction *theoretically* should eliminate the tax on the distribution. Unfortunately the following obstacles often prevent the income tax charitable deduction from wiping out the tax cost of the distribution:

A.   **Percent-of-income limit:** The income tax deduction for charitable contributions is limited to a certain percentage (30% or 50%, depending on the type of property given and the type of recipient charity) of the individual's gross income. § 170(b). If the individual's donations exceed the deduction limit, the excess can be carried forward for a limited number of years.

B.   **Deduction-reduction for high-income taxpayers:** Charitable deductions are an itemized deduction, subject to the "reduction of itemized deductions" that applies to high-income taxpayers under § 68; see ¶ 2.3.07.

C.   **Alternative Minimum Tax:** On the bright side, the charitable deduction is deductible for purposes of the "alternative minimum tax" as well as for purposes of the "regular income tax." § 55, § 56. Thus, the charitable contribution will not increase the donor's exposure (if any) to the AMT, except possibly indirectly (if it increases his state income tax relative to his federal tax; see F). Now for more bad news:

D.   **Split-interest gifts are only partially deductible:** If the gift is made to a charitable remainder or lead trust, to a pooled income fund, or in the form of a charitable gift annuity, the amount of the deduction is only part of the total gift (since a portion of the gift is benefitting individuals, not the charity), even though all of the plan distribution was includible in income.

E.   **Penalty for pre-age 59½ distributions:** If the participant is under 59½ at the time of the distribution, there is a 10 percent penalty (¶ 9.1.02) in addition to the regular income tax, unless an exception applies (¶ 9.2, ¶ 9.4, ¶ 7.6.03). The charitable deduction has no effect on this penalty.

F.   State income taxes. Some states do not allow the charitable deduction in computing their income taxes. A donor in such a state must pay state income tax on the distribution.

G.   Nonitemizers. An individual who uses the "standard deduction" rather than itemizing his deductions would see no income tax benefit from the charitable contribution.

Some drawbacks of making a huge charitable gift (A, B, F) can be minimized by using smaller distributions and smaller gifts (see ¶ 7.6.02–¶ 7.6.03). Also, certain forms of distributions (see ¶ 7.6.04–¶ 7.6.06) are not subject to full normal income tax, and so may offer an opportunity for tax-effective charitable giving.

§ 1201 of PPA '06 creates a temporary way to avoid some of these drawbacks. Under new § 408(d)(8), an IRA (*other than* a SEP or SIMPLE) may (in 2006 and 2007 *only*) make a "qualified charitable distribution" (QCD), which is a transfer directly from the IRA to a charity. QCDs may be made only on or after the date "the individual for whose benefit the plan is maintained has attained age 70½." It's not clear if QCDs can come from an inherited IRA if the beneficiary is over 70½ or if the participant died after age 70½.

QCDs can be made to any type of charity *other than* a donor-advised fund (¶ 7.5.03), a supporting organization (§ 509(a)(3)), or certain private foundations. Also, the contribution must one that would normally be 100 percent deductible. This does not refer to the percentage of income limitations (A, above); rather it means that QCDs may not be made to "split interest" entities (such as charitable remainder trusts, pooled income funds, and gift annuities), or in exchange for any consideration (such as a bargain sale).

The attraction is that up to $100,000 of QCDs are excluded from the gross income of the individual "with respect to" whom the QCD is made, for the year in which the distribution is made. Thus, the gift avoids drawbacks A, B, F, and G in the above list. Of course, there is no deduction for the QCD.

The entire QCD comes out of the pre-tax portion of the individuals' aggregated IRAs; this is an exception to the usual "cream-in-the-coffee rule" regarding recovery of IRA basis. See ¶ 2.1.10, ¶ 2.1.11. A QCD should count towards fulfilling the individual's MRD requirement, since it is a distribution and there is nothing that says that it doesn't count; see ¶ 1.2.02.

7.6.02 *Give your MRD to charity*

A retirement plan participant generally must start taking minimum required distributions (MRDs) annually from his IRAs and other plans after age 70½ (or after retirement in some cases). ¶ 1.3.

If the participant does not need his MRDs for other purposes, this would be an appropriate source of charitable gifts. The drawbacks listed at ¶ 7.6.01 still apply, but since he has to take the unneeded MRD anyway, he might as well give it to charity; and in most cases he will receive some income tax benefit through the charitable gift. In 2006 and 2007, the participant should use QCDs for his IRA MRDs to minimize the drawbacks. A pledge to "give my MRDs to charity" would especially make sense for someone who is planning to leave the balance of the account to charity at his death.

A beneficiary who has inherited a retirement plan is also generally required to take annual MRDs from the plan. See ¶ 1.5, ¶ 1.6. If a beneficiary does not need the distributions from an inherited retirement plan, he might consider giving them to charity. Ideally, the participant should have left the benefits directly to charity rather than to a rich beneficiary who does not want them. However, if that did not happen, and the beneficiary is receiving a stream of unneeded MRDs, the beneficiary could reduce his income tax liability by giving the distributions to his favorite charity as he receives them.

If the participant's estate was subject to federal estate taxes, the beneficiary is entitled to an income tax deduction (the so-called "IRD deduction") as he takes distributions from the inherited plan, for the estate taxes attributable to that plan. ¶ 2.3.04. By giving the distribution to charity, he gets both deductions.

This approach is especially appropriate for a younger wealthy donor, who generally cannot take distributions from his *own* retirement plan without paying a 10 percent penalty; the penalty does not apply to distributions from an inherited plan. ¶ 9.4.01.

7.6.03 *Gifts from a pre-age 59½ "SOSEPP"*

As noted, there is a 10 percent "additional tax" that applies to retirement plan distributions taken before reaching age 59½. See Chapter 9. A young individual who wanted to give some of his retirement benefits to charity would be discouraged from doing so by this penalty—unless he can withdraw from the plan without paying the penalty, by qualifying for one of the exceptions. As it happens, one of the penalty exceptions is well suited for fulfilling a pledge of annual gifts to a charity. It is called the "series of substantially equal periodic payments" (SOSEPP). The series must meet extensive IRS requirements; see ¶ 9.2–¶ 9.3.

Cornelia Example: Cornelia, age 52, has $3 million in a rollover IRA. Her net worth outside of the IRA is $10 million, of which more than $9 million is in real estate and closely-held business stock. She has pledged $100,000 a year for 10 years to her favorite charity. She would like to take this money out of her IRA rather than diminish the smaller pool of liquid funds she has outside her retirement plans. Working with her accountant, she determines that an IRA of $1.6 million would support a "SOSEPP" of approximately $100,000 a year for someone her age, based on the IRS-prescribed methods, interest rates, and actuarial assumptions. ¶ 9.2.04. She divides her $3 million IRA into two separate IRAs, one holding $1.6 million and the other $1.4 million. She starts taking annual distributions of $100,000 from the $1.6 million IRA and uses those distributions to fund her charitable pledge.

7.6.04 *Gift of NUA stock*

The Code gives special favorable treatment to distributions of employer securities from a qualified plan. Any growth in value of such securities which has occurred between the time the plan originally acquired the securities and the time of the distribution is called "net unrealized appreciation" (NUA). Under certain circumstances, NUA is not taxed at the time of the distribution; rather, taxation is postponed until the stock is later sold. ¶ 2.5.

A retired employee who holds stock with not-yet-taxed NUA apparently has the same options that other individuals owning appreciated stock have when they wish to diversify their investments and/or increase the income from their portfolios: Either sell the stock, pay the capital gain tax, and reinvest the net proceeds; or, contribute the stock to a Charitable Remainder Trust (¶ 7.5.04) reserving a life income, thus avoiding the capital gain tax and generating an income tax deduction besides. It is advisable to obtain an IRS ruling if using this technique (see ¶ 2.5.04); see PLRs 1999-19039, 2000-38050, and 2002-15032 for examples of use of this technique.

7.6.05 *Gift of other low-tax lump sum distribution*

"NUA" is not the only special tax deal available for qualifying lump sum distributions (LSDs). An LSD to a participant who was born before January 2, 1936 (or to the beneficiaries of such a participant) qualifies for a special tax treatment under which the distribution is excluded from the recipient's gross income and taxed under a separate rate schedule. This schedule would typically produce a lower-than-normal tax on LSDs up to a few hundred thousand dollars. ¶ 2.4.06.

The special tax treatment for LSDs has a mixed effect on charitable giving. The effect may be favorable: Since the LSD is excluded from the recipient's gross income, the recipient may be able to pay the low LSD rate on the distribution, give the distribution to charity, and deduct the gift from his other income, thus saving taxes at his regular income tax rate. Or the effect may be unfavorable: If the distribution is large enough, excluding it from gross income may cause a large charitable gift to exceed the percentage-of-AGI limits on charitable deductions (¶ 7.6.01(A)).

7.6.06 *Give ESOP qualified replacement property to CRT*

The Code allows a business owner, if various requirements are met, to sell stock of his company to an "employee stock ownership plan" (ESOP), then reinvest the proceeds in marketable securities ("qualified replacement property"), without paying income tax on the sale. § 1042. This book does not cover ESOPs. The untaxed gain carries over to the qualified replacement property and the capital gain tax thus deferred will be paid when the taxpayer "disposes of" the qualified replacement property.

A disposition of the qualified replacement property "by gift" does not trigger this recapture provision, but since the Code doesn't define "gift," there is some question whether transferring qualified replacement property to a Charitable Remainder Trust (which is not totally a gift if the donor retains an income interest) is considered a gift for this purpose. PLR 9732023 answered this question favorably to the taxpayer involved in that ruling, concluding that "the contribution of the qualified replacement property to the charitable remainder unitrust will not cause a recapture of the gain deferred by the Taxpayers under section 1042(a)...."

Unfortunately, even aside from the fact that a private letter ruling cannot be relied on as precedent, the language of the ruling is ambiguous and limited. It says: "In the present case, the transfer of the [qualified replacement property] to the charitable remainder unitrust constitutes a disposition of such property with the meaning of section 1042(e) of the Code. However under the facts of the present case, no gain is realized by the Taxpayers on the transfer...," with no indication of *why* no gain is realized. Presumably the rationale is that the transfer is a gift, and therefore excepted from the recognition of gain.

7.6.07 *Lifetime gifts made directly from an IRA*

Charities dream of passage of a "charitable IRA rollover" law that would allow lifetime transfers directly from an IRA to a charity or charitable remainder trust under certain conditions. This would enable the charitably-inclined individual to fund his charitable intentions immediately with IRA funds; he would get no tax deduction, but also would not have to report the IRA distributions as gross income.

Though PPA '06 does allow, temporarily, some limited direct IRA-to-charity transfers (see ¶ 7.6.01 for details), this is a far cry from the law envisioned by charities, under which (if ever enacted) a charitably-inclined participant could transfer his IRA to a charitable remainder trust (CRT; ¶ 7.5.04). The CRT would receive the funds income tax-free, then pay a unitrust or annuity income to the participant for his life, then to his spouse for her life. When both spouses died, the funds would pass to the participant's chosen charity.

The participant and spouse would get a life-long stream of income that would be somewhat steadier than an MRD payout from an IRA (and also would be longer-lasting, if they live into their mid 90s or beyond), and satisfy their charitable intent. *No income or estate taxes would ever be paid on the IRA balance* (though the annual distributions from the CRT would be taxable). The spouses could provide a replacement asset for their descendants by buying life insurance (via gifts to an irrevocable trust) with some of the income stream they received from the CRT. The life insurance also would never be subject to income tax or estate tax.

However, this is still just a pipe dream. Since we don't know when, if ever, the "charitable IRA rollover" will become available, stick with the preceding methods (¶ 7.6.01–¶ 7.6.06) for lifetime gifts of retirement benefits to charity for now.

7.7 Putting it All Together

Here are the planning principles that emerge from the discussion in this Chapter:

1.   If a client wants to make charitable gifts as part of his estate plan, consider using retirement benefits as a tax-efficient way to fund such gifts. ¶ 7.1.02(B).

2.   If part of the client's IRA is to be paid to individuals and part to charity, and use of the "life expectancy payout method" is an important goal for the individual beneficiaries, consider establishing separate IRAs, one payable to the charity and one to the individuals. ¶ 7.2.02(C).

3.   If benefits are left to a trust that has both individual and charitable beneficiaries, determine which is the more important goal, the "life expectancy payout" or the charitable gifts. It may be necessary to sacrifice one goal to achieve the other, or to establish separate trusts to achieve both. ¶ 7.3.03.

4.   If benefits are to be left to a charity through a noncharitable trust or through the client's estate, care must be taken, both at the drafting and the administrative stages, to assure that the trust or estate does not become liable for income taxes on the benefits intended to go to the charity. ¶ 7.4.

5.   Consider leaving retirement benefits to a public charity, a private foundation, a charitable remainder trust, a gift annuity, or a donor-advised fund; generally do not name a charitable lead trust or pooled income fund as beneficiary of a retirement plan. ¶ 7.5.

6.   Consider lifetime gifts to charity using "NUA" stock, ESOP stock, minimum required distributions, or a series of substantially equal payments; and be on the alert for possible eventual passage of the "charitable IRA rollover bill." ¶ 7.6.

8

Investment Insights

Tax and estate planning issues raised by investments held in retirement plans.

Certain retirement plan investments have particular tax and/or estate planning consequences for the participant or beneficiary.

8.1 Investment Issues: In General

8.1.01 *What practitioners must know*

Estate planners need to know:

✓ The tax treatment of IRA litigation winnings, investment losses, and expenses. ¶ 8.1.02–¶ 8.1.04.

✓ The income tax consequences to the participant and beneficiaries of retirement plan-owned life insurance. ¶ 8.2.

✓ The options for disposition of a plan-owned life insurance policy when the participant retires. ¶ 8.3.

✓ The estate tax treatment of plan-owned life insurance, reasons to buy life insurance in a plan, why IRAs cannot invest in life insurance, and planning principles for plan-owned insurance. ¶ 8.4.

✓ How the income tax on "unrelated business taxable income" (UBTI) can apply to an IRA that operates, or owns an interest in, a business, or borrows money. ¶ 8.5.

✓ How the "prohibited transaction" (PT) rules apply to IRAs. ¶ 8.6–¶ 8.7.

8.1.02 *Restoring lawsuit winnings to IRA*

When an IRA owner has a claim against an investment advisor or firm for losses in connection with products or services provided to the IRA, perhaps the lawsuit should be brought by the IRA custodian as plaintiff rather than by the IRA owner. However, apparently, the IRA owner often or always is the named plaintiff. When the IRA owner recovers, he seeks to have the money restored to the IRA; how can this be done without constituting an excess IRA contribution?

In 11 apparently related PLRs, the IRS ruled that the IRA owners' net proceeds from such a lawsuit (which they received in their individual names) could be deposited in their respective IRAs, and these deposits would be treated as tax-free rollovers. Apparently the date the defendant coughed up the money was considered the date of the "distribution" from the IRAs, because the IRS said the owners had 60 days from that date to complete the rollover. PLRs 2004-52043–2004-52046, 2004-52048–2004-52054. The rulings did not discuss the tax treatment of attorneys' fees. PLR 2005-34026 is similar.

The principle of allowing litigation winnings to be contributed to the IRA is similar to the holding in Rev. Rul. 2002-45, 2002-2 I.R.B. 116 (followed in PLR 2006-04039), where the IRS ruled that amounts recovered from a plan fiduciary (representing the damages caused to the plan by its breach of fiduciary duties) can be added to the plan without violating any Code provision.

See also PLR 2005-21034, in which the IRS allowed an IRA owner to replace investment losses in her IRA with cash from her outside funds, using the late-rollover procedure (¶ 2.6.06).

The IRS was not so generous in PLR 2001-51051, in which, due to a financial institution's malfeasance, there was a "shortfall" of assets in the institution's clients' accounts, including IRAs. Under a court-supervised reorganization of the institution's business, each IRA customer was offered the option of replacing the shortfall in his IRA from other funds, with the proviso that (if the shortfall was later recovered from the malfeasant institution) the recovery would be paid directly to the IRA owner. An IRA owner sought a ruling that depositing his personal funds in his IRA to replace the losses caused by the financial institution's malfeasance would not be considered a contribution to the IRA. The IRS said to the contrary, it WOULD be considered a contribution to the IRA and accordingly subject to the penalty for excess IRA contributions. § 4973.

8.1.03 *Investment losses and IRAs*

The good news is that investment gains inside an IRA are not taxed. ¶ 2.1.02. The bad news is that investment losses inside an IRA are not deductible. The only way a traditional IRA loss could *become* deductible is if the account owner cashes out *all* of his traditional IRAs, and the resulting proceeds are less than his basis (¶ 2.1.09). Similarly, to recognize a loss in a Roth IRA, the taxpayer would have to cash out all of his Roth IRAs; if the resulting proceeds are less than his basis (¶ 5.2.03), he has recognized a loss.

A loss resulting from cashing out all of the individual's traditional (or Roth) IRAs is deductible as a miscellaneous itemized deduction, says IRS Publication 590 (2005), p. 38. Miscellaneous itemized deductions are deductible only to the extent the total of such losses for the year exceeds two percent of the individual's adjusted gross income (§ 67(a)), and are subject to the reduction of itemized deductions for high-income taxpayers under § 68(a) (¶ 2.3.07).

8.1.04 *Payment of IRA investment expenses*

If the IRA owner pays, from his own (taxable) funds, investment expenses that are properly attributable to the IRA, does such payment constitute a contribution to the IRA?

The general principle is that ordinary and necessary expenses incurred for the management of the IRA's investments are deductible as business expenses under § 162, and are *not* considered contributions to the IRA if billed separately to the IRA owner and paid by the IRA owner from his outside assets. Rev. Rul. 84-146, 1984-2 C.B. 61. As a miscellaneous itemized deduction, the deduction is subject to § 67 and § 68(a); see ¶ 8.1.03. However, the IRA's brokerage commissions and similar transaction costs are not considered management expenses. If the IRA owner pays the IRA's brokerage commissions from his outside assets, such payment is considered a contribution to the IRA. Rev. Rul. 86-142, 1986-2 C.B. 60.

With a so-called "wrap" investment account, offered by some brokerage firms, the customer does not pay any separate brokerage commissions. The commissions for trades are included in the "wrap" fee, which is a percentage of the assets in the account. In PLR 2005-07021, the IRS ruled that the wrap fees charged to the applicant-firm's IRA clients could be paid by the IRA owners using outside assets, without causing a deemed contribution, because the wrap fee was "calculated as a percentage of the...assets," included an unlimited number of transactions, and did not "vary with the frequency of the transactions performed."

If the IRA itself has already paid the investment manager's fee, the IRA owner cannot *reimburse* the IRA for that expense. There is no longer a debt to the provider of the investment management services. As a voluntary payment to the IRA, the "reimbursement" would be treated simply as an IRA contribution.

Though an individual can pay his IRA's (or Roth IRA's) separately billed investment management expenses from his own (nonretirement) assets, it would not be proper for the individual to cause the investment expenses of his *Roth IRA* to be paid by his *traditional IRA*. The IRS could attack this as a Roth IRA contribution (¶ 8.7.04(C)) and/or a taxable distribution from the traditional IRA.

The IRA's payment of its own expenses (such as an investment management fee) is not a distribution, and accordingly does not count towards fulfilling the minimum required distribution (Chapter 1).

8.2 Plan-Owned Life Insurance: Income Taxes

This ¶ 8.2 explains the *income tax* rules applicable to the plan participant and his beneficiaries when life insurance is held in a qualified retirement plan (QRP). ¶ 8.3 discusses the choices regarding the policy that arise at the participant's retirement. See ¶ 8.4 for the *estate tax* consequences and other planning considerations with respect to plan-owned life insurance.

For life insurance in IRAs or 403(b) plans, see ¶ 8.4.05. For UBTI aspects of a loan on a plan-owned life insurance policy, see ¶ 8.5.04(D). For life insurance and spousal pension rights, see ¶ 3.4.03.

This book discusses plan-owned life insurance only from the perspective of the participant and beneficiaries. Rules that are of concern only at the plan level (such as the limits on how much life insurance may be purchased in a QRP, and ERISA fiduciary investment rules) are beyond the scope of this book. For other sources, see the Bibliography. Similarly, the analysis of insurance products is beyond the scope of this book.

8.2.01 *Income tax consequences to participant: During employment*

When a retirement plan owns a life insurance policy on the participant's life, payable to the participant's beneficiary, the participant must pay income tax, each year, on the portion of the employer's plan contribution (or of the plan earnings) that is deemed to be providing pure life insurance protection for him (as opposed to adding cash value in the policy). Reg. § 1.402(a)-1(a)(3); § 1.72-16. This is an exception to the normal rule that an employee pays no income tax on his employer's contributions to a retirement plan, or on plan earnings, until these are actually distributed to him. ¶ 2.1.02. The participant can avoid the imputed income by paying the cost of the pure insurance protection himself, rather than having it paid by the plan.

In this book, **Current Insurance Cost** means "the amount the participant is required to include in gross income (or pay himself) because of the plan-held life insurance." The Current Insurance Cost is determined, each year the policy is held in the plan, in two steps. The first step is determining the <u>amount of life insurance protection</u>. The second step is to determine the <u>amount applied to purchase</u> such life insurance protection. § 72(m)(3)(B); Reg. § 1.72-16(b).

A.   **How to determine the amount of life insurance deemed provided.** The amount of life insurance protection that the plan is deemed to have purchased for the employee in any year is the amount of the *death benefit* payable under the policy ("at any time during the year"), minus the *cash surrender value* (CSV) of the policy (determined as of the end of the year). Reg. § 1.72-16(b)(3). It is not clear how to determine this amount (which is sometimes called the "net amount at risk" or "pure insurance") if the death benefit changes during the year.

B.   **How to determine the amount applied to purchase the pure insurance.** Once the amount of "pure insurance" is thus determined, the IRS next tells us how much of the employer contribution and plan earnings are deemed to be applied to purchase this life insurance protection. According to Notice 2002-8, 2002-4 I.R.B. 398, the cost of the pure insurance may be determined using Table 2001 (¶ 8.2.02), *or* (if certain conditions are met) may be based on the insurer's actual term insurance rates, if lower (¶ 8.2.03).

8.2.02 *Background: From P.S. 58 to Table 2001*

The rules for determining the Current Insurance Cost have changed over the years.

Originally, Rev. Rul. 55-747, 1955-2 C.B. 228, provided a table, called "P.S. 58," to calculate the amount includible in the participant's gross income. This ruling was later modified by Rev. Ruls. 66-110, 1966-1 C.B. 12, and 67-154, 1967-1 C.B. 11, which expanded Table P.S. 58 and also provided that the insurer's lowest published rate for one-year term insurance available on an initial issue basis for "all standard risks" could be used if that rate was lower than the "P.S. 58 cost." Although the "P.S. 58-or-insurer's-actual-rates-if-lower" regime lasted for several decades, there was a continuing problem: The P.S. 58 table rates were unrealistically high, while some parties were tempted to use alleged "insurer's actual rates" that were unrealistically low, in the sense that the insurer rarely if ever sold one-year term insurance at such rates.

In Notice 2001-10, 2001-5 I.R.B. 459, the IRS revoked Rev. Rul. 55-747, thus killing Table P.S. 58; published a new table, "Table 2001," with considerably lower rates; and announced its intention to issue further rules on this subject, and to prevent abuse of the "insurer's actual rates" alternative.

Notice 2002-8, 2002-4 I.R.B. 398, revoked Notice 2001-10 (except for Table 2001, which was re-issued), and announced that the IRS would issue proposed regulations providing "further guidance" on the tax treatment of insurance held in QRPs. In the meantime, Notice 2002-8 (Part III, 2) provides "interim guidance" on the tax treatment of life insurance held by a QRP, summarized in the next paragraph. Though the IRS has since issued extensive guidance on other aspects of employment-related life insurance (including split-dollar, § 79, § 83, and distribution of policies by QRPs), it has issued no further guidance on how to determine the amount applied to purchase pure insurance in QRP-owned life insurance since Notice 2002-8.

Under Notice 2002-8, for 2002 and later years (unless and until changed by the promised future "guidance"), the amount reportable as the value of the employee's current insurance protection under a plan-owned policy must *either* be determined under Table 2001 *or* (if certain conditions are met) be based on the insurer's actual term rates, if lower.

8.2.03 Using insurer's actual rates instead of Table 2001

Taxpayers may determine the Current Insurance Cost using the insurer's lower published premium rates "that are available to all standard risks for initial issue one-year term insurance" instead of the Table 2001 rates. However, the IRS reserves the right to take away this option, in future regulations, for "arrangements entered into" after the effective date of such future regulations. For arrangements entered into before the effective date of future regulations, the insurer's actual term rates can be used, but only if the following requirements are met:

For any arrangement entered into after January 28, 2002, the IRS (for years after 2003) "will not consider an insurer's published premium rates to be available to all standard risks who apply for term insurance unless (i) the insurer generally makes the availability of such rates known to persons who apply for term insurance coverage...and (ii) the insurer regularly sells term insurance at such rates to individuals who apply for term insurance...through the insurer's normal distribution channels." Thus, post-January 28, 2002, "arrangements" must meet this stricter standard, beginning in 2004, if the parties want to use the insurer's lower term rates. If this standard is not met, the employee will have to report income (or pay a share of the premium himself) based on the Table 2001 rates.

Policies already in place prior to January 29, 2002, will apparently not have to meet this strict standard of proof. However, it is not clear what standard of proof will apply to such policies, since there was no IRS definition of "insurer's one-year term rates" prior to Notice 2002-8. Also, it is not clear whether modifying an existing plan-owned policy, or swapping it for a replacement policy, would be considered entering into a new arrangement.

8.2.04 Term life insurance

The discussion at ¶ 8.2.01–¶ 8.2.03 deals with life insurance policies that have a cash surrender value, such as "whole" or "universal" insurance. A "term" life insurance policy has no cash value; thus, it provides only the "pure insurance protection" that is considered taxable when provided by a QRP.

In the case of group term life insurance, the actual annual premium paid, rather than the Table 2001 cost, is considered the Current Insurance Cost; see Rev. Rul. 54-52, 1954-1 C.B. 150.

It is not clear whether the Notice 2002-8 rules apply to individual *term* life insurance policies, or only to policies that provide something (such as cash value or annuity benefits) in addition to the pure insurance protection. Possibly, the actual premium of a term life policy, rather than the Table 2001 cost, is considered the Current Insurance Cost, as is true for a group policy under Rev. Rul. 54-52.

8.2.05 *Current Insurance Cost: Basis, MRDs, 10% penalty*

Generally, the amount included in the employee's gross income over the years on account of the Current Insurance Cost is considered his "investment in the contract" and in effect becomes his "basis" in the policy. The exception to this rule is that an owner-employee (¶ 10.1.09) does not get to treat even the Current Insurance Cost as an investment in the contract. Reg. § 1.72-16(b)(4).

The employee is entitled to recover this basis income tax-free, but only if the policy itself is distributed to him. If the policy lapses, or is surrendered for its cash value at the plan level, this basis disappears and cannot be offset against other plan distributions. If the policy is sold to the employee (¶ 8.3.04), he may not be able to reduce the price he pays by the amount of his basis, depending on how the bargain sale (¶ 8.3.03) and prohibited transaction (¶ 8.3.05, #2) rules apply to the purchase. Thus, the payment of income taxes (or a share of premiums) over the years generates a basis that may or may not be recouped later. On the other hand, since the Current Insurance Cost is supposed to represent the annual cost of pure insurance protection, it is surprising the IRS allows it to be used as basis at all; it is really an expense.

For what happens to the basis if the policy is sold to the beneficiaries, see ¶ 8.3.06; on the participant's death, see ¶ 8.2.06.

The Current Insurance Cost that the employee must include in his gross income each year is not treated as a distribution to him for purposes of either the 10 percent penalty on premature distributions (¶ 9.1.03(C)) or the minimum distribution rules (¶ 1.2.02(B)).

8.2.06 *Income tax consequences to beneficiaries*

Normally, life insurance proceeds are income tax-free to the policy beneficiaries. § 101(a). However, when proceeds of *plan-owned* life insurance are paid to the beneficiaries, § 72(m)(3)(C) dictates that, to the extent of the policy's cash surrender value (CSV) immediately prior to the participant's death, the distribution is treated as a "retirement plan distribution" (taxable under § 402; ¶ 2.1.02) rather than as a distribution of "life insurance proceeds." Thus, to the extent of the pre-death CSV, life insurance proceeds are treated the same as all other retirement plan distributions, and are subject to income tax when paid out to the beneficiaries. Only the "pure insurance protection" portion of the distribution is tax-exempt under § 101(a).

Despite the fact that the participant might have been taxable on *more* than the CSV if the policy had been distributed to him during life (see ¶ 8.3.02), only the CSV is treated as gross income to the beneficiaries. Also, the beneficiaries are entitled to deduct the amount of the participant's basis in the policy (¶ 8.2.05) from the amount otherwise includible in their gross income. See Reg. § 1.72-16(c)(3), Example 1; Rev. Rul. 63-76, 1963-1 C.B. 23.

8.3 Life Insurance: The "Rollout" at Retirement

If the participant does not die while still employed, he must make some choices regarding the life insurance policy when he retires.

8.3.01 *Options for the policy when the participant retires*

The IRS generally requires that life insurance policies be either converted to cash or distributed to the participant at retirement. This is one of the constellation of plan qualification requirements known as the "incidental death benefits rule," the gist of which is that a retirement plan is supposed to provide retirement benefits, and may provide death benefits only to the extent they are "incidental." See ¶ 1.4.06, and Rev. Rul. 54-51, 1954-1 C.B. 147, as modified by Rev. Ruls. 57-213, 1957-1 C.B. 157, and 60-84, 1960-1 C.B. 159.

Disposing of the plan-owned policy at or before retirement is popularly referred to as the "rollout" of the policy (not to be confused with a "rollover!"). There are three ways the plan can dispose of the policy: distribute it to the participant; surrender it to the insurance company; or sell it to the participant or beneficiary.

If the life insurance policy is <u>distributed</u> to the participant, the policy's fair market value (¶ 8.3.02), less the amount of his basis (¶ 8.2.05), becomes gross income to him. ¶ 2.1.02. He can not roll over the policy to an IRA; an IRA cannot own life insurance. ¶ 8.4.05.

If the policy is <u>surrendered</u> to the insurance company, the plan receives the cash value from the insurance company. The participant could then leave those proceeds in the plan, or roll them over to an IRA, thus continuing tax deferral on the policy's value. However, he would lose the insurance protection provided by the policy. His income tax basis in the policy disappears under this scenario; he cannot apply it to subsequent cash distributions from the plan. ¶ 8.2.05.

<u>Selling</u> the policy to the participant or to the beneficiaries requires the parties to navigate the "transfer for value" (¶ 8.4.02) and "prohibited transaction" (¶ 8.3.05, ¶ 8.3.07) rules.

In contrast, if the employee buys his life insurance *outside* of the plan to begin with, the issues at retirement simply do not arise.

8.3.02 How to determine policy's FMV: Rev. Proc. 2005-25

When a QRP distributes a life insurance policy to the insured participant, the value of the policy (minus the participant's basis, if any; ¶ 8.2.05) is includible in the participant's income. Reg. § 1.402(a)-1(a)(iii). Prior to February 13, 2004, the "value" of a life insurance policy for this purpose was either the policy's cash surrender value (CSV) or in certain cases the policy reserves. See Reg. § 1.402(a)-1(a)(2) (pre-amendment), Notice 89-25, 1989-1 C.B. 662, A-10. For policy distributions after February 12, 2004, the amount includible is the policy's fair market value (FMV). The "policy cash value and all other rights under such contract (including any supplemental agreements thereto and whether or not guaranteed) are included" in determining FMV. Reg. § 1.402(a)-1(a)(1)(iii), as amended 8/29/2005.

Rev. Proc. 2005-25, 2205-17 I.R.B. 962, provides a safe harbor formula for valuing a life insurance policy distributed by a QRP for purposes of Reg. § 1.402(a)-1(a)(1)(iii). There is one version of the formula for nonvariable contracts and one for variable contracts (as defined in § 817(d)). For both types of policies, the safe harbor value is "the greater of A or B."

"A" is the same for both types of contracts: It is the sum of the interpolated terminal reserve (a number which must be obtained from the insurance company) and any unearned premiums, plus a pro rata portion of a reasonable estimate of dividends expected to be paid for that policy year based on company experience. "B" differs depending on the type of policy; it is a formula which can be summarized as "PERC" (<u>P</u>remiums + <u>E</u>arnings - <u>R</u>easonable <u>C</u>harges) times a certain permitted factor for surrender charges. The formulas basically disallow excessive, waivable, or "disappearing" surrender charges as an offset against value.

The "greater of A or B" formula determines the FMV of the policy. Two other items must then be added to the value so determined, to arrive at the full amount includible in the participant's gross income if the policy is distributed to him:

❑   "Dividends held on deposit with respect to an insurance contract," though not included in the FMV of the contract, "are taxable income to the employee...at the time the rights to those dividends are transferred to that individual." Rev. Proc. 2005-25, § 4.01.

❑   If any loan made to the employee "in connection with the performance of services...is terminated upon distribution or transfer of the collateral, the terminated loan or debt amount constitutes an additional distribution to the employee...." Rev. Proc. 2005-25, § 4.02.

Valuation game-playing by some insurance companies necessitated the change in the rules reflected in the August 2005 amendment of Reg. § 1.402(a)-1(a)(1)(iii). The IRS is determined to end such game-playing. Accordingly, the formulas in Rev. Proc. 2005-25 "must be interpreted in a reasonable manner, consistent with the purpose of identifying the fair market value of a contract."

"Furthermore, at no time are these rules to be interpreted in a manner that allows the use of these formulas to understate the fair market value...For example, if the insurance contract has not been in force *for some time*, the value of the contract is best established through the sale of the particular insurance contract by the insurance company (i.e., as the premiums paid for that contract)." Rev. Proc. 2005-25, § 3.05 (emphasis added). How long is "some time?" It is not defined. In other words, the sum of premiums paid since date of issue is the only REALLY safe harbor. This IRS "fudge factor" makes these formulas just "semi-safe harbors."

Rev. Proc. 2005-25 supersedes Rev. Proc. 2004-16, 2004-10 I.R.B. 559; however, the safe harbor valuation method in Rev. Proc. 2004-16 can still be used to value contracts distributed between

February 13, 2004, and May 1, 2005. The Rev. Proc. 2005-25 safe harbor may also be used for policy distributions before May 1, 2005.

On the bright side, the IRS does not require that the participant's actual health be taken into account in valuing the policy.

Taxpayers are not required to use the valuation formula of Rev. Proc. 2005-25; that formula is just a safe harbor. Another approach, not discussed by the IRS, would be to get an appraisal of the policy from an independent company that is in the business of evaluating insurance policies, if such a company can be found.

8.3.03 Tax code effects of sale below market value

The final version of Reg. § 1.402(a)-1(a)(1)(iii) provides that, for transfers on or after August 29, 2005, where a QRP "transfers property to a plan participant or beneficiary in exchange for consideration and where the fair market value of the property transferred exceeds the value of the consideration" the excess value "is treated as a *distribution to the distributee* under the plan for all purposes under the Internal Revenue Code." Emphasis added.

For the implications of this new rule regarding bargain sales, see ¶ 8.3.04 (sale to the participant) or ¶ 8.3.06 (sale to a beneficiary). For how to determine FMV of an insurance policy see ¶ 8.3.02.

Although the excess policy value distributed through a bargain sale is treated as a distribution for all purposes of the Code, the regulation does *not* say that the plan-owned policy must be valued at FMV "for all purposes of the Code." Thus, for gift tax purposes, Reg. § 25.2512-6(a), which provides that life insurance policies are generally valued at "interpolated terminal reserve, plus unearned premium," is still controlling.

8.3.04 Plan sells the policy to the participant

If the policy is distributed to the participant, then all opportunity to defer income taxes on the amount represented by the policy value is lost. For this reason, the participant may decide to purchase the policy from the plan. Although this requires the participant to come up with some cash, it does allow him to continue deferring income tax on the amount represented by the policy value. Following the purchase, the participant will own the policy, which he can transfer to an irrevocable trust if he wants to remove the proceeds

406 Life and Death Planning for Retirement Benefits

from his gross estate; and the plan will own cash, which can then be distributed to the participant and rolled over to an IRA for maximum continued deferral.

Sale of the policy to the participant creates a prohibited transaction issue. See ¶ 8.3.05.

Sale of the policy to the participant is considered to be partly a "distribution" to him if the consideration he pays to the plan is less than fair market value; see ¶ 8.3.03. Such a deemed distribution has two Code consequences. First, the excess value is gross income to the participant. However, if the participant has basis in the policy equal to the amount of the "bargain element," there will be no gross income generated by the transaction. See ¶ 8.2.05.

Second, the bargain sale could be a plan qualification issue if the plan is prohibited from making a distribution to the participant at the applicable time. For example, a 401(k) plan is not allowed to distribute to the employee prior to severance from employment or certain other events. § 401(k)(2)(B)(i). Pension plans have similar restrictions on pre-retirement distributions. Reg. § 1.401-1(b)(1)(i). Thus, if the plan is not allowed to make a distribution to the participant at the applicable time, the participant will have to pay the plan the full fair market value of the policy, and not reduce the purchase price by the amount of his basis, to avoid a plan-disqualifying distribution.

8.3.05 Sale to participant: Prohibited transaction issue

Buying the policy from the plan may create a prohibited transaction (PT) problem. ERISA § 406(a), 29 U.S.C.§ 1106(a), prohibits the sale of plan assets to a "party in interest." The definition of "parties in interest" includes categories one would expect, such as plan fiduciaries, the employer, and officers, directors, and 10 percent owners of the employer. It also includes, surprisingly, any *employee* of the employer. ERISA § 3(14), 29 U.S.C. § 1002(14). Thus, as an initial proposition, the sale of a life insurance policy from the plan to the insured employee is a PT.

IRC § 4975 has its own set of PT rules, prohibiting sales between a plan and a "disqualified person" (DQP; see ¶ 8.6). An employee of the employer is not *per se* a DQP under § 4975; however, if the insured participant has more relationships with the employer than merely being an employee (for example, if the participant *is* "the employer," or directly or indirectly owns more than 50 percent of the employer, or is an officer of the employer), then the plan's sale to him of an insurance contract would be a PT under IRC § 4975 as well as under ERISA § 406.

The Department of Labor (DOL) has issued a class Prohibited Transaction Exemption (PTE; ¶ 8.6.09) which exempts such sales if certain requirements are met. PTE 1992-6, 2/12/92, 57 FR 5190; amended 9/3/02, 67 FR 56,313. The PTE exempts the transaction from both IRC § 4975 and ERISA § 406. Thus, if the desired approach is to have the participant buy the policy from the plan, the transaction must comply with PTE 1992-6 if the participant is a party-in-interest.

To comply with PTE 1992-6 when the *insured participant* is buying the policy from the plan, the following two requirements must be met. If the purchaser is someone *other than* the participant-insured, there are additional requirements; see ¶ 8.3.07.

1. The contract would, but for the sale, be surrendered by the plan. PTE 92-6, II(c). This requirement is not a problem, if the participant is retiring, for the type of QRP that is *required* to sell or surrender the policy at that point (¶ 8.3.01).

2. The price must be "at least equal to the amount necessary to put the plan in the same cash position as it would have been [sic] had it retained the contract, surrendered it, and made any distribution owing to the participant on [sic] his vested interest under the plan." PTE 92-6, II(e). This requirement does not permit any price reduction for the participant's basis (¶ 8.2.05).

Prior to the 2005 IRS policy-valuation rule changes (¶ 8.3.02), it was most common for these sales to take place at CSV. The participant can still pay just the CSV as far as the DOL is concerned. However, if the price he pays is less than the FMV, he will have to deal with the tax Code consequences described at ¶ 8.3.04.

8.3.06 *Plan sells policy to the beneficiary(ies)*

Sometimes, instead of selling the policy to the participant, the rollout is accomplished by having the plan sell the policy to the beneficiaries. This is usually done for estate tax-planning reasons, to avoid the "three-year rule" (¶ 8.4.02). As with the sale of the policy to the participant, this raises both tax and PT issues.

For tax purposes, if the policy is sold to the beneficiary at its FMV (¶ 8.3.02) there is no income tax consequence; note, however, that the FMV standard allows no reduction of the purchase price to reflect the participant's basis (¶ 8.2.05).

If the price paid by the beneficiary is less than the FMV, Reg. § 1.402(a)-1(a)(1)(iii) provides that the bargain element will be includible in the gross income *of the beneficiary who buys the policy.* This treatment seems questionable. The plan account belongs to the participant, who is the only person entitled to receive distributions during his lifetime. See *Bunney,* ¶ 2.1.05. A bargain sale from his account to his beneficiary can only occur with his consent. ¶ 8.3.07, #3. Thus, such a bargain sale would more properly be treated as a distribution of the bargain element *to the participant,* followed by a gift of the bargain element to the beneficiary.

A more serious problem with a QRP's distributing part of the participant's benefits, while the participant is still alive, to *someone other than the participant* is disqualification of the plan, since this would be a violation of the terms of the plan.

Because of the risks associated with sale of an insurance policy to the participant's beneficiaries caused by the final version of Reg. § 1.402(a)-1(a)(1)(iii), it may be better to avoid this approach. Instead, have the plan sell or distribute the policy to the participant. Once the participant has the policy (either because he bought it from the plan or because he took it as a distribution from the plan), the participant can sell it to the beneficiary to avoid estate tax inclusion (but see ¶ 8.4.02). Reg. § 1.402(a)-1(a)(1)(iii) would not apply to a sale by the insured to the beneficiary; it applies only to sales by a QRP. There would be no income tax consequences; the valuation concerns would be solely for gift and estate tax purposes.

8.3.07 *Sale to beneficiary: Prohibited transaction aspects*

The DOL's class exemption PTE 1992-6 exempts the sale of a life insurance policy by the plan from various PT rules if certain requirements are met. The requirements that must be met if the purchaser of the policy is the participant-insured himself are described at ¶ 8.3.05. If the sale is to someone *other than* the participant, and would be a PT if not exempted, the following three *additional* requirements must be met:

1.   The buyer is a "relative" of the insured participant, or a "trust established by or for the benefit of" the insured participant or a relative. PTE 92-6, I(a), I(b).

2.   The buyer is the beneficiary of the policy. PTE 92-6, II(b).

3.   The participant is "first informed of the proposed sale and is given the opportunity to purchase such contract from the plan, and delivers a written document to the plan stating that he or she elects not to purchase the policy and consents to the sale by the plan of such policy to such" relative or trust. PTE 92-6, II(d).

        "Relative" for purposes of the exemption means either a relative as defined in § 3(15) of ERISA, 29 U.S.C. § 1002(15), and IRC § 4975(e)(6) (spouse, ancestor, lineal descendant, or spouse of a lineal descendant), *or* a sibling or a spouse of a sibling. PTE 92-6, II(b).
        Note that the PTE's definition of permitted buyers does not mention partnerships. If the strategy is for the plan to sell the policy to a partnership, the plan's ERISA counsel must determine whether the transaction is a PT and, if it is, seek a DOL exemption. ¶ 8.6.10.

8.4 Plan-Owned Life Insurance: Other Aspects

        This ¶ 8.4 explains the estate tax aspects of holding life insurance in a retirement plan, planning principles regarding such insurance, and the rules regarding IRAs and life insurance.

8.4.01 *Estate tax avoidance: The life insurance subtrust*

        For the estate tax-conscious client, an important consideration in buying life insurance is to keep the insurance proceeds out of the insured's estate (and the estate of his spouse, if any), to increase the value of the benefits for subsequent beneficiaries (typically the client's children). If the policy is purchased *outside* the retirement plan, it is easy to accomplish this goal: The client creates an irrevocable trust for the benefit of his intended beneficiaries; and the trust buys the policy. The policy proceeds are never part of either spouse's estate. If the policy is bought through a retirement plan, in contrast, it is doubtful whether the proceeds can be kept out of the estate of the participant.

Generally, the estate tax treatment of retirement plan benefits is governed by § 2039. However, § 2042 governs the estate tax treatment of life insurance, even if the insurance is held inside a retirement plan. § 2039(a). Life insurance is subject to estate tax if it is payable to the insured's estate, or if the insured owns any "incident of ownership." § 2042. To keep plan-held life insurance out of the participant's estate, therefore, it is necessary to deprive the participant of such "incidents of ownership" as a five percent or more reversionary interest in the policy and the powers to name the beneficiary of the policy or surrender or borrow against the policy. § 2042(2); Reg. § 20.2042-1(c)(2).

Some practitioners believe this goal can be accomplished by establishing a "subtrust," defined as "an irrevocable life insurance trust slotted within the trust otherwise used to fund the pension or profit sharing plan" (from "The Qualified Plan as an Estate Planning Tool," by Andrew J. Fair, Esq., published by Guardian Life Insurance Company of America, New York, NY, 1995, Pub. No. 2449).

The merits of the subtrust have been debated in numerous publications. See Zaritsky, H., and Leimberg, S.R., *Tax Planning with Life Insurance* (see Bibliography), sections 6.08[2][f] and 6.08[4][b], and articles cited in the Bibliography. Some authors conclude that the subtrust works to keep policy proceeds out of the estate, without disqualifying the underlying retirement plan. Others argue that either the existence of the subtrust disqualifies the plan, or, if the plan *is* qualified, it is impossible for the participant not to have estate-taxable incidents of ownership in the policy. To date, there is no ruling or case either upholding or denying estate tax exclusion for life insurance held in a retirement plan subtrust. Thus, use of this device must be considered risky; if the subtrust does not work, a substantial portion of the policy proceeds could be lost to estate taxes.

The bottom line: If estate tax avoidance is important to the client, buy the life insurance outside of the retirement plan. If the insurance must be bought inside the plan, or is already inside the plan, consider using the subtrust technique, which may work to keep the proceeds out of the gross estate.

Even if the subtrust device does keep the death benefit out of the estate if the participant dies prior to retirement, new problems arise once the participant reaches retirement. If he then either buys the policy out of the plan or receives it as a distribution the participant is right back in the position of owning the policy.

8.4.02 *Avoiding estate tax inclusion and "transfer for value"*

As discussed at ¶ 8.3, the normal course is for the retirement plan to sell or distribute the policy to the participant at retirement. The participant may wish at that point to transfer the policy to his intended beneficiaries (or to an irrevocable trust for their benefit) to get the proceeds out of his estate for estate tax purposes. Since giving away the policy would not remove the proceeds from the participant's estate until three years after the gift (§ 2035(a)), practitioners look for an alternative way to get the policy into the hands of the beneficiary(ies) without the three-year waiting period. The obstacles to success in this endeavor are discussed in this ¶ 8.4.02; for further discussion of ways to deal with what its authors call this "vastly over-exaggerated problem," see the article by Ratner, C.L., and Leimberg, S.R., "Planning Under the New Split-Dollar Life Insurance Prop. Regs., Part 2," 29 *Estate Planning* 12 (Dec. 2002), p. 603, at 606.

Since the plan cannot distribute benefits to anyone other than the participant during the participant's lifetime, the only ways the policy can be moved from the plan to the intended beneficiaries without triggering the three-year rule are for the plan (1) to sell the policy directly to the beneficiaries, or (2) distribute or sell the policy to the participant who then sells it to the beneficiaries. *The second method is safer, due to the IRS rule changes discussed at ¶ 8.3.03.*

Another problem with selling the policy to the beneficiary (regardless of who is the seller) is the transfer-for-value rule of § 101(a)(2). Life insurance proceeds (net of consideration paid for the policy) are taxable income to a recipient who acquired the policy in a transfer for value unless an exception applies. The beneficiaries' purchase of the policy from the participant, or from the plan, would be a transfer for value, causing the eventual death benefit to be taxable income instead of tax-exempt income.

Techniques practitioners use to avoid the transfer-for-value problem include selling the policy to a partnership in which the insured is a partner (see § 101(a)(2)(B), PLR 2001-20007), or to a "grantor trust" (see § 671–§ 677, Rev. Rul. 85-13, 1985-C.B. 184, and PLRs 2005-14001, 2005-14002, 2002-47006). This subject is beyond the scope of this book. See Bibliography for other resources.

8.4.03 *Second-to-die insurance*

A plan's ownership of a "second-to-die policy" (insuring the lives of the participant and the participant's spouse) introduces additional complexity.

A.   **Estate tax minimization.** If a second-to-die insurance policy is purchased *outside* the plan, the only legal paperwork required to avoid estate and gift tax is the drafting of one irrevocable trust to buy the policy, plus "Crummey" notices. If the policy is bought *inside* a retirement plan, on the other hand, one author recommends using a trust, plus either three or four separate life insurance policies, and possibly a family partnership to deal with all the issues involved trying to keep the policy proceeds out of both spouses' estates.

B.   **Current Insurance Cost.** Table 2001 (¶ 8.2.02) covers only single life policies. Notice 2002-8 provides that "Taxpayers should make appropriate adjustments" to the Table 2001 rates "if the life insurance protection covers more than one life." Insurance experts do not find this computation difficult, despite the absence of an official table.

C.   **Prohibited transaction meets transfer-for-value.** Attempting to sell a second-to-die policy to the participant creates a dilemma. The Department of Labor has indicated that PTE 92-6 (¶ 8.3.05) applies to second-to-die insurance policies on the life of the employee and his/her spouse as well as to single life policies on the life of the employee. PTE 92-6 exempts the plan's sale of a life insurance policy from the PT rules provided that (among other conditions) the sale is made *to the participant or beneficiary*. This would *not* permit a sale of the policy to both the participant *and the spouse*; the spouse is not the beneficiary of the policy (because it is a policy on her own life) nor is she the participant. However, if the participant *alone* purchases the second-to-die policy, this may be considered only partly a sale "to the insured" for purposes of the transfer-for-value rule, because the policy insures *both* spouses.

8.4.04 *Reasons to buy life insurance inside the plan*

Here are some reasons why people buy life insurance inside a retirement plan:

A.   ★ **Client uninsurable.** The client is rated or uninsurable, and wants to buy insurance, and there is a policy available through the plan that the client can purchase without evidence of insurability.

B.   ★ **Favorable group policy available through plan.** The plan may have a negotiated group insurance rate that is lower than the rate the participant would have to pay if he bought the insurance outside the plan.

C.   ★ **Increase defined benefit plan contribution.** It is possible in some cases that the purchase of insurance, as an incidental death benefit, could increase permitted contributions to a defined benefit (DB) plan (or help absorb some funds in an overfunded DB plan). See McFadden, J.J., and Leimberg, S.R., "Fully Insured 412(i) Pension Plans Offer Simplicity and Low Risk," 30 *Estate Planning* 4, p. 155 (April 2003).

D.   ★ **Only available money is in the plan.** The client needs life insurance but has no money to pay for it outside the retirement plan. In this case, however, first consider, instead, taking some money out of the plan to buy the insurance. Unless the client cannot get money out of the plan (due to unacceptable level of tax on plan distributions, creditor or marital problems, or because the plan doesn't permit it), the purchase of insurance outside the plan is usually more tax-effective.

E.   ☹ **Minimize tax on plan distributions.** A discredited planning strategy involved pouring plan assets into a life insurance policy, which (due to inflated surrender charges and other valuation gimmicks) had a cash value that was much less than the amount the participant had invested. The policy would then be distributed or sold to the participant at the depressed value, he would give the policy to a trust for his family, and the trust would exchange the policy for another policy on the participant's life. The new policy miraculously would have a much higher value than the original policy. This was the type of valuation "game" that cause the IRS to change the policy valuation rules in 2004–2005. See ¶ 8.3.02.

F.   ⊗ **Buy policy with tax-deductible dollars.** Some advocate buying insurance inside a retirement plan because this mode of purchase enables the participant to "buy insurance with tax-deductible dollars." This is not a valid reason to buy life insurance. *Any* investment bought inside a retirement plan is bought with "tax-deductible dollars." There is nothing special about buying insurance as opposed to stocks, bonds, or mutual funds with the tax-deductible dollars inside the retirement plan. In fact, buying life insurance makes the "dollars" in the plan *less* "tax-deductible" than they otherwise would be, because insurance necessitates the participant's paying income tax on the Current Insurance Cost (¶ 8.2.01).

8.4.05 *Life insurance and IRAs and 403(b)s*

403(b) plans may legally be invested only in annuity contracts and/or mutual funds; however, a 403(b) annuity can provide "incidental life insurance protection." Reg. § 1.403(b)-1(c).

A requirement of a valid IRA is that "No part of the [IRA's] funds will be invested in life insurance contracts." § 408(a)(3).

The guaranteed death benefit under an annuity contract generally does not violate § 408(a)(3). Specifically, "An individual retirement account may invest in annuity contracts which provide, in the case of death prior to the time distributions commence, for a payment equal to the sum of the premiums paid or, if greater, the cash value of the contract." Reg. § 1.408-2(b)(3). Thus, an IRA can hold an annuity contract that provides this type of incidental death benefit.

When a participant wants to buy life insurance, and the only money he has available to use for this purchase is inside an IRA, he has the following choices:

A.   **Roll money to a QRP.** One approach is to roll over money from the IRA into a QRP, where it can be used to buy insurance. This solution helps an IRA owner who happens to participate in a QRP that accepts rollovers and permits insurance purchases. If the IRA owner has no QRP available, but does have a business, some planners recommend having the business start a QRP so that the IRA owner can roll his IRA money into it (and buy insurance). In view of the many drawbacks of plan-owned insurance, and the costs and burdens of starting a QRP the participant would not otherwise want, it is hard to believe that it would not be more cost-effective to simply take the money out of the IRA, pay tax on it, and use what's left to buy the life insurance.

B.   **Own the policy through an IRA-owned entity.** Another approach is for the IRA not to own the insurance directly, but rather to own an interest in an entity (such as a partnership) which in turn owns the insurance policy. There is no authority regarding what degree of control by the IRA (or other factors) might be considered sufficient to cause an entity-held life insurance policy to be deemed held by the IRA, causing disqualification of the IRA. Though there are "look-through" rules that apply to IRA-owned entities for PT (¶ 8.6.11) and UBTI (¶ 8.5.03) purposes, the IRS has not spelled out any look-through rule for purposes of § 408(a)(3). However, if such transactions become common, or get some publicity, the IRS is bound to crack down on them with strict rules, as it has done with other life insurance schemes.

C.   **Take a taxable distribution.** Finally, the participant could simply take the money out of the IRA, pay income tax on the distribution, and buy the insurance with what's left. If the participant is under age 59½, the distributions could be arranged as a "series of substantially equal periodic payments" to avoid the 10 percent premature distributions penalty. ¶ 9.2. This solution is simpler than "A," and less risky than "B."

8.4.06 *Planning principles with plan-owned life insurance*

Here are some estate planning ideas for a client who has life insurance in his QRP account.

A.   **Use insurance to fund credit shelter trust.** The "pure insurance portion" of a life insurance policy held by a QRP is income tax-free to the death beneficiary. ¶ 8.2.06. So, if it is possible under the plan to designate one beneficiary for the life insurance policy proceeds, and a different beneficiary for other plan death benefits, determine how much of the life insurance proceeds would be subject to income tax if the client died today, *i.e.*, the cash surrender value (CSV) of the policy (less the participant's basis if applicable). If the income-taxable CSV is relatively small, and the client has insufficient other assets to fully fund a credit shelter trust, consider naming the credit shelter trust as beneficiary of the plan-held policy. Since most of the proceeds would be income tax-free, the usual drawbacks of funding a credit shelter trust with plan benefits would be minimized. The rest of the plan benefits, being fully income-taxable, could be left to the surviving spouse, who could roll them over to an IRA and continue to defer income taxes.

B.   **Leave the cash surrender value to the participant's spouse (for tax-free rollover), and the "pure death benefit" portion to the credit shelter trust.** It's not clear whether you can do this; although there is no IRS pronouncement on the subject, the IRS might require the taxable and tax-free parts of the policy proceeds to be allocated among the recipients in proportion to what each receives from the contract.

C.   **Buy favorable group insurance in plan.** If the client is not insurable at standard rates, investigate the availability of group insurance through his retirement plan (and elsewhere).

D.   **Consider subtrust for plan-held insurance.** If the client's retirement plan owns life insurance, investigate the "subtrust" (¶ 8.4.01) as a way of keeping the policy proceeds out of the gross estate.

E.   **Plan ahead for rollout.** Be sure the client is aware of, and develops a realistic plan for, the issues that will arise regarding "rollout" of the policy at retirement. ¶ 8.3. Consider ways to get/keep the policy out of the client's gross estate following rollout, without triggering the "three year rule" of § 2035, while avoiding a "transfer for value" or "prohibited transaction."

8.5 IRAs and the Tax on UBTI

This ¶ 8.5 explains how the unrelated business income tax applies to IRAs, including Roth IRAs. Every statement here about an IRA applies equally to a Roth IRA unless otherwise noted.

Normally, IRAs are tax-exempt entities; however, like other tax-exempt entities, IRAs are subject to tax under § 511 on "unrelated business taxable income" (UBTI). § 408(e)(1).

The UBTI tax also applies to other types of retirement plans, not just IRAs. However, for other types of plans, the employer's ERISA counsel or the plan's third-party administrator (TPA) should be dealing with UBTI issues, using a pension resource geared to employer plan compliance; see Bibliography. This book is intended for the estate planner, CPA, or financial planner who is advising an individual participant, and who may be the participant's or beneficiary's only line of defense against incurring UBTI tax (since IRAs typically do not have ERISA counsel or a TPA).

The purpose is to provide an *overview* of the tax, emphasizing rules that estate planners and personal (as opposed to plan) investment advisers typically are not aware of. An IRA owner and his adviser must seek UBTI-expert help (or become UBTI experts) if the IRA invests in nontraditional investments. For more on the UBTI tax, see IRS Publication 598, *Tax on Unrelated Business Income of Exempt Organizations*; or Freitag, C.N., *Unrelated Business Income* Tax (T.M. 874-2) and *Debt-Financed Income* (T.M. 875).

8.5.01 *UBTI: Rationale, exemptions, returns, double tax, etc.*

The idea of the UBTI tax is that a tax-exempt organization (such as a charity or retirement plan) is granted its tax exemption to foster its exempt purposes, not to enable the entity to compete with tax-paying businesses. Reg. § 1.513-1(b). If the tax-exempt entity has UBTI, it must pay income tax on that income. § 511.

However, the tax also applies to "income from debt-financed property," which has nothing to do with competing with tax-paying businesses. § 512(b)(4).

The UBTI tax can require not only the complications of figuring out the tax, and filing returns (Form 990-T, 990-W) but also paying estimated taxes (if "adjusted" UBTI exceeds $500), with associated penalties if any of these filings or payments are late. If the UBTI for the year is under $1,000 there is no tax, because there is a $1,000 deduction. § 512(b)(12). Form 990-T must be filed if gross unrelated business income is $1,000 or more.

If an IRA is subject to the tax on UBTI, the UBTI will be taxed twice. First the IRA pays tax on the income, then the income is taxed again when it is ultimately distributed to the participant or beneficiary. Nothing in the Code allows the IRA owner to treat the already-taxed UBTI as part of his basis. ¶ 2.1.09.

An IRA does not have to actually operate a business to become subject to this tax. Rather, an IRA must contend with this tax if it either: conducts a trade or business (¶ 8.5.02); receives certain types of rental income (¶ 8.5.03(A)); receives certain types of passive income from a business entity it controls (¶ 8.5.03(B)); invests in a partnership or other pass-through entity that conducts a business (¶ 8.5.03(C)); or uses borrowed money (such as a margin account or real estate mortgage) to finance investments (¶ 8.5.04).

The UBTI tax is not a concern if the IRA sticks to traditional investments such as publically-traded corporate stocks, bonds, and mutual funds, and never borrows money.

8.5.02 Income from an IRA-operated trade or business

UBTI includes gross income (minus permitted deductions) from the conduct of an "unrelated trade or business" that is "regularly carried on" by the exempt organization. § 512(a)(1).

A.   **Definition of "trade or business."** This term "includes any activity which is carried on for the production of income from the sale of goods or the performance of services." § 513(c). "[T]he term 'trade or business' has the same meaning it has in section 162" (the Code section that allows a deduction for business expenses). Reg. § 1.513-1(b). There is extensive material, which would be collected under § 162 in any good tax service, on the subject of what constitutes a trade or business.

B.   **Definition of "unrelated" trade or business.** "Unrelated" trade or business means "any trade or business the conduct of which is not substantially related (aside from the need of such organization for income or funds or the use it makes of the profits derived) to the exercise or performance by such

> organization of its charitable, educational, or other purpose or function constituting the basis for its exemption...." § 513(a).

The question of what is a "related" business for a *charity, trade association, or credit union* is not easily answered; see, *e.g.*, 18 pages of squibs summarizing cases and rulings on this issue (many of which seem to contradict each other) in the *RIA Checkpoint* tax service, Ann. ¶ 5135.01(5). In contrast, *any* business conducted by an IRA is an "unrelated" business, subject to the tax on UBTI. See § 513(b), which provides that, for a QRP, "unrelated trade or business" means "any trade or business regularly carried on by such [plan]...or by a partnership of which it is a member." Though there is no comparable specific rule for IRAs, which are tax-exempt under § 408(e)(1) not § 401, it appears prudent to assume that any "trade or business" conducted by an IRA (or by a partnership or LLC of which it is a member) is unrelated to its exempt purpose.

Under § 513(a)(1), unrelated trade or business "does not include any trade or business—(1) in which substantially all the work in carrying on such trade or business is performed for the organization without compensation...." This might make it appear that, if the IRA owner is the only worker in the business conducted by his IRA, and he does not take a salary or withdraw any profits, he could say he is working without compensation, and the IRA should therefore escape UBTI tax on the resulting income.

However, it seems unlikely that this argument would succeed. Presumably a court would not entertain the notion that the IRA owner is serving "without compensation" where 100 percent of the profits of the business flow to him through his ownership of the IRA, even though his compensation is not currently paid out to him. § 513(a)(1) was meant to cover individuals who work as volunteers for a charity, not an entrepreneur who is trying to avoid tax on his business income by shifting it to a tax-exempt entity.

8.5.03 *When investment income becomes UBTI*

Most types of investment income are specifically excluded from the definition of "trade or business" income. Thus, the owner of an IRA that receives interest and dividends, capital gains, and options profits *generally* has no UBTI worries. § 512(b)(1), (5). Also, royalties are not UBTI. § 512(b)(2). However, there are exceptions that can make even these types of "passive" investment income subject to the UBTI tax. One such exception involves income from debt-financed property; see ¶ 8.5.04. The other three are:

A.   **Rent can be UBTI.** Rental income from real estate is generally treated as investment income, rather than as income from a trade or business. However, <u>real estate</u> rental income is treated as UBTI if the amount of rent is determined as a percentage of the tenant's profits. Even stricter rules apply to rental income from <u>personal property</u>. § 512(b)(3).

B.   **Investment income from a controlled entity.** Passive investment income can become UBTI when it is paid to the IRA by a controlled entity. Specifically, if rent, interest, or royalties are received from an entity that is more than 50 percent controlled by the IRA, and such payments have the effect of reducing the business income of the controlled entity, such payments are UBTI to the IRA. § 512(b)(13).

Steve Example: Steve's IRA owns 60 percent of a C corporation. The corporation operates a business. The corporation (having obtained a prohibited transaction exemption for the deal; see ¶ 8.6.10) borrowed money from Steve's IRA, and pays interest on that loan. The interest deduction reduces the business income of the corporation. Though interest payments normally are not UBTI, the interest payments Steve's IRA receives from the controlled corporation are UBTI.

C.   **Business operated by pass-through entity.** If an IRA owns an interest in a business that is a "pass-through" entity for income tax purposes (such as a partnership or an LLC taxed as a partnership), the IRA's share of the partnership's (or LLC's) income from the trade or business is UBTI. This is true regardless of whether the IRA controls the pass-through entity. § 512(c)(1). If the IRA-owned entity is not a pass-through, for example if it is a "C" corporation, then the entity's net income from its trade or business does not pass through as UBTI to the IRA; the corporation itself will pay the corporate income tax on the business income. The IRA-owned entity cannot be an "S" corporation, because an IRA is not a permitted shareholder of an "S" corporation. § 1361(b)(1).

8.5.04 *Income from debt-financed property*

Don't be fooled by the term "unrelated *business* taxable income" into thinking that the UBTI tax applies only if the IRA runs a business. An IRA can have UBTI even without owning or operating a business, because income from "debt-financed property" is UBTI regardless of whether there is a trade or business. § 512(b)(4), § 514.

"Debt-financed property" is property acquired with borrowed funds and held to produce income. § 514(b). Here are guidelines regarding some common investment activities:

A.   **Margin accounts create UBTI.** An investor may have a loan from his brokerage firm, secured by his securities account, that is used to increase the securities investment activity. This is called a margin account, and if the margin account is held in a retirement plan or IRA, a portion of the plan's investment income will be taxed as UBTI. *Bartels Trust*, ¶ 8.5.05.

B.   **Short sales do not create UBTI.** Selling securities short involves two investors at the "selling" end: One investor (the lender-seller) lends its securities (through the brokerage firm) to the second investor, and the second investor (the borrower-seller) sells the borrowed securities to the buyer. The lender-seller receives various payments in connection with this transaction, but generally is treated as if he still owns the securities. The lender-seller is exempted from the UBTI tax by § 514(c)(8)(A) and § 512(a)(5), assuming various requirements are met. Short selling also does not create debt-financed income (or loss) for the borrower-seller. Even though it does involve borrowing the securities to be sold, this borrowing creates an "obligation" but it does not create "indebtedness." Rev. Rul. 95-8, 1995-1 I.R.B. 107.

C.   **Real estate mortgages create UBTI for IRAs.** A qualified retirement plan (QRP) gets the benefit of an exception for certain mortgages used to finance the plan's purchase of investment real estate. § 514(c)(9). This exception does not apply to IRAs. § 514(c)(9)(C).

D.   **Life insurance loans**. An IRA cannot invest in life insurance, so the question of whether borrowing against a life insurance policy creates UBTI is moot for an IRA. § 408(a)(3). If a QRP carries a life insurance policy to provide incidental death benefits, and the plan borrows on the policy in order to invest the loan proceeds in a different investment, the policy loan generates debt-financed income that is taxable as UBTI, according to PLR 7918095. If the borrowing against the policy is solely for the purpose of financing the policy premiums, presumably the loan thus incurred would not create debt-financed income because it is incurred in an essential function of the exempt purpose of the plan; compare *Elliot Knitwear* (¶ 8.5.05). However, there is no ruling on this point.

8.5.05 *Exception for property used for exempt purpose*

There is an exception to the debt-financed property rule for property that is more than 85 percent used for the exempt entity's exempt purpose (other than its need for funds). § 514(b)(1)(A)(i), Reg. § 1.514(b)-1(b)(1)(ii).

One could argue that the purpose of a retirement plan is to invest and accumulate funds for the owner's future retirement, and therefore the use of a margin account (or other debt incurred to increase investment return) is in furtherance of the plan's exempt purpose. However, this argument was rejected in *Elliot Knitwear Profit-Sharing Plan*, 614 F. 2d 347 (3d Cir. 1980), which was followed in *Henry E. & Nancy Horton Bartels Trust*, 209 F. 3d 147 (2d Cir. 2000); Cert. Denied 531 U.S. 978 (2000), on the basis that "in furtherance" of the exempt purpose means inherent in or essential to the fulfilment of the exempt purpose, and, while borrowing for investment purposes may be useful for the accumulation of funds, it is not essential.

8.6 IRAs and Prohibited Transactions

Because many tax- and estate-planning proposals being floated for our clients' consideration involve transactions with parties who are not "arm's length," estate planners need to have prohibited transactions (PTs) on their radar screens. This ¶ 8.6 helps the planner set up the "radar," by explaining the basic PT rules applicable to IRAs.

Unfortunately, some promoters of unconventional IRA investment and tax-saving ideas offer misleading and simplistic advice on this topic. Congress, the IRS, the courts, and the Department of Labor (DOL) have added to the confusion by enacting, promulgating, and issuing unclear laws, regulations, and opinions on the subject of PTs and IRAs. For more on the background of the PT rules, and discussion of various problematic issues, see ¶ 8.7.

In this Chapter, as in the rest of this book, regulations issued by the Treasury are cited as "Reg. §." Regulations issued by the Department of Labor are cited as "29 CFR...."

This Chapter covers the PT rules only with respect to IRAs, other than SEPs or SIMPLEs (¶ 10.1.13). More extensive rules apply to other types of retirement plans, including (at least to some extent) SEPs and SIMPLEs. For SEPs, SIMPLEs, and all other types of retirement plans, the employer's ERISA counsel or the plan's third-party administrator (TPA) should be dealing with PT issues, using a resource geared to employer plan compliance; see Bibliography. This book is intended for the estate planner, CPA, or financial planner who may be the individual IRA owner's or beneficiary's only line of defense against involvement in an IRA-disqualifying PT (since IRAs typically do not have ERISA counsel or a TPA).

8.6.01 *What the practitioner must know about IRA PTs*

To advise a client regarding IRAs and PTs, the practitioner must know the following things:

✓   What transactions are prohibited. There are three types of IRA PTs: direct PTs, ¶ 8.6.02; self-dealing PTs, ¶ 8.6.03; and conflict-of-interest PTs, ¶ 8.6.04. Though this breakdown of the types of PTs is not in the statute in this manner, and there is overlap among the categories, it is useful for analyzing PTs.

✓   Who are "disqualified persons" (DQPs) with respect to the client's IRA. DQPs with respect to an IRA are basically, the IRA owner, his spouse, ancestors, and descendants, spouses of the IRA owner's descendants, and any entity 50% or more owned by any of the foregoing. ¶ 8.6.05.

✓   The punishment for violating the PT rules, which is generally disqualification of the entire IRA. ¶ 8.6.06.

✓   The exemptions (statutory, implied, "class," and individual) that may make an otherwise-prohibited transaction "ok." ¶ 8.6.07–¶ 8.6.10.

✓   The three look-through rules that sometimes cause a transaction with an IRA-owned entity to be treated as a transaction with the IRA itself. ¶ 8.6.11.

✓   How to test a transaction for PT problems. ¶ 8.6.12, ¶ 8.6.13.

8.6.02 *Direct prohibited transactions*

Three categories of transaction are prohibited for an IRA. Everybody knows about the first type, called here "direct" PTs. A direct PT is basically any transfer of property between the IRA and a DQP. Here is the detailed list of direct PTs:

A.   A direct or indirect <u>sale, exchange, or leasing</u> of property between the IRA and a DQP. § 4975(c)(1)(A).

B.   The direct or indirect <u>lending of money or other extension of credit</u> between the IRA and a DQP. § 4975(c)(1)(B).

C.   The direct or indirect <u>furnishing of goods, services, or facilities</u> between the IRA and a DQP. § 4975(c)(1)(C).

D.   The direct or indirect <u>transfer to, or use by, a DQP of the income or assets</u> of the IRA. § 4975(c)(1)(D).

The key points to remember about direct PTs are:

First, a direct PT is prohibited regardless of whether the IRA is "harmed." For example, if the IRA buys a piece of real estate from the IRA owner, that is a PT (sale; type A) *regardless* of whether the price is fair…in fact, even if the sale provides a bargain to the IRA!

Second, there are exemptions that protect many essential and/or commonplace transactions that would otherwise be direct PTs, such as paying benefits to the IRA owner; see ¶ 8.6.07.

Third, even if the transaction takes place with an entity owned by the IRA, rather than with the IRA directly, there is a PT if a look-through rule applies. See ¶ 8.6.11.

Fourth, some advisers mistakenly conclude that direct PTs are the only type of PT there is. That false assumption may be fatal to your IRA. A transaction may not fall into any of the above categories and still be a PT. See ¶ 8.6.03, ¶ 8.6.04.

8.6.03 *Self-dealing PTs*

The second category of PT is self-dealing. What makes this type of PT different from the direct PT is that with this type there must be some possible benefit to (or receipt of consideration by) the DQP. The taxpayer has the burden of proving there was no benefit to a DQP.

A fallacy of some IRA-investing scheme promoters is to believe that if there is no direct PT there is no PT at all. As the following discussion shows, a self-dealing PT can occur even if no funds or assets move directly between the IRA and any DQP.

Here are the two types of self-dealing PTs:

A. **Transactions benefitting a DQP.** Any direct or indirect use of the income or assets of the IRA "for the benefit of" a DQP is a PT. § 4975(c)(1)(D). Also, because the IRA owner is considered a "fiduciary" of his IRA (¶ 8.6.05(A)), the IRA owner's dealing with the IRA's income or assets "in his own interests or for his own account" is a PT. § 4975(c)(1)(E).

A use of plan assets for the benefit of a DQP does not refer to the benefit the IRA owner receives from an increase in the value of the plan's investments. It refers to a personal benefit that the individual receives or could receive *outside* the plan, from the plan's investment.

The *Rollins* case, although it did not involve an IRA, illustrates this type of PT. In *Rollins*, T.C. Memo 2004-260 (2004), Mr. Rollins, as sole trustee of his firm's profit sharing plan, caused the plan to make loans to three businesses that he managed and in which he and his wife held shares. Each business was majority owned by unrelated outside investors. All the loans were paid back.

Mr. Rollins contended that the loans were not PTs because the borrowers were not DQPs. In order to be a DQP, a corporation must be

50 percent or more owned by DQPs (¶ 8.6.05(A)), and the DQPs' ownership of these borrowers was well under that level.

The Tax Court disagreed. It was not necessary for the borrowers to be DQPs. All that was needed to trigger a PT was a use of plan assets that *benefitted* a DQP. As a "significant part owner" of the borrowing corporations, Mr. Rollins *could have* benefitted by these loans. For example, the loans could have enhanced the value of Mr. Rollins' equity interests in the borrowing businesses. Also, the borrowing businesses were spared the necessity of borrowing from a possibly-less-friendly lender. Finally, the borrowing businesses might expect to benefit from Mr. Rollins' leniency in delaying foreclosing the loans (in case of any problem) since he partly owned the borrowers. Since Mr. Rollins failed to demonstrate that he did *not* personally benefit from the loans, the loans were PTs.

See also PLR 9119002, in which the IRS found a PT where a pension plan trustee caused a plan loan to be made to a business entity in which the trustee individually owned a "significant" interest (39%), though not a large enough interest to cause the entity to be a DQP.

In DOL Advisory Opinion 93-33A, an IRA owner proposed to have his IRA purchase real estate from a school that was founded by his "daughter and son-in-law, who are the sole directors and officers of the School. The purchase would be made at fair-market value. Subsequently, the IRA would lease the land and building to the School at a fair market rent or below market rent, depending on the School's ability to pay." The DOL opined that the proposed purchase and leaseback would be a PT because it "would constitute a use of plan assets for the benefit of disqualified persons...." § 4975(c)(1)(D).

This ruling was not based on the daughter's or son-in-law's ownership of the School. The DOL said it had no information on that point. Rather, this conclusion was based on the fact that the transaction would benefit the school (by giving it easy rent terms), and the school employed the daughter, so *even though the school was not a DQP*, the proposed transaction between the IRA and the school would indirectly benefit a "person in whom such fiduciary had an interest."

Though the fact that an entity is majority-owned by outside investors does not guarantee that an IRA transaction with that entity is not a PT, having outside investors, plus an independent plan fiduciary to make the investment decision, *might* work to beat the PT charge. It worked in *Greenlee,* T.C. Memo 1996-378. However, having outside investors, plus a review of the investment by disinterested fiduciaries, did not help the IRA owner avoid a PT in DOL Advisory Opinion 2006-01A.

B.   IRA owner's receipt of consideration outside the IRA.
Because the IRA owner is considered a "fiduciary" of his IRA (¶ 8.6.05(A)), the IRA owner's direct or indirect receipt of consideration, outside the IRA, for a transaction involving the income or assets of the IRA, is also a PT. § 4975(c)(1)(F); see Allen Example at the end of the PT Tester Quiz, ¶ 8.6.12.

8.6.04 *Conflict-of-interest PTs*

The position of the IRS and DOL is that any transaction in which the plan fiduciary has a conflict of interest (i.e., where the fiduciary's interests in other parties to the transaction would affect his judgment as fiduciary) is in itself a separate PT under § 4975(c)(1)(D), (E), or (F). This rule appears in an unlikely place: Reg. § 54.4975-6(a)(5)(i), which deals with the statutory PT exemption for furnishing office space and services to a plan (§ 4975(d)(2); ¶ 8.6.08).

According to the agencies, this regulation applies to IRAs, even though the office space/services exception itself probably does *not* apply to IRAs (see ¶ 8.6.08) and even though the anti-conflicts rule contained in the ERISA rules applicable to QRPs (ERISA § 406(b)(2), 29 U.S.C. § 1106) is not repeated in § 4975 (which is the only PT rule applicable to IRAs; ¶ 8.7.02). See DOL Advisory Opinion 2000-10A, in which the DOL ruled that an IRA's purchase of units in a family partnership would not constitute a direct PT, but refused to rule on whether an indirect PT (under § 4975(c)(1)(D) or (E)) "would occur if the transaction was part of an agreement, arrangement or understanding in which the fiduciary caused plan assets to be used in a manner designed to benefit such fiduciary (or any person in which such fiduciary had an interest which would affect the exercise of his best judgment as a fiduciary)"; and PLR 2001-28011, in which the IRS ruled that a particular transaction was not a PT, but commented that "if the facts were such that the IRA owners' interests in the transaction because of their ownership of [a corporation that would be doing business with a company owned by the IRAs] affected their best judgments as fiduciaries of the IRAs, the transaction would violate section 4975(c)(1)(E)."

The agencies' position on this point has never been tested in court. The Tax Court (though not ruling on the issue) has expressed doubt regarding whether the anti-conflicts rule applies at all to an enforcement under § 4975: "...[I]t appears that a conflict of interest involving a fiduciary's obligations to the other party in a transaction may be actionable under the labor title, but it may be that such a conflict of interest by itself may not be actionable under section 4975(c)(1)(E)." *Rollins,* ¶ 8.6.03(A).

8.6.05 *Fiduciaries and other disqualified persons (DQPs)*

The people to whom the PT rules apply are called **disqualified persons** in § 4975, **DQPs** in this book. ERISA § 406, 29 U.S.C. § 1106, uses the term "party in interest" rather than DQP for the "labor law" PT rules; however, since ERISA § 406 doesn't apply to IRAs (¶ 8.7.02), we will be concerned only with DQPs.

§ 4975(e)(2)(A)–(I) contains the lengthy list of DQPs. Some of the categories do not apply to IRAs (other than SEPs and SIMPLEs; ¶ 10.1.13), such as: an employer any of whose employees are covered by the plan, an employee organization any of whose members are covered by the plan, and 50 percent owners of the foregoing.

Categories that do apply to an IRA are: a fiduciary (§ 4975(e)(2)(A), (3)), and a person providing services to the plan (§ 4975(e)(2)(A)). In this Chapter, we focus only on the IRA owner and beneficiary and their related parties; this Chapter does not cover considerations that may apply to a person providing services to the plan who is neither the IRA owner nor beneficiary nor a person related to the IRA owner or beneficiary. Thus, service-providers such as bank-custodians, investment advisors, brokers, and insurance agents need to consult other sources regarding their duties and liabilities.

As will soon be apparent, it is not always easy to test whether the parties to a particular transaction are or are not DQPs. Threading your way through all the categories and attribution rules can be a lengthy and complex process.

A.   **The IRA owner/fiduciary and related parties.** The main "hook" is the fiduciary. Once a fiduciary is found, numerous parties who are related to the fiduciary also become DQPs.

Assuming the IRA owner is a "fiduciary" of his IRA, he is a DQP in that capacity, and the following parties related to the IRA owner also become DQPs under :

1.   The IRA owner's "family members," i.e., his spouse, ancestors, lineal descendants, and any spouse of a lineal descendant. § 4975(e)(2)(F), (6).

2.   A corporation, partnership, or trust or estate of which (or in which) 50 percent or more of—(i) the combined voting power of all classes of stock entitled to vote or the total value of shares of all classes of stock of such corporation, (ii) the capital interest or profits interest of such partnership, or (iii) the beneficial interest of such trust or estate, is owned *directly or indirectly* by the IRA owner. § 4975(e)(2)(G).

3.   An officer, director (or an individual having powers or responsibilities similar to those of officers or directors), a 10 percent or more shareholder, a highly compensated employee (earning 10 percent or more of the yearly wages of an employer), or a 10 percent or more (in capital or profits) partner or joint venturer of such a corporation, partnership, trust, or estate. § 4975(e)(2)(H), (I).

In determining whether an entity is more than 50 percent owned "directly or indirectly" by the IRA owner (or any other fiduciary), the attribution rules of § 267(c) are used, with some modification. For example, in applying § 267(c), "family member" is limited to spouse, ancestors, descendants, and spouses of descendants. § 4975(e)(4), (5).

See, *e.g.*, PLR 9725029, in which the participant was a plan fiduciary and therefore he was a DQP, and therefore a corporation more than 50 percent owned "directly or indirectly" by him was also a DQP. In determining how much stock the participant "indirectly" owned, his wife's stock was counted as owned by him. § 4975(e)(4), § 267(c).

Is the IRA owner always necessarily a "fiduciary" of his IRA? A "fiduciary" of a retirement plan is a person who "exercises any discretionary authority or discretionary control respecting management of such plan or exercises any authority or control respecting management or disposition of its assets," or "has any discretionary authority or discretionary responsibility in the administration of such plan." (There are other ways to be a fiduciary; these are the most relevant to the typical IRA owner. For more on the definition, see 29 CFR § 2509.75-8, Q. D-2–D-5.)

For purposes of analyzing a potential PT, it is prudent to assume that the IRA owner is a fiduciary of his IRA. Even if the IRA owner has no investment responsibility, the IRS asserts that the IRA owner is a fiduciary if he has the power to decide who does have the investment responsibility. PLR 2003-24018 ("Ruling Requests 4, 5, and 6"). Also see "B."

B.   **The IRA owner *qua* owner.** One category not listed in § 4975(e)(2) is the IRA owner *qua* owner, leading some to argue that an IRA owner is not a DQP as to his own IRA unless he is "fiduciary" of the IRA. Some planning proposals are based on the notion that the IRA owner can be positioned so that he is not a fiduciary (by giving investment control to the bank-trustee of the IRA), and therefore he is not a DQP.

However, the Tax Court believes that the IRA owner is per se disqualified. *Gerald M. Harris*, T.C. Memo 1994-22. Most treatises similarly conclude that IRA owners should be considered DQPs as to their own IRAs (regardless of their fiduciary status) because the legislative history of ERISA makes clear that Congress intended them to be such. See, *e.g.*, Krass, Steven J., *The Pension Answer Book 2004* (Panel Publishers, New York NY), Q 30:42, p. 30-36; *Kleinrock's TaxExpert* (CD-ROM edition, 2006), Section 33.14, "Prohibited Transactions" ("Observation"); Kathryn J. Kennedy, *IRAs, SEPs and SIMPLEs* (T.M. 355-6th), Part IV(A) and Note 691.

The IRS has endorsed both interpretations; compare PLR 8849001 (stating that the "legislative intent is clear" that the IRA owner is disqualified) with PLR 9725029 (ruling that an IRA owner could not transact with his own IRA because he was a fiduciary).

While this point can be debated, the outcome will make no difference if the IRA owner is (as most or possibly all IRA owners are) a "fiduciary" of his IRA (see "A"), because then he (and the long list of related parties and entities) is a DQP in that capacity *regardless* of whether he is automatically a DQP merely by owning the account.

However, if it is possible to position the IRA owner so that he is *not* a fiduciary with respect to the IRA, then (even if the IRA owner is considered a per se DQP, as the *Harris* court concluded), the IRA owner's family members (other than the IRA beneficiary; see "C") and related entities apparently would not be DQPs. While the Code does mention the "IRA owner and beneficiary," it never ties them in to the family member-related party provisions of § 4975.

C.   **The IRA beneficiary.** § 408(e)(2) disqualifies the IRA if the IRA owner "or his beneficiary" engages in a PT. ¶ 8.6.06. Does "beneficiary" mean the person named as beneficiary during the participant's life? Or does it apply only after the participant's death to the person who then, as beneficiary, owns the account?

Application post-death would make sense; the beneficiary, after the participant's death, should be subject to the same restrictions that applied to the participant during his life. However, § 408(e)(2) applies only "during any taxable year of the individual for whose benefit" the account is established—i.e., only during the participant's life. Therefore, "beneficiary" must mean the named beneficiary during the participant's life (which makes no sense, because during the participant's life the beneficiary has no control of the account and may not even know he is named as beneficiary); and after the participant's death the beneficiary (now the owner of the account) is apparently no longer subject to § 408(e)(2).

D.   **The IRA itself.** The IRA itself is a DQP, according to PLR 2003-24018.

8.6.06 *Penalties for violating the PT rules*

Though the penalty for a PT is generally an excise tax (see § 4975(a), (b)), § 408(e) provides special punishments for PTs involving IRAs:

❑   If the IRA owner uses his IRA (or part of it) as *security for a loan*, the IRA (or the part used as security for a loan) is deemed distributed to him. § 408(e)(4); see ¶ 2.1.03(A).

❑   "If, during any taxable year of the individual for whose benefit
        any [IRA] is established, that individual or his beneficiary
        engages in any transaction prohibited by section 4975 with
        respect to such account," the IRA ceases to be an IRA. The
        individual is taxed as if the entire account had been distributed
        on the first day of the taxable year. § 408(e)(2); Reg. § 1.408-
        4(d)(1). For the meaning of "his beneficiary," see ¶ 8.6.05(C).

There is no authority on the meaning of "engages" here, so what
level of involvement of the IRA owner or beneficiary in the PT would
constitute "engaging" in the transaction is unknown. If the IRA owner
is not a party to the PT, but as fiduciary he authorized it, did he
"engage" in it? If the owner or beneficiary did not engage in the PT, the
excise taxes apply instead of § 408(e)(2).

If § 408(e)(2) applies, the IRA loses its income tax exemption
entirely, even if only part of the IRA was involved in the PT. If the IRA
owner was under age 59½ on January 1 of the year the PT occurred,
there is also a 10 percent penalty. § 72(t); see Chapter 9. If the IRA
owner made a rollover contribution to the IRA after the deemed
disqualification date, the rollover is not qualified, so the distribution
that was rolled over becomes retroactively taxable as of the date it was
distributed. PLR 9725029. Disqualification could have the further
effect of increasing the individual's penalty for underpayment of
estimated taxes.

The good (?) news is that if the IRA is disqualified under
§ 408(e)(2), the other § 4975 penalties (excise taxes) do *not* apply to
the IRA owner. § 4975(c)(3).

Despite the fact that § 408(e)(2) requires disqualification of the
entire account, the taxpayer may get away with paying tax only on the
amount involved in the PT. In *Gerald M. Harris* (¶ 8.6.05(B)), the
taxpayer's IRA had invested $23,611 in a house that the taxpayer
intended to use as a personal residence. The court held that this was a
PT. However, the Tax Court inexplicably ruled that there was a deemed
distribution of only $23,611 to Mr. Harris, not of the entire account.

8.6.07 *Essential exemptions (statutory and implied)*

Clearly, not every transaction between a plan and a related party
is "bad" for the participants and beneficiaries. For example, a
transaction could be a good investment for the plan, even though it is

"prohibited" because the person on the other side of the transaction is a DQP. In fact, there are some transactions between the plan and DQPs that are actually legally required, such as paying to a DQP benefits he is entitled to receive under the plan.

Accordingly, Congress provided for three types of exceptions (called "exemptions") to the PT rules: statutory (those spelled out in § 4975 itself), class (¶ 8.6.09), and individual (¶ 8.6.10). In addition, certain "implied exemptions" have become apparent.

This ¶ 8.6.07 discusses the statutory exemptions that are essential to allow a retirement plan to operate and the implied exemptions that have developed for the same reason.

A.   **Payment of benefits to IRA owner or beneficiary.** One essential statutory exemption is the "receipt by a disqualified person of any benefit to which he may be entitled" under the plan. § 4975(d)(9). Thus, when the IRA owner takes a distribution from his IRA, that is not a PT, even though it is the transfer to a DQP of the assets of the plan (¶ 8.6.02(D)).

B.   **Implied exemption for settlor functions.** The DOL recognizes that "there is a class of discretionary activities which relate to the formation, rather than the management, of plans. These so-called 'settlor' functions include decisions relating to the establishment, termination and design of plans and are not fiduciary activities subject to Title I of ERISA." DOL "Information Letter" to John N. Erlenborn, 3/13/86 (www.dol.gov/ebsa/regs/ils/il031386.html). Although no authority discusses the concept of settlor function in the IRA context, the participant's choice of beneficiary, and his contributions to the IRA, would presumably be considered "settlor functions" in the exercise of which he is not a fiduciary.

C.   **Implied incidental benefit exemption.** A fiduciary's receipt of an incidental benefit from a transaction is not a PT, according to DOL Advisory Opinion 2000-10A. Reg. § 53.4941(d)-2(f)(2) discusses the incidental benefit concept in connection with charitable foundation grants (charities are subject to similar anti-PT rules), indicating that such "incidental or tenuous benefits" as public recognition, or improvement of the community in which the foundation manager lives, do not constitute forbidden self-dealing.

D.   **Implied exemption for divorce.** The IRS has privately ruled that the division of an IRA in connection with divorce under § 408(d)(6), although not listed as a statutory exemption in § 4975(d), cannot be a PT, because to rule otherwise would make § 408(d)(6) a nullity. Therefore, IRA divisions in connection with divorce that fit within § 408(d)(6) are an implied exception to the PT rules of § 4975. PLR 2002-15061.

8.6.08 Other statutory exemptions; do they apply to IRAs?

The structure of the statutory exemptions is confusing. § 4975(c) lists the transactions that are prohibited. Then, § 4975(d) contains a list of 16 transactions (the "statutory exemptions") to which the prohibitions of § 4975 do not apply. Finally, § 4975(f)(6) (the "exceptions to the exemptions") says that certain transactions between an owner-employee and his plan *really are* prohibited after all, because the statutory exemptions in § 4975(d) are not available in these cases.

Most of the statutory exemptions are to allow commonplace business transactions to occur. Few would have any relevance to the investment of IRA funds in a business, real estate, or a family partnership. Some could not possibly apply to IRAs, such as the exemptions for: loan from the plan to the participant, § 4975(d)(1)—an IRA cannot lend to the participant (IRS Publication 590 (2005), p. 41); loan to a leveraged ESOP, § 4975(d)(3); and certain life insurance contracts (an IRA cannot invest in life insurance; ¶ 8.4.05). Most of the remaining statutory exemptions are designed to protect institutional fiduciaries, for example by allowing a plan fiduciary that is a bank to invest plan funds in the bank's own deposit accounts (§ 4975(d)(4)) or collective trust funds (§ 4975(d)(8)).

Probably the only statutory exemption that is of conceivable relevance is § 4975(d)(10), "receipt by a disqualified person of any reasonable compensation for services rendered, or for the reimbursement of expenses properly and actually incurred, in the performance of his duties with the plan...."

A.   **Compensation for plan-related services.** Does § 4975(d)(10) allow the IRA owner to receive reasonable compensation from the IRA for services that are necessary for the operation of the IRA, such as investment management? The answer to that question depends on whether § 4975(f)(6) applies to IRAs.

Under § 4975(f)(6), which provides the "exceptions to the exemptions," the statutory exemptions are generally *not* available for loans, sales, or compensation transactions between a plan and an "owner-employee." It appears that Congress intended that § 4975(f)(6) would prohibit an IRA owner from receiving compensation from his IRA. However, due to an error in the statute, it is impossible to say whether § 4975(f)(6) applies to IRAs.

The statutory exemption for payment of reasonable compensation does not apply to "owner-employees." Owner-employee for this purpose is defined to include a "participant or beneficiary" of an IRA. § 4975(f)(6)(B)(i)(II), § 7701(a)(37). Thus, it appears prudent to conclude that the statutory PT exemption for reasonable compensation is simply not available for compensation paid by an IRA to the IRA participant or beneficiary, regardless of whether the compensation is "reasonable" and regardless of whether the compensation is for services necessary for the establishment or operation of the IRA.

However, it must also be said that technically § 4975(f)(6) does not apply to IRAs! § 4975(f)(6), by its terms, applies only to "a trust described in section 401(a) which is part of a plan providing contributions or benefits for employees some or all of whom are owner-employees...." § 4975(f)(6)(A). An IRA is definitely *not* "a trust described in section 401(a)."

So the statute is ambiguous. Congress either forgot to list IRAs in § 4975(f)(6)(A) (as one of the types of plans to which § 4975(f)(6) applies) or forgot to delete the mention of IRAs in § 4975(f)(6)(B)(i)(II) (which includes IRA owners and participants in the definition of owner-employee). In the over 30 years since the enactment of ERISA, Congress has not seen fit to correct this mistake.

How should planners and IRA owners respond to this statutory mistake? Prudence dictates that, in planning mode, an IRA owner or beneficiary should assume that the statutory exemptions do NOT protect his transactions with the IRA. Thus, it is prudent to assume that an IRA cannot pay even "reasonable" compensation to an IRA owner for plan-related services.

However, in "cleanup mode" (when a transaction has already occurred, and the parties are looking for arguments as to why the transaction was permissible), if the transaction would fit into a statutory exemption under § 4975(d), argue that § 4975(f)(6) does not apply to IRAs. For what it's worth, the IRS suggests there is a PT only if a DQP receives *un*reasonable compensation for managing the IRA. IRS Publication 590 (2005), p. 41.

B.   **Compensation for other services.** Some of the more exotic proposals floated for IRAs suggest conducting a business inside the IRA. The IRA owner's working for, and receiving a salary from, a business owned by his IRA would (unless § 4975(d)(10) provides an exemption) constitute a PT under § 4975(c)(1)(C) (furnishing services to the plan) and § 4975(c)(1)(D) (transfer of income or assets of plan to a DQP).

Even if the statutory exemption for reasonable compensation is available for IRAs (see "A"), the exemption would *not* extend to payment of compensation for working in an IRA-owned business. The exemption applies only to compensation for services "necessary for the establishment or operation of the plan." Reg. § 54.4975-6(a)(1). Thus it applies, if at all, only to such services as investment management or plan-related administrative work.

8.6.09 *PT class exemptions*

Congress authorized the IRS to establish an exemption procedure pursuant to which the agency could "grant a conditional or unconditional exemption of any...class of disqualified persons or transactions, from all or part of" the PT rules (§ 4975(c)(2)), and gave similar authority to the DOL. Such class exemptions must meet the various criteria established by Congress, primarily that the exemption is in the best interest of the plan and participants. For an example of a class exemption relevant to estate planning, see discussion of PTCE 1992-6, dealing with sale of a life insurance policy by the plan to the employee (¶ 8.3.05) or his beneficiaries (¶ 8.3.07).

A number of class exemptions relate to such routine transactions as allowing an IRA balance to count, along with the IRA owner's nonIRA assets, as part of the IRA owner's balance with a particular bank (PTE 93-2) or broker-dealer (PTE 93-33) for purposes of establishing minimum balance requirements and fee levels. Class exemptions that have been granted by the DOL are posted at http://www.dol.gov/ebsa/Regs/ClassExemptions/main.html.

8.6.10 *Individual exemptions; DOL Advisory Opinions*

ERISA § 408(a), 29 U.S.C. § 1108(a), allows the DOL to grant individual exemptions from the PT rules of ERISA § 406. Code § 4975(c)(2), in substantially similar language, allows the IRS to grant exemptions from the provisions of § 4975. So which agency should you apply to? That's a good question. See ¶ 8.7.03.

Alternatively, a person can obtain an "advisory opinion" from the DOL that a proposed transaction is *not* a PT. For information about applying to the DOL for an exemption or advisory opinion, see Horahan, E.B., *et al.*, *ERISA Fiduciary Responsibility and Prohibited Transactions*, T.M. 365-2d T.M at p. 58(3), or visit the DOL website, http://www.dol.gov/ebsa/compliance_assistance.html.

Individual PT exemptions are not like IRS private letter rulings. IRS rulings are issued as interpretations of the tax law, confirming how the law applies to a particular taxpayer's fact situation. PLRs are not intended to provide *exceptions* to the rules for particular individuals. In contrast, the PTE procedure is purely for the sake of allowing people to engage in an otherwise-prohibited transaction.

Also, unlike a PLR, a PTE is not "private." A PTE requires notice in the Federal Register and to interested parties. A PLR is published only after it has been issued to the applicant, and is published with the names of the parties deleted; the DOL does not delete the names of the parties from its Advisory Opinions and Exemptions.

8.6.11 *The three look-through rules*

When a transaction is not done directly with the IRA, but rather is done with an entity in which the IRA has an ownership interest, an additional step becomes necessary: determining whether the entity is ignored under one of the three look-through rules. If one of these rules causes the entity to be ignored, then the entity's assets are deemed to be assets *of the IRA* for PT purposes.

Here are the three look-through rules under which a transaction with an IRA-owned entity may be treated as a transaction with the IRA itself:

A.   **Plan assets rule.** The PT rules protect "the income or assets of a" retirement plan. § 4975(c)(1)(D), (E), (F). Under the plan assets rule, if a significant percentage of a privately-held investment entity is owned by IRAs and/or other retirement plans:

1.   The assets held by the entity are considered *assets of the retirement plans* for purposes of the PT rules, even though they are not held directly by any retirement plan.

2.   The managers of the entity are considered *retirement plan fiduciaries* for purposes of the PT rules. 29 CFR § 2510.3-101(a)(2).

The definition of plan assets is the subject of extensive regulatory material and even litigation; yet many planning proposals offered to IRAs ignore this subject. Unlike the ERISA "fiduciary rules," which do not apply to IRAs, the plan assets rule *does* apply to IRAs. 29 CFR § 2510.3-101(a)(1), (f)(2)(ii); DOL Advisory Opinion 2000-10A.

Laura Example: Bank X, as custodian of Laura's IRA, owns 100 percent of Alpha LLP, an investment partnership. Laura is the managing general partner of Alpha. Alpha makes a loan to Laura's son. Under the plan assets rule, Alpha's assets are deemed owned directly by the IRA (because a significant percentage of Alpha is owned by a retirement plan), and therefore Laura is deemed to be a fiduciary *of the IRA*, even if she is only "really" a fiduciary of Alpha. Because she is a fiduciary, her son is a DQP. Accordingly, the loan is a PT under § 4975(c)(1)(B). The fact that the transaction was between the son and Alpha, rather than between the son and the IRA, does not "shield" the transaction, because of the plan assets rule.

The plan assets rule is not a concern with "traditional" IRA investments. If a retirement plan owns shares of a publically traded stock, the shares of stock (not the underlying assets of the corporation) are the "plan assets" the PT rules apply to. The same is true for mutual fund shares—the mutual fund shares themselves (not the investments held inside the mutual fund) are the "plan assets" for purposes of the fiduciary and PT rules. 29 CFR § 2510.3-101(a)(2).

There is an exception to the plan assets rule for "operating companies." Thus, the rule would not apply to an IRA-owned entity that is primarily engaged in the production or sale of a product or service (other than the investment of capital). This exception also applies to a "venture capital" or "real estate" operating company. 29 CFR § 2510.3-101(a)(2)(i) and (c)–(e). Also, the plan assets rule applies to an entity only if the investment of "benefit plan investors" in that entity is "significant." 29 CFR § 2510.3-101(a)(2)(ii) and (f)(1). Specifically, an entity's assets are not treated as "plan assets" unless at least 25 percent of the entity is owned by benefit plan investors (as defined at 29 CFR § 2510.3-101(f)(2)).

It is not advisable to rely any of the above exceptions without either hiring or becoming an expert on the plan assets rule. The DOL regulation on this topic is 10 pages, single spaced, with many unexpected twists. For example, in determining the 25 percent ownership level, all ownership by *any* retirement plan (not just the particular IRA you are testing) must be counted; and the ownership interests of the entity's managers are excluded from the base. 29 CFR § 2510.3-101(f)(1)–(3).

B. **Sufficient control rule.** A transaction between a party-in-interest and an entity that is partly owned by the plan is a PT if the plan has sufficient control of the entity to, by itself, cause the transaction to occur. 29 CFR § 2509.75-2(c).

This DOL regulation never states what statutory sections it is interpreting. It refers to sections of ERISA, uses ERISA terminology ("parties in interest"), and never mentions IRC § 4975 or DQPs. So an argument could be made that this particular look-through rule, unlike the plan assets rule, does not apply for purposes of IRC § 4975 and therefore does not apply to IRAs.

However, in Notice 2004-8, 2004-4 I.R.B. 333, the IRS stated that the DOL's position is that this rule *does* apply to IRAs, a statement confirmed by the DOL's applying the rule to an IRA in DOL Advisory Opinion 2006-01A. Under the sufficient control rule, a transaction between the IRA owner and a company controlled by the IRA could be a PT, *even if the entity's assets are not considered plan assets under the plan assets rule.*

C.   **Arrangement or understanding rule.** The DOL will ignore the separate existence of a plan-owned entity for PT purposes if the plan's investment in the entity was part of an arrangement or understanding under which it was expected that the entity would engage in a transaction with a DQP. 29 CFR § 2509.75-2(c). The DOL's position is that this rule does apply to IRAs. Notice 2004-8, op. cit.; DOL Advisory Opinion 2006-01A (where the DOL also confirmed that, like the "sufficient control" rule, this doctrine has no exception for "operating companies").

8.6.12 *The Prohibited Transaction Tester Quiz*

As estate planners, we are not PT experts. However, we need not be helpless when the client calls regarding a proposed transaction and asks "can I do this," or at the mercy of a promoter who offers an unorthodox tax-saving or investment proposal and promises that "this works." This quiz is designed for a preliminary analysis of a proposed transaction, to determine whether it may be a PT.

The quiz is not designed to be used for every possible transaction, just some of the more common proposed IRA business transactions the author has encountered. Nor is this quiz intended to replace the practitioner's own research (or consultation with an ERISA expert). Rather, the purpose is to help the practitioner quickly identify a prohibited transaction, and show why it is prohibited. If the quiz says that the transaction is a PT, the client and practitioner can then decide whether to drop the idea or to pursue the matter further by consulting with a PT expert.

To use the quiz, you must first identify the transaction you are testing. This may involve breaking a series of transactions into separate transactions so that each can be tested. Identify the parties to the particular transaction you are testing, who are called here "Party X" (which is either the IRA itself, an IRA-owned entity, or the IRA owner) and "Party Y" (the other party to the transaction). Then begin the quiz:

Question 1: Is Party X the IRA itself or an entity wholly or partly owned by the IRA? If no, go to Question 2. If yes, go to Question 4.

Question 2: Is Party X the IRA owner? If no, go to Answer A. If yes, go to Question 3.

Question 3: Is the IRA owner personally receiving consideration, from any party dealing with the IRA, in connection with a transaction involving the income or assets of the IRA? If no, go to Answer D. If yes, the transaction is a PT. ¶ 8.6.03(B). Go to Answer C.

Question 4: Is the transaction the formation of a brand new entity such as a corporation or partnership, which (at the time the IRA is contributing to it) has no owners? If no, go to Question 5. If yes, go to Quasi-Answer B.

Question 5: Is Party Y a DQP? See list of DQPs at ¶ 8.6.05. If no, go to Question 6. If yes, go to Question 7.

Question 6: Your answers to the preceding questions have established that the proposed transaction does not involve a "direct" PT (¶ 8.6.02). Is it possible that the proposed transaction could provide a benefit to a DQP, other than mere increase in the value of the IRA's investments? If the answer is "no," (i.e., you can prove there is no possible benefit from the transaction to any DQP), go to Question 9. If the transaction does benefit a DQP (or you cannot prove that it will not benefit a DQP), the transaction is a PT; see ¶ 8.6.03(A). Go to Answer C.

Question 7: Does the transaction involve: the sale or exchange, or leasing, of any property; the lending of money or other extension of credit; or the furnishing of goods, services, or facilities between Parties X and Y? Does the transaction constitute a transfer of the IRA's income or assets to, or use of such income or assets by, Party Y? If the answer to either question is yes, go to Question 8. If the answer to both questions is no, the transaction does not involve a "direct" PT (¶ 8.6.02). Go back to Question 6.

Question 8: Is Party X the IRA, or is it an entity in which the IRA has an ownership interest? If Party X is the IRA, go to Answer C. If Party X is an entity in which the IRA has an ownership interest, go to Question 10.

Question 9: Does the transaction involve any conflict of interest between (1) the IRA and (2) a person in which or in whom the IRA owner has an interest which may affect the exercise of his best judgment as a fiduciary? If no, go to Answer D. If yes, the transaction is a PT according to the IRS and DOL; see ¶ 8.6.04. Go to Answer C.

Question 10: Does the IRA have sufficient control over the entity to, by itself, cause the transaction to occur? See ¶ 8.6.11(B). If yes, go to Answer C. If no, go to Question 11.

Question 11: Was the IRA's investment in the entity part of an arrangement or understanding under which it was expected that the entity would engage in a transaction with a DQP? If yes, the transaction is a PT according to the DOL; see ¶ 8.6.11(C). Go to Answer C. If no, go to Question 12.

Question 12: Is 25 percent or more of the entity (excluding the ownership interests, if any, of the entity's managers) owned by benefit plan investors? See ¶ 8.6.11(A). If no, go to Answer D. If yes, go to Question 13.

Question 13: Is the entity an "operating company?" See ¶ 8.6.11(A). If yes, go to Answer D. If no, go to Answer C.

Answer A: This quiz tests transactions in which one party to the transaction is either the IRA, an entity wholly or partly owned by the IRA, or the IRA owner. If the transaction in question involves none of the foregoing, this quiz will not work. For example, if the transaction is between the IRA owner's spouse and a third party, or involves the beneficiary of the IRA rather than the IRA owner, this quiz will not be useful in determining whether the transaction is a PT. Sorry, I can't do everything. End of test.

Quasi-Answer B: You have arrived at this Quasi-Answer because your transaction is the formation of a new entity. If, following the IRA's transfer of property to the newly-forming entity, the IRA is the sole owner of the entity, then the transaction is not a PT. ¶ 8.7.01. Similarly, if the IRA is not the sole owner, but *none* of the other owners of the new entity is a DQP, then the transaction is not a PT. In either case proceed to the Bonus Questions (¶ 8.6.13). If any of the other owners of the new entity is a DQP, then you need to determine whether formation of the entity involves a shift of value from the IRA to any DQP, and also whether the formation of the entity or the IRA's investment in it provides a benefit to a DQP (for example by enabling other owners of the entity who are DQPs to qualify to invest in a hedge fund whose minimum investment they could not meet without the IRA's funds). If the answer to either of those question is yes, then the formation of the entity is a PT; proceed to Answer C. If there is still no PT, then the formation of the entity is probably not a PT, but you will need to continually test thereafter for a potential PT every time the entity engages in a transaction with the IRA or any DQP-owner (for example, redeeming stock of a DQP, or paying premiums on insurance on the life of a DQP), paying particular attention to Questions 10–12; see also Answer D and ¶ 8.6.13.

Answer C: Your answers to the quiz indicate that the proposed transaction is either definitely a PT or may be (in the view of the IRS or DOL) a PT, unless an exemption (see ¶ 8.6.07–¶ 8.6.10) applies. If no exemption applies, either do not engage in transaction, or consult an ERISA expert before proceeding. This quiz uses conservative interpretations regarding whether a transaction is prohibited; for example, the quiz assumes the IRA owner is always a fiduciary (see ¶ 8.6.05(A)). Consultation with an ERISA expert could lead to the conclusion (based on a more sophisticated analysis and/or a decision to challenge some of the DOL's or IRS's positions) that the transaction is not prohibited, or to a way to restructure the transaction to avoid the PT problem, or to obtaining a DOL exemption.

Answer D: Your answers to the quiz indicate that the proposed transaction is not a PT or may not be a PT. Now ask yourself why you were concerned that the transaction might be a PT; your answer may reveal that you did not test the right parties or the right aspect of the proposed transaction. It would be unwise to conclude that the transaction is not a PT based on an exception to the plan assets rule (¶ 8.6.11(A)) without becoming, or consulting, a PT expert. If there is any reason to be concerned about the transaction (i.e., because it involves any related party, or any possible outside-the-IRA benefits to the participant or any related parties), do not rely on this quiz. Consult with an ERISA expert. If you are convinced there is no PT, proceed to the Bonus Questions at ¶ 8.6.13.

Quiz examples:

Allen Example: Allen's IRA invests in second mortgage loans. Allen interviews the borrowers, investigates the collateral, prepares the paperwork, oversees the loan closings, and monitors repayments. Allen also personally invests in such loans. When he is personally making the loan, he charges the borrowers a "finder's fee." He asks you whether he can personally charge a finder's fee for the loans made by the IRA. The transaction we test: payment of a fee from the borrower (Party Y) to Allen (Party X) personally.

Question 1: No, Party X is neither the IRA nor an IRA-owned entity.
Question 2: Yes, Party X is the IRA owner.
Question 3: Yes, the IRA owner is personally receiving consideration for a transaction involving IRA assets. This is a PT under § 4975(c)(1)(F). ¶ 8.6.03(B).

Beatrice Example: Beatrice has a $3 million IRA, all liquid. In addition she owns a home worth $1.5 million and has $1 million in a variety of liquid and illiquid securities outside her retirement plans. She is joining the board of a public company. The company requires each director to purchase at least $250,000 of stock in the company on the open market. Beatrice can well afford this, but to buy the stock outside her IRA she would have to either sell some of her illiquid securities, mortgage her home, or tie up all of her liquid nonretirement assets. She would prefer to buy the stock inside her IRA. We test the IRA's proposed purchase of publically-traded stock on the open market.

Question 1: Yes, Party X is the IRA.
Question 4: No, the transaction is not the formation of a new entity.
Question 5: No, Party Y is not a DQP. The IRA would be buying the stock from an anonymous unknown seller on the New York Stock Exchange.
Question 6: Yes, the transaction provides a benefit to Beatrice personally (beyond mere increase in value of the IRA's investment). The transaction would provide an indirect benefit to Beatrice (who is a DQP) by enabling her to fulfill her obligation to purchase stock of the company without mortgaging her house, liquidating investments, or tying up all her liquid funds. The transaction is a PT unless an exemption applies.

8.6.13 *PT Tester Quiz: Bonus Questions*

If you obtained a clean bill of health in the PT Tester Quiz, congratulations. Now answer the following additional questions. As a result of or following the proposed transaction:

❏   Will the IRA have business income, passive income from a controlled business entity, business income from a pass-through entity, or income from debt-financed property? If yes, see ¶ 8.5 (UBTI).

❏   Is any value being transferred to objects of the IRA owner's bounty? If yes, see ¶ 8.7.04(A).

❏   Is anything being contributed to the IRA other than cash, or in excess of the limits on IRA contributions? If yes, see ¶ 8.7.04(C).

❏   Will any person or entity be claiming business expense deductions for payments to the IRA or any entity owned by it? If yes, see ¶ 8.7.04(D).

❏   Is income that properly belongs to another entity being shifted into the IRA? If yes, see ¶ 8.7.04(D).

8.7 IRAs and PTs, Continued

In this ¶ 8.7, we look at some even more difficult and confusing issues regarding IRAs and PTs, and how the state of IRA-PT law got to the state it is in today.

8.7.01 *How the PT rules apply on formation of an entity*

In *Swanson*, 106 T.C. 76 (1996), the taxpayer caused his IRA to form a "domestic international sales corporation" (DISC). Upon formation and at all times thereafter the IRA was the sole stockholder of the DISC. Another company owned by the taxpayer, H & S Swansons' Tool, then paid commissions to the DISC, which in turn paid dividends to its sole owner, the IRA.

The IRS asserted a deficiency against Mr. Swanson based on (among other, unrelated, issues) PTs in the IRAs arising out of the DISC transactions. Later the IRS dropped its PT attack, consenting to a partial summary judgment on that point, and the taxpayer sought compensation from the IRS for the attorneys' fees incurred defending this issue. In trying to ward off the attorneys' fees claim, the IRS argued that *the formation of the DISC,* and *the payment of dividends* from the DISC to the IRA, were PTs.

The Court ruled that the IRS's argument that these two events were PTs was unreasonable. The Court held that the issuance, to an IRA, of stock in a newly formed corporation, *which was wholly owned by the IRA following such issuance*, did not constitute a PT. The basis for this holding was the Court's finding that a corporation that has no shareholders at the time of the transaction in question cannot be a DQP. This was hardly surprising; the DOL similarly ruled that an IRA's contribution of property to an entity in exchange for an ownership interest in the entity was not a PT where, at the time of the transaction, the entity was not a DQP. DOL Advisory Opinion 2000-10A.

The Court also held that payment of dividends to the IRA from its wholly-owned corporation was not a PT, because such payment benefitted solely the IRA (and benefitted Mr. Swanson personally only in his capacity as IRA owner, which is permitted).

Swanson certainly stands for the proposition that an IRA's contribution of assets to an entity that, following the transaction, is wholly owned by the IRA is not a PT. However, some promoters erroneously cite *Swanson* for the proposition that a PT cannot possibly occur upon the formation of a new entity, regardless of how many owners the new entity has.

Walker Example: Walker's IRA contributes $1 million to a newly-forming LLC, while Walker contributes $100 from his personal account. The LLC issues 100 shares of stock to Walker's IRA and 100 shares to Walker. Walker's IRA has contributed 99 percent of the capital but receives only 50 percent of the stock. In effect, half the capital contributed by the IRA has been indirectly transferred to Walker personally through the disproportionate stock issuance. Does anyone doubt that the formation of the LLC constitutes a PT, namely, a transfer of plan assets to a DQP (§ 4975(c)(1)(D))?

In *Swanson* the whole point was that there were no other parties to the "transaction" (formation of the DISC), so there was no DQP. That rationale does not apply to formation of a partnership, LLC, or any other entity when, following such formation, the IRA is not the sole owner of the entity. The *Swanson* court did not make this distinction; it had no need to, since the issue of other owners was not before it. Nevertheless, the *Swanson* case is cited (even by the IRS! See ¶ 8.7.04(A)) as standing for the proposition that, so long as the entity is newly forming, there cannot possibly be a PT.

However, even if the formation of a new entity is not itself a PT, the PT potential begins rather than ends upon formation of the entity. Every subsequent transaction between the entity and its owners or other related parties gives rise to new potential PTs (and other concerns; see the "Bonus Questions" at ¶ 8.6.13). See DOL Advisory Opinion 2000-10A, in which the DOL "blessed" an IRA's purchase of units in a family partnership. The partnership was not a DQP at the time of the purchase (it was less than 50% owned by DQPs), but became a DQP (and also became subject to the plan assets rule) as a result of the purchase. Thus, the DOL was careful to limit its Opinion just to whether the purchase itself was a direct PT; it refused to rule on the possibility of "indirect" PTs, and warned that future "conflict of interest" PTs could arise in administration of the partnership.

8.7.02 *IRAs and PTs, background: The statutory mess*

ERISA's PT rules are contained in similar wording in Internal Revenue Code § 4975 and the "labor law" part of ERISA (ERISA § 406; 29 U.S.C. § 1106). The labor law PT rules apply only to "employee benefit plans." ERISA § 3(14), 29 U.S.C. § 1002(14). To be an "employee benefit plan," the plan must be "established and maintained" by an employer or by an employee organization. ERISA § 4(a), 29 U.S.C. § 1003(a). An IRA is not an employee benefit plan. 29 CFR § 2510.3-2(d). Therefore the labor law rules do not apply to IRAs (except that they do apply to SEPs and SIMPLEs, ¶ 10.1.13, which are employee benefit plans).

The purpose of the PT rules is to prevent self-dealing with the assets of a retirement plan. Similar rules had been applied to private foundations by the Tax Reform Act of 1969, and had worked so well in cleaning up that area that Congress decided to adapt the rules to retirement plans. See Conf. Committee Joint Explanation for § 2003 of ERISA, "Excise Tax on Prohibited Transactions: In General."

The rules were written primarily with "real" retirement plans (i.e., employer-sponsored plans for the benefit of rank and file employees) in mind. A typical abuse that these rules are designed to prevent, in the case of that type of retirement plan, is: The employer is in financial trouble, so it borrows money from the retirement plan.

Unfortunately, the rules that work so well for "real" retirement plans make no sense when applied to IRAs. The gist of the PT rules as applied to charities and "real" retirement plans is to prevent the big guys (plan fiduciaries, employer, employees' union, managers, and donor) from stealing from the employees or charity. The manager of a charity (or retirement plan) is in a position of trust, and must be prevented from benefitting himself and his relatives at the expense of the helpless employees or the charity.

In contrast, the IRA owner is both the manager and beneficial owner of his IRA. He has no incentive to "steal" from the plan, since he would be just stealing from his own pocket. In fact his incentive often goes in the opposite direction—he wants to put MORE money into the plan than he is supposed to.

Another, less global, error that Congress embedded in ERISA in 1974, and has never bothered to fix in the more than three decades that have since elapsed: § 408(e)(2)(A) (¶ 8.6.06) says that "For purposes of this paragraph—(i) the individual for whose benefit any account was established is treated as the creator of such account...." But there is never any other reference, either in § 408(e) or in § 4975, to the "creator of the account!" See ¶ 8.7.05(E).

8.7.03 *IRAs and PTs, background: The regulatory mess*

For many years, neither the IRS nor the DOL seemed interested in enforcing the PT rules regarding IRAs, though this may be changing. Here is how IRA PT enforcement became a no-man's land.

ERISA granted jurisdiction of PTs to both the DOL and the IRS. The agencies cooperated and issued numerous regulations. But because the PT provisions of ERISA § 406 and IRC § 4975 were virtually identical, and applied mostly to the same parties and the same plans, the overlapping jurisdiction of enforcement, interpretive power, and exemption-granting power was deemed wasteful, and accordingly a division of powers between the two agencies was effected by Reorganization Plan No. 4 of 1978 ("1978 Plan"), 1979-1 C.B. 480.

The 1978 Plan slices and dices § 4975, almost word by word, transferring exclusive jurisdiction over most clauses to the DOL. Among the sections of 4975 that are NOT transferred to the exclusive jurisdiction of the DOL are: imposition and computation of the tax on PTs (§ 4975(a), (b)), and the provision (§ 4975(c)(3)) that the excise tax does not apply to an IRA owner whose IRA was disqualified under § 408(e)(2). On those issues, the IRS retains exclusive jurisdiction.

In addition, the Treasury retains interpretive powers regarding the following matters "to the extent necessary for" enforcing the tax imposed by § 4975(a) and (b): joint and several liability of taxpayers (§ 4975(f)(1)); determination of the "taxable period" and "amount involved" (§ 4975(f)(2), (4)); what it takes to "correct" a PT ((§ 4975(f)(5)); and the fact that certain statutory exemptions do not apply to plans covering "owner-employees" (§ 4975(f)(6)). "To the extent necessary" implies that interpretive power over these sections for some other (unspecified) purposes is transferred to the DOL.

Section 105 of the 1978 Plan provides that "[t]he transfers [of exclusive jurisdiction over certain issues to the DOL] provided for in Section 102...shall not affect the ability" of the Treasury to audit plans, enforce the excise tax, and disqualify plans; however, "in enforcing such excise taxes and...in disqualifying such plans the...*Treasury shall be bound by the regulations, rulings, opinions, and exemptions issued by the Secretary of Labor* pursuant to the authority transferred to" the DOL under Section 102 of the 1978 Plan (emphasis added).

The 1978 Plan abruptly ended the productive IRA-DOL cooperation in PT enforcement. Following issuance of the 1978 Plan, the IRS announced that henceforth all requests for rulings, opinions, and exemptions on the PT rules should be submitted only to the DOL, with one exception: "With respect to *individual retirement accounts* defined in section 408(a) of the Code...*all* requests for opinions and rulings under the prohibited transactions provisions of section 4975 of the Code should be submitted *only to the Internal Revenue Service*....pursuant to Rev. Proc. 72-3, 1972-1 C.B. 698, [and]...*all* requests for administrative exemptions from the prohibited transactions provisions of section 4975 of the Code should be submitted *only*" to the IRS, following the procedures set forth in Rev. Proc. 75-26, 1975-1 C.B. 722. IRS Announcement 79-6, 1979-4 I.R.B. 43; emphasis added.

However, the DOL's interpretation of the 1978 Plan was directly contrary to the IRS view. The DOL concludes that its "authority to issue interpretations involving certain prohibited transaction provisions of section 4975 of the Code *extends to transactions involving individual retirement accounts which are not plans and over which the Department would not normally have any jurisdiction.*" DOL Advisory Opinion 93-33A (emphasis added). The DOL sees itself excluded only from ruling on § 4975(c)(3) (the provision that says that the excise tax of § 4975 does not apply to an IRA owner if the IRA is disqualified by virtue of § 408(e)(2)). So, notwithstanding IRS Announcement 79-6, the DOL issues advisory opinions regarding the application of § 4975 to IRAs!

DOL Advisory Opinion 93-33A (¶ 8.6.03(A)) illustrates the confusion caused by the overlapping jurisdiction. The participant wanted to know (1) whether his proposed purchase-leaseback would be a PT under § 4975, and (2) if so, whether it would result in a deemed distribution under § 408(e)(2). The DOL opined that the proposed purchase would be a PT, but refused to discuss § 408(e)(2) because "the Department has no jurisdiction" with regard to this Code section.

What does the future hold? DOL Advisory Opinion 2006-01A may herald a new era of more vigorous IRA-PT enforcement. In this Opinion, the DOL applied all its weapons to hold that a proposed lease between an LLC that was 49 percent owned by an IRA, as lessor, and a corporation (as lessee) that was 68 percent owned by the IRA owner, was a PT. It is recommended reading.

8.7.04 *The PT rules may be the least of your problems*

In many cases the IRS doesn't need the PT rules to go after a questionable IRA transaction. It can use, instead, UBTI (¶ 8.5), or:

A.   **Gift taxes.** In PLR 2001-28011, multiple IRAs (owned by a father and his children) formed a foreign sales corporation (FSC) to handle foreign sales for the father's business. The IRS ruled there was no PT on formation of the FSC, citing *Swanson* (¶ 8.7.01)—even though the FSC had several owners, unlike the entity in *Swanson* which was solely owned by the IRA. The IRS imposed gift tax instead of PT penalties, on the grounds that the father had transferred significant value to the children by issuing shares of the FSC to their IRAs.

B.   **Listed transactions.** In a blatant abuse of the Roth IRA vehicle, some individuals attempted to shift income into their Roth IRAs by such means as having the Roth IRA form a wholly-owned business entity (such as an LLC), then shifting value into that entity by (for example) selling property to it at bargain prices. The goal of these schemes was to shelter gains and income in the tax-exempt Roth. In Notice 2004-8, 2004 I.R.B. 333, the IRS declared war on these devices, attacking them as (among other things) listed transactions for purposes of the anti-tax-shelter regulations (see Reg. § 54.6011-4). TIPRA gives the IRS new and greater powers to go after "tax shelter" transactions involving exempt entities, including IRAs.

C.   **Improper IRA contributions.** In Notice 2004-8, the IRS also warned it would treat any attempt to inappropriately shift value into a Roth IRA as a disguised IRA contribution, in violation of the limits on annual IRA contributions (§ 219(b)) and of the requirement that only cash may be contributed to an IRA (§ 408(a)(1)). This attack could be used against traditional IRAs too. An excess IRA contribution results in a cumulative six percent annual excise tax under § 4973. Violation of the cash-only rule would presumably disqualify the IRA.

D.   **Reallocation of income and deductions.** In Notice 2004-8, the IRS also warned that it would attack attempts to inappropriately shift value into a Roth IRA by dismantling the transactions through denial of business expense deductions under § 162 (for, *e.g.*, excessive payments from a business to the IRA-owned entity) or re-allocation of income and deductions among the persons and entities involved to more clearly reflect each person's or entity's proper income, pursuant to § 482. Though Notice 2004-8 dealt only with a particular abusive Roth IRA scheme, the IRS does not need to issue a new notice to go after any type of IRA- or Roth IRA-owned business under § 482.

Paul Example: Paul has his IRA buy an old house, which he fixes up in his spare time. The IRA then sells the house at a profit. The IRS could use § 482 to reallocate the profit (which resulted from Paul's personal efforts) from the IRA to Paul, meaning that it should have been reported on his personal income tax return. Thus, Paul owes income tax, self-employment tax, and interest and penalties for failure to report that income. Then Paul could be deemed to have contributed that profit to his IRA, resulting in an excess IRA contribution.

8.7.05 *Putting it all together*

Here are guidelines for practitioners confronting the subject of prohibited IRA transactions.

A.   **Don't dabble; become, or hire, an expert.** PT law takes up an entire chapter of *The Pension Answer Book*. No estate planner should advise regarding a transaction between an IRA and any related party unless (1) there is a class exemption that clearly applies, or (2) the planner devotes the time to study the applicable rules (see Bibliography for sources), or (3) an ERISA expert opines that the PT rules are not violated.

B.   **Use the "PT Tester" to get started.** The PT-Tester Quiz at ¶ 8.6.12 will help with a preliminary determination of whether the transaction is prohibited.

C.   **Get a DOL opinion or exemption.** If there is a PT issue with a proposed transaction, it may be solvable by obtaining an exemption from the DOL, or a DOL advisory opinion that the transaction is not a PT. ¶ 8.6.10.

D.   **Use separate IRA for questionable transaction.** Since the potential penalty for a PT is disqualification of the IRA, use one, separate, IRA for the proposed transaction and a different IRA to hold the owner's other, less controversial, investments. If the separation of the two accounts occurs prior to the year in which the questionable transaction occurs, a PT in one account presumably would not put the other IRA at risk.

E.   **Take advantage of government mistakes.** When defending against a PT attack by the IRS or DOL, you may be able to use the confused state of the IRA-PT law to construct a defense. See ¶ 8.6.05(B), (C); ¶ 8.6.08(A); ¶ 8.7.02; ¶ 8.7.03; and ¶ 8.7.06, last paragraph.

9

Distributions Before Age 59½

What distributions the 10 percent penalty under § 72(t) applies to, and how to avoid it.

9.1 10% Penalty on Pre-Age 59½ Distributions

§ 72(t) imposes a 10 percent penalty on retirement plan distributions made to a participant who is younger than age 59½. This ¶ 9.1 describes the penalty. ¶ 9.2 and ¶ 9.3 discuss the most useful exception to the penalty, the "series of substantially equal periodic payments" (SOSEPP). ¶ 9.4 explains the other 12 exceptions.

For application of the penalty in connection with Roth IRAs, see ¶ 5.5. See ¶ 3.2.02 for penalty considerations in connection with the spousal rollover. For special rules for certain hurricane victims, see § 1400Q, IRS Notice 2005-92, 2005-51 I.R.B.1165, IRS Publication 4492, and IRS Form 8915.

9.1.01 *What practitioners must know*

Estate planners need to know:

✓ What the "premature distributions" penalty is and what plans and distributions it applies to. ¶ 9.1.02–¶ 9.1.04.

✓ How to use the "series of substantially equal periodic payments" (SOSEPP) exception to the penalty. ¶ 9.2.

✓ Why "modification" of the SOSEPP must be avoided for a certain period of time, and what changes do or do not constitute a forbidden "modification." ¶ 9.3.

✓ How to qualify for the other exceptions to the penalty. ¶ 9.4.

9.1.02 *The § 72(t) penalty and which plans it applies to*

§ 72(t) imposes a 10 percent additional tax on retirement plan distributions. The penalty does not apply to distributions made after the participant reaches age 59½. § 72(t)(2)(A)(i); PLR 2004-10023. This additional tax is usually referred to as the 10 percent penalty on "early distributions" or "premature distributions." The tax is 25 percent rather than 10 percent on certain premature distributions from "SIMPLE" (§ 408(p)) retirement plans; § 72(t)(6).

The § 72(t) penalty was added to the Code in 1986 and has been amended several times since. The IRS has not issued regulations under § 72(t), perhaps because it gave up trying to keep up with Congress's changes. The Service's position is revealed in IRS publications, IRS Notices, cases, and private letter rulings. However, many aspects of the penalty (and its ever-growing list of exceptions) are not clear.

The 10 percent "additional tax" is not intended to be a punishment for wrongdoing, but merely a disincentive for early distributions (to encourage saving not only *for* but *until* retirement). The idea is to remove some of the benefits of tax-free accumulation if the accumulated funds are not used for their intended purpose.

§ 72(t)(1) says that the penalty applies to any distribution from a "qualified retirement plan (as defined in § 4974(c))." § 4974(c)'s definition of "qualified retirement plan" includes 401(a) plans (true "qualified" retirement plans) as well as 403(b) arrangements and IRAs (both of which are not normally included in the term "qualified retirement plan"). It also includes other types of plans not dealt with in this book. *Although § 72(t) includes all of these plans in the term "qualified retirement plan," in this Chapter the term "qualified retirement plan" (QRP) refers only to plans qualified under § 401(a), as distinguished from 403(b) arrangements and IRAs.*

Note that the plan in question does not have be "qualified" at the time of the distribution for the penalty to apply, as long as it was once a qualified plan. *Powell*, 129 F.3d 321 (4th Cir. 1997).

9.1.03 *How the penalty applies to particular distributions*

The penalty is not necessarily 10 percent of the total distribution. Rather, the 10 percent is calculated only with respect to "the portion of [the distribution] which is includible in gross income." § 72(t)(1); Notice 87-16, 1987-1 C.B. 446, Question D9. To the extent the distribution is income tax-free because (for example) it represents the return of the participant's own after-tax contributions (¶ 2.1.07), or because it is rolled over in a qualifying rollover (¶ 2.6.01), it is also penalty-free. See, *e.g.*, PLR 9253049 (because a pre-age 59½ IRA distribution was excluded from the taxpayer's gross income by virtue of the U.S.-U.K. tax treaty, it was also not subject to the 10% penalty); PLR 9010007 (tax-free rollover not subject to penalty).

Other than the fact that the penalty applies only to the portion of a distribution that is included in gross income, the 10 percent penalty has nothing to do with the income tax treatment of the distribution. Nevertheless, the § 72(t) exceptions are a source of confusion to clients and practitioners who wrongly conclude that distributions that are *penalty-free* under § 72(t) are also *income tax-free*.

Here is how the 10 percent penalty applies to various types of distributions and deemed distributions:

A. **Employer stock and NUA.** An employee who receives employer stock in a lump sum distribution from a QRP is entitled to certain favorable tax treatment regarding the "net unrealized appreciation" in the stock. ¶ 2.5. If the employee is under age 59½ at the time of the distribution, the 10 percent penalty will apply to the portion of the distribution that is includible in the employee's gross income (unless an exception applies; see ¶ 9.4). It will not apply to the income resulting from later sale of the stock (¶ 2.5.01).

B. **IRA contributions withdrawn before return due date**. If an IRA contribution for which no deduction has been taken is withdrawn from the account (together with the net earnings on that contribution) before the due date (including extensions) of the participant's tax return for the year for which the contribution was made, the withdrawal of the *contribution* is not a taxable distribution (§ 408(d)(4); ¶ 2.1.06(H)) and accordingly is also not subject to the penalty. See ¶ 5.6.01(A). However, any *earnings on the contribution* that are included in the corrective distribution will be subject to the penalty (unless it qualifies for an exception; ¶ 9.4). Notice 87-16, 1987-1 C.B. 446, Question C2; *Hall*, T.C. Memo 1998-336.

C.   **Deemed distribution due to plan-owned life insurance.**
      When a QRP purchases life insurance on the life of a plan
      participant, § 72(m)(3) generally requires that the cost of the
      insurance protection be included currently in the participant's
      gross income. ¶ 8.2.01. This deemed income is not treated as a
      distribution for purposes of the 10 percent penalty. See IRS
      instructions for Form 1099-R (2005), p. 1.

D.   **Deemed distribution from failed plan loan.** If an employee
      borrows, from a QRP, a loan that fails to meet the requirements
      of § 72(p), the loan is treated as a taxable distribution rather
      than a loan, and the resulting gross income is subject to the
      penalty if the employee is under age 59½. ¶ 2.1.03(F); Notice
      87-13, 1987-1 C.B. 432, A-20; *Plotkin*, T.C. Memo 2001-71.

E.   **Deemed distribution resulting from prohibited transaction.**
      The penalty applies to deemed distributions resulting from
      prohibited transactions (¶ 8.6.06). IRS Publication 590 (2005).

F.   **Community property.** The taxable income from an IRA
      distribution, and the 10 percent penalty if applicable, are
      imposed on the IRA owner solely (not on the IRA owner's
      spouse), even if the IRA is community property. *Bunney*, 114
      T.C. 259, 262 (2000); *Morris*, T.C. Memo 2002-17.

9.1.04 *Overview of exceptions to the penalty*

If an under-age 59½ participant takes money from a retirement
plan, and does not qualify for any of the very precise and limited
exceptions (see ¶ 9.2–¶ 9.4), the penalty is imposed, regardless of the
taxpayer's ignorance of the rules, good intentions, or other excuse.
Amazingly, many taxpayers litigate their liability for this penalty when
they do not even have a colorable argument as to why they qualify for
an exception. The IRS and the courts will never waive the penalty
unless the requirements for an exception are met.

There are 13 exceptions to the penalty, so many individuals are
able to withdraw funds from their plans prior to age 59½ without
penalty. The exceptions are not the same for all types of retirement
plans. Some exceptions available for qualified plans and 403(b)
arrangements are *not* available for IRA distributions. Other exceptions

apply *only* to IRAs. Some exceptions apply differently depending on the type of plan involved.

Most of the exceptions have limited usefulness for planning purposes because they are triggered only in particular hardship situations (such as disability) or depend on a particular use of the funds distributed (such as college tuition or "first time" home purchase). However, there is no "hardship exception" *per se* to this penalty; *Reese*, T.C. Summ. Op. 2006-23; *Gallagher*, T.C. Memo 2001-34; *Deal*, T.C. Memo 1999-352. See, *e.g.*, *Baas*, T.C. Memo 2002-130, and *Czepiel*, T.C. Memo 1999-289, aff'd. by order (1st Cir., Dec. 5, 2000), in which participants who had been incarcerated due to failure to pay child support, and withdrew funds from their retirement plans in order to get out of jail, had to pay the 10 percent penalty on their withdrawals; and *Robertson*, T.C. Memo 2000-100 (need to withdraw funds for "subsistence" is not an exception to the penalty).

One exception stands out as a useful planning tool: the "series of substantially equal periodic payments."

9.2 Exception: "Series of Equal Payments"

9.2.01 Series of substantially equal periodic payments (SOSEPP)

The penalty does not apply to a distribution that is "part of a series of substantially equal periodic payments (not less frequently than annually) made for the life (or life expectancy) of the employee or the joint lives (or joint life expectancies) of such employee and his designated beneficiary." § 72(t)(2)(A)(iv). While at first this exception sounds rather rigid, in fact it is highly flexible because:

1. Rollovers (¶ 2.6) can be used to create an IRA of exactly the desired size to support the series. See ¶ 9.2.04.

2. The payments do not in fact have to continue for the entire life or life expectancy period. The distributions must continue only until the participant reaches age 59½, or until five years have elapsed, whichever occurs later. ¶ 9.3.02.

3. The IRS allows several methods for determining the size of the "equal payments" (which do not in fact have to be equal). See ¶ 9.2.05.

This is the most significant exception for planning purposes. All the other exceptions are tied to a specific use of the money (home purchase, college tuition), or to some type of hardship situation (death, disability), or are otherwise narrowly limited. In contrast, everyone who has an IRA (or who can get one via a rollover from some other type of plan) can use the SOSEPP exception.

A participant in a qualified plan (QRP) can also use this exception to take a series of payments *from* the QRP, but only if he has separated from service. § 72(t)(3)(B). If the participant is still employed, and the QRP permits in-service distributions he can roll a distribution over to an IRA and take the SOSEPP from the IRA. Separation from service is not required for a SOSEPP from an IRA.

Alternatively, if he is terminating employment and wants to take his SOSEPP from the QRP for some reason, he can take the SOSEPP from the QRP based on his entire QRP account balance, or he can roll over to an IRA a one-time "independent" payment from the QRP and take a SOSEPP from the QRP based on the remaining balance. Reg. § 1.402(c)-2, A-6; PLR 2005-50039.

There is one significant limitation on the SOSEPP exception: Drastic consequences generally ensue if the series is "modified" before the end of the five year/age 59½ minimum duration; see ¶ 9.3.01.

9.2.02 *How this exception works*

The SOSEPP exception starts from the premise that there is a fund of money (the retirement plan account) that will be gradually exhausted by a series of regular distributions over the applicable period of time, which is (1) the life expectancy of the participant or (2) the joint life expectancy of the participant and his beneficiary. Thus, the SOSEPP must be designed so that, *if* it continued for that period of time (which it won't; see ¶ 9.3.02), it would exactly exhaust the fund.

Note that § 72(t)(2)(A)(iv) itself does not say that the SOSEPP must be designed to *exhaust* the account over the applicable time period; it says only that the equal payments must be "made for" such period. This wording precludes a series of equal payments that would exhaust the fund *before* the end of the period, but does not preclude a series of equal payments that would be too small to exhaust the fund. For example, if payments of $50,000 per year would exhaust the account over the applicable period, why can't the participant take equal annual payments of any amount *up to* $50,000 per year?

However, the IRS's interpretation of this exception is that the SOSEPP must be designed to exhaust the fund over the applicable time period. See Notice 87-16, 1987-1 C.B. 446, A-12, and PLR 9805023. The participant cannot take annual distributions that are too small to exhaust the account, even if they are equal, regular, payments designed to continue over the applicable time period. Fortunately, it is easy to get around this limitation; see ¶ 9.2.12.

9.2.03 *Notice 89-25 (A-12) and its successor, Rev. Rul. 2002-62*

Notice 89-25, 1989-1 C.B. 662, A-12, laid out three methods a participant could use to compute the payments in his SOSEPP. The three methods are usually called the "required minimum distributions" (RMD) method (i.e., any method that "would be acceptable" for computing required distributions under § 401(a)(9)), the "amortization" method (similar to a level payment mortgage amortized over the applicable life expectancy) and the "annuitization" method (annuitizing the retirement account over the applicable life expectancy).

Revenue Ruling 2002-62, 2002-42 I.R.B. 710, which supercedes Notice 89-25, A-12, continues the same three methods but changes the rules regarding which life expectancy tables, interest rate, and account balance may be used in designing a SOSEPP. In Notice 2004-15, 2004-91 I.R.B. 526, the IRS confirmed that the same rules apply in applying the SOSEPP exception to nonqualified annuities under § 72(q)(2)(D). Under the new regime, greater specificity in the rules comes at the price of some loss of flexibility.

Rev. Rul. 2002-62 applies to any SOSEPP commencing after 2002, and "may be used for distributions commencing in 2002." Shortly after issuing the Ruling, the IRS posted a document called "FAQs regarding Revenue Ruling 2002-62" at its web site, which is "for general information only and should not be cited as any type of legal authority." You can find these "IRS Frequently Asked Questions" at www.rothira.com or at www.irs.gov/retirement/article.

9.2.04 *Steps required to initiate a SOSEPP*

The first step in initiating a SOSEPP is to decide what size payments the participant wants to take. Ideally, the payments desired will not require the participant to use his entire plan balance. With the help of an actuary, the participant determines what size of IRA would be required to support a SOSEPP of the amount he wants, and that amount is transferred into a separate IRA from which the SOSEPP payments are made. See Cornelia Example at ¶ 7.6.03.

This leaves the balance of his funds in a plan or IRA that is not involved in the SOSEPP and which is available for the participant's later needs to, *e.g.*, take an extra payment (on which he would pay the 10 percent penalty unless he qualifies for another exception) without being deemed to have impermissibly "modified" the SOSEPP (¶ 9.3.01) or even to start another SOSEPP (¶ 9.2.13).

In some cases, the participant just wants the largest possible payments he can get based on the amount of money he has in his IRA or plan, and asks the actuary simply to determine which combination of life expectancy, interest rate, and permitted method will extract the largest possible payments.

The participant must make several choices about the design of the series:

A.   Choose one of the three permitted methods. ¶ 9.2.05.

B.   Choose a life expectancy table. ¶ 9.2.07–¶ 9.2.09.

C.   If using the amortization or annuitization method, choose an interest rate (¶ 9.2.10) and decide whether or not to use "annual recalculation" (¶ 9.2.06).

D.   Choose an initial account balance valuation date. ¶ 9.2.11.

E.   Decide whether payments will be monthly, quarterly, or annually. The "periodic payments" must be paid at regular intervals at least annually. Rev. Rul. 2002-62, § 1.02(b). Though Rev. Rul. 2002-62 and its follow-up "FAQs" use only annual payments in their examples, monthly payments are apparently also popular (see, *e.g.*, PLRs 2002-14029, 2002-14034, 2002-03072).

The big decisions are *choice of method* and *choice of life expectancy table*. These choices are interrelated, not sequential. For example, if the participant's highest priority is might say certainty of payment size he would choose the amortization or annuitization method and the Single Life or Uniform Lifetime Table. Conversely, if the ability to vary payments is his major goal, he would lean towards the RMD method, or one of the other two methods with annual recalculation, and the Joint and Survivor Life Table, ¶ 9.2.08. The other choices (interest rate and initial valuation date) are then interwoven with these to arrive at the exact payment amount.

Although the IRS methods for calculating the payments appear easy, and software programs (see Appendix C) make them appear even easier, consider engaging an actuary to design the series if the amounts involved are substantial. Actuarial calculations can easily be bungled by non-actuaries; see, *e.g.*, PLR 9705033 (penalty imposed because the required payments were improperly calculated by the client's financial advisor). Also, a good actuary can design a series that will most precisely achieve the client's goals (such as small or large payments and the ability to add another series later).

9.2.05 *The three methods: RMD, amortization, annuitization*

The participant has a choice of three IRS-approved methods for the design of his SOSEPP:

A. **RMD method.** Under the RMD method, the "series" payments are calculated in the same manner as required distributions under § 401(a)(9): The account balance (revalued annually) is divided by a life expectancy factor each year to produce the required payment. See Chapter 1.

"Under this method, the account balance, the number from the chosen life expectancy table and the resulting annual payments are redetermined for each year." Rev. Rul. 2002-62, § 2.01(a). Because this method requires annual revaluation of the account, payments fluctuate (both up and down) with investment performance. The advantage of annual revaluation is that the account will never be wiped out by the SOSEPP payments, as can occur with the fixed payments usually used under the other two methods.

The drawback of the RMD method (or any method that employs annual recalculation) is the unpredictability of the payments. Smaller payments might be required just when the participant needs more income, or higher payments when he is in a high bracket. Once the participant has chosen the RMD method, he cannot later change to another method. The only control the participant can maintain over the size of the payments is through his choice of beneficiary, *if* he elected to use the Joint and Survivor Life Table (¶ 9.2.08).

B.   **Amortization method:** Under this method, the participant chooses a reasonable interest rate (¶ 9.2.10), and a life expectancy table (¶ 9.2.07–¶ 9.2.09.), then takes regular payments as if the account were a self-amortizing level payment mortgage (except that he is receiving, rather than making, the payments). Once the amount of the first payment is determined, the payments never vary, regardless of the investment performance of the account (unless annual recalculation is used; see ¶ 9.2.06). If using the amortization method, the participant has the option, in any year after the first year, of switching to the RMD method. See ¶ 9.3.04.

C.   **Annuitization method:** Under this method, the participant chooses a reasonable interest rate (¶ 9.2.10), and single or joint life expectancy, then divides the account balance by an annuity factor, as if the account were being annuitized over the applicable life expectancy. "The annuity factor is derived using the mortality table in Appendix B [of Rev. Rul. 2002-62] and using the chosen interest rate." Once the amount of the first payment is determined, the payments never vary, regardless of the investment performance of the account (unless annual recalculation is used; see ¶ 9.2.06). If using the amortization method, the participant has the option, in any year after the first year, to switch to the RMD method. See ¶ 9.3.04.

Note that there is little difference between the amortization and annuitization methods:

❏   It is easier to calculate the payments under the amortization method. The annuitization method requires an actuary or math whiz, unless you use one of the excellent software programs that perform these calculations such as NumberCruncher® or Brentmark® (Appendix C).

❏   The hypothetical 10-years-younger beneficiary concept is available with the amortization method; it is not clear whether it also applies to the annuitization method. See ¶ 9.2.07(B).

However, beyond these minimal differences, both these methods are pretty much the same, providing permanently fixed payments year after year (though some participants have gotten IRS approval to use annual recalculation with these methods; see ¶ 9.2.06). There *is* a significant difference between these two methods, with their *fixed* payments (unless annual recalculation is elected; see ¶ 9.2.06), and the RMD method, which always has *variable* payments. If the participant wants variable payments he selects the RMD method, or one of the other methods with annual recalculation (¶ 9.2.06). If the participant wants fixed payments, he selects the annuitization or amortization method, without annual recalculation, knowing he can always switch later to the RMD method if he needs to reduce the payments to avoid wiping out the account.

> **Expert tip: End-of-year vs. beginning-of-year payments**
>
> Guerdon Ely, MBA, CFP, President of Prudent Investors, Chico, CA, an investment advisor and IRA expert, points out that, when computing series payments using either the amortization or annuitization method, payments will be larger if you assume end-of-period rather than beginning-of-period payments. In Notice 89-25 and rulings based on it, the IRS clearly allowed use of an end-of-period payment assumption. It is not clear whether this attitude continues under the stricter regime of Rev. Rul. 2002-62. Pending further guidance, use of a beginning-of-period payment assumption would appear more prudent.

9.2.06 *Variations on the three methods*

The three methods are not the only possible ways to design a SOSEPP; however, if varying from these pre-approved models it is necessary to obtain advance approval from the IRS via a private letter ruling. See IRS FAQs (¶ 9.2.03), last question.

Although Rev. Rul. 2002-62 stated that, under the annuitization and amortization methods, "the account balance, …[the other factors] and the resulting annual payment are determined once for the first distribution year and the annual payment is the same amount in each succeeding year," the IRS has since issued several letter rulings approving SOSEPP designs that incorporate various annual adjustments, despite using the amortization or annuitization method. In PLR 2004-32021, the IRS approved two SOSEPPs (one each for a husband and a wife; they obtained a joint ruling, thereby saving one "user fee") using the amortization method. Each spouse's SOSEPP used that spouse's life expectancy (from the IRS single life table), an interest rate of 120 percent of the Federal mid-term rate (the highest rate allowed under Rev. Rul. 2002-62), and the prior year-end account balance. The spouses proposed to recalculate their "fixed" amortization payments annually, using each year's then-current life expectancy, prior year-end account balance, and 120 percent-of-Federal-mid-term-rate interest rate. An identical SOSEPP design was approved for another taxpayer in PLR 2004-32024.

In PLR 2004-32023, the IRS approved an annuitization-method SOSEPP that provided for annual recalculation of the payments in the same manner. Each year's payment would be calculated using the account balance and Federal mid-term rate as of December 31 of the year prior to the distribution year, and the annuitization factor would be based on the participant's age in the distribution year. More recalculation rulings have followed; see PLRs 2005-51032, 2005-51033, 2005-44023. The key to the IRS's approval in these rulings is that, even though the payments will vary in amount, the payment is determined exactly the same way each year.

The flexibility offered by annual recalculation is a welcome addition to the SOSEPP menu. As a reminder, to qualify for the SOSEPP exception, all elements of the SOSEPP design must be fixed at the outset. Thus, someone who has already launched a fixed-payment SOSEPP using the amortization or annuitization method cannot later change to the annual recalculation method of determining his payments. Annual recalculation is available only if it is part of the SOSEPP design from the outset.

Should people use annual-recalculation SOSEPPs modeled on these PLRs without getting their own PLRs? That's not clear. The IRS has stated as a matter of "general information" that any variation not explicitly blessed in Rev. Rul. 2002-62 would require an advance ruling. On the other hand, it is hard to see how the IRS could argue that a SOSEPP that follows a method explicitly blessed in one of these PLRs does not qualify for the penalty exception.

The next question is whether someone will now seek a PLR approving a SOSEPP with an annual cost-of-living adjustment, similar to those approved prior to Rev. Rul. 2002-62 in PLRs 9816028, 9747045, 9723035, and 9536031. For a rejected SOSEPP design, see PLR 2004-37038.

9.2.07 *Choose single or joint life expectancy*

The participant must choose a single or joint life expectancy period for the hypothetical duration of his SOSEPP. The choice is among three life expectancy tables if the participant is using the RMD or amortization method ("A"), or among two (three?) "factors" if using the annuitization method ("B"). The choice of payout period is irrevocable if the SOSEPP commenced after 2002. Rev. Rul. 2002-62, § 2.02(a), last two sentences. For other SOSEPPs, see ¶ 9.3.05, #3.

A. **Three tables for RMD or amortization method.** Rev. Rul. 2002-62 provides that a taxpayer using the RMD or amortization method must select one of three life expectancy tables for calculating his SOSEPP: the Single Life Table, the Joint and Survivor Life Table, or the Uniform Lifetime Table. Rev. Rul. 2002-62, § 2.01(a), (b), § 2.02(a).

The Single and Joint and Survivor Life Tables are contained in Reg. § 1.401(a)(9)-9, A-1, A-3. The Uniform Lifetime Table (showing the joint and survivor life expectancy of the participant and a hypothetical beneficiary who is 10 years younger than the participant) is contained in Appendix A of Rev. Rul. 2002-62. It is an expanded version of the Uniform Lifetime Table contained in Reg. § 1.401(a)(9)-9, A-2, extended down to age 10. The Single Life and Uniform Lifetime Tables are also in Appendix A of this book (Tables 2 and 3).

The choice of a table is not only a choice regarding the hypothetical duration of the series, but also between a predictable life expectancy factor (as provided by the Single Life Table or Uniform Lifetime Table, ¶ 9.2.09) or a variable life expectancy factor (as potentially provided by the Joint and Survivor Life Table, ¶ 9.2.08).

B. **Only two choices for annuitization?** For an annuitization-method SOSEPP, the annuity period is "the life of the taxpayer (or the joint lives of the individual and beneficiary)." Notice 89-25 permitted use of any "reasonable mortality table" under the annuitization method. Rev. Rul. 2002-62 took away that option, and supplies its own table of mortality factors that must be used in determining payments under the annuitization method. Rev. Rul. 2002-62, § 2.02(a).

Under the amortization and RMD methods, distributions are determined using the "chosen life expectancy table," and any of the three life expectancy tables may be used "to determine distribution periods"; see "A." However, the life expectancy tables and the "distribution period" concept do not apply to the annuitization method, so it is not clear whether a participant using the annuitization method can use his joint life expectancy with a hypothetical 10-years-younger beneficiary or only with his actual beneficiary.

9.2.08 *Notes on Joint and Survivor Life Table*

If the participant elects the Joint and Survivor Life Table, then the factor used to determine the first payment in the series is based on the joint life expectancy of the participant and his ACTUAL beneficiary. Rev. Rul. 2002-62, § 2.02(b). If the participant is using the RMD method, then the beneficiary (for purposes of determining the factor under the Table) is redetermined every year.

Under the annuitization or amortization method, subsequent changes of beneficiary will have no effect on the payments so long as the participant continues using that method—but if he switches in mid-stream to the RMD method (¶ 9.3.04), and is required to or chooses to continue using the Joint and Survivor Life Table, then his subsequent payments would be determined using the joint life expectancy of himself and his actual beneficiary.

Under the Joint and Survivor Life Table, the participant's actual beneficiary is determined as of January 1 of the distribution year, using the same rules as apply for determining the beneficiary for minimum distribution purposes. For example, naming an estate as beneficiary would be treated as having "no Designated Beneficiary," or if multiple beneficiaries are named the oldest one's life expectancy is used. See ¶ 1.7. When the participant has elected the Joint and Survivor Life Table, but has no Designated Beneficiary on January 1, the Single Life Table is used for that year's payment(s). Rev. Rul. 2002-62, § 2.02(b).

The participant who wants maximum control over the size of his payments, and who can tolerate risk and complexity, would gravitate towards the Joint and Survivor Life Table, because with this table (combined with the RMD method) the participant can affect the size of his payments by naming a different beneficiary.

9.2.09 *Notes on Single, Uniform Lifetime Tables*

The only difference between the Single Life Table and the Uniform Lifetime Table is the size of the annual payment relative to the size of the account. A participant who wants larger payments would choose the Single Life Table. A participant who wants smaller payments would use the Uniform Lifetime Table. When using the "separate IRA" SOSEPP recommended at ¶ 9.2.04, the Single Life Table should always be used, to generate the largest possible payments relative to the account size. Under both of these tables, there is no possibility of changing to a different table later, and there is no possibility of affecting the size of the payments by changing the designated beneficiary (compare ¶ 9.2.08).

With both these tables, you find the appropriate factor for the first year's payment based on the participant's age on his birthday in that year. Rev. Rul. 2002-62, § 2.02(a). If using the RMD method, you then go back to the originally-chosen table every year to get that year's factor, based on the participant's new age. If using the amortization or annuitization method, you don't go back to the table every year because the payments are fixed in amount (unless your series design is based on annual recalculation; see ¶ 9.2.06).

If the participant elects to use the Single Life or Uniform Lifetime Table, it will make no difference (either at the commencement of the series or at any time thereafter) who is designated as beneficiary of the retirement account. Thus, the Single Life or Uniform Lifetime Table should be selected if the participant wants the greatest possible predictability as to how his distributions will be calculated, and wants to be able to change his beneficiary without having that change impact the size of his SOSEPP payments.

9.2.10 *What interest rate assumption is used*

There is no interest rate assumption under the RMD method. The RMD method involves annual revaluation of the account balance, so investment performance is taken into account only in retrospect.

For the amortization and annuitization methods, it is necessary to choose an interest rate (representing the hypothetical projected investment return on the account during the period of the SOSEPP). The participant may use "any interest rate that is not more than 120 percent of the federal mid-term rate (determined in accordance with section 1274(d) for either of the two months immediately preceding the month in which the distribution begins)." Rev. Rul. 2002-62, § 2.02(c). You can find the monthly federal mid-terms rates at the IRS web site www.irs.gov/tax_regs/fedrates.html, or at www.tigertables.com or www.leimbergservices.com.

Prior to Rev. Rul. 2002-62, the IRS did not prescribe either a safe harbor or a maximum interest rate. Notice 89-25 (A-12) required only that the participant use a rate "that does not exceed a reasonable interest rate on the date payments commence." In pre-2003 letter rulings the IRS had approved rates as high as 120 percent of the applicable federal long-term rate (PLR 9747045). *The flexibility to use "any reasonable rate" does not exist for SOSEPPs commencing after 2002; 120 percent of federal mid-term is now the ceiling.*

9.2.11 *What account balance is used*

Whichever method the participant is using, he must apply a certain factor to an account balance. The account balance "must be determined in a reasonable manner based on the facts and circumstances." Rev. Rul. 2002-62, § 2.02(d).

Under all three methods, the participant must select a valuation date for the first year's payment. The IRS provides an example the gist of which is that any date from the last prior year end to the day before the distribution would be fine. There is no specific prohibition against using a date earlier than the last prior year-end, but it would seem that the prior year-end (or any subsequent valuation date, up to the date of the first distribution) would be a safe harbor.

This reasonable approach gives participants time to do their planning based on a particular valuation date (such as the last prior year-end) without having to rush to get the payments started before the next monthly valuation arrives, while also giving them the flexibility to make a last minute change in the valuation date (prior to the first SOSEPP payment) if violent market fluctuations make the last prior year-end value no longer realistic.

Under the *amortization* and *annuitization* methods, the account balance is determined only once, at the beginning of the series. Since the payments do not fluctuate, there is no need to look at the account balance again after the first year (unless annual recalculation is part of the series design; see ¶ 9.2.06).

Under the *RMD method* the account balance is always redetermined annually. Must the participant use the same valuation date for this purpose every year? No, according to Rev. Rul. 2002-62: From the IRS example of a SOSEPP commencing on July 15 of year 1 using the RMD method from an IRA that had daily valuations: "For subsequent years, under the required minimum distribution method, it would be reasonable to use the value *either* on the December 31 of the prior year *or* on a date within a reasonable period before that year's distribution." § 2.02(d) (emphasis added).

However, the subsequently-issued IRS FAQs (¶ 9.2.03) contain an entirely different statement: "The account balance may be determined in any reasonable manner *that is used consistently.*" (Emphasis added.) The FAQs provide an example ("Mr. B") suggesting that the same valuation date used in the first year (*e.g.*, prior year-end balance) must be used in subsequent years. It is outrageous that the IRS issues an authoritative pronouncement (a Revenue Ruling), then almost immediately issues "informal" guidance that directly contradicts its own authoritative guidance.

9.2.12 *Applying the SOSEPP exception to multiple IRAs*

Generally, all of an individual's IRAs are aggregated (treated as one account) for purposes of determining how much of any distribution is *included in gross income.* ¶ 2.1.10; IRS Notice 89-25, A-7. However, no provision requires IRAs to be aggregated for purposes of the *penalty* under § 72(t), or the SOSEPP exception.

For purposes of structuring a SOSEPP, the participant has several choices: The series can be based on all of his IRAs, aggregated; or on some of the IRAs aggregated, with others excluded; or on one IRA to the exclusion of others. As the IRS said in PLR 9747039, "If a taxpayer owns more than one IRA, any combination of his or her IRAs may be taken into account in determining the distributions by aggregating the account balances of those IRAs. *The specific IRAs taken into account are part of the method of determining the substantially equal periodic payments....*" (Emphasis added.)

All IRAs aggregated: In each of PLRs 9830042, 9824047, and 9545018, all of the participant's IRAs were aggregated for purposes of computing the series payments.

Some IRAs aggregated, others excluded: In PLRs 9816028, 9801050, and 2000-31059, the participant had several IRAs, some of which were aggregated to form the basis of his proposed SOSEPP and the rest of which were not to be counted. The IRS ruled favorably in all cases, requiring only that the series payments be made from the aggregated IRAs and not from the other accounts.

Take series from one IRA, not aggregated with others: In PLR 9818055 the participant was taking a SOSEPP from one of her two IRAs. In PLR 9812038 the participant was taking a SOSEPP from one of his three IRAs and wanted to start a second SOSEPP from a new, fourth, IRA, to be created by transfer of funds from one of the other IRAs (not the IRA that was already supporting the first SOSEPP). The IRS permitted this, and the ruling stated more than once that the taxpayer's IRAs were not aggregated. In PLRs 9747045 and 2001-22048, the participant's IRS-approved SOSEPP was taken from one of two rollover IRAs; the two were not aggregated.

Whichever accounts are included in the initial design of the SOSEPP must be the sole source of payments in the series. Once the SOSEPP begins, funds must not be transferred *out of* the IRAs that are being used to support the series (except to make the SOSEPP payments), or *into* any IRA that is part of the support for the series. See ¶ 9.3.09 regarding rollovers *among* IRAs supporting a SOSEPP.

The ability to choose which IRAs will be aggregated in determining the size of the periodic payments gives the client tremendous flexibility. This flexibility is not unlimited, however. Although it is acceptable to have two IRAs, and use only one of them to support the SOSEPP, the IRS forbids using only *part* of an IRA to support a series. PLR 9705033. Since the participant can easily get to the same result by dividing one IRA into two, this prohibition is little more than a trap for the unwary.

The author has found no rulings or other sources dealing with the aggregation of 403(b) arrangements or qualified retirement plans for purposes of applying the SOSEPP exception.

9.2.13 Starting a second series to run concurrently

A participant receiving a SOSEPP from one or more IRAs may initiate a *second* series of equal payments from a different IRA or set of IRAs. See, *e.g.*, PLR 9812038, discussed at ¶ 9.2.12. PLR 9747039 also permitted starting a second SOSEPP from a different IRA. See PLR 2003-09028 for a good model of exactly how to do this.

However, the participant may not start a second SOSEPP from *the same IRA* (or plan) that is already supporting the first SOSEPP; such a second series would constitute an impermissible "modification" of the first series (see ¶ 9.3.01).

9.2.14 *Procedural and reporting requirements*

There is no specific format for electing one of the three methods. There is no requirement that any of the elections or choices be in writing, or that notice of any choices be delivered to anyone in particular. The usual procedure is for the participant and his professional advisor to prepare detailed worksheets showing the design of the series and how the distributions are calculated. This normal approach is certainly recommended, as the best safeguard for ensuring that the series qualifies for the SOSEPP exception and that such qualification can be proved to the IRS.

However, this approach is not required; a participant who takes distributions from his IRA is exempt from the penalty if the payments he takes coincidentally happen to meet the requirements of Rev. Rul. 2002-62. Similarly, if a participant has obtained a SOSEPP design from his professional advisor, but then fails to comply with it (for example, by taking payments larger or smaller than the advisor recommended, or taking the payments from the wrong IRA), the participant will still qualify for the SOSEPP exception *if* the payments he took could be justified as a SOSEPP under Rev. Rul. 2002-62.

In other words it's possible to be "wrong but lucky." The statute does not require that, in order to avoid the penalty, you take a series of payments "as recommended by a professional advisor"; it requires only that you take a series of substantially equal periodic payments that meets the requirements of Rev. Rul. 2002-62

The plan or IRA will file Form 1099-R each year, reporting the distribution(s) to the IRS. If the plan is aware that the SOSEPP exception applies, the plan can enter distribution code "2" ("Early distribution, exception applies"), in which case the participant does not have to file Form 5329. If the plan enters distribution code "1" on the Form 1099-R ("Early distribution, no known exception"), the participant must file Form 5329 with his income tax return (Form 1040) for the year. On Form 5329, the participant enters the taxable portion of the distribution(s) in Part I, and enters "02" as the exception number in the space provided. There is no requirement to attach any demonstration of compliance with the requirements of the exception. It is advisable to retain documentation of the participant's choices and computations, to demonstrate that any distribution qualifies for the SOSEPP exception, because the burden of proof is on the taxpayer.

In *Evans*, T.C. Memo 1999-33, here is what the IRS asked the participant to produce to prove that his payments qualified for the SOSEPP exception: "[W]e need...worksheets that you prepared (or an explanation) concerning your determination of the period over which the periodic payments would be made and the statements reflecting the periodic payments that were made from the date first made to the present. ...We need to see the documents between 1993 and the present to ensure that the distributions still qualify for the exception."

9.2.15 How professionals use SOSEPPs

The SOSEPP exception can help a client under age 59½ achieve financial, investment, and estate planning goals.

Actuary and retirement expert Bruce Temkin suggests the following program for an under-age 59½ client who needs money to start a business: The client refinances his residence and uses the loan proceeds to cover the immediate financial need. Then he takes from his IRA a SOSEPP (with the size of the payments matched to the mortgage payments) to repay the mortgage. The tax-deductible mortgage interest will reduce the income tax on the IRA distributions.

Individuals have used pre-age 59½ distribution programs to finance early retirement, or just to achieve a better estate balance when IRA assets constituted a disproportionate share of the estate. One individual believed that making capital gain-generating investments *outside* his IRA would be more favorable than continuing to make tax-deferred ordinary income-generating investments *inside* the IRA, so he took a SOSEPP to finance these capital gain investments. A SOSEPP may also be used to fund life insurance premium payments.

Another Temkin idea: Suppose your clients are a young couple. Right now, their estates consist mainly of large IRAs, but they expect to inherit substantial sums in the future from their parents. In view of their eventual expected estate tax problem, they would like to begin making annual gifts to their own children. § 72(t) allows them to take out enough from their IRAs each year to fund their annual gifting program, without penalty.

9.3 Making Changes after SOSEPP Has Begun

9.3.01 *Effects of a forbidden modification of series*

If the participant "modifies" his SOSEPP before a certain period of time has elapsed, he is severely punished. His qualification for the SOSEPP exception is retroactively revoked, and he owes the penalty for all series payments he took prior to age 59½, with interest. As the Code puts it, his "tax for the 1st taxable year in which such modification occurs shall be increased by an amount, determined under regulations, equal to the tax which (but for paragraph (2)(A)(iv)) would have been imposed [under § 72(t)], plus interest for the deferral period." § 72(t)(4)(A).

§ 72(t)(4)(B) defines the "deferral period" over which interest must be calculated, but the definition doesn't make much sense. It is: "the period beginning with the taxable year in which (without regard to paragraph (2)(A)(iv)) [which contains the SOSEPP exception] the distribution *would have been includible in gross income* and ending with the taxable year in which the modification" occurs (emphasis added). This shows that even Congress is confused between "penalty-free" (what the § 72(t) exceptions are all about) and "income tax-free" (which § 72(t) has no bearing on), since *any* distribution from the retirement plan "would have been includible" in the participant's gross income, regardless of whether it qualified under § 72(t)(2)(A)(iv).

Once the participant has modified his series, he cannot start a new SOSEPP from the same plan until the following calendar year, according to PLR 2000-33048.

For how to measure the no-modification period, see ¶ 9.3.02. For death and disability exceptions to the no-modification rule, see ¶ 9.3.03. For how to switch to the RMD method in mid-stream without having a modification, see ¶ 9.3.04–¶ 9.3.05. For other events that have been found to be or not to be a modification, see ¶ 9.3.06–¶ 9.3.07. For the effect of: divorce, see ¶ 9.3.08; rollovers, see ¶ 9.3.09.

9.3.02 *When the no-modification period begins and ends*

The beginning date of the no-modification period is the date of the first payment in the series. The ending date is the fifth anniversary of the date of the first payment in the series, or, *if later*, the date on which the participant attains age 59½. § 72(t)(4)(A). Once this ending date is passed, payments may be freely taken from the plan without penalty (or the series may be suspended—*i.e.*, the participant can STOP taking payments).

Note that the ending date of the five years is not simply the date of the fifth year's payment. The five years ends on the *fifth anniversary of the first payment*. In *Arnold*, 111 T.C. No. 250 (1998), the participant, at age 55, took the first of a series of equal annual payments of $44,000 in December 1989. He took the second, third, fourth, and fifth payments in the series in January 1990, 1991, 1992, and 1993, respectively. In September 1993 he turned 59½, and, thinking he had now completed his greater-of-five-years-or-until-age-59½ requirement (because he had taken all five of the annual required payments and was over age 59½), he took another distribution of $6,776 in November 1993 from the same IRA.

The Tax Court, citing legislative history regarding how to calculate the five-year period, held that this $6,776 distribution was an impermissible modification of the SOSEPP because it occurred less than five years after the date of the first distribution. Therefore, the participant's qualification for the SOSEPP exception was retroactively revoked, and he owed the 10 percent penalty, plus interest, on all five of his $44,000 distributions!

9.3.03 *Exceptions for death or disability*

If the series is modified "by reason of death or disability" there is no penalty. § 72(t)(4)(A). IRS Publication 590 (2005), p. 50, echoes this, saying that a modification does not result in penalty if the "change is made because of your death or disability." Presumably death automatically ends the requirement of continuing the series, since death benefits are exempt from the penalty. ¶ 9.4.01.

"Disability" presumably must be the type of total disability that justifies penalty-free distributions (see ¶ 9.4.02). It is not clear whether the occurrence of such a disability *automatically* ends the requirement of continuing the series, or whether the participant must somehow demonstrate that the series had to be modified *because* of the disability—for example, by showing that he had to increase his distributions because of his disability.

9.3.04 *Changing to RMD method is not a modification*

Rev. Rul. 2002-62 allows a participant using the annuitization or amortization method to change to the RMD method. Because the RMD method requires annual revaluation of the account balance, a downturn in the account value will translate into a reduction in the subsequent year's payment. Thus, the series payments will shrink along with the account value and the account will never run dry.

Similarly, if the investments perform substantially better than the growth assumption used in designing the SOSEPP, switching to the RMD method allows the participant to increase his payments. Also, a participant who elected to use the Joint and Survivor Life Table can, if using the RMD method, manipulate the size of his payments by changing his designated beneficiary; see ¶ 9.2.08.

9.3.05 *How to switch to RMD method*

Here are the requirements for a participant who is using the annuitization or amortization method to switch to the RMD method, from Rev. Rul. 2002-62, § 2.03(b):

1.   He must have used the annuitization or amortization method for the first year's SOSEPP payment(s). He can then switch to the RMD method in the second or any subsequent year.

2.   The switch, once made, is irrevocable. The switch is effective for the year in which it is made and all subsequent years. Any further changes will be considered "modifications."

3.   When he switches, it appears probable that he must continue to use the same life expectancy table (¶ 9.2.07) that his series was originally based on, if his SOSEPP commenced in 2003 or later. A person whose SOSEPP commenced *prior to 2003* can switch to the RMD method at any time, "including use of a different life expectancy table." Rev. Rul. 2002-62, § 3.

What if the participant wants to switch to the RMD method in mid-year, after he has already taken out more money (pursuant to his originally chosen SOSEPP method) for that year than would be required if the payments were calculated using the RMD method? In

PLR 2004-19031, the IRS allowed a participant in this situation to roll back the excess payments into the IRA, so that her net distribution for the year would comply with the newly-elected RMD method. The IRS did not discuss the fact that a distribution that is part of a SOSEPP is not an eligible rollover distribution (¶ 2.6.02(C)).

9.3.06 *What other changes do NOT constitute a modification?*

Receipt of a qualified hurricane distribution from a SOSEPP-paying plan does not constitute modification of the SOSEPP. § 1400Q, IRS Notice 2005-92, 2005-51 I.R.B. 1165, IRS Publication 4492. Converting to a Roth IRA does not constitute a modification; see ¶ 5.5.03. The following other types of changes in a SOSEPP have either been ruled not to be modifications, or have occurred without negative comment in cases or rulings involving other issues:

A.   **Computer system change.** When the paying agent, as part of a change in its computer systems, changed the date of monthly payments in a series to the first day of the month (instead of the last day of the preceding month), the change was ruled to be "ministerial," and not a "modification," even though the change meant that the recipient's income would include one fewer payment for the year the switch was made. PLR 9514026.

B.   **Plan termination.** The participant in PLR 9221052 was receiving monthly payments from a pension plan. When that plan terminated in the middle of his SOSEPP, he sought to roll over the termination distribution to an IRA and continue taking the same monthly payments from the IRA. The IRS ruled that this change would not constitute a modification.

C.   **Payments not on anniversary date.** In the case of annual payments, it does not appear to be required that each year's payment occur on the anniversary of the first payment. See Rev. Rul. 2002-62, § 2.02(d). See PLR 9747039, in which the IRS ruled that the participant would qualify for the exception "if [he] received at least five annual payments of $510,000 from IRA Y (at least one during each of the years 1997, 1998, 1999, 2000 and 2001) and does not otherwise modify his IRA distribution scheme." See also *Arnold*, discussed at ¶ 9.3.02, where the participant took his first annual payment in December of 1989 and his subsequent annual payments in January each year, and this was apparently acceptable.

D.   **Plan exhausted.** If investment performance is poor, fixed payments under the amortization or annuitization method might exhaust the account. Running out of money due to taking the payments called for by the SOSEPP will not be considered a modification of the series. Rev. Rul. 2002-62, § 2.03(a).

E.   **IRA provider error.** A participant attempting to take his annual series payment was thwarted by the IRA custodian's failure to send a distribution on time, despite the participant's diligence in requesting the distribution. The IRS ruled that the late payment did not constitute a modification because it was beyond the participant's control. PLR 2005-03036.

F.   **Participant error.** In PLR 2006-01044, the participant started an amortization method SOSEPP from four IRAs, but due to a math error his first payment was too small by less than 2/10ths of one percent. The IRS ruled that the underpayment (and subsequent "catch up distribution" to correct the error) did not constitute modifications of the series.

9.3.07 *What changes DO constitute a modification?*

Examples of prohibited modifications of a SOSEPP include:

A.   **Stopping the payments.** See PLR 9818055, in which the participant terminated the series because she went back to work; she had to pay the penalty.

B.   **Taking extra payment.** Taking a payment that is over and above the payments required as part of the series is a modification. See *Arnold*, discussed at ¶ 9.3.02. Except in the case of a Qualified Hurricane Distribution (§ 1400Q), there is no authority for the proposition that an extra distribution would not constitute a modification of the SOSEPP merely because the extra distribution itself qualifies for an exception to the penalty.

C.   **Changing the "period" of periodic payments.** Presumably, changing from annual payments to quarterly or monthly payments (or vice versa), even if the total payments for the year add up to the right amount, would be considered a modification. There is no authority for the proposition that the size of individual payments in the series does not matter so long as the total is the same each year.

D.   **Additions to the account; transfers into, out of, the account.** "Under all three methods, substantially equal periodic payments are calculated with respect to *an account balance* as of the first valuation date selected…. Thus, a modification to the series of payments will occur if, after such date, there is (i) any addition to the account balance other than gains or losses, [or] (ii) any nontaxable transfer of a portion of the account balance to another retirement plan…." Rev. Rul. 2002-62, § 2.02(e)(ii). See ¶ 9.3.08 for effect of this rule on a divorce-related split of the benefits. See ¶ 9.3.09 regarding tax-free transfers among multiple IRAs that are supporting a SOSEPP, or transfer of an entire IRA to a new IRA provider.

E.   **Changing how the payments in the series are determined.**

In PLR 9821056, the participant retired at age 47 and started a series of equal annual payments from his IRA. These payments were based on his then-life expectancy, existing account balance, and projected rate of return. Five years later he wanted to recalculate the rest of the required payments, based on his new life expectancy and account balance and a new projected rate of return that reflected the actual investment experience of the account (which had been much more favorable than originally projected).

He sought a ruling from the IRS that this would not be a "modification," on the theory that the change amounted to merely an adjustment to reflect actual experience, and the series was in fact continuing exactly as before. Unfortunately for him, the IRS ruled that "such a proposed change in payments…would be a modification." The IRS ruled similarly in PLR 1999-43050 for another participant who wanted to add a cost of living adjustment (or one-time catch-up payment) after the fact to reflect much higher-than-expected returns in the IRA supporting his SOSEPP.

Ironically, these participants could have designed their series initially to build in the flexibility the IRS did not allow them to add later, by using annual recalculation (see ¶ 9.2.06). Alternatively, each participant could have kept some of his IRA money in another account, separate from the account supporting the SOSEPP, and used the second IRA to start a second SOSEPP later (¶ 9.2.13). Especially with younger clients, it is desirable to build flexibility into the program.

9.3.08 *Effect of divorce on the SOSEPP*

If the participant gets divorced in the middle of his SOSEPP, the divorce court may award a share of the retirement plan that is supporting the SOSEPP to the participant's ex-spouse. Usually the spouse's share is given to her by means of a tax-free transfer to the spouse's account, under a QDRO (§ 414(p)) or the IRA equivalent (§ 408(d)(6)). What happens to the SOSEPP in that case?

Prior to Rev. Rul. 2002-62, the IRS had dealt sensibly with this situation in letter rulings. In PLR 9739044, a participant got divorced after commencing his SOSEPP. The IRAs supporting the series were community property. The divorce court divided the IRAs and gave half of each to the participant's ex-wife. Both spouses then apparently continued the SOSEPP, with each of them taking (from his or her respective share of the formerly unified IRAs) one half of the required annual distribution. The IRS ruled that, because the division of the IRA between the spouses was nontaxable under § 408(d)(6), and in view of the "continuous compliance with the requirements of § 72(t)(2)(A)(iv)," there was no modification.

In PLR 2001-16056 (another community property case), the participant was taking four separate SOSEPPs from four IRAs, A, B, C, and D. The IRS allowed him to cease taking payments from IRAs C and D (which were transferred to his ex-wife pursuant to § 408(d)(6)), without penalty, so long as he continued taking, from IRAs A and B, the same payments he had been taking from IRAs A and B prior to the divorce. Unlike in PLR 9739044, there is no indication that the wife would continue taking the payments from the IRAs transferred to her. In PLR 2000-27060 the IRS ruled that a wife who received part of her ex-husband's IRA in the divorce was not required to continue taking any SOSEPP payments just because he had been taking them.

The three taxpayers in PLRs 2002-02074, 2002-02075, and 2002-02076 were receiving SOSEPPs from their IRAs. They were losing respectively 50, 40, and 45 percent of their IRAs to their spouses in divorce proceedings. The IRS allowed them to reduce their SOSEPP payments by 50, 40, and 45 percent respectively, without such reductions being considered a modification. A similar proportionate reduction of SOSEPP payments upon divorce was allowed in PLRs 2000-50046, 2002-14034, and 2002-25040.

Rev. Rul. 2002-62 gave the IRS the perfect opportunity to say that, in the event of a tax-free divorce-related transfer of a portion of a SOSEPP-supporting IRA or other plan to the participant's spouse, the participant could reduce his SOSEPP payments by the same proportion as the amount of the account transferred to the spouse, as was done in PLRs cited above. Or that a participant could switch to the RMD method in that event, so his payments would automatically adjust downwards.

Unfortunately the IRS did not say either of those things. Instead they said just the opposite: "[A]ny nontaxable transfer of a portion of the account balance to another retirement plan" WILL be a modification of the series. ¶ 9.3.07(D). Thus, every participant in this situation must seek a letter ruling (with attendant filing fees and legal fees—extra costs people do not need when they are getting divorced), not only to change the amount of their SOSEPP payments, but even to avoid having the divorce-triggered transfer itself be considered a modification.

9.3.09 *Transfers among IRAs supporting a SOSEPP*

As explained at ¶ 9.2.12, two or more IRAs can be aggregated for purposes of calculating and paying a SOSEPP. Once the SOSEPP commences, it is essential that no assets be transferred into or out of those IRAs from any other plan, because of the rule discussed at ¶ 9.3.07(D).

However, this rule does not preclude moving assets *among the IRAs that are included in the SOSEPP account balance*, nor does it preclude *moving the entire SOSEPP-supporting IRA to a new IRA provider* (for the purpose of changing investment vehicles or advisors) as long as the funds in the SOSEPP-supporting IRA(s) are not commingled with funds of any other IRA or plan.

Rev. Rul. 2002-62 decrees that a transfer of a "portion of the account balance to another retirement plan" is a forbidden modification of the SOSEPP. The "account balance" referred to is the account balance used to determine and pay the SOSEPP payments—i.e., it is the collective balance of the aggregated IRAs that are supporting the SOSEPP. The purpose of the anti-transfer rule in Rev. Rul. 2002-62 is to prevent the account balance from being augmented or diminished by anything other than investment gains and losses, and SOSEPP distributions. Transferring funds among the accounts that are paying the SOSEPP does not augment or diminish the account balance; there is no forbidden "addition to" the balance being used to compute and pay the SOSEPP distributions, nor is there a transfer of part of the balance to "another" retirement plan, i.e., a retirement plan outside the circle of IRAs that are the source of the SOSEPP. The IRS specifically so ruled in PLR 2000-31059.

This principle also protects the individual who is taking a SOSEPP from an IRA and wishes to transfer the entire IRA to a different custodian, just for investment reasons, without altering the amount or timing of his SOSEPP payments. (Needless to say, the IRA into which the SOSEPP-supporting IRA is being transferred cannot have in it any other funds.) In this case, the "IRAs supporting the SOSEPP" would be the old IRA and the new IRA, with no commingling of funds from any *other* IRA or plan.

PLR 2006-16046 supports this conclusion. This ruling dealt primarily with an inadvertent commingling of the SOSEPP IRA with other IRA funds (due to a financial institution error). In providing the factual background for its ruling regarding the institutional error, the IRS noted without comment that, during the SOSEPP (and prior to and unrelated to the occurrence of this financial institution error), the taxpayer had rolled the entire SOSEPP-paying IRA ("IRA M") into a different IRA ("IRA P"), from which he continued taking the SOSEPP payments. The fact that the IRS ruled that he still had a valid SOSEPP after this rollover shows that merely transferring the SOSEPP IRA to a different custodian does not violate the no-transfers-in-or-out rule.

9.4 Other Exceptions to the Penalty

We now turn to the other exceptions to the § 72(t) penalty. Although these lack the broadly applicable planning possibilities of the SOSEPP, each can be useful in particular situations.

9.4.01 *Death benefits*

A distribution "made to a beneficiary (or to the estate of the employee) on or after the death of the employee" is exempt from the penalty. § 72(t)(2)(A)(ii). This exception applies to distributions from all types of plans. Thus death benefits may be distributed penalty-free from any type of plan or IRA, regardless of whether the *beneficiary* is under age 59½ and regardless of whether the *participant* had attained age 59½ at the time of his death.

Despite the unique clarity of this exception, it generates confusion for the following reason: If a surviving spouse rolls over benefits inherited from the deceased spouse to the surviving spouse's *own* IRA, the rolled-over funds cease to be death benefits; they become simply part of the surviving spouse's own retirement account. Thus, distributions from the rollover IRA will once again be subject to the § 72(t) penalty rules if the surviving spouse is under age 59½—even if the deceased spouse was over age 59½ when he died. See ¶ 3.2.02 for planning implications.

9.4.02 *Distributions attributable to total disability*

A distribution from any type of plan that is "attributable to the employee's being disabled" is not subject to the penalty. § 72(t)(2)(A)(iii).

Disabled is defined in § 72(m)(7): It means "unable to engage in any substantial gainful activity by reason of any medically determinable physical or mental impairment which can be expected to result in death or to be of long-continued and indefinite duration." Note that the definition requires *total* disability. In PLR 2002-14029, a disabled participant sought approval for a SOSEPP (¶ 9.2); presumably he was not disabled enough to qualify for the disability exception.

Reg. § 1.72-17A(f)(1), (2), (interpreting § 72(m) as it applies to lump sum distributions to self-employed persons) provides the following further elaboration on this definition: "In determining whether an individual's impairment makes him unable to engage in any substantial gainful activity, primary consideration shall be given to the nature and severity of his impairment. Consideration shall also be given to other factors such as the individual's education, training, and work experience. The substantial gainful activity to which section 72(m)(7) refers is the activity, or a comparable activity, *in which the individual customarily engaged prior to the arising of the disability* or prior to retirement if the individual was retired at the time the disability arose." Emphasis added. Although the IRS's own regulation says that the "gainful activity" referred to is the individual's customary activity or a comparable one, IRS Publication 590 (2005), p. 50, says you "are considered disabled if you can furnish proof that you cannot do *any* substantial gainful activity because of your physical or mental condition." Emphasis added.

§ 72(m)(7) also states that "An individual shall not be considered to be disabled unless he furnishes proof of the existence thereof [sic] in such form and manner as the Secretary may require." IRS Publication 590 (2005) states that "A physician must determine that your condition can be expected to result in death or to be of long continued and indefinite duration." This requirement is not waived for those whose religious beliefs prohibit them from consulting physicians; the Tax Court points out that the requirement does not impair the free exercise of religion, it just makes such exercise more expensive in some cases. *Fohrmeister*, 73 T.C. Memo 2483, 2486 (1997).

Reg. § 1.72-17A(f) also lists certain impairments, such as "Damage to the brain or brain abnormality which has resulted in severe loss of judgment, intellect, orientation, or memory," which are said to "ordinarily," but not "in and of themselves," result in the necessary impairment. An individual suffering from depression was not "disabled" where he continued his normal occupation (securities trading). *Dwyer*, 106 T.C. 337 (1996). Earning a salary and starting an engineering business are both activities that are "inconsistent with the exigencies of the statutory definition of disability." *Kovacevic*, 64 TCM 1076 (1992) (another depression case). A chemical engineer who stayed on the job with apparently reduced duties and reduced pay was not disabled. *Haas*, T.C. Summ. Op. 2005-172.

What does it mean that the distribution must be "attributable" to the disability? Contrast this wording with § 402(e)(4)(A) (the definition of "lump sum distribution"), which gives lump sum distribution status to an otherwise-qualifying distribution made "after the employee has become disabled," without any requirement that the distribution be "attributable to" the disability.

If the distribution is from an employer plan, and is specifically triggered by a provision in the plan calling for distribution of benefits in case of disability, then the distribution is clearly "attributable" to the employee's being disabled. If the plan does not specifically provide for disability benefits, but does provide for distribution of benefits upon termination of employment, and the cause of the termination of employment was the employee's disability, once again it would appear the distribution is "attributable" to the employee's being disabled.

But what if the termination of employment occurred long before the disability struck? Or what if the distribution is from an IRA, distributions from which can be taken at any time without regard to either disability or termination of employment? In Publication 590 (2005), p. 50, the IRS reiterates that the distribution from an IRA must be "because" of the disability to qualify for this exception. However, in PLR 2001-26037 the IRS said any distributions that commenced after the participant was disabled would be exempt from the penalty.

9.4.03 *Distributions to pay deductible medical expenses*

Distributions after 1996 from any type of plan are penalty-free "to the extent such distributions do not exceed the amount allowable as a deduction under § 213 to the employee for amounts paid during the taxable year for medical care (determined without regard to whether the employee itemizes deductions for such taxable year)." § 72(t)(2)(B). "During the taxable year" presumably means "during the taxable year in which the distribution is received."

This exception may increase the medical problems of the participant by giving him a severe headache. Medical expenses are deductible under § 213 only to the extent such expenses exceed 7.5 percent of adjusted gross income. § 213(a). But the plan distribution *itself* is includible in gross income and thus decreases the "amount allowable as a deduction."

To avoid the penalty, while still taking advantage of the ability to withdraw from the plan to pay deductible medical expenses, the individual would have to perform a circular calculation, so that the distribution does not exceed [total medical expenses] minus 7.5 percent of [distribution plus other adjusted gross income]. This assumes he can determine his adjusted gross income and medical expenses to the penny before the end of the year, since a distribution must be matched with medical expenses incurred in the same year as the distribution.

9.4.04 *QRPs, 403(b), government plans: Early retirement*

A distribution made to an employee "after separation from service after attainment of age 55" is exempt from the penalty. This exception is available for qualified, 403(b), and government plans, but not for IRAs. § 72(t)(2)(A)(v), (3)(A). Under § 828 of PPA '06, for post-PPA '06 government plan distributions to firemen, policemen, and emergency medical personnel, the age is 50 not 55. § 72(t)(10).

Although § 72(t) limits the exception to distributions made after a separation from service occurring after the employee's 55th birthday, Notice 87-13, 1987-1 C.B. 432, A 20, provides that the separation from service can occur on or after *January 1* of the year the employee reaches age 55. See PLR 2002-15032.

An employee who separates from the company's service *before* the year he reaches age 55 is not entitled to use this exception; he cannot simply wait until age 55 and then take a penalty-free distribution. The exception is available only for distributions "after your separation from service in or after the year you reached age 55." IRS Publication 575, "Pension and Annuity Income" (2004), p. 28; *Humberson*, 70 TCM 886 (1995).

9.4.05 *QRPs, 403(b) plans: QDRO distributions*

Distributions from a qualified retirement plan or 403(b) arrangement made to an "alternate payee" under a qualified domestic relations order (QDRO; see § 414(p)(1)) are exempt from the early distributions penalty. § 72(t)(2)(C). This allows a divorcing spouse who is under age 59½ to receive penalty-free distributions from the share of her ex-spouse's QRP or 403(b) plan that is awarded to her in the divorce proceedings (if the QDRO procedures are followed properly).

However, even though, in § 408(d)(6), Congress provided a means for the tax-free division of IRAs between divorcing spouses, analogous to the QDRO procedures for qualified plans, Congress did NOT extend the penalty exception of § 72(t)(2)(C) to IRAs. Thus, a divorced spouse who receives part of her ex's IRA under § 408(d)(6) cannot withdraw from the account prior to reaching age 59½ unless she pays the 10 percent penalty or qualifies for some other exception.

9.4.06 ESOPs only: Dividends on employer stock

Under § 404(k), a company can take a tax deduction for dividends paid on stock that is held by an employee stock ownership plan (ESOP), and the ESOP can pass these dividends out to the plan participants, if various requirements are met. Such dividend payments are not subject to the 10 percent penalty. § 72(t)(2)(A)(vi).

9.4.07 IRAs only: Unemployed's health insurance

An unemployed individual can take penalty-free distributions from his IRA (but NOT from a qualified plan or 403(b) arrangement) to pay health insurance premiums. § 72(t)(2)(D).

To qualify for this exception, the person must have separated from his employment, and, as a result of that separation, must have "received unemployment compensation for 12 consecutive weeks under any Federal or State unemployment compensation law." The distributions must be made during the year "during which such unemployment compensation is paid or the succeeding taxable year." Presumably this phrase does not imply that the 12 consecutive weeks' worth of unemployment compensation must all be received in the same taxable year, but presumably it does mean that the unemployed person does not become eligible for the exception until the year the 12 consecutive weeks are completed.

Does this clause mean that the unemployed person can take penalty-free distributions only in one year—*either* the year he completes the 12 weeks of unemployment benefits *or* the following year? Or does it mean that penalty-free distributions may be taken in both years? The IRS has offered no enlightenment.

The maximum distribution under this exception in any taxable year is the amount paid for "insurance described in § 213(d)(1)(D) [medical and long term care insurance] with respect to the individual and the individual's spouse and dependents." The distribution must be made either while the individual is still unemployed or, if he becomes employed again, less than 60 days after he has been re-employed.

The IRS, in regulations, can permit a self-employed individual to use this exception "if, under Federal or State law, the individual would have received unemployment compensation but for the fact the individual was self-employed." No such regulations have been issued.

9.4.08 *IRAs only: Expenses of higher education*

The 10 percent penalty will not apply to IRA distributions that do not exceed the participant's "qualified higher education expenses" for the taxable year of the distribution. § 72(t)(2)(E).

This exception is for IRAs only. It does NOT apply to distributions from QRPs or 403(b) arrangements. That distinction trips up taxpayers at all levels, from Mr. *Jones*, T.C. Summ. Op. 2005-173 (a CPA studying for his Ph.D.) to Mr. *Uscinski*, T.C. Memo 2005-124 (who was in jail), both of whom had to pay the penalty when they withdrew from the wrong kind of plan to pay education expenses.

The distribution does not actually have to be used to pay the education expenses; the exemption applies to the extent the distribution does not exceed the education expenses incurred in the same year the distribution occurs. IRS Publication 590 (2005), p. 50. Using the distribution to repay a loan does *not* qualify for the exception, even if the loan proceeds were used to pay education expenses, if the education expenses were not paid in the same year as the distribution. *Lodder-Beckert*, T.C. Memo. 2005-162. Transfer of funds from an IRA to a § 529 account would not qualify for the same reason.

The distribution must be made after 1997 and be to pay for education provided in "academic periods" beginning after 1997; see Notice 97-53, 1997-40 I.R.B. 6, for full details. The distribution must be to pay for education furnished to the participant or his spouse, or to any child or grandchild of either of them. (It's pretty fast work for a participant under age 59½ to have college-age grandchildren!)

This exception borrows definitions from the Code section allowing various tax breaks to "qualified state tuition programs" (§ 529(e)(3)) for the type of expenses covered ("tuition, fees, books, supplies, and equipment required for the enrollment or attendance of a designated beneficiary at an eligible educational institution") and eligible institutions. The cost of providing the student's computer, housewares, appliances, furniture, and bedding are not qualified expenses. *Gorski*, T.C. Summ. Op. 2005-112.

"Eligible Institutions" include "virtually all accredited public, non-profit, and proprietary post-secondary institutions," according to Notice 97-60, 1997-46 I.R.B. 1, § 4, A-2, which provides many other details regarding this exception, including the fact that room and board are among the covered expenses if the student is enrolled at least half-time.

To the extent the education expenses in question are paid for by a scholarship, federal education grant, tax-free distribution from an Education IRA (§ 530), tax-free employer-provided educational assistance, or other payment that is excludible from gross income (other than gifts, inheritances, loans, or savings), they cannot also be used to support a penalty-free IRA distribution. § 72(t)(7)(B), § 25A(g)(2); Notice 97-60, § 4, A-1.

9.4.09 *IRAs only: First-time home purchase*

"Qualified first-time homebuyer distributions" from an IRA are not subject to the penalty. § 72(t)(2)(F). An individual can withdraw from his IRA (but not from a qualified plan or 403(b) arrangement) up to $10,000, without penalty, if the distribution is used "before the close of the 120th day after the day on which such payment or distribution is received to pay qualified acquisition costs with respect to a principal residence of a first-time homebuyer who is such individual, the spouse of such individual, or any child, grandchild, or ancestor of such individual or the individual's spouse." § 72(t)(8)(A).

The "date of acquisition" is the date "a binding contract to acquire" the home is entered into, or "on which construction or reconstruction of such a principal residence is commenced"—but, if there is a "delay or cancellation of the purchase or construction" [what about *re*construction?] and, solely for that reason, the distribution fails to meet the 120-day test, the distribution can be rolled back into the IRA; AND the rollover back into the IRA will be a qualified tax-free rollover, even if it occurs more than 60 days after the distribution, so long as it occurs within 120 days of the distribution, AND the rollover back into the IRA will not count for purposes of the one-rollover-per-year limit of § 408(d)(3)(B). § 72(t)(8)(E). See ¶ 2.6.06, ¶ 2.6.07.

The $10,000 is a lifetime limit. It applies to the person making the withdrawal (the IRA owner), not the person buying the home.

"Principal residence" has the same meaning as in § 121 (exclusion of gain on sale of principal residence). § 72(t)(8)(D)(ii). § 121 itself does not contain a definition of "principal residence"; Reg. § 1.121-1(b) says the determination depends on all the "facts and circumstances."

"Qualified acquisition costs" are the costs of "acquiring, constructing, or reconstructing a residence," including "usual or reasonable settlement, financing, or other closing costs." § 72(t)(8)(C).

A "first-time homebuyer" is not someone who has never owned a home before. It is a person who has had no "present ownership interest in a principal residence during the 2-year period ending on the date of acquisition of the" residence being financed by the distribution. If the homebuyer is married, both spouses must meet this test. § 72(t)(8)(D).

Finally, to the extent the distribution in question qualifies for one of the *other* exceptions (*e.g.*, a distribution to pay higher education expenses), it will not count as a "first-time homebuyer" distribution (so it will not count towards the participant's $10,000 limit) even if it is used to pay expenses that would qualify it for the first-time homebuyer exception. § 72(t)(2)(F).

9.4.10 *IRS levy on the account*

Generally, even an involuntary distribution is subject to the penalty. Notice 87-13, 1987-1 C.B. 432. However, the Tax Court has excused certain taxpayers from the penalty when their benefits were seized by the government. See *Murillo*, 75 T.C. Memo 1564 (1998); this case contains references to earlier cases on point. Forced distributions after 1999 resulting from an IRS levy under § 6331 will not be subject to the penalty. § 72(t)(2)(A)(vii).

9.4.11 *Return of certain contributions*

Certain excess contributions to "cash-or-deferred-arrangement" plans (such as 401(k) plans) may be distributed penalty-free if various requirements are met. See § 401(k)(8)(D) and § 402(g)(2)(C). Regarding return of an IRA or Roth IRA contribution prior to the due date of the tax return for the year for which such contribution was made, see ¶ 9.1.03(B).

9.4.12 *Qualified reservist distributions*

PPA '06 added a new temporary exception for "qualified reservist distributions" (QRDs). A QRD is a distribution from an IRA or from the elective-deferral portion of a QRP, that is made after September 11, 2001, to an individual reservist who is ordered or called to active duty. The active duty call or order must be for more than 179 days or for an indefinite period, and occur after September 11, 2001, and before December 31, 2007. The distribution must occur on or after the date the participant is called up and before the end of the active duty period.

In addition to being penalty-free, a QRD may be rolled into an IRA at any time during the 2-year period that begins: (1) on the day after the end of the active duty period; or (2), if later, on the date of enactment of PPA '06. Such rollovers may be made without regard to the usual limits on IRA contributions. § 72(t)(G), added by PPA '06 § 827.

9.5 Putting it All Together

1.   Be aware that distributions (even inadvertent distributions) to a participant under age 59½ generally trigger a 10 percent penalty in addition to income taxes.

2.   If a client wants to take money from a retirement plan prior to age 59½, refer to this Chapter to determine whether he qualifies for an exception. Note carefully the requirements of any possibly applicable exception (e.g., make sure it is available for the type of plan involved). Do not expect the exceptions to operate in a logical, fair, or consistent manner.

3.   If a client has an IRA (or can create one by rollover from another type of plan), consider the highly flexible SOSEPP exception as a possible funding source for gifting programs, life insurance premium payments, and other expenditures. Consider hiring an actuary to help design a substantial or creative SOSEPP. In general, create the smallest possible separate IRA to support the desired size of payment, and preserve as much flexibility as possible for future changes in the client's needs.

4.   The penalty does not apply to post-death distributions, but a surviving spouse who rolls over death benefits to her own retirement plan loses the exemption for death benefits. See ¶ 3.2.02.

10

Defined Benefit and Other Plans

Types of retirement plans; minimum distribution rules for defined benefit plans; how to choose a form of benefit.

This Chapter explains what the estate planner needs to know about various types of tax-favored retirement plans (¶ 10.1) and the minimum distribution rules applicable to Defined Benefit plans (¶ 10.2). It concludes with tips for choosing a form of benefit (¶ 10.3).

10.1 Types of Retirement Plans

10.1.01 *Overview of types of plans*

What's most confusing about the various types of retirement plans is that there is not one set of mutually exclusive categories; instead, there are different overlapping classifications for different purposes. For example, Qualified Retirement Plans (QRPs) are divided into two types (Defined Benefit and Defined Contribution) for purposes of the limits (under § 415) on what may be contributed or accrued for a participant, but into three types (pension, profit-sharing, and stock bonus) for purposes of plan aggregation under § 402 (definition of lump sum distribution; ¶ 2.4.04(b)). Profit-sharing and stock bonus plans must be Defined Contribution plans, but a pension plan may be either a Defined Contribution or a Defined Benefit plan. A Keogh plan can be any type of QRP other than a stock bonus plan or ESOP.

An in-depth discussion of the rules applicable to the different types of retirement plans is beyond the scope of this book. The purpose of this ¶ 10.1 is to explain the differences among the various types of plans only to the extent such differences are likely to have an impact on individual planning choices.

10.1.02 *401(k) plan*

A 401(k) plan is an **elective deferral** plan (also called a **cash-or-deferred arrangement** or **CODA**), meaning that the plan is at least partly funded by voluntary salary reduction (or bonus reduction) contributions. Under a CODA, the participant agrees to have part of his compensation contributed to a retirement plan account for his benefit instead of being paid to him in cash. The portion of the account that is funded with the employee's elective deferral contributions is subject to additional rules (over and above the rules that apply to all retirement plan benefits), such as a restriction on distributions prior to age 59½; see § 401(k). 403(b) plans, SEP-IRAs, and SIMPLEs are other examples of plans that are often funded by means of elective deferrals.

Though elective deferral contributions (unless contributed to a designated Roth account; see ¶ 5.7) are excluded from the participant's gross income for income tax purposes, they are nevertheless considered "wages" for purposes of the Federal Insurance Contributions Act (FICA). § 3121(a)(5)(C), (D), (H), (v)(1)(A). Thus, the employer must withhold, from the employee's wages that are *not* being contributed to the plan, Social Security and Medicare taxes with respect to the elective deferral contribution.

The employer that sponsors the 401(k) plan may make additional "matching" or other contributions to the participant's account. A 401(k) plan is a type of QRP and may be a Keogh plan.

10.1.03 *403(b) plan*

403(b) plans (also called "403(b) arrangements" or "TSAs," which stands for tax-sheltered annuities) are available only to tax-exempt employers. Some 403(b) arrangements are funded exclusively by means of elective deferrals (see ¶ 10.1.02). Others are funded partly or solely by employer contributions; these latter plans must meet the same requirements as QRPs.

403(b) plan assets are held in the name of the employee (like an IRA), not in the name of the plan itself (the way QRP assets are held). 403(b) plans may be invested *only* in annuity contracts purchased by the employer and issued in the name of the employee and/or in "regulated investment companies" (mutual funds) held by a bank (or other approved institution) as custodian for the employee.

A 403(b) plan distribution is never eligible for treatment as a lump sum distribution under § 402 (¶ 2.4.02). Also, the minimum distribution rules apply slightly differently; see ¶ 1.4.06.

Deemed IRA, deemed Roth IRA. See ¶ 5.1.04.

10.1.04 Defined Benefit plan

A Defined Benefit (DB) plan is a type of QRP. Under a DB plan, also called a "defined benefit pension plan," the employer promises to pay the employee a specific pension, starting at retirement, and continuing for the employee's life. Social Security is similar to a DB plan.

DB plans have their own separate set of minimum distribution rules; see ¶ 10.2.

A.   **"Classic" DB plan.** Under the classic type of DB plan, the amount of the pension is based on a formula, such as "a monthly pension for life, beginning at age 65, equal to 1/12th of 1 percent of final average compensation times years of service, reduced by 10 percent for each year of service less than 10 if the employee has less than 10 years of service, and up to an annual maximum of 40 percent of career average compensation."

The formula may award a lower percentage for compensation below the Social Security tax wage base than for compensation in excess of such base. This is called the "permitted disparity." The formula will contain adjustments for early or late retirement.

The employer hires an actuary to tell it, each year, the minimum amount it *must* contribute to the plan (and how much extra it *may* contribute) (both limits being set by the tax Code) in order to amortize the employer's future obligations to retiring employees under the plan.

Classic DB plans generally are of greater value to older employees (older than approximately age 50) than to young employees, just because of the time value of money. Even if their eventual projected pensions are the same amount, say $36,000 per year starting at age 65, the value is greater to the employee who will be receiving that sooner. $36,000 a year starting in 10 years (how the pension looks to the 55 year-old employee) is a more significant asset than $36,000 a year starting in 30 years (how the pension looks to a 35 year-old employee). The older employee's pension looks more valuable to the employer too, who has to contribute more for the older employee than for the younger.

Classic DB plans were once the normal form of retirement plan for American businesses. Their popularity has declined (especially among small businesses) due to the increasingly complex tax and administrative rules applicable to these plans and due to the lower cost of Defined Contribution (DC) plans. However, classic DB plans remain attractive to the one-person business as a way of maximizing tax-deductible retirement contributions. If the business owner/sole employee is over age 50, approximately, a classic DB plan will give him a much larger annual tax-deductible contribution is permissible under a DC plan.

B.   **Cash balance DB plans.** There is another type of DB plan, called a **cash balance plan**, which uses a different type of formula. "A cash balance plan is a defined benefit plan that defines benefits for each employee by reference to the employee's hypothetical account. An employee's hypothetical account is determined by reference to hypothetical allocations and interest adjustments that are analogous to actual allocations of contributions and earnings to an employee's account under a defined contribution plan." Reg. § 1.401(a)(4)-8(c)(3)(i). Under a cash balance plan, contributions are more uniform across age groups, making cash plans more attractive than classic DB plans for younger employees (and less generous for older employees).

C.   **Estate planning features.** From an *estate planning perspective*, the DB plan has the following distinctive features.

First, the participant does not have an "account" in a DB plan the way he does in a DC plan. Even under a cash balance DB plan, though the plan's funding formula is determined by reference to a hypothetical "account" for each employee, the participant does not have an actual account in the plan.

The benefit statement for a classic DB plan will typically say the employee's "accrued benefit" under the plan is (*e.g.*) "$1,450 a month," of which (say) "80 percent is vested." What this means is that the employer has already obligated itself to provide for this employee (if the employee *keeps on working* until retirement age) a pension of $1,450 per month for life starting at the employee's "normal retirement age" under the plan (usually, 65); and if the employee *quits right now*, he's vested in 80 percent of that, meaning that at normal retirement age he would receive 80 percent of $1,450 per month.

The benefit statement may or may not contain more details such as: how much of a pension the employee would receive if he retired early; and (of great significance in estate planning), whether the employee will be permitted upon retirement to withdraw the lump sum equivalent of the accrued pension, or what death benefit, if any, would be available for the employee's beneficiaries. This brings us to the second significant factor in planning for DB pension benefits: Many DB plans do not offer the option of taking a lump sum equivalent in cash (or the client may have already chosen an annuity option and foreclosed his ability to take a lump sum equivalent). Thus under some DB plans there is no ability to "roll over" the benefits to an IRA.

Also, a DB plan may provide no benefits at all after the death of the employee other than the required annuity for the surviving spouse (¶ 3.4). If the participant dies prematurely, the money that was set aside to fund his pension goes back into the general fund to finance the benefits of other employees, rather than passing to the deceased employee's heirs.

D.   **Investment and longevity risks.** Under a DC plan, the participant owns identifiable assets held in an account with his name on it. The value of the account fluctuates depending on investment results, but no party to the proceedings has any money staked on the question of how long the participant will live. With a DC plan, the risk that the participant will outlive his money falls on the participant.

With a DB plan, the plan (or insurance company issuing the annuity contract used to fund the benefits) takes the excess-longevity risk. See Wanda Example, ¶ 10.2.05.

Theoretically, under a DB plan, the plan also takes all the investment risk. If the plan's investments go down in value, the employee's promised benefit remains the same; the employer must contribute more money to the plan to fund that benefit. There are two exceptions to this statement. First, under one type of annuity, the variable annuity, the participant also has investment risk; see ¶ 1.2.07(A). Second, the employee has the risk that the employer will default on its obligation to fund the plan. If the plan becomes insolvent and/or the employer goes bankrupt, the employee may find his benefits limited to the amount insured by the government's pension insurer, the Pension Benefit Guarantee Corporation (PBGC). The employee will not receive the full benefits promised by the plan.

10.1.05 *Defined Contribution plan*

A Defined Contribution (DC) plan is, along with the Defined Benefit plan, one of the two broad categories of QRP. DC plans are also called "individual account plans." § 414(i). IRS regulations use the terms individual account plan and defined contribution plan interchangeably; thus even individual account plans that are NOT QRPs (such as IRAs and 403(b) plans) may be considered DC plans.

Under a DC plan, the employer may commit to making a certain level of contribution to the plan (such as "10% of annual compensation," an example of a Money Purchase plan formula), or (under a profit-sharing plan) may make such contributions periodically on a discretionary basis or based on profit levels. 401(k) plans and ESOPs are other examples of DC plans.

Once the employer has contributed to the DC plan, the contributions are allocated among accounts for the individual participants who are members of the plan. What the participant will eventually receive from the plan is determined by (1) how much is allocated to his account under the contribution formula and (2) the subsequent investment performance of that account. The employer does not guarantee any level of retirement benefits. If the plan's investments do well, the profits will increase the participant's account value. If the plan's investments do poorly, the participant will receive less at retirement.

If the plan is **self-directed**, each participant makes the investment decisions for his own account in the plan, from a menu of alternatives permitted by the plan. The menu may be broad or may be limited to a few mutual funds. If the plan is not self-directed, the investments are determined at the plan level by the trustee of the plan.

Designated Roth account. See ¶ 5.7.

10.1.06 *ESOP (Employee Stock Ownership Plan)*

An ESOP is a QRP primarily designed to invest in stock of the sponsoring employer. § 4975(e)(7). ESOPs have various liberalized rules compared with other retirement plans, most of which are of interest only to the employer-sponsor and not to estate planners. Distributions of company stock to the beneficiary from an ESOP or any other retirement plan are eligible for certain favorable tax treatments if various requirements are met; see ¶ 2.5.

10.1.07 *Individual account plan*

A plan in which individual accounts are maintained on the plan's books for plan participants, with the result that each participant obtains the profits (or bears the losses) of his own account. IRAs, Roth IRAs, SEP-IRAs, and 401(k) plans are individual account plans, but a Defined Benefit plan is not. The terms "individual account plan" and "Defined Contribution plan" may be used interchangeably.

10.1.08 *Individual Retirement Account (IRA)*

An IRA is not a QRP. Rather, it is a private, one-person retirement account that is created under, and given special tax benefits by, § 408. An IRA can be structured either as a custodial account (which is most common) or as a trust (in which case it may be called an **Individual Retirement Trust** or **Trusteed IRA**; see ¶ 6.1.06). § 408(a), (h). An IRA may be funded either by contributions from the participant's own compensation (¶ 5.3.01, ¶ 5.3.02), or by contributions from the participant's spouse's compensation (see § 219(c)), or by contributions from the participant's employer (in which case it is a SEP or SIMPLE; see ¶ 10.1.13). IRAs created under § 408 are called **traditional IRAs** when necessary to distinguish them from Roth IRAs.

10.1.09 *Keogh plan*

A Keogh plan (also called an **H.R. 10 plan**) is a QRP that covers one or more self-employed individuals. Thus, a Keogh plan is a QRP established by an unincorporated employer (partnership or sole proprietor) for the benefit of the partners and employees of the partnership, or for the benefit of the sole proprietor (and his employees, if any). Any type of QRP other than an ESOP or stock bonus plan may be a Keogh plan.

While this term (which never appears in the Code) is still used by self-employed persons to describe their retirement plans, most of the once-numerous distinctions between plans adopted by corporations and plans adopted by the self-employed were eliminated by the Tax Reform Acts of 1984 and 1986, and the Unemployment Compensation Amendments of 1992. To read about what the differences used to be, see Reg. § 1.401(e).

There are still some differences of interest to planners, however. Note that some of the differences are applicable to all "self-employed persons" while others apply only to the "owner-employee."

A.   **Definitions.** A **self-employed** person is an individual who has self-employment income. § 401(c)(1). In contrast, a "common law employee" (or, as the Code calls it, "an individual who is an employee without regard to § 401(c)(1)") is an employee of someone else (not himself).

An **owner-employee** is the sole proprietor of an unincorporated business, or a partner "who owns more than 10 percent of either the capital interest or the profits interest" in the partnership. § 401(c)(3). The author has found no rule as to *when* the 10 percent test for determining owner-employee status is applied; do we test only at the end of the plan year? Or must we determine whether the individual owned more than 10 percent of the capital *at any time during* the year? And is the test applied yearly? Or is the individual considered *forever* an owner-employee if he was *ever* an owner-employee?

B.   **How they differ from other QRPs.** Here are the differences that still remain between Keogh plans and other QRPs that may matter from the self-employed individual's personal planning perspective.

Contributions subject to self-employment tax: The self-employed individual's contributions to his Keogh plan are not deductible for purposes of computing his self-employment tax; this is in contrast to employer contributions to a corporate QRP (other than elective deferral contributions; see ¶ 5.7.02(E), ¶ 10.1.02), which are excluded from the definition of "wages" for FICA tax purposes.

Lump sum distributions: A lump sum distribution (LSD) may qualify for special tax treatment. ¶ 2.4.06. An LSD is a distribution of the participant's entire account balance within one calendar year following the most recent "triggering event." "Triggering events" are: for EVERYBODY, turning age 59½ or dying; for self-employed persons ONLY, becoming disabled; and for common law employees ONLY, separation from service. § 402(d)(4)(A). ¶ 2.4.03.

Premature distributions: A distribution from a QRP made to an employee "after separation from service after attainment of age 55" is exempt from the 10 percent "premature distributions" penalty. ¶ 9.4.04. Although § 72(t) does not specifically exclude the self-employed from using this exception, it is not clear what would constitute "separation from service" for a sole proprietor. Also see ¶ 9.4.07 regarding the penalty exception for IRA distributions to pay health insurance premiums during unemployment.

Life insurance: If a QRP maintains a life insurance policy on the life of a plan participant, the participant must include the cost of the current insurance protection in his income each year. ¶ 8.2.01. Unlike other participants, an owner-employee does not get to treat the accumulated cost that he has paid tax on as an "investment in the contract" for income tax purposes. Reg. § 1.72-16(b)(4); ¶ 8.2.05.

Money Purchase plan. See ¶ 10.1.10.

10.1.10 *Pension plan*

A **pension plan** is a type of QRP under which the employer is *obligated* to make annual contributions, or, as the Code puts it, it is a plan "subject to the funding standards of section 412." The required annual contribution may be determined by an actuarial formula based on the promised benefits (Defined Benefit plan), or may be simply a percentage of employees' compensation each year (**Money Purchase** pension plan). A pension plan is contrasted with a profit-sharing plan, under which the employer's contributions are discretionary or linked to profits.

Pension plans have the following features of interest to estate planners:

1.   Pension plans are generally not permitted to make "in-service distributions," i.e., distributions prior to the employee's

termination from employment or meeting the requirements for "retirement."

2.   Pension plans are subject to the strictest federal spousal-rights rules. See ¶ 3.4.02.

3.   All pension plans are considered "one plan" for purposes of determining whether there has been a distribution, within one calendar year of the recipient, of the employee's entire balance in "the" plan under § 402(d) (lump sum distributions; ¶ 2.4.04(b)), even if they are not the same type of pension plan (*e.g.*, a Defined Benefit plan and a Money Purchase plan).

10.1.11 *Profit-sharing plan*

A profit-sharing plan is a QRP. It is a Defined Contribution plan under which the employer's contributions are either entirely discretionary or are fixed to a certain percentage of profits. Most 401(k) plans are profit-sharing plans. Profit-sharing plans qualify for a limited exemption from the federal spousal-rights rules; see ¶ 3.4.03.

10.1.12 *Qualified Retirement Plan*

In this book, a Qualified Retirement Plan (QRP) means a retirement plan that meets the requirements of § 401(a), i.e., it is "qualified" under § 401(a). (For a different definition used in the Code, see ¶ 9.1.02.) Types of QRPS include the 401(k) plan, Defined Benefit plan, ESOP, Keogh plan, pension plan, and profit-sharing plan.

Since § 401(a) has more than 30 separate requirements, some of which cross reference other lengthy Code sections, it is no mean feat to be qualified under § 401(a). Most of the requirements are of little concern to the estate planner who is advising the individual participant or beneficiary. However, it is helpful to be aware of certain § 401(a) concepts that create the landscape in which all QRPs must function. For example:

A.   A QRP is established and maintained by the "sponsor" of the plan. Normally, the sponsor of the plan is the employer of the employees who are covered by the plan, but it could also be a labor union or an association of employers. The employer could be a sole proprietor or partnership, in which case the plan is also a Keogh plan.

B. The assets of the QRP generally must be kept in a separate trust for the "exclusive benefit" of the employees and their beneficiaries (the "exclusive benefit rule"). § 401(a)(2).

C. § 415 limits how much may be contributed to the plan (or accrued on behalf of a participant) each year. § 404 limits the employer's tax deduction for contributions.

D. The plan must prohibit the assignment or alienation of benefits (the "anti-alienation rule"). § 401(a)(13)(A).

E. The plan must contain provisions required by REA. ¶ 3.4.

Roth IRA. See ¶ 5.1.02.

10.1.13 *SEP-IRA, SIMPLE*

Simplified Employee Pensions (SEP-IRAs, or SEPs) and Simple Retirement Accounts (SIMPLEs) are employer-funded IRAs. SEPs are created under § 408(k). SIMPLEs are created under § 408(p). These plans were designed by Congress to be retirement plans that a small business could adopt without having to hire a lawyer.

From the point of view of the estate planner advising an individual SEP-IRA or SIMPLE participant or beneficiary, the rules are generally the same as the rules for "regular" (traditional) IRAs, with the following exceptions:

The premature distributions penalty for a distribution from a SIMPLE is increased to 25 percent in case of distributions within the first two years of participation in a salary reduction arrangement; see § 72(t)(6), and ¶ 9.1.02. Employer contributions (including the employee's contributions via elective deferral) to a SEP-IRA or SIMPLE have no effect on the participant's personal IRA contribution limits. ¶ 5.3.02.

As employer-funded plans, SEPs and SIMPLEs may be subject to ERISA requirements that generally do not apply to IRAs; see ¶ 8.6 (opening paragraphs)m ¶ 8.6.05, ¶ 8.7.02. ERISA aspects of these and all other plans are beyond the scope of this book.

See also ¶ 2.4.02 (regarding lump sum distributions), ¶ 3.4.04 (regarding spousal rights), and ¶ 5.4.02 (regarding Roth conversions).

Traditional IRA. See ¶ 10.1.08.

Trusteed IRA. See ¶ 10.1.08, ¶ 6.1.06.

10.2 MRDs for Defined Benefit Plans

Chapter 1 explained the minimum required distribution (MRD) rules for Defined Contribution (DC) plans, also called individual account plans. This ¶ 10.2 explains the entirely different MRD rules that apply to (1) Defined Benefit (DB) plans and (2) DC plans that pay benefits in the form of an annuity. For explanation of the difference between DC and DB plans, see ¶ 10.1.04.

As explained at ¶ 1.2.01, #3, the DC plan MRD rules are based on a simple system: Each year, the prior year-end account balance is divided by a factor obtained from an IRS table. The factors (divisors) are designed to liquidate the participant's account through annual distributions over the joint life expectancy of the participant and a beneficiary.

Under a DB plan, in contrast, there is no account balance to be liquidated. Instead, there is simply a promise by the plan to pay a certain monthly amount to the participant for his lifetime, with or without a further promise to pay a monthly amount to the participant's beneficiary after the participant's death. The IRS had to come up with a different approach to insure that DB plans are not used to stretch tax deferral out for too long a period. It accomplished this with Reg. § 1.401(a)(9)-6, issued in 2004 (well after the final MRD regulations for DC plans, issued in 2002).

This explanation of the DB MRD rules is for the guidance of professionals advising individual retirees and small business owners. Most of the work involving DB and annuity MRDs is done by actuaries, plan administrators, and insurance companies, working on behalf of the employer and plan. They should consult a source designed for their use such as *The Pension Answer Book* (see Bibliography).

The DB regulation defines basic terms and concepts, such as "annuity," "payment interval," and "annuity starting date" (ASD). ¶ 10.2.02.

The regulation's core provisions tell us when the distributions must begin (¶ 10.2.06), and how benefits must be paid. The plan can offer the employee a menu of life annuities, fixed-term payouts, and combinations thereof, within limits set by the regulation. ¶ 10.2.03. Generally, the annuity payments cannot increase once the annuity payout has started, but the regulation allows several generous exceptions to that rule. ¶ 10.2.04. Once the form of annuity has been selected and the annuity payout starts, it cannot be changed, except in certain circumstances permitted by the regulation. ¶ 10.2.05.

The regulation also deals with special situations, such as what happens if the employee starts taking annuity payments prior to his RBD, ¶ 10.2.08. The most difficult "special situations" arise when the DC rules and the DB rules interact with each other, for example, when the employee converts his annuity benefit to a cash lump sum (¶ 10.2.07), or annuitizes benefits in a DC plan account (¶ 10.2.10).

The regulation focuses primarily on the type of annuity an employee can elect at or before his RBD, but also provides rules for death benefits paid under a DB plan. See ¶ 10.2.09.

The final regulation applies to distributions in 2006 and later years. For 2003–2005, distributions "based on a reasonable and good faith interpretation" of § 401(a)(9) will satisfy the MRD rules. Reg. § 1.401(a)(9)-6, A-17.

10.2.01 *Differences between DB, DC plan rules*

Here are the differences between the DC and DB plan MRD rules:

A.   **There is no account balance in a DB plan.** See ¶ 10.1.04(C) and Ralph Example, ¶ 10.2.07.

B.   **The annuity payments are the MRD.** Once the participant's plan benefit has been annuitized, each year's payments under the contract *are* the MRD for that year with respect to that benefit. Reg. § 1.401(a)(9)-6, A-1(a). As MRDs, the annuity payments are not eligible for rollover. ¶ 2.6.04. This is true even if the participant could have elected some other form of annuity contract that would have paid him a smaller annuity. See Clyde Example, ¶ 10.2.10.

C.   MRD rules apply after ASD, even if before the RBD. Unlike with a DC plan, the DB MRD rules will apply to the annuity prior to the RBD, if the annuity payments start before the RBD. See ¶ 10.2.08.

D.   Postponing the start of annuity distributions until the RBD does not require a "double distribution" in the second Distribution Year. See ¶ 10.2.06.

10.2.02 Payment intervals; other DB terminology

The DB plan MRD rules contemplate that benefits are paid in the form of an annuity: level payments made at regular intervals over a predetermined period of time. The interval between payments (**payment interval**) may not exceed one year (the usual interval is monthly payments), and must be the same throughout the distribution period. Reg. § 1.401(a)(9)-6, A-1(a).

The annuity may be paid to the participant (or beneficiary) directly from the plan's assets, or the plan may purchase an annuity contract from an insurance company and transfer the contract to the participant or beneficiary. Buying an annuity contract or electing a particular form of annuity benefit (i.e., "annuitizing" the participant's benefits) is an insurance transaction, involving a shifting of investment and/or longevity risk. See Wanda Example, ¶ 10.2.05.

The **annuity starting date** (ASD) is the first day of the first period for which an amount is received as an annuity. § 1.72-4(b). This is the date when the participant's accrued benefit in a DB plan (or account balance in a DC plan) is converted to an annuity payout, that is to say, is "annuitized." The ASD may be difficult to determine if the participant starts payments while still working and accruing further benefits, or starts payments then stops them when he resumes employment, or does not start payments until some time after retiring.

10.2.03 Permitted forms, durations, of annuity

The core provisions of the regulation tell us how long an annuity payout can last. Remember, the point of the MRD rules is to avoid unduly prolonged income tax deferral. Thus, the regulation could not allow a retiring employee to elect to have his benefits paid out over 1,000 years. A thousand-year payout would violate the fundamental concept of § 401(a)(9), which is that retirement benefits must be completely distributed over the life or life expectancy of the participant and (within limits) of the participant's beneficiary. Similarly, the rules could not allow a participant to choose a form of benefit that would defer all distributions until the participant's death; such a payout form would violate the principle that death benefits must be "incidental" to the primary benefit, which is a retirement pension. Reg. § 1.401-1(b)(1)(i).

The regulation permits a variety of different possible payout terms for the annuity payments. Durations can be for life, for a fixed term, or for life with a minimum term. The amount of the employee's monthly pension will vary depending on which form he elects; generally, the more survivor benefits and guarantees the employee opts for, the lower his own monthly pension will be. All forms of benefits are supposed to be of equivalent value (though often they're not; see ¶ 10.3.03); those computations are a function of the plan's benefit formula and actuarial calculations, not the MRD rules.

Here are the forms of payout the IRS allows a DB plan to offer to a retiring employee who is commencing his annuity payout at approximately age 70. If the annuity starts at an earlier age, see ¶ 10.2.08. Regarding the ability to delay "annuitization," see ¶ 10.2.06.

A. **An annuity for the life of the participant, with no minimum guaranteed term.** Reg. § 1.401(a)(9)-6, A-1(a), A-2(a). This would give the participant the largest annuity payments during his life, but would provide no benefits for his beneficiaries.

B. **An annuity for the joint lives of the participant and his spouse, terminating at the death of the surviving spouse, with no minimum guaranteed term.** Reg. § 1.401(a)(9)-6, A-1(a), A-2(b). The monthly payments to the surviving spouse cannot be larger than the payments the participant receives, but can be the same amount or anything less. The spouse's consent would be required in order for her survivor payment to be less than 50 percent of the participant's payment. ¶ 3.4.02. This form of benefit would provide no benefits after the death of the surviving spouse.

C.   **An annuity for the joint lives of the participant and his nonspouse beneficiary, terminating when both of them are deceased, with no minimum guaranteed term.** Reg. § 1.401(a)(9)-6, A-1(a), A-2(c). This option is the same as "B," with one difference: If the nonspouse beneficiary is more than 10 years younger than the participant, the monthly payment to the beneficiary cannot exceed a certain percentage of what the participant was receiving. The percentage depends on the age difference between the participant and the beneficiary, using the Table in Reg. § 1.401(a)(9)-6, A-2(c). (Spousal consent is required in order for the participant to name a nonspouse beneficiary; see ¶ 3.4.) This "minimum distribution incidental benefit" (MDIB) rule, by forcing most of the benefits out during the participant's projected lifetime, assures that distribution of the benefits is not unduly prolonged. See "E" for how this rule interacts with a minimum guaranteed term. See ¶ 10.2.08 for how this rule applies if the participant's annuity starts earlier than age 70.

D.   **An annuity for a period certain, with no life component.** If the ASD is on or after the participant's RBD, the period certain must not be longer than whichever of the following is applicable. (If the ASD is before the RBD, see ¶ 10.2.08.)

   1.   The **General Maximum Period Certain** is the Applicable Distribution Period (ADP) from the Uniform Lifetime Table determined using the participant's age in the calendar year the ASD occurs. Reg. § 1.401(a)(9)-6, A-1(a), A-3(a), first sentence. For example, if the participant's ASD is in the year she turns 71, the General Maximum Period Certain would be 26.5 years; the participant could elect to receive annuity payments for a fixed term of 26.5 years. If she lives longer than 26.5 years? Too bad. Under this option, her payments end after 26.5 years. If she dies in less than 26.5 years, her beneficiary (whoever that may be) would receive the payments for the balance of the 26.5-year term certain.

2.   The **Special Maximum Period Certain** is the ADP determined using the IRS's Joint and Survivor Life Expectancy Table (¶ 1.2.03), based on the ages the participant and spouse attain on their birthdays in the year of the ASD. This Special Maximum Period Certain applies only if the participant's sole beneficiary is his spouse, and only if it provides a longer payout period than the General Maximum Period Certain. Reg. § 1.401(a)(9)-6, A-1(a), A-3(a), last sentence. If either spouse lives past that fixed term, too bad—the payments will stop when the term expires.

E.   **Life annuity with period certain.** The employee can elect a life annuity ("A" above) or a joint and survivor life annuity ("B" or "C" above) with a minimum guaranteed term. The minimum guaranteed term can be any term that does not exceed the General Maximum Period Certain described at "D(1)" above, namely, the ADP determined under the Uniform Lifetime Table using the participant's attained age as of his birthday in the year of the ASD. Reg. § 1.401(a)(9)-6, A-1(b), A-2(d), A-3(a). Note that, even if the employee's sole beneficiary is his more-than-10-years-younger spouse, the joint and survivor life expectancy of the participant and spouse (the Special Maximum Period Certain in "D(2)" above) *cannot* be used as a minimum guaranteed term in conjunction with a life annuity. It can be used as a period certain on its own but not in conjunction with a life annuity.

The "E" option is the most complicated, because of the interaction of the period certain and the MDIB rule.

Which form of benefit should a participant choose? See ¶ 10.3.

10.2.04 *Payments must be nonincreasing, except…*

The other core provision of the regulation is that the annuity payments generally may not increase after the ASD. Reg. § 1.401(a)(9)-6, A-1(a). After all, the purpose of the DB plan MRD rules is to prevent "backloading" the distributions; Congress wants to collect taxes on this pension as soon as possible.

(Payments can be set up so that they *decrease* after the ASD; in fact, in the case of death benefits paid to a nonspouse beneficiary, the MDIB rule may require that payments decrease after the participant's death; see ¶ 10.2.03(C).)

The regulation permits several significant exceptions to the no-increases rule. The pension payable under a DB plan may provide for the following payment increases. All of these represent payout increases that are either built in to the annuity terms from the beginning (A–E), or added later as a result of a plan amendment (F) or the participant's accrual of additional benefits under the plan (G). For other types of changes in the annuity payout after the ASD, see ¶ 10.2.05.

A.   **Cost of living adjustment (COLA).** The payout may provide for an annual adjustment to reflect (or for periodic upward adjustments limited by) increases in certain IRS-approved cost-of-living indices. Reg. § 1.401(a)(9)-6, A-14.

B.   **Elimination of survivor benefit.** If the employee's benefit payments were in a reduced amount to reflect a survivor payment payable to his beneficiary, the contract can provide that the employee's payments will be increased (eliminating the reduction prospectively) if the beneficiary either ceases to be the beneficiary "pursuant to a qualified domestic relations order" (QDRO) or dies. Reg. § 1.401(a)(9)-6, A-14(a)(3). The IRS calls this a "pop up" of benefits. T.D. 9130, 2004-1 C.B. 1082, Preamble.

C.   **Lump sum conversion by beneficiary.** A beneficiary may be allowed to convert his survivor annuity benefit into a lump sum. Reg. § 1.401(a)(9)-6, A-14(a)(5).

D.   **Other permitted increases: contracts purchased from insurance company.** If the benefit is funded with an annuity contract that the plan purchases from an insurance company, the contract can provide for:

     1.   Annual percentage increases in the benefit that are not tied to a cost-of-living index;

2.   A "final payment" at the employee's death equal to the difference between the "total value being annuitized" and the payments made to the employee during his life;

3.   Annual dividends or adjustments reflecting "actuarial gains" in the policy; this allows use of a variable annuity contract (¶ 1.2.07(A)); and/or

4.   "Acceleration" of the annuity.

Generally, the total value of the future expected payments under the contract must be the same, regardless of which of these extras are included. Reg. § 1.401(a)(9)-6, A-14(c). However, the regulation is not overly strict on this point because essentially the IRS is relying on the insurance company that issues the annuity contract to "police" the values. Presumably a rational insurance company would not offer the annuitant a choice of packages that have wildly differing values. If benefits are paid directly from the plan, options are more limited, presumably because the IRS does not trust private employer plans not to try to bend the rules for the benefit of certain individuals; see "E." For definitions of "total value being annuitized," "actuarial gain," "total future expected payments," and "acceleration of payments," see Reg. § 1.401(a)(9)-6, A-14(e).

E.   **Other permitted increases: benefits paid directly from the plan.** If the benefits are paid directly from the plan, rather than being funded with an annuity contract purchased from an insurance company, acceleration of the annuity (D(4) above) is not permitted. The plan may provide for increases similar to those described at D(1)–(3) above, but subject to additional limitations (for example, an annual increase not tied to a cost-of-living index must be less than 5%). Reg. § 1.401(a)(9)-6, A-14(d).

F.   **Plan amendment.** Benefits may be increased to reflect a plan amendment. Reg. § 1.401(a)(9)-6, A-14(a)(4).

G.   **Additional benefits accrued after ASD.** If the employee accrues additional benefits after the ASD, and after his RBD, the distribution of the additional accrued benefit must begin with the first payment interval ending in the calendar year immediately following the calendar year in which such amount accrues. Reg. § 1.401(a)(9)-6, A-5.

10.2.05 *Other changes permitted after the ASD*

The theory of an annuity is that, once the terms of the payout are set, they cannot be changed. That principle is fundamental to an insurance transaction in which one side is taking a risk regarding future events; if one party to the transaction can change his mind after the facts have become known, the system won't work.

Wanda Example: Wanda, age 70, believes she is in the best of health; coming from a long-lived family, she expects to live well beyond average life expectancy. She opts for a life annuity with no minimum guaranteed term, to get the largest possible monthly payments for herself. The insurance company that issues the annuity to Wanda is simultaneously issuing annuity contracts to thousands of other 70-year-olds who want to be protected against the risk of living too long. The insurance company knows that some of them will live longer than average and some will die prematurely; the insurance company will make a "profit" on those who die prematurely, enabling the company to stay in business and pay benefits to those who live "too long." A year later, at age 71, Wanda discovers she has a serious illness and is likely to die prematurely. She would like to change the type of contract she selected, to one that has a minimum guaranteed term. But if all the terminally ill people in the group are allowed to switch to a minimum guaranteed term, while the insurance company is still required to make payments for life to those who live extra long, the insurance company will go out of business.

So the question of whether an annuity payout can be changed after the ASD is usually moot. The annuity issuer usually won't allow such changes. However, in case a particular pension plan or insurance company does allow changes, the MRD rules also recognize the possibility of changes. For example, a payment can be modified in connection with plan termination or the employee's retirement or marriage. For details on permitted post-ASD modifications, see Reg. § 1.401(a)(9)-6, A-13.

10.2.06 *When the annuity payments must commence; the RBD*

The first payment under the annuity must be made not later than the employee's Required Beginning Date (RBD). Reg. § 1.401(a)(9)-6, A-1(c)(1).

Expert Comment: Late Retiree's Dilemma

The final regulations force the DB plan participant to annuitize his benefits starting no later than the RBD. Actuary Ed Burrows (see ¶ 10.3.03) points out that this creates a problem for a business owner who is still working and participating in his DB plan when he reaches age 70½. As a "5-percent owner," he must start taking MRDs by April 1 following the year he reaches age 70½. ¶ 1.4.03. However, typically the entrepreneur does not want to be forced into making annuitization choices prior to retirement, while he is still accruing benefits under the plan. Prior to issuance of the final regulations, the IRS permitted an alternative method of computing MRDs for a DB plan: MRDs could be computed using the DC plan method, treating the lump sum equivalent value of the benefit as the "account balance." Unfortunately, the final regulations removed this option, preserving that concept solely for purposes of certain restrictions on rollovers (¶ 10.2.07). This change has made retirement decisions more difficult for the small business owner who has a DB plan and wants to keep working past age 70½.

The amount that must be paid on or before that date is whatever the regular annuity amount is. For example, if the employee is to receive $6,000 per month, he receives the first $6,000 on or before his RBD, the next $6,000 a month later, and so on until the expiration of the agreed-upon duration of the annuity. In computing the size of the annuity payments the participant is to receive for payment intervals ending on or after the RBD, all the participant's benefit accruals through the first Distribution Year must be included. Reg. § 1.401(a)(9)-6, A-1(c)(1).

Here we have another difference from DC plans. Under a DC plan, if the employee took no distribution from the plan in his first Distribution Year, he would have to take two years' worth of distributions in the second Distribution Year. ¶ 1.4.08(A). This concept does not apply to annuity payouts. As long as the periodic payments start no later than the RBD, there is no need to take some kind of "catch-up distribution" for the first Distribution Year. Under a DB plan, there simply is no MRD for the first Distribution Year—with one major exception: If the participant takes all or part of his benefits in the form of a lump sum distribution rather than as an annuity, in or after his first Distribution Year, then there *is* an MRD for the first Distribution Year; see ¶ 10.2.07.

10.2.07 *Converting an annuity payout to a lump sum*

Under some DB plans, the participant has a choice at retirement. Instead of taking an annuity payout, he can take a lump sum cash distribution. The amount of the lump sum equivalent of the participant's vested accrued pension is determined by the plan's actuary, using interest rates and life expectancy factors dictated by the IRS. Under a cash balance plan, the participant would be made aware of the lump sum equivalent of his benefit every year; under more traditional DB plans, he would not learn this number until he approached retirement.

The lump sum alternative is not the same as an account balance under a DC plan. The value of the lump sum equivalent fluctuates with interest rates; it goes down as interest rates go up, which can be a shock to an employee near retirement:

Ralph Example: Ralph expects to retire at age 65. Rather than take a $3,000 per month life pension, he plans to take the lump sum equivalent value, which the plan projects will be $622,000 when Ralph reaches age 65, using a four percent interest rate. However, by the time Ralph actually reaches age 65, the interest rate used to make these projections has changed to five percent. He can still elect to take a monthly pension of $3,000, but if he wants a lump sum, he will get only $553,000! Ralph is shocked by this decline and thinks he has been cheated, but unfortunately for him this is exactly what is supposed to happen. If it's any consolation, remind him that the plan is not even required to offer him a lump sum distribution; many DB plans require the employee to take the annuity form of benefit. If the applicable interest rate had decreased, the lump sum equivalent value of his pension would have *increased*. [Numbers in this and other examples in this section were made up for purposes of illustration only, and do not purport to represent realistic actuarial values.]

If the plan allows the lump sum option, the plan will tell the employee what the lump sum equivalent value is. The minimum distribution rules have nothing to say about that computation. In fact, if the employee takes the lump sum distribution instead of a pension, the MRD rules are completely finished with him—*unless* the lump sum is to be paid to him in a year for which a minimum distribution is required. Even then, the MRD rules "don't care" about the lump sum distribution—*unless* the participant wants to roll it over!

If the annuity is converted to a lump sum, and the lump sum is paid to the participant in or after his "first Distribution Year" (¶ 1.4), then the MRD rules care about one thing and one thing only: how much of that distribution is treated as an MRD, which is not eligible to be rolled over to another plan. ¶ 2.6.04.

Reg. § 1.401(a)(9)-6, A-1(d), provides two methods whereby a DB plan can compute the nonrollable "MRD portion" of a lump sum distribution.

Method #1: Under Method #1, you compute the MRD portion using the DC plan MRD rules (¶ 1.3), "pretending" that the lump sum distribution the employee receives is the prior year-end balance.

Method #2: Method #2 is more complicated. Essentially you treat one year's worth of pension payments as the MRD for the first year. The regulation permits "expressing the employee's benefit as an annuity that would satisfy" the MRD regulations (apparently *any* annuity that would satisfy the MRD regulations), beginning as of the first day of the Distribution Year for which the MRD is being determined. Reg. § 1.401(a)(9)-6, A-1(d)(2).

Which method is better? Method #1 is easier to calculate, and will always produce a smaller MRD. It seems extremely strange to have a "minimum required" distribution that could be any one of several different possible amounts.

Suppose the participant postpones taking her benefits until her Required Beginning Date (RBD), then receives a lump sum distribution on the RBD. How much of that distribution is treated as a nonrollable MRD? The regulation gives us the same two methods, but in this case we must compute two years' worth of MRDs, since the year of the RBD is actually the second Distribution Year.

Method #1: This is tricky! We must compute two years' worth of MRDs, using the "pretend" DC plan method. That means there are two different divisors, one for the first Distribution Year (the year the participant reached age 70½) and one for the second year (the year he reached age 71½). But the pretend "prior year-end balance" we use for both these computations is the same, the amount of the lump sum distribution. Reg. § 1.401(a)(9)-6, A-1(d)(1).

Any distributions the participant had received in the first Distribution Year would reduce the amount of the MRD for the "first Distribution Year" portion of the second Distribution Year MRD.

Method #2: If the plan uses this method it would treat two years' worth of annuity payments as the MRD for the second Distribution Year. The "annuity payments" for this purpose would be based on an annuity that started on the first day of the first Distribution Year.

10.2.08 *If participant's ASD is prior to the RBD*

If an employee retires before age 70½, at, say, age 65, and starts receiving his pension then, he and the annuity issuer are making their insurance bargain irrevocably at that time. This situation poses another contrast to the DC plan situation, and again required the IRS to come up with different rules for DB plans.

Under a DC plan, any distributions the participant takes prior to his first Distribution Year are irrelevant to the MRD rules. The DC rules kick into action during the first Distribution Year and/or on the RBD or date of death. If the IRS tried to use this same approach for DB plans, then every DB plan participant who retired and started receiving a pension earlier than his RBD would have to calculate everything *again* when he reached age 70½, and annuities issued to participants younger than age 70½ would have to contain different death-benefit rules depending on whether the participant died before or after his RBD. The IRS did not so provide.

If the ASD is prior to the RBD, the annuity contract can provide anything it wants to with respect to distributions prior to the first Distribution Year, but must provide for distributions that satisfy the MRD rules in the first Distribution Year and subsequent years. Reg. § 1.401(a)(9)-2, A-4, last sentence. The ASD is treated as the RBD for certain purposes. Reg. § 1.401(a)(9)-6, A-10, first sentence. For example, if the participant dies after the ASD he is treated as dying *after his RBD*, even if his death occurred prior to April 1 of the year after the year in which he would have reached age 70½. Reg. § 1.401(a)(9)-6, A-10(a), last two sentences.

Treating the ASD as the RBD requires certain adjustments to the computations discussed at ¶ 10.2.03(D). For example, we know that the General Maximum Period Certain is determined using the Uniform Lifetime Table, based on the employee's age as of his birthday in the first Distribution Year, but the ULT does not have factors for ages below 70. Accordingly, the regulation provides that, for an annuity commencing prior to the year the participant reaches age 70, the maximum period certain is 27.4 (which is the ULT factor for age 70) plus the difference in years between 70 and the participant's age as of his birthday in the year of the ASD.

Curt Example: Curt retires from Acme in Year 1, taking his pension in the form of an annuity for a term certain, starting immediately. He will turn age 62 on his Year 1 birthday. The maximum term certain his annuity can last for is 35.4 years ($27.4 + [70 - 62] = 35.4$).

Another adjustment required if the annuity starts before age 70 has to do with the maximum benefit payable to a nonspouse beneficiary under a joint and survivor annuity (see ¶ 10.2.03(C)). Because the participant will be receiving the annuity payments for a longer time (because he is starting the annuity at a younger age), the participant will "automatically" be receiving a larger share of the joint and survivor life annuity, and the survivor's share will "automatically" be less. Accordingly, the IRS allows the survivor benefit to be a larger percentage of the participant's benefit. This is done by "adjusting" the age difference between the employee and the beneficiary for purposes of applying the table in Reg. § 1.401(a)(9)-6, A-2(c)(2).

First, determine the actual age difference between the participant and beneficiary. Then, reduce the age difference so determined by the number of years by which the participant is younger than age 70. For example, if the participant turns age 64 in the year of the ASD, and his nonspouse beneficiary is age 34 (30 years younger than the participant), the 30-year age difference is reduced by six (70 - 64), so the "adjusted age difference" is 24 (30 - 6), and the beneficiary's maximum annuity is 67 percent of the participant's annuity. Reg. § 1.401(a)(9)-6, A-2(c)(1).

10.2.09 *MRD rules for DB plan death benefits*

The regulation provides different rules for death benefits depending on whether the participant died before or after his annuity starting date (ASD).

If the participant died <u>before the ASD</u>, the regulation is a little hazy on the requirements and options. It appears that the beneficiary could take the benefits in a lump sum (if that option is offered by the plan), though that option is not discussed in the regulation. Regarding whether such a lump sum can be rolled over to another plan by the beneficiary, see ¶ 2.6.03 and ¶ 3.2. Alternatively, a Designated Beneficiary (see definition at ¶ 1.7.03) could take the benefits in any of three annuity forms:

A.   **Life annuity with minimum guaranteed term.** He can take a life annuity with a minimum guaranteed term, provided the guaranteed term may not exceed the beneficiary's life expectancy, determined using the Single Life Table. Reg. § 1.401(a)(9)-6, A-3(b)(1); § 1.401(a)(9)-5, A-5(b), (c).

B.   **Life annuity.** He can take a life annuity with no minimum guaranteed term. Although the regulation does not specifically mention this form of benefit, it can be inferred from § 401(a)(9)(B)(iii)(II) and the regulations mentioned at "A."

C.   **Annuity for term certain.** He can take an annuity for a period certain. The period certain may not exceed his life expectancy (see "A").

Whichever of these annuity options is chosen, the first payment must be made no later than the end of the year after the year of the participant's death (or, if later, and if the sole beneficiary is the participant's spouse, the end of the year in which the participant would have reached age 70½). Reg. § 1.401(a)(9)-6, A-1(c)(1), fourth sentence; § 1.401(a)(9)-3, A-3(a), (b).

If the beneficiary is not a Designated Beneficiary, the options are more restricted because all benefits must be distributed within five years after the participant's death. See ¶ 1.5.03(C).

Note that the above discusses the participant's death "before the ASD," rather than "before the RBD." See ¶ 10.2.08.

If the participant died <u>on or after the ASD</u>, the payout to the beneficiary is determined by the type of survivor annuity the participant selected way back when the annuity payout began. See the alternatives listed at ¶ 10.2.03(B)–(E). The survivor annuity can be accelerated (converted to a lump sum), if the beneficiary wishes to do so and the plan permits this option. Reg. § 1.401(a)(9)-6, A-14(a)(5). For whether the lump sum can be rolled over to another plan by the beneficiary, see ¶ 2.6.03 and ¶ 3.2.

Furthermore, "the annuity starting date will be treated as the required beginning date" for purposes of Reg. § 1.401(a)(9)-2 and § 1.401(a)(9)-6. Reg. § 1.401(a)(9)-6, A-10(a). Thus, the employee's death after the ASD is treated as death after the RBD even if it was in fact before the RBD. Similarly, if the participant died before the year he would have reached age 70½, and his surviving spouse starts a regulation-compliant annuity payout *prior* to that year (even though she could have waited *until* that year), distributions after her death must continue to be made over her life expectancy (or whatever other regulation-compliant period she elected). Her death does not trigger a new determination of Designated Beneficiary, as it would have had she died before commencing her payout. Reg. § 1.401(a)(9)-6, A-11. Compare ¶ 1.6.05.

10.2.10 *Buying an immediate annuity inside a DC plan*

Reg. § 1.401(a)(9)-6 applies to defined benefit plans. It also applies to "annuity contracts purchased with an employee's account balance under a defined contribution plan." T.D. 9130, 2004-1 C.B. 1082. Thus, if a retiring employee's 401(k) balance is used directly to purchase an annuity contract, the annuity contract must comply with the DB plan rules, even though a 401(k) plan is a DC plan. The same is true if the employee rolls his 401(k) plan balance over to an IRA (another form of DC plan), and uses part or all of the IRA funds to purchase an annuity contract. Reg. § 1.401(a)(9)-5, A-1(e), second sentence. In the year of the purchase, the account is still subject to the DC plan MRD rules; for that year *only,* distributions under the annuity contract will be taken into account as satisfying the MRD requirement for the account under the DC rules. Reg. § 1.401(a)(9)-5, A-1(e), third sentence.

(Note: Another approach is to take cash out of the DC plan, pay the income tax on the distribution, and use the after-tax proceeds to purchase an annuity outside the plan. That scenario is not what is being discussed here.)

If only *part* of the employee's benefit in a DC plan is used to purchase an annuity, the regulations treat the two portions of the employee's account as two separate accounts, beginning the year *after* the year of the purchase. The annuity contract must comply with Reg. § 1.401(a)(9)-6 (the DB plan rules) and the rest of the account must comply with the DC plan MRD rules (Reg. § 1.401(a)(9)-5). See Reg. § 1.401(a)(9)-5, A-1(e), last sentence, § 1.401(a)(9)-8, A-2(a)(3).

Roz Example: Roz, who turns age 73 in 2005, owns an IRA. The account balance was $2 million as of December 31, 2004, so her MRD for 2005 is $80,972 ($2,000,000 ÷ 24.7, the divisor for age 73 from the Uniform Lifetime Table). In July 2005, she uses $500,000 of the IRA balance to purchase an annuity contract which will pay her $5,000 a month for life, on the first day of each month, starting August 1, 2005. According to Reg. § 1.401(a)(9)-8, A-2(a)(3) (which is made applicable to IRAs by Reg. § 1.408-8, A-1(a)), the IRA will be treated as two separate accounts for MRD purposes, beginning in 2006: The MRDs for the "DC portion" of the IRA will be computed based on the prior year-end account balance excluding the value of the annuity contract; the MRD requirement with respect to the "annuity portion" is satisfied by the payments to Roz under the annuity contract. For the year 2005 *only*, the $25,000 of annuity payments Roz receives from the contract for August–December (five months times $5,000) count towards her $80,972 MRD for 2005; she will have to withdraw the rest of the 2005 MRD ($55,972) from the nonannuity portion of the account by December 31, 2005. Starting in 2006, the payments under the annuity contract will not count towards the MRD requirement for the nonannuity portion of the account (see Clyde Example, below).

Although it does not specifically address this point, it appears that Reg. § 1.408-8, A-9 (allowing the owner of multiple IRAs to take the aggregate MRDs for all IRAs he holds as "participant" from any one or more of such IRAs; ¶ 1.3.04) applies only to IRAs that are DC plans, not to any IRA (or portion of an IRA) that has been annuitized.

Clyde Example: Clyde, age 70, has a $2 million IRA. He uses $500,000 of the balance to purchase a 10-year term-certain annuity that pays him $60,000 per year. Now his IRA holds $1.5 million of securities and a $60,000-per-year 10-year annuity contract. He could have purchased an annuity that would have lasted for up to 27.4 years; see ¶ 10.2.03(D). If he had elected a longer annuity term payout, his annual annuity payment under the contract would have been much smaller. Can Clyde treat the "excess" payments (i.e., the part of the annuity payment in excess of the smallest annuity payment he could have elected) as satisfying the MRD requirement for the remaining IRA balance, under the aggregation rule of Reg. § 1.408-8, A-9?

The answer unfortunately for Clyde is "no." Once the participant has chosen an annuity contract with particular terms, those terms create the MRD under that annuity contract. Thus, the entire $60,000 per year payment to Clyde from his annuity contract *is* the MRD for the annuity, and there is no "excess distribution" to be applied to the DC portion of the IRA (even though he could have chosen a different annuity with smaller payments).

10.3 Putting It All Together

Which form of benefit should the participant choose? That extremely important decision should be made with the advice of a professional such as a financial planner or actuary. The answer depends on a variety of factors including the participant's health, other assets, income, and estate planning objectives, the circumstances of the beneficiary(ies), the financial health of the pension plan, and the degree (if any) to which the plan subsidizes one option or the other.

10.3.01 *Problem with nonspouse survivor annuities*

Retirees choose a life annuity to provide for their own living expenses in retirement and to protect against the danger of living too long, but are often loathe to accept the idea of the insurance company's (or plan's) gaining a "windfall profit" if the retiree dies prematurely. To avoid that result, a retiree may choose an annuity that provides benefits for a minimum guaranteed term. Or the participant may choose an annuity that provides a survivor annuity to his beneficiary, because he wants to provide an inheritance.

Providing a survivor benefit (either through a survivor annuity or through a guaranteed term) to a beneficiary who is not a charity and who is not the participant's spouse has gift and estate tax consequences. The value of the survivor benefit is included in the participant's estate with no offsetting marital or charitable deduction. The estate tax rules for valuing annuity benefits are considered unfavorable; see "The Booby Prize," by Noel C. Ice and Robert W. Goff, in *Trusts & Estates* (May 2006), p. 36. For this reason, a survivor annuity is not the best vehicle for wealth transfer for clients with taxable estates. There may also be a taxable gift involved, if the participant irrevocably elects a joint and survivor annuity with a nonspouse beneficiary.

The participant might better choose an annuity that provides the right level of income for himself (and his spouse, if any). If his plan benefits would provide a larger income than they need, the participant could take the excess as a lump sum distribution, roll that to an IRA, and leave *the IRA* to chosen beneficiaries as an inheritance, rather than leaving them an inheritance in the form of a survivor annuity, or a minimum guaranteed term, under the participant's annuity. This approach treats the annuity as something for the participant and spouse to consume during retirement, and as longevity insurance, and uses other assets for wealth transfer.

10.3.02 Illustrations: Different choices

How do people choose among different forms of plan benefits? The best approach is to get professional advice; see factors discussed at ¶ 10.3.03. Here are examples of some of the approaches people consider.

Hugh, Stu, Lou, and Sue Example: Hugh, Stu, Lou, and Sue are all retiring from Acme Widget. The Acme DB Plan offers every type of annuity or term certain payout permitted by the MRD regulation (minimum term payout ten years), but does not offer the lump sum distribution option.

Hugh views his pension as an asset to be consumed during his life, with his other assets to be used for estate planning objectives. Since he plans to consume the pension, he doesn't mind if his premature death leaves his beneficiaries with no value from the plan; he doesn't intend them to have this particular asset in any case. Hugh chooses a single life annuity, which provides the largest payments to him.

Stu's main concern is to provide for his wife. He chooses a joint and 100 percent survivor life annuity with her as his sole beneficiary.

Lou is primarily interested in providing an inheritance for her children. She decides that the best way to do that is to take a life annuity (thus providing the largest possible payments to herself), and use those annuity payments to buy a life insurance policy (through an irrevocable trust, to keep the proceeds free of estate taxes) that will provide for her children in case of her death. Premature death would cause an economic loss under the annuity, but a gain under the insurance policy. With the combination of a life annuity and a life insurance policy, she has hedged away all risk of both premature death and living too long.

Unlike Hugh, Stu, Stu's wife, and Lou, Sue is not in good health. She would "lose" by choosing a life annuity payout, because she is likely to live less long than the "average" person her age. She is also uninsurable, so she can't use the life insurance technique Lou uses. She will choose a period-certain payout, the shortest one the plan offers so as to move the money out of the plan as quickly as possible. That way it is maximally available for her needs, or for estate planning moves such as lifetime gifts.

10.3.03 *Expert tip: Subsidized plan benefits*

Often the retiree's decision is made complicated not merely by a variety of annuity offerings, but by the additional option of taking a lump sum distribution and rolling it over to an IRA instead of taking any annuity offered by the plan; and also by the issue of subsidized benefits.

Ed Burrows, a pension actuary and consultant in Boston, and President of the College of Pension Actuaries, who reviewed parts of this Chapter prior to publication, reminds us that a retirement plan may subsidize certain options. Typically, for example, a plan may subsidize the joint and survivor spousal annuity option:

Parker Example: Parker is retiring. His plan offers him three options: a life annuity of $1,000 per month; a lump sum cash distribution of $X (which is the actuarial equivalent of a life annuity of $1,000 per month for a person Parker's age); or a joint and survivor annuity with his wife. In order for the joint and survivor annuity to be actuarially equivalent to the straight one-life annuity, the payment to Parker should be reduced to something less than $1,000, to reflect the addition of the survivor annuity. However, this particular plan (like the plan discussed in PLR 2005-50039) provides that a 60 percent survivor annuity can be provided for the participant's spouse without any reduction of the participant's benefit if the spouse is not more than five years younger than the participant. In effect the plan is offering Parker a "free" survivor annuity for his wife.

An early retirement pension is another type of benefit a plan might subsidize. For example, if Parker is 60 years old, and is entitled to a pension of $1,000 a month for life starting at age 65, the plan might offer him the choice of $1,000 a month for life beginning at age 60 (subsidized early retirement benefit) or a lump sum of $Y (the actuarial equivalent of the $1,000-a-month pension starting at age 65). If he takes the lump sum, he is giving up $60,000 (five years' worth of $1,000-a-month payments) and getting nothing in return.

Does this mean the participant should always choose the subsidized benefit, to avoid wasting money? No. If the participant is in poor health, or if the pension plan is in poor financial shape, any life annuity would be a "bad bet," even if it is subsidized. The point is not that one should always take the subsidized benefit; the point is that one should be aware which benefit forms, if any, are subsidized by the plan, in order to properly evaluate the choices. This point can be missed when (for example) a financial advisor who wants to manage the participant's money focuses only on the possibility of rolling over a lump sum distribution to an IRA, without evaluating the plan's annuity options.

10.3.04 *More expert tips: How to evaluate choices*

How can the retiree tell the relative values of different benefit options? Fred Lindgren, Vice President and senior actuary with Fidelity Investments, who reviewed parts of this chapter prior to publication, points out that (starting in 2006) pension plans are required to tell retirees the relative values of the different options the plan is offering them. See Reg. § 1.417(a)(3)-1(c). (This regulation, though it appears to deal with qualified annuity options that must be offered to married participants (see ¶ 3.4), also applies to unmarried employees.)

Unfortunately, Fred says, the plan's use of different interest and mortality assumptions to calculate benefits and/or display the "relative values" of benefits (all as permitted by the IRS regulations) may create additional confusion. Accordingly, the participant should still seek outside help. A professional advisor acting on the retiree's behalf can evaluate the options using "apples to applies" comparisons, and can also consider the individual's own health and financial needs, and the financial health of the plan, factors the plan does not take into account in its "relative value" analysis.

Fred also warns:

❑   **If you delay the start of your pension** (for example, because you are still working), will you get an increased pension when you eventually start taking payments, or are you giving up current monthly payments and getting nothing in return? In this situation, a "cash balance" plan would typically be more favorable than a "classic" DB plan.

❑   **If you want an annuity benefit:** Will the plan buy your annuity from an insurance company, or fund it directly from plan assets? If the latter, and your benefit exceeds the amount insured by the federal pension guaranty program, are you willing to take the risk of the plan's insolvency? Are you better off rolling over a lump sum to an IRA and buying the annuity in the IRA?

If the amount of benefits is not large enough to justify the fee for consulting a professional actuary, a "quick and dirty" method of evaluating the plan's annuity offerings is to compare the prices you would have to pay to purchase each option from an annuity company, *outside* the plan. You can obtain such annuity quotes (free) from the website www.annuityquotes.com.

Appendix A: Tables

1.　　Uniform Lifetime Table

Table for Determining Applicable Distribution Period (Divisor)			
Age	Distribution period	Age	Distribution period
70	27.4	93	9.6
71	26.5	94	9.1
72	25.6	95	8.6
73	24.7	96	8.1
74	23.8	97	7.6
75	22.9	98	7.1
76	22.0	99	6.7
77	21.2	100	6.3
78	20.3	101	5.9
79	19.5	102	5.5
80	18.7	103	5.2
81	17.9	104	4.9
82	17.1	105	4.5
83	16.3	106	4.2
84	15.5	107	3.9
85	14.8	108	3.7
86	14.1	109	3.4
87	13.4	110	3.1
88	12.7	111	2.9
89	12.0	112	2.6
90	11.4	113	2.4
91	10.8	114	2.1
92	10.2	115 and up	1.9

This table must be used by all taxpayers to compute lifetime required distributions for 2003 and later years, unless the sole beneficiary is the participant's more-than-10-years-younger spouse. See ¶ 1.3.01, ¶ 1.4. This table may not be used: by beneficiaries of a deceased participant (except in year of participant's death); or for years prior to 2002 (optional for 2002).

For each Distribution Year, determine: (A) the account balance as of the prior calendar year end (see ¶ 1.2.05–¶ 1.2.07); (B) the participant's age at the end of the Distribution Year (¶ 1.3.01); and (C) the Applicable Distribution Period (divisor) for that age from the above table. "A" divided by "C" equals the minimum required distribution for the Distribution Year.

2.   Uniform Lifetime Table, Younger Ages

For "SOSEPPs" using "RMD Method"; see ¶ 9.2.05(A).

Taxpayer's Age:	Life Expectancy:	Taxpayer's Age:	Life Expectancy:
21	75.3	43	53.4
22	74.3	44	52.4
23	73.3	45	51.5
24	72.3	46	50.5
25	71.3	47	49.5
26	70.3	48	48.5
27	69.3	49	47.5
28	68.3	50	46.5
29	67.3	51	45.5
30	66.3	52	44.6
31	65.3	53	43.6
32	64.3	54	42.6
33	63.3	55	41.6
34	62.3	56	40.7
35	61.4	57	39.7
36	60.4	58	38.7
37	59.4	59	37.8
38	58.4	60	36.8
39	57.4	61	35.8
40	56.4	62	34.9
41	55.4	63	33.9
42	54.4	64	33.0

3.   Single Life Expectancy Table.

For computing MRDs after the participant's death; see ¶ 1.5.

Ages 0 to 57

Age	Life Expectancy	Age	Life Expectancy
0	82.4	29	54.3
1	81.6	30	53.3
2	80.6	31	52.4
3	79.7	32	51.4
4	78.7	33	50.4
5	77.7	34	49.4
6	76.7	35	48.5
7	75.8	36	47.5
8	74.8	37	46.5
9	73.8	38	45.6
10	72.8	39	44.6
11	71.8	40	43.6
12	70.8	41	42.7
13	69.9	42	41.7
14	68.9	43	40.7
15	67.9	44	39.8
16	66.9	45	38.8
17	66.0	46	37.9
18	65.0	47	37.0
19	64.0	48	36.0
20	63.0	49	35.1
21	62.1	50	34.2
22	61.1	51	33.3
23	60.1	52	32.3
24	59.1	53	31.4
25	58.2	54	30.5
26	57.2	55	29.6
27	56.2	56	28.7
28	55.3	57	27.9

Single Life Table, cont.

Ages 58 to 111+

Age	Life Expectancy	Age	Life Expectancy
58	27.0	87	6.7
59	26.1	88	6.3
60	25.2	89	5.9
61	24.4	90	5.5
62	23.5	91	5.2
63	22.7	92	4.9
64	21.8	93	4.6
65	21.0	94	4.3
66	20.2	95	4.1
67	19.4	96	3.8
68	18.6	97	3.6
69	17.8	98	3.4
70	17.0	99	3.1
71	16.3	100	2.9
72	15.5	101	2.7
73	14.8	102	2.5
74	14.1	103	2.3
75	13.4	104	2.1
76	12.7	105	1.9
77	12.1	106	1.7
78	11.4	107	1.5
79	10.8	108	1.4
80	10.2	109	1.2
81	9.7	110	1.1
82	9.1	111+	1.0
83	8.6		
84	8.1		
85	7.6		
86	7.1		

5.   Tax on Various Lump Sum Distributions. Chart prepared by Ed Slott, CPA; see Appendix C for Ed's newsletter, *Ed Slott's IRA Advisor*. For meaning of this chart, see ¶ 2.4.06(B).

If Your Lump Sum Distribution is:	Special Averaging Tax Is:
$100,000	14,471
150,000	24,570
200,000	36,922
250,000	50,770
275,000	58,270
300,000	66,330
318,833	72,733
350,000	83,602
375,000	93,102
400,000	102,602
450,000	122,682
500,000	143,682
550,000	164,682
600,000	187,368
650,000	211,368
700,000	235,368
750,000	259,368
800,000	283,368
850,000	307,368
900,000	332,210
1,000,000	382,210

Appendix B
Forms

Table of Contents

Introduction; Drafting Checklist

This Appendix contains sample forms which can be used by practitioners as a starting point for drafting their own forms for various clients and situations. [Brackets] indicate instructions to the drafter, such as alternative or optional language, or something that needs to be inserted or completed by the drafter. In drafting forms to dispose of retirement benefits, keep in mind the following points:

1.   Impress on the client that the Beneficiary Designation Form is just as important a legal document as a will or trust. Often, more of the client's assets are controlled by this form than by his Will. An improperly drafted (or missing) beneficiary designation form could cost the client's family dearly in taxes and increased settlement costs.

2.   Read the applicable sections of the account documents establishing the client's IRA, to make sure the beneficiary designation and payout method the client desires are permitted. In the case of a qualified retirement plan (QRP) benefit, read the Summary Plan Description or the description of available benefit payout options in the employer-provided beneficiary designation form, then check your conclusions with the Plan Administrator. In case of doubt read the actual plan documents.

3.   Some IRA providers and QRPs cover the following points in their plan documents, but others do not. If these matters are *not* covered in the plan documents, they can be covered in the beneficiary designation form:

A.   Who chooses the form of death benefits, the participant or the beneficiary? In the forms in this Appendix, the beneficiary chooses the form of death benefit.

B.   On the death of the participant, the primary beneficiary is entitled to the benefits. If the beneficiary does not withdraw them immediately, what happens to benefits that are still in the IRA (or QRP) when the *primary beneficiary* dies? See ¶ 1.5.13.

C. In the case of an IRA, can the beneficiary transfer the benefits to another Beneficiary IRA? See ¶ 2.6.01 and Section 3.08 of the IRA/Roth IRA Master Beneficiary Designation Form (Form 2.1).

4. Problems arise when practitioners submit beneficiary designation forms that place unsuitable duties on the plan administrator or IRA provider ("administrator"). Most IRAs are custodial accounts, under which the IRA provider's duties are limited to custodial and tax reporting services, and the provider's fees are nominal. Most administrators cannot be expected to do much more than send out benefit checks in specified proportions to beneficiaries whose names, addresses, and Social Security numbers are listed in the beneficiary designation form. Here are some "do's and don't's" for avoiding problems with the administrator:

A. Don't require the administrator to make legal judgments. A form that says "I leave the benefits to X unless he disclaims the benefits by means of a qualified disclaimer within the meaning of section 2518," appears to require the plan administrator to determine whether the disclaimer is qualified under § 2518 before it can decide who to pay the benefits to. Compare Form 3.1.

B. Don't require the administrator to carry out functions of an executor or trustee. For example, if you say "I designate my son as beneficiary, to receive only the minimum required distribution each year," you are requiring the administrator to control the beneficiary's withdrawals. Some IRAs and plans have a mechanism for restricting the beneficiary's withdrawals, but most do not. If you want to restrict the beneficiary's withdrawals or make them conditional in any way you must either (1) leave the benefits to a trust (so the trustee can enforce the conditions); (2) find an IRA provider that offers accounts which allow restricted withdrawal provisions (and probably charges accordingly); or (3) use an IRT rather than an IRA (see ¶ 6.1.06).

C. Don't require the administrator to determine amounts dependent on external facts. If it is necessary to include, in your beneficiary designation form, a formula that is dependent on external facts (for example, "I leave my grandchild an amount equal to my remaining GST exemption," or "I leave to the marital trust the minimum amount necessary to eliminate federal estate taxes"), do this in a way that does not make the administrator responsible to apply the formula. Provide that a beneficiary or fiduciary will certify the facts to the administrator, who can rely absolutely on such certification. If designating a fiduciary to fulfill this role, be sure the will or trust appointing such fiduciary requires him to carry out this duty.

> D.   <u>Do avoid redundant or contradictory lists of definitions and payout options</u>. The lists of definitions in Forms 2.1 and 2.2 are intended to be used with IRAs and retirement plans which have either no, or incomprehensible, defined terms. If the plan document already has suitable and clear definitions of "primary beneficiary," "death benefit," "the account," and other terms, using a different set of definitions may just create confusion.

5.   Consider whether you wish to alter the applicable presumptions in case of simultaneous death. See ¶ 3.1.02.

6.   If the disposition is intended to qualify for the marital deduction, include language to that effect. See Section 3.07 in Forms 2.1 and 2.2; Form 4.4; and ¶ 3.3.03(B).

7.   Consider the extent to which you need to define any terms such as "issue *per stirpes*," or "income"; and/or specify which state's law shall be used to interpret terms you use in the form. It is highly likely that the QRP or IRA agreement specifies that the law of the sponsor's state of incorporation will be used. Since that may well not be the state in which your client lives (or dies), there is a potential for problems if the client's chosen disposition depends on a definition which varies from state to state. Although you cannot change the governing law of the "plan," a statement that the language *of the beneficiary designation* will be interpreted according to the laws of a particular state should be accepted in the sense that it will lead to the correct determination of the client's intent. See Section 3.04, Forms 2.1, 2.2.

8.   Consider whether different contingent beneficiaries should be named depending on whether the primary beneficiary actually dies before the participant, or merely disclaims the benefits. See Form 3.1, ¶ 4.2.11(E).

9.   Whenever a trust is named as beneficiary, see the Trust Drafting Checklist at ¶ 6.5.01, and be sure to file the required documentation. See ¶ 6.2.08. Some beneficiary designation forms in this Appendix in which benefits are left to a trust describe the trust as "the [TRUST NAME] Trust [optional:, a copy of which is attached hereto]." The phrase "a copy of which is attached hereto" is optional, and would be used solely to identify the trust that is named as beneficiary. Attaching a copy of the trust to the beneficiary designation form does NOT satisfy the "documentation requirement." You could choose to identify the trust by other means (e.g., "under agreement dated 1/1/98") instead of attaching a copy of the trust to the beneficiary designation form. No matter how you choose to identify the trust, you ALSO must comply with the documentation requirement.

10.   Include complete contact information for the beneficiaries, or they and the IRA provider may never find each other.

11.   Require the administrator to provide information to the participant's executor. See Section 3.02, Forms 2.1 and 2.2.

12.   Since separate accounts treatment cannot be used for a gift that will not share in gains and losses post-death, it may be desirable to rework a pecuniary gift into a fractional gift as of the date of death, which should solve the problem. See Form 3.5.

13.   Finally, don't focus on taxes and minimum distributions to the exclusion of basic drafting issues. If the spouse is named as beneficiary, is that only if he/she is married to the participant at the time of death? If a beneficiary predeceases the participant, does his/her share pass instead to the surviving beneficiaries, or to his/her own issue, or to someone else?

1.   SIMPLE BENEFICIARY DESIGNATION FORM

1.1   Simple Beneficiary Designation: Spouse, Then Issue

This form may be suitable for a client who wants to leave benefits outright to his spouse if living, otherwise to his children equally (and issue of deceased children). This form is included primarily for use with (1) retirement plans that are of relatively small value and (2) retirement plans that already contain, in the plan documents, the estate plan-friendly additional provisions included in the longer Master Beneficiary Designation forms (2.1 and 2.2). If the benefit is of substantial value, and the plan documents do not have provisions dealing with the important estate planning issues covered in the longer forms, it would be advisable to use the longer forms.

DESIGNATION OF BENEFICIARY

TO: [Name of IRA or Roth IRA Provider or Plan Administrator]
FROM: [Name of Participant]
RE: [IRA or Roth IRA No._____] or [or Name of Plan]

1.   I hereby designate as my beneficiary, my spouse, [SPOUSE NAME], whose date of birth is [BIRTHDATE], to receive all benefits payable under the above [account] [plan] in the event of my death.

2.   If my spouse does not survive me, I designate as my beneficiaries, in equal shares, such of my children as shall survive me; provided, that if any of my children does not survive me, but leaves issue surviving me, such issue shall take the share such deceased child would have taken if living, by right of representation. My children are:

Name   Address   Date of Birth   Social Security Number   Phone

[alt. 1: pay minor's benefits to a custodian]
3.   Any benefits becoming distributable to a person under the age of twenty-one (21) years shall be distributed to such person's surviving parent, if any, otherwise to my oldest then living child, as custodian for such person under the Uniform Transfers to Minors Act. Such custodian shall be entitled to act for the minor in all respects with regard to the benefits.

[alt. 2: pay minor's benefits to a trust; make sure the trust instrument has suitable provision to receive this payment and hold it for the particular minor beneficiary who is entitled to it]
3.   Any benefits becoming distributable to a person under the age of twenty-one (21) years shall be distributed to the Trustee then serving

as such under the [NAME OF TRUST] created by [Agreement/Declaration/Instrument/my Will] dated [DATE] [optional:, a copy of which is attached hereto], to be held and administered for the benefit of such person as provided therein.

4.   Regardless of who is named as beneficiary above, you shall provide to the executor, administrator, or other duly appointed representative of my estate such information regarding me, my account, or my beneficiary(ies) as such representative may reasonably request in connection with the performance of his, her, or its duties as such representative.

Signed this _____ day of _____, 20 ___.

_____
Signature of Participant

2.   MASTER BENEFICIARY DESIGNATION FORMS

These Master Beneficiary Designation Forms are meant to provide a starting "boilerplate" form, which will be modified by the estate planner when used for a particular client. The modifications will consist of: (1) inserting the names of the beneficiary(ies) in Article II (see sample inserts in Part 3 of this Appendix); (2) deleting superfluous provisions; and (3) such other modifications as are necessary or desirable to reflect applicable state law, the client's intent, and the requirements of the plan. See also the Drafting Checklist at page 530.

Form 2.1 is meant to be used with IRAs (traditional and Roth). Form 2.2 is for QRPs.

Section 3.03 can be omitted if no minors can possibly become beneficiaries. Section 3.05 could be dispensed with if it is not likely there will be multiple beneficiaries. Section 3.07 can be omitted if the participant is not naming his spouse as a beneficiary (see ¶ 3.3.12).

A particular IRA provider or QRP administrator may not be willing to accept some or all of these provisions, or any modifications to its printed beneficiary designation form. In such cases, the client will have to decide whether to move the benefits to another plan (if that is possible) or compromise his estate planning goals.

2.1   Master Beneficiary Designation: Traditional or Roth IRA

DESIGNATION OF BENEFICIARY

TO: _____

     Name of Custodian or Trustee of the Account

FROM: _____

     Name of Participant

RE: Account No. _____

I.   <u>Definitions</u>

The following words, when used in this form and capitalized, shall have the meaning indicated in this Section.

"Account" means the "Individual Retirement Account," "Individual Retirement Trust," "Roth Individual Retirement Account," or "Roth Individual Retirement Trust" referred to above, which is established and maintained under § 408 or § 408A of the Code.

"Administrator" means the IRA custodian or trustee named above, and its successors in that office.

"Agreement" means the account agreement between the Administrator and the undersigned establishing the Account.

"Beneficiary" means any person entitled to ownership of all or part of the Account as a result of my death (or as a result of the death of another Beneficiary), whether such person is a Primary, Contingent, or Successor Beneficiary.

"Contingent Beneficiary" means the person(s) I have designated in this form to receive the Death Benefit if my Primary Beneficiary does not survive me (or disclaims the benefits).

"Death Benefit" means all amounts payable under the Account on account of my death.

My "Personal Representative" means the duly appointed executor or administrator of my estate, who is serving as such at the applicable time.

"Primary Beneficiary" means the person(s) designated in this form to receive the Death Benefit in the event of my death.

"Successor Beneficiary" means a person entitled to receive the balance of another Beneficiary's benefits if such other Beneficiary dies before distribution of all of his or her share of the Death Benefit.

II.   Designation of Beneficiary

[Here insert the name(s) of the primary and contingent beneficiary(ies); this section must be drafted by the estate planning attorney; see sample inserts in Section 3 of this Appendix.]

III.   Other Provisions [dispense with any of these that are not appropriate in view of the choice of beneficiary or that are not necessary because already covered in the IRA provider's documents governing the Account]

3.01   Form of Benefit Payments after my Death. Except as may be otherwise specifically provided herein, or in the Agreement, or by applicable law, each Beneficiary shall be entitled to elect the form and timing of distribution of benefits payable to such Beneficiary.

3.02   Information to be provided to Personal Representative. The Administrator shall provide to my Personal Representative any information such representative shall request in connection with the performance of such representative's duties (including the preparation of any tax return) regarding the benefits, the terms of the account, and the Beneficiary(ies), including information as to matters prior to such representative's appointment, to the same extent and on the same terms that such information would have been provided to me had I requested it. Any Beneficiary, by accepting benefits hereunder, shall be deemed to have consented to the release of information to my Personal Representative as provided in the preceding sentence.

3.03   Payments to Minors. If any Beneficiary becomes entitled to ownership of any part of the Account while under the age of twenty-one (21) years, such ownership shall instead be vested in the name of such Beneficiary's surviving parent, if any, otherwise in the name of my oldest then living child if any, otherwise in the name of some other person selected by my Personal Representative, as custodian for such Beneficiary under the Uniform Transfers to Minors Act of the state of my domicile at death, and such custodian shall have the power to act for such Beneficiary in all respects with regard to the Account.

3.04   Governing Law. The law of the State of _____ shall apply solely for the purpose of interpreting my intent as expressed in this Designation of Beneficiary form. This provision is not intended to amend or supercede any governing law provision in the Agreement with respect to the interpretation and administration of the Agreement.

3.05   Multiple Beneficiaries. If there are multiple Beneficiaries entitled to ownership of the Account simultaneously, the Beneficiaries shall be entitled, by written instructions to the Administrator, to have the Account partitioned into multiple Accounts, corresponding to each Beneficiary's separate interest in the Account, as of or at any time after my death, to the maximum extent such division is permitted by law to occur without causing a deemed distribution of the Account. Following such partition the newly created separated Accounts shall be maintained as if each were an Account in my name payable solely to the applicable Beneficiary; no Beneficiary shall have any further interest in or claim to any Account other than the separate Account representing such Beneficiary's interest.

3.06   Allowing Beneficiary to Appoint Investment Manager. The Beneficiary may designate an Investment Manager for the Account. Upon receipt of written authorization from the Beneficiary, and until receiving notice that such authorization is revoked, the Administrator shall comply with investment instructions of the Investment Manager in accordance with the Beneficiary's authorization.

3.07   Preservation of Marital Deduction. If my spouse survives me, this paragraph shall apply to any portion (or all) of the Account as to which my spouse is the Beneficiary or as to which my spouse becomes the Beneficiary by virtue of another Beneficiary's death or disclaimer. My spouse, as such Beneficiary, shall have the right, exercisable solely by my spouse, annually or more frequently (in my spouse's discretion), to require distribution to my spouse of all income of the Account, and also shall have the power, exercisable by my spouse alone and in all events, at any time or times and from time to time, to appoint all of the principal of the Account (including undistributed income) to my spouse. Rights given to my spouse under this paragraph shall be in addition to and not in limitation of any rights given to my spouse by law, by the Agreement or by other provisions hereof. My spouse shall have sole responsibility for determining the "income" and "principal" of the Account. The Administrator's responsibility under this section is limited solely to distributing to my Spouse any amounts my Spouse has instructed the Administrator to distribute to my Spouse.

       3.08   <u>Transferring Account</u>. The Beneficiary shall have the right to have the Account (or, if the Account has been partitioned pursuant to the preceding provisions hereof, such Beneficiary's separated Account) transferred to a different individual retirement account or trust, of the same type ("traditional" or "Roth") as the Account, still in my name and payable to such Beneficiary, with the same or a different custodian or trustee, if at the applicable time such transfer is permitted by law to occur without causing a deemed distribution of the Account.

      Signed this _____ day of _____, 20 ___.

                  _____
                  Signature of Participant

      Receipt of the above beneficiary designation form is hereby acknowledged this ___ day of _____, 20 ___.

                  _____
                  Name of Custodian or Trustee
                  By:_____
                  Title:

2.2   Master Beneficiary Designation Form: Qualified Plan

DESIGNATION OF BENEFICIARY

TO: _____

       Name of Trustee or Plan Administrator

FROM: _____

       Name of Participant

RE: _____

       Name of Retirement Plan

I.   Definitions

The following words, when used in this form and capitalized, shall have the meaning indicated in this Section.

"Administrator" means the Plan Administrator or Trustee named above, and its successors in such office.

"Beneficiary" means any person entitled to receive benefits under the Plan as a result of my death (or as a result of the death of another Beneficiary).

"Contingent Beneficiary" means the person(s) I have designated in this form to receive the Death Benefit if my Primary Beneficiary does not survive me (or disclaims the benefits).

"Death Benefit" means all benefits payable under the Plan on account of my death.

My Personal Representative" means the duly appointed executor or administrator of my estate, who is serving as such at the applicable time.

"Plan" means the qualified retirement plan or other retirement arrangement described at the beginning of this form.

"Primary Beneficiary" means the person(s) designated in this form to receive benefits under the Plan on account of my death.

"Successor Beneficiary" means a person entitled to receive the balance of another Beneficiary's benefits if such other Beneficiary dies before distribution of all of his or her share of the Death Benefit.

II.   Designation of Beneficiary

[Here insert the name(s) of the primary and contingent beneficiary(ies); this section must be drafted by the estate planning attorney; see sample inserts in Section 3 of this Appendix.]

III.   Other Provisions [dispense with any of these that are not appropriate in view of the choice of beneficiary or not necessary because already covered in the plan documents governing the benefits]

3.01   Form of Benefit Payments After My Death. Except as may be otherwise specifically provided herein, in the Plan, or by applicable law, each Beneficiary shall be entitled to elect the form and timing of distribution of any benefits payable to such Beneficiary.

3.02   Information to be provided to Personal Representative. The Administrator shall provide to my Personal Representative any information such representative shall request in connection with the performance of such representative's duties (including the preparation of any tax return) regarding the benefits, the Plan, and the Beneficiaries, including information as to matters prior to such representative's appointment, and including copies of Plan documents and returns, to the same extent and on the same terms that such information would have been provided to me had I requested it. Any Beneficiary, by accepting benefits hereunder, shall be deemed to have consented to the release of information to my Personal Representative as provided in the preceding sentence.

3.03   Payments to Minors.   If any Beneficiary becomes entitled to benefits under the Plan while under the age of twenty-one (21) years, such benefits shall be instead payable to such Beneficiary's surviving parent, if any, otherwise to my oldest then living child, if any, otherwise to some other person selected by my Personal Representative, as custodian for such Beneficiary under the Uniform Transfers to Minors Act, and such custodian shall have the power to act for such Beneficiary in all respects with regard to the benefits to which such Beneficiary is entitled.

3.04   Governing Law. The law of the State of _____ shall apply solely for the purpose of interpreting my intent as expressed in this Designation of Beneficiary form. This provision is not intended to amend or supercede any governing law provision in the Plan with respect to the interpretation and administration of the Plan.

3.05   Multiple Beneficiaries.   If there are multiple Beneficiaries entitled to ownership of the Death Benefit simultaneously, the Beneficiaries shall be entitled, by written instructions to the Administrator, to have the Death Benefit partitioned into multiple Accounts, corresponding to each Beneficiary's separate interest in the Death Benefit, as of or at any time after my death, to the maximum extent such division is otherwise permitted by the Plan and by law (without causing a deemed distribution of the Death Benefit). Following such partition the newly created separated Accounts shall be maintained as if each were a Death Benefit in my name payable solely to the applicable Beneficiary, and no Beneficiary shall have any further interest in or claim to any Death Benefit other than the separate account representing such Beneficiary's interest.

3.06   Allowing Beneficiary to Appoint Investment Manager. The Beneficiary may designate an Investment Manager for the Death Benefit (or, if the Death Benefit has been divided pursuant to the preceding provisions hereof, such Beneficiary's share of the Death Benefit). Upon receipt of written authorization from the Beneficiary, and until receiving notice that such authorization is revoked, the Administrator shall comply with investment instructions of the Investment Manager in accordance with the Beneficiary's authorization.

3.07   Preservation of Marital Deduction. If my spouse survives me, this paragraph shall apply to any portion (or all) of the Death Benefit as to which my spouse is the Beneficiary or as to which my spouse becomes the Beneficiary by virtue of the death of (or a disclaimer by) a prior Beneficiary. My spouse, as such Beneficiary, shall have the right, exercisable solely by my spouse, annually or more frequently (in my spouse's discretion), to require distribution to my spouse of all income of the Death Benefit, and also shall have the power, exercisable by my spouse alone and in all events, at any time or times and from time to time, to appoint all of the principal of the Death Benefit (including undistributed income) to my spouse. Rights given to my spouse under this paragraph shall be in addition to and not in limitation of any rights given to my spouse by law, by the Plan, or by other provisions hereof. My spouse shall have sole responsibility for determining the "income" and "principal" of the Death Benefit. The Administrator's responsibility under this section is limited solely to distributing to my spouse any amounts my spouse has instructed the Administrator to distribute to my spouse.

3.08   Honoring Disclaimers. Notwithstanding the foregoing, if a Beneficiary disclaims all or any portion of any interest in the Death Benefit to which such Beneficiary would otherwise be entitled under the foregoing provisions hereof, by means of a written disclaimer which either purports to be, or appears to be, a qualified disclaimer within the meaning of § 2518 of the Internal Revenue Code, then that Beneficiary shall be deemed (as to the interest so disclaimed) to have predeceased me, the interest so disclaimed shall pass as if such Beneficiary had predeceased me, and the Beneficiary who takes the interest so disclaimed shall be deemed to be my beneficiary under the Plan for all purposes; This provision shall not be construed to prevent an interest disclaimed by my spouse from passing to my spouse by other means.

Signed this _____ day of _____, 20 ___.

_____
Signature of Participant

Receipt of the above beneficiary designation form is hereby acknowledged this ___ day of _____, 20 ___.

_____
Name of Plan Administrator or Trustee
By:_____
Title:

3.   SAMPLE INSERTS FOR MASTER FORMS

The forms in this section are the actual designation of the primary and contingent beneficiary. These are designed to be inserted into "Article II" of the Master Beneficiary Designation Forms.

3.1   Benefits Payable to Spouse, "Disclaimable" to Credit Shelter Trust; Different Contingent Beneficiary Depending on Whether Spouse Predeceases or Disclaims

This form might be used by a client who does not have sufficient non-retirement plan assets to fully fund a credit shelter trust, but nevertheless wants to leave the benefits to his spouse and allow the spouse to make the ultimate decision whether to keep the benefits and roll them over to an IRA or disclaim some or all of the benefits and allow them to flow to the credit shelter trust. See ¶ 4.2.11(E).

II.   Designation of Beneficiary

A.   Primary Beneficiary

I hereby designate as my Primary Beneficiary my spouse, [SPOUSE NAME], if my spouse survives me.

B.   Contingent Beneficiary in Case of Disclaimer

If my spouse survives me, but disclaims the Death Benefit (or part of it), I hereby designate as my Contingent Beneficiary, to receive the part (or all) of the Death Benefit so disclaimed, [TRUSTEE NAME], as Trustee of the [TRUST NAME] Trust, under agreement dated [TRUST DATE] [optional:, a copy of which is attached hereto]; provided, that with respect to any portion of the Death Benefit that is also disclaimed by the said Trust, or with respect to which my spouse also disclaims all interests passing to my spouse under said Trust, my spouse shall be deemed to have predeceased me.

C.   Contingent Beneficiary in Case of Death

If my spouse does not survive me, or with respect to any portion of the Death Benefit as to which my spouse is deemed (pursuant to the preceding paragraph) to have predeceased me, I hereby designate as my Contingent Beneficiary my issue surviving me, by right of representation.

3.2   Spouse is Primary Beneficiary; Children are Contingent

II.   Designation of Beneficiary

A.   Primary Beneficiary

I hereby designate as my Primary Beneficiary, to receive 100% of the Death Benefit, my spouse, [SPOUSE NAME], if my spouse survives me.

B.   Contingent Beneficiary

If my spouse does not survive me, I hereby designate as my Contingent Beneficiary, to receive 100% of the Death Benefit, my children surviving me, in equal shares; provided, that if any child of mine does not survive me, but leaves issue surviving me, such issue shall take the share such deceased child would have taken if living, by right of representation.

3.3   Designating Children (Or Their Issue) as Beneficiaries

II.   Designation of Beneficiary

    I hereby designate as my Primary Beneficiary, to receive 100% of the Death Benefit, my children surviving me, in equal shares; provided, that if any child of mine does not survive me, but leaves issue surviving me, such issue shall take the share such deceased child would have taken if living, by right of representation.

Name   Address   Date of Birth   Social Security Number   Phone

---

3.4   Trust Is Beneficiary, but Only If Spouse Survives

    See ¶ 6.5.01, #6.

II.   Designation of Beneficiary

    A.   Primary Beneficiary

    I hereby designate as my Primary Beneficiary, to receive 100% of the Death Benefit, if my spouse, [SPOUSE NAME], survives me, [TRUSTEE NAME], as Trustee of the [TRUST NAME] Trust, under agreement dated [TRUST DATE] [optional:, a copy of which is attached hereto].

    B.   Contingent Beneficiary

    If my spouse does not survive me, I hereby designate as my Contingent Beneficiary, to receive 100% of the Death Benefit, my issue surviving me, by right of representation; provided, however, that if any Contingent Beneficiary is under the age of 30 years at the time of my death such Beneficiary's share shall not be paid to such Beneficiary outright, but shall instead be paid to the trustee then serving as such under the separate trust established or to be established for such Beneficiary's benefit under Article [NUMBER] of the [TRUST NAME] Trust, dated [TRUST DATE] [optional:, a copy of which is attached hereto], to be held, administered, and distributed for the benefit of such Beneficiary as provided therein.

3.5   Pecuniary Gift Expressed as Fractional Gift

See ¶ 1.7.06(A).

II.   Designation of Beneficiary

I hereby designate as my Primary Beneficiaries, to receive 100% of the Death Benefit, the following persons in the following proportions; provided, that if either of them does not survive me, the other one shall receive the entire Death Benefit.

A.   There shall be paid to [NAME OF "PECUNIARY" BENEFICIARY] a portion of the Death Benefit determined by multiplying the Death Benefit by a fraction. The numerator of the fraction shall be [HERE INSERT THE DESIRED PECUNIARY AMOUNT, SUCH AS $100,000]. The denominator of the fraction shall be the value of the Death Benefit as of the date of my death.

B.   The balance of the Death Benefit shall be paid to [NAME OF "RESIDUARY" BENEFICIARY].

---

4.   TRUST PROVISIONS DEALING WITH BENEFITS

Definitions of capitalized terms are in Form 4.9. Be sure to use Form 4.9 (modified as necessary to delete unneeded definitions) when using any Form that contains defined (capitalized) terms.

4.1   Administration During Donor's Life; Irrevocability

See ¶ 6.2.06. This form is not suitable for a testamentary trust.

___. Administration During my Life

.01   The Trustee shall distribute to me such amounts of the principal or income of the trust (including all thereof) as I may request from time to time, or (if I am legally incapacitated) as my guardian, conservator, or other legal representative may request on my behalf.

.02   I reserve the right to amend or revoke this trust by one or more written and acknowledged instruments delivered to the Trustee during my lifetime. This trust shall become irrevocable at my death.

4.2   Forbidding Payment of Benefits to Nonindividuals

See ¶ 6.2.10 for why to forbid use of benefits to pay debts, expenses, and taxes of participant's estate. See ¶ 6.3.01(D), ¶ 7.3.02, and ¶ 7.3.03 regarding whether this form is effective with regard to other possible payments to nonindividual beneficiaries.

Notwithstanding any other provision hereof, except as provided in this paragraph, the Trustee may not, after September 30 of the calendar year following the calendar year in which my death occurs, or such earlier date as shall be established by IRS regulations or other guidance as the final date for determining whether this trust meets the requirements for treatment of the trust's beneficiaries as if they had been named directly as beneficiary of any retirement plan payable to this trust ("Such Date"), distribute to or for the benefit of my estate, any charity, or any other nonindividual beneficiary any Deferrable Retirement Benefit. It is my intent that all Deferrable Retirement Benefits held by or payable to this trust as of Such Date be distributed to or held for only individual beneficiaries, within the meaning of § 401(a)(9) of the Code. Accordingly I direct that no Deferrable Retirement Benefit may be used or applied after Such Date for payment of my debts, taxes, expenses of administration, or other claims against my estate; nor for payment of estate, inheritance or similar transfer taxes due on account of my death. This paragraph shall not apply to any bequest or expense that is specifically directed to be funded with Deferrable Retirement Benefits by other provisions of this instrument.

4.3   Excluding Older Adopted Issue

See ¶ 6.2.07(A).

Notwithstanding any other provision hereof or of state law, a person's "issue" shall not include an individual who is such person's "issue" by adoption if such individual (1) was so adopted after my death and (2) is older than the oldest other beneficiary of this trust who was a living member of said class at my death.

4.4   Marital Deduction Savings Language

See ¶ 3.3.04.

> If any marital trust created by this instrument becomes the beneficiary of any Retirement Benefit, the Trustee must withdraw from such marital trust's share of such Retirement Benefit, each year, at least whichever of the following amounts is the greater:
>
> A.   the net income of the marital trust's share of such Retirement Benefit for such year; or
>
> B.   the Minimum Required Distribution for such year with respect to such Retirement Benefit.
>
> This paragraph shall not be deemed to limit the Trustee's power and right to withdraw from the marital trust's share of the Retirement Benefit in any year more than the greater of the said amounts.

4.5   Accounting for Retirement Benefits

See ¶ 6.1.03.

> .01   General Principles. This Article shall govern the Trustee's accounting for Retirement Benefits. In general, a Retirement Benefit shall be deemed an asset of the Trust, increases or decreases in its value shall be allocated to income or principal of the Trust as provided herein, and distributions from the Retirement Benefit shall be accounted for as provided herein.
>
> .02   Certain Individual Account Plans. With respect to any Retirement Benefit which is an individual account plan, for which the Trustee receives such reporting of the investment activity in the account that the Trustee can readily determine the "income" and "principal" of the Trust's interest in the plan in accordance with traditional principles of income and principal, the Trustee shall account for the Trust's interest in the Retirement Benefit as if the applicable plan assets were owned by the Trust directly.
>
> .03   All Other Retirement Benefits. With respect to any other Retirement Benefit, the Trustee shall treat the inventory value of the trust's interest in the Retirement Benefit as principal, and allocate any subsequent increases in value (or charge decreases in value) in such interest to income or principal in accordance with any reasonable

method selected by the Trustee that is consistent with traditional principles of income and principal and is consistently applied to the Trust's interest in such plan, including:

(A)   A method specified in any Uniform Principal and Income Act (UPIA) or other state law governing trust accounting for retirement benefits or deferred compensation, but only if such law provides for a reasonable apportionment, each year, between the income and remainder beneficiaries of the total return of the trust for such year. The "10 percent rule" of UPIA Section 409(c), or any other state law that determines income with respect to a Retirement Benefit by reference to the amount of the retirement plan's required distributions rather than by reference to the return on the applicable investments or other traditional principles of income and principal, or that otherwise departs fundamentally from traditional principles of income and principal, may not be used to determine "income" for any purpose of this trust.

(B)   In the case of a plan similar to the type of plan specified in paragraph .02 above, the method specified in said paragraph .02 adapted as necessary.

(C)   Any method used in the Code or Treasury regulations to distinguish between "ordinary income" and "return of principal" (or corpus) with respect to similar assets.

.04   Treatment of Distributions. When a distribution is received from or under a Retirement Benefit, and, at the time of such distribution, under the foregoing rules, the trust's interest in the Retirement Benefit is composed of both income and principal, such distributions shall be deemed withdrawn first from the income portion.

.05   Definition of Inventory Value. In the interpretation of this Article, the "inventory value" of an interest in a Retirement Benefit shall mean:

A.   In the case of an interest that becomes payable to (or is owned by) this trust as of the date of my death, its "fair market value" determined in accordance with the rules applicable for valuing such interests for purposes of the federal estate tax (as in effect at my death, or, if such tax does not then exist, as last in effect); or,

B.   In the case of an interest that becomes payable to this trust as of a date after the date of my death (for example, by transfer from another fiduciary), its "fair market value" shall be its value as of my death determined as provided in the preceding subparagraph, adjusted as necessary for distributions, expenditures, and receipts that occurred between the date of my death and the date of transfer to this trust; or, if the trustee cannot determine its value in that manner, its "fair market value" shall be its value as of the date it becomes an asset of this trust, determined as provided in the preceding subparagraph, provided, in the case of an interest transferred to this Trust from another fiduciary (such as my Personal Representative) accrued income so transferred shall be treated as income and shall not be included in "inventory value."

4.6   Establishing a Conduit Trust for One Beneficiary

See ¶ 6.3.05.

From and after my death, this trust shall be held for the benefit of [NAME OF INDIVIDUAL TRUST BENEFICIARY] (hereinafter referred to as the "Beneficiary"). Each year, beginning with the year of my death, my Trustees shall withdraw from any Deferrable Retirement Benefit the Minimum Required Distribution for such Deferrable Retirement Benefit for such year, plus such additional amount or amounts as the Trustee deems advisable in its sole discretion. All amounts so withdrawn (net of expenses properly charged thereto) shall be distributed to the Beneficiary, if the Beneficiary is then living. Upon the death of the Beneficiary (or upon my death if the Beneficiary does not survive me) all remaining property of this trust shall be paid to [NAME OF TRUST REMAINDER BENEFICIARY].

4.7   Conduit Provision Included in "Family Pot" Trust

See ¶ 6.3.12(B). As a reminder, this approach will not work for a trust that is not established until the death of a prior beneficiary; see ¶ 6.3.10(A). This approach works only for benefits that pass to the Family Trust on the death of the participant.

Administration of Family Trust

From and after my death, the trustee shall hold and administer all amounts then held by the trust, or that become payable to this trust as a result of my death, for the benefit of my children surviving me, upon the following terms.

A.   While there is any child of mine living who is under the age of thirty years, the Trustee shall hold, administer, and distribute Deferrable Retirement Benefits as provided in Paragraph B and shall hold, administer, and distribute all other property as provided in Paragraph C.

B.   Each year, beginning with the year of my death, my Trustees shall withdraw from any Deferrable Retirement Benefit the Minimum Required Distribution for such Deferrable Retirement Benefit for such year, plus such additional amount or amounts as the Trustee deems advisable in its sole discretion. The Trustee shall distribute each amount so withdrawn (net of expenses properly charged thereto) to (or apply it for the benefit of) such one or more individuals as the Trustee shall select from the class consisting of all my issue then living, and in such proportions among them as the Trustee deems advisable in its discretion.

C.   With respect to all other property of the trust, the Trustee shall pay such amounts of the income and/or principal of such property to (or apply it for the benefit of) such one or more individuals as the Trustee shall select from the class consisting of all my issue then living, and in such proportions among them as the Trustee deems advisable in its discretion.

D.   At such time as there is no child of mine living who is under the age of thirty years, the trust shall terminate and be distributed outright and free of trust to my issue then living by right of representation, or, if there are no such issue then living, shall be distributed to [NAME OF DEFAULT REMAINDER BENEFICIARY].

4.8   Conduit Trusts to Avoid GST Problem

See ¶ 6.3.15.

Article [NUMBER]
Provision for Deferrable Retirement Benefits

[modify this paragraph if there is no spouse]

Notwithstanding any other provision hereof, this Article shall apply, if my spouse does not survive me, to any Deferrable Retirement Benefit payable at my death to this trust, any share of this trust, or any separate trust established under this instrument. If my spouse does survive me, this Article shall apply, notwithstanding any other provision hereof, to any Deferrable Retirement Benefit payable at my death to this trust, any share of this trust, or any separate trust established under this Instrument if and only if my spouse, as of the date of my death, is not a beneficiary of this trust (for example, as a result of a qualified disclaimer(s)).

A.   Establishment of Separate Share Benefits Trusts

Article [NUMBER] requires creation of separate trusts or shares (the "Share Trusts") for each of my children then living (and the issue of any deceased child). If, as of the date of my death, the value of Deferrable Retirement Benefits payable to all the Share Trusts, collectively, exceeds [INSERT MINIMUM DOLLAR AMOUNT OF BENEFITS REQUIRED TO MAKE ESTABLISHMENT OF SEPARATE TRUSTS WORTHWHILE, SUCH AS $500,000], then, rather than being added to such Share Trusts, the portion of Deferrable Retirement Benefits payable to each such Share Trust shall instead be held in a separate trust (the "Separate Share Benefits Trust") for the benefit of the beneficiary of such Share Trust. The Separate Share Benefits Trust for each beneficiary shall be held on all the same terms and conditions as those of the Share Trust for the same beneficiary, with the following exceptions:

B.   Separate Share Benefits Trust for Child

In the case of a Separate Share Benefits Trust held for the benefit of a Child of mine, Article [NUMBER], Section [NUMBER] [*i.e., the article dictating terms for administering such share during the child's life*], shall not apply, and shall instead be replaced by the following new Article [NUMBER], Section [NUMBER]:

"([NUMBER]) Distributions During Life of My Child:

Each year, beginning with the year of my death, and continuing so long as such Child is living, my Trustees shall withdraw from any Deferrable Retirement Benefit payable to such Trust the Minimum Required Distribution for such Trust's share of such Benefit for such year, plus such additional amount or amounts, if any, as my Trustees deem advisable in their sole discretion. All amounts so withdrawn (net of applicable expenses) shall be distributed to (or applied for the benefit of) such Child as soon as reasonably practicable."

C.   Separate Share Benefits Trust: Deceased Child's Issue

In the case of a Separate Share Benefits Trust held for the benefit of a descendant of a deceased child of mine, Article [NUMBER], Section [NUMBER] [i.e., the article dictating terms for administering the share of issue of a deceased child], shall not apply, and shall instead be replaced by the following new Article [NUMBER], Section [NUMBER]:

"([NUMBER]) Distributions During Life of Beneficiary:

Each year, beginning with the year of my death, and continuing so long as the beneficiary of such Separate Share Benefits Trust (the "Beneficiary") is living, my Trustees shall withdraw from any Deferrable Retirement Benefit payable to such Trust the Minimum Required Distribution for such Trust's share of such Benefit for such year, plus such additional amount or amounts, if any, as my Trustees deem advisable in their sole discretion. All amounts so withdrawn (net of applicable expenses) shall be distributed to (or applied for the benefit of) such Beneficiary as soon as reasonably practicable."

4.9　　Definitions for Trust Forms

This Form is designed to be used with Form 4.2 and Forms 4.4–4.8. The optional definition of Taxable Retirement Benefits can be deleted; it is not used with any of the Forms in this Appendix. That definition is included here as an example of a definition that could be used if the trust instrument directs that taxable benefits are to be used to fund particular shares, such as a marital trust or a charitable bequest.

The following definitions shall apply in administering this Trust:

1. The "Code" means the Internal Revenue Code of 1986, as amended.

2. A "Retirement Benefit" means the Trust's interest in one of the following types of assets if payable to this Trust as beneficiary or owned by this Trust: a qualified or nonqualified annuity; a benefit under a qualified or nonqualified plan of deferred compensation; any account in or benefit payable under any pension, profit-sharing, stock bonus, or other qualified retirement plan; any individual retirement account or trust; and any and all benefits under any plan or arrangement that is established under § 408, § 408A, § 457, § 403, § 401, or similar provisions of the Code. "Retirement Benefits" means all of such interests collectively. A "Deferrable Retirement Benefit" means any Retirement Benefit that meets the following two requirements: First, it is subject to the Minimum Distribution Rules. Second, the terms of the plan or arrangement that governs such Benefit permit a trust that is named as beneficiary of such Benefit to take distribution of such Benefit in annual instalments over the life expectancy of the oldest trust beneficiary. Benefits payable under a plan or arrangement that is not subject to the Minimum Distribution Rules (such as, under current law, a "nonqualified deferred compensation plan") are not Deferrable Retirement Benefits. Benefits payable under a plan that does not permit the trust the option of withdrawing the benefits over the life expectancy of the oldest trust beneficiary (such as a retirement plan that offers "lump sum distribution" as the only permitted form of death benefit) are not Deferrable Retirement Benefits.

[optional additional definition] A "Taxable Retirement Benefit" is any Retirement Benefit other than a Roth IRA, deemed Roth IRA, or designated Roth account within the meaning of § 408A or § 402A of the Code.

3. The "Minimum Distribution Rules" mean the rules of Section 401(a)(9) of the Code, including Regulations thereunder.

4. The "Minimum Required Distribution" for any year means, for each Retirement Benefit: (1) the value of the Retirement Benefit determined as of the preceding year-end, divided by (2) the Applicable Distribution Period; or such greater amount (if any) as the Trustee shall be required to withdraw under the laws then applicable to this Trust to avoid penalty. Notwithstanding the foregoing, the Minimum Required Distribution for the year of my death shall mean (a) the amount that was required to be distributed to me with respect to such Benefit during such year under the Minimum Distribution Rules, minus (b) amounts actually distributed to me with respect to such Benefit during such year.

5. The terms "life expectancy," "Applicable Distribution Period," and "designated beneficiary" shall have the same meaning as under the Minimum Distribution Rules.

5.   OTHER FORMS

5.1   Power of Attorney Dealing with Retirement Benefits

This clause could be added to the client's power of attorney or set up as a separate power of attorney just dealing with benefits. The form and formalities of execution need to be appropriate for the applicable jurisdiction and the participant's circumstances. For any significant retirement plan benefit, determine in advance whether the plan will honor this form; some IRAs, for example, require customers to use a particular form prepared by the IRA provider.

My Agent shall have the power to establish one or more "individual retirement accounts" or other retirement plans or arrangements in my name.

In connection with any pension, profit-sharing, or stock bonus plan, individual retirement arrangement, Roth IRA, § 403(b) annuity or account, 457 plan, or any other retirement plan, arrangement, or annuity in which I am a participant or of which I am a beneficiary (whether established by my Agent or otherwise) (each of which is hereinafter referred to as "such Plan"), my Agent shall have the following powers, in addition to all other applicable powers granted by this instrument:

1.   To make contributions (including "rollover" contributions) or cause contributions to be made to such Plan with my funds or otherwise on my behalf.

2.   To receive and endorse checks or other distributions to me from such Plan, or to arrange for the direct deposit of the same in any account in my name or in the name of [NAME OF CLIENT'S LIVING TRUST].

3.   To elect a form of payment of benefits from such Plan, to withdraw benefits from such Plan, to make contributions to such Plan, and to make, exercise, waive, or consent to any and all elections and/or options that I may have regarding the contributions to, investments or administration of, or distribution or form of benefits under, such Plan.

4.   To designate [NAME OF PARTICIPANT'S PRIMARY BENEFICIARY, SUCH AS "my spouse, [SPOUSE NAME]"], if living, otherwise [PARTICIPANT'S CONTINGENT BENEFICIARY, SUCH AS "my issue surviving me by right of representation"], as beneficiary of any benefits payable under such Plan on account of my death.

5.2   Fiduciary Letter Transferring Plan Account to Beneficiary

See ¶ 6.1.05. Use either Alt. 1 or Alt. 2, plus either Alt. A or Alt. B.

To the Plan Administrator of the [NAME OF RETIREMENT PLAN] (hereinafter "the Plan"):

Re: Benefits of [NAME OF DECEASED PARTICIPANT], deceased (hereinafter "the Participant")

[Alt. 1: From executor, if benefits were payable to the participant's estate]:

I am the [FIDUCIARY'S TITLE SUCH AS EXECUTOR, ADMINISTRATOR, OR PERSONAL REPRESENTATIVE] of the estate of the Participant, who was a participant in the Plan. I enclose a certificate evidencing my appointment. In that capacity, I am transferring the Participant's interest in the Plan to the beneficiary/ies of Participant's estate who is/are entitled to receive it under ["THE TERMS OF PARTICIPANT'S WILL" or "APPLICABLE INTESTACY LAW"].

[Alt. 2: From trustee of trust named as beneficiary]:

I am the Trustee of the [NAME OF TRUST] ("the Trust") which was the named beneficiary of the Participant under the Plan. In my capacity as such Trustee, I am transferring the Participant's interest in the Plan to the beneficiary/ies who is/are entitled to receive it under the terms of the Trust.

[Alt. A: Transfer to one beneficiary]

Accordingly, I hereby instruct and direct you to change the titling of this plan benefit to "[NAME OF BENEFICIARY TO WHOM THE BENEFIT IS BEING TRANSFERRED] as successor beneficiary of [NAME OF DECEASED PARTICIPANT]." The beneficiary's address and Social Security number are [INSERT].

[Alt. B. Transfer to several beneficiaries, in separated accounts]

Accordingly, I hereby instruct and direct you to divide the benefit into [NUMBER OF SEPARATED ACCOUNTS TO BE ESTABLISHED] separate accounts of equal value, and to change the titling of each such account to the name of one of the beneficiaries to whom the benefit is being transferred "as successor beneficiary of [NAME OF DECEASED PARTICIPANT]." The names, addresses, and Social Security numbers of the individual beneficiaries of the separated accounts are: [INSERT].

In accordance with the instructions for IRS Form 1099-R (page R-3), this transfer is to be treated as a plan-to-plan transfer and is not to be treated or reported as a distribution from the Plan. Please advise what if any further information or documentation you required to complete this transfer.

Very truly yours,

[SIGNATURE OF EXECUTOR OR TRUSTEE]

5.3   Letter to Administrator Who Won't Provide Information

To the Plan Administrator of the [NAME OF RETIREMENT PLAN] (hereinafter "the Plan"):

Re: Benefits of [NAME OF DECEASED PARTICIPANT], deceased (hereinafter " the Participant")

I am the executor of the estate of the Participant, who was a participant in the Plan. I enclose a certificate evidencing my appointment.

I have requested from you certain information in order that I may fulfill my responsibility to prepare and file a federal estate tax return for the Participant's estate. You have informed me that you will provide no information regarding the Participant's benefits under the Plan to anyone other than the Participant's designated beneficiary. You will not tell me the name of the Participant's designated beneficiary.

As required by § 6018(b) of the Internal Revenue Code, I will include with the estate tax return I will file for the Participant's estate a statement that I am unable to make a complete return regarding the Participant's interest in the Plan, and I will submit your name and address as the person holding legal title to this property. The Internal Revenue Service will then require you to prepare and file an estate tax return regarding this asset on behalf of the Participant's estate.

Very truly yours,

[SIGNATURE OF EXECUTOR]

Appendix C

Resources

This Appendix lists resources available to help professionals in planning for their clients' retirement plan benefits. For books, see the Bibliography. Prices, ordering information and features change constantly, so check with the vendor before placing an order.

Ataxplan Website

Updates to this book, when available, may be downloaded free from the publisher's website, www.ataxplan.com. A Table of Authorities for this book will also be posted there for free download.

Occasionally this book refers to earlier editions of itself for more detail on various expired or otherwise obscure tax rules. Since earlier editions are out of print, most of these sections will eventually be collected and posted as a free download called *Ancient History*.

You can also order and/or download through the website (though these are not free): the forms from Appendix B in 8.5" X 11" format in Word or WordPerfect format, for use in your word processor; additional copies of this book; the author's other book, *The QPRT Manual*; and (coming soon) Special Reports on various topics regarding planning for retirement benefits, such as *The 100 Best & Worst Planning Ideas for Your Client's Retirement Benefits*.

Software

Most providers offer a downloadable demo at their web sites.

Brentmark Pension & Roth IRA Analyzer (version 2005.02). $395. Includes 6 months' free maintenance; $129 annual update fee. Powerful feature-filled software to help planners analyze proposed plan distribution strategies from QRPs, IRAs, and Roth IRAs (comparing up to 4 scenarios simultaneously), including income tax, estate tax and spousal rollover aspects. Also analyzes whether it is worthwhile to convert a traditional IRA to a Roth IRA and computes pre-59½ SOSEPP distributions. The ideal user is an experienced planner with some training to understand the impact that changing assumptions has on outcome. For just running MRD and SOSEPP calculations (including MRDs for multiple beneficiaries), use Brentmark's Pension Distribution Planner ($249). Brentmark Software, Inc., 3505 Lake Lynda Drive # 212, Orlando FL 32817-8327; 1-800-879-6665 or 407-306-6160; www.brentmark.com. The Brentmark web site has lots of free information and useful links; a top web site for professionals on retirement distributions planning.

Steve Leimberg's MRD (Minimum Required Distributions) Calculator. $99. Calculates MRDs from IRAs and QRPs, and pre-59½ SOSEPPs using all three IRS methods. The program is fast and extremely easy to use. The printout shows the assumptions used in making the calculations, which is extremely helpful. The more expensive (but worth it) NumberCruncher also does "almost 100" other estate planning calculations and is an indispensable tool for estate planners. Leimberg & LeClair Inc., PO Box 1332, Bryn Mawr, PA 19010, (610) 924-0515. Order at www.leimberg.com.

WealthCounsel, LLC. WealthCounsel offers WealthDocs, a complete estate plan-drafting system, as well as educational conferences and other resources for its estate planning lawyer-members. They are licensed to use the forms from this book as part of the WealthDocs product. See Www.wealthcounsel.com.

Newsletters

Ed Slott's IRA Advisor. Ed Slott, CPA, is one of America's most knowledgeable retirement benefits experts, plus he writes beautifully and is a great speaker. Each issue has in-depth discussion of practical retirement tax info by top practitioners. $125 for twelve 8-page issues per year (includes all back issues). Sent by mail (800-663-1340), or download, you can order it (and find lots of other useful info) at www.irahelp.com.

Choate's Notes, by Natalie B. Choate. Published irregularly, free for now, sent by regular mail to professionals who request it by handing in business card at a Natalie Choate seminar (or sign up at www.ataxplan.com, where back issues are posted). Each issue contains a short article on some aspect of planning for retirement benefits, plus other info of interest to estate planning and investment professionals.

Steve Leimberg's Employee Benefits and Retirement Planning Newsletter. E-mail-only. Expert analysis of breaking news "as it happens," such as rulings, cases, and legislation. Written by IRA pros such as Bob Keebler, Barry Picker, and yours truly, edited by the incomparable Steve Leimberg, Esq. Includes "LawThreads," which summarizes recent exchanges from estate planning listservs; and 24-hr access to extensive database. $24.95 per month (includes all four of Steve's newsletters). Indispensable. Visit one-time free or subscribe at www.leimbergservices.com. Access is provided free through membership in some Estate Planning Councils and possibly other professional associations, so check with yours. In addition to being a nationally recognized expert on estate planning, retirement benefits, and life insurance, and a major supplier of helpful tools for our industry, Steve also has ready-to-go seminars for estate planners at www.Leimberg.com.

Other Resources

Jack McManemin, CFP, a financial planner in Salt Lake City, has created a wonderful handy quick reference tool for the minimum required distribution rules. It is a laminated card, 9" X 11.5", with color charts summarizing the rules: Lifetime distributions on one side, post-death on the other. $19.85 for one (includes shipping). For info, call 801-273-3310 or e-mail jackmcm@unidial.com.

Bibliography

Estate Planning magazine is published by Warren Gorham & Lamont, 31 St. James Ave., Boston, MA 02116. Single issues are available from Wm. S. Hein & Co., 800-828-7571, ext. 162.

"T.M." refers to the Tax Management Portfolio series published by the Bureau of National Affairs, Inc., 1231 25th St., N.W., Washington, D.C. 20037. A publication date is not provided for books in this series because they are kept up to date by annual supplements.

"CCH" is Commerce Clearing House, Inc., 4025 W. Peterson Ave., Chicago, IL 60646-6085. www.cch.com or 800-449-8114.

ACTEC Journal is published by the American College of Trust and Estate Counsel, 3415 S. Sepulveda Boulevard Suite 330, Los Angeles, CA 90034, 310-398-1888; www.actec.org.

IRS Publications can be downloaded free from the IRS website, http://www.irs.gov/formspubs/lists/0,,id=97819,00.html.

General note on sources: All statements in this book are based on the author's research using primary sources supplemented by secondary sources, with the exception of several aspects of the income tax treatment of trusts, as to which I have relied on Blattmachr, J.G., and Michaelson, A.M., *Income Taxation of Estates and Trusts*, 14th Ed. (2000), (Practicing Law Institute Press, 810 Seventh Ave., New York, NY 10019) (cited as "*Blattmachr*") and Zaritsky, H. and Lane, N., *Federal Income Taxation of Estates and Trusts*, (third Edition, 2000; Warren, Gorham & Lamont) (cited as "*Zaritsky*").

Introduction; Retirement Plans and Estate Planning Generally

The best book for lawyers on tax-oriented estate planning is *Estate Planning Law and Taxation* (4th ed., 2002–2003, with 2005 Supplement) by Professor David Westfall and George P. Mair, Esq., published by Warren, Gorham & Lamont (RIA), Boston. Obtain the paperback "Financial Professionals' Edition."

The best one-volume reference work for ERISA questions is *The Pension Answer Book,* by Stephen J. Krass, Esq. Mainly deals with "employer" issues such as the design, funding and qualification of retirement plans, but several chapters have material on distributions. Also covers prohibited transactions. A Panel Publication of Aspen Publishers, Inc., 7201 McKinney Circle, Frederick, MD 21704, 800-

638-8437; www.panelpublishers.com. Current price is $199 per year, discount available if purchased at a trade show.

Estate and Gift Tax Issues for Employee Benefit Plans (T.M. 378) and *An Estate Planner's Guide to Qualified Retirement Plan Benefits* (American Bar Assoc., Section of Real Property, Probate and Trust Law, 1992), both by Louis A. Mezzullo, Esq. are excellent overviews of the subject. The former also covers subjects not covered in this book, including nonqualified deferred compensation plans and QDROs.

Chapter 1: Minimum Distribution Rules

Practical Application of the Retirement Distribution Rules, by Seymour Goldberg, CPA, MBA, JD (IRG Publications, 2001) is written by the MRD expert who started it all. $59 (includes shipping) plus NY state tax if applicable. 800-808-0422.

Choate, N., "The 'Estate' As Beneficiary Of Retirement Benefits," *Trusts & Estates*, Vol. 138, No. 10 (Sept. 1999), p. 41.

Chapter 2: Income Tax Matters

For more about IRD, see Alan S. Acker, *Income in Respect of a Decedent*, 862-2nd T.M., and two articles by Christopher R. Hoyt, Esq., "Inherited IRAs: When Deferring Distributions Doesn't Make Sense," *Trusts & Estates*, Vol. 137, No. 7 (June 1998), p. 52, and "Sometimes It's Better to Avoid Stretch IRAs," *Trusts & Estates*, Vol. 142, No. 3 (March 2003), p. 38.

For more on lump sum distributions, see Frederick J. Benjamin, Jr., Esq., *Qualified Plans: Taxation of Distributions*, T.M. 370-2d, and *Taxation of Distributions from Qualified Plans*, by Diane Bennett *et al.*, Warren, Gorham & Lamont, ch. 5.1.

For more on what to do for clients who have company stock in their retirement plans, get the audiotape "Sophisticated Tax Planning Opportunities with Employer Securities Held Within Qualified Plans" (with written materials), by Robert Keebler CPA, $29.95 plus $4 shipping, plus WI tax if applicable; send check to Virchow Krause & Co., LLP, PO Box 11997, Green Bay, WI 54307-1997; call 920-490-5607 for further information.

Chapter 3:　Marital Matters

For more on spousal waivers under REA, see Lynn Wintriss, Esq. "Practice Tips: Waiver of Rights Under the Retirement Equity Act and Premarital Agreements," 19 *ACTEC Journal*, no. 2, Fall 1993.

For more on community property issues regarding retirement benefits, see "Practicalities of Post-Mortem Distribution Planning for Community Property Retirement Benefits and IRAs—Trusts as Beneficiaries, Separate Shares and Aggregate Theory Agreements," by Edward V. Brennan, Esq., *California Trusts and Estates Quarterly*, Vol. 5, No. 4 (Winter 1999).

Chapter 4:　Disclaimers

See, generally, on disclaimers, the CCH *Federal Estate and Gift Tax Reporter;* or the RIA *Federal Tax Coordinator 2d;* or Mary Moers Wenig, Esq., *Disclaimers* (T.M. 848).

Chapter 5:　Roth IRAs

Mervin M. Wilf, Esq., authored several articles regarding Roth IRAs in *Estate Planner's Alert* (newsletter published by Research Institute of America): "The Roth IRA: A New Estate Planning Opportunity,", October 1997, page 11; "Roth IRAs: Second Chance for Distribution Planning after Age 70½ (Nov. 1997, p. 9); "Roth IRA AGI Threshold: Per Spouse or Per Couple?" (Dec. 1997, p. 6); and "Roth IRA Rollover Amounts should be Limited" (Jan. 1998, p. 5). See also his "Innovative Estate Planning Strategies Using Roth IRAs," *Estate Planning* March/April 1998 (Vol. 25, No. 3) page 99.

M.M. Wilf, Esq., "Regs Ignore 'Repeal' of Incidental Death Benefit Rule for Roth IRAs," *Pension & Benefits Week* 10/5/98, p. 5.

Michael J. Jones, CPA, "Roth IRA Gifts May Terminate Income Tax Benefits," *Tax Notes*, 6/1/98, p. 1156,

For a financial analysis of Roth IRAs, see R.S. Keebler, CPA, MST, *A CPA's Guide to Making the Most of the New IRAs* (AICPA). Also visit www.RothIRA.com or read *Roth to Riches* by John D. Bledsoe (Legacy Press, $19.95).

Chapter 6:   Trusts as Beneficiaries of Retirement Benefits

For fiduciary income tax, see Blattmachr and Zaritsky books recommended at the beginning of the Bibliography, and *Preparing Fiduciary Income Tax Returns*, by Jeremiah W. Doyle IV, Esq., *et al.* MCLE, 10 Winter Place, Boston, MA 02108, 1997.

The problem of trust accounting for retirement benefits is the subject of "IRA Distributions to a Trust After the Death of the IRA Owner—Income or Principal?" by Jeremiah W. Doyle, Esq., *Trusts & Estates*, Vol. 139, No. 9, p. 38 (Sept. 2000).

Golden, A.J., "Total Return Unitrusts: Is This a Solution in Search of a Problem?," 28 *ACTEC Journal* Vol. 2, p. 121 (Fall 2002).

Jones, Michael J., "Transferring IRAs," 145 *Trusts & Estates* No. 4 (April 2006), p. 38.

Chapter 7:   Charitable Giving with Retirement Benefits

Books:

The Harvard Manual on Tax Aspects of Charitable Giving, by the late David M. Donaldson, Esq., Carolyn M. Osteen, Esq., et al.(8th edition, 1999) is a magnificent summary of charitable giving techniques, with citations, written from the point of view of counsel for the charitable donee. The Harvard University Office of Planned Giving, Cambridge, MA 02138, 800-446-1277 (donation of $105).

Conrad Teitell, Esq., is one of the country's top experts in the tax law of charitable giving, and fortunately for the rest of us he is also a prolific author and superb public speaker. For a complete catalogue of his books, newsletters and amazing seminars, call 800-243-9122.

Articles and seminar outlines:

Babitz, M.S., et al., "The IRA Double Tax Trap: The Private Foundation Solution," 29 *Estate Planning* 8 (Aug. 2002), p. 411.

Blattmachr, J.G., "Income in Respect of a Decedent," 12 *Probate Notes* 47 (1986). This excellent article discusses numerous strategies for reducing taxes on retirement benefits and other IRD, including charitable dispositions.

Burke, F.M., "Why Not Allow Lifetime Charitable Assignments of Qualified Plans and IRAs?" *Tax Notes* 7/7/97.

Hicks, Z.M., "Charitable Remainder Trust may be more Advantageous than a Qualified Plan," *Estate Planning* (5-6/90, p. 158).

This is about using a CRUT *instead of* a qualified plan as an accumulation/payout vehicle for retirement.

Hoyt, C.R., "Solution for Estates Overloaded with Retirement Plan Accounts: the Credit Shelter CRUT," 141 *Trusts & Estates* 5 (May 2002), p. 21.

Hoyt, C.R., "Stretch This: Using a CRT to help heirs of employees of companies that liquidate retirement accounts at death," 145 *Trusts & Estates* (Feb. 2006), p. 50.

Mezzullo, L.A., "Using an IRA for Charitable Giving," March/April 1995 *Probate & Property*, the Journal of the ABA Section of Real Property, Probate and Trust Law, p. 41.

Mulcahy, T.W., "Is a Bequest of a Retirement Account to a Private Foundation Subject to Excise Tax?," *Journal of Taxation*, August 1996.

Newlin, Charles F., "Coping With the Complexity of Separate Shares Under the Final Regs.," *Estate Planning*, July 2000 (Vol. 27, No. 6, p. 243).

Shumaker, R.L., and Riley, M.G., "Strategies for Transferring Retirement Plan Death Benefits to Charity," 19 ACTEC Journal, no. 3, p. 162 (1993), and follow-up comments published in 20 ACTEC Journal, p. 22 (1994). Compares the economic effects of various ways of funding a $1 million charitable gift from a $4 million estate, including the use of retirement benefits.

Shumaker, R.L. (with Riley, M.G.), "Charitable Deduction Planning with Retirement Benefits and IRAs: What Can Be Done and How Do We Do It?," American Bar Association Section of Real Property, Probate and Trust Law meeting outline, August 1995.

Chapter 8:   Investment Issues

LIFE INSURANCE: See generally, Zaritsky, H., and Leimberg, S.L., *Tax Planning with Life Insurance*, Warren, Gorham & Lamont.

For an excellent discussion of life insurance in the retirement plan, see Beverly R. Budin, Esq., *Life Insurance*, T.M. 826.

Regarding "subtrusts," see: "The Qualified Plan as an Estate Planning Tool," by Andrew J. Fair, Esq., booklet distributed by Guardian Life Insurance Co. Of America, 201 Park Ave. South, New York, NY 10003; "Estate Tax on Life Insurance Held in Qualified Plans," by Mervin M. Wilf, Esq., in *Retirement Plan Trio* seminar 6/22/95, materials published by ALI-ABA, 4025 Chestnut St.,

Philadelphia, PA 19104-3099 (Publ. No. Q239); "IRS opens the way toward favorable estate and income tax treatment of plan distributions," by Kenneth C. Eliasberg, Esq., *Estate Planning* (7/83, p. 208); "Subtrusts and Reversionary Interests: A Review of Current Options," by I. Meyer Pincus, L.L.B., *Journal of the American Society of CLU & ChFC* (9/92, p. 64); "Excluding Qualified Plan Insured Incidental Death Benefits from the Participant's Gross Estate; Minority and Non-Stockholders," by Jonathan Davis, Esq., *The Estates, Gifts and Trusts Journal* (9-10/83, p.4); "Excluding Defined Benefit Plan Insured Death Benefits from the Gross Estate -- Sole and Majority Shareholders," by Jonathan Davis, Esq., *Tax Management Compensation Planning Journal* (5/84, p. 123).

PROHIBITED TRANSACTIONS: For thoughtful discussion of PT issues, see materials by Noel C. Ice, Esq., published at his web site www.trustsandestates.net.

The Department of Labor web site, www.dol.gov/ebsa/, has posted copies of the DOL's advisory opinions (back through 1992 only), PT exemptions (1996 to date) and interpretive bulletins, and the "Presidential Reorganization Plan #4 of 1978." Generally this excellent government web site is easy to use. An oddity of the web site is that it clumps several exemptions together into one document; for example, if you click on the exemption for Dr. Smith's IRA, you will find yourself reading about the DeutscheBank Pension Plan...just keep scrolling down until you come to Dr. Smith. For older PT exemption requests and advisory opinions, you must use one of the pension services as these are not posted at the DOL web site.

Chapter 9:   Pre-Age 59½ Distributions

Toolson, Richard B., "Structuring Substantially Equal Payments to Avoid the Premature Withdrawal Penalty," *Journal of Taxation*, Nov 1990, page 276.

Index

Page number in **bold** indicates the page where the term is defined and/or that contains complete cross-referencing to other sections relevant to the term being defined. If a term is used on multiple consecutive pages, this index generally cites only the first of such pages.

Pension Protection Act of 2006

This book was at the printer when Congress enacted the Pension Protection Act of 2006 (PPA '06). I stopped the press and made changes throughout the text as necessary to reflect the new realities created by stroke of a pen. Most of the new law deals with pension plan funding and administration (which are not the subject of this book), but some provisions affect individual estate and distribution planning:

Rollover by nonspouse beneficiary: After, 2006, a nonspouse individual Designated Beneficiary, including a trust, can roll over a QRP or 403(b) plan distribution to an "inherited IRA." See ¶ 2.6.03.

Sunset of the sunset: Most provisions enacted as part of EGTRRA (2001) are scheduled to expire after 2010, but PPA repeals this "sunset" for EGTRRA's pension and IRA provisions. Thus, the following are now permanent: Liberalized rollover rules (¶ 2.6.01), hardship waivers for the 60-day rollover deadline (¶ 2.6.06(B)), deemed Roth IRAs (¶ 5.1.04), increased IRA contribution limits (¶ 5.3.02), and DRACs (¶ 5.7.09). Other income, estate, and gift tax changes made by EGTRRA are still subject to the "sunset" after 2010. PPA '06 § 811.

Rollover from QRP to Roth IRA: Post-2007 QRP, 403(b), and 457 distributions may be rolled over to a Roth IRA, if the distribution is otherwise rollover-eligible and the individual is eligible to make a rollover contribution to a Roth IRA. ¶ 5.4.02.

COLA for certain Roth IRA income limits: See ¶ 5.3.03(A).

72(t) premature distributions: PPA expanded the early retirement exception (¶ 9.4.04), and added a temporary exception for reservists called to active duty (¶ 9.4.12), to the 10% penalty on pre-age 59½ distributions.

More spousal annuities: Plans subject to REA must offer more types of spousal annuities; see ¶ 3.4.02.

Regulation of DAFs: See ¶ 7.5.03.

Temporary "charitable IRA rollover" law: For 2006 and 2007 only, up to $100,000 per year may be transferred from an IRA directly to a charity. See ¶ 7.6.01 for details.

Investment advice: PPA added new provisions regarding providing investment advice for retirement plans, including new prohibited transactions exemptions. Since these changes did not seem to bear directly on the matters discussed in Chapter 8, they are not covered in this book.

HOW TO ORDER BOOKS, FORMS

To order more copies of this book, *Life and Death Planning for Retirement Benefits* (6th ed., 2006), or Natalie Choate's other best-selling estate planning book *The QPRT Manual*, call 1-800-247-6553 or order online at www.ataxplan.com. Each book is $89.95 plus shipping.

You can order all the forms in Appendix B of this book, plus several more that didn't fit into the book, in 8.5" x 11" page size, ready to plug into your word processor (either Word or WordPerfect) and use in your practice, by visiting www.ataxplan.com, or by mailing the following order form to Ataxplan Publications, P.O. Box 961093, Boston, MA 02196-1093. These forms are provided solely for your convenience, to save typing, and are meant to be used in conjunction with this book, so no instructions are included. Price: $49.95 (includes shipping), plus $2.50 sales tax for Mass. delivery.

Name: _____

Company name:_____

Address:_____

City: _____ State: _____ Zip: _____-_____

Telephone: (___) _____

Form of payment:

Check payable to Ataxplan Publications, or VISA, Mcard, or AmExp.

Card number: _____

Name on card: _____ Exp. date_____/__

Signature (required for credit card orders):

_____